Profess

Microsoft® Virtual Server 2005

Professional
Microsoft® Virtual Server 2005

Ben Armstrong

Wiley Publishing, Inc.

Professional Microsoft® Virtual Server 2005

Published by
Wiley Publishing, Inc.
10475 Crosspoint Boulevard
Indianapolis, IN 46256
www.wiley.com

Copyright © 2007 by Wiley Publishing, Inc., Indianapolis, Indiana

Published simultaneously in Canada

Library of Congress Control Number: 2007006575

ISBN: 978-0-470-10917-5

Manufactured in the United States of America

10 9 8 7 6 5 4 3 2 1

No part of this publication may be reproduced, stored in a retrieval system or transmitted in any form or by any means, electronic, mechanical, photocopying, recording, scanning or otherwise, except as permitted under Sections 107 or 108 of the 1976 United States Copyright Act, without either the prior written permission of the Publisher, or authorization through payment of the appropriate per-copy fee to the Copyright Clearance Center, 222 Rosewood Drive, Danvers, MA 01923, (978) 750-8400, fax (978) 646-8600. Requests to the Publisher for permission should be addressed to the Legal Department, Wiley Publishing, Inc., 10475 Crosspoint Blvd., Indianapolis, IN 46256, (317) 572-3447, fax (317) 572-4355, or online at www.wiley.com/ go/permissions.

LIMIT OF LIABILITY/DISCLAIMER OF WARRANTY: THE PUBLISHER AND THE AUTHOR MAKE NO REPRESENTATIONS OR WARRANTIES WITH RESPECT TO THE ACCURACY OR COMPLETENESS OF THE CONTENTS OF THIS WORK AND SPECIFICALLY DISCLAIM ALL WARRANTIES, INCLUDING WITHOUT LIMITATION WARRANTIES OF FITNESS FOR A PARTICULAR PURPOSE. NO WARRANTY MAY BE CREATED OR EXTENDED BY SALES OR PROMOTIONAL MATERIALS. THE ADVICE AND STRATEGIES CONTAINED HEREIN MAY NOT BE SUITABLE FOR EVERY SITUATION. THIS WORK IS SOLD WITH THE UNDERSTANDING THAT THE PUBLISHER IS NOT ENGAGED IN RENDERING LEGAL, ACCOUNTING, OR OTHER PROFESSIONAL SERVICES. IF PROFESSIONAL ASSISTANCE IS REQUIRED, THE SERVICES OF A COMPETENT PROFESSIONAL PERSON SHOULD BE SOUGHT. NEITHER THE PUBLISHER NOR THE AUTHOR SHALL BE LIABLE FOR DAMAGES ARISING HERE-FROM. THE FACT THAT AN ORGANIZATION OR WEBSITE IS REFERRED TO IN THIS WORK AS A CITATION AND/OR A POTENTIAL SOURCE OF FURTHER INFORMATION DOES NOT MEAN THAT THE AUTHOR OR THE PUBLISHER ENDORSES THE INFORMATION THE ORGANIZATION OR WEBSITE MAY PROVIDE OR RECOMMENDATIONS IT MAY MAKE. FURTHER, READERS SHOULD BE AWARE THAT INTERNET WEBSITES LISTED IN THIS WORK MAY HAVE CHANGED OR DISAP-PEARED BETWEEN WHEN THIS WORK WAS WRITTEN AND WHEN IT IS READ.

For general information on our other products and services please contact our Customer Care Department within the United States at (800) 762-2974, outside the United States at (317) 572-3993 or fax (317) 572-4002.

Trademarks: Wiley, the Wiley logo, Wrox, the Wrox logo, Programmer to Programmer, and related trade dress are trademarks or registered trademarks of John Wiley & Sons, Inc. and/or its affiliates, in the United States and other countries, and may not be used without written permission. Microsoft is a registered trade-mark of Microsoft Corporation in the United States and/or other countries. All other trademarks are the property of their respective owners. Wiley Publishing, Inc., is not associated with any product or vendor mentioned in this book.

Wiley also publishes its books in a variety of electronic formats. Some content that appears in print may not be available in electronic books.

About the Author

Ben Armstrong hails from Brisbane, Australia. He relocated to California in 2001 to start working on virtualization software being developed by Connectix Corporation. When Microsoft acquired the Connectix technology in 2003, he worked as a Program Manager on Microsoft's new virtualization team. Ben has been working with virtualization for over five years and has been involved in the release of five major virtualization products (from both Connectix and Microsoft).

In his spare time, Ben messes around with virtual machines, plays computer games, messes around playing computer games in virtual machines, and apparently writes books.

Ben maintains a blog as Virtual PC Guy at `http://blogs.msdn.com/virtual_pc_guy`.

Credits

Executive Editor
Chris Webb

Development Editor
Ami Frank Sullivan

Technical Editor
Steve Jain

Production Editor
Kathryn Duggan

Copy Editor
Nancy Rapoport

Editorial Manager
Mary Beth Wakefield

Production Manager
Tim Tate

Vice President and Executive Group Publisher
Richard Swadley

Vice President and Executive Publisher
Joseph B. Wikert

Graphics and Production Specialists
Denny Hager
Rashell Smith
Alicia B. South

Quality Control Technician
John Greenough

Project Coordinator
Lynsey Osborn

Proofreading and Indexing
Aptara

Anniversary Logo Design
Richard Pacifico

Acknowledgments

I give my love and appreciation to my wife, Werona, and my children, Isaac and Elizabeth, for their patience and support while I worked on this book. I would also like to thank my father, Joe, for putting up with late-night calls from me to complain about minor technical details.

Contents

Acknowledgments	ix
Introduction	xxi

Part I: Getting Started with Virtual Servers   1

Chapter 1: Why Virtualize?   3

Benefits of Virtualization	**3**
Increased Hardware Utilization	3
System Isolation	4
Rapid Provisioning	4
System Flexibility	4
High Availability	5
Drawbacks of Virtualization	**5**
Performance	5
Scalability	6
Hardware Abstraction	6
Common Uses for Virtualization	**7**
Server Consolidation	7
Development and Testing	7
Server Resiliency	8
Dealing with Legacy Applications	8
Training	9
Demonstration	9
Web-Based Systems	10
Conclusion	**10**

Chapter 2: Getting Started with Microsoft Virtual Server 2005   11

Configuring the Host Environment	**12**
Configuring IIS on Windows Server 2003	13
Configuring IIS on Windows XP Professional	13
Configuring IIS on Windows Vista	13
Configuring IIS on Windows Codenamed Longhorn Server	14
Installing Virtual Server	**14**
Website Configuration	15
Firewall Configuration	15

Contents

Advanced Installation Options	**16**
Custom Installation	16
MSI-Based Installation	16
Command Line–Based Installation	17
Creating the First Virtual Machine	**17**
Starting the First Virtual Machine	**19**
Conclusion	**20**

Chapter 3: Virtual Server Basic Concepts   21

Emulated Devices	**21**
Storage	22
Networking	29
How Virtual Networks Work	**31**
Video	32
COM and LPT Ports	32
BIOS	32
Virtual Machine Additions	**33**
Advanced Performance Improvements Provided by Virtual Machine Additions	33
Conclusion	**33**

Chapter 4: Installing Guest Operating Systems   35

Using the Virtual Machine Remote Control Client	**35**
Installing Windows Server 2003	**36**
Installing Virtual Machine Additions for Windows	40
Installing Red Hat Enterprise Linux 4	**41**
Installing Virtual Machine Additions for Linux	44
Configuring Linux After Installation	46
Conclusion	**47**

Part II: Optimizing Virtual Machine Management and Usage   49

Chapter 5: Creating a Virtual Machine Library   51

Different Types of Libraries	**51**
Casual Virtual Machine Library	51
Formal Virtual Machine Library	52
Centralized Virtual Machine Library	52
Automated Virtual Machine Library	53
Differencing Disks versus Full Copies	**54**
Determining What Should Be in Your Base Virtual Machines	**54**

xii

Contents

Base Image Preparation	**55**
Windows Base Virtual Machines	55
Useful Post-Deployment Commands	71
Linux Base Virtual Machines	72
Storing Virtual Hard Disks on the Network	**74**
Conclusion	**75**

Chapter 6: Understanding Virtual Machine Performance   77

32-Bit versus 64-Bit Host Operating Systems	**77**
Hardware Virtualization	**78**
Networking	**81**
Network Performance Recommendations	87
Internal Networking	88
Storage	**88**
Storage Performance Recommendations	92
Keeping an Eye on Fragmentation	93
Other Devices	**93**
Configuring Memory	**94**
Selecting the Right Amount of Memory	94
Understanding the Impact of Non-Uniform Memory Architecture	95
Configuring Resource Allocations	**97**
Finding the Best Candidates for Virtualization	**98**
Conclusion	**99**

Part III: Maintaining Virtual Machines   101

Chapter 7: Monitoring and Managing Virtual Machines   103

Virtual Server Web Interface	**103**
Virtual Server Scripts	105
Windows Event Log	**106**
Performance Monitor	**107**
Microsoft Operations Manager 2005	**108**
Virtual Server Tasks	109
Virtual Server Health Information	110
Virtual Machine Diagram	111
Virtual Machine Performance Monitoring	111
Virtualization Reports	111
System Center Virtual Machine Manager	**112**
Conclusion	**113**

xiii

Contents

Chapter 8: Keeping Virtual Machines Up-to-Date — 115

Don't Update — **115**
Manual Updating — **116**
Automated Updating — **116**
    Using a Windows Server Update Server — 117
    Installing Windows Server Update Server 2.0 — 118
    Configuring Windows Server Update Server 2.0 — 119
    Using a Linux YUM Server — 137
Handling Base Virtual Machines — **144**
Conclusion — **144**

Part IV: Security and Backup for Virtual Machines — 145

Chapter 9: Keeping Virtual Machines Secure — 147

Antivirus for Virtual Machines — **147**
Network Security for Virtual Machines — **148**
    Virtual Machine Firewall Configurations — 148
    Routing Network Connections — 149
Conclusion — **161**

Chapter 10: Securing Virtual Server — 163

Isolating Network Adapters — **164**
Restricting Access to Virtual Machines — **165**
    Example 1: Limited Administrator Rights — 167
    Example 2: Maintenance Needs — 167
    Example 3: A Different Limit on Administrator Duties — 167
    Example 4: Virtual Machine User — 168
Securing Virtual Machines by Using EFS — **169**
Configuring IIS and Virtual Server on Separate Computers — **169**
Securing IIS for Virtual Server — **171**
    Using IIS Lockdown Tool — 172
    Using URLScan Tool — 172
    Removing the Default Website from IIS 6.0 — 173
Configuring Secure Sockets Layer — **174**
    Configuring SSL on the Virtual Server Administrative Website — 174
    Configuring SSL on VMRC — 177
    Using a Self-Signed SSL Certificate — 179
Securing VMRC — **181**

Contents

Using an External Firewall	**182**
Choosing the Right Authentication Type	**183**
Conclusion	**185**

Chapter 11: Backing Up Virtual Machines   187

Introducing VHDMount	**187**
Backing Up Virtual Machine Files	**189**
Problems with Virtual Machine File Backup	190
Shut Down or Save State?	191
Backing Up Inside the Virtual Machine	**193**
Backing Up Inside Windows Server 2003 and Windows XP	194
Backing Up Inside Windows 2000	203
Backing Up Inside Windows NT 4.0	203
Backing Up Inside Vista	204
Backing Up Inside Red Hat Enterprise Linux 4	205
Backing Up from a Remote Backup Server	**208**
Using VSS to Back Up Virtual Machines	**209**
Backing Up Virtual Server Itself	**210**
Determining the Best Back Up Strategy	**211**
Conclusion	**212**

Part V: Physical to Virtual Migration   213

Chapter 12: Physical to Virtual Migration of Servers   215

How Does VSMT Work?	**215**
Source Computer Requirements	**216**
Setting Up the ADS/VSMT Server	**217**
Configuring DHCP	**219**
Configuring Virtual Server	**221**
Preparing the Source Computer	**222**
Performing the Migration	**222**
Gather Information About the Source Server	222
Check for Compatibility	223
Generate Script Files	223
Capture the Source Computer	226
Deploy the Image to a New Machine	227
Check Yourself	227
Troubleshooting P2V Problems with VSMT	**227**
Software Incompatibilities	228
Boot Failures and Crashes	230

xv

Contents

No Boot Policy Received	231
Unsupported HAL Type	231
Administrative Website Doesn't Display	231
Wrong IP Address	231
No Enabled Network Cards	232
SCSI Adapters Not Enabled in the Guest OS	232
Long Migration Process	233
Failures During Migration	233
Advanced Options for VSMT	**234**
Using VSMT to Convert a Vmware Virtual Machine to a Virtual Server Virtual Machine	234
Loading Virtual Machine Additions into the ADS Deployment Agent	234
Enabling Image Encryption for the Migration Process	235
P2V in System Center Virtual Machine Manager	**235**
Conclusion	**236**

Chapter 13: Manual Physical to Virtual Migrations — 237

Migrating Windows with Backup Software	**238**
Using ASR with Windows Server 2003 and Windows XP	238
Using a Full System Backup with Windows Server 2003, Windows XP, and Windows 2000	241
Using a Complete PC Backup with Windows Vista	244
Imaging Physical into Virtual	**245**
Tips for Imaging Windows Systems	**247**
Offline Editing of the Windows Registry	247
Finding the Right Files	248
Migrating with a Prepared System Image	**249**
Migrating Windows Systems	249
Red Hat Enterprise Linux 4	256
Migrating with an Unprepared System Image	**256**
Migrating Unprepared Windows Server 2003, Windows XP, and Windows 2000 Servers	256
Migrating an Unprepared Windows NT 4.0 Server	261
Migrating an Unprepared Red Hat Enterprise Linux 4 Server	264
Cleaning Up After the Migration	**264**
Windows Server 2003, Windows XP, and Windows Vista	264
Windows 2000	265
Windows NT 4.0	265
Conclusion	**266**

Contents

Part VI: Virtual Machines and Clustering — 267

Chapter 14: Clustering Virtual Machines — 269

Clustering with Emulated SCSI — **269**
Preparing Virtual Server — 269
Setting Up the Domain Controller — 271
Preparing the Cluster Nodes — 272
Setting Up the Cluster — 275

Clustering with iSCSI — **282**
Understanding iSCSI — 282
Preparing the Environment for iSCSI Clustering — 283
Setting Up a Software-Based iSCSI Target — 284
Configuring Shared Data Drives — 284
Configuring the Cluster — 285

Conclusion — **286**

Chapter 15: Clustering Virtual Server — 287

Preparing the Physical Cluster — **288**
Installing Virtual Server — **290**
Creating the Clustering Script — **291**
Creating a Virtual Machine — **291**
Configuring the Virtual Networks — **292**
Creating the Cluster Group — **293**
Configuring the Virtual Machine on Each Cluster Node — 294
Configure the Cluster Resource Script — 294
Testing the Cluster Group — 295

Conclusion — **295**

Part VII: Automating Virtual Machine Operations — 297

Chapter 16: Using the Virtual Server COM Interface — 299

Understanding the COM Objects — **299**
Requirements for Accessing COM — **300**
COM Security — 300
Threading Apartment Models — 301

Accessing COM from VBScript — **301**
Accessing COM from Native Code — **302**

xvii

Contents

Accessing COM from Managed Code	**305**
Sample Visual Basic .NET Code	307
Sample C# Code	310
Sample Visual Basic .NET Code	316
Sample C# Code	319
Accessing COM from Windows PowerShell	**323**
Accessing COM from ASP.NET	**325**
Sample Visual Basic .NET Code	326
Sample C# Code	329
Accessing Virtual Server Remotely	**331**
Conclusion	**333**

Chapter 17: Scripting Virtual Server   335

VBScript Best Practices	**336**
Use Option Explicit	336
Do Not Use "On Error Resume Next"	336
Check Your Execution Environment	337
Running VBScripts	**337**
VM Task Objects	**338**
The Virtual Server Object	**341**
Manipulating Virtual Machines	341
Manipulating Virtual Networks	342
Creating Virtual Hard Disks	343
Removable Storage	344
Configuring VMRC	346
Read-Only Properties	348
Managing Paths	349
Managing Virtual Server Scripts	350
Virtual Machines	**352**
Virtual Machine State Management	352
Adding and Removing Devices	353
Configuring Virtual Machine Properties	355
Read-Only Virtual Machine Properties	356
Managing a Virtual Machine Saved State or Undo Disk	358
Virtual Machine Identification	360
Virtual Machine Scripts	362
Virtual Machine Automatic Start	363
SCSI Controller	**364**
Virtual Hard Disks	**365**
Virtual Hard Disk Connections	**368**
DVD Drive	**370**
Floppy Drive	**372**

xviii

Contents

Virtual Networks	**373**
DHCP Virtual Network Server	**375**
Network Adapter	**377**
Serial Port	**379**
Parallel Port	**380**
Display	**381**
Keyboard	**383**
Mouse	**384**
Guest OS	**385**
Accountant	**387**
Security and Access Rights	**389**
Host Information	**391**
Events	**392**
Get and Set Configuration Values	**395**
Samples	**396**
Create and Configure a Virtual Machine	396
Clone a Base Virtual Machine	398
Virtual Machine Automation	401
Conclusion	**404**

Chapter 18: Using PowerShell to Control Virtual Server	**405**
Setting Up the PowerShell Environment	**405**
Configuring Set-ExecutionPolicy	406
Configuring Basic Scripts	406
Accessing Virtual Server Directly from the PowerShell Command Line	**408**
Objects, Properties, and Methods	**408**
Understanding Pipelining	**411**
Variable Declaration and Error Handling	**412**
Functions and Script Parameters	**413**
Sample Scripts	**414**
Conclusion	**420**

Part VIII: Developing Software for Virtual Server	**421**

Chapter 19: Developing Managed Applications for Virtual Server	**423**
Creating a VMRC Client	**423**
Specifying the Server and Virtual Machine	425
Handling Display Size Changes	438
Locking Down the VMRC Client	440
Handling the Virtual Machine State	443

xix

Contents

Creating a Management Application	**457**
Adding Virtual Machine Information	464
Launching the VMRC Client	468
Integrating with the Virtual Server Administrative Website	470
Conclusion	**476**

Chapter 20: Developing ASP.NET Applications with Virtual Server — **477**

Creating Template Virtual Machines	**479**
Understanding ASP.NET Thread Identity	**482**
IIS and Application Pools	**483**
ASP.NET Application Overview	**485**
Default.aspx	**485**
CreateNewVM.aspx	**504**
ChangeState.aspx	**522**
VMRC.aspx	**536**
Conclusion	**541**

Part IX: Development and Debugging in Virtual Machines — **543**

Chapter 21: Application Debugging with Virtual Server — **545**

Application Debugging	**545**
Manual Remote Debugging	546
Automated Remote Debugging	547
Kernel Debugging	**548**
Configuring the Guest Operating System for Kernel Debugging	549
Connecting the Virtual Serial Port to a Named Pipe	550
Connecting a Kernel Debugger from Another Virtual Machine	551
Connecting a Kernel Debugger from the Host Operating System	552
Conclusion	**552**

Appendix A: Common Problems and Solutions — **555**

Appendix B: Virtual Server Clustering Script: HAVM.VBS — **561**

Index	**567**

Introduction

Welcome to *Professional Microsoft Virtual Server 2005*. This book is all about using Virtual Server in a number of different configurations and roles, and taking a close look at how to get the most out of Microsoft Virtual Server.

Microsoft Virtual Server 2005 was first released in August 2004, and was the first server virtualization solution to be released by Microsoft. This was followed by the release of Microsoft Virtual Server 2005 R2 in November 2005. Microsoft Virtual Server 2005 R2 added support for 64-bit host operating systems, support for Linux guest operating systems, new clustering capabilities, and significant performance improvements. Finally, in early 2007, Microsoft released Virtual Server 2005 R2 SP1, which added support for the use of new hardware virtualization technology.

This book focuses on Microsoft Virtual Server 2005 R2 SP1, which is now available as a completely free download from Microsoft. I hope that by the time you have finished reading this book you will have a wealth of knowledge about Microsoft Virtual Server 2005 R2 SP1 and how to use it effectively.

Whom This Book Is For

This book is targeted at system administrators who will be implementing solutions with Virtual Server, and at developers who are trying to build end-to-end solutions with Virtual Server. This book is written for people who have a fair amount of experience with computing in general, and may even have some basic knowledge of virtualization, but who are trying to figure out how to get the most from Virtual Server.

The programming samples in this book assume that you are familiar with how to create a basic application with Visual Studio 2005.

> *If you are experienced with Virtual Server, you may want to skim over the first four chapters of this book, as they are intended for users with less experience with Virtual Server. I don't recommend that you skip them entirely, as I expect that there will be a few hints and tips in there that you do not know about yet.*

What This Book Covers

This book focuses on setting up, maintaining, and developing Virtual Server environments. Much of what is discussed in this book can be applied to any version of Microsoft Virtual Server, but this book is specifically written about Microsoft Virtual Server 2005 R2 SP1. This book looks only at the use of Virtual Server when running operating systems that are officially supported by Microsoft, and using the tools that are provided by Microsoft.

Introduction

Virtual Server is capable of running a large number of operating systems. However Microsoft officially supports only Windows NT 4.0, Windows 2000, Windows XP, Windows Server 2003, Windows Vista, and a select number of Linux distributions (from Red Hat and Novell).

A fair number of third-party tools are available for Virtual Server that help with management and migration of virtual machines. I will not be looking at any of these tools in this book.

How This Book Is Structured

This book is written so that it can be read from cover to cover, or you can skip directly to the chapters that interest you. It is broken into nine parts:

❏ **Getting Started with Virtual Servers:** This part discusses how to get up and running with Virtual Server and covers the basics of virtual machines. By the end of the part, you should know how to get Virtual Server installed, virtual machines configured, and know how it all works.

❏ **Optimizing Virtual Machine Management and Usage:** This part is divided into two chapters. The first chapter focuses on creating a library of virtual machines that can be used for rapid and flexible deployment of virtual machines, while the second chapter is all about getting the best performance out of your virtual machines.

❏ **Maintaining Virtual Machines:** Here you get to read about how to keep track of your existing virtual machines, how to gather information and identify problems, and how to make sure that your virtual machines are always kept up-to-date with the latest software patches.

❏ **Security and Backup for Virtual Machines:** This part outlines everything you need to know about securing virtual machines and Virtual Server.

This part does not discuss how to configure the guest operating systems in a secure fashion.

❏ **Physical to Virtual Migration:** Physical to Virtual (P2V) refers to the process of taking a physical computer and migrating all the software installed on it to a virtual machine. This part looks at how to perform a P2V migration using the tools provided by Microsoft, and how to perform one by hand.

❏ **Virtual Machines and Clustering:** Clustering of virtual machines is a relatively complex object as there are many possible ways to configure such a cluster. This part looks at each of the ways, details the process involved in configuring them, and looks at the advantages and disadvantages involved.

❏ **Automating Virtual Machine Operations:** This part describes how to connect to the Virtual Server COM API and how to automate virtual machine operations using VBScript and PowerShell scripting.

❏ **Developing Software for Virtual Server:** Building on the previous section, this part looks at how to build applications that control and interact with Virtual Server using Visual Basic .NET, C#, and ASP.NET.

❏ **Development and Debugging in Virtual Machines:** This part looks at how to use Virtual Server to help with general development and debugging of applications.

xxii

What You Need to Use This Book

To work your way through most of this book, you need only a single copy of Virtual Server (on Windows XP or Windows Server 2003). Some of the more advanced configurations (such as clustering or automated patching of virtual machines) require that you run Virtual Server on top of a Windows Server 2003 computer that is joined to a domain.

Throughout this book, I use Red Hat Enterprise Linux 4 for any chapters that discuss how to configure Linux virtual machines for specific uses. (It should be relatively easy to adapt these directions for other Linux distributions.)

Finally, the chapters that discuss developing software to control Virtual Server require that you have a copy of Visual Studio 2005 installed.

Conventions

To help you get the most from the text and keep track of what's happening, a number of conventions are used consistently throughout the book.

> **Boxes like this one hold important, not-to-be forgotten information that is directly relevant to the surrounding text.**

Tips, hints, tricks, and asides to the current discussion are offset and placed in italics like this.

As for styles in the text:

- ❑ New terms and important words are *italicized* when introduced.
- ❑ Keyboard strokes look like this: Ctrl+A.
- ❑ Keywords and text that appear in the interface of software are bolded like this: open the **Action** menu.
- ❑ URLs and code within the text look like this: `persistence.properties`.
- ❑ Code blocks are presented two different ways:

```
New and important code is highlighted with a gray background.
```

```
The gray highlighting is not used for code that's less important in the present
context, or has been shown before.
```

Source Code

As you work through the examples in this book, you may choose either to type in all the code manually or to use the source code files that accompany the book. All of the source code used in this book is available for download at `www.wrox.com`. Once at the site, simply locate the book's title (either by using the

xxiii

Introduction

Search box or by using one of the title lists) and click the Download Code link on the book's detail page to obtain all the source code for the book.

Because many books have similar titles, you may find it easiest to search by ISBN; this book's ISBN is 978-0-470-10917-5.

Once you download the code, just decompress it with your favorite compression tool. Alternately, you can go to the main Wrox code download page at www.wrox.com/dynamic/books/download.aspx to see the code available for this book and all other Wrox books.

Errata

We make every effort to ensure that there are no errors in the text or in the code. However, no one is perfect, and mistakes do occur. If you find an error in one of our books, like a spelling mistake or faulty piece of code, we would be very grateful for your feedback. By sending in errata you may save another reader hours of frustration and at the same time you will be helping us provide even higher quality information.

To find the errata page for this book, go to www.wrox.com and locate the title using the Search box or one of the title lists. Then, on the book details page, click the Book Errata link. On this page you can view all errata that has been submitted for this book and posted by Wrox editors. A complete book list including links to each book's errata is also available at www.wrox.com/misc-pages/booklist.shtml.

If you don't spot "your" error on the Book Errata page, go to www.wrox.com/contact/techsupport .shtml and complete the form there to send us the error you have found. We'll check the information and, if appropriate, post a message to the book's errata page and fix the problem in subsequent editions of the book.

p2p.wrox.com

For author and peer discussion, join the P2P forums at p2p.wrox.com. The forums are a Web-based system for you to post messages relating to Wrox books and related technologies and interact with other readers and technology users. The forums offer a subscription feature to e-mail you topics of interest of your choosing when new posts are made to the forums. Wrox authors, editors, other industry experts, and your fellow readers are present on these forums.

At http://p2p.wrox.com you will find a number of different forums that will help you not only as you read this book, but also as you develop your own applications. To join the forums, just follow these steps:

1. Go to p2p.wrox.com and click the Register link.
2. Read the terms of use and click Agree.
3. Complete the required information to join as well as any optional information you wish to provide and click Submit.
4. You will receive an e-mail with information describing how to verify your account and complete the joining process.

xxiv

Introduction

You can read messages in the forums without joining P2P but in order to post your own messages, you must join.

Once you join, you can post new messages and respond to messages other users post. You can read messages at any time on the Web. If you would like to have new messages from a particular forum e-mailed to you, click the Subscribe to this Forum icon by the forum name in the forum listing.

For more information about how to use the Wrox P2P, be sure to read the P2P FAQs for answers to questions about how the forum software works as well as many common questions specific to P2P and Wrox books. To read the FAQs, click the FAQ link on any P2P page.

Part I
Getting Started with Virtual Servers

Chapter 1: Why Virtualize?

Chapter 2: Getting Started with Microsoft Virtual Server 2005

Chapter 3: Virtual Server Basic Concepts

Chapter 4: Installing Guest Operating Systems

Why Virtualize?

Before diving in to a discussion of using and understanding Microsoft Virtual Server 2005 R2 SP1, I would like to address a fundamental question: Why Virtualize?

You picked up this book, so chances are good that you already have ideas about why and how you want to use virtual machines, and you may be tempted to skip this section. I advise against this. Before you get started, it is important to fully understand the benefits and drawbacks associated with virtualization.

Furthermore, while you might have a specific use in mind for virtualization, you may be surprised to find out all the potential that is available in server virtualization.

Benefits of Virtualization

Take a look at the benefits Microsoft Virtual Server 2005 R2 SP1 brings to the table.

Increased Hardware Utilization

Most server administrators today could easily identify a plethora of servers in their organization that are not being fully utilized. In fact, with the usual recommended best practice of having a single server for a single function, many servers are struggling to reach even 10 percent of their capacity. This problem is only going to get worse as hardware continues to get more powerful, and as multi-core processors become commonplace in the server market.

Virtualization allows you to consolidate low utilization systems in order to have fewer systems, with higher hardware utilization, while still maintaining the best practice of having a single server for a single function.

Part I: Getting Started with Virtual Servers

System Isolation

One of the key tenets of virtualization is that the virtual machines should be isolated from one another. When running multiple virtual machines on Virtual Server 2005 there is nothing that a virtual machine can do to negatively affect other virtual machines. In fact, a virtual machine can even suffer an operating system crash without affecting the other virtual machines.

This makes virtualization a great method for managing unreliable or untrustworthy servers in your computing environment.

> The management of print servers provides an excellent example of utilizing the isolation capabilities of virtualization. Printer drivers from different manufacturers often cause problems if installed on the same system. Similarly, a problematic printer or printer driver can negatively affect the performance and availability of an entire server. By grouping printers into separate virtual machines you can greatly reduce the impact of the failure of a single print queue.

Rapid Provisioning

If you need a new server in the physical world, the process of provisioning it can be quite arduous. Most companies do not keep an inventory of spare servers, so you need to acquire the new hardware (which may involve getting financial approval) and wait for delivery. Once the new hardware arrives you then have to invest time to get the appropriate software loaded and ensure that there are no hardware compatibility issues. All of this combines to mean that, for most people, it is weeks between when they decide to get a new physical server and when the server is ready for use.

In a virtual world there is no need to acquire new hardware for a single new server (although should you create enough virtual servers you will need to get more hardware eventually), and there is no need to wait for financial approval or physical shipping. Furthermore, each virtual machine exposes the same set of emulated hardware (irrespective of the physical hardware being used), which allows you to have a standard set of images ready to be deployed. All of this means that provisioning a new virtual server can be as quick as copying a file.

System Flexibility

Virtual machines provide amazing operational flexibility. As already mentioned, virtual machines can be rapidly provisioned, but they can also be destroyed with similar ease. They can have CPU resources changed dynamically while they are running. They can have memory, storage, and network resources quickly reconfigured with a simple reboot of the virtual machine. They can be paused, or even put into a saved state, which stops the virtual machine from using any system resource but allows it to be restored to its current state at a later point in time.

Virtual machines are also fully abstracted from the physical hardware. This means the virtual machines can be moved around amongst physical servers with different hardware configurations without your needing to reconfigure the virtual machines themselves.

All of this combines to mean that virtualization can give you a huge amount of flexibility and responsiveness in your server infrastructure.

Chapter 1: Why Virtualize?

High Availability

In earlier releases of Microsoft Virtual Server, availability was actually a drawback and not a benefit. Many people looked at server virtualization and felt like they were putting all of their eggs in one basket. In response to this, Microsoft has invested a lot of time in developing various clustering and high availability options for R2 SP1.

The net result of this is that now Virtual Server can be used to provide higher availability for systems through the combined use of clustering technology and the ability to move to new, highly available hardware.

> *Clustering technology is covered in depth in Chapters 14 and 15.*

Virtual machines can be clustered together over a shared iSCSI infrastructure, and perform just like a cluster of physical computers. Otherwise, entire instances of Virtual Server can be clustered, and each of the virtual machines can be treated as highly available cluster objects.

With clustering support, it is now even possible to provide high availability to applications that have no native support for clustering themselves, with no need to modify the applications.

Drawbacks of Virtualization

Now that you know all the wonderful things Virtual Server 2005 can do, you probably want to know what the catch is. There are a number of drawbacks to keep in mind.

Performance

No matter how you slice it, virtualization adds a certain amount of performance overhead to the system. For the vast majority of uses this overhead is completely acceptable and is more than justified by the benefits of virtualization.

However, the performance impact of virtualization needs to be acknowledged and taken into consideration before you attempt any major virtualization project.

Defining the overall performance impact of using Virtual Server is very hard to do. Generally speaking, Virtual Server adds a negligible overhead to CPU and memory performance. It adds a more significant overhead to storage and networking performance, and it adds a very steep overhead to video performance inside of the virtual machine.

Even with this knowledge in hand it is hard to accurately predict how a specific custom configuration will perform, as there are some esoteric edge cases in virtualization that can result in excessively slow performance.

With all of this in mind, you should learn all you can about the performance characteristics of virtual machines (covered in Chapter 6), and you should make a frank assessment of the expected performance of your virtualization environment.

5

Part I: Getting Started with Virtual Servers

Finally, I recommend that you always test the performance before deploying virtualization solutions. This way, you can be sure to avoid performance pitfalls, and you may be pleasantly surprised to find out how well the system performs.

Scalability

Virtual Server itself is designed to be a scalable application, with the ability to run up to 128 virtual machines (on a 64-bit host operating system, 64 virtual machines on a 32-bit host operating system). Virtual Server can utilize multiprocessor hardware with large amounts of memory.

However, the virtual machines provided by Virtual Server have a number of limitations. All virtual machines are uniprocessor only, can support only up to 3.6GB of memory, and can run only 32-bit operating systems.

When considering virtualization you need to assess whether your virtualized workloads can run in such an environment. If you have a physical server that is already fully utilizing multiple processors, or large amounts of memory, you should most likely leave that system on physical hardware.

You may be wondering whether Virtual Server will be able to deliver the performance you require, especially given my last two points. So I would like to pause and explain that Virtual Server does provide sufficient performance and scalability for many server scenarios. I just want to make sure that you make a realistic assessment of your performance and scalability expectations.

If you had a departmental Microsoft Exchange server with several hundred users, I would have no hesitation in recommending that you run it inside of a virtual machine. If, on the other hand, that Exchange server had several thousand users, you would be better off keeping it on physical hardware that had sufficient resources to provide the performance you need.

Hardware Abstraction

Hardware abstraction is both a blessing and a curse when it comes to virtualization. It is hardware abstraction that allows for many of the benefits of virtualization (such as rapid provisioning and system flexibility). However, it also has its drawbacks.

Each Virtual Server virtual machine has the same set of fixed hardware:

❏ Intel 440BX–based motherboard (with IDE controllers, serial and parallel ports)

❏ Adaptec 7870 SCSI controller

❏ Intel 21440 network adapter

❏ S3 Trio 32/64 video adapter

If the server that you want to virtualize is not capable of running on this set of hardware, or requires access to a specific piece of hardware that is not in the preceding list, then you are simply out of luck. There is no way to add new or different hardware to a virtual machine.

Common Uses for Virtualization

In my position as a Program Manager on the Microsoft virtualization team I get to see a lot of fascinating applications of Microsoft Virtual Server. Now that you have a good understanding of the benefits and drawbacks of virtualization, here are some typical reasons that people are using virtualization.

Server Consolidation

This is very simple and straightforward. Run more servers on less hardware. Reduce the amount of new hardware that you have to buy. Reduce the amount of power and space being used by your server infrastructure.

Server consolidation is by far the leading reason for using Virtual Server, but it has many variations on its implementation. Most people invest in new, high-end server hardware and consolidate older server systems into virtual machines on the new hardware, and then retire the older hardware. But some people are able to take their existing hardware and use Virtual Server to consolidate "in place" — allowing them to reduce their physical server footprint without the need to buy any new hardware.

Server consolidation can take place in a large data center or server room where large numbers of servers are being reduced to a smaller, but still sizable, amount of servers.

Server consolidation can take place in branch office scenarios where a small number of servers that are required to support a single small office can be consolidated down to one single computer capable of providing multiple roles to local users.

Server consolidation can also be used to help centralize the management of disparate departmental servers while allowing each department to maintain control of their systems.

Development and Testing

Use of virtualization in development and testing environments is usually undertaken for the same reasons as standard server consolidation — the desire to get higher hardware utilization out of less hardware resources and to reduce operating costs. However, virtualization has a lot more to offer to development and testing environments than this.

The rapid provisioning and flexibility aspects of Virtual Server can drastically decrease the overhead associated with developing and testing software. Developers can quickly create the infrastructure necessary to develop complex server solutions. Testers can repeatedly test software inside of a virtual machine with the ability to quickly return to a clean, known state after each test.

For more complex scenarios, virtual machines can be controlled programmatically in order to allow for tests to be executed in an automated and unattended manner.

The use of virtual machines can also help developers to perform quick validation tests on clean copies of all of the operating systems that they intend to support, which enables them to detect any obvious issues before handing the software over to testing.

Part I: Getting Started with Virtual Servers

Development and test environments can cover a broad range of actual uses. In some cases Virtual Server is used by software development companies to reduce the development and test cycle with the use of automation. In other cases, Virtual Server can be used by systems administrators who need to test new programs to ensure that they integrate correctly with an existing environment.

One of my favorite uses of virtualization for development and testing is performing "dry runs" of planned system changes. In one case, a user was preparing for an Active Directory migration. He was able to recreate his production environment inside of virtual machines and attempt a dry run of the migration before doing it with the real systems. In this case, the dry run uncovered a number of issues that the user was then able to be prepared for when he finally attempted the migration. These issues had the potential to be catastrophic if they had been encountered in a high-pressure, time-constrained migration.

Server Resiliency

If you need to be able to provide a server infrastructure that can be rapidly redeployed or rebuilt in another location, virtual machines can help you to do this in a cost-effective manner. With virtual machines it is easy to perform full system backups and then restore them on potentially different hardware.

Higher resiliency to system failures can be achieved in a number of ways. Microsoft Virtual Server can be installed on top of any fault tolerant hardware that is supported by Microsoft Windows Server 2003. Alternatively Microsoft Virtual Server can be configured in a number of clustering configurations that provide high availability across a number of physical computers.

Finally, running virtual machines can be periodically backed up to remote sites and be ready for recovery in the case of an entire site failure.

Dealing with Legacy Applications

Many people have pockets of legacy servers in their company. These are small servers running custom solutions serving a small group of people. Often these are systems that are impossible to upgrade, as the software they are using does not run on the latest hardware and the company that produced the software no longer exists, or does not produce that product any more. These servers are essentially ticking time bombs. If they suffer a hardware or software failure the impact could be serious, but there seems to be little to do to mitigate this problem.

Virtual Server allows you to move these systems off of their old, potentially unreliable hardware onto newer hardware. Once the system is inside of a virtual machine it is now much easier to monitor and manage. It is also much easier to make backups of the environment in case any problems arise.

One of the biggest challenges faced when virtualizing legacy applications is how to get the system in question into a virtual machine, as quite often you will no longer have the expertise (or even media) to be able to perform a clean installation of the system and guarantee that it will continue to function as desired. Chapters 12 and 13 cover the process of migrating physical computers to virtual machines.

Virtualizing legacy applications certainly provides some short-term relief, but it is not a long-term solution. Any security concerns that may exist with the legacy operating environment are still present and unmitigated. As such, virtualization of legacy applications should be viewed as the first step in retirement of the application, and you should continue to investigate replacing or upgrading the system in question.

Chapter 1: Why Virtualize?

Training

For both personal and formal situations, virtual machines are great tools for training and learning. Typically, teaching people about a new computer technology involves extensive amounts of time and hardware.

You have to acquire enough hardware to supply isolated systems and infrastructure to provide an authentic training environment. You then have to configure the systems appropriately, and create full system backups such that if any student should happen to destroy their environment you could restore the systems to a known state.

In fact, in many training situations even if the student does not accidentally do anything wrong, by the time he has finished a training course he has irreparably changed the system configuration. This means that the maintainer of the training environment needs to rebuild the computer systems after each student. Needless to say, this can be very time consuming.

Virtualization can help on many levels in training environments. First, virtual machines can be used to drastically reduce the amount of hardware needed in order to replicate the necessary computing environment. Next, virtual machines can be used to allow for instant re-provisioning of training environments. Through the use of technologies such as undo disks and differencing disks, any changes a student makes can be instantaneously discarded when he is done, leaving a pristine environment for the next student. Best of all, this can be done in an automated fashion with no need for interaction from the lab manager.

Finally, virtual machines allow for training computers to be easily and quickly repurposed for other training courses. In most situations, a lab of computers would be configured for one specific training course, and if people were interested in other courses these computers would go unused. With virtual machines you can have all the potential courses you are interested in loaded on each computer. Students can then bring up the specific environment they need to use.

> *One interesting technique is to incorrectly configure "broken" virtual machines. It is then up to the students to diagnose the problem and fix the system. Once again, Virtual Server allows the virtual machine to be returned to its original (in this case "broken") state once the student has completed his session.*

Demonstration

When developing software or systems solutions one of the biggest challenges you can face is demonstrating the value of your solution to other people. Often a proper demonstration requires significant server infrastructure and a lot of time to configure and initialize.

This can be even more problematic when you need to demonstrate your solution outside of the development environment, and potentially need to have non-technical users demonstrating your solution.

Virtualization can help with all of this. Using Virtual Server, you can create a complete server infrastructure on a single laptop or desktop computer. You can then bundle up this environment and replicate it for other users to demonstrate with ease.

Part I: Getting Started with Virtual Servers

> Microsoft has recently announced a new program where they are allowing customers to download evaluation virtual machines that contain preconfigured Microsoft server software. Microsoft is also extending this capability to other software developers and allowing them to redistribute evaluation virtual machines that contain their software. To find out more about this program go to www.microsoft.com/vhd.

Web-Based Systems

Virtual Server is typically administrated through a web-based interface. By building a custom web interface, you create a number of interesting uses for web-based systems. Users can connect over the Internet to virtual machines, through their web browsers.

This is great for remote training, online demonstration, or centralizing computer resources for development and test environments.

The best thing about using virtual machines for web-based systems is that it is possible to configure them such that while a user connects over the Internet to interact with a virtual machine, the virtual machine itself remains isolated from the general network so there are fewer security concerns.

Conclusion

By now you should have a fair idea of why people and organizations are using virtualization, and understand the benefits and drawbacks of virtualization. With all of this now in your back pocket, the next chapter gets you familiar with Microsoft Virtual Server.

2

Getting Started with Microsoft Virtual Server 2005

Now it is time to get your first Microsoft Virtual Server 2005 system running.

The first thing to know is that Virtual Server is a hosted virtualization solution. This means that Virtual Server runs on top of another operating system and in turn provides virtual machines that additional operating systems can be installed inside of. The operating system that Virtual Server runs on top of is usually referred to as the "host" operating system, while the operating systems that run inside of the virtual machines are referred to as the "guest" operating systems.

Figure 2-1 illustrates the relationship of the operating systems to each other.

Virtual Server can be installed on top of Windows XP Professional, Windows Server 2003 (all editions except Windows Server 2003 Web Edition), Windows Vista Professional and Ultimate, and the Windows Server codenamed "Longhorn." Virtual Server can run on 32-bit and 64-bit versions of these operating systems, but it does not support running on the Itanium family of processors.

There are only a few operational differences between using either a desktop or server operating system as the host operating system (these differences will be highlighted in this book whenever they are encountered). The biggest difference is in Microsoft's support policy. Microsoft fully supports Virtual Server in all configurations when it is hosted on a server operating system. If Virtual Server is hosted on a desktop operating system, then Microsoft will support only non-production uses of Virtual Server. The primary reasoning behind this logic is that Microsoft wants developers and individual users to be able to develop and test software using Virtual Server on top of their desktop operating systems, but they do not want to have people expect to be able to run large production servers on top of desktop operating systems and receive full support.

Part I: Getting Started with Virtual Servers

The second thing to know is what the physical hardware requirements are for using Virtual Server. The minimum requirements are a 550 MHz processor and 512MB RAM, but if you use a computer like this your experience will be pretty terrible. For personal evaluation purposes, I recommend using a 1.5 GHz processor (or higher) with at least 1GB of RAM and 50GB of free hard disk space. For production uses you will want server-level systems.

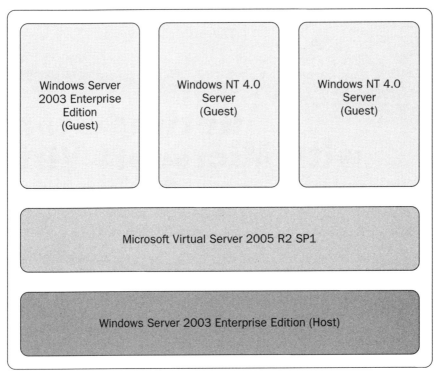

Figure 2-1

Configuring the Host Environment

Once you have installed your host operating system, there is only one prerequisite to be aware of. Virtual Server uses a web-based interface and, as such, requires an instance of IIS (Microsoft's Internet Information Server) to be present. It is possible to install and configure Virtual Server such that it utilizes a remote IIS instance to drive the web interface. This is very useful for reducing the number of IIS instances you need; however, for the purposes of this chapter we will be installing IIS on the same system that we will be using to run Virtual Server.

Configuring Virtual Server to use a remote instance of IIS to host the web interface will be discussed further in Chapter 10.

The necessary steps to install the minimum IIS configuration on each of the supported host operating systems are outlined in the following sections.

Chapter 2: Getting Started with Microsoft Virtual Server 2005

Configuring IIS on Windows Server 2003

To install IIS on a computer running Windows Server 2003 you will need to do the following:

1. From the **Start** menu, select **Control Panel** and **Add or Remove Programs**.

2. Select **Add/Remove Windows Components** from the left of the **Add or Remove Programs** dialog box.

3. From the Windows Component Wizard page, select **Application Server** and continue with the wizard.

4. While the wizard is progressing, it will require you to have your Windows Server install media. Click **Finish** when prompted.

Once the wizard has completed, IIS will be ready for Virtual Server to be installed.

Configuring IIS on Windows XP Professional

To install IIS on a computer running Windows Server XP you will need to do the following:

1. From the **Start** menu, select **Control Panel**.

2. Select **Add or Remove Programs**.

3. Select **Add/Remove Windows Components** from the left of the Add or Remove Programs dialog box.

4. From the Windows Component Wizard page, select **Internet Information Services (IIS)** and press the **Details** button.

5. Clear the **SMTP Service** check box.

6. Select **World Wide Web Service** and press the **Details** button.

7. Clear the **Printers virtual directory** and **Remote desktop web connection** check boxes.

8. Press the **OK** button twice and complete the Windows Component Wizard.

9. While the wizard is progressing, it will require you to have your Windows XP install media. Click **Finish** when prompted.

Once the wizard has completed, IIS will be ready for Virtual Server to be installed.

Configuring IIS on Windows Vista

To install IIS on a computer running Windows Vista, you will need to do the following:

1. From the **Start** menu, select **Control Panel**.

2. Select **Programs**.

3. Select **Turn Windows features on or off**.

4. Check **Internet Information Services**.

13

Part I: Getting Started with Virtual Servers

5. Expand **Internet Information Service**, expand **Web Management Tools**, expand **IIS 6 Management Compatibility**, and check **IIS Metabase and IIS 6 configuration compatibility**.

6. Expand **Internet Information Service**, and open **World Wide Web Services**. Then open **Application Development Features**, and check **CGI**.

7. Expand **Internet Information Service**, and open **World Wide Web Services**. Then open **Security**, and check **Windows Authentication**.

8. Press **OK**, and IIS will be installed.

IIS is now configured and ready for Virtual Server to be installed.

Configuring IIS on Windows Codenamed Longhorn Server

To install IIS on a computer running Windows Codenamed Longhorn Server you need to do the following:

1. From the **Start** menu, right-click **Computer** and select **Manage**.

2. Select **Add Roles** under the **Roles Summary**. This will launch the Add Roles Wizard.

3. Under **Select Server Roles**, check **Web Server (IIS)**.

4. In the **Application Development** section of **Role Services**, select **CGI**.

5. In the **Security** section of **Role Services**, select **Windows Authentication**.

6. Under **IIS 6 Management Compatibility**, select **IIS Metabase Compatibility**.

   Once the Add Roles Wizard is complete, IIS will be installed.

IIS is now configured and ready for Virtual Server to be installed.

Installing Virtual Server

You are now ready to install Virtual Server. This can be done simply by running Setup.exe. The first thing you see is a welcome dialog box with two options: install Virtual Server or view the release notes. While it is probably the last thing you want to do at this stage, I recommend that you do review the release notes as they contain last-minute updates and information about the product. Quite often, this information has to do with potential issues around installation, so it is good to know ahead of time. Once you have reviewed the release notes, you can click "Install Microsoft Virtual Server 2005 R2" to begin the installation.

The first couple of pages are fairly standard installer pages. Review the EULA and accept the terms (or decline, in which case I guess you can stop reading this book now) and enter your user and company name. Then you get to decide whether to perform a complete or custom installation. Select a complete installation for now, and you'll learn the reasons for doing a custom installation in a moment.

Chapter 2: Getting Started with Microsoft Virtual Server 2005

Website Configuration

Next you are presented with a configuration page. Here you will see a different set of options depending on whether you are installing on a desktop operating system or on a server operating system.

For desktop operating systems (Windows XP, Windows Vista) this page is purely informational. The version of IIS in these operating systems allows for only a limited set of configurations, so the installer has to set up the website on port 80. For server operating systems (Windows Server 2003, Windows Server codenamed "Longhorn") there are some decisions to be made here. The first is which port should be used by the Virtual Server administration website. The installer will default to using port 1024. The reason for doing this is that there is no way that is 100 percent reliable for the installer to know if you already have a website configured on this server or not (or if you intend to configure a separate website in the future). If you have no intention of ever using this installation of IIS for anything but Virtual Server, you may want to change the port value from 1024 to 80. This will make it easier to enter in the URL in the future, but you can also leave it at 1024 with no real harm done.

> On a normal install of IIS, a default website will be created and configured to use port 80. Because you can have only one website per port, you will need to either delete or reconfigure the default website if you want to configure Virtual Server to use port 80 for its website. (This applies to server operating systems only; on desktop operating systems the installer will handle the default website automatically.)

The other option that you will have to configure on server operating systems is whether the administration website should be configured to run as an authenticated user or as local system. Running the administration website as an authenticated user is preferable from a security perspective (and is the recommended default). You need to configure the administration website to run as a local system only for special configurations that require constrained delegation (discussed in Chapters 5 and 10).

Firewall Configuration

After this page you are asked if you want the installer to enable appropriate exceptions in the Windows firewall so that you can access al the features of Virtual Server over the network. If you leave this option checked, the installer makes an exception for vssrvc.exe (the Virtual Server service). It also makes an exception for port 135 for Remote Procedure Calls. Finally, it makes an exception for the port being used by the Virtual Server administration website, unless the website is configured to use port 80. Port 80 is the default port for normal websites, and as such Microsoft did not want to be opening this port automatically as part of the installer. If you have configured Virtual Server to use port 80 for its administration website, and you want to access it remotely from another computer, you will need to manually make an exception in the Windows firewall for port 80.

> The entire firewall configuration that I have just mentioned is specific to the Windows firewall. If you are using a third-party firewall you will need to manually configure it appropriately. If you are using an external firewall you will need to read Chapter 10 for details on how to configure it.

Once you have finished on this page, the installer begins installing Virtual Server.

If everything goes correctly you should finally be presented with the installation summary page. This is an HTML page that contains links to the installed files, documentation, and to the master status page on your Virtual Server administration website.

Part I: Getting Started with Virtual Servers

> Be aware that as part of the installation of Virtual Server, a network service is installed onto the host operating system. This causes Windows to momentarily disable and then re-enable its networking so that it can load this new service. This does not negatively affect the installation of Virtual Server, but it can be problematic if you are using other network services while you are installing Virtual Server.

Advanced Installation Options

You have just completed a fairly standard installation of Virtual Server. This section highlights some of the more advanced installation options that you may want to consider at a later time.

Custom Installation

During the installation of Virtual Server you were given the option of doing a complete or a custom installation of Virtual Server. If you select to do a custom installation you get to choose from the following components to install:

❑ **Virtual Server Service:** This component installs the Virtual Server service and all of the necessary components to run the Virtual Server service. This is the heart of Virtual Server, and the component that is responsible for allowing you to create and run virtual machines. This is also the component that causes the network to disconnect during install — so if you do not need this component you do not need to worry about network connectivity during install.

❑ **Documentation and Developer Resources:** This component contains the Virtual Server administrators guide, programmers guide, release notes, and getting started guide. It also contains a few key libraries and headers needed by developers in order to develop programs that interact with Virtual Server.

❑ **Virtual Machine Remote Control Client:** This component installs the standalone virtual machine remote control client that allows you to interact with virtual machines without needing to go through the Virtual Server administration website.

❑ **Virtual Server Web Application:** This component contains all the necessary files and configuration to set up the Virtual Server administration website on a computer running IIS.

The default installation of Virtual Server installs all four of these components. If you want to use Virtual Server in a development and test environment, where you have centralized servers and the developers access them remotely, you may wish to do a custom install on the developers' workstations where you just installed the Documentation and Developer Resources and the Virtual Machine Remote Control Client. On the other hand, if you want to set up Virtual Server to use a remote web server for its web interface, you do a custom install with all the components except the Virtual Server Web Application.

MSI-Based Installation

Some deployment methods, such as using Microsoft SMS or other automated deployment tools, require that you provide an MSI (Microsoft installer package) in order to install a product. The Virtual Server install does use an MSI file, but it is packaged inside of setup.exe by default. To extract the MSI file you will need to run the following command:

Chapter 2: Getting Started with Microsoft Virtual Server 2005

```
Setup.exe /c /t [Full path to extract .msi to]
```

For instance, if I were to run

```
Setup.exe /c /t C:\Temp
```

I would end up with a file called Virtual Server 2005 Install.msi in my C:\Temp directory.

Command Line–Based Installation

Another option for installation is to perform an unattended installation from the command line. You will want to do this if you use batch files for automated installation and configuration of your computers. If you want to perform a default installation you can simply run the following:

```
Setup.exe /v" /qn"
```

Alternatively, if you want to perform a custom installation you can use the following command:

```
Setup.exe /v" ADDLOCAL=VirtualServer,VMRCClient,DevAndDoc,VSWebApp /qn"
```

There should be no spaces in between ADDLOCAL= *and the comma-separated options; otherwise, the installation will not work correctly.*

Don't forget to remove the appropriate parameter from the ADDLOCAL section for each component that you do not wish to have installed. VirtualServer stands for Virtual Server Service, DevAndDoc stands for Documentation and Developer Resources, VMRCClient stands for Virtual Machine Remote Control Client, and VSWebApp stands for Virtual Server Web Application.

Note that all of these command line parameters can also be used with the MSI file and the msiexec command line utility.

Creating the First Virtual Machine

Now that you have installed Virtual Server, you can create your first virtual machine. To start, go to the Virtual Server administration website. You can get to this website either by clicking on the link on the installation summary page, or by selecting **Virtual Server Administration Website** from the **Microsoft Virtual Server** section in the **Start** menu.

You may be prompted to enter your user credentials, depending on the configuration of your system. To avoid getting prompted for credentials, you can either add the Virtual Server website to your trusted sites under Internet Explorer, or you can try going to http://localhost:1024/VirtualServer/VSWebApp.exe (on Windows XP or Windows Vista, go to http://localhost/VirtualServer/VSWebApp.exe) instead of using your full computer name in the Virtual Server URL.

Once you have loaded the Virtual Server administration website you should see an entry stating that no virtual machines have been defined. You can create a new virtual machine by using the navigation pane on the left side of the web page. You will need to click **Create** in the **Virtual Machines** section of the navigation pane.

17

Part I: Getting Started with Virtual Servers

> ### Running Internet Explorer as Administrator
>
> When running on a Windows Vista host operating system you may receive an error message stating that you do not have permission to access the server. If this happens you will need to run Internet Explorer "as Administrator" by right-clicking the **Internet Explorer** icon and selecting **Run as administrator**. You will then need to type in the URL displayed on the installation summary page.
>
> This happens because the Windows Vista security model does not allow Internet Explorer to identify if you are a member of the administrators group or not. To correct this you need to do the following:
>
> **1.** Grant your user account administrative privilege for Virtual Server. Select Server Properties from the Virtual Server section of the navigation pane on the Virtual Server Administrative website. Then select **Virtual Server security** ⇨ **Add entry**, and create a new entry for your user account with full control.
>
> **2.** Add the Virtual Server website to your trusted websites. Press the Alt key while running Internet Explorer, open the Tools menu, and select Internet Options. Then change to the Security tab and select the Trusted sites icon. Click on the Sites button and add the URL for your Virtual Server website to the trusted sites.

You will then be asked to define details about how the new virtual machine should be configured. Fill in the following information.

❑ **Virtual machine name:** The virtual machine name can be specified in two forms. You can specify a simple name, such as "Windows Server 2003," in which case Virtual Server creates a new folder with the name that you have just specified. It will then create a virtual machine configuration file (.vmc) in that folder with the same name. This folder is created in the defined virtual machine location as specified in the Virtual Server Server Properties. By default, this folder is called Shared Virtual Machines and is in the documents folder for the All Users user profile. Alternatively, you can specify a full path and file name for a configuration file, such as C:\VMs\WindowsVM\ Windows Server 2003.vmc. In this case, Virtual Server does not create any new folders and just creates the virtual machine configuration file exactly where you told it to.

The location where the virtual machine configuration file is stored is also used to store various temporary files associated with the virtual machine. Given that these files can get quite large, it is important to ensure that your virtual machine configuration files are created in a location that has a fair amount of free space available.

❑ **Memory:** This setting specifies how much memory the virtual machine will receive. This is defaulted to 128MB and you will be provided with some guidance as to what the recommended maximum is for memory on this computer. Chapter 6 covers the methods for determining the appropriate amount of memory to assign to a virtual machine. As this setting can be easily changed at a later point you can leave it as is, or set it slightly higher if desired (I am setting mine to 256MB).

❑ **Virtual hard disk:** Here you are given three options. You can create and attach a new virtual hard disk, use an existing virtual hard disk, or not configure any hard disk and do this later. Because this is your first virtual machine, go with creating a new virtual hard disk. By default

18

Chapter 2: Getting Started with Microsoft Virtual Server 2005

Virtual Server will create a 127GB dynamically expanding virtual hard disk and attach it to the IDE bus. The next chapter covers the different types of hard disks and compares IDE to SCSI. For now, just go with the default option here.

Virtual Server 2005 R2 SP1 creates 127GB virtual hard disks by default; earlier versions create only 16GB virtual hard disks by default.

❑ **Virtual network adapter:** Each new virtual machine is created with one virtual network adapter. At this stage, you can choose to leave this virtual network adapter disconnected, or connect it to one of the automatically created virtual networks. Once again, this setting can be easily changed later so you can just go with the default value of not connected. On the other hand, if you know that your virtual machine is going to need access to a specific network (especially during installation of the operating system) you should configure it here.

The web page also displays a note about the importance of installing Virtual Machine Additions. Chapter 3 covers Virtual Machine Additions further.

Once you have filled out all of the fields to your satisfaction, click the **Create** button. This creates the virtual machine and takes you to the virtual machine configuration page.

Starting the First Virtual Machine

Now that you are at the virtual machine configuration page you can start the virtual machine simply by clicking on the virtual machine thumbnail (the gray square in the upper-left section of the display). Alternatively, you can hover your mouse over the virtual machine name to the right of the thumbnail and a contextual menu should appear with the option to start the virtual machine. Once you have started the virtual machine, the web page will reload once or twice and the virtual machine state should change from off to running.

If, for any reason, the virtual machine should not start, you can click on the event viewer entry at the bottom of the navigation pane. This should provide you with a quick view of all errors and warnings that have happened recently.

Now that the virtual machine is running you can interact with it directly by clicking on the thumbnail again. At this stage, surprisingly, you will not see the web page that allows you to interact with the virtual machine, but another configuration page.

Virtual Server uses a protocol called the Virtual Machine Remote Control (VMRC) protocol to enable you to interact with virtual machines. However, this protocol is disabled by default. So when you try and connect to your first virtual machine you will be redirected to the VMRC properties page. Here you have to enable VMRC before you can continue (there are a myriad of other options, but those are discussed in Chapter 10). After you have enabled VMRC, you can click **OK** to continue to the virtual machine.

The first time you load this page on a computer, you need to install the VMRC ActiveX control. Internet Explorer should prompt you to do this.

Once the virtual machine remote control page has loaded, you will most likely be presented with one, or maybe two, warning dialog boxes. The first dialog box informs you that as you have not configured VMRC to use SSL (discussed in Chapter 10) any information you exchange with the virtual machine is not encrypted and could be captured and analyzed by a malicious third party.

19

Part I: Getting Started with Virtual Servers

> **It is very important to understand that if you are not using SSL you should ensure that you are operating on a private, trusted network.**

The second dialog box will be displayed only if you have connected to the virtual machine using NTLM authentication. This happens when you are working in a workgroup environment. If you are working in an Active Directory environment, VMRC should connect with Kerberos. The risk involved with using NTLM is that it is possible for a malicious third party to pretend to be the server you are talking to and to try and steal data from you. Once again, this is not a big concern if you are on a private trusted network, but it is something you should be aware of.

After all of this, you should finally see the display of your new virtual machine. At this stage, it is behaving just like a physical computer with a blank hard disk and asking for you to provide installation media for a new operating system. It should be displaying a black screen with the text "Reboot and Select proper Boot device or Insert Boot Media in selected Boot device."

Conclusion

In this chapter you have read how to prepare all the supported host operating systems for an installation of Virtual Server, how to install Virtual Server, and how to create and start your first virtual machine.

You also read about the various advanced installation options that are available, and the reasons why you would want to choose each option.

3

Virtual Server Basic Concepts

This chapter provides background information that is very useful to have when working with Virtual Server virtual machines. It primarily covers the emulated devices used by Virtual Server and drills down into each of the devices and the specific features and options available. You will also learn about Virtual Machine Additions and why you should care about it so much.

Emulated Devices

Each Virtual Server virtual machine comprises a set of predetermined emulated hardware. This means that no matter what physical hardware you are running your virtual machine on, it will always have its own set of hardware.

The hardware that is emulated by Virtual Server is as follows:

- ❏ Intel 440BX motherboard (with AMI Bios)
- ❏ Adaptec 7870 SCSI controller
- ❏ Intel 21140 network adapter
- ❏ S3 Trio 32/64 video adapter

So no matter what sort of video card your physical server has, the virtual machine will always have an S3 Trio 32/64 (even if your server has no physical video card).

Emulation of hardware is one of the areas of virtualization that adds the largest performance overhead today. Chapter 6 covers the performance best practices for the emulated devices.

Part I: Getting Started with Virtual Servers

Storage

Each virtual machine is created with two IDE controllers (a primary and secondary controller). In addition, the virtual machine can be configured to have up to four SCSI controllers. Whether your physical server is using IDE or SCSI (or some other form of storage) has no impact on how you should configure your virtual machine. There are some key differences between the capabilities of IDE and SCSI controllers under Virtual Server. Things to know about the virtual IDE controller include the following:

❑   Virtual CD/DVD drives can only be attached to IDE controllers (not SCSI controllers).

❑   The virtual IDE controllers are limited to two devices each (so four IDE devices total).

❑   The virtual IDE controllers can only support the use of drives that are up to 127GB in size.

❑   You cannot remove the virtual IDE controllers from the virtual machine.

Things to know about the virtual SCSI controller include the following:

❑   Each virtual SCSI controller can have up to seven devices attached.

❑   The virtual SCSI controller can support the use of drives that are up to 2TB in size.

❑   Virtual SCSI controllers can be configured to use a shared SCSI bus, allowing you to cluster virtual machines that are running on the same host operating system.

It's not always straightforward to decide which virtual disk controller should be used. There are definitely times when you will want to use the virtual IDE controller and times when you will want to use the virtual SCSI controller. In addition to the points just mentioned, there are performance issues to be considered when deciding which controller you should use (discussed in Chapter 6).

Virtual Hard Disks

No matter whether you are using a virtual IDE controller or a virtual SCSI controller, you will be attaching virtual hard disks to the controller. Virtual hard disks are very different things depending on whether you look at them from the host operating system's perspective, or from the guest operating system's perspective. To the host operating system, virtual hard disks are files (VHD files) and are no more special than a Word document or a text file. The VHD is just another file that some program (in this case Virtual Server) uses to store data. However, when Virtual Server opens a virtual hard disk and presents it to the guest operating system, it looks and acts like an entire separate hard disk (see Figure 3-1).

Any operation that the guest performs against its virtual hard drive is mapped by Virtual Server back to the data being stored in the VHD file. This is even true of low-level operations such as partitioning and formatting of the virtual hard drive. All changes are made to the VHD file and are completely encapsulated.

There is no way for the guest operating system to escape and accidentally affect the physical hard disks in the host computer, and the guest operating system has no dependence on the host operating system's disk configuration.

You can create a new virtual hard disk when you create a virtual machine, or you can create virtual hard disks by selecting Create under the Virtual Disks section of the navigation page. Virtual hard disks come in a number of different varieties, which are covered in the following sections.

Chapter 3: Virtual Server Basic Concepts

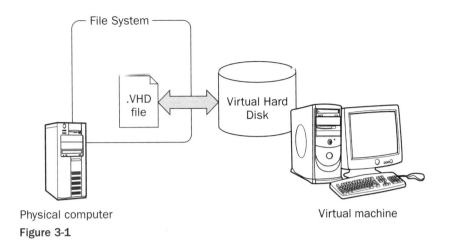

Figure 3-1

Fixed-Size Virtual Hard Disk

The term "fixed-size" virtual hard disk is a bit misleading, as all virtual hard disks have a fixed size of some sort. In Virtual Server, a fixed-size virtual hard disk is one that always uses a fixed amount of space on the host operating system. When you choose to create a fixed-size virtual hard disk, you will be asked to specify the name and location of the new virtual hard disk, as well as to specify the size of the virtual hard disk. Whatever size you specify for the virtual hard disk will also be the size of the VHD file. If you choose to create a 20GB fixed size virtual hard disk, a 20GB VHD file is created on your host operating system.

Once the fixed-sized virtual hard disk is created, nothing done inside of the virtual machine will affect the size of the VHD file. It always remains the same size as what it was when it was created.

Fixed-size virtual hard disks are used when performance is critical (as they have the best performance characteristics of any of the virtual hard disk types). Fixed-size virtual hard disks are also used when it is important to guarantee that all the hard disk space that could possibly be used by the virtual machine is reserved ahead of time.

Fixed-size virtual hard disks can be converted into dynamically expanding virtual hard disks by selecting **Inspect** in the **Virtual Disks** section of the navigation pane and selecting to convert the virtual hard disk. When you convert a fixed-size virtual hard disk to a dynamically expanding virtual hard disk the maximum size of the virtual hard disk (as seen by the guest operating system) remains the same. Fixed-size virtual hard disks are usually converted to dynamically expanding virtual hard disks in order to save space. For example, if you needed to take a production virtual machine that was using fixed-size virtual hard disks and copy it onto a development system, you would probably want to convert any fixed-size virtual hard disks to reduce the amount of space that was used on the development system.

Dynamically Expanding Virtual Hard Disk

Dynamically expanding virtual hard disks are quite different from fixed-size virtual hard disks. When you create a dynamically expanding virtual hard disk, you are asked to specify a name, location, and virtual hard disk size (just as you are with fixed-size virtual hard disks). However, with dynamically expanding virtual hard disks, the virtual hard disk size only specifies the size of the virtual hard disk as it is seen by the guest operating system.

Part I: Getting Started with Virtual Servers

If you created a 20GB virtual hard disk it would appear to be a 20GB disk to the guest operating system, but the VHD file on the host operating system would be less than a megabyte in size. As the guest operating system writes data to the virtual hard disk, the VHD on the host operating system grows in size accordingly. The VHD file will never exceed the size specified when creating the dynamically expanding virtual hard disk.

> **Dynamically expanding virtual hard disks allow you to over-commit your actual physical hard disk space. What this means is that if you had only 30GB of hard disk space available on your physical computer, you could create three 40GB dynamically expanding virtual hard disks. Each of these disks would take up less than a megabyte — and would work perfectly well. However, if the virtual machine tried to write more than 30GB of data to these three virtual hard disks, there would be a problem.**
>
> **If Virtual Server detects that a virtual machine is growing its dynamically expanding virtual hard disk and it is about to run out of space on the physical computer, the virtual machine will be paused (and an error message filed).**
>
> **If Virtual Server does not detect this, or you resume the virtual machine without making more space available, and the physical computer runs out of free space entirely, any new write requests to the virtual hard disk will fail. The guest operating system will handle and report this as it would a physical disk write failure.**

As dynamically expanding virtual hard disks need to clear out space on the physical hard disk whenever data is written to a new area of the virtual hard disk, there is a slight performance penalty involved with dynamically expanding virtual hard disks when compared to their fixed-size counterparts. One other issue that you need to be aware of is that as dynamically expanding virtual hard disks grow the size of the VHD file a little bit at a time, there is a tendency for the VHD file to get fragmented, which potentially can result in a performance loss.

Dynamically expanding virtual hard disks are the default type of virtual hard disk that is created by Virtual Server. They're very useful for development and testing environments and other scenarios in which virtual machines are not expected to fully utilize their hard disk space, and performance is not critical.

> ### Compacting a Dynamically Expanding Virtual Hard Disk
>
> While dynamically expanding virtual hard disks grow in size as data is written to them, they do not automatically shrink as data is deleted. This issue is made more complex by the fact that most operating systems do not actually delete your data when you ask them to. When you delete a file, what usually happens is that the operating system removes the information about the name and location of the file, leaving the data intact and marking the space that used to be used by the file as free. This makes a lot of sense on a physical computer, where it allows for quick deletion of files with no real drawbacks. However this does make it very hard for Virtual Server to know which data needs to be preserved and which data can be fully deleted.
>
> There are a couple of ways to compact a dynamically expanding virtual hard disk.

Chapter 3: Virtual Server Basic Concepts

The most efficient method (from a space-reduction point of view) is to create a new virtual hard disk and to copy all of the data across. For virtual hard disks that contain only data this can be as simple as just copying the files. For virtual hard disks that contain operating systems, it is usually necessary to use a disk imaging tool that will copy partition and boot record information as well.

Not all disk imaging programs are useful for compacting virtual hard disks. If an imaging program performs a 'block level' clone of the virtual hard disk, you will end up with a new virtual hard disk that is exactly the same size as your old virtual hard disk, as it will have copied all of the old "deleted" data as well. You need to use an imaging program that performs a file system–level copy. Disk imaging programs from Symantec, PowerQuest, and Microsoft all perform file system–level copies.

Another way to compact a dynamically expanding virtual hard disk is to select **Inspect** from the **Virtual Disks** area of the navigation pane, clicking **Compact virtual hard disk**, and then clicking the **Compact** button.

In order for this compaction method to be useful you need to take some steps first:

1. Defragment the virtual hard disk from inside the guest operating system. Most operating systems contain a disk defragmentation program, but not all defragmentation programs are created equal. Ideally you want a defragmentation program that not only defragments the files but defragments the free space as well. I find DisKeeper for Windows to be very effective here.

2. "Zero out" free space on the virtual hard disk. As mentioned before, old deleted data is still being stored on your virtual hard disk. You will need to run a program inside of your virtual machine to overwrite this old data with zeros so that Virtual Server can safely compact it.

3. Virtual Server ships with a virtual hard disk precompactor tool that can be used to do this on Windows-based virtual machines. To use the virtual hard disk precompactor, open the Virtual Server Administrative website, select **Configure** from the **Virtual Machines** section of the navigation pane, and select a running (and logged in) Windows virtual machine. Then go to the **CD/DVD Drive Properties** page, select the option to use a **Known image file**, and choose **Precompact.iso** from the drop-down list. Once you have pressed OK, the virtual hard disk precompactor CD image will be attached to the virtual machine and should automatically begin zeroing out the free space on the virtual hard disk. If you have disabled CD autorun, you will need to manually launch the virtual hard disk precompactor inside of the virtual machine by running precompact.exe off of the virtual machine's CD drive.

For Linux-based virtual machines, you can zero out the free space on the hard disk by running the following command as root:

```
cat /dev/zero > zero.dat ; sync ; sleep 1 ; sync ; rm zero.dat
```

This will create a file and fill it with zeros until the virtual machine runs out of space. It will then synchronize the file system and delete the file that is made of zeros.

Once you have completed these steps, compacting the virtual hard disk through Virtual Server will provide the best results possible.

Part I: Getting Started with Virtual Servers

Dynamically expanding virtual hard disks can be converted into fixed-size virtual hard disks by selecting **Inspect** under the **Virtual Disks** section of the navigation pane and selecting to convert the virtual hard disk. When you convert a dynamically expanding virtual hard disk to a fixed-size virtual hard disk, the maximum size of the virtual hard disk (as seen by the guest operating system) remains the same. As dynamically expanding virtual hard disks are the default format, you may create a virtual machine with dynamically expanding virtual hard disks and later realize that you really should have used fixed-size virtual hard disks (for performance or space guarantees).

There is no way to change the maximum size of a dynamically expanding or fixed-size virtual hard disk once it has been created. If you create a virtual hard disk and later find that you need more space, your options are to either create a new virtual hard disk and attach it to the virtual machine for use as a secondary data disk, or create a new, larger, virtual hard disk. Attach it to the virtual machine and then use a disk imaging program to transfer the data from the old virtual hard disk to the new virtual hard disk.

Linked Virtual Hard Disk

Linked virtual hard disks are virtual hard disks that point to a physical hard disk that is in your host computer. It is not possible to use a linked virtual hard disk directly with a virtual machine in Virtual Server. The purpose of the linked virtual hard disk is to enable you, once you have created one, to convert it into either a dynamically expanding virtual hard disk or a fixed-size virtual hard disk.

Converting the linked virtual hard disk will copy all of the data off of the physical hard disk into a new virtual hard disk, which you can then use inside of a virtual machine. You can do this by selecting **Inspect** under the **Virtual Disks** section of the navigation pane and selecting the option to convert the virtual hard disk to either a dynamically expanding or fixed-size virtual hard disk.

When you are converting a linked virtual hard disk, it is best to have no volumes mounted on the host operating system that belong to the physical disk that the linked disk is pointing to. The reason for this is that if the host operating system writes data to the physical hard disk while the conversion is being performed, you can end up with a corrupt virtual hard disk.

To unmount a volume on the host operating system, go to **Control Panel** ➪ **Administrative tools** ➪ **Computer Management** ➪ **Disk Management**, and right-click any volumes on the desired physical hard disk, select **Change Drive Letter and Paths**, and remove any drive letters or paths assigned to the volume.

If you are planning to convert a linked virtual hard disk to a dynamically expanding virtual hard disk you should perform the defragmentation and zeroing out steps previously. This will result in a smaller virtual hard disk being created as Virtual Server will not need to copy any old deleted data.

Differencing Virtual Hard Disk

When you create a differencing virtual hard disk, you are asked to specify an existing virtual hard disk to be used as the "parent" disk. The new differencing disk then gets created with a pointer to this parent virtual hard disk. If you then configure a virtual machine to use this differencing hard disk, it will look just like the parent disk. But any changes that are made to the differencing hard disk remain there and do not affect the parent disk.

Here's an example to demonstrate how this works.

Chapter 3: Virtual Server Basic Concepts

Say I started with a 16GB dynamically expanding virtual hard disk (called BensDisk.vhd). Then I installed Windows Server 2003 on this virtual hard disk. By this stage, BensDisk.vhd would be about 2GB in size. I then create a new differencing disk (BensDiffDisk.vhd), which uses BensDisk.vhd as its parent. To begin with, BensDiffDisk.vhd is under a megabyte in size, but if I try to boot a virtual machine off of it, it will boot into the copy of Windows Server 2003 that is installed on BensDisk.vhd. Finally I install a copy of Microsoft Office on top of BensDiffDisk.vhd and shut down the virtual machine.

After all of this I have two files. BensDisk.vhd is still 2GB in size and contains only Windows Server 2003. BensDiffDisk.vhd is now about 700MB in size and contains all the differences involved when Microsoft Office is installed on the virtual machine (see Figure 3-2). I can continue to use BensDiffDisk.vhd if I want — and access the installation of Microsoft Office that I put there — or I can delete BensDiffDisk.vhd and go back to using BensDisk.vhd, and use my virtual machine in exactly the state it was before I installed Microsoft Office.

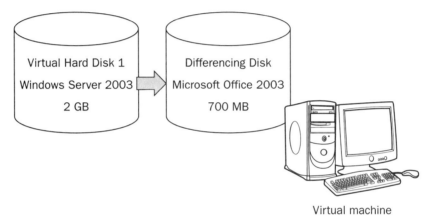

Figure 3-2

At this stage, you might be wondering why you should care about differencing virtual hard disks. Well, there are at least two really good ways to use differencing disks that you should think about.

The first way is to use differencing disks as a check pointing mechanism. If you are building a complex virtual machine and want to have the ability to roll back a change if something goes wrong, differencing disks are invaluable. This is because of the ability to create a differencing disk with another differencing disk as its parent disk. You can install an operating system, create a differencing disk, install your programs, create a differencing disk, apply any service packs or patches, create a differencing disk, and so on. By doing this, you will have the ability to return to any point in your setup process, without having to start over again from scratch.

The second way to use differencing disks is to create master virtual hard disks for all of your virtual machines. For example, if you need to have a large number of Windows Server 2003 virtual machines that all have slightly different configurations or programs installed on them, you could create a single virtual hard disk that had Windows Server 2003 installed on it (and any common programs) — this becomes your master virtual hard disk. You could then create a differencing disk for each of the virtual

Part I: Getting Started with Virtual Servers

machines (all of which had the master image as their parent virtual hard disk). This way you reduce the amount of hard disk space you need to use, as there will be only one copy of Windows for all of these virtual machines. You can also greatly speed up the process of creating any new virtual machines as you will already have the master virtual hard disk configured and ready to go.

So having explained what a differencing disk is and why you would want to use one, it is now time to go through some of the basics of using differencing disks. The first thing to know is that once you have created a differencing disk, you should never make any changes to the parent virtual hard disk. If you do make any changes to the parent virtual hard disk you will immediately invalidate any children differencing disks. The biggest cause of accidental changes to parent disks is that people forget to update any virtual machines that used to use the parent disk to now use the differencing disk.

> **Whenever you create a new differencing disk, you should check all of your virtual machines and make sure that none of them are configured to use the parent virtual hard disk. It is also advisable to go and mark the parent virtual hard disk as read-only on the host operating system. This will stop Virtual Server from making any changes to the virtual hard disk even if you did try to turn on a virtual machine that was configured to use it.**

The second thing to know about differencing disks is that if you ever want to take a differencing disk and make it into a standard dynamically expanding or fixed-size virtual hard disk, you can do so by using the **Inspect** option in the **Virtual Disks** section of the navigation pane. There you can choose whether to merge the differencing disk directly into its parent virtual hard disk, or to merge the differencing disk and the parent virtual hard disk into a new virtual hard disk. Please note that merging a differencing disk back into its parent virtual hard disk will invalidate any other differencing disks that are referring to the same parent disk as your current differencing disk.

Undo Disks

Once you understand how differencing disks work, undo disks are a very simple concept. An undo disk is a differencing disk that gets created automatically when you turn on a virtual machine. All changes that you make are written to this undo disk. When you turn off the virtual machine you have the choice of keeping the undo disks for the next time you use the virtual machine, discarding the undo disks and reverting the virtual machine to how it was before you turned it on, or committing the undo disks and saving the changes made back to the virtual machines virtual hard disks.

Undo disks can be enabled on the hard disks section of the virtual machine configuration page. The undo disk files are always created in the same location as the virtual machine configuration file (VMC).

It is not possible to enable undo disks only on a subset of virtual hard disks in a virtual machine. This setting is enabled or disabled for the entire virtual machine and for any virtual hard disks attached to it.

CD/DVD Drives

CD/DVD drives can only be attached to the virtual IDE controller, which means that you are limited to having up to four of these per virtual machine. For most situations this should be more than adequate. For each CD/DVD drive there are three possible configuration options.

❏ **No media:** This should be fairly obvious; you basically have a virtual CD/DVD drive with no media inserted.

Chapter 3: Virtual Server Basic Concepts

❑ **Physical CD/DVD drive:** This allows you to select one of the physical CD/DVD drives in the host computer that is then mapped to the virtual CD/DVD drive, allowing you to directly access any CD/DVD media that you may need to use.

❑ **Image file:** This allows you to specify an ISO image of a CD/DVD to be used in the virtual CD/DVD drive. The advantage of using an ISO image is that it is much faster than using a physical CD/DVD. However, you have to invest the time (and hard disk space) up front to create such an image.

If you regularly need to install applications or operating systems into virtual machines, creating ISO images of the CD/DVDs being used can greatly reduce the amount of time that these installations can take.

Floppy Drive

The final stop on the tour of storage inside of virtual machines is the floppy drive. Each virtual machine has one, and only one, virtual floppy drive. You can configure this floppy drive to use a physical floppy disk or to use a floppy disk image. Virtual Server allows you to create blank virtual floppy disk images by selecting Create ➪ Virtual Floppy Disk under the Virtual Disks section of the navigation pane.

If you want to create a floppy disk image from an existing physical floppy disk you will need to use an imaging tool such as WinImage (`www.winimage.com`).

Networking

Moving on from storage, it's time for networking. Virtual Server emulates an Intel 21140 network adapter and allows you to have up to four virtual network adapters per virtual machine. When you add a virtual network adapter to a virtual machine you get to configure two things: how the virtual network adapter's MAC address will be managed and what the virtual network adapter will be connected to.

The Intel 21140 network adapter was originally developed by DEC, which then sold the technology to Intel. As such, some operating systems will identify the emulated network adapter as an Intel 21140 network adapter, while other operating systems will call it a DEC 21140 network adapter or a DEC21X4 network adapter. These are all the same network adapter, just with different names depending on when the network driver for the guest operating system was written.

Configuring MAC Addresses

Virtual network adapters are connected to your physical network at OSI layer 3 and from an external point of view are indistinguishable from physical network cards. There is no way to tell from network analysis whether you have four physical computers or one physical computer with three virtual machines running on top of it.

Each virtual network adapter has its own MAC address. This is what is used to uniquely identify this virtual network card on the network. When configuring the MAC address for a virtual network adapter you have two options: static or dynamic.

Configuring a static MAC address is straightforward. Select the **Static Ethernet (MAC)** address option and type your desired MAC address into the field provided. The MAC address should be unique and should consist of six hexadecimal couplets separated by dashes, in the form of AA-BB-CC-DD-EE-FF.

When configured to use a dynamic MAC address, Virtual Server will automatically generate a MAC address that begins with 00-03-FF (this MAC address range is reserved for use by Virtual Server). It will

Part I: Getting Started with Virtual Servers

then check whenever the virtual machine is powered on to make sure that no other virtual machines on this host instance of Virtual Server are using this MAC address. If another virtual machine is using the MAC address configured for this virtual machine, Virtual Server will generate a new MAC address to use.

Using dynamic MAC addresses is definitely more convenient than using static MAC addresses, but you should look at using static MAC addresses for two reasons.

The first issue to consider is that some software programs use the MAC address of a computer's network card to uniquely identify it. This can be problematic if you are using dynamic MAC addresses, and the potential exists that Virtual Server might change the MAC address without your knowing.

The second issue is that while Virtual Server will try to ensure that each virtual machine, on a given host system, will have a unique MAC address, it does not make any guarantees of MAC address uniqueness across multiple physical servers. For this reason, you may want to use static MAC addresses in large installations of Virtual Server in order to guarantee that you have no MAC address conflicts.

Configuring Network Connections

Each virtual network adapter can be configured to be connected to a virtual network or to be disconnected. In most situations you want to connect the virtual network adapter to the virtual network that is associated with the physical network card that you want the virtual machine to communicate over.

Understanding Virtual Networks

So what are these virtual networks? The easiest way to think of a virtual network is to picture it as a virtual network switch that you connect your virtual network adapter to. For each virtual network you can configure the following options:

❑ **Virtual network name:** This is the name that will be displayed for the virtual network.

❑ **Network adapter on physical computer:** This is the physical network adapter that will be used to transmit any network traffic for the virtual network. This option may also be set to "none" if you want to create a virtual network that is used only by virtual machines with no connection to the outside world.

❑ **Connected virtual network adapters:** This is a list of all of the virtual network adapters in the various virtual machines that are connected to the virtual network.

❑ **Virtual network notes:** Here you can enter any notes that you want to associate with the virtual network. This is very useful if you need to remember specific configuration details of a virtual network, or if you need to keep a reminder as to why you created this virtual network and what you are using it for.

❑ **Virtual DHCP Server:** Virtual Server provides a lightweight virtual DHCP server that you can enable on a virtual network. The purpose of this virtual DHCP server is to allow for easy and rapid networking of virtual machines in a development or testing environment. If you need to provide IP addresses to physical computers as well, or if you need to utilize more advanced DHCP features than those provided by the virtual DHCP server, you should install a full DHCP solution (such as the DHCP server that is part of Windows Server 2003).

When you install Virtual Server, it will create a virtual network for each physical network adapter in your computer. It will also make one virtual network with no physical network adapter connected. You can edit the configuration of these virtual networks by selecting the **Configure** option from the

30

Chapter 3: Virtual Server Basic Concepts

Virtual Networks section of the navigation pane. You can create new virtual networks by selecting **Create** from the **Virtual Networks** section of the navigation pane.

If you add a new physical network adapter to your computer after installing Virtual Server, you will need to manually create a new virtual network that connects to the new physical network adapter.

How Virtual Networks Work

When you install Virtual Server, it installs a network service on each of your physical network computers, called the Virtual Machine Network Services service. This service allows Virtual Server to take Ethernet packets that are generated by the emulated network adapter and to deliver them directly to the physical network adapter. It also allows Virtual Server to receive Ethernet packets that are destined for the virtual network adapter and redirect them appropriately. All of this is done at OSI layer 3, which is below conventional protocols like TCP/IP. This means that the virtual machines have their own isolated connections to the physical network and are not affected by any software firewalls or other such programs on the host operating system. It also means that virtual machines can connect only to physical network adapters that use the 802.3 (Ethernet) standard. You cannot use 802.5 (Token Ring) or any other networking standards.

Although the easiest way to think of a virtual network is to picture it as a virtual network switch, it is actually more like a virtual network hub with a switched connection to the physical network adapter, which in turn bridges the virtual network hub to the outside world. This means if you installed a network protocol analyzer in one of the virtual machines you would be able to observe network traffic destined for any of the virtual machines connected to the same virtual network as your virtual machine, but you would not be able to observe network traffic destined for the host operating system or for any other computers on the network (see Figure 3-3).

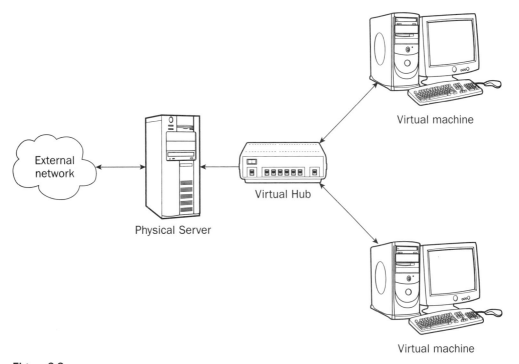

Figure 3-3

31

Part I: Getting Started with Virtual Servers

Video

Each virtual machine has an S3 Trio 32/64 video adapter. This simple 2D video card is configured with 4MB of video RAM (the emulated video card supports resolutions up to 1600×1200 at 16-bit color depth). All video display from the virtual machine is accessed over the network via a protocol called VMRC (Virtual Machine Remote Control protocol); this is true even when you are running the Virtual Server web interface on the same computer as the virtual machine.

Together, this means that graphical performance of virtual machines is not spectacular, but it should be more than sufficient for most server scenarios. The S3 Trio 32/64 is a well-supported video card, and most operating systems contain built-in drivers for it.

COM and LPT Ports

Virtual Server virtual machines always have two COM ports and one LPT port. Configuration of the LPT port is very simple. It can either be disconnected or connected to the physical LPT1 port in the host computer. For the COM ports there are a few more options:

- ❏ **None:** The virtual COM port is not connected to anything.

- ❏ **Physical computer serial port:** The virtual COM port is connected to the specified COM port on the physical server. With this option, you can also select to **Wait for modem command to open port**. When this option is checked, Virtual Server waits until the virtual COM port receives an AT0 command before it attempts to connect the virtual COM port to the physical COM port. If this option is not checked, Virtual Server attempts to connect the virtual COM port to the physical COM port when the virtual machine is started. Only one virtual COM port can be connected to a given physical COM port at a specific point in time.

- ❏ **Text file:** This connects the virtual COM port to a text file on the host operating system. There is no way to access the data in the text file from the virtual machine, but any data written to the virtual COM port from inside of the virtual machine is saved in the text file. This is very useful for logging purposes.

- ❏ **Named pipe:** You can specify a named pipe (in the form of \\physicalServerName\pipe\ namedPipeName) to connect the virtual COM port to. This can be used in two different ways. You can configure the virtual COM port to use a named pipe that is accessed by an external program, such as a kernel debugger. Alternatively, you can configure two different virtual COM ports on different virtual machines to connect to the same named pipe. In this case, the virtual COM ports behave like they had a virtual null modem cable connected between them.

BIOS

You can access the virtual machine's BIOS by pressing the DEL key while it is booting (just like you would for a physical computer). Realistically there are not many reasons why you would want to change any settings under the virtual machine's BIOS—with one exception. You can set the boot order here and specify whether the virtual machine should boot off of the floppy, hard disk, CD, or network adapter first.

Virtual Machine Additions

Virtual Machine Additions is a collection of components that you need to install inside of the guest operating system running on top of Virtual Server. Microsoft provides Virtual Machine Additions for Windows, Linux, and OS/2. Virtual Machine Additions is provided on CD image files (ISOs). Once you have installed your guest operating system you should install Virtual Machine Additions as soon as possible. Virtual Machine Additions installs optimized drivers that improve performance for the virtual machine as well as providing a number of integration features (such as integrated mouse pointer, guest operating system shutdown support, and more).

> **You may be thinking that I have my grammar all wrong in the preceding paragraph. Confusing as it is, "Virtual Machine Additions" is a singular feature name under Virtual Server. This means that the following sentence structure needs to be used: "Make sure Virtual Machine Additions is installed." In casual use, most people will write "Make sure the Virtual Machine Additions are installed" as this is easier to read and write, but it is technically incorrect.**

Advanced Performance Improvements Provided by Virtual Machine Additions

For Windows NT 4.0, Windows 2000, Windows XP, Windows Server 2003, Windows Vista, and Windows Server "Longhorn" virtual machines. Virtual Machine Additions provide an extra level of performance improvements. Typically, when a virtual machine is running, any user mode code is run directly on the physical CPU. However, kernel mode code is run inside of an emulator that runs in the host operating system user mode context. This happens because it is not safe to run arbitrary kernel mode code directly on the physical CPU as it might damage the host operating system.

When Virtual Machine Additions is loaded on the aforementioned operating systems, it examines the virtual machines kernel mode code and makes strategic changes in order to make it safe to run directly on the physical CPU. Once this is done, Virtual Server can run both the user mode and kernel mode code for the virtual machine directly on the physical CPU, greatly increasing the performance of the virtual machine.

Conclusion

You should now understand about all of the components that make up a virtual machine. Specifically, you should know the differences between fixed size, dynamically expanding, linked, and differencing virtual hard disks and why you would want to use one over the others.

You should also understand how virtual networking works inside of virtual machines.

Finally, you should have a good knowledge of the various emulated devices that are available inside the virtual machine and how they can be configured.

33

Installing Guest Operating Systems

Now it is time to install an operating system into a virtual machine. This chapter walks through the process for setting up basic Windows Server 2003 and Red Hat Enterprise Linux 4 virtual machines.

Using the Virtual Machine Remote Control Client

Up until now, you have been using the Virtual Server administrative website to interact with Virtual Server and its virtual machines. The website is useful as it provides a single interface where you can perform all necessary tasks that you need to with Virtual Server. It does, however, have some downsides.

The web interface is a bit clumsy for actually interacting with the virtual machine. Your web browser takes up a fair amount of screen space that you want to use for the virtual machine's display. The web interface is also problematic if you find yourself switching between interacting with a virtual machine and changing configuration values regularly (as you do while installing an operating system or applications) because you have to wait for web page reloads each time you switch.

This is where the virtual machine remote control client comes to the rescue. The Virtual Machine Remote Control client (VMRC client) is a standalone windows application that allows you to directly interact with a virtual machine, without the need to have a web browser open. This allows for a much nicer experience and allows you to utilize your desktop real estate more effectively. The VMRC client does not provide any method for configuring virtual machines, however, so you will still need to use the web interface to do this. The best thing to do is to use the VMRC client and web interface in tandem, using one to control the virtual machine and the other to configure it. You can quickly and easily switch between the two, and there are no reload times.

Part I: Getting Started with Virtual Servers

Installing Windows Server 2003

In order to use the virtual machine you created in Chapter 2, a couple of changes need to be made. First, reconfigure the virtual machine to use SCSI instead of IDE.

You could leave the virtual machine configured to use IDE, but there are some details about SCSI installations that I would like to highlight in this chapter.

To do this you need to:

1. Open the Virtual Server Administrative website.
2. Select **Configure** from the **Virtual Machines** section of the **Navigation** page.
3. Select **SCSI Adapters** and then select **Add SCSI Adapter** and click **OK**.
4. Return to the configuration page and select **Hard disks**.
5. Change the virtual hard disks attachment from **Primary channel (0)** on the IDE controller to **SCSI 0 ID 0** on the SCSI adapter, and then click **OK**.

The second thing you need to do is configure the Install CD for Windows Server 2003. For this you will need to select **CD/DVD** on the virtual machine configuration page. There are two options: You can install off of a physical CD-ROM and select to connect the virtual CD/DVD drive to the physical CD/DVD drive that contains your install media; or you can install off a CD image file (ISO), in which case you need to specify the full name and path of the CD image that you will be using, such as **C:\MyCDImages\WindowsServer2003.ISO**.

> I personally prefer to install operating systems off of CD image files over using physical CDs because image files tend to be faster and result in a shorter installation time.

As a web-based interface, Virtual Server does not allow you to browse for files. If you are using a CD image file you will either need to type in the full path and name of the CD image file or add the location of the CD image file to the Virtual Server search paths and use the drop-down list provided. To add a location to the Virtual Server search paths you should select Server Properties from the Virtual Server section of the navigation pane. Then you should select Search Paths and add the locations where you store your CD image files.

Now that the virtual machine is configured and ready to go you should open the VMRC client. You can launch this from the Virtual Server folder on the Start menu. The VMRC client asks you to enter the address for the virtual machine in the format **vmrc://full computer name:virtual server port/virtual machine**. However, if you left VMRC configured for the default port of 5900 you can simply enter the Virtual Server computer name here with no other formatting (or you can just put in **localhost**). This will connect to Virtual Server and show you a list of the available virtual machines. Clicking the Windows Server 2003 virtual machine will cause it to be started and connect you to it immediately.

As you do not have Virtual Machine Additions installed at this stage, Windows is using standard drivers for everything and has no idea that it is running inside of a virtual machine. One of the downsides of this is that when you click your mouse inside of the virtual machine, it will be captured by the

Chapter 4: Installing Guest Operating Systems

guest operating system. When this happens, you can move your mouse freely inside the virtual machine, but you cannot escape from the virtual machine. In order to release your mouse so you can use it on the host operating system, you will need to press the "host key." The host key is a special key on your keyboard the Virtual Server uses specifically for allowing you to release the mouse. By default, the host key is set to the right ALT key on your keyboard.

When the virtual machine starts, you should see the initial BIOS display, followed by Windows Server 2003 starting to boot off of the CD. Very early in the boot process, you will see a text screen with **Press F6 if you need to install a third-party SCSI or RAID driver** displayed. Press F6 because Virtual Server comes with an optimized SCSI driver that can be used during Windows installation. Press S to specify additional storage devices, and Windows will ask you to provide a floppy disk with the driver that you want to load on it. Go to the virtual machine configuration on the Virtual Server Administrative website and select **Floppy drive**. Open the drop-down list for known floppy disks, select **SCSI Shunt Driver.vfd**, click **OK**, and return to the VMRC client to continue with installation. You then need to press Enter to continue. Windows installation will present you with the options displayed in Figure 4-1. Select the option to load the **(Windows Server 2003) Additions Accelerated SCSI driver** and press Enter.

On most systems, using the F6 floppy driver will decrease installation time by a couple of minutes. However, on some systems, not using the F6 floppy driver can result in the installation taking hours. If you ever see unusually long times during a Windows installation under Virtual Server, ensure that you are using the F6 floppy driver.

> **The F6 floppy driver is needed only if you are installing Windows on a SCSI controller. If you are installing on IDE you can skip this step.**

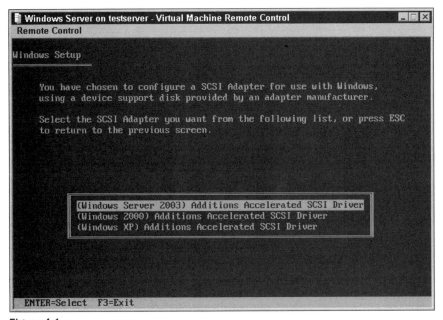

Figure 4-1

Now you can continue with the Windows installation like you would on a physical computer by accepting the end user license agreement. The next step to take is one that might give you some level of consternation if you are new to virtualization. It is time to partition your virtual hard disk (see Figure 4-2).

Remembering the information about virtual hard disks from Chapter 3, you know that the virtual hard disk appears to be an actual hard disk to the virtual machine's guest operating system, and that no changes made inside the virtual machine to the virtual hard disk can affect the physical hard disk. With this in mind it is time to partition and format your disk.

Virtual hard disks are created blank by default with no existing partitions. It is up to you how you will partition your virtual hard disk, but in this chapter you create a single partition that uses all the available space. You then need to choose how to format the virtual hard disk. I recommend that you select the "quick" format option.

Most operating systems provide the capability for a quick or a full format. Quick formats write just the necessary structures for the new partition and file system to the hard disk. Full formats go through and write new values to every sector on the disk (most of which will be written to with blank data). The primary reasons for performing a full format over a quick format are to ensure that any data that may have previously been on the computer is properly erased and cannot be recovered and to ensure that the disk is functioning correctly by writing to every sector.

Virtual hard disks will never suffer from a failure like a physical hard disk would, so you do not need to perform a full format to determine the health of the virtual hard disk.

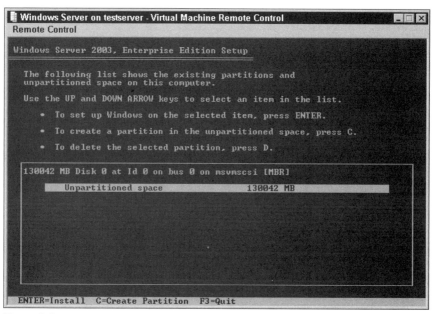

Figure 4-2

Chapter 4: Installing Guest Operating Systems

As for clearing out old data, when you create a new fixed-size virtual hard disk, Virtual Server blanks out the disk contents as part of the creation so this is already guaranteed. In the case of dynamically expanding virtual hard disks, they expand only when actual data is written to them. Any requests to write blank data to an area on a dynamically expanding virtual hard disk that is already believed to be blank will be ignored by Virtual Server.

Given this, there is no advantage to performing a full format in a new virtual hard disk, and you may as well choose the quick option to save yourself some time. Note that if you ever need to reformat an existing virtual hard disk you may want to use the full format option to delete old data, but it is probably easier just to delete the virtual hard disk in question and create a new one.

Once you have partitioned and formatted the virtual hard disk, and Windows copies across all the files, you should return to the virtual machine configuration and remove the floppy disk image from the floppy drive. When the first phase is complete, the virtual machine will reboot to continue with installation. At this stage, the virtual machine will fail to boot if you do not remove the F6 driver floppy from the virtual floppy drive — and you will need to go ahead and remove the virtual floppy disk and press any key inside the virtual machine to continue booting.

When the virtual machine boots into the second phase of the installation you will need to answer the usual installation questions about regional location, username, computer name, and Windows serial number.

> **Once you have completed installing Windows, you will also need to use the host key in order to log in to your virtual machine. Windows requires you to press Ctrl+Alt+Delete to login; however, if you press this key combination on your keyboard, it will always be sent to the host operating system. To send a Ctrl+Alt+Delete message to your virtual machine you will need to press your host key (right ALT)+Delete.**

One detour I would like to take at this stage is to look at the custom networking options (see Figure 4-3). This is the first time that you will notice the emulated hardware used by Virtual Server. No matter what sort of physical network card you have in your computer the virtual machine always has an Intel 21140-Based PCI Fast Ethernet Adapter.

From this point on you can continue to install Windows just as you would on a physical computer. Once you have completed the installation of Windows you may want to begin configuring the operating system and installing appropriate security updates and patches. But before you do that there is something even more important that needs to be done: installing Virtual Machine Additions.

39

Part I: Getting Started with Virtual Servers

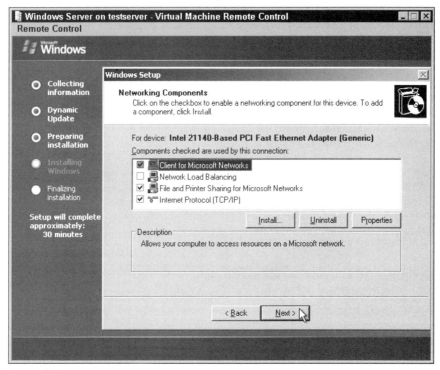

Figure 4-3

Installing Virtual Machine Additions for Windows

Installing Virtual Machine Additions on your Windows virtual machine makes it run much faster, and makes the experience of using the virtual machine much more enjoyable. For these reasons it is advisable to install them as soon as you have finished installing the operating system. In fact, without Virtual Machine Additions installed, installing security updates and patches can take significantly longer.

There are two ways to install Virtual Machine Additions. If you are using the web interface to interact with the virtual machine, there should be a link at the bottom of the web page that states **Click here to start Virtual Machine Additions startup**. If you are using the VMRC client, you will need to go to the virtual machine configuration on the web interface and select **Virtual Machine Additions**, check the check box, and click OK.

Once you have done this, you should see the Virtual Machine Additions installer start inside of the virtual machine (see Figure 4-4). Proceed through the installer (it is fairly basic) and select to reboot the virtual machine once it is complete. Now you are ready to configure Windows any way you want to, and you can install any updates and patches that need to be installed.

Chapter 4: Installing Guest Operating Systems

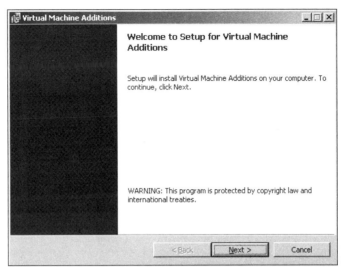

Figure 4-4

> When you select to install Virtual Machine Additions, Virtual Server actually connects a CD image that contains the Virtual Machine Additions installer to your virtual machine. As long as you are currently logged in with an administrative account, and have CD autorun enabled, the installer starts without any further interaction from you. However, if you disable CD autorun, or if you select to install Virtual Machine Additions before you log into the virtual machine, you need to manually go to the CD/DVD drive in the guest operating system and run setup.exe.

Installing Red Hat Enterprise Linux 4

The original release of Virtual Server 2005 did not officially support the use of any Linux distributions. However, with the release of Virtual Server 2005 R2, Microsoft announced support for a number of the Linux distributions that are currently provided by Red Hat and Novell. In this book, I will be using Red Hat Enterprise Linux 4, which is the most recent version of Red Hat Enterprise Linux available at the time of this writing. However, the majority of information documented is applicable to most Linux distributions.

Installing Red Hat Enterprise Linux is also fairly straightforward. You should create a new virtual machine with at least 256MB memory and a new virtual hard disk connected to the IDE controller.

> While Virtual Machine Additions for Linux does provide an accelerated SCSI driver, it is not possible to boot Linux off of a SCSI disk using this driver. For this reason, I recommend installing Linux on an IDE disk and then configuring a second SCSI disk to contain any applications you may have that have high disk performance needs.

41

Part I: Getting Started with Virtual Servers

Once you have created the virtual machine, you will need to attach your installation media (in the same way as discussed for installing Windows) and start the virtual machine. Soon you will see the Red Hat Enterprise Linux boot screen shown in Figure 4-5. Here you will need to type in **linux clock=pit** to begin the installation.

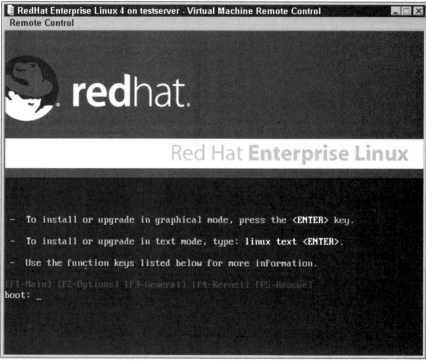

Figure 4-5

> Specifying the `clock=pit` option is required only for Linux distributions that are based off of the 2.6 revision of the Linux kernel. This version of the Linux kernel attempts to use the Time Stamp Counter (TSC) and the Programmable Interval Timer (PIT) in order to track time as reliably as possible. Unfortunately, the TSC inside of a virtual machine is not a reliable time source, and using it can result in a number of timing issues. Specifying the `clock=pit` option gets Linux to rely only on the PIT, which is relatively accurate inside of virtual machines.
>
> I discuss how to permanently enable this option later in this chapter.
>
> Linux distributions that are based on the 2.4 kernel (or earlier) do not need to have this option specified as they use the PIT by default.

Chapter 4: Installing Guest Operating Systems

After this, you can proceed with the Linux installation just as you would on a physical computer. As with the Windows virtual machine, you will need to partition and format the virtual hard disk for your Linux virtual machine. Figure 4-6 shows the options for manually partitioning the virtual hard disk. One thing to note here is that I have created a larger than normal swap partition for a computer that only has 256MB of RAM.

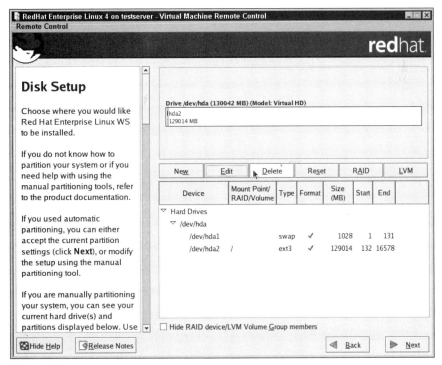

Figure 4-6

I am doing this because it is much easier to increase the amount of memory assigned to a virtual machine than it is to increase the amount of memory in a physical computer. I want to give myself enough swap space that if I decide to increase the amount of memory for this virtual machine at a later point in time, I won't need to recreate my swap partition.

Once this is done, you can proceed through the rest of the installation, selecting the options you would normally choose during an installation of Red Hat Linux.

> *If you opt to customize the packages that are installed you will need to make sure that you have both the GCC and Kernel Development packages selected.*
>
> *While this is not an issue for Red Hat Enterprise Linux 4, some Linux distributions attempt to configure the emulated video card to display a 24-bit color mode (or "millions of colors"). Virtual Server does not support 24-bit color modes so you should make certain that Linux is configured to use 16-bit color mode (or "thousands of colors"). If Linux tries to use 24-bit color mode, you will end up with a dark, corrupted display on the screen.*

43

Part I: Getting Started with Virtual Servers

Installing Virtual Machine Additions for Linux

Now that you have Red Hat Linux installed in a virtual machine you will need to install Virtual Machine Additions for Linux. Virtual Machine Additions does not provide as great a performance benefit for Linux as it does for Windows, but it still makes a big difference for usability.

The differences between Virtual Machine Additions for Windows and for Linux will be discussed further in Chapter 6.

Virtual Machine Additions for Linux is not included with Virtual Server. You will need to download Virtual Machine Additions for Linux from the Downloads section of `www.microsoft.com/windowsserversystem/virtualserver/default.mspx`. Once you have downloaded and installed Virtual Machine Additions for Linux on the host operating system, you should have a CD image file named VMAdditionsForLinux.ISO.

Boot your Red Hat Linux virtual machine and attach this CD image file to the virtual machine's CD/DVD drive. The CDROM should appear in the virtual machine at either /mnt/cdrom or /media/cdrom. Virtual Machine Additions for Linux files are stored in a directory named VMAdditionsForLinux on the CDROM. There are three possible ways to install Virtual Machine Additions for Linux.

The first and easiest way to install Virtual Machine Additions for Linux is to install the vmadd-full-0.0.1-1.i386.rpm package (as shown in Figure 4-7). You can do this by either double-clicking on this file and following the prompts, or by running `rpm -ivh vmadd-full-0.0.1-1.i386.rpm` from a command window that is running as root.

If you are using KDE as your window manager, double-clicking on the RPM will just open the Archive Manager. You will then need to browse for the RPM to install.

The second method for installing Virtual Machine Additions for Linux is to use the individual RPM packages to install the components separately. You may want to do this if you are building a single purpose Linux virtual machine and do not need to have all of the components that are normally installed with Virtual Machine Additions for Linux. The available components are as follows:

❑ **vmadd-kernel-module-0.0.1-1.i386.rpm:** This component is required by all of the other components in order to function correctly. This is the first component to install in a custom installation.

❑ **vmadd-heartbeat-0.0.1-1.i386.rpm:** This component provides Virtual Server with the ability to detect whether the virtual machine is running correctly or not.

❑ **vmadd-shutdown-0.0.1-1.i386.rpm:** This component allows Virtual Server to cleanly shut down the virtual machine through the Virtual Server web interface and through the Virtual Server COM API.

❑ **vmadd-timesync-0.0.1-1.i386.rpm:** This component ensures that the virtual machine is always synchronized to the same time as is set on the physical computer.

❑ **vmadd-x11-0.0.1-1.i386.rpm:** This component contains an accelerated video driver for Linux and a custom mouse driver that provides you with an integrated mouse pointer.

❑ **vmadd-scsi-0.0.1-1.i386.rpm:** This component installs an accelerated SCSI driver.

Chapter 4: Installing Guest Operating Systems

Each of these packages can be installed by either double-clicking on them or by running `rpm -ivh <component file name>` from a command window that is running as root. Note that for the X11 package you need to run `rpm -ivh vmadd-x11-0.0.1-1.i386.rpm --force` to install it.

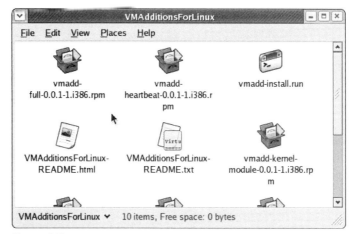

Figure 4-7

The third option is to use the vmadd-install.run shell script to install Virtual Machine Additions for Linux. You can do this by opening a command window as the root user and changing directory to Virtual Machine Additions for Linux CD. You can then run this command: `./vmadd-install.run all`.

Once Virtual Machine Additions for Linux have been installed, you can either restart the virtual machine, or you can manually start the Virtual Machine Additions services by running `/etc/init.d/vmadd start` and `/etc/init.d/vmadd-scsi start` as the root user. You can start using the new video and mouse drivers by restarting X11 if it is running.

> *If you install the accelerated SCSI driver on a virtual machine that has no SCSI disks attached, you will see two error messages during Linux boot as this driver will fail to load. These errors can be safely ignored.*

Installing Virtual Machine Additions for Linux on the 2.4 Kernel

Installing Virtual Machine Additions for Linux involves building and installing kernel modules. In order to do this, you need to have the kernel header files and GCC installed on your Linux virtual machine (the default installation of Red Hat Linux includes both of these items).

For versions of Linux based on the 2.4 kernel, some extra steps need to be taken:

1. Get to a command prompt, running as the root user.
2. Change the directory to usr/src/linux-2.4.*xx* (where *xx* is the kernel version specific to your installation).
3. Run the command `make mrproper`.
4. Copy the kernel configuration file to /usr/src/linux-2.4.*xx* using the following command:

   `cp /usr/src/linux-2.4.xx/configs/kernel-2.4.xx-i686.config /usr/src/linux-2.4.xx/.config`

Part I: Getting Started with Virtual Servers

Depending on the physical CPU you have, a different config file might need to be copied.

5. Modify /usr/src/linux-2.4.*xx*/Makefile. Change the line that reads EXTRAVERSION = -27.ELcustom so it reads EXTRAVERSION = -27.EL.

6. Run `make oldconfig && make dep` from the /usr/src/linux-2.4.xx directory.

Configuring Linux After Installation

After installing Linux in a virtual machine there are a couple of important configuration changes to make. During installation, you specified a kernel argument of `clock=pit`. In order to make sure that this argument is always applied, you will need to get to a command prompt running as the root user and edit /boot/grub/menu.lst. You should then locate the line that begins with `kernel` and add `clock=pit` to the end of this line.

/boot/grub/menu.lst is the file you need to edit if your Linux installation is using the GRUB boot loader (as is the case for Red Hat Enterprise Linux 4). For details on how to configure the LiLO boot loader, read the Microsoft knowledgebase article # 918461 (http://support.microsoft.com/?kbid=918461).

The other configuration change to make is removing the desktop background image. Red Hat Linux Enterprise 4 defaults to being configured with a very nice background image. Unfortunately, this image slows down the graphical performance of the Linux virtual machine. Changing the background to a single solid color (as shown in Figure 4-8) drastically increases the responsiveness of the Linux desktop.

Linux allows you to specify two colors for the desktop background. These colors are displayed in a gradient from one side of the desktop to the other. This is bad from a performance perspective and should be avoided inside of virtual machines.

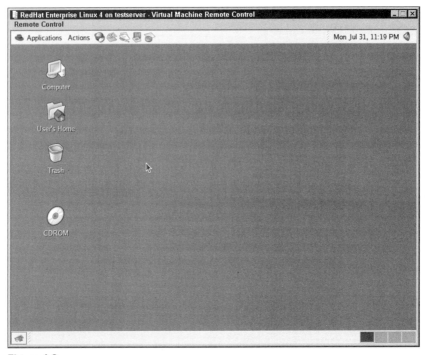

Figure 4-8

Chapter 4: Installing Guest Operating Systems

Conclusion

You now have configured two virtual machines and installed guest operating systems on them. You know how to set up Windows and Linux inside of virtual machines, and you have seen how to install Virtual Machine Additions.

By now you should have a fair understanding of how to perform the necessary basic tasks to use Virtual Server. It is time to start talking about some more advanced topics.

Part II

Optimizing Virtual Machine Management and Usage

Chapter 5: Creating a Virtual Machine Library

Chapter 6: Understanding Virtual Machine Performance

5

Creating a Virtual Machine Library

Now that you are starting to become familiar with Virtual Server, and have installed a couple of guest operating systems, it is time to talk about how to get away from installing guest operating systems ever again. The reality is that unless you are an operating system developer, installing operating systems is a necessary evil that you perform to allow you to do some other task. Virtual Server can help you reclaim the lost time and energy that you would normally spend installing and reinstalling operating systems.

This can be done through something known as a *virtual machine library*.

The concept is to create a set of base virtual machines that you use as a starting point for all new virtual machines. These base virtual machines contain the operating system, Virtual Machine Additions, and any other common tools that you want. Once you have created your base virtual machines, you will never need to install an operating system again (except if you want to add a new operating system to your set of base virtual machines).

Different Types of Libraries

There are a number of different types of virtual machine libraries — each of which has its advantages and disadvantages. The following sections detail some of the common virtual machine library strategies.

Casual Virtual Machine Library

The casual virtual machine library is what most people begin with. They create virtual machines as needed, and over time, end up with a set of virtual machines that they use for most of their tasks. Users with casual virtual machine libraries usually make heavy use of undo disks so that short-term experiments can be discarded without affecting their base images.

Part II: Optimizing Virtual Machine Management and Usage

Advantages of the casual virtual machine library are:

- ❏ Little upfront planning required; the library just grows organically.
- ❏ Easy for a single user.

Disadvantages of the casual virtual machine library are:

- ❏ Cannot scale beyond a single user.
- ❏ Difficult for long-term projects or multiple simultaneous projects that require the same virtual machine to be used.
- ❏ Base images tend to accumulate unwanted software and configuration changes, which can in turn have unpredictable effects on tasks that you try to attempt at a later date.

This type of virtual machine library is most useful for people who are using Virtual Server by themselves and have only a small range of environments and configurations they need access to.

Formal Virtual Machine Library

The formal virtual machine library is where you decide to create an official set of base virtual machines. Once created, you do not run these virtual machines again. Rather, you either copy them to create new virtual machines or you use differencing disks to base new virtual machines off of your original virtual machines.

Advantages of the formal virtual machine library are:

- ❏ New virtual machines are created rapidly with no need to install an operating system.
- ❏ New virtual machines are always in a known, clean state.
- ❏ Easy for a single user.

Disadvantages of the formal virtual machine library are:

- ❏ Difficult to scale beyond a single user
- ❏ Requires a fair amount of preparation and planning
- ❏ Requires more space than a casual library, as separate base images need to be maintained

Formal virtual machine libraries are useful for people who are working by themselves but are serious about getting the most out of Virtual Server and have a sizable number of environments and configurations that they need to have easily accessible.

Centralized Virtual Machine Library

The centralized virtual machine library takes the concept of a formal virtual machine library and pushes it a step further. Here, base virtual machines are created and then stored in a central location for access by multiple people/computers.

52

Chapter 5: Creating a Virtual Machine Library

Advantages of the centralized virtual machine library are:

- ❑ New virtual machines are created rapidly with no need to install an operating system.
- ❑ New virtual machines are always in a known, clean state.
- ❑ Easy for multiple users.
- ❑ Does not require excessive space usage on each individual computer.

Disadvantages of the centralized virtual machine library are:

- ❑ Requires a lot of upfront planning and preparation
- ❑ Requires a central server to store all base virtual machines
- ❑ Need to manage access to avoid accidental user conflicts

Centralized virtual machine libraries are most often used by small to medium groups of servers where consistent virtual machines need to be able to be rapidly deployed to any of the physical computers. There is usually a single person who is the designated owner of the virtual machine library, and he or she is responsible for ensuring that it is kept up-to-date with the appropriate base virtual machine.

Automated Virtual Machine Library

The automated virtual machine library builds on the concept of the centralized virtual machine library, but adds software automation for the creation and destruction of new virtual machines from the library of base virtual machines. Clearly this is the most complicated of all the library types and involved the most upfront work and planning. However, when implemented properly, an automated virtual machine library can reduce creation of new virtual machines, including configuration or the guest operating system, to a single mouse click. Creation of a lightweight, automated virtual machine library is discussed in Chapter 20.

Advantages of an automated virtual machine library include the following:

- ❑ New virtual machines are created rapidly with no need to install an operating system.
- ❑ New virtual machines are always in a known, clean state.
- ❑ Easy for multiple users.
- ❑ Does not require excessive space usage on each individual computer.
- ❑ Users do not need to have any knowledge of how to create virtual machines with Virtual Server.

Disadvantages of an automated virtual machine library include the following:

- ❑ Requires a lot of upfront planning and preparation
- ❑ Requires a central server to store all base virtual machines
- ❑ Requires development of custom software to manage automation
- ❑ Need to manage access to avoid accidental user conflicts

Part II: Optimizing Virtual Machine Management and Usage

Automated virtual machine libraries usually have at least one developer who is responsible for implementing them and maintaining them. These types of libraries are very effective for large-scale deployments of Virtual Server where there will be people who need to create and use virtual machines but who may not necessarily understand how to use Virtual Server itself.

With all virtual machine library strategies it is important that you understand the licensing implications for the software that you are running inside of the virtual machines and ensure that you have the appropriate licenses for your software.

Differencing Disks versus Full Copies

For any library approach you will have to make a decision as to whether you will create a new virtual machine by making an entirely separate copy of one of your base virtual machines or by creating a differencing disk that references the base virtual machine. There are a number of issues to consider when making this decision, and many times there is no clear choice as to what the best option is.

Unfortunately, copying the virtual machine and its virtual hard disk requires a large amount of space and also requires that you wait for the file to copy before you can start a new virtual machine (this is usually 5 to 10 minutes). However, with a full copy of the virtual machine there are fewer management issues because each virtual machine is completely separate and able to be managed as a single entity.

Using differencing disks allows you to create new virtual machines practically instantaneously. Differencing disks also use less space to begin with, but they soon grow to be close to the size of the parent disk. (With a standard Windows virtual machine, the differencing disk will usually match the parent disk in size within 20 boot cycles.) The problem to consider with differencing disks is that once they have been created, you need to track the dependency that they have on their parent disks. This can be particularly problematic in environments with multiple users. Remember that if anyone modifies a parent virtual hard disk, all of the differencing disks based off of it will be invalidated.

Determining What Should Be in Your Base Virtual Machines

The next decision is what should be in your virtual machines. At an absolute minimum, you want to have an operating system and Virtual Machine Additions installed on your base virtual machine. Other things to consider are service packs, security updates, and any other patches. You may also want to install applications and utilities that you need to have in all of your virtual machines. You should give special consideration to what you put in your base virtual machines. If you do not include something that you will need in all of your virtual machines, you will always have to install that specific application whenever you create a new virtual machine. On the other hand, if you include an application that you do not need all the time you will need to uninstall that application from time to time.

If you need to have multiple base virtual machines that are very similar, you can make effective use of differencing disks to reduce the amount of space that you use. A common situation for using differencing disks is to allow for the creation of multiple base virtual machines that are running the same operating system but using a different service pack level.

Chapter 5: Creating a Virtual Machine Library

You can install the operating system and Virtual Machine Additions in the first base virtual machine. You can then use differencing disks to create a second base virtual machine with the same operating system, but a specific service pack installed.

Base Image Preparation

Once you have set up a virtual machine to be a base for new virtual machines, there is a final set of work that needs to be done. As this virtual machine is going to be copied numerous times you need to ensure that there are going to be no problems as a result of this copying. For the most part the only problem that you will encounter will be network identification of the operating system and applications installed in the virtual machine.

If your virtual machines will never be connected to the network, you can probably just leave the base virtual machine as is. If, as is usually the case, you connect your virtual machines to the network, you need to ensure that each new virtual machine has a unique identity on the network and is configured appropriately for the network.

If you are working in a Windows domain–based networking environment, the other issue to be aware of is that of duplicated security identifiers (SIDs). A SID is a unique value used to identify your computer in the domain. If you manually copy a virtual machine and change its network name, you will be unable to join it to the same domain as the original virtual machine because both have the same SID. Thankfully, there are tools for generating new unique SIDs.

Windows Base Virtual Machines

Microsoft provides a tool for the specific purpose of allowing you to prepare an operating system installation to be copied to another computer. This tool is called Sysprep (which stands for "System Preparation tool"). It will ensure that the operating system has a unique network name and SID, is configured correctly for the network, and is licensed correctly. You can use Sysprep to effectively prepare your base virtual machines.

Some third-party tools provide similar functionality to Sysprep, such as NewSID. Because they are not officially supported by Microsoft, I use only Sysprep in this book.

It should be noted that Sysprep prepares Windows only. If you have other applications installed, such as Microsoft SQL Server or Microsoft Exchange Server, you need to take extra steps to prepare the virtual machine.

Only use Sysprep on a virtual machine once you are certain that you have made all the necessary changes to your virtual machine and are ready to turn it into a base virtual machine.

Using Sysprep 2.0 with Windows Server 2003 and Windows XP

Windows Server 2003 and Windows XP both use the same version of Sysprep (2.0) and as such follow a near identical process for configuration. Sysprep is available off of the Windows installation CD and is stored in the deploy.cab file under the support\tools directory on the CD. To install Sysprep you need to navigate to this file on the CD and double-click it. This shows you all of the files inside deploy.cab. Then select all of the files and copy them. You can then paste them into any standard folder on the computer.

55

Part II: Optimizing Virtual Machine Management and Usage

Generally speaking, it is recommended that you place these files in a folder named sysprep in the root of the system drive. The reason for this is that Sysprep will look in this location for its answer file. Sysprep is also designed to delete the SYSPREP folder once the process is complete to ensure that these tools are not left lying around for users to try and use.

> *An answer file is a configuration file that contains the answers to the questions that Windows asks during setup. It is used by Sysprep to store the information about how you want the computer configured.*

Once you have copied the files, you should run setupmgr.exe (Setup Manager). This tool provides an easy graphical method for creating a Sysprep answer file. When it is started, Setup Manager asks you whether you are creating a new answer file or modifying an existing one. Once you select to create a new answer file, you are then asked if you are performing an unattended setup, Sysprep setup, or Remote Installation Services setup. After this, you are asked which operating system you will be using this answer file for, and finally whether you want a fully automated setup or not.

Selecting to perform a fully automated setup means that no user interaction is needed when creating a new virtual machine. However, using the fully automated option does come with a number of compromises, as you are not able to prompt the user to provide appropriate input (such as computer name, domain to join, and so on). As such, you should weigh carefully whether you are okay with having to answer a couple of questions when creating a new virtual machine or not.

At this stage, you are be presented with a page with 15 (or 16, depending on which version of Windows you are using) categories that you can configure:

- ❑ **Name and Organization:** This option allows you to specify the name and organization to be used for this setup of Windows. You will probably want to set this to something generic. Leaving these fields blank will result in Windows prompting for this information whenever you create a new virtual machine off of this image.

  When running Sysprep under Windows XP, this category is called "Customize the Software." Under Windows Server 2003 it is called "Name and Organization."

- ❑ **Display Settings:** Here you specify what resolution and color depth should be used for this setup. I usually leave these settings at "Use Windows default."

- ❑ **Time Zone:** If you do not specify a time zone, the setup will use your current time zone — which for most cases will be completely acceptable.

- ❑ **Product Key:** Entering a product key to be used during setup is mandatory if you selected the "fully unattended" option. (Annoyingly enough, you can't move off this page without entering a product key, so make sure you have it handy.) While having the product key handled automatically is definitely convenient, you should do this only if you have a license that allows you to use the same product key on multiple installations. If you do not have such a license, you should leave this option blank and enter the appropriate product key whenever you create a new virtual machine.

  When running Sysprep under Windows XP this category is called Providing the Product Key. Under Windows Server 2003, it is called Product Key.

56

Chapter 5: Creating a Virtual Machine Library

❑ **Licensing Mode:** Licensing Mode appears only when creating an answer file for Windows Server 2003. It allows you to specify how connection access licenses will be managed (per device or per server).

❑ **Computer Name:** Here you have two options. The first option is the have an automatically generated computer name. The advantage of this option is that you can rapidly create multiple virtual machines from this base image and have each come up with a unique name on the network. The disadvantage is that you probably do not want to keep the automatically generated name for long, as they tend to be nonsensical and hard to remember. The second option is to specify a static computer name to be used after the Sysprep process. The obvious downside is that you aren't allowed to bring up multiple virtual machines at the same time, as they would have conflicting network names.

I usually opt to have an automatically generated computer name, but then change the name soon after creating a new virtual machine (either by hand or by using a script).

❑ **Administrator Password:** This category is a bit complex. Here you can either specify to have the user enter an administrator password during setup or you can specify a specific administrator password to be used. You can also specify whether the administrator password should be encrypted when it is stored in the answer file (otherwise it is stored in plain text). Finally, you can configure the virtual machine to automatically log in as administrator a set number of times after setup (which can be very useful for running any post-setup scripts).

However, there are a number of problems to be aware of when looking at this category. In order for any of the options for setting the administrator password to work, the administrator password must be blank when you run Sysprep. In addition, if you select to have the user specify the administrator password, or you select to encrypt the administrator password, the automatic log-on option will not work (although you can still select it through the configuration user interface). Conversely, if you specify the administrator password and do not encrypt it, the potential exists for another user to determine your administrator password by examining the virtual hard disk before the virtual machine is booted (the answer file that stores the administrator password is deleted after the first boot of the virtual machine).

If you have already created an administrator password on your base virtual machine, you can set it back to blank by opening a command prompt and running `net user Administrator *`. *You will be prompted to define the new password for the administrator account, and you can hit Enter twice to set it to blank.*

The option to have the user specify the administrator password will be disabled if you selected to perform a fully automated setup.

❑ **Networking Components:** Networking Components allows you to set a custom configuration for the network clients, services, and protocols on the virtual machine.

❑ **Workgroup or Domain:** Here you can specify the workgroup or domain that the virtual machine should be configured to use after setup. If you select to have the virtual machine joined to a domain as part of setup, you can either have setup prompt for domain user credentials in order to join the domain, or you can provide a set of domain user credentials so that the virtual machine is joined to the domain with no personal interaction involved.

As with the administrator password, the domain account details are stored in plain text in the answer file, and are susceptible to being read by a malicious user who looks at this file before booting the virtual machine.

57

Part II: Optimizing Virtual Machine Management and Usage

In order to join a domain during setup, you will need to have a network that supports the use of DHCP. Even if you select to have a custom network configuration with a static IP address, the first phase of setup uses DHCP, and this is when the computer will be joined to the domain.

❏ **Telephony:** This category allows you to configure the country, area, and dialing codes to be used by the virtual machine after setup.

❏ **Regional Settings:** The Regional Settings category enables you to specify the language and regional preferences to be used by the virtual machine after setup. If you are not creating a fully automated setup script, you can choose to have the user specify the regional settings during setup.

❏ **Languages:** Here you specify the language groups to be enabled in the virtual machine after setup.

This does not actually install the necessary fonts and files for these languages. If you do not have the files installed the user will be prompted for installation media when they try to use the extra languages.

❏ **Install Printers:** This category is a bit interesting; it allows you to specify a list of network printers that should be configured inside of the virtual machine as part of setup.

❏ **Run Once:** Run Once is a very powerful tool when used in combination with a fully automated setup script and the ability to have the administrator automatically log on. You specify a list of commands to be run on the first log on to the virtual machine after setup. These commands are run synchronously and are never run again after the first log on. This can be used to great effect to allow you to perform specific post-setup customizations to the virtual machine, such as installing specific programs or updates depending on the planned use of the virtual machine.

❏ **Additional Commands:** Unlike Run Once, Additional Commands allows you to specify a set of commands to be run at the end of setup, but before a user logs on. I do not tend to use this very much as the commands specified here are not run in a standard user context, and there is no chance for user interaction, which limits the flexibility of what you can do here.

❏ **Identification String (OEM Duplicator String):** The final category is actually quite useful. Here you can specify an identification string. This string will get stored in the virtual machines registry under HKLM\System\Setup. Setting this string will help you to figure out which base virtual machine was used to create a specific virtual machine at a later date.

When running Sysprep under Windows XP this category is called OEM Duplicator String. Under Windows Server 2003, it is called Identification String.

Once you have filled in all of the categories and pressed Finish you will be asked where you want to save the answer file to. You should save it to \Sysprep\sysprep.inf on your system drive.

It's annoying that once you have saved your answer file you are presented with a page labeled "Completing Setup Manager" where the correct thing to do is to hit the Cancel button. Don't worry: Your answer file has already been created, and you will not lose anything by hitting Cancel.

Looking at the Answer File

You may want to look at the contents of the Sysprep answer file that is created by Setup Manager. Here is a sample file from one of my virtual machines:

Chapter 5: Creating a Virtual Machine Library

```
;SetupMgrTag
[Unattended]
    OemSkipEula=Yes
    InstallFilesPath=C:\sysprep\i386

[GuiUnattended]
    AdminPassword="Password"
    EncryptedAdminPassword=No
    AutoLogon=Yes
    AutoLogonCount=1
    OEMSkipRegional=1
    TimeZone=4
    OemSkipWelcome=1
    OEMDuplicatorstring="My base virtual machine"

[UserData]
    ProductKey=XXXXX-XXXXX-XXXXX-XXXXX-XXXXX
    FullName="User Name"
    OrgName="Organization"
    ComputerName=*

[LicenseFilePrintData]
    AutoMode=PerServer
    AutoUsers=10

[SetupMgr]
    DistFolder=C:\sysprep\i386
    DistShare=windist

[Identification]
    JoinWorkgroup=WORKGROUP

[Networking]

    InstallDefaultComponents=Yes
```

If you look at this file, it is fairly easy to see how the information maps to the options specified in Setup Manager. There are a couple of extra options that you can add to your answer file that are not configurable via Setup Manager:

❑　KeepPageFile: Setting KeepPageFile = 0 causes Windows to delete and regenerate the page file during setup. This makes the process slightly longer, but it also means that if you create a new virtual machine with a different amount of memory than your base virtual machine, your new virtual machine will have an appropriately sized page file.

❑　ResetSourcePath: This option allows you to change the default path where Windows looks for installation files when installing optional components and drivers. I usually make a copy of the i386 directory off of the Windows installation disc on my virtual machines system drive. I then set ResetSourcePath = %SystemDrive%\i386. This way I do not have to worry about having the install media handy for reconfiguring Windows inside of future virtual machines.

Part II: Optimizing Virtual Machine Management and Usage

Running Sysprep

You are now ready to run Sysprep and finish preparing your virtual machine to be a base virtual machine. However, before you do this, I advise you to shut down and make a backup copy of your virtual machine. If, after running Sysprep, you find that you are not happy with the configuration options you chose, it is quite difficult to get back to your pre-Sysprep state without a backup of the virtual machine.

Once you have backed up your virtual machine and then booted it up again, it's time to run Sysprep. When you launch Sysprep you are presented with an introductory dialog that lets you know that this tool will modify security parameters of your system. After pressing OK you will be presented with the main Sysprep user interface (shown in Figure 5-1).

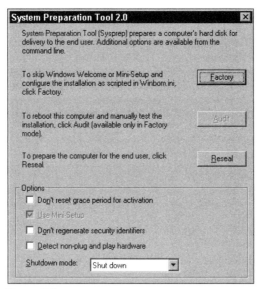

Figure 5-1

Here you will see a number of options:

- **Factory and Audit:** The Factory and Audit options are used for advanced image customization such as that performed by large hardware companies like DELL, HP, IBM, and so on. Because you do not need to do anything as advanced as this, it is best to leave these options alone.

- **Reseal:** This button kicks off the whole Sysprep process. Before you press this, make sure you have the correct options set for everything else.

- **Don't reset grace period for activation:** For installations of Windows that have already been activated, you can select this option to make it so that you do not need to reactivate the virtual machine after setup.

    If you select this option you should be very careful to ensure that you are correctly licensed to run multiple versions of Windows inside of different virtual machines.

Chapter 5: Creating a Virtual Machine Library

This option is labeled "Don't reset grace period for activation" when using the version of Sysprep that comes with Windows Server 2003. Under the Windows XP version, it is labeled "Pre-activated."

❑ **Use Mini Setup:** This option allows you to specify whether Windows XP virtual machines should use the "mini-setup" user interface or the full graphical setup user interface that is used by Windows XP normally. This option is required if you want to perform a fully automated setup. It is also disabled on Windows Server 2003 virtual machines, as you have no choice but to use the mini-setup.

This option is labeled "Use Mini-Setup" when using the version of Sysprep that comes with Windows Server 2003. Under the Windows XP version it is labeled "MiniSetup."

❑ **Don't regenerate security identifiers:** Generating new security identifiers is one of the main reasons why you want to use Sysprep in a virtual machine, so it does not make much sense to select this option.

This option is labeled "Don't regenerate security identifiers" when using the version of Sysprep that comes with Windows Server 2003. Under the Windows XP version it is labeled "NoSIDGen."

❑ **Detect non–plug and play hardware:** This option makes Windows scan for non–plug and play hardware as part of setup. Given that this makes the setup process longer, and none of the non–plug and play hardware will ever change because you are running inside of a virtual machine, you should leave this option unchecked.

This option is labeled "Detect non–plug and play hardware" when using the version of Sysprep that comes with Windows Server 2003. Under the Windows XP version, it is labeled "PnP."

❑ **Shutdown mode:** Finally you can specify whether the virtual machine should shut down, reboot or just exit Sysprep after being resealed. Choose the default, Shutdown.

This option is labeled "Shutdown mode" when using the version of Sysprep that comes with Windows Server 2003. Under the Windows XP version, it is labeled "Shutdown."

After selecting the desired options and hitting **Reseal** the virtual machine should shut down. Now your virtual machine is completely ready to be used as a base virtual machine. You can test this by making a copy of your virtual machine and starting it up to confirm that the setup process goes as you intended. The base virtual machine now needs to be protected so that it is not accidentally started (which would cause the setup process to complete and mean that you would have to run Sysprep again on your base image). You can do this by either marking the VHD file as read-only or by editing the security settings on the file to restrict who can write to it.

If you do not want to use the Sysprep user interface, you can run it from the command line with the following command:

```
Sysprep -activated -mini -quiet -reseal
```

The `-quiet` **option will stop Sysprep from confirming that you want to prepare your virtual machine. The other options map to their respective options in the user interface.**

61

Part II: Optimizing Virtual Machine Management and Usage

Using Sysprep with Windows 2000 Server

As with Windows Server 2003 and Windows XP, Sysprep is available on the Windows 2000 installation CD and is stored in the deploy.cab file under the support\tools directory on the CD. To install Sysprep, you will need to navigate to this file on the CD and double-click on it. This shows you all of the files inside deploy.cab. You should then select all of the files and select to copy them. You can then paste them into a folder named sysprep on the system drive of the virtual machine.

Unlike Windows Server 2003, Windows 2000 Server uses earlier versions of Sysprep and Setup Manager, which have their own set of quirks. The Windows 2000 Server version of Setup Manager functions like a (very long) wizard where you are presented with a sequence of questions to answer. With that in mind, it is time to dive in and start setupmgr.exe to create the Sysprep answer file.

After launching Setup Manager and clicking through the welcome page, you are asked if you want to create a new answer file or modify an existing one. Select the option to "Create an answer file that duplicates this computer's configuration." Next, specify that you are creating the answer file for a Sysprep installation, and that you are creating this for either Windows 2000 Professional or Windows 2000 Server. You are then presented with a series of questions, including a number of granular items such as the license agreement and display settings. Most of these questions are fairly self-explanatory but there are a couple of critical spots. Items to be aware of include the following:

❑ **Customize the Software:** Enter in the details for the user name and organization to be used for this base virtual machine.

With this setting it is possible to leave the user name and organization fields blank. However, this will then require that you enter these details during the virtual machine setup. As such, it is advisable to fill in these fields. (This is also true for many other options in this wizard.)

❑ **Licensing Mode:** This option is displayed only if you are creating an answer file for Windows 2000 Server. It allows you to specify how client access licenses will be managed for this base virtual machine.

❑ **Computer name:** If you enter a computer name here, all of your virtual machines that are based off of this virtual machine will have the same computer name (which is problematic from a networking perspective). You can leave this blank and be prompted during installation to enter a computer name. However, this is not an option if you are performing a fully automated installation. Ideally, you want Windows to generate a random computer name during installation. Unfortunately, the Windows 2000 version of Setup Manager does not allow you to configure this. As such, you need to enter a computer name and then fix up the answer file once you are done.

❑ **Administrator Password:** Here you can either specify an administrator password to be set during installation or choose to be prompted for an administrator password during installation (once again, you cannot choose to be prompted during installation if you opted to perform a fully automated installation). You can also enable automatic logon to enable the execution of post-installation scripts.

Unlike Windows Server 2003 and Windows XP, with Windows 2000 there is no option to encrypt the administrator password that is stored in the Sysprep answer file. This means that it is always stored in plain text — and a malicious user could get to it if he managed to manipulate the virtual hard disk offline before it is booted the first time.

Chapter 5: Creating a Virtual Machine Library

Sysprep requires that the administrator password be blank. If you have already created an administrator password on your base virtual machine, you can set it back to blank by opening a command prompt and running `net user Administrator` *. You will be prompted to define the new password for the administrator account, and you can hit Enter twice to set it to blank.*

❑ **Network Settings:** If you select to have custom settings here you will be asked how many network adapters you are planning to have, and you will be given the option to configure network clients, services, and protocols for each adapter. Selecting typical settings will result in TCP/IP being installed and configured to use DHCP, as well as installing the Client for Microsoft Networks. I usually go with the typical settings option, as this is compatible with my environment.

❑ **Workgroup or Domain:** You can specify whether the virtual machine should be part of a workgroup or a domain after installation. If you choose to make the virtual machine part of a domain you can either provide domain account credentials to automatically join the virtual machine to the domain or you can have it so you are prompted for domain credentials after installation.

As with the administrator password, the domain account details are stored in plain text in the answer file — and are susceptible to being read by a malicious user who looks at this file before booting the virtual machine.

In order to join a domain during setup, you will need to have a network that supports the use of DHCP. Even if you select to have a custom network configuration with a static IP address, the first phase of setup uses DHCP, and this is when the computer will be joined to the domain.

❑ **Sysprep Folder:** Here you will be asked if you want to create a Sysprep folder. If you copied the Sysprep files to a folder named SYSPREP on your system drive, then you already have this folder. But even if you do already have this folder, it doesn't hurt to tell the wizard to create one, so you should select "Yes, create or modify the Sysprep folder."

❑ **Additional Commands:** Additional Commands are run after installation is complete, but without requiring a user to log on. These commands are not run in a standard user context, and are relatively hard to diagnose if something goes wrong. As such I find it more convenient to use the Run Once scripts over this option.

❑ **OEM Branding:** This is not really necessary for your purposes, but if you want to get creative you can specify your own custom background and logo to be displayed during the installation phase when the virtual machine is first booting.

❑ **OEM Duplicator String:** Here you specify an identification string that will get stored in the virtual machines registry under HKLM\System\Setup. Setting this string will help you to figure out which base virtual machine was used to create a specific virtual machine at a later date.

❑ **Answer File Name:** This should be defaulted to \Sysprep\sysprep.inf on your system drive. You should accept this value, as this is where Sysprep will look for the answer file.

And now you are done with the Setup Manager Wizard. But before you run Sysprep, you need to look at the answer file and fix up a few things.

Looking at the Answer File

If you open your answer file using Notepad, it should look something like this.

```
;SetupMgrTag
[Unattended]
```

63

Part II: Optimizing Virtual Machine Management and Usage

```
    OemSkipEula=Yes
    InstallFilesPath=C:\sysprep\i386
    TargetPath=\WINNT

[GuiUnattended]
    AdminPassword=password
    AutoLogon=Yes
    AutoLogonCount=1
    OEMSkipRegional=1
    OEMDuplicatorstring="Windows 2000 Server Base VM-Professional Microsoft ⮐
Virtual Server 2005 R2"
    TimeZone=4
    OemSkipWelcome=1

[UserData]
    FullName="The User"
    OrgName="The Organization"
    ComputerName=ChangeMe

[Display]
    BitsPerPel=32
    Xresolution=800
    YResolution=600
    Vrefresh=60

[LicenseFilePrintData]
    AutoMode=PerServer
    AutoUsers=5

[TapiLocation]
    CountryCode=1
    Dialing=Tone
    AreaCode=425

[RegionalSettings]
    LanguageGroup=1

[SetupMgr]
    DistFolder=C:\sysprep\i386
    DistShare=win2000dist

[GuiRunOnce]
    Command0=c:\postinstall.cmd

[Identification]
    JoinDomain=test
    DomainAdmin=DomainUser
    DomainAdminPassword=DomainPassword

[Networking]
    InstallDefaultComponents=Yes
```

Chapter 5: Creating a Virtual Machine Library

This looks good, but it needs a couple of changes before it can be used with Sysprep:

❏ **ComputerName:** This should be changed from ComputerName=ChangeMe to ComputerName=*. This causes Sysprep to generate a random computer name each time this image is used.

❏ **ProductID:** You may have noticed that the Setup Manager did not ask you to provide a product key. If you are using Select media to build your Windows 2000 virtual machine you will not need to specify a product key. If you are using retail, MSDN, or OEM media, you need to add the line ProductID=XXXXX-XXXXX-XXXXX-XXXXX-XXXXX to the end of the [UserData] segment of the answer file.

The Windows 2000 version of Sysprep does not support the KeepPageFile *or* ResetSourcePath *options.*

Running Sysprep

Now that the answer file is in place, it's time to run Sysprep. Before you do this, shut down your virtual machine and make a backup copy so you can quickly restore your virtual machine if something isn't quite right with your Sysprep configuration.

Unlike the Windows Server 2003 and Windows XP version of Sysprep, this version of Sysprep has no configuration user interface. If you run it, it asks you to confirm that you want it to run and then shut down the virtual machine. Sysprep defaults to using the appropriate set of options for preparing a base virtual machine, so there's no need to specify any custom command-line parameters.

Now your virtual machine is completely ready to be used as a base virtual machine. Test this by making a copy of your virtual machine and starting it up to confirm that the setup process goes as you intended. The base virtual machine now needs to be protected so that it is not accidentally started (which would cause the setup process to complete and mean that you would have to run Sysprep again on your base image). You can do this by either marking the VHD file as read-only or by editing the security settings on the file to restrict who can write to it.

Using Sysprep with Windows NT Server 4.0

Windows NT 4.0 uses a very early version of Sysprep. The following steps walk you through the setup.

1. Download this version of Sysprep by searching www.microsoft.com for the file WIN_DEPLOY .EXE. (The direct link to such a search is www.microsoft.com/downloads/results.aspx? freetext=WIN_DEPLOY.exe.)

2. Once you have downloaded WIN_DEPLOY.EXE, extract it by double-clicking it.

3. After extracting WIN_DEPLOY.EXE you should change the directory to the Winnt40\English\I386 subdirectory and run Nt4prep.exe. This asks you where you want to extract Sysprep to. You should select to extract the files to a folder named Sysprep in the root of your system drive.

   When you look in this folder, notice that there is no Setup Manager. With Windows NT 4.0, you need to make your own answer file manually

   You should also be aware that it is only possible to run Sysprep on Windows NT Workstation 4.0 and Windows NT Server 4.0 (when the server is configured to be a standalone server). It is not possible to run Sysprep on an installation of Windows NT Server 4.0 when it is configured to run as a primary or backup domain controller. Nor is it possible to run Sysprep on Windows NT Server 4.0 Enterprise Edition, Terminal Edition, or BackOffice Small Business Server.

Part II: Optimizing Virtual Machine Management and Usage

Sysprep on Windows NT 4.0 is far more limited than Sysprep on Windows 2000, XP, and 2003 Server. Here is a sample answer file:

```
[NT4Preinstall]
OemSkipEula = YES
ProductID = XXX-XXXXXXX
FullName = "The User"
OrgName = "The Organization"
ComputerName = "auto"
AdminPassword = "password"
OEMNoWaitAfterGUIMode = 1
OEMSkipWelcome = 1
```

As you can see there is only one section in this answer file. The file begins with [NT4Preinstall] and then has the following entries:

❑ OemSkipEula = YES: This tells Sysprep to not ask you to accept the EULA during setup.

❑ ProductID = XXX-XXXXXXX: Here is where you enter the product key for Windows NT 4.0. Without this entry you will have to provide the product key during setup. This key can be formatted XXX-XXXXXXX or XXXXX-OEM-XXXXX-XXXXX depending on whether you used retail, select or OEM media to install Windows NT 4.0.

❑ FullName = "The User": This is the name of the user to be displayed in registration information.

❑ OrgName = "The Organization": This is the name of the organization to be displayed in registration information.

❑ ComputerName = "auto": ComputerName: This is where you specify the computer name to be used for the virtual machine after setup. Entering a value of "auto" will get Windows to generate a random computer name during setup.

❑ AdminPassword = "password": This sets the value for the administrator password after setup.

Unlike Windows Server 2003 and Windows XP, with Windows 2000 there is no option to encrypt the administrator password that is stored in the Sysprep answer file. This means that it is always stored in plain text, and a malicious user could get to it if she managed to manipulate the virtual hard disk offline before it was booted the first time.

Sysprep requires that the administrator password be blank. If you have already created an administrator password on your base virtual machine, you can set it back to blank by opening a command prompt and running net user Administrator *. *You will be prompted to define the new password for the administrator account, and you can hit Enter twice to set it to blank.*

❑ OEMNoWaitAfterGUIMode = 1 Setting: This setting tells Sysprep to reboot automatically after completing setup. Without this value, setup would stop on the last page and wait for you to hit Finish.

❑ OEMSkipWelcome = 1: OEMSkipWelcome tells Sysprep to skip the welcome page of the setup process.

66

Chapter 5: Creating a Virtual Machine Library

Other potential, but less interesting, options to put in your answer file include:

- ❏   `OEMBannerText = "Insert your string here"`: OEMBannerText is a string value that will get displayed in the background while the automated setup is running. You can specify multiple lines to be displayed by using * as a carriage return.

    Interestingly enough, this option will be ignored unless the phrase "Windows NT" is included somewhere in the string specified.

- ❏   `OEMLogoBitmapFile = "FileName.BMP"`: This is the name of a BMP file to be displayed in the upper-right corner of the display while setup is running.

- ❏   `OEMBackgroudBitmapFile = "FileName.BMP"`: OEMBackgroundBitmapFile specifies a bitmap to be used for the background graphic during setup.

    While there is a certain attraction to using these three options to customize the look and feel of the setup process, my experience has been that the setup phase completes so quickly that it is hardly worth the effort to make this visually interesting.

- ❏   `NoSidGen = YES`: Setting `NoSidGen` to yes will stop Sysprep from generating a new security identifier for the computer (which is contrary to our needs from Sysprep).

Filling in the Gaps

At this stage you have noticed that the Windows NT 4.0 Sysprep has a few notable gaps. It does not provide you with any way to enable automatic logon, to run post-setup scripts, or to join the virtual machine to a domain. In order to fill in these gaps, we are going to need to do some extra work before running Sysprep.

First, configure a script to be run the first time this virtual machine is logged into after setup. This can be done by specifying a string value in the registry under [HKLM\Software\Microsoft\Windows\Current Version\RunOnce]. Here is a sample REG file that executes the file C:\InstallScript.cmd the next time the virtual machine is started.

```
REGEDIT4

[HKEY_LOCAL_MACHINE\SOFTWARE\Microsoft\Windows\CurrentVersion\RunOnce]
"PostSysprepScript"="C:\\InstallScript.cmd"
```

REG files are plain-text files. They can be loaded into the registry by either double-clicking on them, or by running regedit /s filename.reg. All REG files need to begin with REGEDIT4.

Pay special attention to the fact that any backslashes need to be escaped with another backslash.

Once you have a script configured to run after setup, you are well on your way to being able to do everything you need to. The next half of the puzzle is to get Windows to log on automatically just once, so you can get the script to run. To enable automatic logon you need to create a string in the registry under [HKLM\Software\Microsoft\Windows NT\CurrentVersion\Winlogon] called `AutoAdminLogon` and set it to 1. Next, make string entries called `DefaultUserName` and `DefaultPassword` with values of the user name and password to be used for the automatic logon. Here is a REG file that will do just that:

```
REGEDIT4

[HKEY_LOCAL_MACHINE\SOFTWARE\Microsoft\Windows NT\CurrentVersion\Winlogon]
```

67

Part II: Optimizing Virtual Machine Management and Usage

```
"DefaultUserName"="Administrator"
"DefaultPassword"="password"
"AutoAdminLogon"="1"
```

The only problem with this is that unlike Windows 2000 and later there is no way to tell Windows NT 4.0 to log on automatically only once. In the current configuration it will automatically log on as the user you just specified forever. To remedy this, you will need to create a REG file to remove the keys and run it in the logon script that you just added by using REGEDIT -S FILENAME.REG. Here is the REG file you will need:

```
REGEDIT4

[HKEY_LOCAL_MACHINE\SOFTWARE\Microsoft\Windows NT\CurrentVersion\Winlogon]
"DefaultPassword"=-
"AutoAdminLogon"=-
```

Now that you have automatic logon and post-installation scripts working, you can handle other tasks (such as joining the domain) in your post-installation script. This means that you are ready to run Sysprep.

Running Sysprep

This version of Sysprep should be given the name of the answer file as a parameter when you start it (for example, Sysprep.exe C:\Sysprep\sysprep.inf). After starting, Sysprep asks you to provide your organization name and licensing details. The licensing details are stored in the registry of the computer for auditing purposes. As such, if you do not have this information handy you can put stub entries, but be sure you are correctly licensed for Windows NT 4.0. Once you have filled out this information, you're asked to confirm it. Then you are given one last confirmation dialog box before Sysprep shuts down Windows.

> *If you see a dialog box that states "Use of this utility with the Microsoft products detected on this system is prohibited," you will need to start Sysprep with the -defeat command-line parameter. This message will be displayed if you did not use OEM or Select media to install Windows NT 4.0. If this is the case, you should ensure that you are correctly licensed.*
>
> *Like all versions of Sysprep, this one will delete the Sysprep folder off of your system drive if it detects one.*

Now your virtual machine is completely ready to be used as a base virtual machine. You can test this by making a copy of your virtual machine and starting it up to confirm that the setup process goes as you intended. The base virtual machine now needs to be protected so it is not accidentally started (which would cause the setup process to complete and mean that you would have to run Sysprep again on your base image). You can do this by either marking the VHD file as read-only or by editing the security settings on the file to restrict who can write to it.

Using Sysprep with Windows Vista

The Sysprep process has been changed heavily with Windows Vista. For one, Sysprep is now included with the standard operating install and can be found at Windows\System32\Sysprep on the system drive. The Windows Vista version of Sysprep takes an XML-formatted answer file that you need to create with the Windows System Image Manager.

68

Chapter 5: Creating a Virtual Machine Library

Windows System Image Manager is a fairly complex tool for creating unattended installation answer files. With Windows Vista, the same answer file format is used whether you are performing an unattended installation or a network-based deployment, or using Sysprep on an existing installation. The Windows System Image Manager is included as part of the Windows Automated Installation Kit (Windows AIK), which can be downloaded from www.microsoft.com/downloads/results .aspx?freetext=Windows%20AIK.

> The Windows AIK is provided on a CD image file (.img). If you rename this file to .iso it can be attached directly to the Windows Vista virtual machine without the need to burn the data to a physical CD or DVD.

Once you have opened Windows System Image Manager you first need to select a Windows image for which you wish to build your answer file (which, technically, you don't have because you want to create a Sysprep answer file for your current installation, and you don't have a Windows image file of it yet). Thankfully you can get around this by basing your Sysprep answer file off of the Windows Vista installation image. To do this, execute the following steps:

1. Insert your Windows Vista installation media and choose **Select Windows Image** from the File menu.

2. Browse to the \Source directory on your installation media and select install.wim. When you do this, you are prompted to select the version of Windows Vista that you want to use (Home, Business, Ultimate, and so on).

3. Now that you have a Windows Image selected, you can create an answer file. To do this, go to the **File** menu and select **New Answer File**.

4. The process for adding configuration options to your new answer file is to expand the **Components** section and drag and drop the component that you want on to one of the stages listed under the **Components** section for the answer file. To create an answer file for a base virtual machine, you will need to configure the following components:

   ❏ **x86_Microsoft-Windows-PnpSysprep**: This component belongs in **3 generalize** and you need to set **PersistAllDeviceInstalls** to **true**. If you do not do this, the Sysprep will cause problems if you have Virtual Machine Additions installed. This option tells Sysprep to leave the current device driver configuration as it is.

   ❏ **x86_Microsoft-Windows-Shell-Setup**: There are a number of components to drag to different places here.

   ❏ Drag entire component to **4 Specialize**. Then set **ComputerName** to your desired computer name (or to * to have a random name generated). Also, enter your Windows product key in the **ProductKey** field, and put the appropriate data in the **RegisteredOrganization** and **RegisteredOwner** fields. Then enter an appropriate value in the **TimeZone** field. Finally, you need to delete all of the subitems under the root setup node, as you won't be using them here.

   *The **TimeZone** field takes a string for the time zone to be used; for example, I am using Pacific Standard Time. The Windows System Image Manager help documentation provides a full list of the time zones.*

   ❏ Drag **OOBE** to **7 oobeSystem**. Then set **HideEULAPage** to **true**, **NetworkLocation** to **Work** (if appropriate for your situation), **ProtectYourPC** to **3**, SkipUserOOBE to **true**, and **SkipMachineOOBE** to **true**.

69

Part II: Optimizing Virtual Machine Management and Usage

The Windows System Image Manager will display a warning about using SkipMachineOOBE, *but this is necessary to avoid any user interaction in the Sysprep process.*

❑ Drag **AdministratorPassword** from under **UserAccounts** to **7 oobeSystem**. You can then configure the Administrator password to be used after Sysprep has run.

❑ Drag **AutoLogon** to **7 oobeSystem**. Here you can configure a user account to automatically log on for a specified number of times.

❑ Drag **FirstLogonCommands** to **7 oobeSystem**. Now you will need to right-click **FirstLogonCommands** and select **Insert New SynchronousCommand** and specify the name of the command that you want to run.

❑ **x86_Microsoft-Windows-UnattendJoin**: Drag this to **4 specialize**. You can then configure your virtual machine to join a domain or a workgroup as you want.

You can configure a plethora of options on top of this, but this is the basic configuration that you need to get going. Once you have set up these options, you can save your answer file as sysprep.xml. Here is what your answer file should look like after following all of these steps:

```xml
<?xml version="1.0" encoding="utf-8"?>
<unattend xmlns="urn:schemas-microsoft-com:unattend">
    <settings pass="generalize">
        <component name="Microsoft-Windows-PnpSysprep" ⤵
processorArchitecture="x86" publicKeyToken="31bf3856ad364e35" ⤵
language="neutral" versionScope="nonSxS"
xmlns:wcm="http://schemas.microsoft.com/WMIConfig/2002/State"
xmlns:xsi="http://www.w3.org/2001/XMLSchema-instance">
            <PersistAllDeviceInstalls>true</PersistAllDeviceInstalls>
        </component>
    </settings>
    <settings pass="specialize">
        <component name="Microsoft-Windows-Shell-Setup" ⤵
processorArchitecture="x86" publicKeyToken="31bf3856ad364e35" ⤵
language="neutral" versionScope="nonSxS" ⤵
xmlns:wcm="http://schemas.microsoft.com/WMIConfig/2002/State" ⤵
xmlns:xsi="http://www.w3.org/2001/XMLSchema-instance">
            <ComputerName>*</ComputerName>
            <ProductKey>XXXXX-XXXXX-XXXXX-XXXXX-XXXXX</ProductKey>
            <TimeZone>Pacific Standard Time</TimeZone>
        </component>
        <component name="Microsoft-Windows-UnattendedJoin" ⤵
processorArchitecture="x86" publicKeyToken="31bf3856ad364e35" ⤵
language="neutral" versionScope="nonSxS" ⤵
xmlns:wcm="http://schemas.microsoft.com/WMIConfig/2002/State" ⤵
xmlns:xsi="http://www.w3.org/2001/XMLSchema-instance">
            <Identification>
                <Credentials>
                    <Domain>test</Domain>
                    <Password>Administrator</Password>
                    <Username>Password</Username>
                </Credentials>
                <JoinDomain>true</JoinDomain>
            </Identification>
        </component>
```

Chapter 5: Creating a Virtual Machine Library

```xml
        </settings>
    <settings pass="oobeSystem">
        <component name="Microsoft-Windows-Shell-Setup"
processorArchitecture="x86" publicKeyToken="31bf3856ad364e35"
language="neutral" versionScope="nonSxS"
xmlns:wcm="http://schemas.microsoft.com/WMIConfig/2002/State"
xmlns:xsi="http://www.w3.org/2001/XMLSchema-instance">
            <OOBE>
                <HideEULAPage>true</HideEULAPage>
                <NetworkLocation>Work</NetworkLocation>
                <ProtectYourPC>3</ProtectYourPC>
                <SkipUserOOBE>true</SkipUserOOBE>
                <SkipMachineOOBE>true</SkipMachineOOBE>
            </OOBE>
            <UserAccounts>
                <AdministratorPassword>

<Value>RgBvAG8AQQBkAG0AaQBuAGkAcwB0AHIAYQB0AG8AcgBQAGEAcwBzAHcAbwByAGQA</Value>
                    <PlainText>false</PlainText>
                </AdministratorPassword>
            </UserAccounts>
            <FirstLogonCommands>
                <SynchronousCommand wcm:action="add">
                    <CommandLine>C:\Windows\System32\Notepad.exe</CommandLine>
                    <Order>1</Order>
                </SynchronousCommand>
            </FirstLogonCommands>
        </component>
    </settings>
    <cpi:offlineImage cpi:source="wim:d:/sources/install.wim#Windows Vista
ULTIMATE" xmlns:cpi="urn:schemas-microsoft-com:cpi" />
</unattend>
```

Once you have you answer file (and have made a backup of your base virtual machine) you start Sysprep by running C:\Windows\System32\Sysprep\Sysprep.exe /generalize /oobe /shutdown /unattend:*Name and path of answer file*. Once the virtual machine has shut down, it is completely ready to be used as a base virtual machine. Test this by making a copy of your virtual machine and starting it up to confirm that the setup process goes as you intended. The base virtual machine now needs to be protected so that it is not accidentally started (which would cause the setup process to complete and mean that you would have to run Sysprep again on your base image). You can do this by either marking the VHD file as read-only or by editing the security settings on the file to restrict who can write to it.

Useful Post-Deployment Commands

With all versions of Windows it is possible to run a post-installation script file. You can do a number of useful things with this script file:

❑ **Join the virtual machine to a domain:** If you did not join the virtual machine to the domain as part of Sysprep you can do so in the post-installation script by using a tool called NetDom. The following command joins a virtual machine to a domain:

```
netdom join %ComputerName% /domain:[DOMAINNAME] /userd:[USERNAME]
/passwordd:[USERPASSWORD]
```

71

Part II: Optimizing Virtual Machine Management and Usage

Alternatively if you replace [USERPASSWORD] with * you are prompted to provide the password when the script runs.

❑ **Rename the virtual machine:** Once the virtual machine is joined to a domain you can also use NetDom to change the virtual machine's name via the following command:

```
netdom renamecomputer %computername% /NewName:[NEWNAME] /userd:[DOMAIN\USER]
/passwordd:*
```
NetDom can be downloaded for Windows 2000, XP, and 2003 as part of the Windows Server 2003 Resource Kit Tools (available from www.microsoft.com/downloads/results.aspx?free-text=rktools.exe).

To use NetDom with Windows NT 4.0, you will need to have the Windows NT 4.0 Resource Kit.

❑ **Add users to the local administrators group:** You can add specific users to the local administrators group by using the command net localgroup administrators /add [DomainName\ UserName].

❑ **Change the password on user accounts:** If you need to have a password changed on one of the accounts after the new virtual machine has been made you can use the net user command. You can set a new password by running net user username newPassword. Alternatively, you can prompt for a new password to be specified for a given account by running net user username *.

❑ **Run a network-based script:** One option to consider is to have your post-installation script launch another script from a known network location. This way if you find that you need to perform any customizations after making your base virtual machine, you have an easy way to do so. One great strategy is to have a network-based script that installs any hotfixes and security patches that were released after you made your base virtual machine.

❑ **Rebooting the virtual machine / logging the user out:** By running shutdown -r to reboot, or shutdown -l to log off, at the end of your script you can make sure that any configuration changes are properly applied. You can also reduce the chance that the initial automatic logon will be misused.

It is still possible for a malicious user to cancel your script and to use the first automatic logon session, so you should be careful to ensure that this is not exposed in untrusted environments.

Shutdown is not included with Windows NT 4.0 — but it is part of the Windows NT 4.0 Resource Kit.

Linux Base Virtual Machines

Unlike Windows, Linux does not have the concept of a central security identifier (SID). The amount of configuration necessary to make your Linux virtual machine unique from a network perspective depends largely on which networking packages you have installed. As there is definitely not enough space in this entire book to discuss all of the different network options available for Linux and how to configure them all, this section focuses on a generic method for handling most Linux networking packages.

A number of tools are available on the Internet that allow people to automate Linux deployment. For the purposes of creating a Linux base virtual machine most of these tools are far too heavy weight. All you need to do is to take an existing installation of Linux and programmatically change its network identity on the next boot.

72

Chapter 5: Creating a Virtual Machine Library

This task is made easier by the two facts that almost all Linux networking packages use plain-text configuration files, and that Linux provides some very powerful text parsing tools.

On a standard installation of Linux, configured to act as a standalone workstation, the primary network identifier is the host name. (As mentioned, with other network packages installed there would be other values that needed to be changed.) Under Red Hat Enterprise Linux 4, the host name is stored in two files: /etc/hosts and /etc/sysconfig/network.

Different versions of Linux store the host name in different files. If you are unsure, a quick Web search on changing the host name for the specific version of Linux that you are using should quickly let you know which files need to be changed.

So you need to create a shell script to edit these two files. You should create this file as /root/change HostName.sh:

```
#Backup configuration files
cp /etc/hosts /etc/hosts.old
cp /etc/sysconfig/network /etc/sysconfig/network.old

#Generate new random hostname
newHostName="newHostName-"$RANDOM

#Use sed to parse backup files and create new files with the new values
sed 's/oldHostName/'$newHostName'/g' /etc/hosts.old > /etc/hosts
sed 's/oldHostName/'$newHostName'/g' /etc/sysconfig/network.old >
/etc/sysconfig/network

#Delete backup files
rm /etc/hosts.old
rm /etc/sysconfig/network.old

#Rename script and reboot virtual machine
mv /root/changeHostName.sh /root/changeHostName.old
/sbin/shutdown -r now
```

As you can see, this script backs up the configuration files, generates a new random host name, substitutes the new host name for the old host name, and then deletes the backups. Finally, the script changes its file name (so it won't run again) and reboots the system. After creating this file, you need to make it executable by running `chmod +x /root/changeHostname.sh`.

You also need to manually edit your existing configuration files to set the current host name to `oldHostName` so that this text can be replaced by the script.

It would be nice to do this without resetting the system. However, at the stage that Linux initializes its host name, the file system is mounted read-only. This means that the only way to change this value without rebooting the virtual machine is to edit the file offline.

> **In order to create a file in /root you will need to be logged in as the root user (either directly or via su).**

Part II: Optimizing Virtual Machine Management and Usage

To have this script run on the next boot, add the following text to your /etc/rc.local file.

```
if [ -f /root/changeHostName.sh ]; then
    . /root/changeHostName.sh
fi
```

This causes Linux to run the script before the first user logon, unless the file no longer exists.

Once you have made these changes, your virtual machine is completely ready to be used as a base virtual machine. You can test this by making a copy of your virtual machine and starting it up to confirm that the setup process goes as you intended. The base virtual machine now needs to be protected so that it is not accidentally started (which would cause the setup process to complete and mean that you would have to run Sysprep again on your base image). You can do this by either marking the VHD file as read-only or by editing the security settings on the file to restrict who can write to it.

This method can be easily modified to allow for the modification of other configuration files if needed.

Storing Virtual Hard Disks on the Network

Now that you have all of these base virtual machines ready to be used to create new virtual machines, you probably want to store them in a central network location. There is one big issue to be aware of before you do this — and that is the "three machine problem."

To understand this, you need to really understand how Virtual Server security works. Under Virtual Server, each virtual machine runs as a separate thread. The thread runs in the user context of the person who started the virtual machine. This user context is in turn used by the virtual machine to be able to access resources on the host computer, such as the virtual hard disk. (For what it is worth, this is called "impersonation.") Now, when you have only one computer involved (for example, you are running Virtual Server and the Web interface on the same computer as the virtual hard disks are stored on) or when you have two computers involved (for example, you have Virtual Server and the virtual hard disks on one computer and are accessing the Web interface on a second computer) everything works just fine. However once you get three computers involved you hit a problem. There are two common configurations where you have three computers involved:

❑ You could have Internet Explorer running on your first computer, accessing Virtual Server on your second computer, which is in turn accessing network-based VHD files on the third computer.

❑ You could have Internet Explorer running on your first computer, accessing the Web interface, which is running on a second computer, which is in turn talking to Virtual Server on a third computer.

It is also possible to have a four-computer setup, but it has exactly the same configuration requirements as a three-computer setup.

The problem is that once you have three (or more) computers involved, the first computer can use your user credentials to talk to the second computer, but the second computer cannot then use those same credentials to talk to the third computer. When you encounter this sort of environment you usually see a generic "access denied" error message when trying to configure or start a virtual machine.

74

Chapter 5: Creating a Virtual Machine Library

In order to get this configuration to work, you need to set up a configuration known as *constrained delegation*. This is an option under Windows that allows the second computer to reuse the user credentials provided from the first computer. In order to enable constrained delegation you must be running in a Microsoft Windows Server 2003 native domain, and you must be running Virtual Server on Windows Server 2003. (It is not possible to enable constrained delegation on a computer that is running Windows XP.)

You can check the functional level of your domain by opening the Active Directory Domains and Trusts item of the Administrative tools on your domain controller. You should then select your domain and select Raise Domain Functional Level from the Action menu. If your current level is Windows 2000 mixed or Windows 2000 native you need to select Windows Server 2003 and press Raise.

> *If you have any Windows NT Server 4.0 or Windows 2000 Server instances in your domain, do not raise the functional level. This stops these older servers from being able to participate in the domain. Furthermore this action cannot be reversed.*

Once you have done this, follow these steps:

1. Open **Active Directory Users and Computers** from the **Administrative tools** on your domain controller.
2. Select the **Computers** node under your domain.
3. Select the computer that is running Virtual Server, right-click it, and select **Properties**.
4. Select the **Delegation** tab.
5. Select **Trust this computer for delegation to specified services only** and **Use any authentication protocol**.
6. Click **Add**.
7. Click **Users or Computers**.
8. Enter the name of the server that is storing the virtual machine files and click **OK**.
9. Select **cifs** from the **Service Type** column and click **OK** twice.

Your Virtual Server is now configured for constrained delegation and will be able to access virtual hard disk and virtual machine files on the remote file server without any problems. You need to repeat the preceding steps for any extra instances of Virtual Server, or for any extra file servers, that you may have.

> *A slightly different configuration for constrained delegation is required if you are running the Virtual Server Web Application on a separate computer to the Virtual Server service. This configuration is discussed in Chapter 10.*

Conclusion

Creating a functional virtual machine library can greatly increase your productivity while using Virtual Server, as you will be able to create new virtual machines much more rapidly and ensure that they are always created in the same fashion.

75

Part II: Optimizing Virtual Machine Management and Usage

In this chapter you have learned about the concept of a virtual machine library and read about the different types of virtual machine libraries that can be used.

You have seen the advantages and disadvantages of using differencing disks or full virtual hard disk copies.

You have also learned how to create base virtual machines that can be used to rapidly create new virtual machines. This can be done by using the various versions of Sysprep for Windows, or by using custom shell scripts for Linux.

Finally, you have learned how to configure Windows to allow Virtual Server access to virtual machine files that are stored on a remote file server.

6

Understanding Virtual Machine Performance

Virtual machine performance optimization is a relatively complex topic, and many people struggle with it. This chapter steps through each of the areas involved and explains the performance issues and implications to consider. By the end of this chapter, you should understand all the factors that determine how a virtual machine performs.

32-Bit versus 64-Bit Host Operating Systems

Virtual Server 2005 R2 added the ability to run Virtual Server on a 64-bit host operating system. But what does this mean from a performance perspective?

While Virtual Server runs as a native 64-bit application when you are using a 64-bit host operating system, it still provides only 32-bit virtual machines. Having a 64-bit host operating system does not generally affect the performance of CPU operations inside the virtual machine, or the performance of the emulated hardware devices inside the virtual machine. Where a 64-bit host operating system makes the most difference is in memory performance and scalability.

Whenever Virtual Server turns on a virtual machine it needs to allocate kernel memory in order to back the various emulated devices inside the virtual machine. This means that the amount of kernel memory required to start a virtual machine varies greatly depending on the number of devices you have configured inside the virtual machine. On a 32-bit host operating system, 2GB of virtual address space is available for managing kernel memory. A portion of kernel memory space will be

Part II: Optimizing Virtual Machine Management and Usage

used by any device drivers that are loaded on the host operating system. All of this means that while Virtual Server supports up to 64 virtual machines running at the same time, it is not always possible to do this on a 32-bit host operating system because the kernel memory has been exhausted.

Windows supports the use of a boot parameter called /3GB. 32-bit operating systems have 4GB of addressable memory, which Windows usually divides into 2GB user mode memory and 2GB kernel mode memory. The /3GB option causes Windows to assign 3GB of memory to user memory and only 1GB of logical memory to kernel memory. Given that Virtual Server has a tendency to exhaust kernel memory, enabling /3GB will significantly reduce the number of virtual machines that can be running at the same time.

A 64-bit host operating system has 2TB of virtual address space. Windows assigns 1TB of this memory space to be used for kernel memory, which means that it is practically impossible for Virtual Server to exhaust the kernel memory. In fact, with Virtual Server 2005 R2 SP1, Microsoft has raised the maximum number of virtual machines that can be run at the same time from 64 to 128, but only for 64-bit host operating systems.

With this increase in kernel memory space, Virtual Server is able to use a much simpler memory management method. On 32-bit host operating systems Virtual Server constantly scans kernel memory that it has allocated to see if it can free any of it up for use by other virtual machines. On 64-bit operating systems, Virtual Server just statically allocates kernel memory and frees it when the virtual machine is turned off. This results in a minor improvement in memory performance on 64-bit host operating systems.

As you can see, a 64-bit host operating system does not offer huge advantages over a 32-bit host operating system, but if your computer is capable of running a 64-bit host operating system there are no downsides to doing so.

Hardware Virtualization

Both AMD and Intel have recently released CPUs with support for hardware virtualization. Virtual Server 2005 R2 SP1 was the first release of Virtual Server to support the use of this new hardware virtualization technology. In order to understand what this means for virtual machine performance you need to know a few key things. First, in its first iteration, the hardware virtualization support from AMD and Intel is focused on processor virtualization. This means that while it helps with the problem of CPU virtualization, it makes no difference for the performance of the emulated devices inside the virtual machine.

The second thing to know is how Virtual Server manages the virtual machine's CPU when hardware virtualization support is not present. When you install Virtual Server, a driver called vmm.sys is installed on your host operating system. This is the virtual machine monitor driver. It runs at kernel mode (also known as ring 0) on the processor. Virtual Server in turn runs as a user mode service on top of Windows.

As a multitasking operating system, Windows is responsible for scheduling the execution of all currently running processes. It does this by letting each process run, one at a time, for a very small period of time (this is known as *time slicing*). When Virtual Server receives its time slice from Windows, it makes a determination as to whether any of the currently running virtual machines have CPU operations that

Chapter 6: Understanding Virtual Machine Performance

need to be performed. If one does, Virtual Server will call into the virtual machine monitor driver and perform a *context switch*. Performing a context switch involves backing off the host operating system state that is on the physical CPU and applying the virtual machines state to the physical CPU. Once the virtual machine is running on the CPU, the virtual machine monitor watches for any attempts by the virtual machine to perform operations that are not supported (such as accessing hardware). If it detects such an attempt from the virtual machine it returns the CPU context back to that of the host operating system and lets the Virtual Server service decide what to do.

By default, the virtual machine monitor only allows a virtual machine to run user mode code (also known as *ring 3 code*). Any attempts to talk to the virtual machine's hardware are handled by the Virtual Server service. And any kernel mode code is run inside of a binary translator inside of the Virtual Server service (see Figure 6-1).

For Windows NT, Windows 2000, Windows XP, Windows Server 2003, and Windows Vista virtual machines there is a second mode of operation. Once Virtual Machine Additions has been installed in the virtual machine, there is a kernel mode driver in the virtual machine that makes strategic changes to the guest operating system's kernel. Once these changes have been made, the virtual machine monitor will allow the virtual machine to run kernel mode code, but it does so at ring 1 (ring 0, or kernel mode, is reserved for the virtual machine monitor), as shown in Figure 6-2.

When Virtual Server is running on a system with hardware virtualization support, it is able to utilize a new mode of execution that is more privileged than kernel mode. By running the virtual machine monitor in this new mode it is possible to allow all virtual machines to run user mode and kernel mode code directly on the processor at all times (without the need to have Virtual Machine Additions installed).

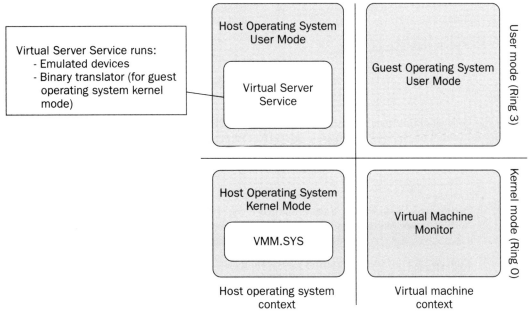

Figure 6-1

Part II: Optimizing Virtual Machine Management and Usage

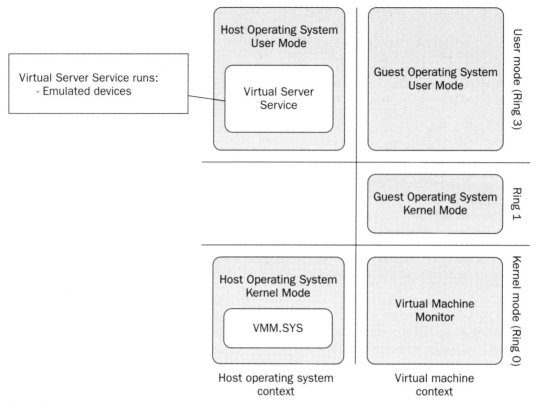

Figure 6-2

However, all hardware access is still handled via the emulated devices in the Virtual Server service (see Figure 6-3).

So what does all of this mean for performance? The critical thing to know is that the performance of a Windows virtual machine with Virtual Machine Additions loaded is pretty comparable to that of a Windows virtual machine running on a system with hardware virtualization support. In both cases both user and kernel mode code is running directly on the processor. The real performance advantages of hardware virtualization are:

- **Operating system installations are much faster.** It is not possible to load Virtual Machine Additions before you install the guest operating system. Hardware virtualization allows for kernel mode code to be run directly during the operating system installation.
- **Non-Windows–based operating systems are much faster.** While Microsoft provides Virtual Machine Additions for Linux, and Virtual Server is capable of running numerous operating systems, Virtual Server only supports direct execution of kernel mode code (without hardware virtualization) for Windows-based operating systems. If you are intending to run virtual machines with Linux (or any other non-Windows–based operating systems) then having a physical computer that supports hardware virtualization should be considered a must.

Chapter 6: Understanding Virtual Machine Performance

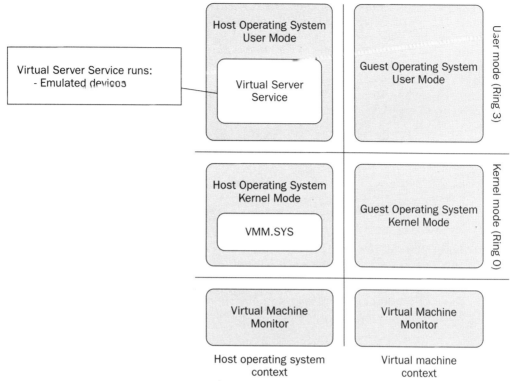

Figure 6-3

Networking

For server environments, network performance is one of the most critical things to look at. Virtual Server emulates an Intel 21140 network card, which you in turn connected to a virtual network associated with one of the physical network cards in your computer. Even though the Intel 21140 network card is a 100-Mbit card in the real world, this restriction does not apply to the emulated version of the Intel 21140. Rather, a number of different factors come into play when trying to determine how much bandwidth a virtual machine is capable of.

The first, and easiest, thing to consider is how much physical network bandwidth is available. If a single virtual machine is connected to a physical network card that is only capable of 100 Mbits, then the bandwidth of the virtual machine will be limited by the capabilities of the physical network card.

The next thing to look at is how your physical networking resources are being shared amongst different virtual machines. When you have multiple virtual machines connected to a single physical network card, the network bandwidth is allocated dynamically to whichever virtual machine needs it at the moment. If multiple virtual machines are trying to utilize more network bandwidth than is available, then the networking resource will be divided equally between the virtual machines. For example, if you had two virtual machines connected to a single 100-Mbit physical connection, each virtual machine would be able to get 100 Mbits of bandwidth, if the other virtual machine was not doing anything on the network. If both virtual machines attempted to perform a network intensive task at the same time they would get only 50 Mbits of bandwidth each.

Part II: Optimizing Virtual Machine Management and Usage

Another important factor to consider is available CPU resource. On a physical computer system some amount of CPU resource is required to sustain a high network load. With Virtual Server even more CPU resource is required. The reason for this is that Virtual Server needs to use the CPU to run the code necessary to emulate the Intel 21140 network card so that the virtual machine can access the network. This is one of the biggest hidden costs of network performance in Virtual Server.

Figure 6-4 shows some performance information about Virtual Server running with a single 100-Mbit physical network connection. The information is provided for Virtual Server running on both a single processor and a dual processor physical computer. In both cases a different number of virtual machines were run at the same time (one, two, four, and eight virtual machines), and each virtual machine was configured with a network bandwidth testing tool.

While the tests were being run, the following information was recorded:

❏ **Bandwidth used:** Measured on the left axis, this value displays the network bandwidth that was achieved by the virtual machines.

❏ **Host CPU load:** This value displays the amount of CPU resource that Virtual Server used on the physical computer during the test. It is measured on the right side with a scale of 0 to 200 percent, where 100 percent equals the total capacity of a single CPU.

❏ **Guest CPU load:** Guest CPU load is the amount of CPU resource that the guest operating system thinks it is using. This is measured on the same axis as host CPU load, with the same scale.

For all of these values there is a total number for all running virtual machines and an average number per running virtual machine.

You may be wondering why both the host and guest CPU values are recorded, and how these values would ever be different. But, these values are almost always different. Unlike the guest CPU value, the host CPU value includes the processing time necessary for emulating any hardware devices inside the virtual machine. This causes the host CPU value to usually be higher than the guest CPU value. There are also times when the guest CPU can be higher than the host CPU. This happens when the host is running out of CPU resource and is unable to give the virtual machine all of the processing resource it asks for. In this situation, the guest operating system believes that it is using all of its available CPU power, but is only being given a fraction of the physical CPU resource.

With all of this in mind it is time to look at the results. In Figure 6-4 you can see that with one, two, four, or eight virtual machines running, on either a single or dual processor computer, the total network bandwidth was close to the theoretical limit of 100 Mbits. This shows that with a single 100-Mbit connection, the main limitation for networking performance is that of the network card. However, if you look closely you will see that by the time eight virtual machines are running, the single processor computer is using less total host CPU, and has a guest CPU value that is very close to that of the host CPU value. This indicates that the single processor computer is close to running out of CPU resource, but that does not appear to affect the performance in this test.

> **Why does the single processor system never get to 100 percent?** In all of the network performance charts in this section, you see that the single processor system never gets above 80 percent host CPU utilization, even when it is clearly in need of more processing power. The reason for this is that on a single processor system there are others tasks (such as the Virtual Server web interface) running on the same physical processor and reducing the amount of resource available.

Chapter 6: Understanding Virtual Machine Performance

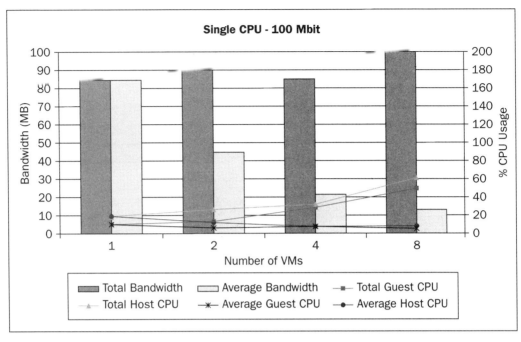

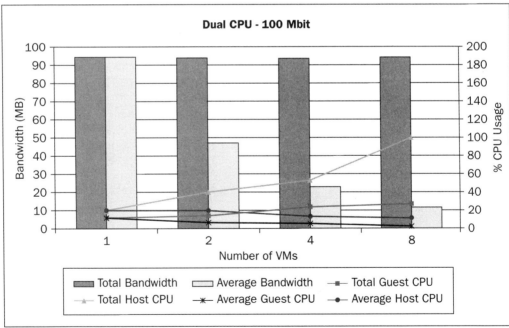

Figure 6-4

Part II: Optimizing Virtual Machine Management and Usage

Moving on to Figure 6-5, you can see the results for the same systems, running the same tests, but this time the computers are configured with two 100-Mbit network cards. As you can see, the dual processor computer is able to utilize the two network cards with no problems. However the single processor computer starts to falter once four or more virtual machines are running.

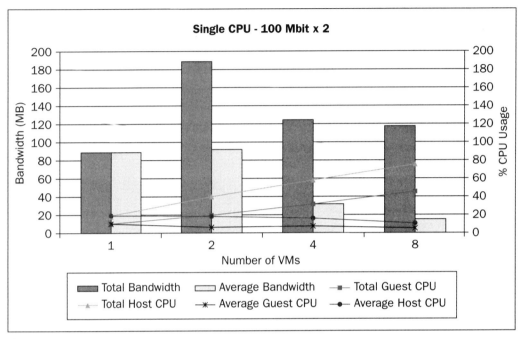

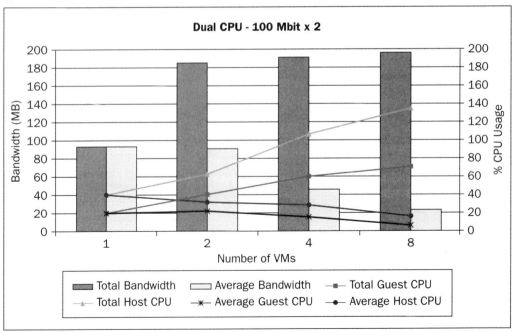

Figure 6-5

Chapter 6: Understanding Virtual Machine Performance

Clearly in this test, the processor resource is the bottleneck for the single processor computer. For the dual processor computer, physical network bandwidth remains as the main limitation for network performance.

In Figure 6-6, the same computer systems are tested again, but this time with a single 1-Gbit physical network card.

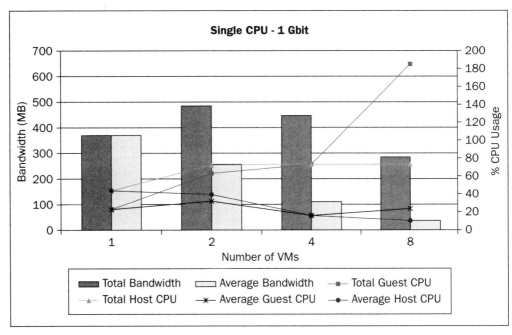

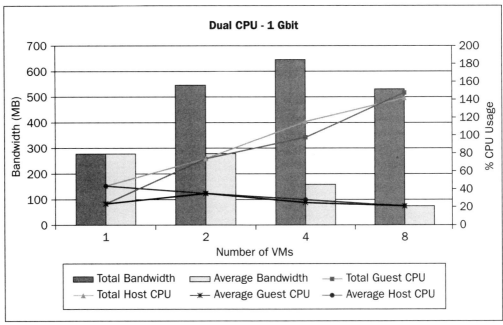

Figure 6-6

Part II: Optimizing Virtual Machine Management and Usage

Some things to highlight from this information include:

- You can see that with a single virtual machine, Virtual Server is capable of getting close to 400 Mbits in throughput. This is mostly limited by the speed of the physical CPU being used. A faster CPU is able to achieve higher throughput.

- The single processor computer is clearly struggling here. The dual processor computer achieves better performance when running two, four, and eight virtual machines. When the single processor computer is running eight virtual machines you can see that the guest CPU usage is much higher than the host CPU usage, indicating that the virtual machines are desperately out of CPU resource.

- The dual processor computer begins to run out of processing power when running eight virtual machines. The total bandwidth achieved is lower than with four virtual machines, and you can see that the guest CPU usage is slightly higher than the host CPU usage.

> **When performing the network tests displayed in this book I was using computers with AMD Opteron 246 (2.0 GHz) processors. Using a slower or faster processor will yield different results.**

The next factor that can influence the networking performance of a virtual machine is the type of data being sent and received. Figure 6-7 shows the network bandwidth achieved by a single virtual machine, connected to a physical 1Gbit network card, when it is configured to use different network packet sizes.

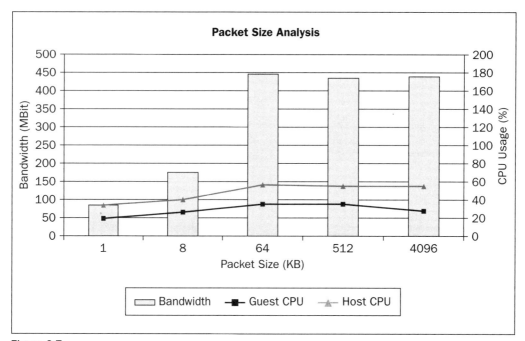

Figure 6-7

Chapter 6: Understanding Virtual Machine Performance

Once the network packet is 64KB or larger, the performance is fairly constant, but when the packet size drops under 64KB you can see that the overall throughput achieved drops rapidly.

CPU usage inside of the virtual machine can also affect the networking performance of the virtual machine. In all of the network tests that you have just reviewed, the virtual machine was doing nothing but utilizing the network card. In this setup, a single virtual machine was able to achieve 450-Mbit throughput on a 1-Gbit network card. If, however, the same virtual machine is configured to run a CPU intensive program at the same time as running the network test, throughput drops down to 150 Mbits. This happens because as the virtual machine uses more CPU time for actual processing, there is less CPU time available to emulate the Intel 21140 network card.

One final thing to consider is the impact of the quality of the physical network card you use. In gathering the network performance data for this chapter, the different physical network cards all had different impacts on the CPU. On one network card I could sustain 100 Mbits inside the virtual machine with 20 percent host CPU usage, but another network card would require 40 percent host CPU in order to achieve the same results.

Network Performance Recommendations

By now you might feel a little overwhelmed by the amount of data and variables to consider when looking at network performance. You have now seen that when determining the expected network performance for a virtual machine you need to consider the following:

- ❑ The physical network bandwidth available
- ❑ The physical processing resources available
- ❑ The number of virtual machines that will be running
- ❑ The nature of the network activity that the virtual machine performs
- ❑ The impact of any other CPU-based activities inside of the virtual machine
- ❑ The quality of the physical network card being used

So at this stage, let's pause and consider some basic guidelines that can be drawn from all of this information:

- ❑ Avoid single-processor computers if at all possible. Having multiple processors will help increase networking performance significantly.
- ❑ If you are using a 100-Mbit network infrastructure, plan to have one physical network card for each processor in your computer. If you are planning to run only two or three network intensive virtual machines for each processor, you may consider adding more physical network adapters, but this will not be usual.
- ❑ If you are using 1-Gbit network infrastructure, plan on having one physical network card for each pair of processors in your computer.

87

Part II: Optimizing Virtual Machine Management and Usage

❑ To achieve the highest possible network performance for a virtual machine, plan on having a dedicated processor and a 1-Gbit network adapter for that virtual machine.

❑ Always have a spare physical network card that is not used by any virtual machine. It is possible for virtual machines to completely utilize any physical network card, and you should always have one physical network card solely for the purpose of connecting to the host operating system and performing administrative tasks.

For the purposes of the preceding guidelines, processors with multiple cores should be viewed as multiple processors. For example, if I were configuring a Virtual Server instance on a quad-core processor, I would want to have two 1-Gbit physical network cards installed. Hyper-threaded processors should still be treated as a single processor.

Internal Networking

An interesting area to look at is *internal networking*. Internal networking refers to the practice of performing network activity between a virtual machine and its host operating system, or between two virtual machines that are connected to the same virtual network. I call this internal networking because in these scenarios Virtual Server handles all network traffic internally without involving the physical hardware. On my test computers, a single virtual machine was able to communicate with the host operating system at 360 to 400 Mbits, even when the host was configured to use a 100-Mbit network card. Similarly, two virtual machines were able to communicate with each other at 420 to 520 Mbits, even when the virtual network was connected to a 100-Mbit network card.

Storage

When thinking about the performance of storage inside of Virtual Server, you need to consider many of the same factors that you need to consider for networking. The performance of storage depends heavily on the capabilities of the underlying physical storage capabilities and the amount of physical processing power available to emulate the storage controllers provided by Virtual Server.

There are also some things that need to be considered that are unique to storage. Unlike networking, when you are running multiple virtual machines on the same physical storage device, the throughput of the storage device will not be divided evenly. The performance of virtual machines in these cases will depend largely on the ability for the physical storage device to support concurrent disk access. This means that for running multiple virtual machines, SCSI or RAID configurations should be preferred over standard IDE configurations. Furthermore, if you are configuring RAID storage it is better to use more, smaller drives than to use fewer, larger drivers as this will enable your RAID storage to sustain a higher number of concurrent accesses.

Chapter 6: Understanding Virtual Machine Performance

You also need to consider the impact of the different types of virtual hard disk:

❑ **Fixed-size virtual hard disk:** This is the best option for performance. Using a fixed-size hard disk means that you have to dedicate all of the space needed for the virtual hard disk at creation time, but in many cases this is worthwhile for the performance benefit.

❑ **Dynamically expanding virtual hard disk:** With a dynamically expanding virtual hard disk, there is a performance impact whenever data is written to a new block on the hard disk. When this happens Virtual Server needs to initialize the new block before the data can be written. Once a block has been initialized, writing different data to that block in the future does not have a performance impact.

❑ **Differencing virtual hard disk:** A differencing virtual hard disk has the same performance issues as a dynamically expanding virtual hard disk, but it also has the overhead of needing to read from both the parent and child virtual hard disks when reading data. This overhead is relatively small but increases if you chain a number of differencing virtual hard disks.

❑ **Undo disks:** Undo disks have all the performance characteristics of differencing disks. It is important to note that if you enable undo disks on a virtual machine that is configured to use fixed-size virtual hard disks, you are effectively negating any performance benefit that you would have gained from using fixed-size virtual hard disks.

One more issue to consider is the type of virtual disk controller that you use inside the virtual machine. Virtual Server allows you to configure a virtual machine with either an IDE controller or a SCSI controller.

Figures 6-8 and 6-9 provide a comparison of the performance of the different types of emulated hard disk controllers as compared to the host performance. Figure 6-8 illustrates a system that uses a single physical standard IDE hard disk; Figure 6-9 illustrates a system that uses two SATA disks configured in a RAID 0 array. Both figures show data for the host, IDE virtual hard disk, SCSI virtual hard disk, and VM-SCSI virtual hard disk. The difference between the SCSI and VM-SCSI virtual hard disks is that the SCSI virtual hard disk is configured to use the standard Adaptec 78xx driver while the VM-SCSI virtual hard disks is configured to use the optimized virtual machine SCSI driver that is included with Virtual Machine Additions.

As you can see, the performance of the SCSI controller without the optimized driver is truly woeful, because the hardware involved in an Adaptec SCSI controller is much more complex than the hardware involved in an IDE controller, which means it takes more processing power to produce slower performance. You can also see that, generally speaking, the IDE controller and VM-SCSI controller provide comparable performance. The key difference between these two controllers is in the amount of processing power needed to sustain a high load.

89

Part II: Optimizing Virtual Machine Management and Usage

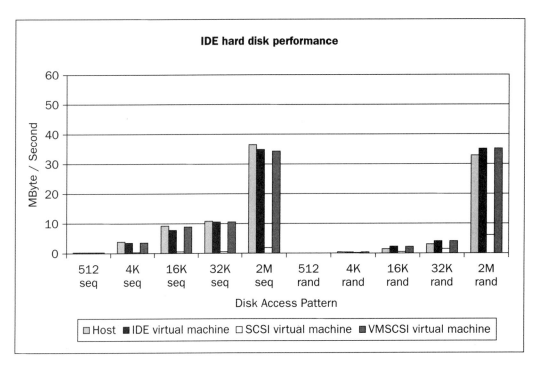

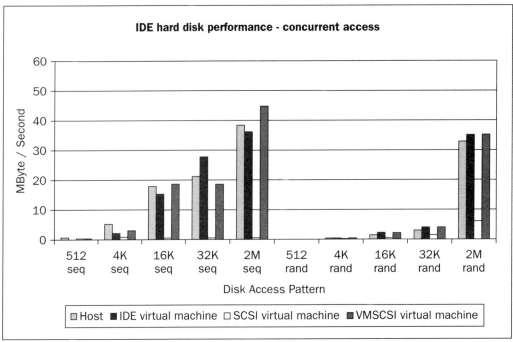

Figure 6-8

Chapter 6: Understanding Virtual Machine Performance

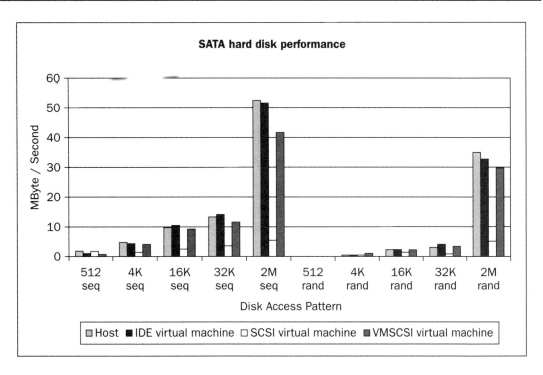

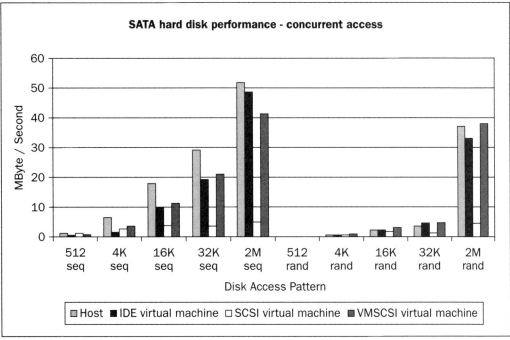

Figure 6-9

Part II: Optimizing Virtual Machine Management and Usage

Figure 6-10 shows that under a heavy load, the IDE controller uses up to twice the amount of CPU resource compared to the VM-SCSI controller. (The standard SCSI controller uses very little CPU resource, but its performance is so low that it is not worth considering.) It is this reduced CPU requirement that means that the VM-SCSI controller delivers better performance in most real-life configurations (as opposed to static disk benchmarks that are not utilizing the processor or other devices at the same time as testing the hard disk).

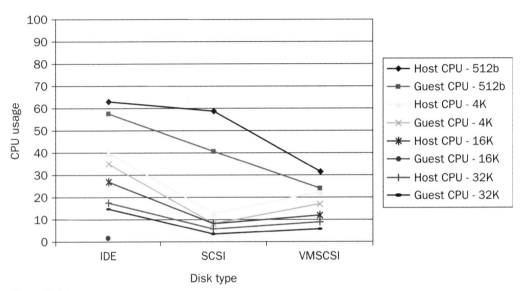

Figure 6-10

Storage Performance Recommendations

Here are some key recommendations for improving storage performance inside of virtual machines:

- ❑ If you are running a guest operating system that has a virtual machine–optimized SCSI driver available via Virtual Machine Additions you should use SCSI for everything. Otherwise, you should use IDE. Never use SCSI without the virtual machine–optimized drivers.

  If you create a virtual machine with IDE virtual hard disks, install Virtual Machine Additions, and then add a virtual SCSI controller, the virtual machine–optimized SCSI drivers will not be used, thus causing the virtual machine to use the emulated SCSI drivers, which have terrible performance characteristics. To avoid this, either add the SCSI controller prior to installing Virtual Machine Additions or reinstall Virtual Machine Additions after adding the SCSI controller to the virtual machine.

- ❑ For high-performance virtual machines, consider using fixed-size virtual hard disks with undo disks disabled.

- ❑ If you need to use undo disks, use dynamically expanding virtual hard disks. It will not cost you anything in performance and is convenient.

Chapter 6: Understanding Virtual Machine Performance

❑ If you are using differencing virtual hard disks extensively, do not allow yourself to build a difference virtual hard disk chain that involves more than five or six virtual hard disks.

❑ Use SCSI or RAID configurations for your physical storage

Keeping an Eye on Fragmentation

One final note about storage performance is that you need to keep an eye on file fragmentation. Whenever you have heavy file fragmentation, you will see slower performance on storage-related tasks. When it comes to virtual machines you can have fragmentation inside the virtual machine, and the virtual hard disk file can be fragmented on the host operating system itself. In fact, the dynamically expanding virtual hard disk is particularly susceptible to file fragmentation because of the way it grows a little bit at a time, as more space is needed. To combat this, you should regularly run defragmentation programs both on the host operating system and inside the virtual machine.

You should not run a defragmentation program on the host operating system while a virtual machine is still running because it conflicts with Virtual Server when it tries to access the virtual hard disk file.

Many defragmentation programs will flag any file with more than one fragment and claim that they need to be defragmented. As virtual hard disks are regularly several gigabytes in size, expecting to have them all stored in one extent is unreasonable. The reality is that as long as the fragments are over 10MB in size, there should be no noticeable performance impact.

Other Devices

Beyond storage and networking, there are some other areas to be discussed. Virtual Server provides virtual machines with access to emulated floppy drives, serial ports, and parallel ports. All of these devices are fairly slow in the physical world, and as such are not noticeably slower inside of virtual machines.

For video display, each virtual machine has an emulated S3 Trio video adapter. The performance of the emulated video card is very slow compared to the performance of the average physical video adapter; however for most server scenarios the video performance is more than adequate.

> **While not strictly a device, there is important information to know about the processor inside the virtual machine. As a general rule of thumb, the virtual machine's processor is able to run at close to native speed. However, there are a small handful of operations that can be up to 10 times slower than native. These operations are usually rare enough that they're not a cause for concern, but every now and then there are programs that rely heavily on these operations. If you have a program that is excessively slow inside of a virtual machine, and you have ruled out any bottlenecks apart from CPU, it is possible that you have hit one of these rare situations. Unfortunately, there is no solution for this problem other than to run the program in question on a physical computer.**

Part II: Optimizing Virtual Machine Management and Usage

Configuring Memory

Another aspect of virtual machine performance to look into is configuring memory appropriately for your virtual machines. Virtual Server adds relatively little overhead to memory performance, and as such, faster physical memory translates directly to faster memory access in the virtual machine. From a performance point of view, there are two areas that you need to focus on: making sure that your virtual machines are configured with the appropriate amount of memory and making sure you are effectively using NUMA memory.

Selecting the Right Amount of Memory

You may be tempted to think that throwing large amounts of memory at your virtual machines will make them run faster. While this is sometimes the case, it is not true the majority of the time, and there are a number of things to consider here.

You need to leave enough memory for the host operating system. Unlike most Windows applications, when Virtual Server reserves memory for a virtual machine it locks it down so Windows cannot reclaim it for other uses until the virtual machine is stopped. This means that if you assign too much memory to running virtual machines it is possible to starve the host operating system and slow down the performance of the whole system (virtual machines included) as the host will use its page file excessively.

> *There is a fair amount of confusion as to the purpose of the page file in Windows. It is true that a system that is using its page file a lot will perform badly, but I would never recommend that you disable paging. When Windows is configured with enough memory, the presence of a page file helps with memory management and improves performance overall. If Windows is paging heavily, it is because the system does not have enough physical memory. In both situations disabling paging results in worse performance at the end of the day.*

Do not assign too much, or not enough, memory to your virtual machines. If you do not assign enough memory to your virtual machines they will need to page heavily, which reduces overall performance. If you assign too much memory to a virtual machine, it may not be able to effectively utilize it all, and you will be wasting memory that could be used for other virtual machines or for the host operating system.

As you can see, the real issue comes down to figuring out what amount of memory is just right for both the virtual machines and for the physical computer. There are a couple of ways to do this. One quick and easy method is to use the Windows Task Manager. On the system that you are trying to determine memory needs for, open the Task Manager while it is running under a typical load. Go to the **Performance** tab of the Task Manager and you should see statistics about the physical memory in your computer. There are three figures here: total, available (or free), and cache. When you look at the amount of available memory, you are seeing the amount of memory that is not being used for anything. It is essentially being wasted. To be clear, you do not want to configure your systems to have no available memory as you should have some buffer space available to allow for new programs to open and the system to remain responsive. On a system that remained under a fairly even load I would be comfortable configuring it to have 100 to 150MB of available memory. So if I looked at a virtual machine and saw that it had 300MB of available memory I would consider dropping the amount of memory assigned to that virtual machine by 150MB.

> *Taking the amount of memory that is being used for cache into account can be challenging. Memory that is being used for cache is helping system performance, but Windows will stop using this memory*

Chapter 6: Understanding Virtual Machine Performance

for cache if there is a shortage of available memory in the system. Windows Vista uses memory for cache far more extensively than previous versions of Windows. If you look at Task Manager and see a small amount of available memory but a large amount of memory being used for cache, you should consider dropping the amount of memory assigned to the system and seeing how performance is affected by the smaller amount of cache.

If the system in question is subject to variable loads you will want to give yourself more buffer space, and hence leave more available memory assigned to the virtual machine. To get a better picture for how much memory a system is actually using you can turn to PerfMon. PerfMon provides you instantaneous information about the system, but it can also log data over an extended period of time. This can give you a better picture of how the system is actually using its memory. Some useful PerfMon counters to look at include:

❑ **Memory: Available MBytes:** This counter allows you to measure the levels of available memory.

❑ **Paging File: %Usage:** Here you can see how much of your page file is being actively used.

If available memory is consistently high while page file usage is low you should decrease the amount of memory available. Conversely, if available memory is low and page file usage is high, you will need to increase the amount of memory for the system. These techniques can be used in both the virtual machine and the host operating system.

Understanding the Impact of Non-Uniform Memory Architecture

NUMA, which stands for Non-Uniform Memory Architecture, is a form of memory architecture for systems with multiple processors. In standard multiprocessor systems, all processors are connected to the same bank of memory. This means that any given processor can access the entire amount of memory in the physical computer. The problem: As you add more processors and run more tasks there is a high rate of contention for access to physical memory and for access to the memory bus. This causes systems to scale poorly as you add more processors.

With a NUMA system, the computer is broken down into nodes. Each of these nodes may include 0 to n processors in it. Each node also has its own memory bank associated with it. Processors in a given node are able to access the memory associated with that node at high speed and with low contention. The problem arises with NUMA systems when a processor needs to access memory that is associated with another node. When this happens, a back channel is used to access the memory. The speed of this back channel is never as fast as direct access and can range from 15 to 90 percent of the performance when accessing memory local to the node.

The overhead of accessing memory that is not local to a node is known as the NUMA ratio. This is expressed in the form of a ratio of the performance of local memory to non-local memory. A computer with a NUMA ratio of 1:1.3 takes 30 percent longer to access non-local memory. A computer with a NUMA ration of 1:6 takes 600 percent longer to access non-local memory. Unfortunately there is no standard way to determine the NUMA ratio of a computer system, but hardware vendors are usually able to provide this information if requested.

Any multiprocessor AMD system is inherently NUMA because the AMD CPU architecture embeds the memory controller in the processor itself — so multiprocessor AMD systems will be NUMA systems with one processor per node.

95

Part II: Optimizing Virtual Machine Management and Usage

For Virtual Server, the best performance is achieved when all of the memory for a virtual machine is allocated from a single NUMA node.

Virtual Server attempts to do this automatically, but there are situations in which this is not possible — for example, if you have NUMA nodes that have processors but do not have any memory associated with them. If Virtual Server detects that you have a NUMA node with no memory present, it will file a warning in the event log when it starts to inform you of this. If you are seeing this event log entry on your computer you should immediately check the configuration of the physical memory in your computer and consult the computer documentation to ensure that you have memory configured for each NUMA node.

If you are seeing this event log entry and are certain that you have configured your memory correctly it is possible that there is a BIOS issue with your system. In order to determine which NUMA nodes have memory, Virtual Server checks the information stored in the system BIOS. There have been known cases where the BIOS reported incorrect information so that Virtual Server filed this event log even though all nodes had local memory. Updating to the latest available BIOS for your computer will sometimes correct this.

Another situation occurs when there is not enough available memory on any one NUMA node. In this case, Virtual Server will split the virtual machine memory across multiple nodes. Once again, in this situation Virtual Server files an event log entry to inform you that this has occurred.

Depending on the NUMA ratio of your computer you may or may not want to keep an eye out for this. The NUMA system I use for testing has a NUMA ratio of 1:1.3 and the performance impact of having a virtual machine split across multiple nodes is barely noticeable. However, on systems with higher NUMA ratios, the performance impact can be very severe.

As mentioned, Virtual Server will try to allocate virtual machines and their memory within the same NUMA node. Having said that, there are times when it will not do this as efficiently as possible. In these cases, it is possible for you to hand-tune the allocation of virtual machines to NUMA nodes. You can specify a preferred NUMA node to run a given virtual machine in by finding the virtual machine's VMC file, opening it with a text editor (I use Notepad), and adding the following text to the `<settings>` section of the file:

```
<Numa>
    <Memory>
        <Preferred_Node type="integer">1</Preferred_Node>
    </Memory>
</Numa>
```

Note that this setting is "preferred" node. This means that Virtual Server will attempt to place the virtual machine in this node to start with, but if there is not sufficient resource in the preferred node Virtual Server will schedule the virtual machine in another node.

96

Chapter 6: Understanding Virtual Machine Performance

Configuring Resource Allocations

Virtual Server allows you to configure CPU resource allocations for each virtual machine. You can do this by selecting **Resource Allocation** from the **Virtual Server** section of the navigation pane. For each virtual machine you can set a relative weight, reserved capacity, and a maximum capacity. The effects of these allocations are as follows:

❑ **Reserved capacity:** This allows you to specify the percentage of a single processor that should be reserved for a specific virtual machine. Setting this value has two effects on how virtual machine resources are managed. First, if you have multiple virtual machines with a reserved capacity set, you are not able to launch more virtual machines than you have CPU resources for. For example, if you had four virtual machines and each had a reserved capacity of 30 percent, you would be able to run only three of the virtual machines at a time. Even if the three running virtual machines were completely idle, you would be unable to launch the fourth virtual machine as Virtual Server would be unable to guarantee the reserved capacity that you have requested. The second effect is that the virtual machine will always be guaranteed access to the amount of CPU resource specified by the reserve, if needed.

If a virtual machine has a reserved capacity set, but is not using the CPU resource, Virtual Server will allow other virtual machines to use this resource. However, as soon as the virtual machine in question needs to use the CPU, Virtual Server will guarantee that it gets at least the reserved amount of CPU capacity.

❑ **Maximum capacity:** This resource setting allows you to specify the maximum percentage of a single processor that a specific virtual machine can use. There is not much more to say about this option as it is fairly straightforward, without any complications involved.

❑ **Relative weight:** Here you can specify what weighting a virtual machine should be given when there is a competition for CPU resource. If you have three virtual machines running with a relative weight of 100 each, they each get 33 percent of the available CPU resource. However, if you change one of the virtual machines to have a relative weight of 300, it gets 60 percent of the CPU resource while the other two virtual machines received 20 percent each. It is important to note that the relative weight value is only used when there is contention for CPU resource. If you have a virtual machine with a relative weight of 400 that is completely idle, and a virtual machine with a relative weight of 100 that is trying to use 100 percent of the CPU resources, then the second virtual machine can use all of the CPU resources (until the first virtual machine needed resource, in which case it would have priority). Another thing to know about relative weight is that it is overruled by the reserved and maximum capacity settings. If a virtual machine is operating at its maximum capacity (as defined in the maximum capacity setting) increasing its relative weight does not allow it to access more CPU resource.

Each of these settings influences the way the virtual machine is scheduled for resource by Virtual Server. It is important to understand from a scheduling point of view that a virtual machine is either running or not running. Setting a maximum capacity of 50 percent means that the virtual machine is only allowed to run on the processor for up to 50 percent of the time available; it does not mean that the virtual machine runs at 50 percent of the literal performance of the native processor. Also, Virtual Server is not absolute in the enforcement on these values. It is not unusual to see a virtual machine sneak slightly over its maximum or to be pushed slightly under its reserve. In both these cases the virtual machine should remain within at least 5 percent of its set maximum or reserve.

97

Part II: Optimizing Virtual Machine Management and Usage

Using these three settings or a combination thereof, you can employ a number of resource management strategies:

❑ **Default settings:** By default, each virtual machine has a relative weight of 100, a reserved capacity of 0 percent, and a maximum capacity of 100 percent. If you leave the virtual machines configured this way each virtual machine is treated as an equal peer. Each virtual machine is capable of utilizing as much resource as is available, and in the case of resource contention, the resource is divided evenly between the virtual machines involved.

❑ **Relative weight based:** If you leave the reserved and maximum capacities at 0 and 100 percent respectively, and modify the relative weights of the virtual machines according to their priorities, you end up with a weight-based scheduling system. The advantage of this approach is that it is very flexible. When you add or remove virtual machines, you do not have to change any settings as the relative weights are dynamically calculated. The problem with this approach is that there is no absolute guarantee about how much resource a virtual machine is given.

❑ **Reservation based:** This approach involves leaving your virtual machines with a relative weight of 100 and modifying the reserved and maximum capacities for each virtual machine. With this approach, it is possible to provide guarantees. If you are obligated to ensure that a given virtual machine will always have 50 percent of a single CPU available for use, you can do it. The problem here is that as you add and remove virtual machines, you will need to review the settings for all of your virtual machines to make sure that the reserves and maximums that are set still make sense.

❑ **Mixed:** The final strategy is to use all of the settings available so that you can provide guarantees about the virtual machine's ability to access resource while still having some level of flexibility in the system. Having said that, very few people actually do this because it is too confusing to figure out exactly what is going to happen with a virtual machine that has a relative weight of 400, a reserve of 30 percent, and a maximum of 60 percent.

These settings affect the CPU allocation for everything on the main virtual machine thread. The majority of this thread is for the virtual machine's CPU, but it also includes time spent emulating the various hardware devices in the virtual machine. This means that when you change the resource allocation you affect the performance of networking, storage, and other subsystems, in addition to affecting the virtual machine's CPU.

Finding the Best Candidates for Virtualization

Now that you know all about the different aspects of virtual machine performance, how do you go about determining which physical computers are the best candidates to be virtualized? First, look for things that clearly rule out a system. Any physical computer that needs to access custom hardware devices, more than 4GB of RAM, or more than one processor is not appropriate for virtualization as virtual machines are limited to one processor with less than 4GB RAM and the emulated devices provided by Virtual Server.

Chapter 6: Understanding Virtual Machine Performance

Next, gather information about the CPU, network, and storage usage patterns for the system in question. You can do this using PerfMon or other monitoring tools. Once you have this information, compare it against the expected performance inside of a virtual machine. If any one of these items is consistently requiring higher performance than can be delivered inside a virtual machine you should reconsider virtualizing that system.

Conclusion

In this chapter, you learned about the performance characteristics of all of the different subsystems of a virtual machine. You now know what the effects are of 32- and 64-bit host operating systems and hardware virtualization support.

Remember the details of how to optimize the performance of networking and storage, and that you need to make sure that the processor requirements are accounted for when tuning these devices.

Finally, it is important to correctly configure the memory and CPU for virtual machines so that you can get the best performance possible.

Part III

Maintaining Virtual Machines

Chapter 7: Monitoring and Managing Virtual Machines

Chapter 8: Keeping Virtual Machines Up-to-Date

7

Monitoring and Managing Virtual Machines

As soon as you have more than one installation of Virtual Server, you start wondering how you will effectively monitor and manage your virtual machines. With Virtual Server, virtual machines can be easily created at any time, and without a clear management strategy you may soon lose track of what virtual machines are where, what they are doing, and whether they are working correctly. In this chapter, you read about the different tools that Microsoft provides for you to be able to manage and monitor your virtual machines.

A number of third-party management tools are available for Virtual Server. Some of them are tools built specifically for the management of virtual machines (such as the tools provided by PlateSpin and LeoStream) while others are traditional computer management systems that have been extended to provide extra functionality when used with Virtual Server (such as the management suites available from IBM or HP). However, I will be focusing on the tools provided by Microsoft in this book.

Virtual Server Web Interface

One often-overlooked management tool for virtual machines is the Virtual Server web interface. With the Virtual Server web interface, it is possible to manage multiple servers, view virtual machine status information, and access event log information — not to mention that you can control and configure virtual machines as well. One of the biggest advantages of the web interface is that you can use it from any computer with Internet Explorer 5.5 or later, with no need to install any client software.

To configure the Virtual Server web interface to manage multiple instances of Virtual Server, select Virtual Server Manager from the Navigation section of the navigation pane, and then select Switch Virtual Server. Now enter the computer name for the instance of Virtual Server installation that

Part III: Maintaining Virtual Machines

you want to manage. You can also specify whether you want this instance of Virtual Server to be added to the Virtual Server Manager list. Adding the computer to the Virtual Server Manager list enables you to quickly and easily switch to that computer in the future (without the need to type in the computer name).

One of the biggest flaws with using the Virtual Server web interface to manage multiple instances of Virtual Server is that you can only view information from one instance of Virtual Server at a time.

The default configuration of the Virtual Server web interface allows you to see a thumbnail of the virtual machine's display, and the name, status, running time, and CPU usage for up to 10 virtual machines. It also displays the last five entries to the system event log. All of these options are configurable by selecting **Website Properties** from the **Virtual Server** section of the navigation pane. On the website properties page you can configure the following:

❑ **How regularly the administrative website should refresh itself:** The Virtual Server web interface refreshes itself every 60 seconds by default. You can increase or decrease this value, but you should be aware that refreshing the Virtual Server web interface takes a fair amount of CPU resource, which will not be available for virtual machines to use. If you set this value to an excessively low number (say 5 seconds) you can hurt the performance of your virtual machines. This is especially true when you are running Virtual Server on a computer that has only one processor.

❑ **The number of virtual machines to display per page:** As mentioned, you will see 10 virtual machines by default, but you can increase or decrease this value to your preference. Each extra virtual machine displayed on the page increases the amount of time and CPU resource that is required to load the page, so if you set this value very high you could hurt the performance of Virtual Server.

❑ **The columns that should be displayed for each virtual machine:** Here you can selectively disable any of the columns that are displayed for each of the virtual machines. The Remote View and CPU Usage columns require the most server CPU resource to display and take up the most visual space on the page. If you disable these columns, you can easily display many more virtual machines per page, with less impact on CPU resources for page refreshes.

When you are on the main page of the Virtual Server web interface, you can choose to sort the virtual machines by any of the columns. Sorting by status, uptime, or CPU usage provides interesting information about the state of your virtual machines in a very easy-to-absorb way.

❑ **Whether event log entries should be displayed:** If you want to maximize the amount of web page space that you can use to list virtual machines, you may want to disable this option.

❑ **The specific classes of events that should be displayed:** Typically, all events that are filed to the event log are displayed on the main page of the Virtual Server web interface. Virtual Server files a lot of event log entries that are informational only (for example, configuration changes to virtual machines) and this can cause serious errors to be missed. If you want to highlight only the more critical entries, uncheck the informational class of events and choose to see only warnings and errors.

❑ **The number of event log entries that should be displayed:** Finally you can configure how many event log entries should be displayed on the main page.

Chapter 7: Monitoring and Managing Virtual Machines

The default configuration of the Virtual Server web interface is primarily geared toward the creation and configuration of a small number of virtual machines. To use it for monitoring a larger set of existing virtual machines, consider a configuration where you disable the display of the virtual machine display thumbnail, CPU usage, and informational events. You can then increase the number of virtual machines and events to be displayed. This gives you a lightweight page allowing you to see the status of your virtual machines and any recent warning or error events that had been logged.

Another section of the Virtual Server web interface to look at when you are trying to monitor large numbers of virtual machines is the **Event Viewer** option under the **Virtual Server** section of the navigation pane. This page allows you to look through all the events logged for an instance of Virtual Server. You can also select to filter the events so that you see only events related to a specific virtual machine.

Virtual Server Scripts

By selecting **Server Properties** from the **Virtual Server** section of the navigation pane, and then selecting **Virtual Server Scripts**, you will get to the Virtual Server Script Settings page.

Calling this page Virtual Server Scripts is very misleading as it really has very little to do with scripting directly. This page allows you to configure a command to be executed on the host operating system in response to a specific event occurring under Virtual Server. The events that you can use to launch a command are:

❑ Virtual Server starts.

❑ Virtual Server stops.

These first two events are referring to the Virtual Server service starting and stopping, as opposed to the web interface or a specific virtual machine.

❑ Any virtual machine is turned on.

❑ Any virtual machine is restored from a saved state.

❑ Any virtual machine is put into a saved state.

❑ Any virtual machine is turned off.

❑ Any virtual machine is turned off within the guest environment.

This event allows you to differentiate between a virtual machine that was turned off through the Virtual Server web interface (or an external script) and a virtual machine that was turned off because the guest operating system was shut down.

❑ Any virtual machine is reset.

❑ No heartbeat is detected for any virtual machine.

❑ Any virtual machine experiences a guest processor error.

When a virtual machine experiences a guest processor error it will be reset by Virtual Server. The primary situation where you see this error is if the guest operating system has performed an illegal series of processor operations that would cause a physical computer to crash. Guest processor errors are very uncommon.

Part III: Maintaining Virtual Machines

❑　Any virtual machine receives a warning as a result of low disk space on the physical computer.

❑　Any virtual machine receives an error as a result of low disk space on the physical computer.

When you look at this list, you might think that the Virtual Server Scripts would be a very useful feature. However, you should be aware of some issues with this page because they greatly limit the functionality provided. The first issue is that the command you specify will be launched in the context of the Virtual Server service, which runs as Network Service. Running as Network Service means you will not be able to access many of the resources on the computer. It also means you won't be able to interact directly with any program that you launch via these options, which makes troubleshooting problems difficult. The next issue is that for events that will launch a command for "any virtual machine" there is no way to tell which virtual machine it was that caused the event. This means that it is not possible to tell which virtual machine caused the command to be launched.

You can work around both of these issues by using the **Scripts** option under a virtual machine configuration; however, in order to use this you will need to configure the script for each virtual machine that you want to monitor.

Except for very basic uses, it is usually more effective to write a separate script that watches for the specific event externally and then performs the action that you want.

Virtual Server scripts are disabled by default, and you will need to enable them on the Virtual Server scripts page.

As mentioned, Virtual Server Scripts executes a standard command. If you want it to actually launch a script you will need to provide a command that includes the script parser — for example, cscript.exe C:\myVirtualServerScript.vbs.

Windows Event Log

Everything that happens under Virtual Server gets written to the Windows event log. In fact, most other monitoring and management tools for Virtual Server build themselves on top of the information that is available in the Windows event log. If you open up the Event Viewer and go to the Virtual Server section, you should see all the events related to your installation of Virtual Server.

Now, the information that gets stored here is really far too verbose for most purposes. But luckily the Event Viewer provides excellent filtering capabilities. If you select to filter the events (from the View menu) you will see a number of options. The first thing to look at filtering is the category. Virtual Server uses six different categories to log events under:

❑　**Remote Control:** This category is used for logging information specific to VMRC sessions. If you examine the informational entries in this category, you will be able to tell who connected to which virtual machine at a specific time.

❑　**Setting Change:** This category is used for any settings change, either to a virtual machine or to Virtual Server as a whole. One important thing to know is that there are settings changes that get logged that are not the direct result of user action. For instance, when you shut down a virtual machine, Virtual Server changes an internal setting value to let it know that the virtual machine was stopped cleanly. This setting change is also logged to the event log.

106

Chapter 7: Monitoring and Managing Virtual Machines

❑ **Virtual Disk Operation:** Creating, compacting, merging, converting, and inspecting virtual hard disks will cause event log entries to be created under this category.

❑ **Virtual Machine:** The virtual machine category is used to store information about the operations (stopping, starting, and so on) of virtual machines. Note that any configuration change for a virtual machine is stored under the setting change category and not this category.

❑ **Virtual Server:** This category is used to store event information that is not a setting change and is not associated with a virtual machine or a virtual hard disk. An example of an entry you could expect to see in this category is information about whether Virtual Server failed to locate any virtual machine configuration files.

❑ **VSS Writer:** The final category is used to log any events that are pertinent to the volume shadow copy services support in Virtual Server 2005 R2 SP1.

Unlike most applications, Virtual Server will use the same Event ID in different categories to have different meanings. So an event #1024 that is in the Setting Change category is created for an entirely different reason than an event #1024 that is in the Virtual Disk Operation category.

In addition to filtering for category, you can also filter for event type (error, warning, or informational) and for the date range in which you believe the event occurred. Unfortunately the one thing you cannot filter for is the machine. In other words, you can't see only the event log entries that are related to one specific virtual machine.

Remember that the Virtual Server web interface provides a way to view the events filtered on a per-virtual-machine basis.

Performance Monitor

The next management tool to look at is the Windows Performance Monitor (or PerfMon). This tool can be used in two ways. It can be used to provide a quick glance at the status of your system, or it can be configured to gather statistical logs over a longer period of time to help you identify how the workload on your system changes. Virtual Server exposes a number of data points to PerfMon. You can view these data points by selecting to add a new counter and then selecting either the **Virtual Machines** or **Virtual Processors** performance objects.

*Sometimes the Virtual Machines and Virtual Processors performance objects do not appear when you first try to add new counters. If this happens, just close the **Add New Counter** dialog box and try again; they should appear the second time.*

If you are viewing performance counters on the local computer use the "local computer" option rather than specifying the network name of your computer.

Virtual Server provides the following performance counters:

❑ **Virtual Machines: Allocated MB.** Allocated MB tells you how much memory (in megabytes) is allocated to each running virtual machine. Notice that the number is always slightly higher than the amount you specified in the virtual machine settings. This extra memory is used to store program information that Virtual Server needs to store in order to run the virtual machine (registers and information for emulated devices, and so on).

107

Part III: Maintaining Virtual Machines

Because Virtual Server assigns memory to the virtual machines through the VMM driver, there is no other way than using PerfMon to determine how much memory is being used by a specific virtual machine and by Virtual Server as a whole.

❑ **Virtual Machines: Allocated Pages.** This is similar to Allocated MB, with the only difference being that rather telling you about the amount of memory being used in megabytes, it tells you the amount of memory being used in pages.

❑ **Virtual Processors: Cumulative Guest Run Time.** Cumulative Guest Run Time is a counter that lets you know how long (in microseconds) the virtual machine has actually been able to run on the physical processor. When graphed under PerfMon this gives you a highly accurate image of how much CPU is being used by the virtual machine. Unfortunately when you try and log this value you just see a list of ever increasing very large numbers, which is not really that interesting or useful.

❑ **Virtual Processors: Host-to-VMM context switches.** This counter allows you to track how often Virtual Server switches from the host operating system context to the virtual machine monitor context per second. For an idle virtual machine you would expect this to happen about 600 times a second. For an active virtual machine this will happen anywhere from 1,000 to 10,000 times a second. The higher the rate of context switches, the lower the overall performance of the virtual machine will be.

❑ **Virtual Processors: Guest External Interrupts.** Guest External Interrupts displays how many interrupts were delivered to the virtual machine in the last second. Generally, interrupts are delivered into the virtual machine in response to activity on the emulated hardware.

❑ **Virtual Processors: VMM Exceptions.** VMM Exceptions records the number of times that the VMM needed to handle processor exceptions from inside the virtual machine.

❑ **Virtual Processors: HVM-VP is in HVM mode.** This counter indicates whether the virtual machine is using hardware virtualization technology or not. If the virtual machine is using hardware virtualization technology, this returns 1; if not, it returns 0.

Microsoft Operations Manager 2005

Microsoft Operations Manager (MOM) 2005 is Microsoft's centralized server management solution. MOM allows you to not monitor servers with a variety of different server software and roles installed, through the use of plug-in management packs. One of the greatest strengths of MOM is that it provides you with a single console that you use to manage all of your servers, no matter the role for which they are configured. When it is used with Virtual Server, this is even more powerful as you can manage the host operating system, guest operating systems, and any other software installed inside the virtual machines from a single location.

MOM 2005 comes with a basic management pack for Virtual Server, but an updated management pack with improved functionality is available as a free download from www.microsoft.com/mom. Once you have updated the management pack and installed the MOM agent on your Virtual Server instances, you can do a number of things.

If you are not familiar with how to install and configure MOM you should review the Microsoft Operations Manager 2005 Deployment Guide, which can be downloaded from www.microsoft.com/downloads/results.aspx?freetext=Microsoft%20Operations%20Manager%202005%20Deployment%20Guide.

Chapter 7: Monitoring and Managing Virtual Machines

Virtual Server Tasks

MOM provides a number of built-in tasks that can be performed on an instance of Virtual Server. Once you have selected your Virtual Server host computer under the MOM Operator console, you can open the Virtual Server Administration website, and start and stop Virtual Server. You can also select to stop, start, pause, reset, save, or resume virtual machines.

With each of these virtual machine operations you will be presented with a wizard that allows you to perform the specified operation on multiple virtual machines at the same time. All of these tasks are built using VBScript and can be customized under the MOM Administrator Console. For example, while there is a task to stop a virtual machine, there is not one to shut it down cleanly. To create a new task to do this, you will need to open the MOM Administrator Console and follow these steps:

1. Select your MOM server instance, and then select **Management Packs and Scripts**.

2. Select **Virtual Server – Stop Virtual machine**; right-click it and select **Copy**.

3. Right-click on the empty space and select **Paste**.

4. Right-click **Copy of Virtual Server – Stop Virtual machine**, and select **Properties**.

5. Change the name to **Virtual Server – Shutdown Virtual Machine**, and change the description as appropriate.

6. Click the **Script** tab.

7. Go to the end of the script and locate the following line:

    ```
    oVM.TurnOff()
    ```

    Change it to this:

    ```
    oVM.GuestOS.Shutdown()
    ```

8. Select **Tasks** and then **Microsoft Virtual Server** under the **Management Packs** section.

9. Select **Create Task** from the **Action** menu. This starts the Create Task Wizard.

10. On the **Task Run Location and Type** page, select to run on the **Agent-managed computer** and to use a **Script**.

11. On the **Task Configuration** page, specify a **Target** role of **Virtual Machine**, and select the script you created in steps 2 through 7.

12. Change the value for **SaveVMState** from 1 to **0**.

    The original script that you copied to stop the virtual machine has an option to save state the virtual machine before stopping. This does not make sense for the shutdown script, as the virtual machine cannot be shut down after being saved. Changing this value disables the save state option.

13. Change the value for **VMName** to **$Name$**.

14. Set the **Name** and **Description**, and finish the wizard.

You can now go to the MOM Operator Console and choose to shut down a running virtual machine. A number of useful tasks could be created to be used here; it all depends on what you feel you need to be able to do.

109

Part III: Maintaining Virtual Machines

Virtual Server Health Information

MOM provides detailed health information about Virtual Server. It does this by examining the event logs generated by Virtual Server, and by checking the configuration of Virtual Server and the virtual machines directly. You can use MOM to review the Virtual Server event logs directly, or you can look at the specific alerts that are raised by MOM. The advantage of using the MOM alerts is that you see a filtered view of the event log, so you only see issues that are really important. MOM also provides valuable information and prescriptive guidance on how to resolve the problem.

MOM will alert you about configuration issues that normally would not be identified as errors by Virtual Server, but that could be problematic in a production environment. For example, MOM will raise an error alert if it detects any virtual machine that is not currently running. MOM will also raise a warning alert if it detects a virtual machine where the guest operating system is configured to use a different network name than the virtual machine name under Virtual Server, which can make network-based management confusing. As with the tasks, you can create your own alerts to be created in response to specific events. To do this, go to the MOM Administrator Console and select your MOM server, followed by selecting **Management Packs** ➪ **Rule Groups** ➪ **Microsoft Virtual Server**. For example, you might want to receive an alert whenever someone makes a connection to a virtual machine via VMRC (this would be useful if you were expecting people to connect via Remote Desktop only). To do this, follow these steps:

1. Select **Event Rules** under the **Microsoft Virtual Server** section.

2. Select **Create Event Rule** from the **Action** menu.

3. Select **Alert on or Respond to Event (Event)**.

4. On the **Data Provider** page, change the **Provider** name to **Virtual Server**.

5. On the **Criteria** page, check **from source** and enter **Virtual Server** into the text entry box.

6. Check **with event id** and enter **1024** into the text entry box.

   In order to determine the event id, category, and type, just use the Windows event viewer to locate the event that you want to monitor.

7. Check **of type** and select **Information** from the drop-down menu.

   This step is not strictly necessary, but it is a good practice to fill out as much information as you can as this will reduce the potential for false positives.

8. Click the **Advanced** button.

9. Set **Field** to **Category**, **Condition** to **equals**, and **Value** to **Remote Control**. Then click **Add to List**.

   As mentioned earlier in this chapter, Virtual Server reuses the same event IDs under different categories. This means that whenever you create an event-based rule, it is critical to specify the category that you want to monitor.

10. On the **Schedule** page, select **Always process data**.

11. On the **Alert** page, check **Generate alert**, set the **Alert severity** to **Information**, and fill out any other data that you want to provide.

12. Complete the wizard and save your new rule.

Chapter 7: Monitoring and Managing Virtual Machines

Now when this event occurs, you will be notified under the MOM Operator Console.

> The preceding steps didn't discuss a number of advanced features of MOM rules. For instance, you can configure this rule to not file an alert when you connect via VMRC but only do so when someone else connects. You can specify specific hours during which to monitor for this event or you can configure a script to be launched when the event occurred.
>
> By putting information into the knowledge base section of the rule, other users will be able to understand why this rule was created and what they should do when it occurs.

Virtual Machine Diagram

As mentioned at the beginning of the chapter, once you have a large number of virtual machines on a number of Virtual Server instances, it is very easy to lose track of the location of a specific virtual machine. This can be problematic if you need to perform maintenance and know exactly what the dependencies are.

I have, on occasion, been contacted by frantic systems administrators who needed to reconfigure a virtual machine but could no longer figure out where it was. They could access it over the network but did not know which host it was residing on.

To see a map of virtual machines and their hosting computers, open the MOM Operator Console and select the Diagram option. Then select to view the **Virtual Machines on Hosts** diagram from under the **Microsoft Virtual Server** folder. This provides you with all the information you need in an easy-to-understand graphical display.

Virtual Machine Performance Monitoring

The MOM Operator Console also provides an easy way to view performance information about your virtual machines. Unlike PerfMon, MOM only provides information about the CPU usage, disk usage, and RAM usage. However it is much easier to view performance information under MOM than under PerfMon, especially when multiple host computers are involved. To view performance data under the MOM Operator Console, select the **Performance** option, and then select **Virtual Machine** under **Microsoft Virtual Server**. Select the performance counter that you are interested in, check the virtual machines you want to see information about, and click **Draw Graph**.

The MOM performance graph also has the advantage that MOM automatically keeps a historic log of performance information. This means that the instant you choose to look at a performance counter you will have a large amount of historic performance data at hand. With PerfMon, you need to configure it to manually log information over a period of time.

Virtualization Reports

MOM also provides reporting capabilities, and you can use this to build your own online reports about virtual machine status and activity. One of the cool features of the Virtual Server MOM Management pack is that it comes with a report that is not aimed at virtual machines at all. Rather, this report profiles any existing hardware servers that you have and identifies which ones would be the best candidates to migrate to running inside of a virtual machine.

Part III: Maintaining Virtual Machines

System Center Virtual Machine Manager

Microsoft is also currently working on a dedicated management tool for its virtualization products. This tool is called System Center Virtual Machine Manager (SCVMM). At the time of this writing SCVMM is currently in public beta with an expected release in the second half of 2007.

SCVMM is designed to provide a single location where you can perform all necessary tasks to use and maintain a large number of Virtual Server instances. SCVMM uses a Microsoft Management Console (MMC)–based user interface, and aims to provide sufficient functionality such that you do not need to use the Virtual Server web interface as well. Where MOM is aimed at allowing you to monitor and maintain existing virtual machines, SCVMM is much more focused on creating and interacting with virtual machines.

Some of the key features of SCVMM include:

❑ **Single user interface for managing multiple instances of Virtual Server:** SCVMM allows you to view and manage virtual machines that are running on multiple instances of Virtual Server without your needing to switch from one server to another.

❑ **Automatic grouping of virtual machines:** All virtual machines (on all host computers) can be viewed in a number of ways. You can group virtual machines by their current state (running, stopped, and so on), by the guest operating system that is installed on them, by when they were created, or by the designated owner for each virtual machine. All of these views are maintained dynamically and reflect up-to-date information.

❑ **Managed virtual machine library:** SCVMM provides a managed virtual machine library. This allows you to store base virtual machines, virtual machine templates, virtual hard disks, CD image files, and scripts in a central location that can then be easily deployed to any instance of Virtual Server.

Virtual machine templates differ from base virtual machines in that they just contain the configuration information about the virtual machine, and not the virtual hard disks.

❑ **Advanced virtual machine creation methods:** When creating virtual machines, you can specify all of the normal configuration options, but you can also choose where a virtual machine should be created: on a specific instance of Virtual Server, or directly to the virtual machine library to be used as a base virtual machine in the future.

❑ **Support for cloning of virtual machines:** You can select an existing virtual machine and clone it, copying all of the configuration data as well as the virtual hard disks. You can even choose to clone a virtual machine from one physical computer to another, in which case SCVMM coordinates copying the virtual hard disks over the network.

❑ **Support for virtual machine migration:** With SCVMM, you can select a virtual machine and easily move it from one instance of Virtual Server to another. If the virtual machine is stored on a form of shared storage then the migration will be relatively fast as it only involves saving the virtual machine state and then restoring it on the target system. If the Virtual Server instances do not have any shared storage, SCVMM will shut down the virtual machine and transfer all of the virtual hard disks, virtual machine state, and virtual machine configuration data over the network.

112

Chapter 7: Monitoring and Managing Virtual Machines

❏ **Support for virtual machine checkpointing:** By integrating with Windows Volume Shadow Copy Services, SCVMM can quickly take checkpoints of a virtual machine, which you can then roll back to at a later point in time.

❏ **Improved physical to virtual migration tools:** SCVMM includes a new set of tools to allow you to take existing physical computers and change them into virtual machines with a minimal amount of downtime and configuration.

❏ **Intelligent placement technology:** One of the key strengths of SCVMM is its intelligent placement technology. When you are creating a new virtual machine, or migrating an existing virtual machine, SCVMM is able to profile all of your Virtual Server instances and provide recommendations as to which servers would make the best possible host for your virtual machine.

❏ **Self-service provisioning tool:** SCVMM provides a web-based tool that allows end users to provision their own virtual machines from a set of base virtual machines that you define. They can do this without needing SCVMM or Virtual Server installed, and they do not need to have any administrative privileges on any of the server systems involved.

❏ **Windows PowerShell integration:** By using Windows PowerShell to execute all of its tasks, it is possible for SCVMM to provide you with full PowerShell scripts for any action that you perform. It is easy for you to automate any task that you perform on a regular basis.

To find out more about SCVMM, go to `www.microsoft.com/scvmm`.

Conclusion

In this chapter you have read about all of the tools that are available to help you manage and monitor your virtual machines. These tools range from the free solutions that exist with a standard installation of Virtual Server, such as the Virtual Server web interface, Windows event viewer, and PerfMon, to the higher scale management solutions such as Microsoft Operations Manager and the upcoming System Center Virtual Machine Manager.

You have seen the capabilities of these tools to provide statistical and event-based information and should now understand what each tool can be used for.

8

Keeping Virtual Machines Up-to-Date

When maintaining any sort of computing infrastructure you need to ensure that it is kept up-to-date with the latest security patches and updates. Using virtual machines can complicate the process of keeping systems up-to-date in a number of ways:

- ❑ With virtual machines, a larger number of systems need to be kept up-to-date.

- ❑ Virtual machines may be turned off for long periods of time, and not receive regular updates that other computers receive.

- ❑ Virtual machines created from older base virtual machine images don't have the latest patches and updates installed.

- ❑ The use of undo disks and differencing disks can cause updates to inadvertently be removed after they have been applied to a system.

This chapter covers the different methods and strategies for ensuring that your virtual machines are always updated with the right software.

Don't Update

The first strategy to consider is to not update your virtual machines. At this stage you are probably thinking that I have lost touch with reality, but there are a number of cases in which you can consider using virtual machines and never updating them. For example, you might consider not updating under the following circumstances:

- ❑ If the virtual machine is running legacy software for which the software vendor is no longer providing security updates, such as a Windows NT 4.0 virtual machine.

Part III: Maintaining Virtual Machines

❏   If your virtual machines will always run in an isolated, trusted environment. If you will not be using network connectivity inside of the virtual machine, or you will be networking only with a select number of other, trusted, virtual machines you could consider not updating the software.

In either of these cases you would have to be very careful to ensure that the virtual machines were not exposed to public networks or the Internet, as these environments would pose significant security risks.

Manual Updating

In small environments, a good option might be just manually installing updates on virtual machines as appropriate. This involves the least amount of upfront work but is also the least reliable option. As new updates come out, you need to be vigilant about ensuring that you have applied them to your virtual machines. You also need to be careful about reapplying updates after using undo disks or deleting a differencing disk.

The manual updating strategy can be very effective in environments where the majority of your virtual machines are made by conscientious administrators, who are guaranteed to apply the appropriate patches to their virtual machines. You can improve the process for manual updating by making "update CD images" for administrators to use. You can do this by periodically downloading appropriate updates from the Microsoft Windows Update catalog (`http://go.microsoft.com/fwlink/?linkid=8973`). The Microsoft Windows Update catalog allows you to download specific update packages for use in a standalone fashion on other computers at a later date; it even allows you to download updates for operating systems other than the one you are currently running.

Once you have all of the appropriate update files, you can use one of many available programs to create an ISO image containing the updates.

> *ISORecorder* (`http://isorecorder.alexfeinman.com/isorecorder.htm`) *and WinISO* (`www.winiso.com`) *are examples of two programs that are designed solely for the purpose of creating ISO images. Many CD/DVD burning programs also provide the functionality to create ISO images.*

This image file can then be placed in a central location where everyone can use it. Using an update CD image has a couple of advantages. The first is that it reduces the amount of external network bandwidth required, as every person does not need to download the updates themselves. It can also prove very useful in situations where Internet connectivity is not available, but you want to keep systems up-to-date. Another advantage is that in most situations this approach is faster for installing updates than downloading them over the Internet each time.

Automated Updating

Most modern operating systems also provide methods for automatically installing the latest updates and patches. These are very effective when used in a virtual machine, and for virtual machines that are always connected to the Internet these capabilities provide an excellent solution. The biggest issue when using automated update solutions is managing the potential for any given update to cause a compatibility issue with the software that you are running. Different automated update solutions provide you with different levels of flexibility in managing this risk.

Chapter 8: Keeping Virtual Machines Up-to-Date

There are a couple of situations where relying on Internet-based automatic updating can be problematic.

❑ If you are only powering virtual machines occasionally, you can end up in a situation in which your virtual machine presents a security risk until it has been able to successfully download and install an update. This window of risk can be a number of hours, depending on the configuration used.

❑ You need to operate the virtual machine while it is not connected to the Internet because you do not have a guaranteed Internet connection, or because you are running software inside of the virtual machine that is not appropriate to expose to the public network (for example, you could be creating a test DHCP server and not want to connect it to your normal public network).

❑ You have more complicated update requirements than can be addressed by standard automatic update services. For various reasons you might need to install a subset of available updates, either because you have a known application incompatibility or because you are trying to replicate an environment that has a specific update configuration.

All of these scenarios can be effectively addressed by creating your own automated update infrastructure, which is thankfully much easier than it sounds.

Using a Windows Server Update Server

Microsoft provides Windows Server Update Server (WSUS) as a free download from www.microsoft.com/windowsserversystem/updateservices. The current version of Windows Server Update Server is WSUS 2.0 Service pack 1. WSUS 3.0 is in beta at the time of this writing. WSUS can be used effectively for Windows virtual machines to provide custom automated update installation, or to provide updates to virtual machines that are not directly connected to the Internet.

Preparing to Install Windows Server Update Server 2.0

To set up WSUS using a Windows Server 2003 virtual machine, you need to create a virtual machine with two virtual hard disks, configure it with two virtual network adapters and the appropriate amount of memory, and install Windows Server 2003, Microsoft .NET Framework 1.1 Service Pack 1, Background Intelligent Transfer Service (BITS) 2.0, and IIS 6.0.

One virtual hard disk should be used to install Windows on, while the second should serve as the data disk for WSUS. Microsoft recommends having approximately 30GB available on your data disk.

You can configure WSUS to not store the updates locally, but in such a configuration the clients need to be able to connect to the Internet directly to download the updates. This is not desirable in most uses, so I will not discuss this sort of configuration.

While Microsoft recommends having 30GB of storage available on your data disk, the actual amount needed will depend heavily on how many operating systems and products you want to update. In my case, I selected to have updates for all versions of Windows, Windows Live, SQL, and Office in all available languages. This used just over 60GB of space.

One virtual network adapter should be configured to connect to a public network with access to the Internet. The other network adapter should be configured to connect to the private network that is being used for your virtual machine. It is possible to configure WSUS to operate in a completely offline mode. This is discussed later in this chapter.

117

Part III: Maintaining Virtual Machines

It is also possible to configure a WSUS instance to refer to another WSUS instance (this is called chaining). Chaining is most often used in branch office scenarios, or multi-administrator scenarios. WSUS chaining will not be discussed in this chapter, and you should refer to online WSUS resources if you want to know more about this configuration.

In terms of the appropriate amount of memory, WSUS documentation recommends a minimum of 512MB RAM for a server with 500 or fewer clients (1GB RAM for a server with 500 to 15,000 clients). Given that you are likely to have far fewer than 500 clients, you probably want to drop this as far as possible. I had no problems servicing a dozen clients with a WSUS virtual machine that had 256MB RAM.

Download the .NET Framework from `http://go.microsoft.com/fwlink/?LinkId=35326`, or install it by running Windows Update on your WSUS computer and installing the latest updates available.

Next, download BITS from `http://go.microsoft.com/fwlink/?LinkId=47251`, or install it by running Windows Update on your WSUS computer and installing the latest updates available.

Finally, you need to install IIS 6.0 in the virtual machine by executing the following steps:

1. From the **Start** menu select **Control Panel** and **Add or Remove Programs**.

2. Select **Add/Remove Windows Components** from the left of the **Add or Remove Programs** dialog box.

3. From the **Windows Component Wizard** page, check **Application Server** and continue with the wizard. Note that while the wizard is progressing it will require you to have your Windows Server install media.

   Once the wizard has completed, IIS will be ready.

WSUS also requires a database to store information in. You can use a Microsoft SQL Server 2000 server or an installation of the Microsoft SQL Server 2000 Desktop Engine (MSDE). However, the WSUS installer will automatically install and configure the Microsoft Windows SQL Server 2000 Desktop Engine (WMSDE) if you are installing on a Windows Server 2003 computer.

SQL Server 2000 should be used for large installations of WSUS. MSDE should be used for installations of WSUS on Windows 2000 Server computers. For the purpose of this chapter I use the default WMSDE option, as this should be more than enough to service a small number of virtual machines (less than 500).

Installing Windows Server Update Server 2.0

Now that you have everything configured and ready to go, you can launch the WSUS installer inside of the virtual machine. In order to complete the installation, you need to do the following:

❑ After accepting the EULA you will need to specify that you do want to store updates locally and provide WSUS with a location on your second virtual hard disk to use for this storage.

❑ You will need to select to either install a copy of the Windows Microsoft SQL Server desktop engine or provide the name of another computer that is running a copy of SQL that will be used by WSUS.

118

Chapter 8: Keeping Virtual Machines Up-to-Date

❏ You will also need to configure whether WSUS should use the default website under IIS or create a new one. Unless you are intending to run other Web-based applications on this server, using the default website makes the most sense.

❏ You can select to name another WSUS server to mirror. If you do not have an existing WSUS server, you can just skip over this step.

After this final step you can leave the installation to complete itself.

Configuring Windows Server Update Server 2.0

After installing WSUS, you can configure it through the WSUS administrative website (a shortcut to this website is available in the **Administrative Tools** folder off of the **Start** menu). Before doing anything, you need to add the WSUS administrative website to your trusted sites under Internet Explorer (loading the WSUS administrative website without doing this will display the steps necessary to add the site to your trusted sites). Once you have loaded the WSUS administrative website, you may be tempted to start it downloading updates straight away, but it is much easier if you perform some basic configuration first.

*As WSUS uses a website for its administration, it is easy to accidentally lose a settings change by clicking on another page without applying options. You should always be certain to click **Save settings** in the task pane on the left of the WSUS administrative website after making any changes.*

Configure Computer Groups

By selecting **Computers** from the top-right section of the WSUS administrative website and then selecting **Create a computer group,** you create multiple groups by which to define your computers. The advantage of doing this is that you can then define different update policies for each group. This allows you to have one group of virtual machines where all updates are installed automatically, while another group gets only a subset of the available updates.

Set Computer Options

Select **Options** in the top-right section of the WSUS administrative website, and then select **Computer Options**. Here you will have a choice of two settings:

❏ **Use the Move computers task in Windows Server Update Services.** This setting requires that you use the WSUS administrative website to assign computers to computer groups manually. Any computer that you have not explicitly put in a group will be placed in the Unassigned Computers group. This setting is appropriate for use in a relatively static computing environment, where computers do not get created or deleted regularly. It has the advantage that there is no way that an administrator on the remote computer can change the group that the other computers are in.

❏ **Use Group Policy or registry settings on computers.** This setting allows each client computer to define which group it is in through the use of a specific registry key/group policy setting. This setting is best for environments where computers are rapidly created and destroyed, as it does not require a central administrator to keep track of each new computer and configure WSUS for it. The downside of this approach is that an administrator on the virtual machine could change which computer group they were in.

Part III: Maintaining Virtual Machines

Even if you are using the option to have each computer define which group it is in, you still need to create the groups using the WSUS administrative website. If a computer defines a group that does not exist it will be put in the Unassigned Computers group.

These two options are mutually exclusive. If you select to manage computer groups on the WSUS administrative website, any client-side settings will be ignored. Similarly if you choose to configure this on the client, the option to place a computer in a computer group will be disabled on the WSUS administrative website.

Set Automatic Approval Options

Select **Options** in the top-right section of the WSUS administrative website, and then select **Automatic Approval Options**. Configure the following settings:

❑ **Approve for Detection:** By checking this option you can specify which types of updates, on which computer groups, should be detected automatically. Specifying that an update should be detected means that the client computers will check to see if they need an update and log this information on the WSUS server.

❑ **Approve for Installation:** This option allows you to specify which types of updates, on which computer groups, should be installed automatically. An update that is configured to be installed automatically will be installed without prompting the end user for consent, if the client computer is configured to allow this.

❑ **Revisions to Updates:** From time to time, Microsoft releases an updated version of an existing update. By selecting **Automatically approve the latest revision of the update** the new update will be automatically approved if you had already approved the old update. Selecting **Continue using the older revision and manually approve the new update revision** means that you will need to approve each update as it occurs.

❑ **Windows Server Update Services Updates:** Some updates that need to be installed are specifically for Window Server Update Services itself. Without these updates, WSUS may have problems correctly detecting and installing updates as needed. For this reason, you should enable the option to automatically approve WSUS updates.

Configuring automatic update approval is a double-edged sword. On one hand, it reduces the amount of administrative overhead involved with running a Windows Server Update Server, but on the other hand, it increases the risk of installing an update that causes compatibility issues in your environment.

Unfortunately, the automatic approval option in WSUS is not very sophisticated. You cannot set different automatic approval options for different computer groups, nor can you set different automatic approval options for different products. If you want to have an advanced configuration like this, you are going to need to manually approve updates.

Windows Update Server Classifications

Windows Server Update Server breaks updates into a number of classifications:

❑ **Critical updates:** These are updates that address a critical, non–security-related bug. For an update to be regarded as critical, it will usually need to address a dire issue such as system crashes, data loss, or completely broken functionality. Critical updates are one of the two classifications that are enabled by default for download on WSUS.

120

Chapter 8: Keeping Virtual Machines Up-to-Date

❏ **Definition updates:** Definition updates are used for programs that maintain internal data stores for pattern matching or checking. Examples of this include Windows Defender (for detecting spyware and other malicious software) or Microsoft Outlook (for detecting junkmail).

❏ **Drivers:** Updated and new drivers are regularly made available through Windows Update. However, as virtual machines have a static hardware set and the virtual machine drivers are not released through Windows Update, selecting to download these updates does not make much sense (unless you are using WSUS for your physical computers as well).

❏ **Feature packs:** This is new functionality that is being released between major product releases. An example of this would be Windows Movie Maker, which was released via Windows Update after Windows XP was released. Feature-pack items are almost always included in the next official update of the product in question.

❏ **Security updates:** Microsoft rates security updates as critical, important, moderate, or low. Unfortunately, you cannot specify which level of security update to use when configuring Automatic Approval Options. If you want to install only critical and important security updates, you will need to manually approve security updates.

❏ **Service packs:** Service packs are the big rollups of security updates, critical updates, non-critical updates, feature packs, and sometimes even new functionality for a product. Service packs have the highest chance of causing compatibility problems of all the update categories. You should think carefully before selecting to automatically install these on all your computers. Given the relatively low volume in service pack releases, it is quite reasonable to approve service packs by hand only, after testing them on your computers.

❏ **Tools:** These are small, standalone applications that are designed to help you perform a specific task. An example of a tool that has been distributed through Windows Update is the Network Diagnostic Tool.

❏ **Update rollups:** This is a collection of updates that have been released separately in the past for a specific product or feature. Update rollups often include critical updates, security updates, and standard updates.

❏ **Updates:** Finally, there are the plain, non-critical, non-security–related updates that address minor bugs.

Set Synchronization Options

Select **Options** in the top-right section of the WSUS administrative website, and then select **Automatic Approval Options**. There are then a number of options to configure for synchronization.

Schedule

You can configure WSUS to synchronize its update database on a manual basis, or daily at a time that you specify. Even if you specify that you want WSUS to synchronize daily you can start a manual synchronization at any time by selecting **Synchronize now** from the task pane (or from the home page of the WSUS administrative website).

Products and Classifications

You can also specify the products and update types to be provided by this instance of WSUS. WSUS 2.0 allows you to store updates for Microsoft Exchange, Forefront, Internet Security and Acceleration Server, Max, System Center Data Protection Manager, Office, SQL, Windows Live, Small Business Server, and Windows itself (supported versions of Windows are Windows 2000, XP, and Server 2003).

Part III: Maintaining Virtual Machines

Proxy Server

If you connect to the Internet through a proxy server, you can configure this for WSUS. As WSUS receives all information over standard http, you only need to specify a Web proxy address. If needed, you can also provide user credentials to use when connecting to the proxy server.

Update Source

By default, WSUS will connect to Microsoft's update servers to download new updates. If you have an internal corporate WSUS installation already in place, you can configure your installation of WSUS to reference that instead.

Update Files and Languages

There are more options here than meet the eye, so it is worth pressing the **Advanced** button to configure this properly.

The first option to select is whether you want to store update files locally on your server or whether clients should install the updates directly from the Microsoft servers. As discussed before, one of the main benefits of configuring WSUS for virtual machines is that the virtual machines do not need to be connected to the Internet. This makes the option of having clients connect to the Microsoft servers a non-starter. Once you select to have updates stored locally on your system, you have two very interesting options:

❑ **Download update files on this server only when updates are approved.** This option is checked by default and means that updates will be downloaded only once they are approved (either automatically or manually). This conserves the amount of data that is downloaded to WSUS but means that there is a delay between update approval and update deployment, as you have to wait for WSUS to download the update first. Otherwise, you can uncheck this option and have WSUS download updates immediately. This means that WSUS may download updates that you do not intend to install, but it also means that the updates are more likely to be ready to go the moment you approve them.

❑ **Download express installation files.** Normally, WSUS downloads full update packages that are, in turn, deployed to the client computers. Using express installation files requires WSUS to download more data from the Internet, but it can then deploy a smaller package to the client computers. As such, the decision to use express installation files or not depends on whether you want to reduce the amount of Internet bandwidth needed or the amount of internal bandwidth needed.

The other option you can configure is which languages to download updates in. You can choose to have updates downloaded in only the language that is used by the Windows Server Update Server, in a select number of languages, or in all possible languages. Increasing the number of languages that are supported by your WSUS server directly affects the amount of storage space you need to store the updates.

Using Windows Server Update Server 2.0

Now that you have installed and configured WSUS, you can begin the first synchronization of updates. You can do this from either the Synchronization options page or from the home page. Once WSUS has synchronized the update database, go to the **Updates** page to view information about the currently available updates on WSUS. By default, WSUS displays a filtered list of updates. You can change the filter that is used by modifying the options under the **View** panel on the left side of the WSUS administrative website.

Chapter 8: Keeping Virtual Machines Up-to-Date

Selecting a single update gives you more information about that update. Three tabs are displayed on the WSUS administrative website for each update. The **Details** tab allows you to see the update title, description, classification, and release date. You can also see which product it applies to as well as any online resources that provide more information about the update. The **Status** tab allows you to see which computers have had this update installed, which computers need to have this update installed, and which computers do not need the update at all (because of having the appropriate software). Finally, the **Revisions** tab allows you to see if this specific update has been released multiple times, and if so, when it was released.

The updates page is also where you can manually approve or decline an update. When you select an update from the list, you should see a number of tasks appear in the **Update Tasks** panel on the left side of the WSUS administrative website. The tasks that are offered depend on the current state of the update. If the update has not yet been approved, you will see the option to **Approve for installation** or to **Approve for detection**. Both of these tasks bring up the same dialog box, but with a different default setting (**Install** and **Detect**, respectively). This dialog box allows you to specify an approval action for all computers, and individually for each computer group. This is the location where you can configure updates to be applied for one group of computers, but not to another group. For each computer group, you can specify **Install**, **Detect only**, **Remove**, or **Not approved**.

Install, obviously, installs the update on the virtual machines, according to the update download and installation policy that is set on the virtual machine. Detect simply checks to see if the virtual machines need this update. You can then view information about how many computers need this update through the WSUS administrative website. With this option, the user of the virtual machine receives no prompting to install the update, and the update is not installed automatically. The Remove option uninstalls the update if it is detected on the virtual machines in the specified computer group. Note that this option is not available for all update packages. Not approved is the default state for updates that have not been automatically approved. Nothing is done with these updates.

In addition to setting the approval option, you can also set a deadline for installation of the update. Typically, the deadline is set to None, which means that the update will be installed according to the policy set on the virtual machine. Setting a deadline ensures that the update will be installed on all virtual machines by that date. If you want an update to be installed immediately, you can set a deadline that occurs in the past.

Another option you will have is to **Decline update**. Doing this will stop the update from being installed on any virtual machines and will also remove the update from the default update view (you can see the update again by changing the **View** options). Finally, you can use the **Updates** page to change the approval settings on multiple updates simultaneously by selecting all of the updates in question and choosing a task from the **Update Tasks** panel.

Configuring WSUS Client Virtual Machines

Now that you have your Windows Server Update Server all set up and ready to go, it is time to configure the virtual machines to use this server for their updates. The easiest way to do this is by using Group Policy. If your virtual machines are in an Active Directory environment you can define the Group Policy for your domain and have it deployed to the virtual machines automatically. If you are not in an Active Directory environment, you can use Group Policy locally on the virtual machines to configure the update settings.

Part III: Maintaining Virtual Machines

In an Active Directory environment, you can link the Group Policy object with the WSUS settings to the domain. (Microsoft does not recommend editing the Default Domain or Default Domain Controller Group Policy Objects to add WSUS settings.)

After configuring WSUS Group Policy settings in an Active Directory environment, it can take up to 90 minutes for the policy to be deployed to any given virtual machine. If you want to have a virtual machine immediately download the latest Group Policy settings, you can run gpupdate /force *on a Windows XP, 2003 Server, or Vista virtual machine. On a Windows 2000 virtual machine, you can run* scedit /refreshpolicy machine_policy enforce.

To edit the Group Policy settings for WSUS, do the following:

1. Select **Run** on the **Start** menu.

2. Enter **mmc** into the Run dialog box and press OK.

3. From the **File** menu, select **Add/Remove Snap-in**.

4. Click **Add**.

5. Select the **Group Policy** snap-in and press **Add**.

6. Specify whether you are editing the Group Policy on the local computer or for the Active Directory, and then select **Finish**.

7. Select **Close** and **OK** to return to the console.

You will now need to expand the **Group Policy Object**, and then select **Computer Configuration** ➪ **Administrative Templates** ➪ **Windows Components** ➪ **Windows Update.**

If the Windows Update node is not present in the Windows Components sections, you will need to load the WSUS administrative template. The WSUS template is stored in wuau.adm, which is stored in the INF directory under the Windows directory on your system disk. Follow these steps to load this template:

1. Click the **Administrative Templates** node.

2. Select **Add/Remote Templates** from the **Action** menu.

3. Click **Add**.

4. Select the wuau.adm file and click **Open**; then click **Close**.

If your computer has an older version of the WSUS administrative template, you should still be able to configure the client to use your instance of WSUS. It will then download and install an up-to-date version of the WSUS administrative template.

A number of settings are controlled by policies defined under the **Windows Update** section.

Remove the "Install Updates and Shut Down" Option

This setting is controlled by the "Do not display 'Install Updates and Shut Down' option in Shut Down Windows dialog box" policy. With Windows XP SP2 and later releases, Windows Update will offer to install pending updates as part of Windows shut down. It does this by adding the option to **Install Updates and Shut Down** to the standard Windows Shut Down dialog box.

124

Chapter 8: Keeping Virtual Machines Up-to-Date

The policy has three possible configurations:

❏ **Enabled:** Causes this option to be removed from the Windows Shut Down dialog box.

❏ **Disabled:** Leaves the option to Install Updates and Shut Down in the Windows Shut Down dialog box.

❏ **Not Configured:** Is the same as Disabled.

> The recommended configuration is Not Configured. Being prompted to install updates on shutdown of a virtual machine is not problematic in most cases. Unless you have a specific need to stop this from happening, you should leave this policy off.

Don't Default to "Install Updates and Shut Down"

This setting is controlled by the "Do not adjust default option to 'Install Updates and Shut Down' in Shut Down Windows dialog box" policy. Typically, when Windows Update detects that there are updates that need to be applied, Windows will make **Install Updates and Shut Down** the default option that is selected when a user chooses to shut down Windows. The policy allows you to change this behavior:

❏ **Enabled:** If this policy is enabled, the user will always have a default selection of the last shut down action they performed (Turn off, Restart, and so on).

❏ **Disabled:** The **Install Updates and Shut Down** option will be the default selection for the Windows Shut Down dialog box, if it is available.

❏ **Not Configured:** This is the same as Disabled.

If the "Do not display Install Updates and Shut Down option in Shut Down Windows dialog box" policy is enabled, then the "Do not adjust default option to Install Updates and Shut Down in Shut Down Windows dialog box" policy no longer makes any difference as the option will never be available to be set as a default.

> The recommended configuration is Not Configured. It is good to know if updates are available that need to be applied. Unless you have a specific need to stop this from happening you should leave this policy off.

Configuring Automatic Updates.

This setting is controlled by the "Configure Automatic Updates" policy. Typically under Windows, a user can configure their own settings for how and when automatic updates are performed. The policy allows you to enforce a specific setting for automatic updates. The options for the policy are:

❏ **Enabled:** Enabling this policy allows you to specify automatic update settings to be used by Windows. It also disables the user interface used to configure this by the end user under Windows.

❏ **Disabled:** This will stop any automatic updating from ever happening. All updates will have to be installed manually by the end user. This is obviously an undesirable option after going to the effort of setting up your own Windows Server Update Server.

❏ **Not Configured:** This option will leave configuration of automatic updates to the end user through the standard user interface.

125

Part III: Maintaining Virtual Machines

If this policy is enabled, a number of settings need to be configured:

❑ **Configure automatic updating:** This setting has four choices:

> **2 - Notify for download and notify for install:** This means that the computer will check with the Update Server and notify the user when updates are available. The user will then need to select to download the updates and will be notified again once the updates are downloaded so that the user can install them.

> **3 - Auto download and notify for install:** With this option, the computer will check with the Update Server and automatically download any new updates that are available. The user will only be notified once the updates are downloaded, so that they can then be installed.

> **4 - Auto download and scheduled install:** Here the computer checks with the Update Server, automatically downloads any new updates, and automatically installs them at the scheduled time. The user will only be prompted if the scheduled installation requires the computer to be rebooted.

> **5 - Allow local admin to choose setting:** With this option, the user on the computer is able to configure the option for automatic updates; however, the user cannot disable automatic updates.

❑ **Scheduled install day:** This setting applies only if **4 - Auto download and scheduled install** is selected as the automatic update setting. Here you can specify a specific day of the week that updates should be installed on. Alternatively, you can specify that any new updates should be installed daily.

❑ **Scheduled install time:** This setting applies only if **4 - Auto download and scheduled install** is selected as the automatic update setting. This allows you to specify the hour in which updates should be installed on the computer.

> The recommended configuration is Enabled with the "Auto download and scheduled install" option selected and a daily installation scheduled. The main purpose of configuring a Windows Server Update Server is to ensure your virtual machines are as up-to-date as possible. Allowing this functionality to be disabled does not make much sense.

Use Intranet Update Server

This setting is controlled by the "Specify intranet Microsoft update service location" policy. This is the critical client setting. This policy allows you to configure the virtual machine to use your Windows Server Update Server instead of trying to contact Microsoft's update servers. You can set the following states for this policy:

❑ **Enabled:** This means that the virtual machine will use the WSUS instance specified.

❑ **Disabled:** If this policy is disabled the virtual machine will continue to contact Microsoft's update servers for automatic updates.

❑ **Not Configured:** This is the same as Disabled.

Chapter 8: Keeping Virtual Machines Up-to-Date

Once you have enabled this policy, you need to configure two additional settings:

❑ **Set the intranet update service for detecting updates:** Here you need to enter the URL for your Windows Server Update Server, in the form of http://servername. This is the server that will be used to download updates.

❑ **Set the intranet statistics server:** WSUS gathers statistics about the update level for each of its client computers. You have to use the same server name that you specified as the update server for the statistics server setting.

> The recommended configuration is Enabled with your Windows Server Update Server specified for both the update and statistics server addresses. It does not make sense to go to all the effort of setting up WSUS if you are going to have your virtual machines download updates from the Internet.

Enabling Client-Side Targeting

This setting is controlled by the "Enable client-side targeting" policy. This policy allows the virtual machine to specify which computer group it should be in on the Windows Server Update Server. The same three settings apply.

As noted earlier in this chapter, in order for client-side configuration of computer groups to work, this option needs to be enabled on the Windows Server Update Server as well, and the computer group specified by the client needs to be defined on the server.

❑ **Enabled:** This means that the virtual machine will be placed in the WSUS computer group specified by this policy.

❑ **Disabled:** If this policy is disabled the virtual machine will be placed in the **Unassigned computers** group, unless it is manually placed in a group via the WSUS administrative website.

❑ **Not Configured:** This is the same as Disabled.

When this policy is enabled, you need to define the "target group name" for that computer. The Target Group Name is the name of the group for which you want this virtual machine to be configured.

> The recommended configuration is Enabled with an appropriate group name specified. You may choose to manage computer group assignment on the Windows Server Update Server, but given the dynamic nature of virtual machines, client-side configuration of computer groups is much easier to manage.

Rescheduling Update Installation

This setting is controlled by the "Reschedule Automatic Updates scheduled installations" policy. It may not be possible for all available updates to be installed on a virtual machine at the same time. This can happen when updates require that they be installed by themselves (like a service pack installation) or

127

Part III: Maintaining Virtual Machines

when one update is dependent on having another update already installed. Normally when this happens any missed updates will not be installed until 24 hours later when Windows checks for updates again (or a week later if you have configured Windows to only check on a weekly basis rather than on a daily basis). If you are regularly bringing new virtual machines online and need to have all patches applied as quickly as possible, this behavior can be quite problematic. Thankfully, this policy allows you to specify that the virtual machine should download and install outstanding updates soon after rebooting because of an update installation. The options for this policy are:

❑ **Enabled:** This means that the virtual machine will attempt to download and install any outstanding updates after rebooting because of an update installation.

❑ **Disabled:** This means that the virtual machine will wait until the next scheduled update check to install outstanding updates.

❑ **Not Configured:** When set to Not Configured, updates will be rescheduled to occur one minute after system startup.

When this policy is enabled there is a single setting that needs to be defined: **Wait after system startup (several minutes)**.

This is the amount of time that the virtual machine should wait after system startup to initiate the installation of any outstanding updates. Normally this value is set to one minute. You will need to increase this value only if you have other programs that perform operations at system startup, and you do not want to disrupt them.

Note that this policy specifies that outstanding updates should be installed within a specified time from system startup, not user login. You do not need to have a user login in order for any updates to be installed on the virtual machine.

> The recommended configuration is Not Configured. As mentioned, enabling this policy will help you to bring newly created virtual machines up-to-date rapidly.

Disable Automatic Restart

This setting is controlled by the "No auto-restart for scheduled Automatic Updates installations" policy. When Windows Update installs a new update that requires that Windows be restarted, Windows Update automatically restarts the virtual machine. This policy allows you to disable this behavior for when a user is currently logged into Windows on the virtual machine. There are three options for this policy:

❑ **Enabled:** With this option, the virtual machine will not restart automatically if a user is currently logged in. Note that if no users are logged into the virtual machine, it will still be restarted automatically.

❑ **Disabled:** Disabling this policy means that the virtual machine will be restarted automatically (if required by the update) even if a user is currently logged in.

❑ **Not Configured:** This is the same as Disabled.

Chapter 8: Keeping Virtual Machines Up-to-Date

> The recommended configuration is Not Configured. Unless you have a specific issue with the normal behavior, it's a good thing to restart virtual machines in order to allow updates to take effect as soon as possible

Configuring Update Detection Frequency

This setting is controlled by the "Automatic Updates detection frequency" policy. While Windows Update can be configured to install updates only on a daily or weekly basis, it can be configured to check for available updates much more frequently. Typically, having a higher update detection frequency than your installation frequency makes no real difference, apart from increasing the load on your Windows Server Update Server. The one place where this can help is if you have configured update installation deadlines on your Windows Server Update Server. If an update installation deadline has been passed, Windows Update will install the update immediately on detection instead of waiting for the designated update installation schedule. The options for this policy are:

❑ **Enabled:** This allows you to specify a custom update detection frequency.

❑ **Disabled:** This means that Windows Update will use the default update detection frequency of 22 hours.

❑ **Not Configured:** This is the same as Disabled.

When this policy is enabled, the "check for updates at the following interval" setting needs to be defined. Here you can define a figure between 1 and 22 to be used as the update detection interval (in hours).

Windows Update does not actually use the exact value that you specify for the update detection interval. Rather, it randomly picks a number that is anywhere from 80 to 100 percent of the number you specified. So if you configured Windows Update to perform update detection every 10 hours, it could be checking as often as every 8 hours.

The reason for doing this is so that when you have a large number of computers that are all configured with the same update detection frequency, they will not all try to check the Windows Server Update Server at the same time.

> The recommended configuration is Enabled with an update interval of one hour. It is unlikely that you will be stressing a Windows Server Update Server that is dedicated to your virtual machines. Having a small update detection interval allows you to be able to push out updates rapidly if needed.

Immediately Install Minor Updates

This setting is controlled by the "Allow Automatic Updates immediate installation" policy. If an update is small enough that it does not require Windows to be restarted, and it is guaranteed to not interrupt any Windows services, it is possible to have Windows Update install the update immediately upon update detection. The options for this policy are:

❑ **Enabled:** This means that the virtual machine will install any non-disruptive updates immediately upon update detection, rather than waiting for the scheduled installation time.

129

Part III: Maintaining Virtual Machines

❑ **Disabled:** Disabling this policy means that all updates, even non-disruptive ones, will be installed only at the scheduled installation time.

❑ **Not Configured:** This is the same as Disabled.

If you enable this policy, increasing the update detection frequency in the prior policy can result in non-disruptive updates being deployed very rapidly.

> **The recommended configuration is Enabled. This just makes sense; getting non-disruptive updates installed as soon as possible is a good idea.**

Restart Delay

This setting is controlled by the "Delay Restart for scheduled installations" policy. This policy allows you to configure how long Windows Update should wait after installing an update to restart the virtual machine, if the update requires a system restart. The options for this policy are:

❑ **Enabled:** This means you will be specifying a custom delay period to be used before restarting the virtual machine.

❑ **Disabled:** Disabling this policy means that Windows update will wait five minutes after installing the updates before attempting to restart the virtual machine.

❑ **Not Configured:** This is the same as Disabled.

When this policy is enabled, the **Wait the following period before proceeding with a scheduled restart** setting needs to be defined. This setting is set to 5 minutes by default. It can be configured for any value between 1 and 30 minutes.

> **The recommended configuration is Not Configured. For most environments the default configuration for this policy will be fine. Enable this only if you have a specific need to address.**

Re-Prompt Delay

This setting is controlled by the "Re-prompt for restart with scheduled installations" policy. If a user is logged in to Windows when an update that requires a system restart is installed, the user will be prompted to restart the virtual machine. When prompted, the user can choose to restart the system immediately or to be asked again in the near future. This policy allows you to define how long Windows Update should wait before prompting the user again. The options for this policy are:

❑ **Enabled:** This means you specify a custom time period to be used before re-prompting the user.

❑ **Disabled:** Disabling this policy means that Windows update will wait 10 minutes before re-prompting the user.

❑ **Not Configured:** This is the same as Disabled.

130

Chapter 8: Keeping Virtual Machines Up-to-Date

When this policy is enabled the **Wait the following period before prompting again with a scheduled restart** setting needs to be defined. This setting is set to 10 minutes by default. It can be configured for any value between 1 and 1,440 minutes.

> The recommended configuration is Not Configured. The default wait of 10 minutes is reasonable, and using a smaller interval will most likely only serve to frustrate the end user. You may consider increasing the interval if you (or the users of your virtual machines) are annoyed by being prompted too often.

Finally there is one last group policy that you should consider configuring, but you'll have to look somewhere else.

Disable Windows Update Links

This setting is controlled by the "Remove links and access to Windows Update" policy. Unlike the other policies, this one is in the **Start Menu and Taskbar** folder under **Administrative Templates**, under **User Configuration**. Windows usually displays links to access the Windows Update website on the Start Menu. This option allows you to remove these links so that only your Windows Server Update Server is used for installing updates. The options for this policy are:

❏ **Enabled:** This means that the links will be removed from the Start menu. It also means that if users try to access Windows Update manually (by going to the appropriate website) they will receive an error message informing them that the system administrator has disabled this feature of Windows.

❏ **Disabled:** Disabling this policy means that the links are left in the Start menu, and everything functions as normal.

❏ **Not Configured:** This is the same as Disabled.

> The recommended configuration is Enabled. As you are using a Windows Server Update Server for update management, there is no need to access the Windows Update website. Furthermore, if you have configured WSUS to not install specific updates, going to the Windows Update website may result in these updates being installed against your wishes.

Configuring WSUS Client Virtual Machines with the Registry

While group policy is the best way to configure a WSUS client virtual machine in an Active Directory environment, for standalone computers you may prefer to just edit the registry settings directly.

Editing the Registry settings is definitely less intuitive than using the group policy configuration options, but it does have one significant advantage: It is easy to script against the registry. One option to consider is that when you create your base virtual machines you could include a script to configure WSUS individually for each virtual machine after it is booted.

131

Part III: Maintaining Virtual Machines

WSUS stores the client configuration details in two places in the Windows Registry. The following table describes the entries are stored under HKEY_LOCAL_MACHINE\Software\Policies\Microsoft\Windows\WindowsUpdate.

Entry Name	Data Type	Values	Description
ElevateNonAdmins	DWORD	0 or 1	If this entry is set to 1, then users who are in the Users security group on the virtual machine will be able to approve or disapprove updates. If it is set to 0, then you will need to be an Administrator to approve or disapprove updates.
TargetGroup	String	The name of the WSUS computer group that this virtual machine should belong to.	This Registry entry corresponds to the **Enabled client-side targeting** group policy, and allows you to specify the name of the WSUS computer group that this virtual machine should belong to.
TargetGroupEnabled	DWORD	0 or 1	This entry dictates whether client-side targeting is enabled or not. A value of 1 means that it is enabled, and a value of 0 means that it is not enabled. For client-side targeting to work, both the TargetGroup and TargetGroupEnabled Registry entries need to be configured correctly.
WUServer	String	The URL of the Windows Server Update Server that is going to be used for update detection and downloads (for example, `http://servername`).	This corresponds to the **Specify intranet Microsoft update service location** group policy. You need to specify the URL for your instance of WSUS.
WUStatusServer	String	The URL of the Windows Server Update Server that is going to be used for recording the update status of the virtual machine (for example, `http://servername`).	This entry needs to be set to the exact same value as the WUServer entry; otherwise both will be treated as invalid.

132

Chapter 8: Keeping Virtual Machines Up-to-Date

The following table describes the entries stored under HKEY_LOCAL_MACHINE\Software\Policies\ Microsoft\Windows\WindowsUpdate\AU.

Entry Name	Data Type	Values	Description
AUOptions	DWORD	2, 3, 4 or 5	This entry corresponds to the **Configure Automatic Updates** group policy. 2 means that Windows will prompt the user before downloading or installing any updates. 3 means that updates will be downloaded automatically, but the user will be prompted before they are installed. 4 means that updates will be downloaded and installed automatically. 5 means that automatic updates must be enabled, but that the user can configure whether to be prompted or not. If this entry is set to 4, both the ScheduledInstallDay and ScheduledInstallTime entries must be configured appropriately.
AutoInstallMinor Updates	DWORD	0 or 1	This entry corresponds to the "Allow Automatic Updates immediate installation" group policy. When this entry is set to 1 minor, non-disruptive updates will be installed immediately. Otherwise, minor updates will only be treated like all other updates.
DetectionFrequency	DWORD	A number from 1 to 22	This entry corresponds to the "Automatic Updates detection frequency" group policy. The value specified for this entry is the number of hours to wait between each attempt to detect new updates.
DetectionFrequency Enabled	DWORD	0 or 1	Setting this entry to 1 means that the value specified in the DetectionFrequency will be used. Otherwise, updates are detected every 22 hours.
NoAutoReboot WithLoggedOnUsers	DWORD	0 or 1	This entry corresponds to the "No auto-restart for scheduled Automatic Updates installations" group policy. If this entry is set to 0, the virtual machine will automatically restart, if needed, after installing an update even if a user it currently logged in. Setting this entry to 1 means that the user will be prompted as to whether the virtual machine should restart or not.

Table continued on following page

Part III: Maintaining Virtual Machines

Entry Name	Data Type	Values	Description
NoAutoUpdate	DWORD	0 or 1	Setting this entry to 1 disables automatic updates.
RebootRelaunch Timeout	DWORD	A number from 1 to 1440	This entry corresponds to the "Re-prompt for restart with scheduled installations" group policy. It specifies how long, in minutes, Windows Update should wait before re-prompting a user to restart the virtual machine, if the user chooses to delay the restart of the virtual machine after updates are installed.
RebootRelaunch TimeoutEndabled	DWORD	0 or 1	If this entry is set to 1, the custom value specified in the RebootRelaunchTimeout entry will be used. Otherwise, the default setting of 10 minutes is used.
RebootWarning Timeout	DWORD	A number from 1 to 30	When Windows Update installs an update that has a deadline or schedule associated with it, and requires that the virtual machine be restarted, the user is not able to delay the restart. The user is, however, given a warning that the virtual machine is going to be restarted. This entry allows you to specify how long, in minutes, the user should have before the virtual machine is restarted.
RebootWarning	DWORD	0 or 1	If this entry is set to 1, the custom value TimeoutEnabled specified in the RebootWarningTimeout entry is used. Otherwise, the default setting of 5 minutes is used.
RescheduleWaitTime	DWORD	A number from 1 to 60	This entry corresponds to the "Reschedule Automatic Updates scheduled installations" group policy. The value for this entry indicates how long Windows Update should wait after system startup before it attempts to install any updates that could not be installed before the virtual machine was restarted.
RescheduleWait TimeEnabled	DWORD	0 or 1	If this entry is set to 1, the custom value specified in the RescheduleWaitTime entry is used. Otherwise, Windows Update waits until the next scheduled update installation time to install any missed updates.

Chapter 8: Keeping Virtual Machines Up-to-Date

Entry Name	Data Type	Values	Description
ScheduledInstallDay	DWORD	A number from 0 to 7	This entry determines on which day Windows Update will automatically install downloaded updates. 0 means that updates should be installed daily. 1 through 7 indicate that updates should be installed weekly on a specific day (1 stands for Sunday, 7 for Saturday, and the other numbers map to the appropriate day of the week).
			For this entry to be used, the AUOptions entry has to equal 4.
ScheduledInstallTime	DWORD	A number from 0 to 23	This entry specifies the hour of the day at which updates should be installed on the scheduled day. This entry uses 24-hour formatting where 0 equals midnight, 12 equals noon, and 23 equals 11 p.m.
			For this entry to be used, the AUOptions entry has to equal 4.
UseWUServer	DWORD	0 or 1	Setting this entry to 1 means that the Windows Server Update Server specified in the WUServer entry will be used. If you do not create this entry or you set it to 0, then the WUServer entry will be ignored and the virtual machine will use Microsoft's update servers instead.

Using WSUS 2.0 Without Any Internet Connection

Thus far, I have been talking about using WSUS when at least the WSUS virtual machine has an Internet connection (even if the client virtual machines do not), but there may be times when you will need to keep virtual machines up-to-date and not have any Internet connection available for WSUS. There are two options that you can consider in this sort of environment.

The first option is to create a WSUS virtual machine that is connected to the Internet, get it to download all the updates for the software that you are running, and then move it to the private network. Once the WSUS virtual machine is disconnected from the Internet, it will not be able to receive new updates, but it will still be able to service all of your virtual machines and provide the updates that it is aware of.

The second option is to maintain two WSUS virtual machines: one that is connected to the Internet and one that is not. You can then migrate update data from one WSUS instance to the other. This is a four-step process:

1. **Make sure that the advanced synchronization options are the same on both Windows Server Update Server installations.** As mentioned earlier in this chapter, under the advanced synchronization options for a Windows Server Update Server you can indicate whether the server

Part III: Maintaining Virtual Machines

should use "express" or "full" updates, and you can specify what languages updates should be downloaded. If either of these settings is different between the two Windows Server Update Servers, then the second server will not offer the updates to its client virtual machines.

2. **Copy the update data from one WSUS instance to the other.** During the installation of WSUS you needed to specify a location in which to store updates. In this location is a folder named WSUSContent. This folder will need to be copied from your source WSUS virtual machine to the target WSUS virtual machine.

3. **Export WSUS metadata from the database.** Next you need to export all of the metadata about the updates from the source WSUS virtual machine. This can be done using a tool called wsusutil.exe, which is stored in the Tools folder where Windows Server Update Server was installed. (This is usually in a folder called Update Services in the Program Files folder.) To export the metadata, you should execute the command:

```
wsusutil.exe export exportCabFile.cab exportLogFile.log
```

This can take quite a while to execute but unfortunately there is nothing that can be done to speed this up.

4. **Import WSUS metadata into the target database.** Finally you need to import the WSUS metadata on the target server. This is done using the same tool (wsusutil.exe) with the following command:

```
wsusutil.exe import exportCabFile.cab exportLogFile.log
```

Before importing the WSUS metadata, you need to ensure that the WSUS update data has already been copied across. When the metadata is imported, WSUS will check to see if the update file is present.

> As the amount of data to be transferred between the two virtual machines is quite sizable, one option to consider is using a third virtual hard disk. You can attach it to the source virtual machine, copy the data on to it, and then attach it to the destination virtual machine.

WSUS 3.0

Windows Server Update Server 3.0 is in beta at the time of this writing. Major changes in WSUS 3.0 include the following:

❑ A native Windows-based user interface that uses the Microsoft Management Console (MMC). There are also a number of usability improvements in the user interface.

❑ Support for more complex and advanced automatic approval rules, including the ability to set automatic approval depending on the product that is being updated.

❑ The ability to receive e-mail notification of new updates that need approval.

Other as yet undefined improvements are expected as well. If you want more details, check out this website: www.microsoft.com/windowsserversystem/updateservices/default.mspx.

Chapter 8: Keeping Virtual Machines Up-to-Date

Using a Linux YUM Server

A number of update distribution servers are available for Linux. This chapter employs the Yellow dog Updater, Modified (YUM) package management tools. YUM is a package management tool that is based on the Red Hat Package Manager (RPM) format used by RedHat, SuSE, and many other Linux distributions. To configure YUM, you need to install the YUM client on your Linux virtual machines. You can configure the YUM clients to use an Internet-based YUM server or you can create your own YUM server to provide updates to virtual machines that are not connected to the Internet.

> **Many commercial Linux distributions base their value proposition on the provision of update services. By configuring your own update server it is possible to avoid paying for these services. Having said that: It is up to you to decide whether this is appropriate for your environment and usage of Linux or not.**

Creating a YUM Server

A YUM server is basically a network-based repository of RPM packages along with a metadata file that describes the contents on the RPM packages. Beyond this there is no specific logic that runs on the YUM server. The YUM clients connect to this repository, access the metadata file, and make their own decisions on installation of packages. There are five steps to creating your own YUM server:

1. Install FTP or HTTP Server for file distribution.
2. Set up a YUM user account.
3. Ensure that FTP access is allowed from remote virtual machines.
4. Download update files for the YUM server.
5. Create the repository metadata file.

The following sections describe each step in detail.

> *The majority of steps in creating a YUM Server require that you are running with root privilege. This can be done by either logging in as root, or by logging in with your normal user account and using* su *to run the necessary commands. Always be careful when running as root to ensure that you do not inadvertently damage the system.*
>
> *I will be using Red Hat Enterprise Linux 4 as my Linux distribution. If you are running a different version of Linux, some of the steps specified may need to be modified as different packages may be installed, and configuration files may be in different places.*

Step One: Install FTP or HTTP Server for File Distribution

This chapter sets up an FTP server (using vsftpd) that is used to distribute updates to the client virtual machines. It is possible to use other FTP servers that are available for Linux, or to use an HTTP server for update distribution. The main reason for using vsftpd is its popularity.

137

Part III: Maintaining Virtual Machines

First, you need to find an RPM for installing vsftpd on the version of Linux that you are using. I was able to find the right RPM for RedHat Enterprise Linux 4 on www.rpmseek.com. Once you have the RPM, you can install vsftpd by running the following command:

```
Rpm -ivh vsftpd-2.0.1-5.EL4.4.i386.rpm
```

The exact name of the RPM file will depend on the version of Linux you are using and the version of vsftpd that you install.

Once vsftpd is installed, you need to configure it. This can be done by using a text editor to open /etc/vsftpd/vsftpd.conf. I will be using VI and opening this file by running the following:

```
vi /etc/vsftpd/vsftpd.conf
```

You need to make the following changes to this file:

1. Disable anonymous user access. To do this, you will need to find the line that says:

```
anonymous_enable=YES
```

and change it to:

```
anonymous_enable=NO
```

It is possible to leave anonymous access enabled, and indeed this does make setting up YUM slightly easier; however, it is not a good practice from a security perspective.

It is important to set anonymous_enable *to* NO *as commenting out this line will leave it enabled.*

2. Set an appropriate FTP banner. While this is a relatively small and cosmetic step, setting an appropriate FTP banner helps you and other users to know what this FTP server is being used for. (The FTP banner is the text that is displayed when anyone logs into the FTP server.) To do this you will need to find the line:

```
#ftpd_banner=Welcome to blah FTP service.
```

and change it to something like:

```
ftpd_banner=Welcome to my YUM FTP server.
```

3. Restrict users to only being able to access files and directories that are under their home directories. As with disabling anonymous access, this is good security practice. You will be creating a user account specifically for the purpose of downloading RPMs via YUM and you want this account to be as restricted as possible. In order to do this, add the following line to the end of the file:

```
Chroot_local_users=YES
```

After saving the changes to vsftpd.conf, restart the vsftpd service and configure it to start automatically when your Linux virtual machine starts. To do this, run the following commands:

```
/sbin/service vsftpd restart
/sbin/chkconfig vsftpd on
```

Chapter 8: Keeping Virtual Machines Up-to-Date

The final step in setting up the FTP server is to create the directory that will be used to store the YUM repository. Vsftpd uses the directory `/var/ftp/pub` as its default public directory, so you should create a directory under this to be used for your repository. I will be creating a directory called `/var/ftp/pub/yum/rhel4/` to store my YUM repository in.

Step Two: Set Up a YUM User Account

You need to create a user account that YUM can use to log into your FTP server. As this user will be used only for this purpose, you want to set the user's home directory to be that of the repository location that you created at the end of Step 1. The YUM user account can only be used to download packages from the YUM repository. You can do this by using the `useradd` and `passwd` commands as follows:

```
/usr/sbin/useradd -d /var/ftp/pub/yum yumuser
passwd yumuser
```

The `-d` *option on* `useradd` *allows you to specify the home directory to be used for the new user account. The preceding* `useradd` *command creates a user account called yumuser.*

`Passwd` *will prompt you to enter the password to be used for the yumuser account.*

To confirm that everything is working after creating this account you should test the FTP server and log in with the yumuser account. To do this, run:

```
ftp 127.0.0.1
```

and then log in using the yumuser account. Once you have confirmed that this works, it is time to quit from FTP and move on to the next step.

Step Three: Ensure That FTP Access Is Allowed from Remote Virtual Machines

Most Linux distributions install and configure a firewall when they are installed. Red Hat Enterprise Linux uses a firewall package called iptables (as do many other versions of Linux). You will need to configure the firewall to allow remote access to your FTP server. With iptables, this is a three-step process:

1. Add appropriate rules to the iptables rule file (`/etc/sysconfig/iptables`). To do this, open the rule file using a text editor:

```
vi /etc/sysconfig/iptables
```

Then add the following line:

```
-A RH-Firewall-1-INPUT -m state --state NEW -m tcp -p tcp --dport 21 -j ACCEPT
```

This should be added after the entry that states:

```
-A RH-Firewall-1-INPUT -m state --state ESTABLISHED,RELATED -j ACCEPT
```

but before the final COMMIT entry. Once you have made these changes, save them and close the file.

2. Configure iptables to load the FTP connections tracking module. This can be done by opening the iptables configuration file (`/etc/sysconfig/iptables-config`) in a text editor:

```
vi /etc/sysconfig/iptables-config
```

139

Part III: Maintaining Virtual Machines

and changing the line that says:

```
IPTABLES_MODULES=""
```

to say:

```
IPTABLES_MODULES="ip_conntrack_ftp"
```

When you are done, save your changes and close the file.

3. Restart the firewall. Now that everything is configured correctly, you can restart the iptables firewall by running the following:

```
/sbin/service iptables restart
```

You should try connecting to the FTP server from another virtual machine to ensure that everything is configured correctly at this stage.

Step Four: Download Update Files for the YUM Server

Now you need to acquire the update files for your YUM server from another public server. You can use a number of public servers. I will be using the DAG archive (http://dag.wieers.com/home-made/apt/). A good tool to use to download the RPM files is rsync. The following command downloads the files for Red Hat Enterprise Linux 4 from the DAG archive to a local directory that I have created in /var/ftp/pub:

```
rsync rsync://apt.sw.be/pub/freshrpms/pub/dag/redhat/el4/en/i386/RPMS.dag/
/var/ftp/pub/yum/rhel4/ -r -v -u --delete
```

This `rsync` command uses a number of handy parameters:

❏ -r: Tells `rsync` to recurse into any subdirectories

❏ -v: Tells `rsync` to be verbose, and display information about the files that are being copied

❏ -u: Tells `rsync` to not download older files, or files that you already have

❏ --delete: Tells `rsync` to delete any files that are on the local computer that are not on the remote computer

This exact command can be run again in the future in order to update your repository, and it will only download new or updates packages.

Step Five: Create the Repository Metadata File

The final step to configuring the YUM server is to create a repository metadata file. This is what clients use to determine what RPMs are available and how they should be installed. To do this, download the latest version of createrepo from http://linux.duke.edu/projects/metadata/generate and then install it with a command like this:

```
rpm -ivh createrepo-0.4.4-1.noarch.rpm
```

Chapter 8: Keeping Virtual Machines Up-to-Date

After installing createrepo, you can generate the repository metadata file for your RPMs by running createrepo with a parameter of the directory where you are storing the RPMs. In my case this means running:

```
Createrepo /var/ftp/pub/yum/rhel4/
```

Once this is completed, your YUM server is ready to go.

> **Now that you have created a YUM repository server you are going to want to keep it up-to-date. The easiest way to do this is to make a simple shell script that runs the `rsync` command (from Step 4) followed by the `createrepo` command (from Step 5). As `rsync` will download only new or changed files, this is a fairly short process.**
>
> **Once you have created this shell script, you can use cron (or a tool of similar functionality) to run it as often as you feel is appropriate.**

Operating a YUM Server with No Active Internet Connection

Compared to a Windows Server Update Server, a YUM server is a much simpler implementation. All of the files required by the YUM server are stored in a single directory and are easily portable. For this reason, operating a completely "offline" YUM server that is not connected to the Internet is quite easy. Once you have all of the appropriate tools installed on your YUM server, you need Internet access only to download new RPM files.

A YUM server with an intermittent Internet connection can download new RPMs while it is connected to the Internet, and it can continue to provide the RPMs it has to clients while it is not connected to the Internet. YUM servers that are never connected to the Internet can also function correctly, as long as RPMs are delivered in some other fashion (either through another virtual machine that is connected to the Internet, or through any other method. For example, new RPMs could be burned to a CD and then copied onto the YUM server).

Configuring a YUM Client

Now that your YUM server is configured, you must set up the client virtual machines to connect to it and download appropriate updates. A second look at www.rpmseek.com quickly reveals a YUM RPM for Red Hat Enterprise Linux 4 that can be installed with the following command:

```
rpm -ivh yum-2.4.2-0.4.el4.rf.noarch.rpm
```

On a standard installation of Red Hat Enterprise Linux 4, I needed the following RPM packages installed before installing YUM:

- ❑ Sqlite (sqlite-2.8.16-1.2.el4.rf.i386.rpm)
- ❑ Python-sqlite (python-sqlite-1.0.1-1.2.el4.rf.i386.rpm)
- ❑ Python-elementtree (python-elementtree-1.2.6-6.2.el4.rf.i386.rpm)
- ❑ Python-urlgrabber (python-urlgrabber-2.9.7-1.2.el4.rf.noarch.rpm)

141

Part III: Maintaining Virtual Machines

I was able to find all of these using `www.rpmseek.com` and similar websites.

After installing YUM, you will need to edit `/etc/yum.conf` by running:

```
vi /etc/yum.conf
```

You then need to make the following changes:

❑   Create a new section at the end of the configuration file by creating a new title. The new title can be any text that you like, as long as it is surrounded by square brackets and consists of one word with no spaces or tabs. For example:

```
[myYUMServer]
```

❑   Under this title, you must define the following:

   ❑   **name:** This is a friendly, human-readable name to be used to identify this YUM repository.

   ❑   **baseurl:** This is the URL used to access the YUM repository. Because the FTP server does not support anonymous access, this URL will need to include the user name and password for the YUM user account.

As this information is stored in plain text, and not protected in any way, it is important to make sure that the YUM user account is treated as untrusted on the YUM server and should be given as few privileges as possible.

   ❑   **enabled:** This value needs to be set to 1 in order for YUM to actually use this server entry.

   This section of the YUM configuration file ends up looking like this:

```
[myYUMServer]
name=My Private YUM Server
baseurl=ftp://yumuser:password@YUMServer/rhel4/
enabled=1
```

Strictly speaking, this is all that you need to do to enable the YUM client, but there are a few other options in the YUM configuration file that you may be interested in setting:

❑   **assumeyes:** This option can be set to 1 or 0. The default setting for this is 0, but setting it to 1 means that YUM will never prompt for confirmation.

❑   **tolerant:** This option can be set to 1 or 0. When this option is set to 0, any error during the installation of any package will stop the installation of any other pending packages. Setting this to 1 means that YUM will continue installing other packages after a failure. The default setting for this is 0.

❑   **exclude:** This is a space-separated list of packages that should be excluded from any updates or installs. This is very useful for handling cases in which you need a specific version of a package and want to ensure that it is never updated.

❑   **retries:** This option sets the number of times a YUM client will attempt to retry downloading a package if an error occurs. The default setting for this is 6. Setting this option to 0 means that YUM will retry infinitely until it succeeds.

❑   **timeout:** This is the amount of time (in seconds) that a YUM client should wait before deciding that a server has failed to respond, and that it should retry. The default value is 30.

142

Chapter 8: Keeping Virtual Machines Up-to-Date

The retries and timeout values are useful for tuning behavior when you have limited bandwidth between the YUM server and the YUM client.

❑ **throttle:** This is a really useful option. It allows you to specify the maximum bandwidth to be used by the YUM client. This way, you can ensure that scheduled updates do not negatively affect other networking activity that is occurring. This option takes a number with a postfix of k, M, or G for kilobytes per second, megabytes per second, and gigabytes per second, respectively. If you want to limit the YUM client to 1.5 megabytes per second, for example, you specify a throttle value of 1.5M.

❑ **proxy:** If you need the YUM client to go through a proxy to access the YUM server, you can configure that here. This option takes a URL for the value. There are two other options, proxy_username and proxy_password, that can be used to specify the user name and password needed to connect to the proxy.

Using the YUM client

Now that everything is configured, you can install updates by going to the command prompt and running yum. This will provide you with some basic details of how to use the YUM client. Some important commands to know are:

❑ yum list: This command connects to the YUM server and provides you with a list of all of the packages that are available to be installed. You should be warned that this list can be very long indeed.

❑ yum check-update: Check-update is primarily used for shell scripts and other automation. If no new packages need to be updated, this program exits with a return code of 0. If there are packages that need to be updated, it will exit with a return code of 100.

❑ yum update: If run with no extra parameters, this updates all packages installed on your Linux virtual machine to the latest available version. Alternatively, you can specify a specific package to update.

❑ yum install: To install a specific package off of the YUM server, you need to run yum install packagename. This is one of the areas where YUM is very handy, as it then determines any dependencies needed for the package you want to install, and installs everything necessary to use that package.

❑ yum remove: Similar to the install command, the remove command takes an extra parameter of the name of the package that you want to remove. It also identifies any other packages that have dependencies on the package you are removing and asks if you want to remove them as well.

When the YUM client is installed, it also configures cron to run a YUM update once a day. If you want to change this behavior, you need to edit the /etc/cron.daily/yum.cron file.

A number of graphical interfaces are available for YUM as well; however, I don't discuss those in this book. If you prefer to use a GUI over the command line it is well worth doing some research on the tools that are available.

143

Part III: Maintaining Virtual Machines

Handling Base Virtual Machines

When trying to keep all of your virtual machines up-to-date, base virtual machines can be one of the biggest problems to deal with. As time passes, your base virtual machines will become more outdated. This means that as you create new virtual machines from your base virtual machines, you will have an ever increasing number of updates that need to be installed.

You may be thinking that you should just install updates on your base virtual machines as they are released, but there are problems with doing this. In order to apply an update to a Windows base virtual machine you will need to complete the SysPrep process, install the update, and re-SysPrep the base virtual machine. The problem with this is that many versions of Windows are limited to having SysPrep run on them only three times.

The second problem is that if you have used differencing disks to create new virtual machines, you cannot apply an update to the base virtual machine without invalidating all the virtual machines that are referencing it.

To deal with these problems, the best approach when you create your base virtual machines is to keep a backup copy that is configured as you need and is ready to run SysPrep. You can then periodically install updates on this backup and recreate your base virtual machines with minimal effort.

If you are using differencing disks you will need to keep existing base virtual machines in place until such a time as when there are no longer any active virtual machines referencing them.

Conclusion

In this chapter, you have read about the different approaches to patch management inside of virtual machines, and you have seen when and why the different strategies are appropriate.

The options are to not update your virtual machines, as they are in a trusted private location, to rely on automated updating over the Internet, or to use your own update installation servers.

You have also learned how to create your own update server virtual machines for both Windows, using Windows Server Update Server, and Linux, using the Yellow dog Updater, Modified (YUM) server, so that you can provide a robust update solution without dependencies on external computers.

144

Part IV

Security and Backup for Virtual Machines

Chapter 9: Keeping Virtual Machines Secure

Chapter 10: Securing Virtual Server

Chapter 11: Backing Up Virtual Machines

9

Keeping Virtual Machines Secure

With any computing infrastructure, it is important to keep it secure from viruses and other network-based dangers. This is also true for virtual machines. Virtual machines act and behave just like physical computers, which means that they, too, can be infected with viruses or be the victim of a network attack, or otherwise be compromised.

This chapter looks at the different issues to consider, and the possible strategies you can employ to keep your virtual machines secure from these threats.

Antivirus for Virtual Machines

Virtual machines cannot be protected by the antivirus or antispyware software running on the host operating system. This software is not aware of the virtual machines and cannot scan either the virtual machines memory or their virtual hard disks. The best way to provide virus protection for your virtual machines is to install antivirus and antispyware software inside of each of the virtual machines.

Even though most antivirus programs do not have the ability to scan the contents of virtual hard disks, a number of them still attempt to receive notification of any writes to these files. This can result in performance degradation, and in some cases can even cause system crashes. It is best to check your antivirus software to see if there is any way for you to exclude VHD files from automatic virus scanning.

When you do this, it is important to make sure that you have appropriate licenses to run the number of antivirus and antispyware installations that you have. It is also important to have a strategy determined for keeping virus and spyware definitions up-to-date for each of the virtual machines. Much like with the update management options discussed in the previous chapter; you can choose to use Internet-based updates, store updates on a central server or virtual machine, or store updates on a CD/CD image and install them manually when you start a virtual machine.

Part IV: Security and Backup for Virtual Machines

You should also check to see if the antivirus and antispyware software that you are using performs scheduled system scans. If it does, you need to configure the virtual machines to perform their scans at different times; otherwise, you will see performance problems when all the virtual machines attempt to perform a system scan at the same moment in time.

> With Virtual Server 2005 R2 SP1, it is possible to scan virtual hard disks using the antivirus software installed on the host operating system without your having to run the virtual machine. Virtual Server 2005 R2 SP1 provides a tool called VHDMount that allows you to mount a virtual hard disk on the host operating system as if it were a physical hard disk.
>
> Using VHDMount, you can mount a virtual hard disk and then scan it with the antivirus software installed on the host operating system. Note that you cannot do this while the virtual machine is running, so you still need to install antivirus software on each of the virtual machines.

Network Security for Virtual Machines

Each virtual machine has its own MAC address, IP address, and network identity. As such, it is as vulnerable to network-based threats as any physical computer. Virtual machines are connected to the physical network through your host operating system.

Virtual Machine Firewall Configurations

Unfortunately, software firewalls installed in the host operating system will not protect any virtual machines. The reason for this is that the virtual machines are connected to the physical network at a lower level in the networking stack than where most firewall software operates.

Virtual machines are connected to the physical network at OSI layer 3. Most firewall software runs at layers 4, 5, or higher.

In order to protect your virtual machines from the network, consider the following approaches:

❑ **You can install and configure firewall software inside each of the virtual machines.** This is the simplest approach to configure, but it relies on the fact that all of your virtual machines are capable of running software firewalls. It also adds a management burden if you ever need to make a change to your firewall configuration, as you will then need to go into each of the virtual machines to make the change.

❑ **You can use an external firewall.** As virtual machines appear like separate physical computers from a networking perspective, firewalls that are external to your physical computer will protect your virtual machines along with your physical computer. Having said that, it is not always practical to have an external firewall, either because you do not have enough computers to justify the overhead of maintaining an external firewall or because you are using a mobile computer and cannot always guarantee that it will be connected to a protected network with firewall infrastructure present.

148

Chapter 9: Keeping Virtual Machines Secure

❏ **Route network connections through a firewall before connecting to the physical network.** It is possible to configure your network such that the virtual machine's network traffic is routed through a firewall before it gets to the physical network. This option requires the most configuration but provides a central point of configuration and will move with your physical computer wherever you go.

Routing Network Connections

At a high level, securing virtual machines by routing their network connections involves the creation of a private trusted network to which your virtual machines are connected, and a public untrusted network that contains your physical network connection. Once you have these two networks, you can configure network traffic to be routed between them, and in the process you can limit the types of connections that are allowed in order to protect the virtual machines on the private network. You can create a private and public network arrangement in a number of ways:

❏ **Create two physically separate networks and use a physical computer to route traffic between the two networks.** This approach requires the most infrastructure and configuration, but it has the advantage of giving you a single network protection solution that can be used to protect multiple physical computers and any virtual machines that are running on top of them. This configuration is essentially equivalent to having an external firewall on your network.

❏ **Create an internal virtual network and use a virtual machine to route traffic between it and the physical network.** You can create a virtual network (with no physical network connection) to which all of your virtual machines are connected. You can then create a single virtual machine that is connected to both the internal virtual network and the physical network. This virtual machine can be responsible for routing the network traffic between the virtual machines and the physical world.

Having an entire virtual machine dedicated to routing network traffic may be considered a very heavy implementation, as this approach will use a lot of memory and disk space for this purpose. However, if you already have this sort of configuration for other purposes (such as maintaining an update server as discussed in the previous chapter) then it is easy to go with this approach.

❏ **Use the Microsoft Loopback Adapter to allow the host operating system to route traffic between an internal virtual network and the physical network.** Windows includes drivers for a special network card called the Microsoft Loopback Adapter. This is a network card driver that can be installed into Windows without any physical network adapter being present. It creates what appears to be an active network connection without any other computers connected to it. The Microsoft Loopback Adapter was originally created to allow people to install and configure the networking features in Windows even when they did not have drivers for their physical network card handy. With virtual machines, the Microsoft Loopback Adapter takes on a whole new dimension of functionality.

By installing the Microsoft Loopback Adapter on your host operating system, and then creating a virtual network that uses the Microsoft Loopback Adapter as its physical connection, you can create a private virtual network that includes only virtual machines and the host computer (but not any external computers). Once you have done this, you can then use the host operating system to route network traffic between this private network and the physical network.

This chapter steps through a number of options and sets them up using the third approach mentioned here (using the Microsoft Loopback Adapter). However, you should be able to apply similar configurations to any of the approaches just discussed.

149

Part IV: Security and Backup for Virtual Machines

Installing the MS Loopback Adapter

The Microsoft Loopback Adapter is available on Windows XP, Windows Server 2003, and Windows Vista. To install the Microsoft Loopback Adapter on Windows Server 2003 and Windows XP you need to do the following:

1. On the host operating system, go to **Control Panel** on the **Start menu.**

2. Start **Add Hardware.**

   *This is under the **Printers and Other Hardware** category of the **Control Panel** if you are using the category view with Windows XP.*

3. In the **Add Hardware Wizard**, click **Next** to get started.

4. When the **Is the hardware connected?** page appears, select **Yes, I have already connected the hardware,** and then click **Next.**

5. In the **Installed hardware** list, select **Add a new hardware device**, and then click **Next.**

6. In the **What do you want the wizard to do?** list, select **Install the hardware that I manually select from a list (Advanced)**, and then click **Next.**

7. In the **Common hardware types** list, click **Network adapters**, and then click **Next.**

8. In **Manufacturer** list, select **Microsoft.**

9. In the **Network Adapter** list, select **Microsoft Loopback Adapter**, and then click **Next** twice.

10. In the Completing the Add Hardware Wizard page, click Finish.

To install the Microsoft Loopback Adapter on Windows Vista execute the following steps:

1. On the host operating system go to **Control Panel** on the **Start menu.**

2. Switch the **Control Panel** to **Classic view** and start **Add Hardware.**

3. In the **Add Hardware Wizard**, click **Next** to get started.

4. In the **What do you want the wizard to do?** list, select **Install the hardware that I manually select from a list (Advanced)**, and then click **Next.**

5. In the **Common hardware types** list, click **Network adapters**, and then click **Next.**

6. In **Manufacturer** list, select **Microsoft.**

7. In the **Network Adapter** list, select **Microsoft Loopback Adapter**, and then click **Next** twice.

8. In the **Completing the Add Hardware Wizard** page, click Finish.

When the Microsoft Loopback Adapter is first installed, it is configured to use DHCP to automatically acquire an IP address. However, as the Microsoft Loopback Adapter is never connected to a physical network, it never receives an IP address via DHCP. If you leave the Microsoft Loopback Adapter with this configuration, you add a noticeable delay to networking being initialized on your computer. As such, you should configure the Microsoft Loopback Adapter to use a static IP address as soon as you have finished installing it.

150

Chapter 9: Keeping Virtual Machines Secure

> When you have installed a Microsoft Loopback Adapter and are configuring a static IP address, you need to be careful to configure it correctly. You should configure the IP address and an appropriate subnet mask, but you should not configure a default gateway. The gateway is the network address of the computer that routes traffic on one network to another. The Microsoft Loopback Adapter connects to an internal network with no gateway. If you configure a gateway address on the Microsoft Loopback Adapter, Windows will believe that it can transmit data over the Microsoft Loopback Adapter and have it reach the outside world. This has the potential to disrupt general network connectivity on your host computer, so in short: Leave the gateway address blank.

After installing the Microsoft Loopback Adapter you will need to create a new virtual network that references it. To do this, go to the Virtual Server administrative website and select **Create** from the **Virtual Networks** section of the navigation pane. Then enter a virtual network name (and notes if you want to) and select the entry for the Microsoft Loopback Adapter for the **Network adapter on physical computer** option.

Using Internet Connection Sharing

Once you have your private and public networks in place, you can route network traffic between the two networks in a number of ways. The first method to look at is to use the Internet Connection Sharing functionality that is built into Windows XP, Windows Server 2003, and Windows Vista. Internet Connection Sharing is a feature of Windows that implements a basic Network Address Translation (NAT) router.

NAT routers work by receiving traffic from computers on the private network, changing it so that it looks like it came from the router itself, and then transmitting the "translated" network traffic. The result of this approach is that it allows all virtual machines that are connected to the private network to be able to access resources on the public network, but computers on the public network cannot access computers on the private network (they can access only the NAT router, which is the host operating system in this case). This is both a blessing and a curse. The benefit of this is that you do not need to worry about installing firewalls on virtual machines, as they are protected from the public network by the NAT router. The downside is that this can cause problems if you actually need computers on the public network to access specific resources on your virtual machines. This can happen when:

❑ Your virtual machines are configured as network servers and you want computers on the public network to access them. For example, you may want to set up a virtual machine as a file server and have computers from the public network access it.

❑ You are using a program on the virtual machine that requires that a remote server be able to connect back to the client computer. This happens with peer-to-peer applications, and many video and voice conferencing programs as well as FTP.

FTP supports two modes of operation: active and passive. Active mode is the default for most FTP programs and requires that the server open a connection to the client that does not work with NAT routers. Passive FTP works correctly with NAT routers.

151

Part IV: Security and Backup for Virtual Machines

> A NAT router protects virtual machines on the private network from computers on the public network, but it does nothing to stop a virtual machine on the private network from attacking a computer on the public network. This might happen if the virtual machine is infected with a virus. For most people, the combination of a NAT router and up-to-date antivirus software provides sufficient protection. If you need more capability than this, you will need to configure a full firewall capable of monitoring both inbound and outbound connections.

To enable Internet Connection Sharing on Windows Server 2003 and Windows XP, follow these steps:

1. On the host operating system go to **Control Panel** on the **Start menu**.

2. Open **Network Connections**.

   *This is under the **Network and Internet Connections** category of the **Control Panel** if you are using the category view with Windows XP.*

3. Right-click on the network connection that is connected to the public network and select **Properties**.

   Do not select the Microsoft Loopback Adapter! Selecting the wrong network card at this stage can cause big problems for your network.

4. Click the **Advanced** tab.

5. Check the option to **Allow other network users to connect through this computer's Internet connection**. If you have multiple network adapters, you need to also specify that you are sharing the Internet connection with the Microsoft Loopback Adapter.

6. Click **OK**.

Follow these steps to enable Internet Connection Sharing on Windows Vista:

1. On the host operating system, go to **Control Panel** on the **Start menu**.

2. Select **Network and Internet** and then select **Network and Sharing Center**.

   *If you are using the classic view of the **Control Panel**, you can just start **Network and Sharing Center** directly.*

3. Select **Manage Network Connections** from the **Tasks** section of the left panel.

4. Right-click on the network connection that is connected to the public network and select **Properties**.

   Do not select the Microsoft Loopback Adapter! Selecting the wrong network card at this stage can cause big problems for your network.

5. Click the **Sharing** tab.

6. Check the option to **Allow other network users to connect through this computer's Internet connection**.

152

Chapter 9: Keeping Virtual Machines Secure

7. If you have multiple network adapters you will need to also specify that you are sharing the Internet connection with the Microsoft Loopback Adapter.

8. Click **OK**.

Once you have enabled Internet Connection Sharing, a number of changes are made to your system:

❑ The private network interface (in this case, the Microsoft Loopback Adapter) is configured with an IP address of 192.168.0.1.

❑ A DHCP server is initiated on the private network interface that provides the virtual machines with an IP address from 192.168.0.2 to 192.168.0.254.

❑ A DNS proxy is configured so virtual machines on the private network can use 192.168.0.1 as their DNS server.

All of this allows you to connect a virtual machine that is configured to use DHCP to the private network and have it instantly be able to gain access to resources on the public network.

> If you change the private network interface to use an IP address other than 192.168.0.1, Internet Connection Sharing will stop working. This can cause problems if your public network is also configured to use 192.168.0.x and, unfortunately, there is nothing that can be done to fix this (except for reconfiguring your public network to use a different subnet).
>
> Internet Connection Sharing aims to provide the basic capabilities needed from a NAT router. If you want to access more advanced NAT routing options, a number of commercial solutions are available. One popular solution for NAT on Windows is **WinGate** (www.wingate.com).

Configuring Port Forwarding with Internet Connection Sharing

One of the biggest problems with NAT routing solutions such as Internet Connection Sharing is that computers (or virtual machines) that are on the private network are unable to provide network services to the public network. One solution to this problem is an approach called port forwarding.

Port forwarding is where the NAT router is configured to direct network traffic bound for a specific network port on the NAT router to another network port on one of the computers attached to the private network. For example, if you want to have a virtual machine act as an FTP server from behind a NAT router, you can configure the NAT router to forward any traffic for port 21 (used by FTP) on the router to port 21 on the virtual machine that was running the real FTP server.

While port forwarding does address some of the issues associated with providing network services from behind a NAT router, it also has some problems of its own.

It can be confusing for people who are connecting to your server, as they will think that they are connecting to one server (the NAT router) but will actually be connected to another server. In some cases, they may even see the names of both servers in the process. Functionality will still be present but if they do not understand why they are seeing a different server name they may think that something has gone wrong.

153

Part IV: Security and Backup for Virtual Machines

Each port on the NAT router can be used by only one server. For instance, you cannot have two virtual machines set up as an FTP server and have port 21 traffic directed to both of them. Also, you cannot redirect a port if the NAT router is using it, so you cannot have an FTP server configured on both the NAT router and a virtual machine and expect them to be accessible from the public network.

Most NAT implementations allow you to forward a port to a different port to get around this issue. So you can forward port 7000 on the NAT router to port 21 on a virtual machine. Unfortunately, many network programs do not handle the use of nonstandard ports, and the ones that do require you to know the port number to configure them correctly. This is not the prettiest solution for this problem.

Some network servers rely on dynamically negotiated network ports. This means that each time a client connects to the server they agree upon a different, random port number to use. This is close to impossible to make work with static port forwarding (unless you manually forward all possible ports to the server in question).

With all of this in mind, if you want to configure port forwarding under Internet Connection Sharing, you can do so by going to the network connection properties page where you enabled Internet Connection Sharing and clicking the Settings button. Here you will be presented with a list of services that you can provide to the public network from the private network. If you select a service and click the Edit button you will see that each service has the following information associated with it:

❑ **Description of service:** This is a friendly name that is used to allow you to easily identify why this service was created.

❑ **Name or IP address of the computer hosting this service on your network:** Here you can specify either the network name or the IP address of the virtual machine that will be running the network server.

> Given that Internet Connection Sharing expects you to configure your virtual machines to use DHCP, there is no guarantee that a specific virtual machine will always have the same IP address. For this reason, you should always use network names when configuring services to be exposed through Internet Connection Sharing.

❑ **External Port number for this service:** This is the port number used on the host operating system by external computers that are trying to connect to the service provided by the virtual machine.

❑ **Internal Port number for this service:** This is the port number that is actually used by the server software on the virtual machine.

❑ **The ability to define TCP or UDP for a service:** TCP and UDP are the two common protocols used on TCP/IP-based networks. If you are not sure, it is most likely that your service is using TCP.

Once configured correctly, you can enable port forwarding by just checking the appropriate service from the list and clicking **OK**.

Chapter 9: Keeping Virtual Machines Secure

Using Routing and Remote Access Services

Windows Server 2003 provides a more advanced routing solution in the form of Routing and Remote Access Services (RRAS). Routing and Remote Access Services is installed by default, but not enabled. There are two ways that RRAS can be configured. The first is as a NAT router (which is similar to Internet Connection Sharing but with more configurability). The second is as a standard router.

To enable RRAS as a NAT router, follow these steps:

1. Select **Administrative Tools** and **Routing and Remote Access** from the **Start** menu.

2. Select the Routing and Remote Access entry for your server.

3. Select Configure and Enable Routing and Remote Access from the Action menu.

4. Proceed through the **Routing and Remote Access Server Setup Wizard** until you get to the **Configuration** page.

5. Select **Network address translation (NAT)** and click **Next**.

6. On the **NAT Internet Connection** page, select the network interface that is connected to your public network and make sure the **Enabled security on the selected interface by setting up Basic Firewall** option is selected.

7. On the **Network Selection** page, select the network interface that is connected to your private network (in this case it will be the Microsoft Loopback Adapter).

8. On the **Name and Address Translation Services** page select to **Enable basic name and address services** and complete the wizard.

You could select to not enable the basic name and address services provided by RRAS, and instead install and configure DHCP and DNS servers on your host operating system. This chapter covers the functionality provided by RRAS.

Disabling Internet Connection Sharing or the Windows Firewall

Routing and Remote Access is not compatible with Internet Connection Sharing or the Windows Firewall. If you have ever enabled either of these features, this step will fail with an error message. To disable these features you will need to do the following:

1. Select **Administrative Tools and Services** from the **Start** menu.

2. Find and select the service entry for **Windows Firewall/Internet Connection Sharing (ICS)**.

3. Select **Properties** from the **Action** menu.

4. Change the **Startup type** to **Disabled**.

5. Click the **Stop** button.

6. Click **OK** and exit the **Services** control.

155

Part IV: Security and Backup for Virtual Machines

Using RRAS for NAT Routing

Now you have a NAT router with similar functionality to the router that is provided by Internet Connection Sharing. There are many advantages when using RRAS for NAT.

You can configure your private network to use any subnet, not just 192.168.0.x. To change the subnet that is used by your private network, you first need to change the IP address and subnet mask that are used by your private interface (Microsoft Loopback Adapter) to one that is your desired subnet. Then you will need to do the following:

1. Select **Administrative Tools** and **Routing and Remote Access** from the **Start** menu.

2. Select the Routing and Remote Access entry for your server.

3. Select **NAT/Basic Firewall** from under the **IP Routing** node.

4. Click **Properties** under the **Action** menu.

5. Change to the **Address Assignment** page.

6. Enter the IP address and Mask that you want to use for your private network and click OK.

   After changing the subnet of the private network you will need to restart RRAS in order for the changes to work properly. You can do this by restarting the service under the services console, or by running `net stop "Routing and Remote Access"` *followed by* `net start "Routing and Remote Access"` *at a command prompt.*

You can also reserve IP addresses to be used for devices with static IP addresses on the private network. Internet Connection Sharing assumes that all devices connected to the private network will be using DHCP, but if you have virtual machines that are configured to be servers connected to the private network you will probably want to use static IP addresses for them instead. With RRAS, you can specify that these IP addresses be excluded from the range of IP addresses that it uses for its DHCP implementation. To do this, go to the **Address Assignment** page of the **NAT/Basic Firewall** properties and click the **Exclude** button. This brings up the **Exclude Reserved Addresses** page, which allows you to keep a list of IP addresses that should not be offered by the DHCP server.

Another advantage of using RRAS for NAT routing is that you can restrict the types of network traffic that are allowed to be sent from computers on the private network. This means that you can set up a private network where the virtual machines connected to it can browse websites on the public network, but not access other services that you want to block. To do this you will need to do the following:

1. Select **Administrative Tools** and **Routing and Remote Access** from the **Start** menu.

2. Select the Routing and Remote Access entry for your server.

3. Select **General** from under the **IP Routing** node.

4. Select the private interface from the list of available interfaces.

5. Click **Properties** under the **Action** menu.

6. You can now use the **Inbound Filters** and **Outbound Filters** buttons to configure static packet filtering on the network interface selected.

156

Chapter 9: Keeping Virtual Machines Secure

Static packet filtering allows you to define a set of static rules that determine whether network packets are allowed through or not. Inbound filters are applied to network traffic coming from the outside world into your network, while outbound filters are applied to network traffic coming from your network headed to the outside world. Once you have opened a configuration page for either inbound or outbound filters, you see the options allowing you to set preferences for receiving or dropping packets and the ability to create, edit, and delete filters.

First is the ability to configure the filters to **Receive/Transmit all packets** except those that meet the criteria below or to **Drop all packets** except those that meet the criteria below. The option that you select depends on whether you want to accept all network traffic by default, and block only specific uses, or whether you want to block all network traffic by default, and allow only specific uses.

The option to configure the filter to receive or drop by default is disabled until at least one filter is defined.

Then there is the ability to create, edit, and delete filters. For each filter you can define the following:

❑ **The source IP address and subnet mask:** This allows you to specify that a filter should only apply network traffic coming from a group of computers (or from one specific computer). Leaving this option not configured will mean that the filter applies to network traffic from any computer.

❑ **The destination IP address and subnet mask:** This allows you to specify that a filter should apply network traffic headings only for a group of computers (or for one specific computer). Leaving this option not configured will mean that the filter applies to network traffic heading for any computer.

❑ **The protocol type to filter:** This can be TCP, TCP [established], UDP, ICMP, Any, or Other. For TCP, TCP [established], and UDP, you can also specify a source and destination port to filter on. For ICMP, you can specify the ICMP type and code. For Other, you can specify the protocol number to filter.

Perhaps the most significant advantage of using RRAS over NAT, in relation to security concerns, is that you have access to a stateful, powerful firewall on the routing computer. To configure it you need to:

1. Select **Administrative Tools** and **Routing and Remote Access** from the **Start** menu.
2. Select the Routing and Remote Access entry for your server.
3. Select **NAT/Basic Firewall** from under the **IP Routing** node.
4. Select the public interface from the list of available interfaces.
5. Click **Properties** under the **Action** menu.
6. Check **Enable a basic firewall on this interface**.
7. You can now use the **Inbound Filters** and **Outbound Filters** buttons to configure static packet filtering on the network interface selected.

Configuration of the basic firewall uses the same user interface as is used for setting filters on general IP routing.

157

Part IV: Security and Backup for Virtual Machines

Configuring Port Forwarding with RRAS

You can also configure port forwarding with RRAS just as you can with Internet Connection Sharing. Follow these steps:

1. Select **Administrative Tools** and **Routing and Remote Access** from the **Start** menu.

2. Select the Routing and Remote Access entry for your server.

3. Select **NAT/Basic Firewall** from under the **IP Routing** node.

4. Select the public interface from the list of available interfaces.

5. Click **Properties** under the **Action** menu.

6. Change to the **Services and Ports** page.

Here you can add, edit, and delete port forwarding. As with Internet Connection Sharing, you can configure the service description, incoming port, outgoing port, and whether TCP or UDP is being used. However, unlike Internet Connection Sharing you can use only the IP address to specify the location of the actual server (and not the network name).

Configuring RRAS as a Standard Router

The other way to configure RRAS is as a standard router. In this configuration, network traffic is freely routed between both the public and private networks, with each network having full access to the other. While this is useful for providing external access to servers that are running on your virtual machines it has its own drawbacks.

You need to configure your private network to use valid public IP addresses. With a NAT router, the IP addresses on your private network are hidden from the public network. This allows you to use any private IP address without conflicting with computers on the larger public network. With standard routing, you need to make sure that your IP addresses will be unique on the public network as well as on the private network.

The other drawback is that your virtual machines will not be protected from unwanted network traffic by default. Thankfully this can be easily addressed by enabling network filtering on the router.

Follow these steps to enable RRAS as a standard router:

1. Select **Administrative Tools** and **Routing and Remote Access** from the **Start** menu.

2. Select the Routing and Remote Access entry for your server.

3. Select **Configure and Enable Routing and Remote Access** from the **Action** menu.

4. Proceed through the **Routing and Remote Access Server Setup Wizard** until you get to the **Configuration** page.

5. Select **Secure connection between two private networks** and complete the wizard.

Unlike setting up a NAT router with RRAS, when you set up a standard router with RRAS it will not handle DHCP and DNS for you. For most people it is easiest to just configure your virtual machines to use the same DNS servers as your host operating system is using. DHCP can be handled in one of two ways.

158

Chapter 9: Keeping Virtual Machines Secure

One option is to use the DHCP server that is provided by Virtual Server for each of the virtual networks. Follow these steps:

1. Open the Virtual Server administrative website.

2. Select **Configure** from the **Virtual Networks** section of the navigation pane, and choose the virtual network that is used for your private network.

3. Click **DHCP server**.

4. Check **Enabled** and configure the **Network address**, **Network mask**, **Starting IP address**, **Ending IP address**, **Virtual DHCP server address**, **Default gateway address**, and **DNS Servers**.

   Be aware of a number of restraints when configuring this page:

   ❑ Virtual Server reserves the first 16 IP addresses in the range for its own use. So the **Starting IP address** must be past the first 16 IP addresses in the range.

   ❑ The **Virtual DHCP server address** must be below the range specified by the **Starting IP address** and the **Ending IP address**.

   ❑ The **Virtual DHCP server address** is the IP address that will be used by Virtual Servers DHCP server. It is different than the **Default gateway address**, which is the address of the Microsoft Loopback Adapter.

5. Press **OK**.

A second option is to use the DHCP server that is part of Windows Server 2003. To do this you need to do the following:

1. Select **Control Panel** and then **Add or Remove Programs** from the **Start** menu.

2. Click **Add/Remove Windows Components**.

3. Select **Networking Services** and click **Details**.

4. Check **Dynamic Host Configuration Protocol (DHCP)** and click **OK**.

5. Complete the **Windows Components Wizard** and close the **Add or Remove Programs** window.

6. Select **Administrative Tools** and then **DHCP** from the **Start** menu.

7. Select your server from the **DHCP** list. If you have multiple network adapters with static IP addresses, you should make certain that you are selecting the server entry that uses the IP address of the network adapter you want the DHCP server to run on. If you do not see the entry you want, try deleting the other entries and manually adding the IP address that you want to use.

8. Click **New Scope** in the **Action** menu.

9. On the **Scope Name** page, define an appropriate name and description for your DHCP scope.

10. On the **IP Address Range** page, specify the starting IP address, ending IP address, and subnet mask that should be used for virtual machines on your private network.

11. Specify any IP addresses that need to be excluded from the DHCP range you just specified on the **Add Exclusions** page.

12. Configure the lease duration for your DHCP server. Unless you have specific needs, the default setting here should work fine for your network.

159

Part IV: Security and Backup for Virtual Machines

13. On the **Configure DHCP Options** page, select **Yes, I want to configure these options now**.

14. Place the IP address that is used for your private interface (Microsoft Loopback Adapter) as the only entry on the **Router (Default Gateway)** page.

Your private interface should be configured with an IP address that is in the same subnet as was used for your IP address range, but it should not be in the IP address range itself.

15. There are a number of options that you can define on the **Domain Name and DNS Servers** page. The most important thing to ensure is that the IP address for at least one DNS server is entered in the list of IP addresses. The other fields can be left blank if you do not want to fill them out.

16. If you have WINS Servers on your network you can enter them on the **WINS Servers** page, but otherwise you can leave this page alone and proceed with the wizard.

17. On the **Activate Scope** page, select **Yes, I want to activate this scope now**.

18. Complete the **New Scope Wizard**.

Filtering Out Undesired Network Traffic

Once you have your router configured and have virtual machines accessing the public network via it, the last important step is to secure the private network by filtering out undesirable network traffic. To do this, you need to do the following:

1. Select **Administrative Tools** and **Routing and Remote Access** from the **Start** menu.

2. Select the Routing and Remote Access entry for your server.

3. Select **General** from under the **IP Routing** node.

4. Select the public interface from the list of available interfaces.

5. Click **Properties** on the **Action** menu.

6. You can now use the **Inbound Filters** and **Outbound Filters** buttons to configure static packet filtering on the network interface selected.

Static packet filtering allows you to define a set of static rules that determine whether network packets are allowed through or not. Inbound filters are applied to network traffic coming from the outside world into your network, whereas outbound filters are applied to network traffic coming from your network headed to the outside world. Once you have opened a configuration page for either inbound or outbound filters, you see options to configure filters to receive or drop packets, and you have the ability to create, edit, and delete filters.

You can configure the filters to **Receive/Transmit all packets** except those that meet the criteria below or to **Drop all packets** except those that meet the criteria defined in the filter. The option that you select depends on whether you want to accept all network traffic by default, and only block specific uses, or whether you want to block all network traffic by default, and allow only specific uses.

The option to configure the filter to receive or drop by default is disabled until at least one filter is defined.

160

Chapter 9: Keeping Virtual Machines Secure

For each filter you can define the following:

❑ **The source IP address and subnet mask:** This allows you to specify that a filter should apply only network traffic coming from a group of computers (or from one specific computer). Leaving this option not configured means that the filter applies to network traffic from any computer.

❑ **The destination IP address and subnet mask:** This allows you to specify that a filter should apply only network traffic heading for a group of computers (or for one specific computer). Leaving this option not configured means that the filter applies to network traffic heading for any computer.

❑ **The protocol type to filter:** This can be TCP, TCP [established], UDP, ICMP, Any, or Other. For TCP, TCP [established], and UDP you can also specify a source and destination port to filter on. For ICMP, you can specify the ICMP type and code. For Other you can specify the protocol number to filter.

Conclusion

In this chapter you have read about how to keep your virtual machines secure from viruses and other network-based attacks. You have read about the different possible network configurations that you can use to create secure, yet functional, networking environments for your virtual machines.

It is important to make sure that you have appropriate firewalls configured to protect your virtual machines.

You have also seen the options that are available for routing virtual machine network connectivity through the host operating system by using the Microsoft loopback Adapter, in order to utilize network security software that is installed there. This can be done using the simple Internet connection sharing or the more advanced Routing and Remote Access Services functionality of Windows Server.

It should be noted that I have focused on the solutions that are available to you "out of the box" with Virtual Server installed on Windows Server 2003. There are many other commercial network security packages (including Microsoft's own ISA server) that can be used to further enhance the network security of your virtual machines.

10

Securing Virtual Server

Now that you know how to keep your virtual machines secure, the next thing to look at is how to keep Virtual Server itself secure. This chapter covers a number of the available options to increase the security of an installation of Virtual Server.

In order to understand many of the configurations discussed in this chapter, you need to know how the Virtual Server security model works in general. The Virtual Server services runs as Network Service. This means that it does not have access to most of the files on the host operating system by default. When you connect to Virtual Server and ask it to do something, it uses your user credentials to access any files that it needs to access. This is called *impersonation*.

Virtual Server uses your credentials to start a virtual machine on your behalf. Once you have started a virtual machine, it continues to run using your credentials, even if someone else accesses it. Your credentials will be used for the virtual machine until it is stopped (either by being turned off, save stated, or shut down).

With Virtual Server, you can also configure a specific user account that should always be used to run a virtual machine. To do this, follow these steps:

1. Hover your cursor over the **Configure** entry in the **Virtual Machines** section of the navigation pane on the Virtual Server administrative website.

2. Select the desired virtual machine from the list.

3. Click on **General Properties**.

4. Check **Run virtual machine under the following user account**.

5. Enter the user name and password that you want the virtual machine to run as.

6. Click **OK**.

Part IV: Security and Backup for Virtual Machines

Once you have configured a user account to be used for running a virtual machine, you can also configure the virtual machine to start automatically whenever Virtual Server is started. You can configure a virtual machine so that it will always be started when Virtual Server starts, or so that it will be started only when Virtual Server starts if it was running when Virtual Server was stopped. Both of these options are very useful as they allow you to ensure that the virtual machines will continue to run even if the host operating system is restarted.

This option is enabled only when you have specified a user account to be used for running the virtual machine because without this information Virtual Server is not able to start the virtual machine without having a user initiate it.

Isolating Network Adapters

One of the recommended best practices for Virtual Server is to always have one network interface in the physical computer that is not used by any virtual machines. This ensures that no matter what the virtual machines do, you will always be able to access the host operating system for administrative purposes. If you allow virtual machines to be configured on every physical network adapter, it is possible for rogue virtual machines to flood the network and stop you from being able to connect to the host operating system.

It is possible to take this a step further and configure your network adapters to be used specifically for the host operating system or for virtual machines, as follows:

1. Go to **Control Panel** on the **Start** menu.

2. Open **Network Connections**.

3. Locate the network adapter that you want to modify and select it.

4. Click the **File** menu and select **Properties**.

You will now see a list of the clients, services, and protocols that are installed on your computer. This will most likely include features such as **Client for Microsoft Networks** and **Internet Protocol (TCP/IP)**. It will also include **Virtual Machine Network Services**. This is the service that Virtual Server uses to communicate to the network through a specific network card. As such, if you want to create a physical network card that is dedicated to the use of virtual machines, you should open the **Properties** for that network card and clear all of the entries except **Virtual Machine Network Services**.

With this, virtual machines can continue to use the network adapter, but the host operating system is completely protected from this adapter. Conversely, if you wanted to ensure that a network adapter was only ever used by the host operating system, and that there was no way for a virtual machine to communicate over it, you should open the **Properties** for that network card and unselect **Virtual Machine Network Services**.

Chapter 10: Securing Virtual Server

Restricting Access to Virtual Machines

Virtual Server is typically configured so that members of the local administrators group have full access to create and administer virtual machines. It is possible to set up Virtual Server to allow specific users to have restricted access to specific virtual machines. This is a two-phase process.

The first thing that needs to be done is to give the user (or user group) the appropriate access permissions to Virtual Server as a whole. To do this, click **Server Properties** in the **Virtual Server** section of the navigation pane on the Virtual Server administrative website. Then select **Virtual Server security**. On this page, you can add and remove entries for users and user groups. For each entry you can define the following set of permissions:

❑ **Full:** This is the combination of all other permissions. Checking this permission for an entry will automatically cause the other permissions to be checked.

❑ **Modify:** The modify permission means that a user can create virtual machines and virtual networks, as well as change the settings for Virtual Machine Remote Control, Virtual Server scripts, and Virtual Server search paths.

❑ **View:** This permission allows the user to read the current Virtual Server configuration, virtual machine and virtual network configuration, and any Virtual Server–specific event log entries. It also gives the user permission to connect to a virtual machine via VMRC and interact with it.

❑ **Remove:** Remove allows the user to remove existing virtual machines and virtual networks from Virtual Server.

❑ **Change permissions:** This allows the user to edit the settings on the Virtual Server security page.

❑ **Control:** The control permission determines whether a user can control Virtual Server via the Virtual Server COM APIs. Now, given that the Virtual Server administrative website relies on the Virtual Server COM APIs, not having this permission effectively blocks usage of the Web interface as well. If a user does not have this permission, he can interact with virtual machines only via VMRC.

❑ **Special permissions:** This permission exists to show you whether the given entry has any extra permission that does not map to the other categories. The checkbox for special permissions is always disabled, as it cannot be set or cleared — it exists only to inform you of the presence of any extra permission that may be assigned to this entry.

> Virtual Server's access model is built on top of file system permissions. The permissions that are configured on this page actually map to the discretionary access control list (DACL) of the Virtual Server folder. This folder is created in Documents and Settings\All Users\Application Data\Microsoft on your system drive by default. You can modify the permissions on this folder directly, but any changes you make this way will not take effect until the Virtual Server service is restarted (whereas changes made through the Virtual Server security page of the Virtual Server administrative website take effect immediately).

New entries will be configured with View and Control permissions by default. This is the minimum required in order to effectively use the Virtual Server administrative website.

165

Part IV: Security and Backup for Virtual Machines

The second part of the process is to set the appropriate access control list (ACL) settings on the virtual machine files themselves. There is no user interface in the Virtual Server administrative website to allow you to set these restrictions. A number of virtual machine files need to be considered when restricting access for users:

❑ **VMC file:** The VMC file contains all the information about the virtual machine's configuration.

   ❑ **Read:** The read permission is needed on the VMC file in order for the user to be able to see the virtual machine and its configuration data. If you do not have read access to the VMC file, the virtual machine will simply not show up on the Virtual Server administrative website.

   ❑ **Execute:** The execute permission is needed to be able to turn a virtual machine on or off.

   When a virtual machine is turned on and off, data is written to the VMC file. This data records information about temporary working files and about the state of the virtual machine when it was turned on or off. Because of this, a user needs both execute and write permissions to be able to turn a virtual machine on or off.

   ❑ **Write:** The write permission is needed to be able to make changes to the virtual machine configuration.

❑ **VMC folder:** The folder in which the VMC file is stored.

   ❑ **Read/Execute/Write:** When a virtual machine is started, it creates temporary files in the same directory as the VMC file. If you want a user to be able to start a virtual machine, she will need to have read, execute, and write permissions on the folder that contains the VMC file.

❑ **VHD file:** This is the virtual hard disk that is used by the virtual machine.

   ❑ **Read:** Without read permission the user will be unable to access the virtual hard disk at all. If you give a user read permission on a VMC file but not on the related .HD files, Virtual Server will report errors when a user tries to look at the virtual machine's configuration, as it will not be able to open the VHD files.

   ❑ **Write:** Write permission is required on the virtual hard disk in order to start the virtual machine.

   If you are using differencing disks, users will also need to have read permission on any parent virtual hard disks. Write permission is not needed as no data is ever written to the parent virtual hard disk.

❑ **VNC file:** The VNC file is used to store configuration information about virtual networks. VNC files are stored in Documents\Shared Virtual Networks under the All Users profile (which is usually \Documents and Settings\All Users on the system drive).

   ❑ **Read:** Read permission on a VNC file allows the user to view the configuration information for that virtual network.

   ❑ **Execute:** Execute permission allows the user to connect a virtual machine to the virtual network.

   ❑ **Write:** Write permission allows the user to change the configuration for the virtual network.

New virtual machine, virtual network, and virtual hard disk files are created with the same permission set as is configured on the folder that they are created in. When you change any setting on the Virtual

Chapter 10: Securing Virtual Server

Server security page, it automatically grants all configured users access to the default location for virtual machines. If you want to configure a user so that he or she does not see any new virtual machines that are created by other users, you should make sure that that user does not have read permission on the folder that contains the virtual machines and just give him or her read permission for the specific virtual machines that you want him or her to see.

All of these permissions work together, and the user ends up having the most restrictive combination of permissions (in other words, you need to have read permission set on all areas to be able to read). All of this can be quite confusing. The following sections demonstrate some example configurations.

Example 1: Limited Administrator Rights

Jim needs to have complete control over three virtual machines that he is the administrator of; however, he does not need to create any other virtual machines, nor should he be able to see, control, or configure any other virtual machines on Virtual Server. For Jim you would need to do the following:

❑ Grant him **View** and **Control** permissions on the **Virtual Server security** page.

❑ Ensure that he has no permissions on the folder that contains all of the virtual machines.

❑ Ensure that he has no permissions on the other virtual machines.

❑ Grant him **Read**, **Execute**, and **Write** permissions on the VMC and VHD files, as well as on the folders that contain the VMC files for the three virtual machines he is responsible for.

❑ Grant him **Read** and **Execute** permissions on the VNC files used by Virtual Server.

Example 2: Maintenance Needs

Alice needs to be able to perform maintenance tasks on a virtual machine, including installing software from CD images from time to time, but she should not be allowed to start or stop the virtual machine, change the virtual machine's network configuration, or have access to any other virtual machines. For Alice you would need to do the following:

❑ Grant her **View** and **Control** permissions on the **Virtual Server security** page.

❑ Ensure that she has no permissions on the folder that contains all of the virtual machines.

❑ Ensure that she has no permissions on the other virtual machines.

❑ Grant her **Read** and **Write** permissions on the VMC and VHD files, as well as on the folder that contains the VMC file for the virtual machines she is responsible for.

❑ Grant her **Read** permissions on the VNC files used by Virtual Server.

Example 3: A Different Limit on Administrator Duties

Jane needs to be able to manage a set of virtual machines, and create new virtual machines as appropriate. However she should be restricted from accessing three virtual machines that belong to a different department. For Jane you would need to do the following:

❑ Grant her **View**, **Control**, and **Modify** permissions on the **Virtual Server security** page.

❑ Grant her **Read**, **Execute**, and **Write** permissions privileges on the folder that contains all of the virtual machines.

167

Part IV: Security and Backup for Virtual Machines

❏ For the three virtual machines that she should not have access to, edit the permissions on the VMC files and their containing folders to explicitly deny permissions for **Read**, **Execute**, and **Write**.

❏ Grant her **Read**, **Execute**, and **Write** permissions on the VMC and VHD files, as well as on the folder that contains the VMC file for the virtual machines she is responsible for.

❏ Grant her **Read**, **Execute**, and **Write** permissions on the VNC files used by Virtual Server.

Example 4: Virtual Machine User

Fred needs to be able to start, stop, and interact with a specific virtual machine. But he should not be able to change any of the settings for the virtual machine, or access any other functionality under Virtual Server. For Fred you would need to do the following:

❏ Grant him **View** and **Control** permissions on the **Virtual Server security** page.

❏ Ensure that he has no permissions on the folder that contains all of the virtual machines.

❏ Ensure that he has no permissions on the other virtual machines.

❏ Grant him **Read** and **Execute** permissions on the VMC file for the specific virtual machine.

❏ Ensure that he has no permissions on the VHD files and on the folder that contains the VMC file for the specific virtual machines he is going to use.

❏ Ensure that he has no permissions on the VNC files used by Virtual Server.

At this stage, Fred has the right set of permissions, but he is unable to start the virtual machine unless you give him write access to the VMC and VHD files. This is undesirable for this scenario, so instead you should create a separate user account called FredsVirtualMachine and give the account a secure password that Fred does not know. Then you should configure the virtual machine to always run using this account. Finally you should configure Virtual Server for the FredsVirtualMachine account by:

❏ Granting it **View** and **Control** permissions on the **Virtual Server security** page.

❏ Ensuring that it has no permissions on the folder that contains all of the virtual machines.

❏ Ensuring that it has no permissions on the other virtual machines.

❏ Granting it **Read**, **Execute**, and **Write** permissions on the VMC and VHD files, as well as on the folder that contains the VMC file for the virtual machine in question.

❏ Granting it **Read** and **Execute** permissions on the VNC files used by Virtual Server.

With this configuration, Fred will be able to start and stop the virtual machine without having access to any of the virtual machine settings or virtual hard disks.

Securing Virtual Machines by Using EFS

Encrypting File System (EFS) is a feature of Windows that allows you to encrypt a file such that only the people you give permission to can access it. EFS goes a step beyond file permissions by actually encrypting the data in the file and provides a higher level of protection. EFS can by used to encrypt virtual machine files, but some tradeoffs need to be considered.

The first issue to consider is performance. Enabling EFS on a virtual hard disk can reduce the performance to one-third of normal. There is no way to avoid this.

The second issue to consider is that it is not possible to effectively enable EFS on a virtual hard disk file and have the virtual machine configured to start automatically. The reason for this limitation is two-fold.

First, if you enable EFS on both the VHD and VMC files, Virtual Server is not able to automatically start the virtual machine. This happens because Virtual Server needs to have your user credentials to access the encrypted VMC file, but it needs to open the VMC file to figure out which user credentials to use.

And second, if you only enable EFS on the VHD file, and configure the VMC file to automatically start with the appropriate user credentials, it will work. But there is now an easy way for a malicious user to access your VHD data by just editing the unencrypted VMC file to add a second unencrypted VHD file. Then the malicious user can copy any data he wants off of your encrypted VHD.

The final issue is that it is not advisable to enable EFS both on the .VHD file on the host operating system, and then on files contained on the VHD in the guest operating system. Doing so drastically reduces performance with no effective gain to the level of protection.

Seriously consider whether you need the level of protection provided by EFS before enabling it on a virtual machine. You should also think about whether it is more appropriate to use EFS to protect the virtual machine files on the host operating system, or to use EFS to protect specific files within the virtual machine under the guest operating system.

Configuring IIS and Virtual Server on Separate Computers

Chapter 5 covered how to set up constrained delegation to allow you to store VHD files on a separate computer. This section discusses the second scenario in which you need to use constrained delegation.

By default, Virtual Server is configured to run on the same computer as the Virtual Server administrative website (which requires IIS). This is problematic from a security perspective as IIS is commonly targeted by viruses and malicious users. As such, it is desirable to separate IIS and Virtual Server, and to reduce the number of IIS installations you need to be able to run Virtual Server. Luckily, it is possible to install the Virtual Sever administrative website on a different computer than Virtual Server itself, and in this configuration you can have one instance of IIS for multiple instances of Virtual Server.

Part IV: Security and Backup for Virtual Machines

The first thing to do when setting up this configuration is to ensure that your Virtual Server servers do not have IIS or the Virtual Server Administrative website installed on them. IIS is not installed with Windows Server 2003 by default. To install Virtual Server without installing the Virtual Server Administrative website, you should select to perform a custom setup during the installation of Virtual Server, and then click the **Virtual Server Web Application** feature and select **This feature will not be available**. If you have an existing installation of Virtual Server that you want to remove the Virtual Server Web interface from, this can be done as follows:

1. From the **Start** menu, select **Control Panel** and then **Add or Remove Programs**.

2. Find **Microsoft Virtual Server 2005 R2 SP1** and click the **Change** button.

    If Virtual Server is running, you will be prompted to shut down any virtual machines and stop the Virtual Server service at this stage.

3. On the **Maintenance Type** page, select **Custom**.

4. Then click the **Virtual Server Web Application** feature and select **This feature will not be available**.

5. Complete the maintenance wizard.

6. Now you can safely uninstall IIS.

Next you need to install the Virtual Server administrative website on the computer that you want to use for IIS. Obviously, you will need to have IIS installed on your computer before installing Virtual Server. You should start the Virtual Server installer like normal, but then select to perform a custom install. On the feature selection page, you should click on the **Virtual Server Service** feature and select **This feature will not be available**. Next, on the **Configure Components** page of the installer, you need to select **Configure the Administration Website to always run as the Local System account (Required for constrained delegation)** and then complete the installation of Virtual Server.

Technically there is no problem with installing the Virtual Server service on your Web server (or installing the Web interface on the Virtual Server server) in this sort of configuration — it just does not make sense to do.

While this configuration runs the Virtual Server Web application as Local System, the Virtual Server service still runs as Network Service. You should never change the account that is used to run the Virtual Server service as this is an unsupported configuration, and there are a number of known problems that will happen if you do this.

Now that you have everything set up, you will need to configure constrained delegation. This is an option under Windows that will allow the Web server to reuse the user credentials provided from the client computers when talking to the Virtual Server server. In order to enable constrained delegation you must be running in a Microsoft Windows Server 2003 native domain, and you must be running Virtual Server on Windows Server 2003. (It is not possible to enable constrained delegation on a computer that is running Windows XP.)

You can check the functional level of your domain by opening the **Active Directory Domains and Trusts** item of the **Administrative tools** on your domain controller. You should then select your domain and select **Raise Domain Functional Level** on the **Action** menu. If your current level is **Windows 2000 mixed** or **Windows 2000 native** you need to select **Windows Server 2003** and press **Raise**.

170

Chapter 10: Securing Virtual Server

If you have any Windows NT Server 4.0 or Windows 2000 Server instances in your domain do not raise the functional level as this will stop these older servers from being able to participate in the domain. Furthermore, this action cannot be reversed.

Once you have completed the previously listed steps, you have to enable constrained delegation for Virtual Server. Do so by executing the following steps:

1. Open **Active Directory Users and Computers** from the **Administrative tools** on your domain controller.

2. Select the **Computers** node under your domain.

3. Select the computer that is running the Virtual Server Web application and right-click it and select **Properties**.

4. Select the **Delegation** tab.

5. Select **Trust this computer for delegation to specified services only** and **Use any authentication protocol**.

6. Click **Add**.

7. Click **Users or Computers**.

8. Enter **Virtual Server service** as the name of the server, and click **OK**.

9. Hold down the Ctrl key and select **cifs** and **vssrvc** from the Service Type column and click **OK**, and then click **OK** again.

If you want to use a single instance of IIS to manage multiple instances of Virtual Server you will need to repeat the preceding steps for each Virtual Server server that you want to manage.

Once everything is in place, you can start using your Web server to control your Virtual Server computers. You can use the default server name (`http://WebServerName:1024/VirtualServer/vswebapp.exe`), in which case you will be prompted to provide the name of the Virtual Server instance that you want to control. Alternatively, you can go directly to the Virtual Server that you want to control by going to `http://WebServerName:1024/VirtualServer/vswebapp.exe?view=1&remoteServer=Virtual ServerName`.

If you want to configure Virtual Server such that you have one server that runs Virtual Server, one server that stores the virtual machine files, and one server that runs the Web application, it is possible. You just need to combine the steps outlined here and in Chapter 5.

Securing IIS for Virtual Server

Microsoft has done a lot of work in increasing the security of IIS. As such, the default installation of IIS on Windows Server 2003 already has close to the best configuration for IIS from a security point of view. If you are running Virtual Server on Windows XP, and hence using IIS 5.1, you can take a number of steps to increase the security of your computer.

Part IV: Security and Backup for Virtual Machines

> All of the steps outlined in this section assume that you are using IIS solely for the purpose of running the Virtual Server administrative website. If you are running other websites, you should refer to documentation that they provide to ensure that these steps will not cause problems.

Using IIS Lockdown Tool

The first tool for a Windows XP user to look at is the IIS Lockdown tool (available from www.microsoft.com/technet/security/tools/locktool.mspx). This tool helps you disable many of the features of IIS 5.1 that are not required for using the Virtual Server administrative website.

The IIS Lockdown tool is neither supported nor required for IIS 6.0 running on Windows Server 2003.

After downloading the IIS Lockdown tool, double-click on iislockd.exe to start the **Internet Information Services Lockdown Wizard**. You then need to do the following:

1. Accept the End User License Agreement.

2. Select **Other (Server that does not match any of the listed roles)** from the **Server templates** list.

3. On the **Internet Services** page, uncheck **File Transfer service (FTP)**, **E-mail service (SMTP)**, and **News service (NNTP)** options.

4. On the **Script Maps** page, ensure that all options are checked.

5. On the **Additional Security** page, ensure that all options are checked.

6. On the **URLScan** page, check the **Install URLScan filter on the server** option.

7. Complete the wizard.

Using URLScan Tool

The second tool is URLScan. This tool acts as a filter on IIS and denies a large number of accesses and responses from IIS that have been known to be dangerous from a security point of view. If you are running Windows XP as your host operating system, and using IIS 5.1 for your Web server, URLScan can significantly improve the security of your computer. However, Microsoft states that with IIS 6.0, URLScan offers only minor improvements in security over the standard installation of IIS. Some of the specific capabilities that URLScan offers over the top of the standard IIS 6.0 installation are the ability to:

❑ Filter out specific URL character sequences or verbs

❑ Remove the server banner from outgoing pages

❑ Specify different maximum lengths for each element of the HTTP client request header

URLScan is installed with the IIS Lockdown tool on Windows XP, but if you want to install it on Windows Server 2003 you will need to download it from www.microsoft.com/technet/security/tools/urlscan.mspx. URLScan comes with an excellent default configuration that provides a high level of protection for IIS. Unfortunately, it will also stop the Virtual Server administrative website from working correctly in the default configuration. In order get the Virtual Server administrative website to work with URLScan installed, you need to do the following:

Chapter 10: Securing Virtual Server

1. Open **urlscan.ini** from the **system32\inetsrv\urlscan** directory in your Windows directory.

2. Find the **[DenyExtensions]** section.

3. Find the entry for **.exe** and change it to **;.exe**.

   This change will stop URLScan from blocking any URL requests that have .exe as the file extension. This is required as the Virtual Server administrative website references vswebapp.exe.

   URLScan is configured to use [DenyExtensions] *by default. It is possible to change this to use* [AllowExtensions], *in which case URLScan will allow only the extensions specified in that section. If you have other software installed that requires that you use this setting you will need to add .exe to the allowed extensions.*

4. Save the changes you have made to **urlscan.ini**.

5. Run **urlscan.exe** from the **system32\inetsrv\urlscan** directory within your Windows directory. This applies your new **urlscan.ini** settings.

Removing the Default Website from IIS 6.0

The final item to discuss around securing IIS for use with Virtual Server applies only to Windows Server 2003 with IIS 6.0. When the Virtual Server administrative website is installed on Windows Server 2003, a new website is created and configured to use port 1024 (or another port that you may have specified in the installer). The Virtual Server administrative website is installed like this to ensure that it does not disrupt any other websites that you may have configured. If, however, you are only using your IIS instance to run the Virtual Server administrative website, you will most likely have a blank "default website" configured on your server, which you do not need. From a management and security point of view it is best to get rid of this website if you have no intentions of using it.

   Windows XP with IIS 5.1 does not support the creation of multiple websites. As such, Virtual Server installs itself into a virtual directory under the default website when it is installed on Windows XP. This means that deleting the default website on a Windows XP computer will cause the Virtual Server administrative website to stop working altogether.

To delete the default website under IIS 6.0 you will need to do the following:

1. On the **Start** menu, select **Administrative Tools** and then **Internet Information Services (IIS) Manager**.

2. Select the **Default Web Site** entry from the **Web Sites** node for your server.

3. Click **Delete** on the **Action** menu.

Once you have deleted the default website it is possible to change the Virtual Server administrative website to use port 80 rather than port 1024. This is convenient because you don't need to specify the port number when navigating to the Virtual Server administrative website. To change the port to 80:

1. Select **Internet Information Services (IIS) Manager** from **Administrative Tools** on the **Start** menu.

2. Select the **Virtual Server** entry from the **Web Sites** node for your server.

3. Click **Properties** on the **Action** menu.

173

Part IV: Security and Backup for Virtual Machines

4. On the **Web Site** properties tab, in the **Web site identification** group box, change the value for **TCP port** from 1024 to 80 and click **OK**.

Once you have done this, you will need to update any shortcuts or links that you have so that they no longer use the :1024 extension on the Virtual Server administrative website address.

Configuring Secure Sockets Layer

Secure Sockets Layer (SSL) is a cryptographic protocol. SSL provides a number of protections for applications that are communicating over a public network. First, SSL encrypts all data that is transmitted, which makes it impossible for third parties to attempt to gain access to any information that is being exchanged. Second, SSL provides a way to guarantee that the server you have connected to is really the server you think it is (and not a malicious server that is pretending to be the server you wanted to connect to).

With Virtual Server it is possible to configure SSL both on the Virtual Server administrative website and on VMRC.

> If you are using VMRC over a public network, you should think of SSL as a mandatory requirement. VMRC does not encrypt any of the keystroke data that is sent over the network. It would be very easy for a malicious third party to intercept information that you type on the keyboard over VMRC—such as your user name and password.

Configuring SSL on the Virtual Server Administrative Website

There are three main steps to enabling SSL on IIS. You start by generating an SSL certificate request. You then take this request to a certificate authority who will, for a small price, generate a certificate that meets the requirements of the certificate request. Finally, you assign this certificate to your website under IIS.

Generating an SSL Certificate Request

To generate an SSL certificate request under IIS:

1. Select **Internet Information Services (IIS) Manager** from **Administrative Tools** on the **Start** menu.

2. Select the **Virtual Server** entry from under the **Web Sites** node for your server.

3. Click **Properties** on the **Action** menu.

4. Change to the **Directory Security** tab.

5. Click **Server Certificate** in the **Secure communications** section. This starts the **IIS Certificate Wizard**.

Chapter 10: Securing Virtual Server

6. On the **Server Certificate** page you should select **Create a new certificate**.

7. On the **Delayed or Immediate Request** page you can select either option. If you choose to **Prepare the request now, but send it later** your request is saved to a text file that you can send to the certificate authority. The option to **Send the request immediately to an online certification authority** will be enabled only if you have a certification authority server on your network.

8. On the **Name and Security Settings** page you should define a name for your certificate that is easy for you to remember. On this page you can configure the **Bit length** of the SSL certificate. This is set to 1024 by default but can range from 512 to 16384. Having a longer bit length increases the strength of the security provided by SSL, but it also increases the load on the server to handle encryption of the data being sent. For most situations 1024 or 2048 is completely acceptable.

9. On the **Organization Information** page, you will need to provide details about your **Organization** name and **Organizational unit** name.

10. On the **Your Site's Common Name** page, it is critical that you enter the name of the server as you will be accessing it. If you will be accessing the server by using the fully qualified domain name, you should enter that here. If you access the server on an intranet using the server's NetBIOS name, you should enter the NetBIOS name here.

11. On the **Geographical Information** page, provide the appropriate data.

12. Finally, specify the file name to be used for saving the certificate request and complete the wizard.

You can now take this file to a certificate authority in order to get a valid certificate.

Assigning the SSL Certificate

Once you have received the certificate back from the certificate authority, follow these steps to load it into IIS:

1. On the **Start** menu, select **Internet Information Services (IIS) Manager** from **Administrative Tools**.

2. Select the **Virtual Server** entry from the **Web Sites** node for your server.

3. Click **Properties** on the **Action** menu.

4. Change to the **Directory Security** tab.

5. Click **Server Certificate** in the **Secure communications** section. This starts the **IIS Certificate Wizard**.

6. The wizard will remember that you have a pending certificate request and ask you whether you want to process the pending request or delete it. Obviously you want to process it.

7. On the **Process a Pending Request** page you will need to specify the location of the certificate file.

You can then complete the wizard and have your certificate loaded.

175

Part IV: Security and Backup for Virtual Machines

Using an Existing SSL Certificate

If you already have an SSL certificate, it is possible to load it onto your IIS server, without generating a certificate request. Follow these steps:

1. Start **mmc.exe**.

2. Select **Add/Remove Snap-in** from the **File** menu, and click **Add**.

3. Select the **Certificates** snap-in and click **Add**.

4. Select **Service account** ➪ **Local computer** ➪ **IIS Admin**, and click **Finish**.

5. Under **Certificates - Service (IIS Admin) on Local Computer**, select **IISADMIN\Trusted Root Certification Authorities** and then **Certificates**.

6. Select **All Tasks** and **Import** from the **Action** menu.

7. Enter the file name for your certificate file.

8. Select **Place all certificates in the following store** and complete the wizard.

9. Close MMC.

10. Select **Internet Information Services (IIS) Manager** from **Administrative Tools** on the **Start** menu.

11. Select the **Virtual Server** entry from under the **Web Sites** node for your server.

12. Click **Properties** on the **Action** menu.

13. Change to the **Directory Security** tab.

14. Click **Server Certificate** in the **Secure communications** section. This will start the **IIS Certificate Wizard**.

15. Select **Assign an existing certificate.**

16. Select your certificate from the list of available certificates and complete the wizard.

Requiring SSL for IIS

The final step for configuring SSL for IIS is that once you have assigned your certificate successfully you need to configure your website to require the use of SSL. If you do not do this, people will be able to connect to your website using insecure network connections. To configure your website to require SSL, execute the following steps:

1. On the **Start** menu, select **Administrative Tools** ➪ **Internet Information Services (IIS)**.

2. Select the **Virtual Server** entry from the **Web Sites** node for your server.

3. Click **Properties** on the **Action** menu.

4. Change to the **Directory Security** tab.

5. Click **Edit** from the **Secure communications** section.

6. Check the option to **Require secure channel (SSL)** and click **OK**.

Chapter 10: Securing Virtual Server

Configuring SSL on VMRC

As with IIS, configuring SSL on VMRC is a three-step process. First you have to generate an SSL Certificate Request, then you have to have a certificate authority issue a certificate to meet the request, and finally you have to assign the SSL certificate to be used by VMRC.

Generating an SSL Certificate Request

Follow these steps to generate an SSL certificate request for VMRC:

1. Select **Server Properties** from the **Virtual Server** section of the navigation pane on the Virtual Server administration website.

2. Select **Virtual Machine Remote Control (VMRC) Server**.

3. Check **Enable** for the **SSL 3.0/TLS 1.0 encryption** option.

4. Select **Request** for the **SSL 3.0 TLS 1.0 certificate** option.

5. Fill in the appropriate details for all of the fields. Once again, ensure that you use the form of your computer name (NetBIOS or FQDN) that you are planning to connect for the **Host name** option. If you use the wrong name, the certificate will not work.

6. Click **OK**.

You are then shown a Web page that has a large text field on it that contains the contents of a certificate request. You need to copy and paste this text into a text file to send to a certificate authority in order to request a real certificate that meets the parameters you have provided.

Assigning the SSL Certificate

Once you have the SSL certificate back from the certificate authority, follow these steps to assign it to the VMRC server:

1. Select **Server Properties** from the **Virtual Server** section of the navigation pane on the Virtual Server administration website.

2. Select **Virtual Machine Remote Control (VMRC) Server**.

3. Check **Enable** for the **SSL 3.0/TLS 1.0 encryption** option.

4. Select **Upload** for the **SSL 3.0 TLS 1.0 certificate** option.

5. Enter the path to the certificate file in the **Upload this certificate** field and click **OK**.

Now VMRC should be ready to use SSL.

Using an Existing SSL Certificate

Using an existing SSL certificate with VMRC can be quite difficult. If you have an existing SSL certificate that was created using an SSL certificate request generated by Virtual Server, you should be able to just follow the steps mentioned in the previous section, "Assigning the SSL Certificate." If you want to use an SSL certificate that was generated any other way there is a significant problem. The issue is that as Virtual Server runs as a Network Service, it needs the certificate to have access permission for Network Service. Most SSL certificates do not have this permission configured.

177

Part IV: Security and Backup for Virtual Machines

Workaround for Using an Existing SSL Certificate

There is an unsupported method for using an existing SSL certificate, but it is a bit complicated. You need to have your certificate in a PFX file with a private key and password. Once you have this, do the following:

1. Open mmc.exe.

2. Select Add/Remove Snap-in from the File menu, and then click Add.

3. Select the Certificates snap-in and click Add.

4. Select Service account ⇨ Local computer ⇨ Virtual Server, and click Finish.

5. In MMC select the Virtual Server\Personal node from under Certificates - Service (Virtual Server) on Local Computer.

6. Select All Tasks and Import from the Action menu.

7. Enter the file name for your certificate file.

8. Select Place all certificates in the following store and complete the wizard.

9. Double-click the new certificate entry and select Details.

10. Copy the values from the Subject and Thumbprint fields. You will need then later.

11. Close MMC.

Now that the certificate is loaded in the correct place, you need to give permission to Network Service. To do this, you will need to use a tool called WinHttpCertCfg. You can download this tool from http://go.microsoft.com/fwlink/?linkid=20506. Once you have downloaded and installed this tool you need to run the following command:

```
winhttpcertcfg -g -c Local_Machine\ My -s [Name] -a "Network
Service"
```

Here, [Name] is the server name of the value you copied from the Subject field of the certificate.

The final step is to configure Virtual Server to use this certificate. Unfortunately, even though the certificate is now in the right place with the right access permissions, you cannot tell Virtual Server to do this through the Virtual Server administrative website. Instead, you will need to stop the Virtual Server service, and open the Virtual Server configuration file directly. This file is called *Options.xml* and is located in *\Documents and Settings\All Users\Application Data\Microsoft\Virtual Server* folder on the system drive. Open this file with notepad and locate the <vmrc> section. If there is a <encryption> section you will need to remove it. Then you will need to add the following XML to the <vmrc> section:

```
<encryption>
    <certificate>
        <id type="bytes">[Thumbprint]</id>
    </certificate>
    <enable type="boolean">true</enable>
</encryption>
```

Chapter 10: Securing Virtual Server

> where [Thumbprint] is the value that you copied from the Thumbprint field of the certificate, with the spaces removed. Once you have done this, you should save the changes to the *Options.xml* file and start the Virtual Server service. SSL should now be enabled on VMRC using your SSL certificate.

Using a Self-Signed SSL Certificate

If you do not want to pay to have a certificate authority create an official certificate for you, you can create a self-signed certificate. Self-signed certificates are useful for test environments, and for more controlled environments. When using a self-signed SSL certificate, your data is still encrypted by SSL but because there is no third-party server that can attest to the authenticity of the SSL certificate, there is no way to guarantee that you are really talking to the right server (and not a malicious server that is trying to look like the server you want to connect to). Furthermore, there are known techniques for compromising a connection that uses a self-signed SSL certificate in order to access the data that is being transmitted.

Creating a Self-Signed SSL Certificate for IIS

With all of this in mind, Microsoft provides a tool called SelfSSL that allows you to generate your own self-signed SSL certificate. SelfSSL is part of the IIS 6.0 Resource Kit (which can be downloaded from `http://go.microsoft.com/fwlink/?linkid=34407`). Once you have installed the IIS 6.0 Resource Kit, you will need to follow these steps to generate your own self-signed SSL certificate:

1. From the **Start** menu, select **All Programs** ⇨ **IIS Resources** ⇨ **SelfSSL,** and finally click on **SelfSSL**.

2. The details of the parameters for the `SelfSSL` command will now be displayed. On the average installation of Virtual Server on Windows Server 2003 you will want to run `selfssl.exe /T /S:2`. On Windows XP you will want to run `selfssl.exe /T /S:1`. You may need to specify other parameters depending on the configuration of your computer.

The `S` parameter is used to define the site ID. Windows XP supports only one website, so this is always `1` on Windows XP. Windows Server 2003 supports multiple websites. In order to determine the site ID for your installation of Virtual Server you should open the **Internet Information Services (IIS) Manager** and select the **Web Sites** node for your computer. You should see a list of the websites that are configured. Each one will have an **Identifier** number, which is its site ID.

Other parameters that you may want to configure include the following:

❑ `/N`: This allows you to specify the name that you will be using to access your server. SelfSSL will use your computer's NetBIOS name if no value is specified.

❑ `/K`: This allows you to specify the key size to be used for the SSL certificate. SelfSSL will use a key size of 1024 if no value is specified.

❑ `/V`: This allows you to specify how long (in days) the SSL certificate should be valid for. SelfSSL will create a certificate that is valid for seven days if no value is specified.

At this stage, SelfSSL has done the entire configuration necessary for IIS. The only thing left to do is follow the steps outlined in the section "Requiring SSL for IIS." You will now be able to use SSL and connect to your website using `https://` on your local computer. If you try and connect to the secure

179

Part IV: Security and Backup for Virtual Machines

website from a remote computer you will receive a warning that the certificate is not trusted, but you will be able to continue to access the website. If you want to get rid of this warning you can do so by exporting the SSL certificate from your Web server and importing it to your client computer. Follow these steps:

1. Start **mmc.exe**.

2. Select **Add/Remove Snap-in** from the **File** menu, and then click **Add**.

3. Select the **Certificates** snap-in and click **Add**.

4. Select **Service account** ⇨ **Local computer** ⇨ **IIS Admin**, and click **Finish**.

5. Under **Certificates - Service (IIS Admin) on Local Computer**, select **IISADMIN\Trusted Root Certification Authorities** and then **Certificates**.

6. Select the certificate for your computer, and then select **All Tasks** and **Export** from the **Action** menu.

7. On the **Export Private Key** page, select **No, do not export the private key**.

8. On the **Export File Format** page, select **DER encoded binary X.509 (.CER)**.

9. Specify the file name to use for the certificate (it should have a .cer extension) and finish the wizard.

10. Copy the .cer file to you client computer and double-click it.

11. Click the **Install Certificate** button.

12. Choose the option to Automatically select the certificate store based on the type of certificate and complete the wizard.

Creating a Self-Signed SSL Certificate for VMRC

Microsoft does not provide a tool for generating self-signed certificates for VMRC. There is a free open source tool that is capable of doing this: OpenSSL. You can download a version of OpenSSL for Windows from www.openssl.org/related/binaries.html. It will install to C:\OpenSSL by default. Once you have downloaded and installed OpenSSL, you should generate a certificate request using the Virtual Server administrative website, and save the request to a text file. To generate the self-signed certificate you need to do the following:

1. Generate a private key to sign the certificate with. To do this you will need to run:

```
C:\OpenSSL\bin>openssl genrsa -des3 -out server.key 1024
```

where `server.key` is the name of the private key file and `1024` is the bit length of the key. When you run this command you will be asked to provide a passphrase that you will need to enter twice.

2. Create the certificate with the private key and the certificate request. To do this you will need to run:

```
C:\OpenSSL\bin>openssl x509 -req -days 365 -in VMRC.txt -signkey server.key -out VMRC.crt
```

180

Chapter 10: Securing Virtual Server

where `VMRC.txt` is the file that contains the certificate request, `VMRC.crt` is the name of the new certificate file, and *server.key* is the name of your private key. The `-days` value specifies how many days the certificate should be valid for. When you run this command you are asked for the passphrase used in Step 1.

Once this is finished you are able to upload the certificate file to the Virtual Server administrative website and enable SSL on VMRC. When you try and connect to a virtual machine with VMRC you see a warning message stating that the server certificate cannot be verified. You can just hit **Yes** in this dialog box, or you can install the certificate into your trusted certificates by following these steps:

1. In the **Untrusted Server** dialog box, click **View Certificate**.

2. Click **Install Certificate**.

3. In the **Certificate Import Wizard** select **Place all certificates in the following store**, and click the **Browse** button.

4. Select **Trusted Root Certification Authorities** and click **OK**.

5. Complete the wizard, read the security warning, and select **Yes**.

Securing VMRC

Besides enabling SSL encryption on VMRC connection, you can take some basic steps to increase the security of VMRC. VMRC is normally configured to accept incoming requests on all network adapters in the physical computer. You can restrict this so that VMRC accepts only incoming requests on a trusted interface. To do this you will need to:

1. Select **Server Properties** from the **Virtual Server** section of the navigation pane on the Virtual Server administration website.

2. Select **Virtual Machine Remote Control (VMRC) Server**.

3. Select the IP address for the trusted interface from the **TCP/IP address** field.

   *The default value of (**All unassigned**) means that VMRC will accept incoming requests on all network adapters. Unfortunately it is not possible to specify multiple trusted interfaces.*

Other options to configure on the **Virtual Machine Remote Control (VMRC) Server Properties** page include the **Authentication** setting and the **Disconnect idle connections** setting.

The **Authentication** setting can be configured for NTLM, Kerberos, or Automatic (Automatic is the default option). Selecting Automatic means that VMRC will first try to use Kerberos and then try NTLM if that fails. If you select Kerberos as your Authentication setting and VMRC fails to authenticate using Kerberos, the entire connection will fail.

The **Disconnect idle connections** setting allows you to specify that if a VMRC session is inactive for a period of time (in minutes) then it should be disconnected. This is a good idea for two reasons: It reduces the load on Virtual Server by reducing unnecessary connections, and it disconnects VMRC sessions where the user has potentially forgotten that the connection was active and has left his computer unattended.

Part IV: Security and Backup for Virtual Machines

VMRC User Authentication

One important detail to understand about VMRC is that when you connect to a virtual machine with VMRC, you are accessing the virtual machine directly and not the guest operating system. This is done by authenticating you against the host operating system. You then need to log in to the guest operating system with appropriate credentials for that environment.

It is possible that another user who is authorized to access the host operating system, but is not authorized to access the guest operating system, could attempt to connect to the virtual machine after you have logged into the guest operating system and use your credentials.

For this reason some people opt to disable VMRC altogether after the virtual machines are configured, and use protocols such as Remote Desktop to connect directly to the guest operating system. If you do not do this, you should keep the risks involved with VMRC in mind and maintain general good security practices, such as logging off the guest operating system or locking the console when you are not actively using the virtual machine.

Using an External Firewall

When it is installed, Virtual Server configures the Windows firewall to allow for external access to the Virtual Server administrative website and to all of the various features of Virtual Server. If you want to be able to access Virtual Server from behind an external firewall you will need to configure the firewall manually to allow this. You will need to allow several network ports through the firewall, depending on the functionality that you want available to external users.

Accessing the Virtual Server administrative website requires that you open the port that the Virtual Server administrative website is using. This is TCP port 1024 by default, but it could be port 80, 443, or any other port depending on how you have configured the Virtual Server Web interface.

The next item to consider is whether you want to be able to access virtual machines through VMRC from external computers. Doing so allows users and administrators to interact with virtual machines remotely, but it increases the potential security risks involved as malicious users could attempt to connect to the virtual machines. If the answer is yes, you will need to open a single TCP port. Normally, VMRC is configured to use port 5900, but you can configure VMRC to use any other port that you want (in which case you would need to open that port instead).

TCP Port 5900 is traditionally used by the Virtual Network Computer (VNC) protocol. VMRC uses this port as it is based on the VNC protocol. Unfortunately, VMRC includes a number of modifications that make it incompatible with standard VNC clients. If you have a VNC Server configured on your host operating system, you will need to configure either VNC or VMRC to use a different port range.

The final item to think about when configuring an external firewall is whether you need to have remote computers accessing the COM interfaces exposed by Virtual Server. In most cases, you will not want this, as it is required only if you are remotely running scripts or custom applications directly against the Virtual Server COM APIs. Remote access to COM interfaces is done via DCOM (Distributed COM).

Chapter 10: Securing Virtual Server

Unfortunately DCOM uses a random port number over 1024 for network communication, which can make access through an external firewall rather tricky. Thankfully there is a way to configure DCOM to use a fixed port for network communication. To do this you will need to;

1. Open the Registry Editor (regedit).

2. Go to **HKEY_LOCAL_MACHINE\Software\Microsoft\Rpc**.

3. Create a new key named **Internet**.

4. Select the new key and create the following entries under it:

   ❑ **A multi-string value named Ports:** The value data for this entry is a list of ports (for example, 5800) and port ranges (for example, 6000–6100) that can be used for DCOM. It is recommended that you open at least 15 to 20 ports, and that you use ports that are over 5000.

If you do not open up enough ports, remote applications will fail with error messages about not having enough resources to complete the operation.

   ❑ **A string value named PortsInternetAvailable:** The value data for this entry should always be set to Y. If this entry is not set to Y. then the data in the ports entry will not be used.

   ❑ **A string value named UseInternetPorts:** The value data for this entry should also be set to Y. If this entry is set to N then DCOM will use all of the ports except the ones specified in the ports entry.

Whenever you change these registry keys you will need to reboot Windows in order for the new values to be used for DCOM.

Once you have made these changes, configure your firewall to allow TCP connections on the ports you have configured. You also need to allow TCP connections on port 135 (this port is used by the Windows Remote Procedure Call protocol).

Virtual Server also exposes a number of WMI interfaces that can be used for gathering statistical data about Virtual Server. WMI is built on top of DCOM and, as such, has the same firewall requirements as DCOM.

Choosing the Right Authentication Type

A number of authentication options are available under Virtual Server, both for the Virtual Server administrative website and for VMRC. It is important to understand the advantages and shortcomings of each option so that you can select the most appropriate configuration for your environment. Four main authentication options are available:

❑ **Integrated Windows Authentication/Automatic:** Integrated Windows Authentication under IIS and Automatic authentication under VMRC implement similar logic. These options allow the server to attempt to connect using Kerberos authentication, but to then fall back to using NTLM authentication if Kerberos authentication is not possible. This is the default option for both IIS and VMRC. This option provides the best user experience and means that you do not need to provide user credentials in order to access Virtual Server when it is configured on an intranet or trusted computer.

183

Part IV: Security and Backup for Virtual Machines

❑ **Kerberos:** VMRC allows you to specify that only Kerberos authentication should be used. Kerberos provides a high level of security on connections and also provides guarantees that the server to which you are connecting is really the server you think it is (and not a malicious server that is pretending to be the server you want to connect to). The biggest downside of Kerberos is that it requires that both the server and client computers be members of the same Active Directory environment. This is not a problem for corporate environments, but is a show stopper for smaller environments or for Internet-based computers.

❑ **NTLM:** VMRC also allows you to specify that only NTLM authentication should be used. NTLM does not require that both computers be members of the same Active Directory environment, and works in workgroup environments. However NTLM does not provide guarantees that the server you are connecting to is really the server you think it is. Furthermore, there are known methods for attacking NTLM connections to determine user name and password being used (usually via a "brute force" attack).

❑ **Basic Authentication:** IIS allows you to configure your website to use Basic Authentication. This authentication method involves the client sending the user name and password in clear text to the server. There are no attempts to protect the user name and password, nor are there any attempts to provide any guarantees about the trustworthiness of the server. Basic Authentication is hideously insecure, but it is compatible with pretty much every Web browser in existence. Basic Authentication also has no problems traversing firewalls and proxies, both of which can cause problems for Kerberos and NTLM.

Configuring Basic Authentication

The use of Basic Authentication with IIS has another interesting advantage. If you have configured Virtual Server such that IIS is on one computer and Virtual Server is on another computer, using Basic Authentication on the IIS server means that you do not need to enable constrained delegation for the IIS server. If, however, you also want to user a third computer to act as a file server for the virtual machine files, you still need to enable constrained delegation on the Virtual Server server.

To enable Basic Authentication under IIS you need to do the following:

1. On the Start menu, select Administrative Tools ➪ Internet Information Services (IIS) Manager.

2. Select the Virtual Server entry from the Web Sites node for your server.

3. Click Properties on the Action menu.

4. Change to the Directory Security tab.

5. Click Edit in the Authentication and access control section.

6. Uncheck Integrated Windows authentication and check Basic authentication (password is sent in clear text).

7. Read the warning and click Yes, and click OK to apply the changes.

Once you have enabled Basic Authentication, users will always be prompted to provide a user name and password when connecting to the Virtual Server administrative website.

Chapter 10: Securing Virtual Server

Be aware that when looking at these options, that NTLM and Basic Authentication are both able to reach a similar level of security as Kerberos when they are combined with SSL. SSL encrypts all network traffic, including user names and password, and SSL provides a guarantee that the server you are talking to is the correct one.

With all of this in mind, there are some general recommendations for when you should use the different types of authentication.

If your Virtual Server server and all planned client computers are expected to be part of the same Active Directory environment, the obvious choice is to use Integrated Windows authentication and Kerberos authentication. This will provide you with an excellent level of security with minimal configuration.

If you are using Virtual Server in a small, trusted workgroup environment, you should use Integrated Windows authentication and NTLM. While it does not provide an absolute guarantee of security, it is easy to configure and it tends to "just work." Note that having a trusted network environment is a must if you go with this option.

If you intend to connect Virtual Server directly to the Internet and have Internet-based clients connecting, you should use Basic Authentication and NTLM combined with SSL. This way, you can be confident in the security of the communication between the server and the clients, and everything will work in a public environment like the Internet.

Conclusion

It is important to make sure that Virtual Server is secured to a level that is appropriate for your networking environment. You should always configure the access rights for your virtual machine files so that each user has the right level of privilege for their needs.

You should also consider the implications of having IIS installed in order to use Virtual Server, and take steps to have a secure configuration of IIS.

SSL should be used for any instances of Virtual Server that are being directly connected to a public, or untrusted, network. SSL should be configured for both the Virtual Server Administrative website and for VMRC.

185

11

Backing Up Virtual Machines

With production environments running inside of virtual machines, creating a backup strategy that allows you to guarantee data recovery in the case of a system failure is critical. In fact, this is more important with virtual machines than with hardware, because with virtual machines a single hardware failure could affect multiple virtual machines.

Unfortunately, backup is quite a bit more complicated with virtual machines than with physical computers, but this chapter explains the various options available for ensuring your virtual machines are always safely backed up in a fashion that integrates with your existing backup infrastructure.

This chapter focuses on using the backup tools that are available with a standard installation of Virtual Server on Windows. If you are using any of the commercially available backup programs you should be able to apply the principles of this chapter to those programs.

> It should be noted that Microsoft has recently started licensing the format for its virtual hard disk file to other software companies and has stated that a number of popular backup vendors have licensed this format. However, at the time of this writing, no commercial backup solutions have been released that provide specific functionality for Virtual Server virtual machines.

Introducing VHDMount

You will see mention of the VHDMount tool a number of times. This is a new tool that Microsoft has provided with the release of Virtual Server 2005 R2 SP1. It allows you to connect (or mount) a virtual hard disk to your host operating system just as if it were a separate physical disk. This is very useful, especially when looking at data backup options.

Part IV: Security and Backup for Virtual Machines

VHDMount is normally installed into a directory with the name "VHDMount" under the directory that Virtual Server itself was installed into. VHDMount is a command-line utility with a simple interface. It takes four possible command-line parameters:

❑ `VHDMount /p [VHDFILENAME]`: The `/p` option will connect the virtual hard disk specified in `[VHDFILENAME]` to the host operating system. On a Windows XP host operating system, any partitions on the virtual hard disk will be automatically mounted by Windows and will have the next available drive letter assigned to them. A Windows Server 2003 host operating system will not automatically mount the partitions on the virtual hard disk, so if you used this option you would then need to open up the disk management console and assign a driver letter or mount point in order to access the data.

❑ `VHDMount /m [VHDFILENAME] [DRIVELETTER]`: The `/m` option is available only on Windows Server 2003. It connects the virtual hard disk specified in `[VHDFILENAME]` to the host operating system and mounts any partitions on the virtual hard disk, using the drive letter specified in `[DRIVELETTER]` for the first partition (any other partitions on the virtual hard disk will get assigned incrementing drive letters appropriately). If no drive letter is specified, the behavior of `/m` on Windows Server 2003 is similar to the behavior of `/p` on Windows XP.

`/m` cannot be used on Windows XP because it utilized the Virtual Disk Service (VDS) to mount the partitions on the virtual hard disk and VDS is not included with Windows XP.

Amusingly enough the Virtual Disk Service has nothing to do with Virtual Server or virtual machines, but rather provides a generic interface to allow programs to manage physical hard disks without needing to know about which specific storage hardware is being used.

❑ `VHDMount /u [VHDFILENAME]`: The `/u` option disconnects a mounted virtual hard disk from the host operating system. You can specify a specific virtual hard disk to be disconnected in `[VHDFILENAME]`, or you can run `VHDMount /u All` to disconnect all currently mounted virtual hard disks.

❑ `VHDMount /q [VHDFILENAME]`: The `/q` option returns the SCSI address of the virtual hard disk specified in `[VHDFILENAME]`. The SCSI address can be used to correlate the virtual hard disk to the mounted hard disk under the Windows Device Manager. Alternatively you can run `VHDMount /q All`, which will return information about the SCSI addresses for all mounted virtual hard disks. This second command is also quite useful if you have forgotten which virtual hard disks you have mounted because it also tells you the file names of the virtual hard disks that have been mounted.

You do not need to have Virtual Server installed to install VHDMount. You can perform a custom installation of Virtual Server in which you only select to install VHDMount. This can be useful if you have a backup server where you do not want to install Virtual Server, but you do want to be able to manipulate virtual hard disks directly.

Chapter 11: Backing Up Virtual Machines

Backing Up Virtual Machine Files

One of the first options to be aware of when backing up virtual machines is the simplicity of just copying the virtual machine files. A virtual machine comprises a virtual machine configuration (.vmc file), virtual hard disks (.vhd files) and potentially undo disks (.vud files), and a saved state (.vsv file). You can use the Virtual Server administrative website in order to find out the files that are used to define a single virtual machine. Follow these steps:

1. In the Virtual Server administrative website, select **Configure** from the **Virtual Machines** section of the navigation pane and then select the virtual machine that you are interested in.

2. Click **General Properties**.

3. Scroll down the page until you see the section entitled **Files Associated with**.

This will show you where the VMC, VHD, VUD, and VSV files associated with the virtual machine are stored. It will also show you the location of any virtual network configurations (VNC files) for the virtual networks that the virtual machine is connected to. Unfortunately, this page will not show you the location of any parent virtual hard disks if you are using differencing virtual hard disks. To find the location of a parent virtual hard disk, follow these steps:

1. Copy the VHD filename and path from the **General Properties** page for the virtual machine.

2. Click **Inspect** from the **Virtual Disks** section of the navigation pane.

3. Enter the VHD filename and path and click **Inspect**. You will see the information about the parent virtual hard disks on the next web page.

   If you back up the virtual machine files but do not include the parent virtual hard disk, you may not be able to start the virtual machine in the future if the parent virtual hard disk is not available.

Once you have a complete list of the files involved, you can use a backup program to back them up, or you can simply copy them to another location. These files represent the entire virtual machine and can be easily restored at a later point in time, even on to a different instance of Virtual Server on a different computer. Indeed, for casual users of Virtual Server, just manually copying the virtual machine files to a network share periodically is a very effective and simple form of backup.

> When moving a virtual machine configuration and associated files, you may wonder if there will be any problems with Virtual Server locating all of the files if they are restored in a different location on another computer. Virtual Server tracks dependencies between files by storing the absolute, or complete, path to the files (for example, C:*Directory**filename*) and the relative path from other files in the virtual machine (for example, ..*Directory**filename*).
>
> The virtual machine configuration (VMC) stores the path information for the virtual hard disk, undo disk, and saved state files. Undo disks and differencing disks store the path information for their parent disks. Saved state files store path information for all of the files involved in the virtual machine.
>
> When Virtual Server is checking for a specific virtual machine file, it will try to use the relative path first, and then the absolute path if the relative path fails. It also updates the path value if one fails and the other succeeds. All of this means that it is okay to move a virtual machine around to different locations, as long as each of the virtual machine files has the same relative location when compared to one another.

Part IV: Security and Backup for Virtual Machines

It should also be noted that the virtual machine configuration file, the saved state file, and any undo disks associated with a virtual machine always have to be together in the same folder.

Problems with Virtual Machine File Backup

Unfortunately there are a number of issues with this approach to backing up a virtual machine:

❑ The virtual machine needs to be stopped in order to back up the virtual machine. Virtual Server holds the virtual hard disk open for exclusive access while the virtual machine is running. This means that it is not possible to just copy the virtual machine while it is running. Some backup programs are capable of making backup copies of the virtual machine while it is running, but they end up making a backup of a corrupted virtual hard disk because the guest operating system is making changes to the virtual hard disk while the backup program is copying it.

> **A number of problems have been reported with virtual hard disks getting corrupted by backup programs that attempt to access them while Virtual Server is running the virtual machine. For this reason, it is important to exclude virtual hard disks from running virtual machines from any automated backup solutions.**

This means that the virtual machine needs to be stopped while a backup is made, which can require a significant amount of offline time for larger virtual machines.

❑ The virtual machine files can be very large. Even a basic virtual machine with a single virtual hard disk and a plain installation of Windows Server 2003 will use over 1GB of space to store. Once you have installed server class applications and added user data to a virtual machine, it can be tens of gigabytes in size. This means that you will need to have a lot of space on your backup media. It also means that it can take a long time to actually back up the virtual machine and copy all of the data.

❑ You have to back up the entire virtual machine. Typically when you back up a computer system, you may decide to back up only data files that you particularly care about, and not to back up system and program files that can be easily regenerated. When backing up the virtual machine files there is no way to back up part of the system.

❑ Incremental backups are ineffective. One of the most common methods for minimizing the amount of space and time needed to back up a system is incremental backup. In an incremental backup, only the files that have changed are backed up. Unfortunately, the bulk of the space used by a virtual machine is stored in the virtual hard disks. These are very large files that get changed whenever the virtual machine is booted. As such, the only time that an incremental backup would be effective would be when the virtual machine had not been powered on between backups.

Incremental backups are slightly more useful when differencing disks are used; because the parent virtual hard disk can never be changed, it needs only to be stored in the first backup made. However, even with differencing disks, the virtual hard disk will be quite large.

❑ It is hard to do a partial restore of the virtual machine. In the event that you lose data only from specific files inside the virtual machine and not the entire virtual machine, it is very hard to restore only the affected files without affecting all other files in the virtual machine. In fact, prior to Virtual Server 2005 R2 SP1 this was not hard, but impossible. Restoring the virtual hard disk files resets the entire state of the virtual machine back to the point in time when it was backed up. To perform a partial restore of a backup with Virtual Server 2005 R2 SP1 you would need to do the following:

Chapter 11: Backing Up Virtual Machines

1. Restore the virtual hard disk needed to a different location than the current virtual hard disk.

2. Use the VHDMount tool to mount the virtual hard disk file directly on the host operating system.

3. Locate the files that you wanted to restore from the backup and copy them off the mounted virtual hard disk.

4. Unmount the restored virtual hard disk and delete the VHD file.

5. Copy the specific files that were restored into the virtual machine.

If the virtual machine is currently running, you can copy the restored files in over the network. If the virtual machine is turned off, you can then mount the virtual hard disk with VHDMount and copy the restored files to the appropriate location on the virtual hard disk.

As you can see, while it is possible to perform a partial restore it is cumbersome and requires a large amount of temporary storage space, as you effectively have two copies of the virtual hard disk on your system while you are restoring the specific files that you want.

❑ There can be problems if you have the virtual machine configured to start automatically or to run under a specific user account and restore the virtual machine to another computer. When you configure a virtual machine to start automatically or to run under a specific user account you need to provide user credentials to use for these operations. Virtual Server does not store this information in the virtual machine files themselves, as this would be a potential security risk. Rather it stores the user credentials in a secure credential store, and places a reference to these credentials in the virtual machine configuration. When you restore the virtual machine files to a different physical computer this reference will no longer point to the same credentials. This can cause problems when trying to start the virtual machine, and might even require you to delete the virtual machine configuration and to recreate it manually.

❑ The guest operating system is unaware that it has been backed up. Some applications and operating systems store specific information as part of the backup process so that when they are restored at a later point in time they will know that they have been restored from a backup and need to operate accordingly. When a virtual machine is restored from a virtual machine file backup, the guest operating system just believes that it has been turned off for a period of time.

There are some cases where this last point can be extremely problematic. For instance, an Active Directory server that is restored from a backup knows that it needs to invalidate all of its directory information and rebuild it from the network and from other Active Directory servers. However, if the Active Directory server was restored by just copying virtual machine files back, this Active Directory server would believe that its directory information was authoritative, and it might even corrupt other Active Directory servers by updating them with out-of-date directory information.

Shut Down or Save State?

As mentioned, in order to back up a virtual machine by backing up the virtual machine files the virtual machine needs to be stopped. There are two possible ways to stop a virtual machine. You can either shut down the guest operating system and turn off the virtual machine, or you can put the virtual machine into a saved state.

191

Part IV: Security and Backup for Virtual Machines

> When a virtual machine is put into a saved state, Virtual Server pauses the virtual machine and writes the contents of the virtual machine's memory to hard disk. The virtual machine can then be restored from the saved state at a later point in time. Because this is done at the virtual machine level, the guest operating system and any applications that are running have no idea that they have been in a saved state. It is even possible to save state a virtual machine while you are halfway through installing a guest operating system and then resume it later and continue with the operating system installation.

There are a couple of factors to consider when trying to decide whether you want to shut down or save state the virtual machine in order to back it up:

❑ **Which option is fastest?** The amount of time that it takes to stop the virtual machine, back up the files, and start the virtual machine again is something that most people want to reduce as much as possible. Unfortunately when it comes to shutting down or saving state, one is not always faster than the other.

The amount of time it takes to shut down the virtual machine depends on the guest operating system running in the virtual machine, and on the applications running on top of it. For instance, an installation of Windows Server 2003 with no applications installed will shut down very quickly. But if you install SQL Server and Exchange on that virtual machine, then it takes a much longer time to shut down, as both of these server applications extend the shutdown time in order to allow them to safely commit all data to disk.

The amount of time it takes to put a virtual machine into a saved state is largely dependent on the amount of memory assigned to the virtual machine (with more memory meaning that it will take longer to save state). However, the amount of assigned memory that is actually being used by the virtual machine also affects the amount of time it will take.

> When saving the state of a running virtual machine, the thing that takes the most time is actually writing the contents of the virtual machine's memory to the hard disk. In order to minimize the amount of data that needs to be written to the hard disk, Virtual Server compresses the contents of the virtual machine's memory before writing it to disk. This means that a virtual machine with 3.6GB of memory assigned to it, but no active programs running, will save state much faster than a similarly configured virtual machine that has programs running that are actually using large sections of the memory.

❑ **How reliable is it?** This is an interesting point to configure. Unfortunately it is not always possible to shut down an operating system cleanly. When things go wrong inside of an operating system it is not impossible to get into a state where it is no longer able to shut down. In the case of Windows, it is also possible for applications running on Windows to veto a system shutdown. Save stating a virtual machine, on the other hand, is guaranteed to work as the guest operating system is not aware that it is being put into a saved state and none of the applications running on the guest operating system can stop a save state from happening.

Chapter 11: Backing Up Virtual Machines

❑ **Can it be automated programmatically**? If you want to develop an automated backup solution you will need a way to programmatically stop the virtual machine. Programmatically shutting down the guest operating system is possible only if you are running a virtual machine that has Virtual Machine Additions installed, or if you are able to shut down the guest operating system over the network. It is always possible to programmatically save state a virtual machine, no matter what is running inside the virtual machine.

❑ **How portable does the backed up virtual machine need to be?** When a virtual machine is placed into a saved state it can be restored only on a physical computer that has a processor with the same set of capabilities as that of the server the virtual machine was saved on. A virtual machine that has been shut down can be restored on any type of computer.

Processor capabilities are things such as MMX or SSE2. A virtual machine in a saved state can usually be restored on a different processor that is part of the same family (for example, Pentium III, Pentium IV, and so on) but this is not always the case.

❑ **Does the virtual hard disk need to be data consistent?** The virtual hard disk of a virtual machine that is in a saved state is not data consistent. The reason for this is that when the virtual machine is placed into a saved state any disk operations that are currently taking place are not allowed to complete, but are just paused. A virtual machine that has been shut down completes all disk operations before it stops. This is important because if you want to use VHDMount to access files on the backed up virtual hard drive, then the virtual hard drive needs to be data consistent and the virtual machine should not be in a saved state.

❑ **Do you want to restore the virtual machine to the exact state it was in, or not?** There are some cases where you want to restore a virtual machine to the exact state in which it was backed up, and there are cases where you do not want this. For example, if you had a development machine and you wanted to back up a set of running programs in their current state, using a saved state would be a good idea. If, however, you had an Exchange mail server with multiple clients you would not want to create a saved state and have it restored to the exact same state. In this case, it would be better to have the virtual machine shut down in order to be backed up.

Backing Up Inside the Virtual Machine

Now that you know all of the issues to consider with performing a virtual machine file–based backup of a virtual machine, it is time to look at backing up a virtual machine by running a backup process from inside the virtual machine, on top of the guest operating system. By using this approach, you can avoid many of the pitfalls of virtual machine file–based backup.

You do not need to stop the virtual machine to back up the files; nor do you need to backup all of the files every time. It is also much easier to perform incremental backups and partial restorations of virtual machines this way. And best of all, if you already have a standard backup strategy, this approach should be easy to incorporate into your existing practices.

However, as with virtual machine file–based backup there are a number of downsides to this approach:

❑ **Full system recovery is more complicated.** When backing up a virtual machine by copying the virtual machine files, recovering the complete system is as simple as restoring the virtual machine files. With a guest operating system–based backup it is usually much harder to restore a full system. You would need to create a new virtual machine, prepare it to have the backup restored, and then go through the backup restoration process.

193

Part IV: Security and Backup for Virtual Machines

❑ **Performing a full system backup will take longer.** Backing up files by using a backup program inside the guest operating system means that you will be accessing emulated storage and network devices in order to back up the data. Virtual machine file–based backups always use the physical hardware directly. As such, if you were performing a full system backup from inside the guest operating system, it would take noticeably longer than performing the same backup by copying the virtual machine files.

This problem is somewhat offset by the fact that you can perform incremental backups, which means that backup sizes will drop significantly after the first full system backup is taken.

❑ **Virtual machines cannot access tape drives.** This means that it is hard to back up directly from a virtual machine, and in most cases the only option is to back up the files to a network share and to then back up the files to tape.

> It is possible to access network-based tape storage from inside of a virtual machine; however, because relatively few people have network-based tape solutions deployed today, this book doesn't cover the use of tapes inside of virtual machines. If you do have network-based tape storage in your environment you can use it inside of virtual machines just as you would on a physical computer.

❑ **Backing up is difficult when the virtual machine is not running.** If the virtual machine is not running when you want to perform a backup operation, you either need to start the virtual machine, or mount the virtual hard disk using VHDMount and back up the files using the host operating system.

❑ **Backups are harder to manage.** When backing up virtual machine files from the host operating system, all backup operations can be performed from a single location. But when the backup is performed inside the virtual machine you need to coordinate backups across multiple systems.

❑ **Backups are potentially more expensive.** If you are using commercial backup software you need to have only a single license in order to back up the virtual machine files on the host operating system. But to back up the files inside of each virtual machine you will need to license the backup software to run inside of each virtual machine.

Backing Up Inside Windows Server 2003 and Windows XP

Windows Server 2003 and Windows XP include a backup tool called NTbackup. This tool has been included with Windows since Windows NT 3.1. Obviously it has evolved over time. NTbackup can be operated in a graphical mode or via the command prompt. Both modes have their strengths. The command prompt can be integrated into batch files and other automated processes. The graphical interface is more intuitive and provides you with the ability to schedule jobs.

This chapter uses the name "ntbackup" as this is the name of the executable file that you need to run, and it is the name that has traditionally been used for this utility. You can start ntbackup by either running ntbackup from a command prompt or from the Windows run dialog box. You can also start ntbackup by opening the Start menu and selecting All Programs ➪ Accessories ➪ System Tools ➪ Backup.

Using the Graphical Interface

NTBackup has two modes of operation: a wizard-based mode and the advanced mode. Both are useful in different situations. The wizard is the easier way to schedule a simple backup, but the advanced mode allows you to edit more of the options.

Chapter 11: Backing Up Virtual Machines

Creating a Backup with the Backup Wizard

To create a backup with the backup wizard you need to do the following:

1. Start **ntbackup**. This will start the **Backup or Restore Wizard** automatically.

2. On the **Backup or Restore** page, select **Back up files and settings**.

3. On the **What to Back Up** page, you can select either **All information on this computer** or **Let me choose what to backup**.

4. If you select **Let me choose what to backup**, you then see the **Items to Back Up** page. On this page, you can select the specific drives, folders, and files that you want to back up.

*In addition to being able to specify local drives and folders, you can select network locations to back up. Unfortunately, you have to browse through **My Network Places** in order to locate the network share that you want to back up. This is one area where using the command-line interface allows you more control as you can specify the network locations manually.*

*Another option that is available is to select to back up **System State**. This option is available under the **My Computer** option and backs up system information such as the registry, system files, and boot files. It also backs up data from many server roles such as the Active Directory database, Cluster database information, and IIS Metabase.*

5. On the Backup Type, Destination, and Name page you can specify the location and name of the backup. You cannot specify the backup type, as file-based backup is the only type that is available inside the virtual machine.

6. At this stage, you can either complete the wizard and have the backup start immediately, or you can click the **Advanced** button to specify extra options.

7. If you select **Advanced**, you end up on the **Type of Backup** page, where there are five possible types of backup that you can select:

❑ **Normal**: This option backs up all of the files you specified and marks them as backed up.

❑ **Copy**: This option backs up all of the files you specified, but does not mark them as backed up. This is useful if you want to make a full system backup without interfering with scheduled incremental and differential backups.

❑ **Incremental**: Incremental backups copy all files that have been changed since the last backup, and then marks the changed files as backed up. When restoring from an incremental backup you need to provide all previous incremental backups until you get to a normal backup.

❑ **Differential**: Differential backups copy all files that have been changed since the last backup, but will not mark the changed files as backed up. When restoring from a differential backup you need to have only the last normal backup present.

❑ **Daily**: This option will back up files that have been created or modified today, but it will not mark them as backed up.

8. On the **How to Back Up** page, you can choose the **Verify data after backup** to provide a guarantee that no data has been lost in the process of creating the backup. However, this will significantly extend the amount of time needed to make the backup.

Part IV: Security and Backup for Virtual Machines

9. On the **Backup Options** page, you can specify whether the back up should be appended to previous backups, or whether it should overwrite any existing backup files.

10. On the **When to Back Up** page, you can specify whether the backup should be performed immediately, or should be scheduled to happen at another time. If you select the **Later** option you will need to set a **Job name** and click the **Set Schedule** button. On the **Schedule Job** dialog box there are a number of options that can be configured. These options are discussed in the "Scheduling a Backup Job" section of this chapter.

Creating a Backup with the Advanced Mode User Interface

Ntbackup normally starts in wizard mode, but the first page of the wizard allows you to change to the advanced mode user interface. It also allows you to configure ntbackup to always start in the advanced mode by unselecting the Always start in wizard mode option. The advanced mode user interface is not as intuitive as using ntbackup in wizard mode, but there are a number of tasks and settings that can be accessed only when running ntbackup in advanced mode.

Once you have opened ntbackup in advanced mode you are presented with a window with four tabs:

❏ **Welcome:** This is just the introductory page, and can be used to launch one of the three backup and restore wizards. But if you had wanted to run wizards, you would have just stayed in wizard mode, right?

❏ **Backup:** On the **Backup** tab, you can select the files that you want to back up from your virtual machine. Once you have selected the files you want to back up, you can start the backup immediately by clicking the **Start Backup** button. Alternatively you can save the selected set of files and folders to a BKS file by selecting **Save Selections** from the **Job** menu. You can load a saved selection at a later date by choosing **Load Selections** from the **Job** menu.

If you choose to start the backup immediately, the backup will be made to the location specified in the **Backup destination** and **Backup media or file name** fields.

There are a number of advanced options that you were able to specify in the backup wizard that are not offered here. Instead, this section covers options that are specified in the Options dialog box as the default settings for a backup job. You should review the configuration of the Options dialog box before performing a backup in this way.

❏ **Restore and Manage Media:** This tab allows you to browse the contents of known backups and select to restore the files to their original location, or to a different location that you specify. Unfortunately it is not possible to add any new backup sets to this page. If you want to restore files from a backup that is not listed here, you will need to run the backup and restore wizard.

When you restore files using this tab, ntbackup will use the restore settings defined in the NTbackup Options dialog box to determine whether existing files will be replaced or not.

❏ **Schedule Jobs:** The **Schedule Jobs** tab will show you a calendar that indicates when any scheduled backup jobs are going to occur. Each job is represented by a small icon with a letter that indicates the type of the backup (normal, copy, incremental, differential or daily).

You can edit the schedule for any job by clicking on the schedule entry. Then you are given the option to delete the scheduled job or to view the properties for the scheduled job. If you click the **Properties** button, you will see the **Schedule Job** dialog box that is discussed in the "Scheduling a Backup Job" section of this chapter.

Chapter 11: Backing Up Virtual Machines

It is possible to add a job to the schedule on this tab, either by clicking the **Add Job** button or by double-clicking on a blank entry on the calendar. This launches the backup wizard and automatically displays the advanced options, as they are required to be able to set the schedule for a backup job.

*Scheduled jobs will appear on the days that they are going to occur on. Jobs that have a repeating schedule will be displayed multiple times in the calendar, on every day that they are going to be run. For backup jobs that are scheduled to occur in response to system events, such as system startup or user login, icons are displayed in the **System Event** box in the lower-right of the calendar.*

In addition to these main tabs, there are also two very useful dialog boxes that can be accessed only when running ntbackup in advanced mode: **Backup Reports** and **Options**.

Select **Report** from the **Tools** menu to open the **Backup Reports** dialog box. This dialog box provides a list of all backup logs that are available on the virtual machine, and sorts the logs by the date and time they were created. This dialog box also shows you the name of the backup job that was used to generate each log file. From this dialog box you can choose the **View** or **Print** option for each log file.

*Backup jobs can be configured to use full logging, summarized logging, or no logging at all. This is configured in the **Options** dialog box.*

*The Backup Reports dialog box just opens the existing log files in Notepad when you choose the View option. You can open these log files yourself by using the Explorer to go to **%userprofile%\Local Settings\Application Data\Microsoft\Windows NT\NTBackup\data**, but by doing it this way there is no easy way to know which log file is associated with a specific backup job (except for opening all of the files and looking at the contents).*

The **Options** dialog box can be accessed by opening the **Tools** menu and selecting **Options**. This dialog box has five tabs with many options to configure. Some of these options can be configured in other locations as well, but others can only be configured here. Either way, the options that are configured here serve as the default values for all backups, whether they are performed with the backup wizard, advanced mode user interface, or the command-line interface. The five option tabs are as follows:

❏ **General:** The **General** tab provides the capability to configure a number of miscellaneous options related to backup. Most of these options are specific to tape-based backups, and hence are not important inside of a virtual machine with no tape access. These options can be ignored for the purpose of running ntbackup in a virtual machine:

   ❏ **Use the catalogs on the media to speed up building restore catalogs on the disk**

   ❏ **Show alert message when I start the Backup Utility and there is recognizable media available**

   ❏ **Show alert message when new media is inserted**

   ❏ **Always allow use of recognizable media without prompting**

   The following options on the **General** tab should be configured appropriately:

   ❏ **Compute selection information before backup and restore operations.** When this option is enabled, ntbackup estimates the number of files and bytes that are backed up and uses this information in the progress dialog box that is displayed during the backup. Unselecting this option slightly reduces the time it takes to back up the files and stop the estimates from being displayed. This option cannot be configured anywhere else.

197

Part IV: Security and Backup for Virtual Machines

❑ **Verify data after the backup completes.** Verifying the data provides a guarantee that no data was corrupted during the backup operation; however, it greatly increases the amount of time that it takes to complete the backup. This option can be overridden for a specific backup job when you use the backup wizard or command-line interface to create the backup job, but not if you are using the advanced mode user interface.

❑ **Back up the contents of mounted drives.** An NTFS-formatted partition can either be mounted using a drive letter, or mounted to a folder that is stored on another drive. If this option is enabled, drives that are mounted to folders on other drives are backed up if the folder that contains the mounted drive is backed up. This option cannot be configured anywhere else.

❑ **Show alert message when I start the Backup Utility and Removable Storage is not running.** Because you will most likely be doing only file-based backups, you do not need to have Remote Storage running in order to use ntbackup; you may wish to uncheck this option.

❑ **Restore:** The **Restore** tab allows you to configure whether existing files should be overwritten when files are being restored from a backup. You can select one of three options:

❑ **Do not replace the file on my computer** (recommended)

❑ **Replace the file on disk only if the file on disk is older**

❑ **Always replace the file on my computer**

This is the only place where you can set this option.

❑ **Backup Type:** On this tab you can configure the default backup type to be performed (normal, copy, differential, incremental, or daily). This is just a default value and both the backup wizard and the command-line interface allow you to override this option. This is the value that will be used if you start a backup from the backup tab of the advanced mode user interface or if you use the backup wizard and do not choose to specify the advanced settings.

❑ **Backup Log:** Here you can select from three logging options:

❑ **Detailed:** This option logs all information, including the names of all files that are backed up. This option results in the generation of very large log files, which probably will have too much information in them to be of much use to you. As such, you should choose this option only if you have a specific need to have this level of information available.

❑ **Summary:** This is the default configuration for logging. It logs information about the start and completion of the backup as well as any errors that occurred during the backup.

❑ **None:** No log file is generated. This configuration is used for all backup operations, and only the command-line interface allows you to specify that a different logging option should be used for a specific backup.

❑ **Exclude Files:** By default, ntbackup will not attempt to back up a number of system files that are known to contain information that is not appropriate to back up (for example, the system page file). On this tab, you can add to or remove from the list of files that are excluded from backup operations. You can specify file exclusion lists that should be applied to all backups attempted on this virtual machine, or only to backups that you attempt on this virtual machine. For each entry you can specify:

Chapter 11: Backing Up Virtual Machines

❏ The file mask to exclude. You can either provide the full name of a specific file that you want to exclude (for example, **MySecretFile.txt**) or you can use standard file wildcards (for example, ***.txt** or **SomeName.***).

❏ The path that the exclusion should apply to.

❏ Whether files in subfolders of the path specified should be excluded as well.

This is the only place that you can configure the excluded files for backups.

Scheduling a Backup Job

When you select to schedule a backup job in either the backup wizard, or the advanced mode user interface, you will see the **Schedule Job** dialog box. This is a very powerful part of ntbackup and allows you to construct quite complex job schedules.

It is only possible to configure backup schedules through the graphical user interface for ntbackup. You cannot configure backup schedules with the command-line interface.

The **Schedule Job** dialog box has two tabs; the **Schedule** and **Settings** tabs. On the **Schedule** tab, you can configure:

❏ **Schedule Task:** This setting allows you to select from a number of schedule routines:

❏ **Daily:** The daily schedule setting allows you to configure that the backup should run at a specific time on a daily basis. You can also use this setting to configure a backup to run every two, three, or more days as you define.

❏ **Weekly:** This schedule setting allows you to configure a backup to be run on specific days of the week at specific times. It also allows you to configure whether backups run every week, every two weeks, or any other interval of weeks.

❏ **Monthly:** Here you can configure a job to either be run on a specific date of each month (for example, the 1st, the 15th, and so on) or on a specific day of each month (for example, the first Monday of each month, the last Friday of each month). You can also configure during which months the backup should be run.

❏ **Once:** This setting simply allows you to specify a date and time to run the backup job.

❏ **At System Startup:** This schedules the backup to be run every time the system is started up. (It does not require that a user log into the virtual machine.) There are no extra options that can be configured with this setting.

❏ **At Logon:** This schedules the backup to run whenever a user logs into the system. There are no extra options that can be configured for this setting.

❏ **When idle:** The **When idle** setting allows you to specify that whenever the system has been idle for a period of time (in minutes) the backup job should be initiated. If the system is sitting idle for an extended period of time, this schedule option will continue to take backups until something happens on the virtual machine. As such, with this option it is advisable to ensure that you have sufficient storage to avoid running out of space.

❏ **Show multiple schedules:** By checking the **Show multiple schedules** option, you will be able to associate multiple different schedules with a single backup job. Once you have checked this option you will see that you now have the ability to create new schedules for this job, and to delete existing ones. Each schedule is configured in the same manner as the first schedule.

Part IV: Security and Backup for Virtual Machines

❏ **Advanced:** For the **Daily**, **Weekly**, **Monthly**, and **Once** backup schedule settings you can also specify advanced settings by clicking the **Advanced** button. This will open the **Advanced Schedule Options** dialog box, which allows you to configure the following options:

 ❏ **Start date:** Here you can create a schedule for a backup, but specify that it only starts after a specific date. Typically this is set to the current date for today so that the backup is scheduled immediately.

 ❏ **End date:** You can also specify that a specific backup schedule should stop being followed after a specific date.

 ❏ **Repeat task:** Typically the shortest repeating period that you can configure for a scheduled backup is once a day. The repeat task section of the advanced settings allows you to specify that the backup just should actually be repeated during the day, at a custom interval that you configure (in either minutes or hours).

On the **Settings** tab, you can configure the following settings:

❏ **Delete the task if it is not scheduled to run again.** This setting is fairly straightforward. If you are scheduling a backup job that you know that you will not use again after it has been used for this schedule, you can request that the job be deleted after it runs for the last time. This way, the backup job scheduler is kept clear of obsolete job data.

❏ **Stop the task if it runs for: (user defined hours and minutes).** The next three settings (this one included) are all about allowing you to manage the impact of scheduled backups on your virtual machines. While files are being backed up, your virtual machine will be heavily accessing disk and network resources, which will in turn reduce the performance of the virtual machine if people try to access it while backups are being performed.

If you are performing a regular incremental, differential or daily backup of your computer system the amount of time required to perform the backup will depend on the number of files that are changed from backup to backup. The amount of time taken to perform a normal or copy backup will depend upon the size of the data you are trying to back up.

By enabling this setting you are able to set a guaranteed window of time for the backup to complete in, and ensure that general usage is not disrupted by a backup that takes too long. You need to be careful to choose a time period that will allow your backup job to complete under normal loads with normal circumstances; otherwise you could always be ending up with an incomplete backup set.

❏ **Only start the task if the computer has been idle for at least: (user defined minutes). If the computer has not been idle that long, retry for up to: (user defined minutes).** This setting allows you to specify that ntbackup should wait for the computer to remain idle for a specified amount of time before running the backup job. The benefit of enabling this setting is that it means for virtual machines that have unpredictable workloads you can make sure that a backup job never interferes with a period of high activity on the virtual machine. You also need to specify the maximum amount of time that ntbackup will wait before giving up and waiting for the next scheduled execution of this job.

❏ **Stop the task if the computer ceases to be idle.** This setting will cause a backup job to stop if you begin to use the virtual machine while the backup is running. This setting, like the prior two settings, allows you to minimize the potential impact that backups have on the system but does so at the risk of not ensuring that you always get a complete system backup.

200

Chapter 11: Backing Up Virtual Machines

❑ **Power management settings.** Three power management settings are available for scheduled backup jobs:

  ❑ **Don't start the task if the computer is running on batteries**

  ❑ **Stop the task if battery mode begins**

  ❑ **Wake the computer to run this task**

But none of these settings need to be enabled inside of a virtual machine. The virtual machine will never report that it is running on a battery (even if the physical computer is) and the virtual machine does not allow the guest operating system to sleep, so enabling these settings will make no practical difference to the backup schedule.

Whenever you configure a backup job to be run on a specify schedule, you will be prompted to provide user credentials that will be used to run the backup process. This is required as it is not possible to guarantee that a user with the right credentials will be logged into the virtual machine when the backup needs to be performed.

Using the Command-Line Interface

To back up a drive inside of a virtual machine to a network location using the command-line interface you just need to run a command like this:

```
Ntbackup backup C:\ /J "Virtual machine backup" /F "\\fileserver\backupshare\
backupfile.bkf" /V:yes /L:s /M incremental /SNAP:on
```

This command uses a number of parameters:

❑ `backup`: This parameter says that you want to perform a backup operation. This is a bit of a strange parameter as ntbackup does not support restoring files via the command line; as such, the only operation that you are going to perform with the command line is to back up.

❑ `C:\`: Here you can specify the path to back up. Ntbackup allows you to specify only one path here and it will back up everything that is underneath that path. If you want to have more control over which files are backed up, you will need to create a BKS file. To create a BKS file you need to do the following:

  1. Run **ntbackup** and start the advanced mode user interface.

  2. Change to the **Backup** tab.

  3. Check the files and folders that you are interested in having backed up.

  4. Open the **Job** menu and select **Save Selections As**.

  5. Save the BKS file to an appropriate location.

Once you have the BKS file, you can specify that it be used for specifying the files to back up by replacing the path in the preceding command with **@TheNameOfTheFile.bks**. For example:

```
Ntbackup backup @C:\BackupSet.bks /J "Virtual machine backup" /F
"\\fileserver\backupshare\backupfile.bkf" /V:yes /L:s /M incremental /SNAP:on
```

If you need to specify a path or backup file name that contains spaces in its name, you should place the path or file name inside double quotes.

201

Part IV: Security and Backup for Virtual Machines

A third option that you can specify here is `SystemState`. This will tell ntbackup to just back up the system state data for the computer.

Once you have created a .bks file, you can open it using Notepad and look at the format of the file. A .bks file is just a plain-text list of all of the paths and specific files that you want to back up. All path entries are automatically recursed during the backup process. If you do not want a specific subdirectory to be backed up, you can add an entry with the path for the subdirectory and the text `/Exclude` after it. Here is the content of a sample .bks file:

```
\\remoteServer\share1
\\remoteServer\share2
C:\
C:\i386\ /Exclude
C:\Windows\ /Exclude
C:\Windows\iis6.log
SystemState
```

This .bks file would back up all of the files on Share1 and Share2 on remoteServer, all of the files on C:\ except for the files under the I386 and Windows directories, but including IIS6.LOG under the Windows directory, and the system state information.

If you want to create a backup job that backs up multiple network locations, hand editing a .bks file is probably the easiest method to use.

❑ `/J "Virtual machine backup"` — This defines the title of the backup job. This should be a descriptive title that you can use to easily identify the purpose of the backup. The backup job title must be placed in quotes, and there must be a space between the /J and the backup job title.

❑ `/F "\\fileserver\backupshare\backupfile.bkf"` — This specifies the file that the backup should be stored in. This should be a file with the .bkf file extension. The backup file can be created locally on the virtual machine, or directly on a network share. Like the backup job title, the backup file must be placed in quotes, and there must be a space between the /F and the backup file.

❑ `/V:yes` — This specifies whether the data should be verified to be correct after it has been backed up. You can use yes or no as the /V: option. The option should not be placed in quotes and there should be no space between /V: and the option you want to use.

❑ `/L:s` — This specifies what level of logging should be performed for the backup. You can specify f for full logging, s for summarized logging, or n for no logging. The option should not be placed in quotes and there should be no space between /L: and the option you want to use.

❑ `/M incremental` — This allows you to define the type of backup that will be performed. You can specify a normal, copy, differential, incremental, or daily option. The option should not be placed in quotes and there should be a space between /M and the option you want to use.

❑ `/SNAP:on` — This specifies whether volume shadow copy services should be used to back up files that are currently being held open by running programs. You can specify on or off. The option should not be placed in quotes and there should be no space between /SNAP: and the option you want to use.

If your backup includes backing up the system state, volume shadow copy services will be used even if the /SNAP: parameter is set to no.

Chapter 11: Backing Up Virtual Machines

> If the /V, /L, /M, or /SNAP **options are not defined, then the default settings from the** **Options dialog box in the advanced mode user interface will be used.**

Backing Up Inside Windows 2000

The version of ntbackup included with Windows 2000 is very similar to the version of ntbackup included with Windows XP and Windows Server 2003. In fact, the only differences between the two versions are:

❑ The Windows 2000 version of ntbackup does not support the use of volume shadow copy services (VSS). This means that none of the options relating to VSS are available on Windows 2000.

❑ The Windows 2000 version of ntbackup does not have a wizard mode; rather, it always starts with the advanced mode user interface and allows you to launch the wizards from the **Welcome** tab.

Backing Up Inside Windows NT 4.0

The version of ntbackup included with Windows NT 4.0 is significantly different to the later versions of ntbackup. In fact, it is so different that it is pretty much useless for the purpose of backing up files inside of virtual machines. The reason for this is that the Windows NT 4.0 version of ntbackup allows you only to back up files to a tape drive, and not to a file or network share. So how can you back up files from inside a Windows NT 4.0 virtual machine? Well, there are two options. The first is to back up the files from a remote backup server (this is discussed later in this chapter). The second is to use an old faithful tool: xcopy.

Most people are familiar with xcopy as a tool for copying files from one location to another. It can also be used to provide a number of basic network backup functionality. Here is an xcopy command that will work well for backing up a Windows NT 4.0 virtual machine:

```
Xcopy "C:\WINNT" "\\fileserver\NTbackup\WINNT" /E /V /C /I /H /R /K /Z /D
```

Now let's look at the specific parameters that were used for this command:

❑ `Xcopy "C:\WINNT" "\\fileserver\NTbackup\WINNT"`: The command starts with simply specifying the source and destination paths for the copy operation.

❑ `/E`: This parameter tells xcopy to copy any subdirectories under the source path.

There are two possible parameters to tell xcopy to include subdirectories. /S is the other parameter to do this, but using /S means that empty directories will not be copied. Some people use both /S and /E, but this has the same effect as using just /E.

❑ `/V`: This tells xcopy to verify the data after it has been copied. This makes the operation take longer, but it provides a guarantee that the data is valid after it has been backed up.

❑ `/C`: With this parameter, xcopy will continue copying even if an error occurs. This is important as xcopy will report an error whenever it encounters a file that is held open by Windows, and hence cannot be copied. In this case, you want xcopy to skip the file and continue copying the other files.

203

Part IV: Security and Backup for Virtual Machines

❑ /I: This parameter tells xcopy to assume that if you tell it a destination that does not exist, that you want it to create a directory with that name to store the files in. Without this parameter, xcopy will prompt you to create the directory.

❑ /H: This tells xcopy to copy hidden and system files.

❑ /R: This tells xcopy to overwrite read-only files if required.

❑ /K: This tells xcopy to include the file attributes when it copies the files. It does not do this normally.

❑ /Z: Causes xcopy to operate in a restartable mode, so that if there are any problems during a network copy the file copy can be resumed without recopying all of the data.

❑ /D: The /D option is very useful. When you just use /D by itself, xcopy will not copy any files that exist on the destination and have not been changed since they were last copied. If you use the form /D:month-day-year then xcopy will copy all files that have been created or modified since the date specified.

Use of the /D option allows you to achieve similar results to performing daily, incremental, or differential backups with ntbackup.

While xcopy can be used as a basic backup tool, it does have a number of shortcomings. It does not copy system state information, and there is no built-in tool to schedule xcopy commands.

Backing Up Inside Vista

Windows Vista has an entirely new backup experience to previous versions of Windows. It does not use the ntbackup tool. In fact, there is no command-line interface for creating a backup under Windows Vista. There are two ways to back up a Windows Vista virtual machine from the inside.

The first way is to take a Windows Complete PC Backup. This will back up all of the files in your virtual machine so that you can perform a full system restoration at a later date. The Windows Complete PC Backup process does not allow you to configure the details of which files should or should not be backed up. Interestingly enough, Windows Complete PC Backup will actually back up your system to a VHD file. So you can see that running Windows Complete PC Backup inside of the virtual machine does not make too much sense when you can just copy the virtual machine files and get a similar result.

The only time that you would want to consider using Windows Complete PC Backup over copying the virtual machine files is if you wanted to generate a full system backup, but did not want to turn the system off to do so.

The second way to back up files from inside a Windows Vista virtual machine is to use the **Backup and Restore Center**. Follow these steps:

1. Open the **Start** menu and click Control Panel.

2. Select **System and Maintenance** and then **Backup and Restore Center**.

If you are using the classic view for the Windows Vista control panel, you can just double-click on the **Backup and Restore Center** *icon.*

3. Click the **Back up files** button next to the **Create backup copies of your files and folders** text.

204

Chapter 11: Backing Up Virtual Machines

You can also launch a Windows Complete PC Backup from this location, but that is not discussed in this chapter.

4. This will start the **Back Up Files** Wizard, where the first thing you will see is the **Where do you want to save your backup?** page. On this page, you can select **On a network** and specify the network path that you want files to be backed up to.

    When you specify the network share, you will be prompted to enter user credentials for accessing the network share.

5. On the **Which file types do you want to backup?** page, you can select the types of files that will be backed up (such as pictures, music, documents, and so on).

    Unlike in NTBackup, with Windows Vista backup you do not need to select specific files and folders to be backed up. Rather, you specify the file types and Windows Vista backs up all files that meet the criteria that you have set.

6. On the **How often do you want to create a backup?** page, you can specify the schedule to be used for running this backup job. In the **How often:** field you can select daily, weekly, or monthly. If you select weekly or monthly you can then specify the day of the week (or month) that the backup should happen on in the **What day:** field. In addition, you can specify when the backup should happen through the **What time:** field.

7. If you want the backup job to be run immediately when you complete the wizard you can check the **Create a new, full backup now in addition to saving settings** option.

When the backup runs, it will create backup files so that you can restore files at a later date through the **Backup and Restore Center**. The backed up files themselves are stored in ZIP files, so you can restore a single file without using the Windows Vista tools if you want to. Once you have created a backup schedule, you can edit it by going to the **Create backup copies of your files and folders** section of the **Backup and Restore Center** and clicking **Change Settings** and then **Change backup settings**.

> The backup capabilities of Windows Vista have been streamlined significantly from those included in Windows XP. The reasoning behind this is that Microsoft wants backup to be something that home users can easily do with their computers. Having said that, a number of features from NTBackup are no longer possible with Windows Vista backup, such as having multiple backup schedules and specifying more advanced backup options.

Backing Up Inside Red Hat Enterprise Linux 4

A number of free and commercial backup tools are available for Linux today. This section describes how to use an established work horse of the Linux backup world: tar. The name *tar* is an abbreviation of *tape archive*. Tar was originally designed for backing up data to tape, but it can be equally well used to back up data to a file or network location.

Interestingly enough the file format used by tar is identical for local file archives as for tape archives. This means that if you want to back up your Linux virtual machines to tape you can run tar on the virtual machine, have it create an archive file on a network share and then have a physical computer copy the archive directly to tape.

205

Part IV: Security and Backup for Virtual Machines

Tar does not contain any capability to schedule archive creation; however, several tools (such as cron) can be used to schedule periodic backups. This book does not discuss the use of scheduling tools for Linux.

Creating and Restoring a Tar Archive

A basic tar archive can be created with the following command:

```
tar cpfW /archive/backup.tar -C / --ignore-failed-read --exclude=proc --exclude=mnt
--exclude=archive --exclude=cache --exclude=*/lost+found --exclude=dev .
```

The following are the arguments used in this command:

❑ cpfW: This is an argument block (multiple arguments put together). Each argument has its own meaning:

   ❑ c: Tells tar to create a new archive. This can also be set by using the argument form --create.

   ❑ p: Tells tar to preserve file permissions when creating the archive. This can also be set by using the argument forms --same-permissions or --preserve-permissions.

   ❑ f: Tells tar that a file name will be provided, and that this file name should be the name of the archive. This can also be set by using the argument form --file.

   ❑ W: Tells tar to attempt to verify the archive after creating it. This can also be set by using the argument form --verify.

❑ /archive/backup.tar: This is the name of the archive file that will be created.

Tar works at a file level so if you want to create a tar archive on a network share, simply mount the network share that you want to use and provide tar with the path to a file on that share.

❑ -C /: This argument tells tar to change directory to the specified directory (in this case /) before creating the archive. This can also be set by using the argument form --directory.

❑ --ignored-failed-read: This will stop tar from exiting if an unreadable file is encountered. We do not want this to happen with a periodic backup operation. There is no other form for specifying this argument.

❑ --exclude=proc --exclude=mnt --exclude=archive --exclude=cache --exclude=*/lost+found --exclude=dev: The --exclude argument allows you to specify directories that should not be included in the archive. All of the directories listed are special system directories that should not be archived. There is no other form for specifying this argument.

Many of the arguments for tar come in multiple forms. There are short forms (such as p), which are intended to be convenient for people who use tar regularly and there are long forms (such as --preserve-permissions), which are easier to read. In this book, I will use short forms when they are available, simply because that is my personal preference. The alternate argument forms are also mentioned whenever they exist.

It is important to note that the arguments for tar are case-sensitive. For example, the W argument will tell tar to verify the archive but the w argument will tell tar to ask for confirmation on every action.

206

Chapter 11: Backing Up Virtual Machines

Once you have a tar archive you can get a file listing of the contents of the archive by running the following command:

```
tar tf backup.tar
```

The t argument tells tar to list the contents of the archive (this has a long form of --list) and once again the f indicates that the archive will be the file specified.

To restore the contents of a tar archive you can run:

```
tar xpf backup.tar -C /
```

The x argument tells tar to extract files from the archive (this has long forms of --extract and --get). The f argument indicates that a file will be used for the archive and the p tells tar to preserve the permissions. -C / is used to change the directory to / before extracting the contents of the archive. This ensures that the files will get extracted to the right place.

Of course, if the archive was created from a different directory than / you would want to change directory to the directory from which the archive was created.

Creating a Differential Tar Archive

Tar provides you with the ability to archive only the files that have been created or modified since a specified date. Here are two examples of how to do that:

```
tar cpfW /archive/backup.tar -C / --ignore-failed-read -N 'yesterday' --
exclude=proc --exclude=mnt --exclude=archive --exclude=cache --exclude=*/lost+found
--exclude=dev .

tar cpfW /archive/backup.tar -C / --ignore-failed-read -N 20050601 --exclude=proc --
exclude=mnt --exclude=archive --exclude=cache --exclude=*/lost+found --exclude=dev .
```

The -N (which can also be --newer or --after-date) tells tar to archive only the files that have been created or modified after the date specified. Tar accepts a dizzying array of formats for specifying dates. As you can see, one command uses the literal string yesterday and another uses a number in the form of year, month, then day. For a detailed list of all the date formats accepted by tar, refer to www.gnu .org/software/tar/manual/html_node/tar_109.html.

Creating an Incremental Tar Archive

Tar also supports the concept of incremental archives, where only the files that have changed since the last archive was created are stored in the new archive. Here is a command that does exactly that:

```
tar cpfW /archive/backup.tar -C / --ignore-failed-read -g=/var/log/backup.snar --
exclude=proc --exclude=mnt --exclude=archive --exclude=cache --exclude=*/lost+found
--exclude=dev .
```

The key difference here is the -g argument (which can also be --listed-incremental). This tells tar to perform an incremental archive using the metadata file /var/log/backup.snar. The metadata file is used to store the information that is necessary to have in order to determine which files have changed from backup to backup. The first time you run the preceding command, tar will detect that the metadata

207

Part IV: Security and Backup for Virtual Machines

file does not exist and create a new one. Each time you run the command after that the metadata file will be updated with new information.

If you want to start a new chain of incremental archives all you need to do is to delete the metadata file.

Creating Compressed Tar Archive

The final capability of tar highlighted in this chapter is the ability to make compressed archives. The standard tar archive is not compressed and takes up a fair amount of space. However, tar includes built-in support for some of the more common compression routines. Here is a command that will create a gzipped tar archive:

```
tar cpfz /archive/backup.tar.gz -C / --ignore-failed-read --exclude=proc --
exclude=mnt --exclude=archive --exclude=cache --exclude=*/lost+found --exclude=dev .
```

The z in the argument block tells tar to gzip the archive after it is created. The archive file name has been changed from backup.tar to backup.tar.gz, as this is the standard naming format for gzipped archives.

> *If you enable one of the archive compression options, you can no longer use the w argument. The reason for this is that while tar is capable of compressing the archive, it does not have any ability to uncompress the archive and cannot verify the contents of the archive.*

Once you have created a compressed archive, tar will be unable to perform any operations on it until you uncompress it. To uncompress a gzipped archive you just need to run the following:

```
gunzip backup.tar.gz
```

Tar also supports creating bzip2 compressed archives through the use of the j argument:

```
tar cpfj /archive/backup.tar.bz2 -C / --ignore-failed-read --exclude=proc --
exclude=mnt --exclude=archive --exclude=cache --exclude=*/lost+found --exclude=dev .
```

This archive can be uncompressed by running the following:

```
bunzip2 backup.tar.bz2
```

> *When creating a compressed archive, tar will actually create the entire archive upfront and then compress it once it is created. This means that while compressing the archive saves space at the end of the day, you still need to have enough space available for all the data that is being backed up in its uncompressed state. It also means that if you are creating an archive on a network location this will cause a lot of network traffic.*

Backing Up from a Remote Backup Server

As I highlighted earlier, two of the biggest problems with backing up files from inside the virtual machine are dealing with the management of so many backup operations and dealing with the fact that virtual machines do not have access to tape devices. Both of these issues can be addressed handily by the use of a remote backup server.

Chapter 11: Backing Up Virtual Machines

The concept here is that rather than having each virtual machine responsible for running its own backup process, you have a central server to manage this. This server would connect to the virtual machines over the network and back up their files remotely (both NTBackup and tar allow you to back up network shares). This gives you a single point of management for backups, and because it's a physical computer the server can just write data directly to tape.

Unfortunately even this solution has its downsides. Configuring the remote backup server and all of the virtual machines so that the backup server can reliably connect to the virtual machine's network resources at the right time and perform the backup operation can be difficult to do. Also, in the case of NTBackup, once you are backing up a virtual machine over the network you are no longer able to back up the virtual machine's system state data. You can only back up the files.

Using VSS to Back Up Virtual Machines

Virtual Server 2005 R2 SP1 includes native support for Volume Shadow Copy Services (VSS). VSS is a new functionality in Windows Server 2003 and Windows XP SP2 that allows backup programs to back up the data from a running computer system with guaranteed data integrity and no noticeable downtime. It does this by creating VSS snapshots, which are point-in-time images of the hard disk. The VSS support in Virtual Server 2005 R2 SP1 allows a backup program on the host operating system to request a virtual machine file–based backup of all running virtual machines. This works in one of two ways:

- ❏ If you are running a virtual machine with a guest operating system that supports VSS, Virtual Server will work with VSS inside the guest operating system and provide a data consisted backup to the host backup program with no downtime for the virtual machine. The resulting backup is equivalent to having shutdown the virtual machine and then having backed up the virtual machine files, but no downtime is involved.

- ❏ If you are running a virtual machine with a guest operating system that does not support VSS, Virtual Server will save state the virtual machine and then restore it immediately. In the brief instance that the virtual machine was in a saved state, the VSS-enabled backup program on the host will have taken a *VSS snapshot*. This allows Virtual Server to restore the virtual machine and let it continue running while the backup program is still copying the virtual machine files from the virtual machine in a saved state. The resulting backup is equivalent to having put the virtual machine in a saved state and then having backed up the virtual machine files, but minimal downtime is involved (the amount of time that it would take to save state the virtual machine and immediately restore it).

Unfortunately, NTBackup does not support the use of VSS except for backing up the Windows system state. If you want to back up Virtual Server virtual machines using VSS you have two options. The first is to use a commercial backup program with VSS support. The second is to download the VSS SDK and use the sample tools provided with it. You can download the VSS SDK from here: `www.microsoft .com/downloads/results.aspx?freetext=VSS%20SDK`.

Once you have downloaded and installed the VSS SDK you can use the vshadow tool. A number of useful commands are available. `vshadow -wm` lists all of the known VSS writers on the system. When you run this command you should see an entry for every virtual machine that is configured under Virtual Server.

209

Part IV: Security and Backup for Virtual Machines

The next command is `vshadow -p X:` (where `X:` is the drive that holds the virtual machines that you want to back up). This command will cause VSS to make a point-in-time image of the drive containing your virtual machines, and Virtual Server will do the necessary work to ensure that all of the virtual machines are in a backup ready state.

At this stage you have a consistent backup of your virtual machines in VSS. You could just leave this and use this as your local backup solution. If you accidentally deleted or corrupted a virtual machine, you could get the disk back to this point in time by running `vshadow -revert={SNAPSHOT ID}`.

> *When the* `vshadow -p X:` *command completes, it displays some information about the VSS snapshot that was just created on the hard disk. The most important piece of information displayed is the snapshot ID as this is needed by many of the other* `vshadow` *commands.*

Alternatively you could run `vshadow -el={SNAPSHOT ID},Y:`. This command tells VSS to mount the point-in-time snapshot that was taken as a drive (in this case `Y:`). Once this has happened, you can copy the virtual machines from the VSS snapshot to a safe location, or even use NTBackup to back them up. Then, once you have the data that you wanted to back up, you can run `vshadow -ds={SNAPSHOT ID}` to delete the snapshot.

The important thing to remember is that all of this is done with almost no disruption to the virtual machines themselves.

> *One thing to keep in mind is that while VSS helps address the issue of virtual machine file–based backup requiring virtual machine downtime, it does not address any of the other issues around virtual machine file–based backups.*

Backing Up Virtual Server Itself

Many people do not think about backing up Virtual Server itself (the application, rather than the virtual machines). There is good reason for this. Virtual Server is a small application that is quick to install and configure, and as long as you have the virtual machines it is relatively painless to set up from scratch in the case of a disaster. However, for the sake of completeness, I list the various files used by Virtual Server so you can back them up if you want to.

Virtual Server stores specific files in the following locations:

❑ **%programfiles%\Microsoft Virtual Server:** This is the location where Virtual Server itself is installed. A number of things are stored here including the following:

  ❑ The Virtual Server service

  ❑ Documentation

  ❑ Drivers

  ❑ VHDMount

  ❑ The Virtual Machine Additions installers

210

Chapter 11: Backing Up Virtual Machines

- ❏ The VMRC client
- ❏ The Virtual Server WebSite

❏ **%allusersprofile%\Application Data\Microsoft\Virtual Server:** This folder contains the main Virtual Server configuration file (Options.xml) and the license file (VSLicense.xml). It also contains two folders: Virtual Machines and Virtual Networks. Each of these folders contains shortcuts (LNK files) for each registered virtual machine and virtual network. Virtual Server uses these shortcuts to track known virtual machines and virtual networks.

❏ **%allusersprofile%\Application Data\Microsoft\Virtual Server Webapp:** This folder contains a single configuration file: ServerPaths.xml. This file contains information about the possible Virtual Server instances that can be administrated by this installation of the Virtual Server Web interface.

❏ **%allusersprofile%\Application Data\Microsoft\Virtual Machine Helper:** There is a single file in this folder called NETWORK SERVICE. This file is owned by the network service account and you will not have appropriate permissions to copy it. This is an encrypted file that contains any user credentials used when configuring virtual machines to start automatically.

❏ **%allusersprofile%\Documents\Shared Virtual Machines:** This is the default location for virtual machines created by Virtual Server. This location can be changed through the Virtual Server administrative website.

❏ **%allusersprofile%\Documents\Shared Virtual Networks:** This is the default location for virtual network configuration files. It is not possible to change this location.

Virtual Server also relies on configuration in the IIS Metabase for the Virtual Server web application and on the presence of two system drivers (vmm.sys and vnetsrv.sys).

Determining the Best Back Up Strategy

By this stage you should see that while many strategies are available for backing up virtual machines, they all come with their own advantages and disadvantages. This makes it very hard to decide on the best strategy to use. Some key points to keep in mind when creating your virtual machine backup strategy are:

❏ It is important to give this consideration and come up with a formal process that you will be using. Otherwise you may find that you do not have enough data protection for your virtual machines.

❏ If at all possible your virtual machine backup strategy should line up with the methods and practices that you use for backing up your physical servers.

❏ The best results can be used by combining the different methods for virtual machine backup. For instance, you may decide to take a full virtual machine file–based backup of your virtual machines once a week (on the weekends when momentary downtime is acceptable) but then use daily backups run from inside the virtual machines during the week.

211

Part IV: Security and Backup for Virtual Machines

Conclusion

There are many options when it comes to backing up virtual machines. You can back up the virtual machine files directly, or you can run backup software inside of the virtual machines. Virtual machines cannot access backup hardware (such as tape drives) directly; however, most operating systems include software that allows you to back up to a network location.

Virtual Server 2005 R2 SP1 adds the ability to back up virtual machines directly from the host operating system using Volume Shadow Copy Services. It also adds the ability to mount virtual hard disks directly on the host operating system and access individual files on the virtual hard disk.

Part V
Physical to Virtual Migration

Chapter 12: Physical to Virtual Migration of Servers

Chapter 13: Manual Physical to Virtual Migrations

12

Physical to Virtual Migration of Servers

Many times when you decide that you want to virtualize an existing server, there is an unforeseen problem. Servers often require extensive configuration in order to get them set up just right. In a best case scenario, this could mean hours of work. In worst case scenarios you may never be certain the new server setup is exactly the same as the original server, or you may not even have the appropriate media or expertise to set up the server again.

In order to deal with this roadblock to virtualization, many physical to virtual (P2V) migration tools have been developed. These tools allow you to take an existing working physical server and migrate it to a virtual machine without the need to install or configure any software inside of the virtual machine.

There are a number of commercial P2V products (such as those offered by PlateSpin and LeoStream). This chapter covers the Virtual Server Migration Toolkit (VSMT), which is a P2V tool provided by Microsoft. VSMT is a free download, but it requires that you have an installation of Windows Server 2003 Enterprise Edition running Automated Deployment Services (ADS). If you do not want to, or cannot, use Windows Server 2003 Enterprise Edition and ADS, you will need to use a third-party P2V product.

How Does VSMT Work?

Using VSMT to perform a physical to virtual migration involves (at least) three computers: the source physical computer, the target Virtual Server server, and the ADS server. VSMT uses ADS to capture an image of the physical computer. It then performs appropriate modifications to this image to allow it to run inside of a virtual machine. And finally it uses ADS to deploy this image to a new virtual machine.

Part V: Physical to Virtual Migration

VSMT is only supported on 32-bit versions of Windows Server 2003. As such, both the ADS server and the Virtual Server server need to be installed on 32-bit versions of Windows Server 2003.

> **All of the computers involved in the migration process do not need to be joined to a domain, but they should be capable of using the same user credentials because they need to communicate with each other. For this reason, you should that you create an administrative "Migration" account on the ADS server, the Virtual Server server, the source physical computer, and any other computers that are involved. If your computers are in a domain, you can create this account on the domain and then add it to the Administrators group on each computer. If your computers are not in the same domain, or in a workgroup environment, you should create a local account with the same name and password on each computer involved.**
>
> **For the rest of this chapter, it is assumed that you are using this account to install and configure the appropriate software.**

Source Computer Requirements

VSMT places a number of requirements on the source computer that you wish to turn into a virtual machine. The first requirement is that VSMT supports only migrating computers that are running the following operating systems:

- ❏ Microsoft Windows Server 2003 Standard or Enterprise Editions
- ❏ Microsoft 2000 Server or Advanced server, with Service Pack 4
- ❏ Microsoft Windows NT Server 4.0, Standard Edition, with Service Pack 6a

In addition to this, VSMT requires that the source computer has:

- ❏ At least 96MB physical memory

There are also some specific requirements for Windows NT Server 4.0 computers:

- ❏ You must have the Windows Management Instrumentation (WMI) CORE 1.5 installed. You can download this from `http://go.microsoft.com/fwlink/?LinkId=35457`. VSMT uses WMI to gather information about the source computer. Windows 2000 and later all include WMI by default, but it has to be installed manually on Windows NT.

- ❏ It is advisable to install the hotfix for KB 872952. During the migration VSMT will upgrade the version of NTFS that is used by Windows NT. For the most part, this causes no problems. There is one known issue, which is that after upgrading the version of NTFS, CHDSK.EXE does not work under Windows NT. To fix this you will need to contact Microsoft product support and request the hotfix for KB 872952. Details on this hotfix are available at `http://support.microsoft.com/kb/872952`.

216

Chapter 12: Physical to Virtual Migration of Servers

Finally, there are a number of configurations that VSMT does not support. You should ensure that your source computer does not have either of the following items; otherwise you may encounter problems when migrating it with VSMT:

❏ **FAT formatted disk partitions:** FAT partitions will not be migrated by VSMT. They should be converted to NTFS before attempting the migration. You can do this without needing to format the partition by using the tool `convert` from a Windows command prompt.

❏ **Multiple boot partitions:** If your source computer has multiple boot partitions, you can migrate each partition as a separate virtual machine, but VSMT will migrate only one boot partition per virtual machine. If the boot partitions are dependent on each other, this can cause problems.

You should also confirm that the source computer does not have any specific hardware requirements that cannot be met inside of a virtual machine. VSMT will not be able to identify this and will migrate the computer, but if it cannot perform its primary functions afterwards then the whole process is just a waste of time.

Setting Up the ADS/VSMT Server

The server that runs ADS and VSMT needs to be a 32-bit version of Windows Server 2003 Enterprise Edition. Once you have a server ready you can download the installer for ADS and VSMT from `www.microsoft.com/downloads/results.aspx?freetext=ADS_VSMT_1.1.exe`. Running this executable extracts the files to a temporary directory and launches the installer.

> If you do not have ADS already present in your environment and you do not have the necessary hardware resources available, it is possible to install ADS and VSMT in a virtual machine that is then used to migrate other computers. This means that the migrations take slightly longer than if they were performed with dedicated hardware, but it is a very convenient trick for reducing the hardware requirements for performing migrations with VSMT.
>
> Another option to consider is that you can have ADS, VSMT, and Virtual Server all installed on the same computer.

But before you do that, there are some configuration decisions that you need to make.

ADS uses a database to store configuration and image information. You can either use a database on the same computer as the ADS server or you can use a remote database. You can also use a full database or the Microsoft SQL Server Desktop Engine. If you are only using ADS for the once-off migration of physical computers to virtual machines, using the Microsoft SQL Server Desktop Engine on the same computer as ADS will most likely be adequate. If you are planning to use ADS for repeated migrations, or for image deployment to new computers, you may want to consider using a full database server on a separate computer.

ADS consists of a number of components (Controller Service, Network Boot Services, Image Distribution Service, and so on). You can install all of these components on one computer, or you can distribute them across multiple computers to increase the performance of ADS. Once again, if you are planning to use

217

Part V: Physical to Virtual Migration

ADS only for the one-time migration of physical computers to virtual machines, it will likely be acceptable to install all components on the same computer.

You will need to decide on a static IP address before starting the installation of ADS. ADS needs to be configured with a static IP address. As a network boot server, ADS should not be configured with a dynamic IP address that could change at some stage in the future. Furthermore, several of the ADS services manually record the IP address and will fail to start if it is changed.

Once you have decided how you will be configuring ADS, you can begin with the installation.

For the purposes of the chapter I will be configuring an ADS server that uses the Microsoft SQL Server Desktop Engine and has all of the components installed on the same computer.

After you have downloaded and executed ADS_VSMT_1.1.exe you will need to do the following:

1. Click **Install Microsoft SQL Server Desktop Engine SP4 (Windows)**. This automatically installs the Microsoft SQL Server Desktop Engine with no further input from you.

2. Click **Install Automated Deployment Services**. This starts the **Automated Deployment Services Setup Wizard**. If you already have existing ADS infrastructure that you are planning to use, skip ahead to Step 10. Please note that VSMT must be installed on the main ADS controller in your environment.

3. Accept the **License Agreement**.

4. On the **Configure the ADS Controller** page, select **Use Microsoft SQL Desktop Engine (Windows)** and **Create a new ADS database**. At this stage, you will receive a warning about the potential for the ADS Network Boot Services (NBS) to interfere with other network boot services (such as Remote Installation Services). For now, just hit OK.

5. On the **Network Boot Service Settings** page, you will need to either specify the path where the Windows setup files are, or choose to be prompted for the files later during the installation. The files that are being asked for specifically are in the I386 directory on the Windows installation media, so you need to have this handy.

    I always make a local copy of the I386 directory on my servers so that I do not need to have the media handy for situations like these. If you have done the same you can enter in the path of your local copy of the I386 directory here.

6. On the **Windows PE Repository** page select **Do not create a Windows PE repository**. VSMT does not require that ADS have a Windows PE Repository configured, as it does not use Windows PE. If you intend to use ADS for other purposes that do require Windows PE you should configure this page appropriately.

7. On the **Image Location** page, you will need to specify a location for ADS to use for the images that will be created in the VSMT migration process. This location needs to have sufficient space for the images of the computers you are planning to migrate. It is advisable to configure the image location on a separate dedicated hard disk to help with performance. If you do not have a separate dedicated disk, it is okay to place it on the system disk (or another shared disk) as long as there is enough space available.

218

Chapter 12: Physical to Virtual Migration of Servers

You cannot use a network location to store images.

8. If you have multiple network adapters in your server, you are asked which one should be used for ADS. Specify the appropriate network card and continue.

9. On the **Installation Confirmation** page, click **Install**. Once this process has completed you are returned to the ADS installation menu and are ready to install the Virtual Server Migration Toolkit.

Installation of ADS can take a little while, so it is not unusual to have to wait for installation to complete.

10. Click **Install Virtual Server Migration Toolkit**.

11. Agree to the **License Agreement**.

12. On the **Setup Type** page, select **Full Installation**.

13. Complete the installation wizard.

Once you have completed the installation of ADS and VSMT, you need to configure one last thing. There is a tool, Gatherhw.exe, which you need to run from a remote computer. To enable this, you should create a folder on the ADS computer called VSMTShare (it could be called anything you want). You should then copy Gatherhw.exe from the Microsoft VSMT folder (in your Program Files folder) to this newly created folder. Finally you should share this folder on the network.

When you configure the folder to be shared on the network, you need to make sure that the account you use on the source computer has full access to the share.

Configuring DHCP

In a network environment, computers that are performing a network-based boot usually receive the location of the network boot server in their DHCP offer. The fact that ADS/VSMT uses a network boot server to perform the virtual machine migration can cause a number of problems:

❏ If you already have a network boot service in your environment (such as Remote Installation Services) it is hard to ensure that the right computers get to the right network boot servers. It is possible to handle this by setting up two DHCP scopes on your DHCP server, each configured with a different network boot server, and then filter the physical computer's MAC address to determine which scope they belong in. Needless to say, this is a lot of work.

❏ You need to configure your DHCP server with the appropriate information about the location of the network boot server. In many large corporate environments it is neither allowed nor appropriate to make such a configuration change to a central DHCP server. As with the boot server, it is possible to configure multiple DHCP servers in the same environment and have them filter on the MAC address of the clients, but this is a lot of work and involves coordination with the administrator of the central DHCP server.

Most people end up setting up a standalone ADS server with VSMT and DHCP installed on it. They then connect this server to a private, physically separate network that is used solely for the purpose of performing physical to virtual migrations.

Part V: Physical to Virtual Migration

If you are manually configuring a separate DHCP server you will need to enable the scope option `060` `PXESTRING` *with a value of* `PXEClient`.

If you decide to install and configure a DHCP server on the ADS/VSMT server you need to do the following:

1. Select **Add or Remove Programs** from **Control Panel** on the **Start** menu.

2. Select **Add/Remove Windows Components**.

3. Select (but do not check) **Networking Services** and click **Details**.

4. Check **Dynamic Host Configuration Protocol (DHCP)** and hit **OK** and then **Next**.

5. Once the **Windows Component Wizard** has completed, close **Add or Remove Programs** and open a command prompt.

6. Change directory to the location where ADS is installed (this is likely to be in the Microsoft ADS folder in your Program Files folder).

7. Change directory into the bin folder.

8. Run **adsdhcpconfig /add**; once this has completed, you can close the command prompt.

This step is necessary as DHCP and ADS both try to use port 67 by default. This tool will reconfigure ADS so there is no conflict.

9. Open the **Start** menu, and select **All Programs ➪ Administrative Tools ➪ DHCP**.

10. Select the entry for your server, open the **Action** menu, and select **New Scope**.

11. On the **Scope Name** page, configure a **Name** and **Description** for this scope.

12. Specify an appropriate **Start IP address**, **End IP address**, and **Subnet mask**. If you are configuring a private network for physical to virtual migrations, this should use a private IP address in the 192.168.x.x range with a subnet mask of 255.255.255.0

13. Pass over the **Add Exclusions** page, unless you specifically need to exclude IP addresses from your DHCP server.

14. Accept the default lease duration on the **Lease Duration** page.

15. On the **Configure DHCP Options** page, you can select whether you want to configure the details for the **DNS** and **WINS** servers for your network.

If you are using a private network you will most likely not have DNS or WINS servers configured. If this is the case you should just leave these values unconfigured.

16. Complete the **New Scope Wizard**.

*If you chose to configure the DNS and WINS servers, you will also be given the option to activate the scope at the end of the wizard. If you did not choose this option you will need to select the scope, open the **Action** menu and select **Activate**.*

Chapter 12: Physical to Virtual Migration of Servers

Configuring Virtual Server

Once ADS and VSMT are ready to go, the next step is to install the ADS Administration Agent on the computer that is running Virtual Server.

In order to work with the ADS Administration Agent, Virtual Server must be running on Windows Server 2003. It is not possible to use an instance of Virtual Server that is installed on Windows XP with ADS and VSMT.

You need to do this so that VSMT can control Virtual Server during the migration process. To do this you will need to run ADS_VSMT_1.1.exe (which you downloaded on the ADS / VSMT server) and follow these steps:

1. Select **Install ADS Administration Agent** from the installation menu.

2. Accept the **License Agreement**.

3. On the **Configure Certificates** page, you need to install the certificate from the ADS controller. This file is called adsroot.cer and is stored in the Certificate folder under the installation location of ADS (usually Microsoft ADS in the Program Files directory). You can locate this file and copy it to a location that can be used by this installation, or you can provide the network path to this file (in the form of \\ADSServerName\C$\Program Files\Microsoft ADS\Certificate\adsroot.cer).

4. On the **Configure the Agent Logon Settings** page, select **None**.

5. Complete the installation wizard.

6. Select **Install Virtual Server Migration Toolkit** from the installation menu.

7. Accept the **License Agreement**.

8. Choose to do a **Tools only** installation

Now that the ADS Administration Agent and VSMT tools are installed on the Virtual Server server, allowing ADS and VSMT to remotely control this server, you will need to go back to your ADS/VSMT server and perform the following steps:

1. Open the **Start** menu, and select **All Programs** ⇨ **Microsoft ADS** ⇨ **ADS Management**.

2. Select the **Devices** node from under the **Automated Deployment Services** node.

3. Open the **Action** menu and select **Add Device**.

4. In the **Name** field you will need to enter the network name used by your Virtual Server server.

   You can enter a description if you want, but this is not necessary.

5. In the **Media access control (MAC) address** field, you will need to enter the MAC address of the network card that you want ADS to use on your Virtual Server server.

   To find the MAC address of your network card, open a command prompt on the Virtual Server server and run ipconfig /all. This will list all of the active network interfaces in your computer. Locate the network adapter you are interested in and look for the Physical Address field. This is the MAC address that you need to enter in this field.

221

Part V: Physical to Virtual Migration

6. Click **OK** and then click **Cancel** to close the **Add Device** dialog box.

7. Select the new entry for your Virtual Server server from the devices list.

8. Open the **Action** menu and select **Take control**.

Preparing the Source Computer

Prior to performing the migration, some basic tasks should be performed on the source computer. You should ensure that:

❑ You have up-to-date backups of the physical computer. While uncommon, there are situations where a physical to virtual migration can fail and damage the source computer. If this happens, you need to have system backups ready.

❑ The latest updates for the operating system and software have been installed on the source computer.

❑ You have deleted any unneeded data off of the source computer. The more data there is, the longer the migration process will take. If data is on the source computer that is not needed, deleting it can speed up the process significantly.

❑ A chkdsk has been performed on the source computer, so that all disks are guaranteed to be in a good state for migration.

❑ The source computer is not being actively managed by ADS. If it is being managed by ADS you should change the ADS configuration so that this is no longer the case, as it can interfere with the migration process.

❑ You have scheduled the system downtime. During the migration process, the source computer will not be available for external access. If you are migrating a production server you need to make sure that the migration is scheduled for a time when the downtime involved is acceptable.

A typical physical to virtual migration with VSMT can take from 30 minutes to multiple hours, depending on the amount of data that is stored on the source computer.

Performing the Migration

Now it is time to actually migrate the physical computer. This is a six-step process, each of which is covered in the following sections.

Gather Information About the Source Server

The first step is to gather information about the source server. To do this you will need to do the following:

1. Log in to the source physical computer.

2. Open a command prompt.

Chapter 12: Physical to Virtual Migration of Servers

3. Connect to the share you created when setting up the VSMT server by running `net use *` `\\ADSServer\VSMTShare`.

4. Change directory to the newly mapped drive letter.

5. Run `GatherHW /t:SourceComputerName.xml`.

6. Change directory back to the system drive.

7. Unmap the network drive that was mapped in Step 3 by running `net use z: /d` (where you use the drive letter that was mapped on your computer for `z:`).

Check for Compatibility

The second step is to analyze the source server information for compatibility issues:

1. Log in to the ADS server.

2. Open a command prompt.

3. Change to the directory you created for the XML files.

4. Run `C:\Program Files\Microsoft VSMT\VmScript.exe -hwvalidate -hwinfofile: SourceComputerName.xml`.

In Step 4, `C:\Program Files\Microsoft VSMT\` *is the location where you installed VSMT on the ADS server.*

Generate Script Files

The third step is to use VmScript.exe to generate the script files if no incompatibilities are found:

```
vmscript.exe /hwGenerateP2V /hwInfoFile:"VSMTShareFolder\SourceServerName.xml"
/name:NewVMName /vmConfigPath:"DefaultVMFolder\NewVMName" /virtualDiskPath:
"DefaultVMFolder\NewVMName" /hwDestVS:VirtualServerFQDN /vmMemory:Memory
/vsHostNet: VirtualNetworkName /postDeployAction:2
```

That is an awful lot of command-line arguments, so I am going to pause and go through each of them (and mention some arguments that are not used in this specific example). Each argument has a long and a short form, where the long form is easy to read and understand but the short form is easier to type. I will list the long form of the argument with its short form in brackets. Most arguments take the form of `/argumentName:parameter` where the parameter is the value that is specified for the specific argument. If any parameter has spaces in it, the entire parameter should be placed inside double quotes. The possible arguments for this command are as follows:

❑ `hwGenerateP2V (p2v)`: This argument tells vmscript that you want to generate the script files needed to perform a physical to virtual migration. No parameters need to be specified for this argument.

❑ `hwInfoFile (i)`: This argument takes a parameter of the path and name of the hardware information XLM file that you generated on the source computer with GatherHW.exe. This argument must be defined.

223

Part V: Physical to Virtual Migration

❑ `name (n)`: This argument is used to define the name of the virtual machine that should be created. This name does not need to match the source computer's network name, or any other name. This argument must be defined.

❑ `vmConfigPath (vmp)`: This argument takes a parameter of the location on the destination Virtual Server server where the virtual machine configuration file will be created. This should be, but does not have to be, in a folder with the same name as the planned virtual machine name that is located in the common virtual machine store for Virtual Server. This argument must be defined.

To determine the common virtual machine store location for an instance of Virtual Server you will need to do the following:

1. Click **Server Properties** in the **Virtual Server** section of the navigation pane on the Virtual Server administrative website.

2. Click Search paths.

3. The value specified for the **Default virtual machine configuration folder** is the value that you need.

❑ `virtualDiskPath (vhdp)`: This argument specifies the location where the virtual hard disks for the new virtual machine should be stored. This is usually in the same location as the virtual machine configuration file, but it does not have to be. This argument must be defined.

❑ `hwDestVS (vs)`: This argument specifies the network name of the Virtual Server server that will be used for the new virtual machine. If the Virtual Server server is part of a domain you should provide the fully qualified domain name; otherwise the NetBIOS name is sufficient. This argument must be defined.

❑ `vmMemory (vmm)`: This argument is used to define the amount of memory that should be assigned to the newly created virtual machine. (The parameter should be a whole number, and indicates the amount of memory to be used in megabytes.) This is an optional argument. If this argument is not defined, VSMT will create a virtual machine with the same amount of memory as the physical source computer.

❑ `vsHostNet (vsnet)`: This argument specifies the name of the virtual network on the Virtual Server server that the new virtual machine should be connected to. This network needs to be connected to a physical network card that can access the ADS/VSMT server, as it will be used to deploy the image of the source computer to the virtual machine. This is an optional argument. If this argument is not defined, the default value that will be used is the value that is set in the vsmt_initenv.cmd file that is in the VSMT installation directory. (If you do not edit vsmt_initenv.cmd this will be VM0.)

❑ `suppressVsConsole (sc)`: This optional argument takes no parameters, but specifies that the Virtual Server administrative website should not be displayed at the end of the migration.

❑ `postDeployAction (da)`: This optional argument defines what should happen to the new virtual machine after the data from the source computer has been deployed to it. There are three possible parameters:

  ❑ 0: Leaves the virtual machine running the deployment agent code

  ❑ 1: Shuts down the virtual machine

  ❑ 2: Restarts the virtual machine

224

Chapter 12: Physical to Virtual Migration of Servers

❑ hwTaskSeqPath (ts): This argument specifies where the script files that are used to migrate the computer should be stored. This is an optional argument. If this is not defined, the scripts will be created in the p2v folder under the directory where VSMT was installed.

❑ hwPatchDir (pd): This argument can be used to specify a custom directory for loading patches that are applied to the computer image before being deployed to the virtual machine. This is an optional argument. If this is not defined, the Patches directory in the VSMT installation directory will be used.

❑ virtualDiskDynamic (vhdd): This argument indicates that the virtual machine should be created with dynamically expanding virtual hard disks. If this argument is not defined, the virtual machine will be created with fixed-size virtual hard disks. This argument is optional and takes no parameters.

❑ adminMac (mac): This argument specifies the MAC address for the physical network adapter that should be used to connect to the ADS server for migration purposes. The parameter for this argument can use one of a number of formats. For example: AABBCCDDEEFF, AA:BB:CC:DD:EE:FF, and AA-BB-CC-DD-EE-FF are all valid parameters. This argument is optional and should be specified only if ADS appears to have problems identifying the correct network adapter to use.

❑ virtualMacDynamic (dmac): Typically, VSMT will configure the new virtual machine to have the same MAC address as the source physical computer. Specifying this argument causes the virtual machine to be created with a dynamic MAC address instead. This argument is optional.

You need to give some thought to how the MAC address will be handled. Changing the MAC address during the migration may cause problems with software that either checks the MAC address for identification purposes or that stores the MAC address, assuming that it will not change. However, leaving the MAC address with the same value as the source computer means that the source computer and virtual machine will never be able to connect to the same network, as this will cause and address conflict.

❑ serviceDriverState (sd): This argument allows you to specify a custom XML file to use for deciding which drivers and services should be disabled as part of the physical to virtual migration. This argument is optional. If this is not defined, the P2Vdrivers.xml file in the Patches directory in the VSMT installation directory will be used.

❑ excludeDrives (ex): This optional argument takes a semicolon-separated list of drive letters (for example, f:;g:;r:). The drive letters specified will then be excluded from the migration process. If a physical disk has all drive letters associated with it excluded, VSMT will not create a virtual hard disk for that specific disk.

❑ fixHAL (hal): One of the biggest problems encountered when migrating a physical computer to a virtual computer is having the wrong HAL installed. HAL stands for "hardware abstraction layer" and this driver is responsible for determining how Windows should interact with the hardware at the most basic level. Having the wrong HAL loaded stops Windows from booting. As such, VSMT changes the HAL that is used by Windows in the migration process. This argument allows you to specify how the HAL should be configured. There are four possible parameters:

    ❑ Auto: This is the default behavior if this argument is not defined. VSMT will make the decision as to which HAL should be used automatically.

    ❑ None: This tells VSMT to not change the HAL and to continue to use the same HAL as was being used on the source computer.

Part V: Physical to Virtual Migration

❑ `ACPI`: This tells VSMT to use the HAL for a single-processor, PIC-based, ACPI-aware computer.

❑ `NACPI`: This tells VSMT to use the HAL for a single-processor, PIC-based, non-ACPI–aware computer.

This argument is optional.

❑ `forceGenerate (fg)`: This argument tells VSMT to create the migration scripts even if an error is encountered while generating the scripts. This is done to allow advanced users to correct the scripts by hand if an error is encountered. This is an optional argument that takes no parameters.

Unfortunately, not only does this command use a large number of arguments, but the error handling on these arguments is very poor. If you mistype any of the argument names or values, vmscript will simply fail without telling you which parameter you got wrong. For this reason, I tend to use the shorter forms of the argument names as it reduces the potential for error.

Once you have successfully run this command, it will generate a number of scripts and command files that you can use to migrate the physical computer to a virtual machine.

Capture the Source Computer

The fourth step is to capture the source computer using ADS. To do this, execute the following steps:

1. Open a command prompt on the ADS server.

2. Change to the directory where the scripts were created in the previous step. By default, this will be under the VSMT installation folder, in the p2v folder, in a folder named after the planned virtual machine name.

3. Run the command file plannedVMName_capture.cmd.

4. Wait for the command file to tell you that it is ready for you to start the source computer.

5. Now you will need to reboot the source computer and get it to boot off of the ADS server by using the PXE boot capabilities on the network card.

If your source computer has a network card that is capable of booting via PXE you can do so by changing the BIOS settings for the computer and ensuring that the network adapter is the first boot device that should be used. Alternatively, many computers allow you to specify that the network adapter should be used to boot by pressing the F12 key during the BIOS section of the boot process.

If your source computer does not have a network that is capable of booting via PXE, you will need to create a PXE boot floppy. To do this, go to your ADS server (or any other Windows Server 2003 computer) and run `C:\Windows\system32\dllcache\ rbfg.exe` **(where** `C:\Windows` **is the location where you have Windows installed). This tool allows you to generate a remote boot disk that you can then use to boot your source computer.**

The dllcache folder is hidden on most systems, but you can still run the files that are inside it.

226

Chapter 12: Physical to Virtual Migration of Servers

6. The source computer should connect to the ADS server, and you should see a progress indicator for the process of capturing an image of the source computer.

7. Once the image has been captured, the source computer should shut down automatically.

Deploy the Image to a New Machine

The fifth step is to deploy the source computer image to a new virtual machine. After capturing the image, the next thing to do is to deploy it to a new virtual machine. To do this, follow these steps:

1. Open a command prompt on the ADS server.

2. Change directory to the location where the scripts were created in the previous step. This will be in a folder named after the planned virtual machine name in the p2v folder in the VSMT installation folder by default.

3. Run the command file plannedVMName_CreateVM.cmd. This will create the new virtual machine on the target Virtual Server service.

4. Run the command file plannedVMName_DeployVM.cmd. This will boot the new virtual machine, which will then connect to the ADS server over the network and deploy the image.

5. Once the image has been deployed, the virtual machine will wait, shut down, or restart, depending on the option you specified when creating the scripts.

Check Yourself

For the final step, check the newly created virtual machine to make sure that everything works.

You should:

1. Check the virtual machine configuration under Virtual Server and change any settings that need to be changed for your environment (changing network settings, startup options, and so on).

2. Boot the virtual machine and confirm that all of the software installed is still functioning correctly.

3. Install Virtual Machine Additions into the virtual machine.

4. Create a backup of the new virtual machine.

Troubleshooting P2V Problems with VSMT

Performing a physical to virtual migration with VSMT is a relatively complex process and there are a number of places where you can encounter problems. The following sections detail some common problems and how to solve them.

227

Part V: Physical to Virtual Migration

Software Incompatibilities

Sometimes, analyzing the source server information reveals software incompatibilities. These will be displayed as part of the hwvalidate step.

In a perfect world you would validate the source server configuration information, and it would tell you that there were no incompatibilities (and, in fact, this is not that uncommon). But sometimes VSMT will report that there are incompatibilities. The most common cause of these incompatibilities is that hotfixes and updates may have been released after VSMT was released. If this is the case, Vmscript will display a message like this:

```
Warning: A required patch file is missing. Refer to the
documentation for more info on how to provide this file.
File     ntdll.dll
Version  5.0.2195.6899
Language 1033
Potential source of this file is KB835732.
```

You will also see messages like this if you are trying to migrate a non-English operating system. VSMT only ships with information about the English versions of Windows.

VSMT alerts you about these files because during the migration VSMT needs to swap certain system files with different versions of these files that are needed to run on the hardware inside a virtual machine. If VSMT did this when you had installed an update that VSMT did not know about, you would end up with the wrong version of the system files, which could have catastrophic results.

When this happens, you need to update VSMT so that it knows how to handle this. To do this, you will need to use a tool called vmpatch.exe, which is installed with VSMT (it is placed in the VSMT installation directory). There are four possible ways to update VSMT with this information. Each of these ways requires that you do the following:

1. Log in to the ADS server.

2. Open a command prompt.

3. Change to the VSMT installation directory.

You can gather the appropriate files and information from:

❑ **The source computer:** To attempt to gather information about the updated files from a Windows Server 2003 source computer run:

```
Vmpatch /s:"\\sourceComputerNetworkName\drive$\Windows\driver cache"
```

To attempt to gather information about the updated files from a Windows 2000 source computer, run the following:

```
Vmpatch /s:"\\sourceComputerNetworkName\drive$\WINNT\driver cache"
```

*In both of these cases **sourceComputerNetworkName** is either the fully qualified domain name or the NetBIOS name of the source computer. **Drive** is the drive letter of the system drive on the source computer.*

Chapter 12: Physical to Virtual Migration of Servers

❑   **The installation CD for the source computer:** To attempt to gather information about the updated files from an installation CD, insert the CD into the ADS server and run:

```
Vmpatch /s:CD
```

CD should be the root path for the CD-ROM—for example, `F:`.

❑   **Hotfix files:** If you can't gather the information from the source system or the installation CD, the next option is to download the hotfix that is suggested by VSMT when it analyzed the source computer information. Once you have downloaded the hotfix to the ADS server, you can unpack it to a temporary location by running:

```
hotfixFileName.exe /x:"TemporaryFolder"
```

and then running:

```
Vmpatch /s:"TemporaryFolder"
```

HotfixFileName.exe should be the actual name of the hotfix file. ***TemporaryFolder*** *is a location that you determine to use for storing the files from the hotfix.*

❑   **Service packs:** If you have installed a service pack that was released after the release of VSMT, you will need to update VSMT with the details of the service pack. To do this, download the full installer for the service pack to the ADS server (you cannot use an express installer for this process). You should then extract it to a temporary folder using a command similar to the one used for a hotfix:

```
servicePackFileName.exe /x:"TemporaryFolder"
```

Then create a new service pack directory in the VSMT patches folder. Typically, the patches folder is located in the VSMT installation directory and is named Patches, but if you are using a custom patches folder you will need to place the service pack files in the custom location. Inside the Patches folder is a folder for each supported operating system that is named after the operating system version number. (For example, the folder for Windows Server 2003 is named 5.2.3790.)

Once you have located the folder for the operating system to which you are migrating, you should create a new folder inside the operating system folder for the new service pack. Service pack folders should be named spX where X is the number of the service pack (that is, the folder for service pack 2 would be named sp2).

Next, copy all of the executable (.exe), dynamic link library (.dll), and system (.sys) files from the temporary folder containing the service pack files to the service pack patch folder that you just created. You also need to copy the XML files from the operating system patch folder to the service pack patch folder.

If the operating system patch folder does not contain any XML files you should copy the XML files from the most recent existing service pack patch folder for that operating system.

Finally, when all the files are in place, you will need to run the following:

```
Vmpatch /s:"TemporaryFolder"
```

229

Part V: Physical to Virtual Migration

When you have completed updating VSMT with the information about the newer files, you can confirm that everything is ready to go by analyzing the source server XML file again. To do this, follow the steps in the "Performing the Migration" section of this chapter. If any incompatibilities remain, you will need to update VSMT with the information about those files. If no incompatibilities are left, you can continue with the migration.

Boot Failures and Crashes

Another problem you might run across is that after performing the physical to virtual migration the virtual machine fails to boot, crashes during boot, or is unstable.

Any of these symptoms can be the result of a system driver or service that is not compatible with the virtual machine environment. When VSMT migrates a system, it disables a number of services and drivers that are known to be incompatible, but it does not have a comprehensive list of all services and drivers that might ever cause a problem. You can extend VSMT to disable other services and drivers, but there are some challenges involved in doing this.

The first, and biggest, challenge is identifying which driver or service needs to be disabled. It is not always obvious which driver or service is causing the problem, and disabling the wrong driver or service may cause further problems. If you are lucky, you will see event log errors or crash messages that signal out a specific driver or service, but many times you need to rely on your instincts.

Once you have decided which drivers and services need to be disabled, you will need to edit the P2Vdrivers.xml file in the patches directory (normally under the VSMT installation directory). This file needs to be saved in UTF-8 format, and is case sensitive. The safest editor to use for editing it is Notepad (more advanced editors can cause problems with formatting of the data).

Three types of entries can be made: service, driver, and program. For service and driver entries, you need to specify a start value, which can be Boot, System, Auto, Manual or Disable. For program entries, you can only specify an action of Remove. Entries should be placed between the `<Configuration>` and `</Configuration>` tags and formatted as follows:

❑ **For service entries:**

```
<Service Name="The name of some service" Start="Disable" />
```

The service name used here should be the name that is listed under the service management user interface in Windows.

❑ **For driver entries:**

```
<Driver Name="SomeDriverName" Start="Disable" />
```

The driver name used here does not match the name that is displayed in the Device Manager. Rather, you have to find the driver name that is used in the system registry. To do this, open regedit.exe and go to HKEY_LOCAL_MACHINE\System\CurrentControlSet\Services and use the name of the registry key for the driver that you want to disable.

Remember that this data is case sensitive, so make sure that you get the capitalization right.

❑ **For program entries:**

```
<Program Name="someProgram" Action="Remove" />
```

The program entry allows you to remove programs from the system autorun section.

Save the XML file when you are done and reattempt the migration. This time, VSMT will disable the extra services and drivers that you specified.

No Boot Policy Received

If you are using an older version of the Windows Remote Boot Floppy you might experience that while booting the source server off of a Remote Boot Floppy it connects to the ADS server but never receives a boot policy. You should create a new boot floppy using the version of RBFG.EXE that is installed on Windows Server 2003.

Unsupported HAL Type

Sometimes, VSMT reports that the source computer has an unsupported HAL type.

Windows has a number of different HAL drivers. (HAL stands for Hardware Abstraction Layer. This driver serves as one of the lowest level interfaces between Windows and the hardware.) VSMT does not support all of the HALs that exists, but it does support the most common HAL drivers. If you are attempting to migrate a physical computer that uses a HAL driver that VSMT does not support, you can do so by using the **/fixHAL** option when generating the migration scripts and specifying **ACPI** or **NACPI** (but not **Auto**). If you do this, VSMT provides no guarantees as to whether the virtual machine will be able to boot correctly after the migration.

Administrative Website Doesn't Display

Sometimes, the Virtual Server administrative website is not displayed after the virtual machine is created.

VSMT will automatically open the Virtual Server administrative website on the ADS server after creating the virtual machine, so that you can continue to configure it (unless you specified the /suppressVSConsole option when creating the migration scripts). If this does not happen it is most likely caused by the Enhanced Security Configuration for Internet Explorer feature of Windows Server 2003. In order for this to work, you need to have added the URL for the Virtual Server administrative website to the Trusted Sites for Internet Explorer on the ADS server.

Wrong IP Address

You might find that the virtual machine has the wrong IP address after it is migrated with VSMT.

VSMT will automatically configure the new virtual machine to use DHCP to obtain an IP address, even if the source physical computer was configured to use a static IP address. Unfortunately, there is no way to change this behavior, so if you rely on the server having a specific IP address, you will need to log in to the virtual machine and reconfigure the IP address manually.

Part V: Physical to Virtual Migration

No Enabled Network Cards

After migrating a Windows NT 4.0 computer, the virtual machine has no network cards enabled in the guest operating system. This always happens with Windows NT 4.0 migrations. Windows NT 4.0 does not support the same level of plug-and-play functionality that later versions of Windows do. It will not automatically detect and configure the network cards inside the virtual machine. To correct this you will need to do the following:

1. On the Virtual Server administrative website, select **Configure** from the **Virtual Machines** section of the navigation pane, and then click on your virtual machine.

2. Click **Floppy Drive**.

3. Select the **NT4 Network Driver.vfd** entry from the **Known floppy disks** drop-down list and click **OK**.

4. Log in to the guest operating system with an administrative user account.

5. Right-click on **Network Neighborhood** on the desktop and select **Properties**.

6. Change to the **Adapters** tab.

7. **Remove** any existing network adapters.

8. Click on **Add** and then click **Have Disk**.

9. Make sure A: is specified and click **OK**.

10. Select DEC PCI Fast Ethernet DECchip 21140 and click **OK** three times.

11. Remove **NT4 Network Driver.vfd** from the floppy drive and reboot the virtual machine.

SCSI Adapters Not Enabled in the Guest OS

After migrating a Windows NT 4.0 computer, the virtual machine has no SCSI adapters enabled in the guest operating system. As with the network card, Windows NT 4.0 will not automatically detect and configure the SCSI adapters inside the virtual machine. To do this:

1. Ensure that Virtual Machine Additions have been installed in the virtual machine.

2. Log in to the guest operating system with an administrative user account.

3. Open the **Start** menu and select **Settings**, and then click **Control Panel**.

4. Double-click on the **SCSI Adapters** icon and change to the **Drivers** tab.

5. **Remove** any entries that should not be there.

   *At this stage the only entry that should be present is the **IDE CD-ROM (ATAPI 1.2)** entry.*

6. Click **Add**.

7. In the **Install Driver** dialog box, select **Microsoft** from the **Manufacturers** list. There should be only one driver entry; select it and click **OK**.

232

Chapter 12: Physical to Virtual Migration of Servers

*If there is no **Microsoft** entry, click **Have Disk** and install the drivers from **Virtual Machine Additions** folder in the **Program Files** folder.*

8. Reboot the virtual machine once the drivers are installed.

Long Migration Process

Sometimes, the migration process seems to take a very long time.

The most common cause of unexpectedly long migration times is badly configured physical networks. Before attempting a migration you should confirm that you are getting the proper throughput on your physical network. You can do this by copying a large file between your computers. Once you have started the file copy, open the Windows Task Manager (this can be done by running `taskmgr`) and change to the **Networking** tab. The utilization should be over 70 percent. If it is only at 6 to 10 percent, your network is not running at the correct speed and you should check your configuration.

Other ways to improve the speed of the migration are to disable any antivirus checking software on the Virtual Server and ADS server computers, or to configure VSMT to use dynamically expanding virtual hard disk for the new virtual machine.

Failures During Migration

Several things can go wrong during migration and deployment; here are some common problems and details on how to handle them:

- ❑ **One of the migrations failed and needs to be attempted again.** Along with the CreateVM and DeployVM scripts, VSMT also provides a script called virtualMachineName_CleanUpVM.cmd. You can run this file to clean up after a failed migration. It will delete the virtual machine, and all associated files, off of the Virtual Server server. It will also remove any reference to the virtual machine from the ADS server.

  This script does not delete any images that are in ADS. If you want to do this you must do it manually through the ADS Management user interface.

- ❑ **Creating the virtual machine fails with a "The device does not exist" message.** This usually happens if you specified the wrong network name for the Virtual Server server or if you did not configure the Virtual Server server to be controlled by ADS. In either case you will need to run the CleanUpVM script, correct the problem, and try again.

- ❑ **The virtual machine deployment fails silently without giving any error messages.** This will happen if you select to use a dynamically expanding virtual hard disk and the Virtual Server server runs out of space. To avoid this, always make sure that you have enough space for the physical system that you are planning to migrate. If this happens, you will need to run the CleanUpVM script, make more space available on the Virtual Server server, and attempt the migration again.

- ❑ **The virtual machine will not boot to the ADS Deployment Agent in order to have the image deployed to it.** The ADS Deployment Agent requires that the virtual machine has at least 96MB of memory assigned to it. If you specified a memory amount that is smaller than 96MB when creating the deployment scripts you are going to need to start over again and specify at least 96MB of memory for the virtual machine.

233

Part V: Physical to Virtual Migration

❑ **You have double checked all of my arguments and parameters, but the migration is failing mysteriously.** A couple of tips to help VSMT along here include:

    ❑ Make sure that any path or parameter that has a space in it is placed inside double quotes.

    ❑ Use the short form of any argument names; it reduces the potential of mistyping something.

    ❑ Do not place a trailing back slash at the end of path names (for example, use C:\Path not C:\Path\).

Advanced Options for VSMT

There are a few advanced configuration options for VSMT. All of these options apply to VSMT itself or to the Deployment Agent (DA). The Deployment Agent is the software that is run on the physical computer and virtual machine to capture and deploy the system image.

Using VSMT to Convert a Vmware Virtual Machine to a Virtual Server Virtual Machine

You can use VSMT to convert a VMware virtual machine to a Virtual Server virtual machine. If the VMware virtual machine is configured to use IDE hard disks you can just go ahead and perform the migration with the VMware virtual machine as the source computer. If, however, the VMware virtual machine is configured to use SCSI drivers you will need to configure these drivers for use with the ADS Deployment Agent.

To do this, you need to download the VMware SCSI drivers from the VMware website. They are usually distributed in a virtual floppy disk format, which means that you need to connect the virtual floppy disk to a VMware virtual machine and copy the files off of it. Once you have the files, you should place them in the %ProgramFiles%\Microsoft ADS\nbs\repository\user\presystem folder on the ADS server.

Finally you will need to restart the ADS Deployment Agent Builder service by running:

```
net stop adsbuilder
net start adsbuilder
```

And now you are ready to migrate VMware virtual machines.

Loading Virtual Machine Additions into the ADS Deployment Agent

Because the ADS Deployment Agent is run inside a virtual machine in order to deploy the image, the migration process can be significantly sped up by loading Virtual Machine Additions into the ADS Deployment Agent. Unfortunately, this is not a straightforward process. To do this, gather the following six separate files:

❑ Msvmscsi.sys

❑ Vmsrvc.sys

Chapter 12: Physical to Virtual Migration of Servers

- ❏ Intelide.sys
- ❏ Pciidex.sys
- ❏ Vsmt_ide.inf
- ❏ Vsmt_scsi.inf

Msvmscsi.sys and Vmsrvc.sys need to be copied from the Windows\System32\drivers directory of a Windows Server 2003 virtual machine that has Virtual Machine Additions installed. Intelide.sys and Pciidex.sys need to be copied from the %ProgramFiles%\Microsoft ADS\nbs\repository\Windows directory on the ADS server. And finally, Vsmt_ide.inf and Vsmt_scsi.inf need to be copied from the %ProgramFiles%\Microsoft VSMT\Samples directory on the ADS server.

All of these files need to be copied into the %ProgramFiles%\Microsoft ADS\nbs\repository\User\ PreSystem directory on the ADS server. After copying these files you will need to restart the ADS Deployment Agent Builder service by running the following:

```
net stop adsbuilder
net start adsbuilder
```

And now the ADS Deployment Agent will have Virtual Machine Additions loaded.

Enabling Image Encryption for the Migration Process

If you are concerned about malicious users trying to gather data from the information being transferred over the network while the system is being migrated, it is possible to encrypt the image data. This option is disabled by default as it does slow down the migration process, and most migrations are performed on private trusted networks. Encryption can be enabled separately for the image capture process and the image deployment process.

To enable encryption on the image capture process you will need to edit the SourceComputerName _captureDisk.xml file. To enable encryption on the image deployment process you will need to edit the SourceComputerName_deployVM.xml file. In both cases, you will need to locate and remove the following entry:

```
<parameter>-nonetencrypt</parameter>
```

For both files mentioned, SourceComputerName should actually be the real name of your source computer. These files will typically be located in %ProgramFiles%\Microsoft VSMT\P2V\virtualMachineName.

P2V in System Center Virtual Machine Manager

Microsoft has announced that the upcoming System Center Virtual Machine Manager will include a new, improved physical to virtual migration tool. However, at the time of this writing, very few details are available about this tool.

To find out more about System Center Virtual Machine, go to www.microsoft.com/scvmm.

235

Part V: Physical to Virtual Migration

Conclusion

By now you should know all the details of how to perform a physical to virtual migration using the Virtual Server Migration Toolkit. It is a relatively complex process but it is a very powerful and useful tool when you need to migrate a number of existing physical computers into virtual machines.

You know that you need to configure Windows Server 2003 Enterprise Edition with ADS and VSMT, you need to have a private network to perform the migrations on, and you need to be familiar with the command-line tools used for the migration. You are also aware of potential issues that might be encountered and how to handle them.

13

Manual Physical to Virtual Migrations

Using the automated physical to virtual migration tools such as VSMT is very useful when you have a large number of physical computers to migrate in a planned fashion. There are, however, times when these tools are not so appropriate. If you only have one or two computers that you want to migrate you may not be able to justify the time and/or money involved in using a physical to virtual migration tool, and you might want to try a manual conversion. Also, you might find that the computer that you want to migrate is not supported by the migration tool that you want to use (either because the operating system is not supported, or because the specific configuration you have installed is not supported).

This chapter details some of the methods that can be used to perform a manual physical to virtual migration of the various operating systems that are supported by Virtual Server. For each of these operating systems, three possible methods are covered:

❑   **Using backup and restore software:** This involves using the built-in backup software on the operating system to make a system-level backup and then restoring it to the virtual machine.

❑   **Using a prepared system image:** In this case, you would go through and make the necessary changes to the operating system on the physical computer to prepare it for the migration. Then you use an imaging tool (such as PQImage or Symantec Ghost) to transfer the system data to the virtual machine.

❑   **Using an unprepared system image:** This is a relatively common scenario. You have a system image of an existing physical computer that you want to deploy to a virtual machine, but no preparation has been done on the image in order to help it run in a virtual machine.

Part V: Physical to Virtual Migration

> Performing manual physical to virtual migrations is not easy, and it is not always guaranteed to succeed. This chapter outlines the steps that will work in 95 percent of migrations, but you may need to perform further configuration for your physical computers.
>
> It should also be noted that a number of the techniques discussed in this chapter are not officially supported by Microsoft. I will attempt to highlight any specific techniques that I know are not supported and explain why they aren't.

Migrating Windows with Backup Software

Migrating systems by using Windows backup software is one of the most reliable methods. At the end of the day, you will always have a virtual machine that is capable of booting and running the operating system that is installed.

Traditionally, one of the biggest problems with this approach has been that some of the programs installed on the source computer may not work correctly after the migration because when using a backup and restore process, the backup program makes decisions about which files actually need to be copied and which files are system files that can be reloaded later. If the backup software makes a bad choice, it can cause problems.

However Microsoft has been working to make their backup programs better in this respect. The chance of encountering problems like this with Windows XP and Windows Server 2003 is very slim. With Windows Vista, you are close to guaranteed that the system will function exactly as you want it to after the migration.

Using ASR with Windows Server 2003 and Windows XP

With NTBackup on Windows Server 2003 or Windows XP, you can create an ASR (Automated System Recovery) system backup by either using the wizard or advanced mode user interface. An ASR backup allows you to restore the backed up system directly on to a blank virtual machine. One problem with an ASR backup is that it will back up all data on the computer. If you need to exclude any disks or locations from the backup process, you will need to perform a non-ASR–based backup.

Creating an ASR System Backup with NTBackup Wizard Mode

To create an ASR system backup with Windows Server 2003 or Windows XP using wizard mode you will need to do the following:

1. Open the **Start** menu and select **All Programs** ➪ **Accessories** ➪ **System Tools** ➪ Backup.

2. The **Backup or Restore Wizard** should start automatically.

   *If you have configured NTBackup to run in advanced mode by default, you can get to this wizard by selecting **Switch to Wizard Mode** from the **Tools** menu.*

238

Chapter 13: Manual Physical to Virtual Migrations

3.   On the **Backup or Restore** page select **Back up files and settings**, and click **Next**.

4.   On the **What to Back Up** page, select **All information on this computer**, and click **Next**.

5.   On the **Backup Type, Destination, and Name** page provide the information on where the backup will be created.

If you are backing up to a network location, it is advisable to have the network location mapped to a drive letter before starting this process. Otherwise, it can be problematic to enter the network location.

6.   Finish the wizard.

7.   At the end of the backup process you are asked to provide a blank, formatted floppy disk. This floppy disk will be used to store the automated system recovery information.

Creating an ASR System Backup with NTBackup Advanced Mode

To create an ASR system backup with Windows Server 2003 or Windows XP using advanced mode you will need to do the following:

1.   Open the **Start** menu and select **All Programs** ➪ **Accessories** ➪ **System Tools** ➪ **Backup**.

2.   Click the **Advanced Mode** link to change into advanced mode.

If you have configured NTBackup to run in advanced mode by default, you will not need to do this step.

3.   On the **Welcome** tab, click the **Automated System Recovery Wizard** button.

4.   On the **Backup Destination** page enter the location and name of the backup file.

If you are backing up to a network location it is advisable to have the network location mapped to a drive letter before starting this process. Otherwise it can be problematic to enter the network location.

5.   Finish the wizard.

6.   At the end of the backup process you will be asked to provide a blank, formatted floppy disk. This floppy disk will be used to store the automated system recovery information.

Restoring an ASR System Backup to a Virtual Machine

Restoring an ASR backup on a virtual machine can be a bit tricky because Windows expects to be able to access a hard disk or removable media that contains the backup data, and does not support loading the data off a network share. To deal with this, you will need to either burn your backup to DVD or a secondary virtual hard disk.

If your backup is small enough to fit on a DVD, you can burn it to a DVD (or create a DVD ISO file with the backup file on it). If your backup file is too large for the DVD approach you will need to put it on a secondary virtual hard disk that you attach to the virtual machine. To get the backup file onto a virtual hard disk you can either:

❑   Attach the secondary virtual hard disk to an existing virtual machine and use the virtual machine to copy the data onto the virtual hard disk.

❑   Use VHDMount to mount the secondary virtual hard disk on the host operating system, and then copy the backup files directly onto it.

Part V: Physical to Virtual Migration

Locating the Backup File

If you are using a DVD or DVD ISO image to provide the backup file, this is simple to do. If you are using a virtual hard disk, things are a bit more difficult. ASR will not automatically assign drive letters to your secondary hard disk. So you will need to do the following:

1. Press `Shift+F10`. This opens a command window.

2. Run `diskpart`.

3. Type **list volume**. This will show you a list of the disk volumes in the system. You should be able to identify the volume that you are using for the backup files. In my case it is Volume 2.

4. Type **select Volume 2** (or the volume that you have your backup files stored on).

5. Type **assign**.

6. Type **list volume** again to see which drive letter was just assigned to your volume.

7. Type **exit** twice.

The ASR process provides you with a browse button for locating the backup file, but in my experience I was never able to get the file browser to work correctly. Let's hope you used a simple enough name for your backup file that it is not a problem to just type the correct file name and location.

Whichever method you choose, do it before starting the ASR backup restore process. When you have completed this you will need to:

1. Create the new virtual machine with the appropriate parameters and boot it off the Windows installation disk for the version of Windows that you want to migrate.

If you are using a secondary virtual hard disk to provide the ASR backup files, you should make sure that it is attached before you start the ASR process.

2. During the boot process, you should see a page that contains the line **Press F2 to run Automated System Recovery (ASR)**. Press **F2** on this page.

3. You will then be asked to insert the Windows Automated System Recovery Disk that was created at the end of the backup process. Insert this floppy and press any key to continue.

You have to wait until this stage to insert the floppy disk, as it is not bootable and will stop you from being able to boot off the CD if you insert it earlier.

4. You will then be asked to confirm that it is okay to delete and recreate all of the partitions on the virtual machine. Press **C** to continue.

240

Chapter 13: Manual Physical to Virtual Migrations

You do not actually have to partition the disk. ASR will automatically do that, and you just need to tell it that it is okay to delete all of the data on the virtual machine's hard disk. If you are using a secondary virtual hard disk to provide the ASR backup files, you should make sure that it is not listed in the disks that will be deleted and repartitioned.

5. After a while the virtual machine will automatically reboot. You need to remove the ASR floppy disk at this stage; otherwise it will stop the virtual machine from booting.

6. If the location of the backup file is not identical to where it was created (which is highly likely) ASR will ask you to locate the backup file.

   The ASR process should now finish and leave you with a virtual machine that is ready to run and is identical to your source computer.

Using a Full System Backup with Windows Server 2003, Windows XP, and Windows 2000

If you do not want to back up the entire system, or you are backing up a Windows 2000 system (which does not support ASR), you will need to perform a full system backup with NTBackup. This can be done using either the wizard mode or the advanced mode.

It is not possible to use the version of NTBackup that was included with Windows NT 4.0 to perform a system migration because that version did not provide any way to back up system state data.

Remember that Windows 2000 has only the advanced mode backup user interface.

Creating a Full System Backup with NTBackup Wizard Mode

To create a full system backup with Windows Server 2003 or Windows XP using wizard mode you will need to do the following:

1. Open the **Start** menu and select **All Programs** ➪ **Accessories** ➪ **System Tools** ➪ **Backup**.

2. The **Backup or Restore Wizard** should start automatically.

   *If you have configured NTBackup to run in advanced mode by default, you can get to this wizard by selecting **Switch to Wizard Mode** from the **Tools** menu.*

3. On the **Backup or Restore** page, select **Back up files and settings**.

4. On the **What to Back Up** page, select **Let me choose what to back up**.

5. On the **Items to Back Up** page, you need to ensure that at least the system drive and the **System State** entries are checked. You can check other drive letters as you want.

6. On the **Backup Type, Destination, and Name** page, provide the information on where the backup will be created to.

   If you are backing up to a network location it is advisable to have the network location mapped to a drive letter before starting this process as otherwise it can be problematic to enter the network location.

7. Click **Finish** to create the backup.

241

Part V: Physical to Virtual Migration

Creating a Full System Backup with NTBackup Advanced Mode

To create a full system backup with Windows Server 2003, Windows XP, or Windows 2000 using advanced mode, execute the following steps:

1. Open the **Start** menu and select **All Programs** ➪ **Accessories** ➪ **System Tools** ➪ **Backup**.

2. Click the **Advanced Mode** link to change into advanced mode.

   If you have configured NTBackup to run in advanced mode by default, you will not need to do this step. This step is not necessary on Windows 2000.

3. On the **Welcome** tab, click the **Backup Wizard** button.

4. On the **What to Back Up** page, select **Back up selected files, drives, or network data**.

5. On the **Items to Back Up** page, you need to ensure that at least the system drive and the **System State** entries are checked. You can check other drive letters as you want.

6. On the next page, specify the location where the backup should be created.

   If you are backing up to a network location, it is advisable to have the network location mapped to a drive letter before starting this process. Otherwise, it can be problematic to enter the network location.

7. Click **Finish** to create the backup.

Preparing a Virtual Machine for the Full System Backup

Unlike with an ASR backup, with a standard full system backup there is no way to apply it to a blank virtual machine. Instead you need to do the following:

1. Create a new virtual machine.

2. Install the same version of Windows as is on the source computer.

   When installing Windows you should just choose the default settings. Most of them will be overwritten when you apply the backup from the source computer.

3. Configure the virtual hard disks and partitions to match those of your source computer.

4. Apply appropriate service packs and updates to bring Windows to the same level of the source computer.

5. Apply the backup set from the source computer to the virtual machine.

As you can see, using a full system backup instead of an ASR backup involves a lot more manual work for you. One of the biggest advantages of the full system backup approach is that the backup files can be restored from a network location (unlike with ASR).

242

Chapter 13: Manual Physical to Virtual Migrations

Restoring a Full System Backup to a Virtual Machine with Wizard Mode

To restore a full system backup with Windows Server 2003 or Windows XP using wizard mode you will need to do the following:

1. Open the **Start** menu and select **All Programs** ⇨ **Accessories** ⇨ **System Tools** ⇨ **Backup**.

2. The **Backup or Restore Wizard** should start automatically.

*If you have configured NTBackup to run in advanced mode by default, you can get to this wizard by selecting **Switch to Wizard Mode** from the **Tools** menu.*

3. On the **Backup or Restore** page, select **Restore** files and settings.

4. On the **What to Restore** page you can browse for the existing backup set (from the source computer) to import. Once you have done this you can check all the entries in the backup set.

5. On the **Completing the Restore Wizard** page, click the **Advanced** button.

6. Leave the **Where to Restore** page set to **Original location**.

7. On the **How to Restore** page, select the option to always replace the exiting files.

8. Complete the wizard to begin the restore process and reboot the virtual machine. The migration is now finished.

Restoring a Full System Backup to a Virtual Machine with Advanced Mode

To restore a full system backup with Windows Server 2003, Windows XP, or Windows 2000 using advanced mode, do the following:

1. Open the **Start** menu and select **All Programs** ⇨ **Accessories** ⇨ **System Tools** ⇨ **Backup**.

2. Click the **Advanced Mode** link to change to advanced mode.

If you have configured NTBackup to run in advanced mode by default, you will not need to do this step. This step is not necessary on Windows 2000.

3. On the **Welcome** tab, click the **Restore Wizard** button.

4. On the **What to Restore** page, you can browse for the existing backup set (from the source computer) to import. Once you have done this, you can check all the entries in the backup set.

5. On the **Completing the Restore Wizard** page, click the **Advanced** button.

6. Leave the **Where to Restore** page set to **Original location**.

7. On the **How to Restore** page, select the option to always replace the existing files.

8. Complete the wizard to begin the restore process and reboot the virtual machine. The migration is now finished.

243

Part V: Physical to Virtual Migration

Using a Complete PC Backup with Windows Vista

Creating a full system backup for the purpose of migrating to a virtual machine is very easy with Windows Vista. To create the backup you will first need to ensure that you have an appropriate location for the backup to be written to. This can be a removable hard disk, secondary hard disk, or CD/DVD media. Once you have your backup media configured you can start a complete PC backup under Windows Vista by following these steps:

1. Select **Control Panel** from the **Start** menu.

2. Select **System and Maintenance**.

   If you are using the classic Control Panel view, you can skip step 2.

3. Select **Backup and Restore Center**.

4. Click **Backup up computer** (this will require you to authorize the action).

5. On the **Where do you want to save the backup?** page of the **Windows Complete PC Backup** wizard, select the media that you will be using.

   Windows Vista Complete PC Backup does not support creating a backup to a network share.

6. If your system has multiple disk partitions, you will be presented with the **Which disks do you want to include in the backup?** page. Check the disks you want to back up.

7. The **Confirm your backup settings** page will allow you to review your settings. Once you have done this, click **Start backup** to begin the backup process.

When the backup process has completed, you need to work on restoring the backup into a virtual machine. Create a new virtual machine with the appropriate settings for your Windows Vista computer and then create new virtual hard disks that will be used by the virtual machine.

While Complete PC backs up to a virtual hard disk file, it is not configured to be bootable. This means that you cannot just use the .vhd file directly under Virtual Server, and instead you have to restore it in a virtual machine just as you would a physical computer.

> Like ASR, Complete PC does not allow you to restore off of a network location. If you created the Complete PC backup on CD/DVD media you can just use that to load the virtual machine. If you created the Complete PC backup on a secondary hard disk, you will need to transfer the backup files to a virtual hard disk, which you will then need to attach to the virtual machine before starting the restoration process.

To restore the Complete PC backup, do the following:

1. Boot the virtual machine using the Windows Vista installation DVD.

2. After specifying your language preferences, click **Repair your computer** (on the page with the **Install now** button).

3. On the **System Recovery Options** page, click **Next**.

244

Chapter 13: Manual Physical to Virtual Migrations

4. On the **Choose a recovery tool** page, select **Windows Complete PC Restore**.

5. Select the backup that you want to restore.

6. Finish the wizard, and confirm that the disk should be formatted.

Once this process has finished, your virtual machine should be good to go. If you find that it is not booting correctly, you can fix it by booting the virtual machine off of the Windows Vista installation DVD and choosing the **Repair your computer** option. This will automatically scan the virtual hard disk and attempt to fix any issues it finds.

Imaging Physical into Virtual

This section refers to *imaging* of physical computers onto virtual machines. There are numerous ways that you can take an image of a physical computer and load it onto a virtual machine.

One way to image a physical computer is to actually use Virtual Server itself to image a physical computer into a virtual machine. In order to do this, follow these steps:

1. Shut down the physical source computer, remove the hard disks, and attach them to the Virtual Server.

The source hard disks can be attached in any manner you want. Many people place the source hard disk in a USB enclosure and use this to attach the hard disk to the Virtual Server server. This way they do not need to shut down and reconfigure their Virtual Server server.

2. Open the Virtual Server administrative website.

3. Select **Create** and then select **Linked Virtual Hard Disk** under the **Virtual Disks** section of the navigation pane.

4. Enter a name and location for the new linked virtual hard disk, select the source physical disk, and click **Create**.

5. In the navigation pane, select **Inspect** from the **Virtual Disks** section.

6. Enter the name and path for the linked virtual hard disk that you just created.

7. Click **Convert virtual hard disk**.

8. Enter the name and path you want to use for the final virtual hard disk (that you will use with the new virtual machine).

9. Also select whether you want to have a dynamically expanding virtual hard disk or a fixed size virtual hard disk, and click **Convert**.

If you choose to convert the linked virtual hard disk into a dynamically expanding virtual hard disk, you should consider compacting the physical hard disk before attempting the conversion (by defragmenting it and using the Virtual Disk precompactor to zero-out unused space); otherwise, the new dynamically expanding virtual hard disk will be very large when it is created.

10. The conversion process will take a while, but when it is finished, you can delete the linked virtual hard disk and use the newly created virtual hard disk that now contains an image of the physical disk.

Part V: Physical to Virtual Migration

Handling Mounted Physical Hard Disks

When selecting the source physical hard disk, you will see a number of entries that look something like this:

```
\\.\PHYSICALDRIVE0 - 149.05GB - Mounted
```

It is a bad idea to make an image of a disk that is mounted by the host operating system, as there is a high potential for data corruption on the new virtual hard disk. To stop a hard disk from being mounted by the host operating system you will need to run diskmgmt.msc. Once the disk management console is open you will be able to do a couple of things.

First, you will be able to figure out which drive letters are assigned to which physical disks. \\.\PHYSICALDRIVE0 under Virtual Server maps to Disk 0 under the disk management console.

Once you have located the disk that you want to image, you can stop Windows from mounting it by doing the following:

1. Select each partition that has a drive letter assigned to it.

2. Right-click the partition.

3. Select **Change Drive Letter and Paths**.

4. Select the drive letters or paths for the disk you don't want to mount.

5. Click **Remove** and then click **OK**.

When all partitions are no longer mounted by Windows, you can return to Virtual Server to continue with the process of imaging the hard disk.

If you have multiple physical hard disks in your source computer you will need to repeat this process for each disk.

At this stage, you will probably want to remove the source computer's disks from your Virtual Server.

Another option for imaging your computer is to use one of the many tools that are available that allow you to create system images of physical computers that can then be deployed to other physical computers. You should be able to follow the standard procedures for creating the system image, and you can use the same process for loading the image into the virtual machine that you would for a physical computer. The one challenge to solve is how to get the image into a location where the virtual machine can load it. Here are a couple of ways to access the image from inside a virtual machine:

❑ **CD/DVD drive:** For many people, it is common practice to put system images onto CDs or DVDs so that they can be installed onto hardware when no network access is possible. These CDs/DVDs work perfectly for loading the system images into virtual machines.

❑ **A second virtual hard disk:** Alternatively, you can create a second virtual hard disk, which you connect to the physical computer with VHDMount. You can copy the system image file onto this virtual hard disk and then connect it to your virtual machine, where the imaging tool would be able to apply it to the primary virtual hard disk.

Chapter 13: Manual Physical to Virtual Migrations

Of course, if your system imaging tool supports being run directly on top of Windows, you can just use VHDMount to mount the primary virtual hard disk and apply the system image directly.

❑ **Over the network:** The final method to consider is to load the system image over the network (this is the approach that I use most often). In this case the system image files are stored on a network share (which may even be on the host operating system) and the virtual machines are configured to connect to the network share and apply the system image directly from there.

For Windows-based imaging tools, you can boot the virtual machine off of a Windows PE boot CD. For DOS-based imaging tools, you can boot off of a network-enabled DOS boot floppy.

DOS-based networking is one of the slowest methods for loading an image into a virtual machine. You should treat DOS-based networking as a "last resort" option when imaging virtual machines.

The website www.netbootdisk.com *provides an excellent tool for quickly creating network-enabled DOS boot floppies that work with Virtual Server.*

Tips for Imaging Windows Systems

Before starting on the actual migration, you need to know some background information about configuring Windows systems.

Offline Editing of the Windows Registry

A number of places in this chapter talk about changes that need to be made to the Windows Registry on a virtual machine that cannot be booted. A little known fact about Windows is that it provides full support for offline editing of the Registry. To edit the Registry of a virtual machine that is not currently running, do the following:

1. On the host operating system, mount the virtual hard disk of the virtual machine in question by using VHDMount.

   For details on how to use VHDMount, refer to Chapter 11.

2. Open **regedit.exe** from the host operating system.

3. Select the entry for **HKEY_LOCAL_MACHINE**.

4. Open the **File** menu and select **Load Hive**.

5. Browse to the **system32\config** folder under the Windows folder for the mounted virtual hard disk.

6. Select the file named system (with no file extension) and click **Open**.

7. You will be asked for a key name; this is just for temporary purposes so it can be anything you want. I will call mine SYSTEM_VM.

8. If you now expand the **HKEY_LOCAL_MACHINE** entry, you will see an entry with the name you just specified.

247

Part V: Physical to Virtual Migration

9. Expand this entry and you will see that it is the **HKEY_LOCAL_MACHINE\SYSTEM** section of the virtual machine's Registry.

10. You can repeat this process and load the **SAM**, **SECURITY**, and **software** files to get access to **HKEY_LOCAL_MACHINE\SAM**, **HKEY_LOCAL_MACHINE\SECURITY**, and **HKEY_LOCAL_MACHINE\SOFTWARE** on the virtual machine's Registry.

You can now interact with the virtual machine's Registry just as if it were the local computer's Registry. Once you have made the changes you need to make you will need to unload the virtual machine's Registry by selecting the node for the virtual machine's Registry and selecting **Unload Hive** from the **File** menu.

Changes are not written to the offline Registry files until they are unloaded, so always remember to do this last step.

Regedit is backward, but not forward, compatible. This means that you can use the version of regedit.exe in Windows XP to edit a Windows 2000 Registry, but not a Windows Vista Registry.

Finding the Right Files

Another thing that you will need to do is to manually load system files into Windows systems. There are two possible locations for obtaining these files: a matching virtual machine or copying files from the installation media.

The preferred approach is to use a virtual machine with the same operating system and updates as the source system. The reason for this is that one of the biggest dangers when manually loading system files is that you use an older version of the file that does not contain the updates that you have installed on your source computer. When this happens, Windows will believe that it is up-to-date with patches and updates, but it will not really be. Using files from a virtual machine with the same operating system and updates as the source system means that you are guaranteed to have the appropriate updates installed.

Another approach is to copy files from the installation media. If you do not have a matching virtual machine handy, you can copy the files off of the original installation media. As noted, these files don't contain any updates or patches, and using this method is the most likely way to end up with a virtual machine that is not officially supported by Microsoft. All the files you need to copy are usually stored in the **I386** directory on your installation media. They are compressed, but the tool to uncompress them is also stored in this directory. This tool is called expand.exe. For example, if I wanted to get a copy of the eventvwr.exe system file from my Windows 2000 installation media (that is in my D: drive) I would need to open a command prompt and run the following:

```
D:\I386\Expand.exe D:\I386\EVENTVWR.EX_ eventvwr.exe
```

In this case, the compressed version of eventvwr.exe was helpfully named eventvwr.ex_; however, the naming of the compressed files is not always this intuitive.

248

Chapter 13: Manual Physical to Virtual Migrations

Some files are also stored inside of a file called driver.cab. If you need to expand a file from this location, you would need to run the following:

```
D:\I386\Expand.exe D:\I386\DRIVER.CAB /F:HIDUSB.SYS .
```

where hidusb.sys is the file to expand, and . is the location where the file will be expanded to.

Migrating with a Prepared System Image

The next method of physical to virtual migration is to use a prepared system image, in which you take your existing physical computer, make configuration changes to it such that the operating system will be able to run under Virtual Server, and then use an imaging tool to transfer the data. Ideally, the preparation that you perform on the source computer will not cause it to stop working on the source hardware.

Migrating Windows Systems

Windows Server 2003, Windows XP, or Windows 2000 have excellent support for automatically detecting changes in hardware and loading the correct drivers as needed. This makes the process of performing a system image–based migration easier. Windows NT 4.0 needs more work, but has similar considerations. A few key items need to be configured correctly.

Windows needs to be configured with the appropriate storage drivers such that it can boot off the hard disk. Without these drivers, Windows will be unable to load other drivers that are needed.

> **Windows has what are referred to as *critical devices*. These are devices that, if they cannot be started, Windows will not attempt to continue booting. In order to boot successfully Windows needs to have information about the storage driver for the hard disk controller it is booting off of in the critical device database.**
>
> **If this information is not there, Windows will crash with the following blue screen error:**
> ```
> STOP 0X0000007B
> Inaccessible Boot Device
> ```

The next area that needs to be configured correctly is the HAL (Hardware Abstraction Layer). This is a driver that Windows uses to talk to the computer hardware on a very basic level. Having the wrong HAL loaded will stop the virtual machine from being able to boot.

The final area is the kernel. Windows has two different kernels: one for uniprocessor computers and one for multiprocessor computers. Virtual Server virtual machines are always uniprocessor computers, so if you are migrating a uniprocessor physical computer, there is nothing that you need to do. If, however, you are migrating a multiprocessor physical computer you will need to configure Windows to use the uniprocessor kernel.

249

Part V: Physical to Virtual Migration

Understanding HALs

Windows includes six standard HALs. The HALs differ in such areas as how the operating system should manage power management, how it should enumerate hardware devices, and how it should interact with the processors.

The six standard HALs are:

- ❑ Standard PC — Non-ACPI PIC HAL (Hal.dll)

- ❑ MPS Uniprocessor PC — Non-ACPI APIC UP HAL (Halapic.dll)

- ❑ MPS Multiprocessor PC — Non-ACPI APIC MP HAL (Halmps.dll)

- ❑ Advanced Configuration and Power Interface (ACPI) PC — ACPI PIC HAL (Halacpi.dll)

- ❑ ACPI Uniprocessor PC — ACPI APIC UP HAL (Halaacpi.dll)

- ❑ ACPI Multiprocessor PC — ACPI APIC MP HAL (Halmacpi.dll)

All of these HALs have different file names on the installation media (as noted in the preceding list) but they are all installed as hal.dll under Windows.

PIC versus APIC

The PIC (Programmable Interrupt Controller) and APIC (Advanced Programmable Interrupt Controller) are both used by the operating system to assign priority levels to interrupts, and to perform other interrupt management. APIC is an extension of PIC, which contains greater functionality and flexibility. Traditionally PIC has been used in uniprocessor computers and APIC has been reserved for multiprocessor computers. However, recent computers have integrated APICs into uniprocessor motherboards, and PIC-based systems are rapidly becoming less common.

With Windows, PIC-based HALs can run on either PIC- or APIC-based systems. But APIC-based HALs can only run on APIC-based systems.

ACPI versus Non-ACPI

ACPI (not to be confused with APIC) stands for Advanced Configuration and Power Interface. ACPI is used by the operating system to manage the power usage and state of the processors and devices in a computer. In addition, ACPI is used by Windows in order to locate the presence of all devices in a computer. If a computer does not support ACPI it most likely uses APM (Advanced Power Management). ACPI is the current standard for the majority of computer hardware.

With Windows, non-ACPI–based HALs can run on either non-ACPI–based or ACPI-based systems. But ACPI-based HALs can only run on ACPI-based systems.

MP versus UP

MP (multiprocessor) and UP (uniprocessor) HALs have a clear distinction. If you have multiple processors, you need the MP HAL; otherwise you can use the UP HAL. With Windows, UP-based HALs can run on either UP- or MP-based systems. But MP-based HALs can only run on MP-based systems.

Chapter 13: Manual Physical to Virtual Migrations

> There are also hardware-specific HALs that are provided by the hardware manufacturer, rather than Microsoft, but these are relatively rare.
>
> Virtual Server virtual machines are always uniprocessor PIC ACPI computers. This means that they can use either the Standard PC or the Advanced Configuration and Power Interface (ACPI) PC HALs.

Apart from these areas, Windows Server 2003, Windows XP, and Windows 2000 are able to automatically detect and install appropriate drivers as needed (for video, networking, and so on). With Windows NT 4.0 you can manually configure other drivers after the migration process.

Preparing Windows Server 2003 and Windows XP Storage Drivers for Migration

When migrating a Windows Server 2003 or Windows XP computer to a virtual machine, you need to load the correct IDE and SCSI drivers.

Load the Correct IDE Drivers

Even if you are migrating an IDE-based physical computer into an IDE-based virtual machine, there can be problems if the incorrect IDE drivers are present. The process for ensuring that the right IDE drivers are present is different for an IDE-based physical computer and a non-IDE–based physical computer. This applies to Windows 2000 as well.

If you physical computer has an IDE controller installed, you can prepare the system for migration by following these steps:

1. Select the **Control Panel** from the **Start** menu.

2. Select **Administrative Tools** and then select **Computer Management**.

3. Select the **Device Manager** node.

4. Expand the **IDE ATA/ATAPI controllers** node.

5. Select one of the controllers, open the **Action** menu, and select **Update driver**.

   You need to select a controller, not a channel.

6. On the first page of the **Hardware Update Wizard**, select to not use Windows Update.

7. On the next page, select **Install from a list or specific location (Advanced)**.

8. On the **Please choose your search and installation options**, select **Don't search**.

9. On the **Select the device driver you want to install for this hardware** page, select the entry for **Standard Dual Channel PCI IDE controller**.

10. Complete the wizard.

251

Part V: Physical to Virtual Migration

Your IDE-based system is now configured with a driver that will work on your current hardware and inside of a virtual machine.

While the standard dual channel PCI IDE controller driver is very compatible, it is not a high-performance driver. As such you should not use it long term or in production. Once you have completed the migration you can get the correct driver loaded by repeating the preceding process, but letting Windows automatically choose the best driver. This applies to Windows 2000 as well.

If your physical computer does not have an IDE controller installed you can prepare the system for migration by following these steps:

1. Select the **Control Panel** from the **Start** menu.

2. Select **Add Hardware**.

3. On the **Is the hardware connected?** page, select **Yes, I have already connected the hardware**.

4. On the **The following hardware is already installed on your computer** page, select **Add a new hardware device**.

5. On the **The wizard can help you install other hardware** page, select **Install the hardware that I manually select from a list (Advanced)**.

6. On the **From the list below, select the type of hardware you are installing** page, select **IDE ATA/ATAPI controllers**.

7. On the **Select a device driver** page, select the **Standard Dual Channel PCI IDE controller**.

8. Complete the **Add Hardware** wizard.

   Your non-IDE-based system is now configured with a driver that will work inside of a virtual machine.

Load the Correct SCSI Drivers

Loading the correct SCSI drivers is much more difficult than loading the correct IDE drivers. In fact, I recommend that you do not attempt this as part of the image preparation. If you do not intend to use SCSI for the virtual machine boot disk, then you will not have to worry about this at all. If you do want to use SCSI for the virtual machine boot disk, but the boot disk is fewer than 128GB in size, you can have Windows do the work automatically for you. All you need to do is to boot the virtual machine with an IDE controller but have a SCSI controller installed. When Windows boots up it will automatically detect the SCSI controller and install the right drivers. You can then shut down the virtual machine and change the configuration to boot off of SCSI instead.

This applies to Windows 2000 as well.

If you absolutely need to have the SCSI drivers configured before creating the image, you should follow the directions for adding the SCSI drivers to an unprepared system image.

Preparing Windows 2000 Storage Drivers for Migration

When migrating a Windows 2000 computer to a virtual machine, changes in IDE and drivers need to be performed.

252

Chapter 13: Manual Physical to Virtual Migrations

Load the Correct IDE Drivers

If your physical computer has an IDE controller installed, you can prepare the system for migration by following these steps:

1. Select **My Computer** and then **Control Panel**.
2. Select **Administrative Tools** and then open **Computer Management**.
3. Select the **Device Manager** node.
4. Expand the **IDE ATA/ATAPI controllers** node.
5. Select one of the controllers, open the **Action** menu, and select **Properties**.

   You need to select a controller, not a channel.

6. Change to the **Drivers** tab and click **Update Driver**.
7. On the **Install Hardware Device Drivers** page select **Display a list of known drivers for this device so that I can choose a specific driver**.
8. On the **Select a Device Driver** page, select the entry for the **Standard Dual Channel PCI IDE controller**.
9. Complete the wizard.

Your IDE-based system is now configured with a driver that will work on your current hardware and inside of a virtual machine.

If your physical computer does not have an IDE controller installed, you can prepare the system for migration by following these steps:

1. Select **My Computer** and then **Control Panel**.
2. Select **Add/Remove Hardware**.
3. On the **Choose a Hardware Task** page, select **Add/Troubleshoot a device**.
4. On the **Choose a Hardware Device** page, select **Add a new device**.
5. On the **Find New Hardware** page, select **No, I want to select the hardware from a list**.
6. On the **Hardware Type** page, select **IDE ATA/ATAPI controllers**.
7. On the **Select a Device Driver** page, select the **Standard Dual Channel PCI IDE controller**.
8. Complete the **Add Hardware** wizard.

Your non-IDE-based system is now configured with a driver that will work inside of a virtual machine.

Preparing Windows NT 4.0 Storage Drivers for Migration

When migrating a Windows NT 4.0 computer to a virtual machine, the changes described in the following sections need to be performed for the storage system.

253

Part V: Physical to Virtual Migration

Load the Correct IDE Drivers

Unlike Windows 2000 and later, Windows NT 4.0 uses a generic IDE driver that is compatible with Virtual Server virtual machines. This means that if you are migrating an IDE-based Windows NT 4.0 computer, things should just work.

If your source computer is not using the generic IDE driver, you can install it by following these steps:

1. Select **My Computer** and then **Control Panel**.
2. Open **SCSI Adapters**.
3. Change to the **Drivers** tab and click the **Add** button.
4. Select the **(Standard mass storage controllers)** entry from the **Manufacturers:** list. Then select **IDE CD-ROM (ATAPI 1.2)/Dual-channel PCI IDE Controller** from the **SCSI Adapter** list.
5. Click **OK** and provide the location of the Windows NT CDROM installation files.

Load the Correct SCSI Drivers

Loading the correct SCSI drivers for Windows NT 4.0 is much easier than with Windows 2000 and later. Simply follow these steps:

1. Select **My Computer** and then **Control Panel**.
2. Select **SCSI Adapters**.
3. Change to the **Drivers** tab and click the **Add** button.
4. Select the **Adaptec** entry from the **Manufacturers:** list. Then select **Adaptec AHA-294X/ AHA-394X or AIC-78XX PCI SCSI Controller** from the **SCSI Adapter** list.
5. Click **OK** and provide the location of the Windows NT CDROM installation files.

Preparing the Windows HAL and Kernel for Migration

Configuring the right HAL and kernel before creating the system image is more difficult than making these changes after the image has been created. The reason for this is that a running copy of Windows actively prevents you from changing these files. But there is a workaround.

The first thing that you need to do is to identify whether you need to change the HAL or kernel in the first place. To check the HAL that is used by your physical system, follow these steps:

1. Open **My Computer** and then navigate to the Windows directory for your computer.
2. Open the **System32** directory.
3. Find and select the file called hal.dll.
4. Right-click on the filename and select **Properties**.
5. Change to the **Version** tab and select the **Internal Name** item.

If the internal name is **hal.dll** or **halacpi.dll**, then you do not need to do anything, because the HAL will work under Virtual Server.

254

Chapter 13: Manual Physical to Virtual Migrations

To check which kernel is being used by your system, repeat the steps for the HAL but look at the file ntoskrnl.exe. If its internal name is **ntoskrnl.exe**, then you do not need to make any changes.

If you have the wrong HAL on your system for a virtual machine, you need to get a copy of the hal.dll file off an existing virtual machine, and expand halacpi.dl_. (Or for Windows NT 4.0, hal.dl_. Windows NT 4.0 had no support for ACPI.). Then copy the file to halvm.dll in the **System32** directory.

> *If you just tried to copy the new file over the top of the existing HAL, Windows will restore the original HAL when you were done. This is also true of the kernel files.*

If you have the wrong kernel on your system for a virtual machine, you need to get a copy of ntoskrnl.exe and ntkrnlpa.exe off an existing virtual machine; expand ntoskrnl.ex_ and expand ntkrnlpa.exe from driver.cab; and copy Ntoskrnl.exe to Ntosvm.exe and Ntkrnlpa.exe to Ntosvmpa.exe in the **System32** directory.

> *Ntkrnlpa.exe does not exist for Windows NT 4.0 and can just be ignored.*

Now that all the files are in place, you need to configure Windows so it can boot with these files. To do this, edit the boot.ini file that is located in the root of the system disk. Before editing boot.ini, change its file attributes. boot.ini is normally marked as a hidden system file, which stops you from editing it. To edit boot.ini you need to change to the root of the system drive (usually C:) and run the following:

```
ATTRIB -S -H BOOT.INI
NOTEPAD BOOT.INI
```

You should then see a file with contents similar to the following:

```
[boot loader]
timeout=30
default=multi(0)disk(0)rdisk(0)partition(1)\WINDOWS
[operating systems]
multi(0)disk(0)rdisk(0)partition(1)\WINDOWS="Windows XP" /FASTDETECT ⤶
/NOEXECUTE=OPTIN
```

You will need to make a copy of the entry under `[operating systems]` that maps to the system you are using. Then you will need to make the following changes to the copy:

❑ Change the entry name (the section in quotes) so that you can differentiate between the original entry and the new entry.

❑ Add `/KERNEL=NTOSVM.EXE /HAL=HALVM.DLL` to the end of the new entry.

When you are done, the file should look like this:

```
[boot loader]
timeout=30
default=multi(0)disk(0)rdisk(0)partition(1)\WINDOWS
[operating systems]
multi(0)disk(0)rdisk(0)partition(1)\WINDOWS="Windows XP" /FASTDETECT ⤶
/NOEXECUTE=OPTIN
multi(0)disk(0)rdisk(0)partition(1)\WINDOWS="Windows XP - VM" /FASTDETECT ⤶
/NOEXECUTE=OPTIN /KERNEL=NTOSVM.EXE /HAL=HALVM.DLL
```

255

Part V: Physical to Virtual Migration

You should then save the file and return it to its original state by running the following:

```
ATTRIB +S +H BOOT.INI
```

Now your physical system is ready to be imaged and migrated.

Red Hat Enterprise Linux 4

When preparing a Red Hat Enterprise Linux system, the main area to look at is kernel configuration. If you are using one of the standard kernels provided by Red Hat there is nothing that you need to do here. If you have compiled your own kernel, it is possible that you have excluded functionality that is needed to run inside a Virtual Server virtual machine. For this reason, you should always keep a copy of the standard Red Hat kernel and configure your boot loader to provide the option of booting off this kernel if needed.

I am not going to provide details on how to configure a second boot option for the standard kernel, as these details are included with most documentation on how to compile your own kernel. So if you need to know how to do this, you should already have access to this information.

Unlike with Windows, the Linux multiprocessor kernel has no problems booting on a uniprocessor computer. So you do not need to worry about this when migrating a Linux system to a virtual machine.

Migrating with an Unprepared System Image

While this option is the hardest to handle, there are times when it is unavoidable. For example, you may need to create a virtual machine from a system backup for a physical computer that is no longer functional (and hence cannot be booted). Migrating with an unprepared system image means that you performed no system configuration to aide the migration process before creating the system image. This will happen most often when the system image was made without the idea of migration to a virtual machine in mind. (It was intended as a backup or for use in deploying to identical physical hardware.) But now that you have the image, you want to use it to build a virtual machine.

Migrating Unprepared Windows Server 2003, Windows XP, and Windows 2000 Servers

As with a prepared system image, you will need to correct the configuration for the IDE drivers, SCSI drivers, HAL file, and kernel files. However, you need to use a completely different technique in this case because the unprepared system image won't boot inside the virtual machine. So you need to be able to correct these configuration issues without booting the virtual machine.

First, create a new virtual machine and load the unprepared system image on to its virtual hard disk. Once you have done this, shut down the virtual machine and mount its virtual hard disk on the host operating system with VHDMount. Then you can perform the following offline modifications: Load the correct IDE drivers, load the correct SCSI drivers, and update the kernel.

256

Chapter 13: Manual Physical to Virtual Migrations

Loading the correct IDE drivers is a two-stage process. You will need to copy the right files to the right locations, and then make appropriate changes to the Windows Registry. You need the following files:

- ❏ atapi.sys
- ❏ intelide.sys
- ❏ pciide.sys
- ❏ pciidex.sys

The first thing you should do is to check if any of these files are already in the system32\drivers directory under the Windows directory for your virtual machine. (It is likely that some, if not all, of these files will already be there.) If any of these files are not on the virtual machine you can do the following:

- ❏ Copy them from another virtual machine that has the same version of Windows.
- ❏ Expand atapi.sy_, intelide.sy_, pciide.sy_, and pciidex.sy_ from the installation media.

When the files are in place, the next step is to update the Registry. I have provided a sample .REG file that can be used when the virtual machine's SYSTEM Registry section is loaded at HKEY_LOCAL _MACHINE\SYSTEM_VM in the host Registry.

```
Windows Registry Editor Version 5.00

[HKEY_LOCAL_MACHINE\SYSTEM_VM\ControlSet001\Control\CriticalDeviceDatabase\
primary_ide_channel]
"ClassGUID"="{4D36E96A-E325-11CE-BFC1-08002BE10318}"
"Service"="atapi"

[HKEY_LOCAL_MACHINE\SYSTEM_VM\ControlSet001\Control\CriticalDeviceDatabase\
secondary_ide_channel]
"ClassGUID"="{4D36E96A-E325-11CE-BFC1-08002BE10318}"
"Service"="atapi"

[HKEY_LOCAL_MACHINE\SYSTEM_VM\ControlSet001\Control\CriticalDeviceDatabase\
*pnp0600]
"ClassGUID"="{4D36E96A-E325-11CE-BFC1-08002BE10318}"
"Service"="atapi"

[HKEY_LOCAL_MACHINE\SYSTEM_VM\ControlSet001\Control\CriticalDeviceDatabase\
*azt0502]
"ClassGUID"="{4D36E96A-E325-11CE-BFC1-08002BE10318}"
"Service"="atapi"

[HKEY_LOCAL_MACHINE\SYSTEM_VM\ControlSet001\Control\CriticalDeviceDatabase\gendisk]
"ClassGUID"="{4D36E967-E325-11CE-BFC1-08002BE10318}"
"Service"="disk"

[HKEY_LOCAL_MACHINE\SYSTEM_VM\ControlSet001\Control\CriticalDeviceDatabase\
pci#cc_0101]
"ClassGUID"="{4D36E96A-E325-11CE-BFC1-08002BE10318}"
"Service"="pciide"

[HKEY_LOCAL_MACHINE\SYSTEM_VM\ControlSet001\Control\CriticalDeviceDatabase\
pci#ven_0e11&dev_ae33]
```

257

Part V: Physical to Virtual Migration

```
"ClassGUID"="{4D36E96A-E325-11CE-BFC1-08002BE10318}"
"Service"="pciide"

[HKEY_LOCAL_MACHINE\SYSTEM_VM\ControlSet001\Control\CriticalDeviceDatabase\↺
pci#ven_1039&dev_0601]
"ClassGUID"="{4D36E96A-E325-11CE-BFC1-08002BE10318}"
"Service"="pciide"

[HKEY_LOCAL_MACHINE\SYSTEM_VM\ControlSet001\Control\CriticalDeviceDatabase\↺
pci#ven_1039&dev_5513]
"ClassGUID"="{4D36E96A-E325-11CE-BFC1-08002BE10318}"
"Service"="pciide"

[HKEY_LOCAL_MACHINE\SYSTEM_VM\ControlSet001\Control\CriticalDeviceDatabase\↺
pci#ven_1042&dev_1000]
"ClassGUID"="{4D36E96A-E325-11CE-BFC1-08002BE10318}"
"Service"="pciide"

[HKEY_LOCAL_MACHINE\SYSTEM_VM\ControlSet001\Control\CriticalDeviceDatabase\↺
pci#ven_105a&dev_4d33]
"ClassGUID"="{4D36E96A-E325-11CE-BFC1-08002BE10318}"
"Service"="pciide"

[HKEY_LOCAL_MACHINE\SYSTEM_VM\ControlSet001\Control\CriticalDeviceDatabase\↺
pci#ven_1095&dev_0640]
"ClassGUID"="{4D36E96A-E325-11CE-BFC1-08002BE10318}"
"Service"="pciide"

[HKEY_LOCAL_MACHINE\SYSTEM_VM\ControlSet001\Control\CriticalDeviceDatabase\↺
pci#ven_1095&dev_0646]
"ClassGUID"="{4D36E96A-E325-11CE-BFC1-08002BE10318}"
"Service"="pciide"

[HKEY_LOCAL_MACHINE\SYSTEM_VM\ControlSet001\Control\CriticalDeviceDatabase\↺
pci#ven_1097&dev_0038]
"ClassGUID"="{4D36E96A-E325-11CE-BFC1-08002BE10318}"
"Service"="pciide"

[HKEY_LOCAL_MACHINE\SYSTEM_VM\ControlSet001\Control\CriticalDeviceDatabase\↺
pci#ven_10ad&dev_0001]
"ClassGUID"="{4D36E96A-E325-11CE-BFC1-08002BE10318}"
"Service"="pciide"

[HKEY_LOCAL_MACHINE\SYSTEM_VM\ControlSet001\Control\CriticalDeviceDatabase\↺
pci#ven_10ad&dev_0150]
"ClassGUID"="{4D36E96A-E325-11CE-BFC1-08002BE10318}"
"Service"="pciide"

[HKEY_LOCAL_MACHINE\SYSTEM_VM\ControlSet001\Control\CriticalDeviceDatabase\↺
pci#ven_10b9&dev_5215]
"ClassGUID"="{4D36E96A-E325-11CE-BFC1-08002BE10318}"
"Service"="pciide"

[HKEY_LOCAL_MACHINE\SYSTEM_VM\ControlSet001\Control\CriticalDeviceDatabase\↺
pci#ven_10b9&dev_5219]
```

Chapter 13: Manual Physical to Virtual Migrations

```
"ClassGUID"="{4D36E96A-E325-11CE-BFC1-08002BE10318}"
"Service"="pciide"

[HKEY_LOCAL_MACHINE\SYSTEM_VM\ControlSet001\Control\CriticalDeviceDatabase\↪
pci#ven_10b9&dev_5229]
"ClassGUID"="{4D36E96A-E325-11CE-BFC1-08002BE10318}"
"Service"="pciide"

[HKEY_LOCAL_MACHINE\SYSTEM_VM\ControlSet001\Control\CriticalDeviceDatabase\↪
pci#ven_1106&dev_0571]
"ClassGUID"="{4D36E96A-E325-11CE-BFC1-08002BE10318}"
"Service"="pciide"

[HKEY_LOCAL_MACHINE\SYSTEM_VM\ControlSet001\Control\CriticalDeviceDatabase\↪
pci#ven_8086&amp;dev_1222]
"ClassGUID"="{4D36E96A-E325-11CE-BFC1-08002BE10318}"
"Service"="intelide"

[HKEY_LOCAL_MACHINE\SYSTEM_VM\ControlSet001\Control\CriticalDeviceDatabase\↪
pci#ven_8086&dev_1230]
"ClassGUID"="{4D36E96A-E325-11CE-BFC1-08002BE10318}"
"Service"="intelide"

[HKEY_LOCAL_MACHINE\SYSTEM_VM\ControlSet001\Control\CriticalDeviceDatabase\↪
pci#ven_8086&dev_2411]
"ClassGUID"="{4D36E96A-E325-11CE-BFC1-08002BE10318}"
"Service"="intelide"

[HKEY_LOCAL_MACHINE\SYSTEM_VM\ControlSet001\Control\CriticalDeviceDatabase\↪
pci#ven_8086&dev_2421]
"ClassGUID"="{4D36E96A-E325-11CE-BFC1-08002BE10318}"
"Service"="intelide"

[HKEY_LOCAL_MACHINE\SYSTEM_VM\ControlSet001\Control\CriticalDeviceDatabase\↪
pci#ven_8086&dev_7010]
"ClassGUID"="{4D36E96A-E325-11CE-BFC1-08002BE10318}"
"Service"="intelide"

[HKEY_LOCAL_MACHINE\SYSTEM_VM\ControlSet001\Control\CriticalDeviceDatabase\↪
pci#ven_8086&dev_7111]
"ClassGUID"="{4D36E96A-E325-11CE-BFC1-08002BE10318}"
"Service"="intelide"

[HKEY_LOCAL_MACHINE\SYSTEM_VM\ControlSet001\Control\CriticalDeviceDatabase\↪
pci#ven_8086&dev_7199]
"ClassGUID"="{4D36E96A-E325-11CE-BFC1-08002BE10318}"
"Service"="intelide"

[HKEY_LOCAL_MACHINE\SYSTEM_VM\ControlSet001\Services\atapi]
"ErrorControl"=dword:00000001
"Group"="SCSI miniport"
"Start"=dword:00000000
"Tag"=dword:00000019
"Type"=dword:00000001
```

Part V: Physical to Virtual Migration

```
"DisplayName"="Standard IDE/ESDI Hard Disk Controller"
"ImagePath"=hex(2):53,00,79,00,73,00,74,00,65,00,6d,00,33,00,32,00,5c,00,44,00,\
   52,00,49,00,56,00,45,00,52,00,53,00,5c,00,61,00,74,00,61,00,70,00,69,00,2e,\
   00,73,00,79,00,73,00,00,00

[HKEY_LOCAL_MACHINE\SYSTEM_VM\ControlSet001\Services\IntelIde]
"ErrorControl"=dword:00000001
"Group"="System Bus Extender"
"Start"=dword:00000000
"Tag"=dword:00000004
"Type"=dword:00000001
"ImagePath"=hex(2):53,00,79,00,73,00,74,00,65,00,6d,00,33,00,32,00,5c,00,44,00,\
   52,00,49,00,56,00,45,00,52,00,53,00,5c,00,69,00,6e,00,74,00,65,00,6c,00,69,\
   00,64,00,65,00,2e,00,73,00,79,00,73,00,00,00

[HKEY_LOCAL_MACHINE\SYSTEM_VM\ControlSet001\Services\PCIIde]
"ErrorControl"=dword:00000001
"Group"="System Bus Extender"
"Start"=dword:00000000
"Tag"=dword:00000003
"Type"=dword:00000001
"ImagePath"=hex(2):53,00,79,00,73,00,74,00,65,00,6d,00,33,00,32,00,5c,00,44,00,\
   52,00,49,00,56,00,45,00,52,00,53,00,5c,00,70,00,63,00,69,00,69,00,64,00,65,\
   00,2e,00,73,00,79,00,73,00,00,00
```

Before you panic too much, this is actually a lot simpler than it first looks.

There are a lot of repeated `CriticalDeviceDatabase` entries, all of which have the same value for `ClassGUID`. (This means that you can quickly copy and paste the values for these keys.)

For the last three sections (under `ControlSet001\Services`) there is a long and confusing `ImagePath`. This is just the hexadecimal representation of a `REG_EXPAND_SZ`, which is actually a readable string when using regedit.exe. The values for the `atapi`, `IntelIde`, and `PCIIde` sections are `System32\DRIVERS\atapi.sys`, `System32\DRIVERS\intelide.sys`, and `System32\DRIVERS\PCIide.sys`, respectively.

These two points combined should make entering this data much easier. Of course, if you have a working virtual machine you could always run regedit.exe on it and export the keys listed so they could be easily imported on the new virtual machine.

> *If you were modifying a running system you would change these values in the HKEY_LOCAL_MACHINE\SYSTEM\CurrentControlSet section of the Registry. But CurrentControlSet does not exist when the computer is not running, so you need to update ControlSet001 instead.*

Now that you've completed loading the correct IDE drives, it's time to load the correct SCSI drivers. Loading the SCSI drivers offline is actually easier than loading the IDE drivers (which is ironic as preloading the SCSI drivers on a running system is very hard to do). You need only one file for this: aic78xx.sys. It needs to be in the system32\drivers directory under the Windows system directory. You can get this file from an existing virtual machine or by expanding aic78xx.sy_ off the installation media.

260

Chapter 13: Manual Physical to Virtual Migrations

Once the file is in place, you will need to load the following Registry information:

```
Windows Registry Editor Version 5.00

[HKEY_LOCAL_MACHINE\SYSTEM_VM\ControlSet001\Control\CriticalDeviceDatabase\
pci#ven_9004&dev_7078]
"Service"="aic78xx"
"ClassGUID"="{4D36E97B-E325-11CE-BFC1-08002BE10318}"

[HKEY_LOCAL_MACHINE\SYSTEM_VM\ControlSet001\Services\aic78xx]
"ErrorControl"=dword:00000001
"Group"="SCSI miniport"
"Start"=dword:00000000
"Tag"=dword:0000001e
"Type"=dword:00000001
"ImagePath"=hex(2):73,00,79,00,73,00,74,00,65,00,6d,00,33,00,32,00,5c,00,44,00,\
   52,00,49,00,56,00,45,00,52,00,53,00,5c,00,61,00,69,00,63,00,37,00,38,00,78,\
   00,78,00,2e,00,73,00,79,00,73,00,00,00
```

As with the IDE Registry keys, the `ImagePath` here is a hexadecimal representation of the REG_EXPAND_SZ, which is actually a string that reads `System32\DRIVERS\aic78xx.sys`.

Finally, you need to load the correct HAL and kernel files. The final step to editing an unprepared system image is getting the correct HAL and kernel files. This is also easier to do offline, as you do not need to worry about Windows protecting these files. So unlike when you are preparing a computer to be imaged, when you are editing an offline virtual machine you can just overwrite the old files with the new files. To get the correct files, you should do the following:

- ❏ Get a copy of the hal.dll, ntoskrnl.exe, and ntkrnlpa.exe files off an existing virtual machine.
- ❏ Expand halacpi.dl_ and ntoskrnl.ex_, and expand ntkrnlpa.exe from driver.cab.

All of these files should be copied into the system32 directory under the Windows system directory.

You may also want to get copies of kernel32.dll, ntdll.dll, win32k.sys, and winsrv.dll from whichever source you choose. It is not strictly required to update these files, but it is a good idea, as this way you can ensure that the core files are all at the same revision level and that there will be no incompatibilities.

Now you can save all the changes, unmount the virtual hard disk, and boot it under Virtual Server.

Migrating an Unprepared Windows NT 4.0 Server

Windows NT 4.0 has a very different driver model from Windows 2000 and later. One of the most notable differences is that Windows NT 4.0 does not support automatic detection of devices via plug and play. But, it still has the same requirements when it comes to fixing an unprepared system image so that it can be run inside of a virtual machine.

The first step to take is to create a new virtual machine and load the unprepared system image onto its virtual hard disk. Once you have done this, shut down the virtual machine and mount its virtual hard disk on the host operating system with VHDMount.

261

Part V: Physical to Virtual Migration

If the Windows NT 4.0 system is using an NTFS formatted hard disk, mounting the virtual hard disk will result in the NTFS being automatically updated to the latest version. When this happens, CHKDSK will stop working under NTFS until you install the hotfix for KB 872952.

Then you can perform the following offline modifications:

❑ **Load the correct IDE drivers.** The Windows NT 4.0 IDE driver needs only a single file: atapi.sys. You can get this file by copying it from an existing virtual machine running Windows NT 4.0 or copying atapi.sys directly off the installation media. (It is not compressed so you do not need to expand it.) You will then need to load the Registry information that follows. (Once again, the virtual machine's SYSTEM Registry section is loaded at HKEY_LOCAL_MACHINE\ SYSTEM_VM in the host Registry for this sample.)

```
Windows Registry Editor Version 5.00

[HKEY_LOCAL_MACHINE\SYSTEM_VM\ControlSet001\Control\Class\{4D36E97B-E325-11CE-↵
BFC1-08002BE10318}\0001]
"InfPath"="scsi.inf"
"InfSection"="atapi_Inst"
"ProviderName"="Microsoft"
"DriverDesc"="IDE CD-ROM (ATAPI 1.2)/Dual-channel PCI IDE Controller "

[HKEY_LOCAL_MACHINE\SYSTEM_VM\ControlSet001\Enum\Root\LEGACY_ATAPI]
"NextInstance"=dword:00000001

[HKEY_LOCAL_MACHINE\SYSTEM_VM\ControlSet001\Enum\Root\LEGACY_ATAPI\0000]
"BaseDevicePath"="HTREE\\ROOT\\0"
"ClassGUID"="{4D36E97B-E325-11CE-BFC1-08002BE10318}"
"Class"="SCSIAdapter"
"DeviceDesc"="IDE CD-ROM (ATAPI 1.2)/Dual-channel PCI IDE Controller "
"Driver"="{4D36E97B-E325-11CE-BFC1-08002BE10318}\\0001"
"Service"="atapi"
"Mfg"="(Standard mass storage controllers)"
"HardwareID"=hex(7):61,74,61,70,69,5f,73,63,73,69,00,00
"Problem"=dword:00000000
"StatusFlags"=dword:00000008
"FoundAtEnum"=dword:00000001
"ConfigFlags"=dword:00000000

[HKEY_LOCAL_MACHINE\SYSTEM_VM\ControlSet001\Services\atapi]
"Type"=dword:00000001
"Start"=dword:00000000
"Group"="SCSI miniport"
"ErrorControl"=dword:00000001
"Tag"=dword:00000019
"ImagePath"=hex(2):53,79,73,74,65,6d,33,32,5c,44,52,49,56,45,52,53,5c,61,74,61,\
  70,69,2e,73,79,73,00
"PlugPlayServiceType"=dword:00000001
```

The `ImagePath` value is a REG_EXPAND_SZ with the contents `System32\DRIVERS\atapi.sys`.

❑ **Load the correct SCSI drivers.** The Windows NT 4.0 SCSI driver also needs only a single file: aic78xx.sys. You can get this file by copying it from an existing virtual machine running

Chapter 13: Manual Physical to Virtual Migrations

Windows NT 4.0 or copying aic78xx.sys directly off the installation media (it is not compressed so you do not need to expand it). You then need to load the following Registry information.

```
Windows Registry Editor Version 5.00

[HKEY_LOCAL_MACHINE\SYSTEM_VM\ControlSet001\Control\Class\{4D36E97B-E325-11CE-
BFC1-08002BE10310}\0002]
"InfPath"="scsi.inf"
"InfSection"="aic78xx_Inst"
"ProviderName"="Microsoft"
"DriverDesc"="Adaptec AHA-294X/AHA-394X or AIC-78XX PCI SCSI Controller"

[HKEY_LOCAL_MACHINE\SYSTEM_VM\ControlSet001\Enum\Root\LEGACY_AIC78XX]

[HKEY_LOCAL_MACHINE\SYSTEM_VM\ControlSet001\Enum\Root\LEGACY_AIC78XX\0000]
"BaseDevicePath"="HTREE\\ROOT\\0"
"FoundAtEnum"=dword:00000001
"ClassGUID"="{4D36E97B-E325-11CE-BFC1-08002BE10318}"
"Class"="SCSIAdapter"
"StatusFlags"=dword:00000020
"Driver"="{4D36E97B-E325-11CE-BFC1-08002BE10318}\\0002"
"Mfg"="Adaptec"
"HardwareID"=hex(7):70,63,69,5c,76,65,6e,5f,39,30,30,34,26,64,65,76,5f,37,31,\
  37,38,00,00
"Service"="aic78xx"
"DeviceDesc"="Adaptec AHA-294X/AHA-394X or AIC-78XX PCI SCSI Controller"
"ConfigFlags"=dword:00000000

[HKEY_LOCAL_MACHINE\SYSTEM_VM\CurrentControlSet\Services\aic78xx]
"ErrorControl"=dword:00000001
"Group"="SCSI miniport"
"Start"=dword:00000000
"Tag"=dword:0000001e
"Type"=dword:00000001
"ImagePath"=hex(2):73,00,79,00,73,00,74,00,65,00,6d,00,33,00,32,00,5c,00,44,00,\
  52,00,49,00,56,00,45,00,52,00,53,00,5c,00,61,00,69,00,63,00,37,00,38,00,78,\
  00,78,00,2e,00,73,00,79,00,73,00,00,00
```

The `ImagePath` value is a REG_EXPAND_SZ with the contents `System32\DRIVERS\aic78xx.sys`.

❑ **Load the correct HAL and kernel files.** The final step to editing an unprepared system image is getting the correct HAL and kernel files. To get the correct files you should do the following:

   ❑ Get a copy of the hal.dll and ntoskrnl.exe files off an existing virtual machine.

   ❑ Expand hal.dl_ and ntoskrnl.ex_.

All of these files should be copied into the system32 directory under the Windows system directory.

You may also want to get copies of kernel32.dll, ntdll.dll, win32k.sys, and winsrv.dll from whichever source you choose. It is not strictly required to update these files, but it is a good idea as this way you can ensure that the core files are all at the same revision level and that there will be no incompatibilities.

Now you can save all the changes, unmount the virtual hard disk, and boot it under Virtual Server.

Part V: Physical to Virtual Migration

Migrating an Unprepared Red Hat Enterprise Linux 4 Server

If you have an unprepared system image of a Red Hat Enterprise Linux 4 computer that was installed on hardware which had an IDE controller, you should be able to just load the image and start the virtual machine. During the first boot, you will see a screen that displays **Welcome to Kudzu**. Press a key so that it does not bypass this tool. Kudzu is used by Red Hat Enterprise Linux to respond to any hardware changes that are detected.

When Kudzu starts, it will list all of the hardware devices that are no longer in the system. You should choose to remove the configuration for each device. It will also detect any new hardware (such as the DEC 21140 network adapter) and allow you to configure it.

If you have a custom-compiled kernel that does not load correctly under Virtual Server, you will need to replace it with one of the standard kernels provided by Red Hat. The easiest way to do this is to attach the virtual hard disk for the migrated system as a secondary disk on an existing Linux virtual machine. You can then overwrite the custom-compiled kernel with the standard kernel from the Red Hat installation media.

> You may have noticed that I have not discussed how to perform a system image-based migration of Windows Vista. The reason for this is that the Windows Vista Complete PC backup process is actually a system image-based backup. If you want to migrate a Windows Vista system using a different imaging tool, you can do so, but the same process should be followed.

Cleaning Up After the Migration

For each of these operating systems, only the basic changes have been made to allow the operating system to boot under a virtual machine. There are still a number of changes that need to be made after the system has been migrated.

Windows Server 2003, Windows XP, and Windows Vista

Windows Server 2003, Windows XP, and Windows Vista should be able to automatically detect and install all of the necessary drivers that are needed inside the virtual machine. You need to make two changes:

❑ Install Virtual Machine Additions.

❑ Remove any drivers that are no longer needed. Drivers for hardware devices that are no longer present can cause system instability and should be uninstalled. In the worst case situations these drivers can cause the operating system to boot. If this happens you should boot Windows in safe mode and disable the unnecessary drivers.

Chapter 13: Manual Physical to Virtual Migrations

Windows 2000

Windows 2000 has the same cleanup requirements as Windows Server 2003, Windows XP, and Windows Vista, but there is one difference to be aware of. With Windows Server 2003, Windows XP, and Windows Vista, Windows is able to detect that the virtual machine has a different keyboard and mouse and install the drivers automatically.

Windows 2000 is able to detect the keyboard and mouse that are used by the virtual machine and install the appropriate drivers. But these drivers will not work until after the virtual machine is rebooted. This means that if you start your Windows 2000 virtual machine and do not have mouse or keyboard input, you need to wait until the drivers are automatically installed and then manually reset the virtual machine.

Unfortunately there is no indication as to when these drivers have been installed. In my experience if you wait at least five minutes after the virtual machine has booted before restarting it, the drivers will be installed on the next boot.

Windows NT 4.0

Windows NT 4.0 does not support automatic detection of new hardware as the later versions of Windows do. As such, when you have finished migrating your Windows NT 4.0 computer, you need to do the following:

❏ Manually uninstall any drivers that were needed on the hardware system that are no longer needed in the virtual machine.

❏ Install Virtual Machine Additions.

❏ Manually configure the network adapter. Follow these steps:

1. On the Virtual Server administrative website, select **Configure** from the **Virtual Machines** section of the navigation pane, and then click your virtual machine.

2. Click **Floppy Drive**.

3. Select the **NT4 Network Driver.vfd** entry from the **Known floppy disks** drop-down and click **OK**.

4. Log in to the guest operating system with an administrative user account.

5. Right-click **Network Neighborhood** on the desktop and select **Properties**.

6. Change to the **Adapters** tab.

7. Remove any existing network adapters.

8. Click **Add** and then click **Have Disk**.

9. Make sure **A:** is specified and click **OK**.

10. Select **DEC PCI Fast Ethernet DECchip 21140** and click **OK** three times.

You will need to, remove **NT4 Network Driver.vfd** from the floppy drive and reboot the virtual machine for these changes to take effect.

265

Part V: Physical to Virtual Migration

Conclusion

Performing a manual physical to virtual migration is not the easiest thing to do, but at times it is the best method to use for getting a system up and running inside a virtual machine. By now, you should know all the ins and outs of manually migrating Windows Server 2003, Windows XP, Windows 2000, Windows NT 4.0, Windows Vista, and Red Hat Enterprise Linux 4 computers.

If you can use the backup tools that are part of the operating system to migrate the physical computer to a virtual machine, this is definitely preferable. But there are also viable options for performing image-based migrations. It is even possible to migrate a physical computer using a completely unprepared system image.

266

Part VI
Virtual Machines and Clustering

Chapter 14: Clustering Virtual Machines

Chapter 15: Clustering Virtual Server

14

Clustering Virtual Machines

Virtual Server supports three different kinds of clustering: virtual machine clustering with emulated SCSI, virtual machine clustering with iSCSI, and Virtual Server clustering. Each of these clustering configurations has its own strengths and weaknesses and different reasons for using it. This chapter discusses how to set up a virtual machine clusters with emulated SCSI and with iSCSI.

Clustering with Emulated SCSI

When using emulated SCSI for virtual machine clustering, you have two virtual machines that are connected to the same virtual hard disk, which operates as a shared SCSI device. The advantage of this configuration is that you can recreate an authentic replication of a clustered computer system on a single computer, without needing any special hardware. The problem with this configuration is that both virtual machines always need to be on the same physical computer, which means that you gain no availability increases with this form of clustering. This configuration is also restricted to have only two virtual machines configured in the cluster.

This clustering configuration should never be used in a production environment because of the requirement that all virtual machines be on the same computer, but it is very useful for development and testing environments. It is also useful for training situations in which you want to teach yourself or others about how to configure clustered applications.

Preparing Virtual Server

This chapter assumes you are setting up a completely isolated clustering environment (which has no access to an external network). This involves setting up some extra virtual machines that you may not need if you were connecting your cluster to an existing network with the necessary infrastructure. This setup has the following requirements:

- ❑ One Windows Server 2003 virtual machine configured as a domain controller
- ❑ Two Windows Server 2003 Enterprise Edition virtual machines to be configured as a cluster

Part VI: Virtual Machines and Clustering

- ❏ One Windows virtual machine to act as a client computer when testing out the cluster
- ❏ One internal virtual network to be used as the "public" network that all virtual machines are connected to
- ❏ One internal virtual network to be used as the "private" network that will be used by the clustered virtual machines
- ❏ One 500MB fixed-size virtual hard disk to be used as the clusters quorum disk
- ❏ One 10GB fixed-size virtual hard disk to be used as shared media for the clustered virtual machines

Both these virtual hard disks will be configured as shared virtual hard disks. Virtual Server only allows you to configured fixed-size virtual hard disks as shared virtual hard disks.

If you consider that as a private cluster configuration, there will be only one user (you) connected to the cluster, it is possible to configure these virtual machines with minimal amounts of memory. The 256MB of RAM per virtual machine should result in acceptable performance, although depending on the application that you are running on the clustered virtual machine you may need to increase the amount of memory for the clustered computers (the domain controller and client computer should not need more memory, however). This means that you need a computer with 1.5 to 2GB RAM for a basic configuration.

Planning for approximately 5GB of storage space per virtual machine, plus the space for the fixed-size virtual hard disk, means that your host computer should have just over 30GB of free storage space.

In order to reduce the amount of time needed to set up the cluster, I recommend that you create a base Windows Server 2003 Enterprise Edition virtual machine that you can quickly copy to make the four virtual machines needed.

Refer to Chapter 5 for information on creating base virtual machines.

To create the two virtual networks, follow these steps:

1. Open the Virtual Server administrative website.
2. Click **Create** in the **Virtual Networks** section of the navigation pane.
3. Fill in the appropriate details for the virtual network name and notes, and leave the **Network adapter on physical computer** setting at **None (Guests Only)**.
4. Click **OK**.

Execute these steps twice. Call one virtual network "Public cluster network" and specify in the notes that this virtual network will be used as the "public" network for the virtual machine cluster (even though it is not really a public network as it is not connected to the real world in any way). Call the other virtual network "Private cluster network" and specify in the notes that this is the private network used for the virtual machine cluster, and that virtual machines that are part of the cluster should be attached to it.

270

Chapter 14: Clustering Virtual Machines

The final preparation is to create the two fixed-size disks:

1. On the Virtual Server administrative website, click **Create** and then **Fixed Size Virtual Hard Disk** in the **Virtual Disks** section of the navigation pane.

2. Enter an appropriate path (the location where you intend the files for the clustered virtual machines to be stored) and name the first virtual hard disk quorum.vhd (as it will be used as the quorum disk).

3. Specify a size of 500MB and click OK.

4. You will be returned to the main status page, with an indicator that the quorum disk is being created. While this is happening you can create the shared data disk (there is no need to wait for the quorum disk to be created).

5. Click **Create** and then **Fixed Size Virtual Hard Disk** under the **Virtual Disks** section of the navigation pane again.

6. Enter the same path as used in Step 2, but this time name the virtual hard disk sharedData.vhd.

7. Specify a size of 10GB and click **OK**.

   This last step will take a while as Virtual Server will need to write out the entire 10GB of the new virtual hard disk.

You now have all the pieces you need; it is time to start setting up the virtual machines.

Setting Up the Domain Controller

For the domain controller, create a virtual machine with a 16GB virtual hard disk and 256MB of RAM. Give it one virtual network adapter that is connected to the Public cluster network. Name the virtual machine **Cluster - Domain Controller**.

Now either install Windows Server 2003, or use a base virtual machine to get Windows Server 2003 ready to go. Under the guest operating system, give the computer a network name of ClusterDC and specify a secure administrative password.

Some people recommend using the same name for the virtual machine name under Virtual Server and the guest operating system's network name. In large virtualization environments this certainly makes it easier to correlate network services with virtual machines, but in small development and test environments I find this to be quite restrictive on the virtual machine name, and as a result I give my virtual machines more descriptive names.

It is a good idea to use a different password for the Domain Administrator account than the password that you use for the Local Administrator account on all the other virtual machines. Not only is this a good security practice, but it will help you to ensure that you always know when you are logging in with the Domain Administrator account of the Local Administrator account.

To configure a static IP address for the domain controller, follow these steps:

1. Open the **Start** menu; then select **Control Panel** ⇨ **Network Connections** ⇨ **Local Area Connection**.

2. Click on **Properties**.

271

Part VI: Virtual Machines and Clustering

3. Select **Internet protocol (TCP/IP)** and click **Properties**.

4. For the **IP address** use 10.0.0.1.

5. For the **Subnet mask** use 255.0.0.0.

6. Leave the **Default gateway** entry blank.

7. For the **DNS** use 10.0.0.1.

It is usually recommended that domain controllers be configured with a static IP address.

After doing this, promote the virtual machine to be a domain controller:

1. Run **DCPromo**.

2. Proceed through the **Active Directory Installation Wizard** until you get to the **Domain Controller Type** page. On this page, select **Domain controller for a new domain**.

3. On the **Create New Domain** page select **Domain in a new forest**.

4. On the **New Domain Name** page enter the name for your test domain. VMCluster.test is a good name to use.

5. On the **NetBIOS Domain Name** page, specify the NetBIOS name to be used for the domain. In most cases you'll be able to accept the default value that is offered here.

6. Accept the default values on the **Database and Logs Folders** and the **Shared System Volume** pages.

7. On the **DNS Registration Diagnostics** page, select **Install and configure the DNS server on this computer, and set this computer to use this DNS server as its preferred DNS server**.

8. On the **Permissions** page, select **Permissions compatible only with Windows 2000 or Windows server 2003 operating systems**.

9. Enter an appropriate restore mode password on the **Directory Services Restore Mode Administrator Password** page.

10. Complete the wizard.

You may be prompted to provide the Windows Server installation media during this process.

The domain controller is now all configured and ready to go.

Usually you would want to configure a DHCP server on your network. However given that you will have only four virtual machines configured on this network, setting up a DHCP server would be overkill. Using static IP addresses for all the virtual machines involved will be easy enough.

Preparing the Cluster Nodes

Computers that are part of a cluster are referred to as cluster nodes. This cluster will have two cluster nodes. Create two virtual machines, one for each node. Each virtual machine should be configured with 512MB of RAM and a 16GB virtual hard disk. One virtual machine should be called **cluster - node 1**, while the other virtual machine should be called **cluster - node 2**.

272

Chapter 14: Clustering Virtual Machines

Each cluster node virtual machine should be configured with two SCSI adapters and two network adapters.

If the cluster node virtual machines are configured to boot off a SCSI adapter, they should have a third SCSI adapter configured. One of the SCSI adapters will need to be used for the quorum disk, while the other SCSI adapter will need to be used for the shared data virtual hard disk. These adapters cannot be used by the boot disk.

To add a SCSI adapter to the virtual machine:

1. On the Virtual Server Administrative Website, click **Configure** from the **Virtual Machines** section of the navigation page, and click the virtual machine you want to configure.

2. Click **SCSI adapters**.

3. Click **Add SCSI Adapter**.

4. Click **OK**.

Follow these steps too add a network adapter to the virtual machine:

1. Open the virtual machine configuration page.

2. Click **Network Adapters**.

3. Click **Add Network Adapter**.

4. Click **OK**.

One of the virtual network adapters should be connected to the private cluster network, while the other one should be connected to the public cluster network.

Boot each of the cluster node virtual machines and configure the following:

1. Create a secure administrator password.

2. Configure the virtual machines to use static IP addresses. Cluster node 1 should have an IP address of 10.0.0.2 on the network adapter that is connected to the public cluster network (and the same subnet mask and DNS settings as the cluster domain controller). Cluster node 2 should have an IP address of 10.0.0.3.

In order to help differentiate the private network connection from a public network connection when you're inside the virtual machine it is a good idea to set a custom name for the network connection:

1. Open the **Start** menu, and select **Control Panel** and then **Network Connections**. Find the entry for **Local Area Connection**.

2. Right-click on **Local Area Connection**.

3. Click on **Rename**, and enter the name that you want to use for the **Local Area Connection**.

You can name the connection for the private network **Private Connection,** and the connection for the public network, the **Public Connection.**

273

Part VI: Virtual Machines and Clustering

Confirming the Correct SCSI Adapter Driver Is Installed

If Virtual Machine Additions is installed when the virtual machine does not have a SCSI adapter configured, it is possible that the wrong driver will be used for the SCSI adapter. This can be very problematic in a clustered environment. To check that the correct driver is being used for the SCSI adapter:

1. Boot the virtual machine and log in to the guest operating system.

2. Open the Start menu, and then open Administrative Tools and Computer Management.

3. Click Device Manager.

4. Expand SCSI and RAID controllers.

5. If you see an entry that reads **Adaptec AIC-7870 PCI SCSI Controller**, Virtual Machine Additions has not installed correctly. If all the entries read **Microsoft Virtual Machine PCI SCSI Controller**, then Virtual Machine Additions is installed correctly.

If you have the wrong driver loaded, you can correct this by either reinstalling Virtual Machine Additions, or by following these steps:

1. Select the Adaptec AIC-7870 PCI SCSI Controller entry from the Device Manager.

2. Open the **Action** menu and select **Update Driver**.

3. In the **Hardware Update Wizard** select **Install the software automatically (Recommended)**.

4. Complete the wizard.

Usually, Windows will use the name Local Area Connection for the first network card in your computer, and Local Area Connection 2 for the second network card (and so on). If you want to confirm that the network connection maps to the network card that you think it does, you can do the following:

1. Open the properties for network connection that you are interested in.

2. Click the **Configure** button that is next to the item that says **Intel 21140-Based PCI Fast Ethernet**.

3. You should see a field called **Location**. The value for this field will read something like **PCI Slot 3 (PCI bus 0, a device 10, function 0)**. The number you are interested in is the function number. The first network card in the virtual machine will have a function number of 0. The second network card in the virtual machine will have a function number of 1 (and so on).

4. Join the cluster nodes to the domain, and configure the NetBIOS name for each to ClusterNode1 and ClusterNode2, respectively.

You are now ready to begin setting up the cluster, after you have installed Virtual Machine Additions on all the machines in this configuration.

274

Chapter 14: Clustering Virtual Machines

Setting Up the Cluster

Setting up a Windows Server cluster is a relatively complex process. A number of steps are involved.

Configuring the Private Cluster Network

With both cluster node virtual machines running, it is time to set up the private cluster network. Inside cluster node 1 do the following:

1. Configure the network card, which is connected to the private cluster network with an **IP address** of 192.168.1.2 and a **Subnet mask** of 255.255.255.0.

2. Ensure that no **Default gateway** or **DNS server** addresses are configured.

3. While on the **Internet Protocol (TCP/IP) Properties** page, click on the **Advanced** button.

4. On the **Advanced TCP/IP Settings** dialog box, change to the **WINS** tab.

5. Make sure that no WINS servers are configured.

6. Select Disable NetBIOS over TCP/IP in the NetBIOS setting area.

   It is important to disable NetBIOS over TCP/IP on the private network connection, as this will stop you from having problems that could occur if the virtual machine tried to communicate over the private network for public network communications.

Repeat this process for the second cluster node virtual machine, but use an **IP address** of 192.168.1.3.

Now test that IP connectivity and name resolution are working correctly on all the virtual machines. To do this, log in to each of the cluster node virtual machines and then ping the other machines, both by their names and by their IP addresses. When pinging the cluster node virtual machines by their names you should ensure that you are connecting via the public IP address (10.0.0.X).

Creating the Cluster User Account

Clustering requires the use of a domain user account that is a member of the local administrators group on all the cluster nodes. As a security best practice, you should not use a domain administrator account for this purpose. To do this you need do the following:

1. Log in to the domain controller virtual machine with a domain administrator account.

2. Select **Start ⇨ Administrative Tools ⇨ Active Directory Users and Computers**.

3. Expand the entry for the VMCluster domain and click the **Users** node.

4. Open the **Action** menu and select **New** and then **User**.

5. Type in **cluster** for the **First name**, and **service** for the **Last name**.

6. For the **User logon name**, enter **cluster**, and click **Next**.

7. Enter a secure password for the account.

8. Uncheck **User must change password at next logon**, and check **Password never expires**.

9. Click **Next** and then **Finish**.

10. Log in to the first cluster node virtual machine.

275

Part VI: Virtual Machines and Clustering

11. Select **Start** menu ⇨ **Administrative Tools** ⇨ **Computer Management**.

12. Expand the **Local Users and Groups** node and click the **Groups** node.

13. Select the **Administrators** group.

14. Open the **Action** menu and select **Add to Group**.

15. Click the **Add** button.

16. Type in **cluster** and click **OK**.

If you are logged in with a non-domain account, you will be prompted to provide domain credentials at this stage.

17. Click **OK** again.

18. Repeat Steps 10 through 17 on the second cluster node virtual machine.

Now shut down both cluster node virtual machines.

Configuring the Shared Disks

It is now time to connect the shared disks to each of the clustered node virtual machines.

> **Do not have both cluster node virtual machines running at the same time when the shared disks are attached, until you have the cluster service installed. If you do this, you will suffer data corruption and possibly worse.**

To connect the shared disks to the first cluster node virtual machine, follow these steps:

1. Open the Virtual Server administrative website and choose to configure the first cluster node virtual machine.

2. Click **SCSI Adapters**.

3. Check the **Share SCSI bus for clustering** option on the first SCSI adapter (or the second SCSI adapter if you are using the first SCSI adapter for your boot virtual hard disk).

4. Do the same for the second SCSI adapter (and the third SCSI adapter if you have three configured).

5. Click **OK**.

> **In order to enable the Share SCSI bus for clustering option, undo disks must not be enabled on the virtual machine. If you have undo disks enabled on your cluster node virtual machines you will need to go to the master status page and select to merge the existing undo disks and then disable undo disks. The option to merge the undo disks is available from the contextual action menu that appears for the virtual machine name.**

276

Chapter 14: Clustering Virtual Machines

6. Return to the virtual machine configuration page and click **Hard disks**.

7. Click the **Add disk** button.

8. On the new virtual hard disk entry, change the **Attachment** to location 0 on the first shared SCSI adapter.

Once the SCSI adapter has been marked as shared it is allowed to have only one virtual hard disk connected to it. This means that location 0 is now the only valid location on the shared SCSI adapter.

9. Enter the full path and file name for the quorum virtual hard disk that you created earlier.

10. Repeat Steps 7 through 9 to attach the shared data virtual hard disk, which you created earlier, to the second shared SCSI adapter.

11. Click **OK**.

Do not power on the first cluster node virtual machine at this stage, but repeat the preceding steps for the second cluster node virtual machine.

Now power on only the first cluster node virtual machine and follow these steps:

1. Log in using a local administrator account.

2. Select **Start ➪ Administrative Tools ➪ Computer Management**.

3. Click the **Disk Management** node. At this stage, the **Initialize and Convert Disk Wizard** should open automatically.

4. On the **Select Disks to Initialize** page, make sure both disks are checked.

5. On the **Select Disks to Convert** page, make sure that both disks are not checked.

If the disks are checked on this page they will be converted to dynamic disks, which are not supported in Windows Server clustering.

After completing the Initialize and Convert Disk Wizard, you should see both of the new virtual hard disks listed.

6. Click the unallocated space on the first new hard disk (it should be approximately 500MB in size).

7. Open the **Action** menu, and select **All Tasks** and then **New Partition**.

8. On the **Select Partition Type** page of the **New Partition Wizard** select **Primary partition** and click **Next**.

9. Accept the default value on the **Specify Partition Size** page.

10. On the **Assign Drive Letter or Path** page, choose to assign the letter Q to the new drive.

It is a standard best practice with Windows Server clustering to assign the letter Q to the quorum drive. Extra shared hard disks should be assigned letters that increase after this (R, S, and so on).

11. On the **Format Partition** page, specify a **Volume label** of "Quorum drive."

Assigning a volume label is very important because it allows you to correctly identify the drive when you are accessing it from either cluster node.

Part VI: Virtual Machines and Clustering

12. Complete the New Partition Wizard.

13. Repeat Steps 6 through 12 for the second new hard disk (although this time the unallocated space should be approximately 10GB in size, the drive letter that should be assigned is R, and the volume label should be "Shared data drive").

Now it is time to test that the shared virtual hard disks are connected to both cluster node virtual machines correctly. As the first cluster node virtual machine is currently running, open Notepad on it and type in a test string. Save this to a new text file on the Q drive, and then do the same for the R drive. Close Notepad and attempt to open both of these text files to confirm that they were saved correctly.

Now shut down the first cluster node virtual machine and power on the second cluster node virtual machine (remember that both virtual machines should not be running at the same time at this stage). Log in to the second cluster node virtual machine and open up **Computer Management** and then **Disk Management**. You should see that both the shared virtual hard disks have partitions on them that have not had drive letters assigned to them. To assign drive letters, follow these steps:

1. Click on the partition.

2. Open the **Action** menu, and select **All Tasks** and then **change drive letter and paths**.

3. Click the **Add** button.

4. Select **Assign the following drive letter** and choose Q for the quorum drive and R for the shared data drive.

Repeat the testing process of creating text files and then confirming that you can open and read their contents on the second cluster node virtual machine. When you're done, shut down the second cluster node virtual machine.

Configuring the Cluster Service

Ensure that the second cluster node virtual machine is not running and power on the first cluster node virtual machine. Then follow these steps:

1. Log in to the first cluster node virtual machine with a domain administrator account.

2. Select **Start** menu ⇨ **Administrative Tools** ⇨ **Cluster Administrator**.

3. On the **Open Connection to Cluster** dialog box, select **Create new cluster** as the **Action**, and click **OK**.

4. This will launch the **New Server Cluster Wizard**.

5. On the **Cluster Name and Domain** page, enter a **Cluster name** of **TestCluster**.

   If you are not logged in with a domain administrator account you, will be prompted to provide domain administrator credentials at this stage.

6. Accept the default values on the **Select Computer** page and click **Next**.

7. Wait while the **New Server Cluster Wizard** analyzes your configuration and identifies any issues.

   If you are using a SCSI boot disk, no issues should be identified. If you are using an IDE boot disk, you can ignore the warning message.

278

Chapter 14: Clustering Virtual Machines

8. On the **IP address** page you need to enter an IP address that will be used for the cluster. Enter 10.0.0.10.

9. On the **Cluster Service Account** page, enter the details of the cluster service account that you created earlier (the user name should be cluster).

10. On the **Proposed Cluster Configuration** page, review the summary that is provided and ensure that all the details are correct. Then click the **Quorum** button.

11. In the **Cluster Configuration Quorum** dialog box, select **Disk Q:** and click **OK**.

12. Complete the wizard to create the cluster.

13. Leave the first cluster node virtual machine running and start the second cluster node virtual machine. Wait until the second cluster node virtual machine finishes booting, but do not log in to it.

14. In the **Cluster Administrator**, on the first cluster node virtual machine, open the **File** menu and select **New and** then **Node**.

15. On the **Select Computers** page of the **Add Nodes Wizard** enter **ClusterNode2** in the **Computer name** field, and click the **Add** button.

16. On the **Cluster Service Account** page, provide the password for the cluster service account.

17. Complete the wizard to join the second cluster node virtual machine to the cluster.

When adding down second cluster node, you'll most likely receive a warning alert in the "Reanalyzing cluster" step of the process. If this is caused by a `Status 0x00138f: The cluster resource` `could not be found` *error, it can be safely ignored. This warning is displayed because when the first cluster node virtual machine and second cluster node virtual machine access the shared storage they see different hardware identifiers on the shared storage. This is expected because of the way Virtual Server handles the shared storage, and Windows Server clustering is able to handle it correctly.*

Now it is time to ensure that the network connections are configured correctly for the cluster:

1. Using **Cluster Administrator**, expand the node for the cluster you have just created.

2. Expand the **Cluster Configuration** node and then select the **Networks** nodes.

3. Choose the network entry for the private cluster network.

4. Open the **File** menu and select **Properties**.

5. In the **Enable this network cluster use** group box, select the option for **Internal cluster communications only (private network)**.

6. Click **OK**.

The network for the public cluster network will be configured to be used for both private and public network communication by default. You can leave it configured like this, or you can go through the preceding steps and configure it to be used for public communication only.

Now you need to ensure that networks are prioritized in the right order:

1. Using **Cluster Administrator**, select the node for the cluster you have just created.

2. Open the **File** menu and select **Properties**.

279

Part VI: Virtual Machines and Clustering

3. Change to the **Network Priority**.

4. The private cluster network should be listed first, and the public cluster network should be listed second. If this is not the case, use the **Move Up** and **Move Down** buttons to correct the order of the network connections.

Setting Up a Simple Cluster Application

You now have a cluster configured and working.

You can test this by going into the **Cluster Administrator**, expanding the TESTCLUSTER node, expanding **Groups**, and selecting **Cluster Group**. You should see **ClusterNode1** listed as the owner for all of the resources is in **Cluster Group**. Right-click the **Cluster Group** node, and select **Move Group**.

The cluster will organize to move the resources for Cluster Group from ClusterNode1 to ClusterNode2. If you open **My Computer** on **ClusterNode1** at this stage, you will see that **ClusterNode1** does not have access to the Q: drive (which is a resource of Cluster Group). If you use the **Cluster Administrator** to move **Cluster Group** again, you will see that **ClusterNode1** regained access to the Q: drive.

This is all very nice, but to really test the cluster configuration you need to set up a simple cluster application. Creating a clustered file share is a good point to start. To do this, follow these steps:

1. Open **Cluster Administrator**.

2. Expand the **Groups** node, and then select **Group 0**.

3. Select **Disk R:**.

4. Open the **File** menu and select **Change Group**, and then select **Cluster Group**.

5. Click **Yes** in the confirmation dialog box.

6. Click **Group 0** again.

   *You need to do this so that **Cluster Administrator** will update the options that are available on the File menu, now that the last resource has been removed from Group 0.*

7. Open the **File** menu and select **Delete**.

8. Now select Cluster Group, open the **File** menu, and select **Configure Application**.

9. On the **Select or Create a New Virtual Server** page, choose the option to **Use an existing virtual server**. Then select the **Cluster Group** space for the **Virtual server** and click **Next**.

   Ironically Windows Server clustering also uses the phrase "virtual server." This actually has nothing to do with Microsoft Virtual Server itself, but is rather clustering's way of referring to the fact that it creates an imaginary server that is backed by different physical servers.

10. On the **Create Application Clustered Resource** page, choose **Yes, create a cluster resource for my application now** and click **Next**.

11. On the **Application Resource Type** page, choose a **Resource type** of **File Share**.

12. Provide an appropriate **Name** and **Description** for the new clustered file share application (I will be calling my application "Clustered File Share").

280

Chapter 14: Clustering Virtual Machines

13. Click on the **Advanced Properties** button.

14. Change to the **Dependencies** tab and click the **Modify** button.

15. In the **Modify Dependencies** dialog box make the **Cluster IP Address**, **Cluster Name** and **Disk R:** dependencies. Click **OK** twice and then click **Next**.

By configuring the dependencies correctly, you are telling Windows Server clustering that these resources need to be brought online before the clustered file share can be brought online.

16. On the **File Share Parameters** page, you will need to specify the **Share name** (I am using clusteredFileShare), the **Path** (this should be R:\), and a **Comment** users see about the share.

If you want to use a subfolder on the R: drive for your file share instead, you will need to manually create it before completing this page.

17. Click the **Permissions** button to configure the permissions for the new file share. You can configure the permissions whichever way you like. I will be leaving the default setting of everyone having read access and granting full control to Domain Admins. After you have configured this, click **Next** and then **Finish**.

18. Click on the new entry for your clustered file share in **Cluster Administrator**.

19. Open the **File** menu and select **Bring Online**.

And now the cluster is actually providing a service to your network.

Setting Up a Client Virtual Machine and Testing the Cluster

The final step with this emulated cluster is to create a client virtual machine that can access it just like client computer would access the cluster in the real world. For this you need to create a fourth virtual machine using the same process that was used to create the three virtual machines.

The client virtual machine does not need to have that much memory so 256MB should be sufficient. It will need only a 16GB virtual hard drive and one network connection. It should be connected to the public cluster network. You will need to:

1. Get a copy of Windows running on the client virtual machine.

You could use any version of Windows for the client virtual machine; however, I will be using Windows Server 2003 Enterprise Edition because it allows me to reuse the base image that I used for the other three virtual machines. It also gives me access to Cluster Administrator from the client virtual machine, so that I can perform various tasks on the cluster while I am testing it.

2. Boot the client virtual machine and log in to Windows.

3. Configure the client virtual machine with an **IP address** of 10.0.0.4, a **Subnet mask** of 255.0.0.0, and a **DNS** of 10.0.0.1.

4. Give the client virtual machine and network the name **ClusterClient** and join it to the **VMCluster** domain.

5. Log in to the client virtual machine with the Domain Administrator account.

6. Open a command prompt and run `net use X: \\TestCluster\clusteredFileShare`.

281

Part VI: Virtual Machines and Clustering

7. Open **My Computer** and copy something to the X: drive (I am copying the I386 directory of my installation media).

8. After the files are copied, open **Cluster Administrator** and choose to connect to the TestCluster.

9. Select the **Cluster Group** node from **TESTCLUSTER**.

10. Open the **File** menu and select **Move Group**.

You should now see all the resources go offline and come back online on the other cluster node. Once all the resources are back online, return to **My Computer**, and you should see that you can still access the files that you copied to the X: drive. Now you have everything configured to use your emulated cluster of virtual machines.

Clustering with iSCSI

iSCSI is a new technology for accessing network-based storage. It involves encapsulating standard SCSI communication over the top of the IP network protocol. Microsoft added support for iSCSI devices to Windows Server 2003 SP1. iSCSI is of particular interest to virtual machines as it is capable of being used by standard computers with no specific hardware requirements, which means that virtual machines can use it, too.

Clustering virtual machines with iSCSI allows you to create a cluster with multiple virtual machines that are connected to an iSCSI disk over a standard network connection. With this approach, you can cluster up to eight virtual machines running on separate host operating systems. Here, you do get the benefits of increased hardware availability, and you can have more than two virtual machines in a cluster. However, this approach requires that you have an iSCSI disk available for use. It also has the lowest performance of all possible cluster configurations because of the overhead involved with networking inside of a virtual machine.

Clustering virtual machines with iSCSI is recommended for production environments that want to increase the availability of their virtual machines but that are not running heavy loads on the virtual machines themselves.

Understanding iSCSI

When working with iSCSI, you need to know a few basic terms. An iSCSI target is any shared storage that is accessible over iSCSI. An iSCSI initiator is the device that allows a computer to connect to an iSCSI target. For both iSCSI targets and iSCSI initiators there are hardware and software versions. Hardware iSCSI initiators come in the form of HBA (Host Bus Adapter) cards that you install into physical computers, which in turn appear like storage controller cards to the physical computer. You cannot use hardware iSCSI initiators directly inside virtual machines. You can, however, use software iSCSI initiators. Windows Server 2003 is the first version of Windows that includes a built-in software iSCSI initiator. You can use this inside of the virtual machines to connect to both hardware and software iSCSI targets.

Using iSCSI for clustering does add one complication. For the standard, the cluster configuration, you have two separate networks. One network is the public network, to which all the computers are

Chapter 14: Clustering Virtual Machines

connected, while the other network is the private network, which is used for internal cluster communication. When you add iSCSI into the picture, Microsoft recommends that you have a third isolated network to be used solely for iSCSI communication.

Preparing the Environment for iSCSI Clustering

As with emulated SCSI disk clustering, you need to have a domain controller and a public and private network (as well as the network for iSCSI communication). However, as you are likely to be configuring multiple virtual machines on separate host operating systems, you need to use a physically separate domain controller and a physically separate public, private, and iSCSI network. Furthermore, you don't need to create any fixed-size virtual hard disks to use the quorum shared data disks.

You need to do the following:

1. Ensure that there is a domain controller that all Virtual Server host operating systems can access, a physically separate private network running between all Virtual Server host operating systems, and a physically separate private network running between all Virtual Server host operating systems for connection to the iSCSI target.

   If you do not have such a domain controller, follow the directions in the "Setting Up a Domain Controller" section of this chapter. While a domain controller should be physically separate from all of the Virtual Server instances that are hosting clustered virtual machines, there is no reason why it cannot be in a virtual machine on another physical computer.

2. Create a virtual network on each Virtual Server instance that is connected to the public physical network (name this virtual network "Public Network").

3. Create a virtual network on each Virtual Server instance that is connected to the private physical network (name this virtual network "Private Network").

4. Create a virtual network on each Virtual Server instance that is connected to the private iSCSI physical network (name this virtual network "iSCSI network").

5. Create a virtual machine for each planned cluster node (you can have up to eight) and configure it with three network cards.

   You do not need to configure in shared SCSI controllers when you are using iSCSI for clustering.

6. Configure the virtual network cards on each virtual machine to be connected to the public, private, and iSCSI networks respectively.

7. Install Windows Server 2003 SP1 Enterprise Edition on each of the virtual machines.

8. Configure the private network connection on each of the virtual machines in a way similar to what is outlined in the "Configuring the Private Cluster Network" section earlier in this chapter.

9. Configure the public network connection on each of the virtual machines in a way that is appropriate for your public network.

10. Configure the iSCSI network connection on each virtual machine with a static IP address on a private subnet.

Part VI: Virtual Machines and Clustering

11. Join each of the virtual machines to the domain, and ensure that they have appropriate network names.

12. Create a clustering user account on the domain (as discussed in the "Creating the Cluster User Account" section earlier on in this chapter).

During this process none of the cluster node virtual machines are connected to any shared storage, so there is no concern about having them all powered on the same time.

Setting Up a Software-Based iSCSI Target

A number of software packages are available that allow you to turn a standard computer into an iSCSI target. There are solutions that run under Windows or under Linux; some are commercial and some open source. For the purposes of this book, I use the StarWind software iSCSI target provided by RocketDivision. You can download a 15-day trial of StarWind from `www.rocketdivision.com`. Installing StarWind is very simple and straightforward. Once you have installed StarWind, you can double-click on the desktop icon to bring up the StarWind management console. You then need to do the following:

1. Click the `localhost: 3260` entry.

2. Open the **Connection** menu and select **Connect**.

3. You will be asked to provide a user name and password. The default user name and password are "test" and "test".

*You should change this user name and password as soon as possible. To do this, open the **Connection** menu and select **Edit Configuration**. In the **Edit Configuration** dialog box you can enter a new user name and password.*

4. Click the **Add device** icon.

5. Select **Image File device** for the **Device type** and click **Next**.

The StarWind iSCSI target supports the use of image-based devices and physical devices. I am using image-based devices in this chapter for convenience.

6. On the **Please specify Image File device parameters** page, click the **New image** button.

7. Specify the name and size of the image file to create.

8. Check the **Allow multiple connections (clustering)** option and click **Next**.

9. Specify a name for the target and click **Next**.

Repeat this process for any other iSCSI targets that you want to create.

Configuring Shared Data Drives

With all the virtual machines correctly configured for the network, and joined to the domain, power on the first cluster node virtual machine. The first thing you need to do is to install the Microsoft software iSCSI initiator. You can download this from `http://go.microsoft.com/fwlink/?LinkId=44352`.

284

Chapter 14: Clustering Virtual Machines

When you install it, you can follow the default settings and you soon have the software initiator installed. After it is installed, double-click the **Microsoft ISCSI Initiator** icon on the virtual machine's desktop.

Now you will need to do the following:

1. On the **Discovery** tab, click the **Add** button and provide the details about your iSCSI target server (the default TCP/IP port number is appropriate and does not need to be changed).

2. Once the iSCSI target server has been configured, you should be able to change to the **Targets** tab and see a list of available targets.

3. Select the iSCSI target, which the cluster will use as its quorum drive, and click the **Log On** button.

4. On the **Log On to Target** dialog box, you can check the option to **Automatically restore this connection when the system boots** and click **OK**.

5. On the **Bound Volumes/Devices** tab, click the **Bind All** button.

   *By configuring the quorum drive as a bound volume, Windows will ensure that this drive is always present and available when it is booted. This is critical for drives that are used by the cluster service. You can configure iSCSI target as bound volumes only if you select the **Automatically restore this connection when the system boots** option when you log on to the target.*

The iSCSI target is now connected to the virtual machine. You now need to do the following:

1. Open the **Start** menu, select **Administrative Tools** and then click **Computer Management**.

2. Click on the **Disk Management** node.

3. If this iSCSI target has never been attached to a computer before, you will need to initialize the partition and format it. Otherwise you'll just need to assign a drive letter to it.

   If you need to initialize the iSCSI target, remember that you should not make it a dynamic disk as this is not compatible with clustering.

   Also remember that it is a best practice to assign the letter Q as the drive letter for the quorum drive, and to assign increasing drive letters to the shared data drives after that.

Repeat this process for any other shared data drives that you want to be part of your cluster.

Configuring the Cluster

To configure the iSCSI-based cluster, you can follow the steps used in the "Configuring the Cluster Service" section from earlier in this chapter. The only difference is that once you have configured the cluster service on the first node, but before you try and add any extra nodes, you will need to log in to each of the separate cluster node virtual machines and use the Microsoft iSCSI software initiator to connect to the shared storage.

Do not connect the other cluster node virtual machines to the shared storage until you have set up the cluster service on the first cluster node virtual machine.

285

Part VI: Virtual Machines and Clustering

When you connect the other cluster node virtual machines to the shared storage you'll find that you will not be able to mount them using **Disk Management**. This is okay because the clustering service will mount them for you.

Your iSCSI-based cluster it is now ready for you to configure cluster-aware applications.

Conclusion

In this chapter you have read about the two methods for clustering virtual machines.

The first method is to use the emulated SCSI controller provided by Virtual Server. You have seen that this provides an excellent replication of the clustering environment contained inside one physical computer. This is ideal for development and testing scenarios and for training yourself on how to configure and use clustered environments.

You have also seen how to configure an iSCSI-based virtual machine cluster. This allows you to cluster production applications across multiple physical computers while running inside of virtual machines. Using a software-based iSCSI solution also allows you to do this in a completely virtualized environment.

15

Clustering Virtual Server

In Chapter 14, you read about how to configure virtual machines in a cluster. In that configuration, the virtual machines were clustered just like physical computers are clustered, and you had to install cluster-aware applications inside the virtual machines. Virtual Server clustering is a significantly different configuration. You configure the host operating systems in a cluster, and Virtual Server then acts as the cluster-aware application, with the virtual machines being clustered, highly available resources.

This presents a completely different set of advantages and disadvantages to virtual machine clustering. As it is the host operating system that is being clustered, there is no overhead from emulation in the cluster and the highest possible performance is provided. Furthermore, because Virtual Server is the cluster-aware application, the guest operating systems and other applications installed inside of virtual machines are completely unaware of the fact that they are clustered. This means that you do not have to invest time or money in making these applications cluster aware.

Virtual Server monitors the state of the virtual machines and detects if one has failed, in which case Virtual Server will migrate it to another node on the cluster. If you need to perform maintenance on a cluster node, you can safely migrate the virtual machine resources off the cluster node onto other nodes on the cluster while you perform maintenance. And finally, if an entire Virtual Server cluster node were to fail, the cluster would automatically start the virtual machines that had been on the failed node on other nodes on the cluster.

There are disadvantages to this configuration. Virtual Server is aware of the health of the virtual machine only to the extent that the guest operating system is running or not. If the guest operating system is still running successfully, but the applications on top of it have failed for some reason, Virtual Server will not detect this failure.

In the case of a planned migration (where you go into Cluster Administrator and select to move a resource in order to prepare for maintenance) the virtual machine will be put into a saved state and then restored on the target cluster node, but in the case of an unplanned migration (where the guest operating system has failed, or the host operating system has crashed) the virtual machine

Part VI: Virtual Machines and Clustering

will be restarted and will behave as if a power failure occurred. This means that to be able to gain the benefit of high availability through clustering, the guest operating system and applications need to be able to recover gracefully from a crash.

Virtual server clustering is best used in production environments where you are trying to provide high availability to applications and operating systems that do not support high-availability configurations themselves. If your guest operating system and application support operation of the clustered configuration then you should consider clustering the virtual machines (as discussed in the previous chapter) for high availability.

> *It is possible to use clustered virtual machines on top of clustered instances of virtual server when you use an iSCSI cluster of the virtual machines.*

Preparing the Physical Cluster

I am not going to go into great detail about how to set up the physical cluster because the details will vary significantly depending on the hardware configuration that you are using for the cluster.

Rather, I am just going to focus on some key things that you need to know about preparing your physical cluster. The first thing to know is that your physical cluster needs to be configured and fully operational before you attempt to install Virtual Server on any of the cluster nodes.

> *If you are not familiar with configuring cluster systems, you can read how to do this inside of virtual machines in Chapter 14 and apply this information to setting up your physical cluster.*
>
> *Microsoft does support the use of iSCSI for creating Virtual Server clusters.*

The next thing to be aware of is how to correctly configure your shared storage for the cluster. When configuring a Virtual Server cluster there are two possible ways to manage the storage of virtual machines:

❑ Store all the virtual machine files on a network share that is available to all notes in the cluster. In this configuration, you need to ensure that your network share provides enough performance for all your virtual machines. You also need to make sure that your network share is configured in a highly available fashion; otherwise it becomes the weakest link in the availability of the entire system.

❑ Store the virtual machine files on some form of shared storage. This option requires custom configuration of the shared storage itself. Because only one cluster node can be accessing any specific LUN (or logical unit number, a LUN is a virtual partition or volume that is offered by shared storage device) at a given time, only one virtual machine can be configured on any given LUN. The reason for this is that when the clustered node detects that the virtual machine has failed, the LUN on which it resides will be disconnected from the current cluster node and reconnected to a new cluster node. If you had multiple virtual machines stored on a single LUN, this would cause the other virtual machines that were running correctly to fail. Thankfully most modern SANs allow you to dynamically configure the size of the LUNs that they offer.

❑ You should configure your SAN (or other shared storage) so that it provides a LUN for each virtual machine. This means that to utilize your shared storage most effectively you are going to have to calculate the exact amount of space needed by each virtual machine. This is easiest to do

Chapter 15: Clustering Virtual Server

when you configure your virtual machines to use fixed-size virtual hard disks. When using a fixed-size virtual hard disk the amount of space needed for a specific virtual machine is the amount of space taken up by its virtual hard disks, plus the amount of memory assigned to the virtual machine, plus about 10MB overhead.

If you use dynamically expanding virtual hard disks, you will have to create a LUN with enough space for the maximum possible size of the dynamically expanding virtual hard disk (or risk running out of space). It is not advisable to enable undo disks on a clustered instance of Virtual Server, as this makes it very hard to calculate the exact amount of space that needs to be available on the line.

Another issue to consider if you are using shared storage is how you are going to manage assignment of drive letters to LUNs. Normally you would attach a LUN to your server and assign a drive letter to it. But with one LUN to a virtual machine you may find that you will quickly run out of available drive letters. The solution to this is to use NTFS mount points. This is a feature of NTFS that allows you to mount the volume as a folder on an existing NTFS volume. The recommended configuration for LUN mounting with the Virtual Server cluster is to create a single folder, which you then mount all your LUNs underneath. To do this:

1. Create the folder that you plan to use to contain all the NTFS mount points (for example, C:\SANVMs).

2. Create subfolders for each of the mount points that you intend to create (for example, VM1, VM2, VM3, and so on).

3. Attach the shared storage device, or LUN, to the physical computer.

4. Open the **Start** menu, select **Administrative Tools** and then **Computer Management**.

5. Click on the **Disk Management** node.

   If the shared storage device has not been initialized, you will need to initialize it here and create a new partition.

6. Select the partition that you are interested in, open the **Action** menu, and select **All Tasks and** then **Change Drive Letter and Paths**.

7. If any drive letters are already assigned, remove them.

8. Click the **Add** button.

9. In the **Add Drive Letter or Path** dialog box, select the **Mount in the following empty NTFS folder** option, enter the path you want to use (for example, C:\SANVMs\VM1), and click **OK**.

Repeat this process for each storage device that you want to mount in this way.

While this is useful for mounting a large number of LUNs for the purpose of clustering Virtual Server, it is important that your quorum disk be assigned a drive letter (preferably Q).

When you are using NTFS mount points for shared storage Windows, clustering does not automatically detect it as an available resource. To configure it as a clustered resource, execute the following steps:

1. Open the **Start** menu and select **Administrative Tools and** then **Cluster Administrator**.

2. Select the entry for your cluster; then open the **File** menu and select **New and** then **Resource**.

289

Part VI: Virtual Machines and Clustering

3. Enter a suitable **Name** and **Description** and specify **Resource type** of the **Physical Disk**.

4. Configure the **Possible Owners** and **Dependencies** pages appropriately.

    All cluster node computers should be listed as possible owners.

5. On the **Disk Parameters** page, you see a list of available partitions. Select the one that corresponds to the mount point that you want to add to the cluster, and click **Next**.

The final item for preparing your cluster for Virtual Server is to ensure that all the clustered nodes are compatible for the purposes of Virtual Server clustering. Normal clustering is fairly lenient about the type of processor that is used in each cluster node (as long as it is of the same general architecture). Virtual Server clustering, on the other hand, relies on the ability to put a virtual machine into a saved state on one cluster node and then restore it on another cluster node. This means that the processors in all the clustered nodes of the cluster need to be from the same manufacturer and from the same family, and have similar CPU features.

For example, you cannot create a Virtual Server cluster that consists of cluster nodes with Pentium III and Pentium 4 processors, or with Intel and AMD processors. Determining whether your cluster node processors have the same manufacturer (Intel or AMD) and family (Pentium III, Pentium 4, Opteron, and so on) is fairly easy. Determining whether they have the same CPU features is harder. CPU features are things such as the SSE2 and SSE3 instruction extensions, or the 3DNow! instruction extension. Generally speaking, if your processors are from the same manufacturer and family and are of the same clock speed, they will have the same feature set. The further apart in clock speed processors get the higher the chances are that they will have the different feature set. The easiest way to confirm that all your cluster nodes have compatible processors, before setting up the cluster, is to install Virtual Server and test the creation of saved virtual machines on one node and then the restoration on the other node by hand.

Installing Virtual Server

To install Virtual Server on the existing physical cluster you will need to go through the cluster nodes one at a time. On each node you will need to first stop the cluster service, and then install Virtual Server, and then start the cluster service again. You need to stop the cluster service first because installing Virtual Server disrupts network connectivity momentarily. If the cluster service is running when this happens it will think that there has been a cluster node failure and try to failover resources inappropriately.

You will need to decide for yourself whether you will be installing IIS and the Virtual Server Administrative website on each cluster node, or whether you will be configuring Virtual Server without the Administrative website and using a remote instance of IIS to administer Virtual Server.

After you have installed Virtual Server on a cluster node, one extra configuration step is advised. When the cluster node is being shut down, there is a potential race condition. If the Virtual Server service is stopped before the cluster service stops, the cluster service may well try to restart the Virtual Server service. This will fail because the system shuts down.

Chapter 15: Clustering Virtual Server

To avoid this you need to do the following:

1. Create a batch file (for example, C:\Cluster\stop_clustering.cmd).

2. In the batch file, type the following line:

```
net stop clussvc
```

and save the changes.

3. Then open the **Start** menu and click **Run**.

4. Run **gpedit.msc**.

5. In the **Group Policy** window, select **Local Computer Policy** ➪ **Computer Configuration** ➪ **Windows Settings**, and then click **Scripts (Startup/Shutdown)**.

6. Double-click on the **Shutdown** script.

7. Click the **Add** button and specify the name of the batch file that you created in Step 1.

Creating the Clustering Script

Virtual Server uses a clustering resource script to enable Virtual Server clustering. Unfortunately Microsoft does not provide this script in its native format. To create the Virtual Server clustering resource script, get a copy of the Virtual Server Host Clustering Step-By-Step Guide for Virtual Server 2005 R2. You can download this guide from Microsoft's website; alternately it should be installed with Virtual Server itself. If you look in the Virtual Server program directory ("Microsoft Virtual Server" in your "Program Files" directory by default) there should be a "Host Clustering" folder, which contains the guide.

Appendix B, at the end of this book, shows the contents of the Virtual Server cluster resource script (havm.vbs). You will need to copy the contents of the script from the end of the guide and save it in the file called havm.vbs. This script needs to be created on each cluster node, and should be created in the same location. You should keep this script in the cluster folder in the Windows folder on the system drive.

This script is also provided in Appendix B of this book, and as an online sample file.

Creating a Virtual Machine

When creating virtual machines on a clustered instance of Virtual Server it is important to make sure that all of the virtual machine files are stored on the same shared storage device. Use the following steps:

1. Click **Create** from the **Virtual Machines** section of the navigation pane on the Virtual Server Administrative website.

2. In the **Virtual machine name** field, specify the full path to the location where you want the virtual machine to be created and the virtual machine name followed by .vmc (for example, C:\SANVMs\VM1\Windows Server 2003.vmc).

3. The rest of the **Create Virtual Machine** page can be filled out according to your requirements.

291

Part VI: Virtual Machines and Clustering

If you need to install the guest operating system, or perform any other configuration on the virtual machine, you should do it now.

*To use an existing virtual machine that you have already created, just copy the virtual machine folder (which contains all of the virtual machine files) to a shared storage location. You can then add it to Virtual Server by using the **Add** option from the **Virtual Machines** section of the navigation pane on the Virtual Server Administrative website.*

Configuring the Virtual Networks

Configuring virtual networks for a clustered Virtual Server environment is actually a bit trickier than configuring the virtual machines themselves. When a virtual machine is moved from one host operating system to another it will attempt to reconnect a matching virtual network. It tries to match the virtual network according to its name. If a virtual network exists on the new host operating system that has exactly the same name as the virtual network on the old host operating system, the virtual machine will use it. Otherwise the virtual machine will disconnect itself from the network.

If a virtual network configuration is moved from one host operating system to another host operating system, it too will try to reconnect itself to an appropriate physical network device. Like the virtual machine, it looks for an appropriate network device by checking the device name. If there is a physical device with the exact same device name as the physical device that was used at the source host operating system, the virtual network will connect to it. Otherwise, the virtual network will disconnect itself from the network.

*The name that is used for the physical network device, is the name that is displayed for the network adapter in **Device Manager** (for example, Intel® PRO/1000 PM Network Connection).*

With all of this in mind, there are two possible configurations for handling virtual networks on a Virtual Server cluster.

The first option is to go to each cluster node and manually create a virtual network that has the same name and is connected to the appropriate network adapter. The virtual machines will always be able to connect to a new virtual network with that name on any computer in the cluster.

The second option is to ensure that all computers in the cluster of physical network adapters share the same device name, and then configure a virtual network that is stored on the shared storage beside the virtual machine files. Follow these steps:

1. Click **Create** from under the **Virtual Networks** section of the navigation pane on the **Virtual Server Administrative** website.

2. Enter a suitable **Virtual network name** (for example, "cluster network") and select the physical network adapter that you want the virtual network to be connected to.

3. Clicking **OK** will bring up the properties of the virtual network that you just created. On the virtual network properties page you can see the name and location of the virtual network configuration file (VNC). Make a copy of the name and location of the virtual network configuration file, as you'll need it in a moment.

292

Chapter 15: Clustering Virtual Server

4. Select **Configure** and then **View All** from the **Virtual Networks** section of the navigation pane on the Virtual Server Administrative website.

5. Click on the virtual network that you just created and then click Remove.

Do not worry. This does not actually delete the virtual network configuration but rather just removes it from Virtual Server's list of known virtual networks.

6. Open **My Computer** and navigate to the location where the virtual network configuration file is stored. Once you have found the virtual network configuration file, move it to the shared storage where the virtual machine is kept.

It is important that you move the virtual network configuration file, and not just copy it.

7. Return to the Virtual Server Administrative website and select **Add** from the **Virtual Networks** section of the navigation pane.

8. On the **Add Virtual Network** page, enter the full path and name for the new location of the virtual network configuration file and click the **Add** button.

Creating the Cluster Group

Now that everything is in place, the final step is to create the cluster group for the virtual machine. To do this, execute the following steps:

1. On one of the cluster node computers, click the **Start** menu, select **Administrative Tools**, and then click **Cluster Administrator**.

2. In **Cluster Administrator**, select your cluster, and then open the **File** menu and select **New** and **Group**.

3. Specify a **Name** and **Description** for the new group that will help you to associate it with the virtual machine.

In a standard configuration, there will be one cluster group for each virtual machine.

4. If there is one, or multiple, cluster nodes that you would prefer that this virtual machine was running on, you can specify this on the **Preferred Owners** page.

If you do not specify a preferred owner, the virtual machine will run on whichever cluster node is available.

5. Locate the physical hard disk resource for the shared storage that contains this virtual machine's files. Click on the resource, open the **File** menu, select **Change Group**, and select the group you just created.

If you do not have a physical hard disk resource configured for the shared storage that you want to use, follow the steps outlined in the "Preparing the Physical Cluster" section of this chapter. Remember that all cluster node computers should be listed as possible owners for the physical hard disk resource.

Part VI: Virtual Machines and Clustering

In order to move a physical hard disk resource from one group to another group, both groups need to be running on the same physical cluster node. If you receive an error when you try to move the physical hard disk resource that states that the cluster node is not the owner of the resource (or group), you need to check to ensure that both the source group and the target group are currently on the same cluster node.

If a virtual machine has multiple physical hard disk resources associated with it, they should all be added to the cluster group. The physical hard disk resource that contains the virtual machine's boot disk should be made to be dependent upon any other physical hard disk resources. This guarantees that all of the physical hard disk resources will be present when the virtual machine attempts to boot.

Configuring the Virtual Machine on Each Cluster Node

Now that you have created the cluster group for the virtual machine, you need to register the virtual machine, and potentially the virtual network, on each cluster node computer in the cluster. Use the following steps:

1. Open **Cluster Administrator** and select your cluster.

2. Select the cluster group that represents your virtual machine, open the **File** menu, and select **Move Group**.

   Should you have more than two cluster nodes in your cluster you may need to manually disable the cluster service on specific cluster nodes during this process to ensure that the cluster group is moved to the right cluster node.

3. Open the Virtual Server Administrative website for the cluster node on which the cluster group now resides.

4. Add the virtual machine and the virtual network if needed.

Repeat this process for each cluster node in the cluster.

Configure the Cluster Resource Script

The final step in setting up the clustered virtual machine is to configure the cluster resource script. To do this, follow these steps:

1. Open **Cluster Administrator**, select your cluster, and select the cluster group that represents your virtual machine.

2. Open the **File** menu, and select **New** and then **Resource**.

3. Enter a suitable **Name** and **Description** and specify a **Resource type** of **Generic Script**.

   Make sure that the resource is assigned to the group that you have selected.

4. On the **Possible Owners** page ensure that all cluster nodes are listed as possible owners.

5. On the **Dependencies** page, configure the script to be dependent on all the physical disk resources that are required for the virtual machine.

294

Chapter 15: Clustering Virtual Server

6. On the **Generic Script Parameters** page, enter the full path and name for the **Script filepath** (for example, C:\Windows\Cluster\havm.vbs).

7. On the same computer, open the **Start** menu, click **Run**, and run the following command:

```
cluster res "ScriptResourceName" /priv VirtualMachineName="VirtualMachineName"
```

where "ScriptResourceName" is the name that you assign to the script resource in step three and "VirtualMachineName" is the name of the virtual machine on Virtual Server.

Your virtual machine is now set up as a clustered resource. You should repeat this process for any extra virtual machines that you want to configure as clustered resources.

Testing the Cluster Group

After all this, you probably want to confirm that the virtual machine is configured correctly on the cluster. To do this, follow these steps:

1. Open **Cluster Administrator**, select your cluster, and select the cluster group that represents your virtual machine.

2. Open the **File** menu and select **Bring Online**.

   If you open the Virtual Server Administrative website at this stage you should see the selected virtual machine powering on and starting to boot.

3. Still in **Cluster Administrator**, open the **File** menu and select **Move Group**.

   Now if you look at the Virtual Server Administrative website, you should see the virtual machine starting to save state, and then be restored on the target server.

Conclusion

Virtual Server host clustering provides a powerful tool to enable high availability for virtual machines. It does not require that the guest operating system, or the applications on top of it, be cluster aware. However, it does have some drawbacks. In this chapter you have read about how to configure Virtual Server host clustering; you have also read that it is best used in production environments with guest operating systems that are not capable of being clusters themselves. If a guest operating system and applications can be clustered natively, they should be.

Creating a Virtual Server cluster requires you to first create a cluster of Windows Server 2003 systems, and then to install Virtual Server, create the clustering script, and create cluster resource objects for each of the virtual machines. You need to pay special attention to the management of shared disk resources if you are not using a network share to store your virtual machines.

Part VII

Automating Virtual Machine Operations

Chapter 16: Using the Virtual Server COM Interface

Chapter 17: Scripting Virtual Server

Chapter 18: Using PowerShell to Control Virtual Server

16

Using the Virtual Server COM Interface

Virtual Server provides a fully documented and fully programmable COM (Component Object Model) API. This is the interface that the Virtual Server Administrative website uses to display information about virtual machines, to allow you to configure and interact with virtual machines and configure all aspects of Virtual Server. Using the COM API that is exposed by Virtual Server, you can automate almost any operation possible with Virtual Server.

There are many situations in which you want to automate Virtual Server. In production environments you want to use scripts to automate regular maintenance operations. In training environments you want to provide customized, limited interfaces for users to use. In development and testing environments you want to automate virtual machines to assist the testing process. Indeed, the possibilities are close to limitless.

Understanding the COM Objects

The Virtual Server COM API is constructed by a set of hierarchical COM objects. The primary COM object is the `IVMVirtualServer` object. This is the first COM object you need to create in any program or script that interacts with Virtual Server. From here you can begin to access the other COM objects provided in the Virtual Server COM interface. You can also access properties and perform global Virtual Server actions. Using the Virtual Server COM object, you can do the following:

- ❏ Create virtual machines, virtual networks, and virtual hard disks
- ❏ Register, unregister, and delete virtual machines and virtual networks
- ❏ Connect to virtual machine, virtual network, and virtual hard disk COM objects
- ❏ Retrieve information about the host operating system
- ❏ Configure server-wide settings

Part VII: Automating Virtual Machine Operations

Some of the other significant COM objects in the Virtual Server COM object model include the following:

- ❏ **The virtual machine COM object:** This object allows you to start, stop, and otherwise control the state of the virtual machine. You can also edit the configuration of the virtual machine.

- ❏ **The virtual hard disk COM object:** With the virtual hard disk object you can create virtual hard disks, attach them to virtual machines, and perform other actions on the virtual hard disks.

- ❏ **The virtual network COM object:** With this object you can connect virtual machines to network adapters on the physical computer. You can also configure the virtual networks and gather statistics about them.

Requirements for Accessing COM

The Virtual Server COM API has some specific requirements of clients that connect to it, which you will not find in many other COM APIs. You should be aware of these requirements and understand the impact they have on your programming.

COM Security

When a program is written to talk to a COM interface it needs to define its security impersonation level. The security impersonation level dictates the extent to which server processes can perform actions on behalf of the client. There are four different security impersonation levels:

- ❏ **SecurityAnonymous:** At this security impersonation level, the server knows nothing about the client. It does not know what user credentials the client is using, nor can it perform any actions on behalf of the client. All actions that are performed by the server need to be done under the server's security credentials.

- ❏ **SecurityIdentification:** This level means that the server can obtain information from the client such as security identifiers and privileged information. It can use this information to make decisions about what the client is allowed to do. It cannot use this information to run code under the identity of the client process.

- ❏ **SecurityImpersonation:** With this level, the server is not only able to obtain information from the client about its security identifiers and privileged information, but it is able to run code under the identity of the client process. However, it is able to do this only on the system on which the server code is running.

- ❏ **SecurityDelegation:** This is the highest impersonation level. It provides all the abilities of SecurityImpersonation, but it also provides the ability to run code under the identity of the client process on a remote computer.

If a program does not define its security impersonation level, it will operate at the SecurityIdentification level by default.

For most programs, and COM APIs, this is sufficient. However, as discussed in Chapter 10, "Securing Virtual Server," Virtual Server uses impersonation as part of its security model. Furthermore, Virtual Server requires impersonation to be able to start a virtual machine, or to access any configuration information about the virtual machine.

Chapter 16: Using the Virtual Server COM Interface

This means that any program that wants to connect to the Virtual Server COM API needs to set its security impersonation level at SecurityImpersonation or higher.

Threading Apartment Models

In order to help developers who are using different development environments and languages, COM supports the concept of threading apartments. The application that hosts the COM object can hold one or more threading apartments. When a client program connects to the COM object, it can request the type of threading apartment to be used. There are two possible types of threading apartments:

❑ **Single threaded apartment model:** In the single threaded apartment model (also known as STA) the client hosts a single threaded COM object. This is easier for the developer of the client, as he/she will not have to worry about any threading issues.

❑ **Multithreaded apartment model:** In the multithreaded apartment model (also known as MTA) the client hosts fully threaded COM objects. This way, the server is able to spin up new threads to respond to requests if necessary.

Most applications that expose COM APIs support both the STA and MTA threading models.

Virtual Server supports only the MTA threading model. The reason for this is that when a client connects using the STA threading model it needs to ensure that it does not block on the single thread that is provided. If an STA client blocks, without running a Windows message pump, it can potentially block all forward progress on the application that is exposing the COM interface. Microsoft decided that it was too dangerous to risk having a poorly written client application block the progress of an entire Virtual Server instance and disabled support for STA clients.

Accessing COM from VBScript

VBScript (and other scripting languages that use the Windows scripting host environment) is lucky. The Windows scripting host environment automatically runs any scripts at the SecurityImpersonate level with an MTA-compatible threading apartment model. This means that VBScript can connect to the Virtual Server COM interface without any special configuration.

Connecting to the virtual server COM interface and VBScript is as simple as running the following code:

```
Option Explicit

Dim virtualServer

Set virtualServer = CreateObject("VirtualServer.Application")

MsgBox virtualServer.Name & " version " & virtualServer.Version
```

This code declares the `virtualServer` variable, uses it to create a connection to the local instance of Virtual Server, and displays a message box with the name and version information of the local instance of Virtual Server.

Part VII: Automating Virtual Machine Operations

To run this script, open Notepad and type in the sample code. Then save the file as sample1.vbs and double-click on sample1.vbs to run it.

Accessing COM from Native Code

This book focuses primarily on scripting and managed languages. But I would like to show you how to connect to Virtual Server from a native program written in C++. The code sample after the table does the following:

❑ The main routine establishes the variables that will be used for the program.

❑ It then calls `SetupCOM`.

❑ `SetupCOM` sets the process to use the correct threading model, by calling `CoInitializeEx(NULL,COINIT_MULTITHREADED)`.

❑ `SetupCOM` then sets the `SECURITY_IMPERSONATION_LEVEL` to impersonate. It does this by calling `CoInitializeSecurity`.

The following table describes the parameters that `CoInitializeSecurity` requires.

Parameter	Description
`PSECURITY _DESCRIPTOR pVoid`	This parameter defines the access permissions that the server will use to receive calls. As you are not writing server code, but rather the client code that connects to a server, you can set this to `null`.
`LONG cAuthSvc`	This parameter is a number that specifies the count of the entries in the next parameter (`asAuthSvc`). If `asAuthSvc` is `null` this parameter should be set to -1.
`SOLE_AUTHENTICATION _SERVICE * asAuthSvc`	This parameter is an array of authentication services that the server is willing to use to receive a call. If this parameter is null, COM will automatically choose which authentication service should be used for the connection.
`void * pReserved1`	This parameter is reserved for future use, it should be set to null.
`DWORD dwAuthnLevel`	This parameter specifies the authentication level to be used. `RPC_C_AUTHN_LEVEL_PKT_PRIVACY` is a constant defined by `_WIN32_DCOM`, which has a value of 6. This is the most secure authentication level that can be used. It means that all data packets will be authenticated, encrypted, and checked for integrity.
`DWORD dwImpLevel`	This is the parameter that actually specifies the security impersonation level that should be used. `RPC_C_IMP_LEVEL_IMPERSONATE` is a constant defined by `_WIN32_DCOM`, which has a value of 3. It sets the security impersonation level to IMPERSONATE.

302

Chapter 16: Using the Virtual Server COM Interface

Parameter	Description
SOLE_AUTHENTICATION _LIST * pAuthList	This parameter specifies which authentication methods are appropriate for this connection. Setting this value to `null` will cause Windows to auto negotiate an appropriate authentication method.
DWORD dwCapabilities	This parameter is used to specify additional capabilities on the client or server. EOAC_DYNAMIC_CLOAKING is a constant defined by _WIN32_DCOM, which has a value of 64. Setting this parameter to EOAC_DYNAMIC_CLOAKING means that the thread token will be used to determine the client's identity when every a connection is made.
void * pReserved2	This parameter is reserved for future use; it should be set to `null`.

Once `SetupCOM` has completed, it then calls `InitVSComInterfaces` to establish a connection to Virtual Server. The connection to Virtual Server is established by using `CoCreateInstance`. The program then displays some basic information retrieved from Virtual Server. Finally the program cleans up the appropriate resources, and exits.

Here is the sample C++ code:

```
#define _WIN32_DCOM
#include "VSComInterfaces.h"
#include <atlbase.h>
#include <comdef.h>

HRESULT SetupCOM()
{
  // Initialize COM to the right threading model
  HRESULT hr = CoInitializeEx(NULL,COINIT_MULTITHREADED);
  if (FAILED(hr)) return hr;

  // Set default security level to IMPERSONATE. This is required by
  // the Virtual Server COM object's security model.
  hr = CoInitializeSecurity(NULL, -1, NULL, NULL,
                        RPC_C_AUTHN_LEVEL_PKT_PRIVACY,
                        RPC_C_IMP_LEVEL_IMPERSONATE,
                        NULL, EOAC_DYNAMIC_CLOAKING, NULL);
  return hr;
}

HRESULT InitVSComInterfaces(IVMVirtualServer** ppIVS)
{
  // Check for required arguments
  if (ppIVS == NULL)
    return E_INVALIDARG;

  *ppIVS = NULL;

  REFCLSID classID = _uuidof(VMVirtualServer);

  // Connect to the local instance of Virtual Server
```

303

Part VII: Automating Virtual Machine Operations

```
  HRESULT hr = CoCreateInstance(classID, NULL, CLSCTX_ALL, ⤵
IID_IVMVirtualServer, (LPVOID*)ppIVS);

  // test connection
  if (SUCCEEDED(hr) && (*ppIVS != NULL))
  {
    // Make a call to the interface and see if it works.
    _bstr_t bVer;
    hr = (*ppIVS)->get_Version(bVer.GetAddress());
  }
  return hr;
}

// COM UNINITIALIZATION routine
HRESULT UninitVSComInterfaces(IVMVirtualServer* pIVS)
{
  HRESULT hr = S_OK;
  if (pIVS != NULL)
  {
    hr = pIVS->Release();
    pIVS = NULL;
  }
  CoUninitialize();
  return hr;
}

// MAIN PROGRAM
int _tmain()
{
  HRESULT hr = S_OK;
  IVMVirtualServer* pIVS = NULL;

  // Initialize the COM layer
  hr = SetupCOM();
  if (FAILED(hr))
    printf("Init error: %01X\n", hr);
  else
  {
  // Create Virtual Server connection
  hr = InitVSComInterfaces(&pIVS);
  if (FAILED(hr))
        printf("Create Connection error: %01X\n", hr);
  else
  {
          // Display name and version number
          _bstr_t bAppName, bVersion;
          hr = pIVS->get_Name(bAppName.GetAddress());
          if (SUCCEEDED(hr))
              hr = pIVS->get_Version(bVersion.GetAddress());
          if (FAILED(hr))
              printf("VSComInterfaces initialized, error %01X when retrieving ⤵
version info\n",hr);
```

Chapter 16: Using the Virtual Server COM Interface

```
        else
                printf("\n%ls version %ls\n", (wchar_t*)bAppName, ⤴
    (wchar_t*)bVersion);
        }
    }
    // Exit gracefully
    hr = UninitVSComInterfaces(pIVS);
}
```

To compile this code, save it to a CPP file, open a Visual Studio command prompt, and run the following:

```
Cl sample.cpp /link VSComInterfaces.lib
```

Note that this assumes that both VSComInterfaces.h and VSComInterfaces.lib are in your current directory. If they are not, you will need to provide full path references to these files.

If you try to build this sample on an x64 host operating system you will need to use the 64-bit version of cl.exe.

Accessing COM from Managed Code

When building a managed application to control Virtual Server the first thing you need to do is add the reference libraries for the Virtual Server COM interface to your project under Visual Studio. You can do this under Visual Studio 2005 by opening your project, and then following these steps:

1. Open the Project menu and select Add Reference.

2. Change to the COM tab and select Virtual Server 2005 R2 Type Library. If the Virtual Server 2005 Type Library does not appear in the list on COM page, change to the Browse tab. Browse to the directory where Virtual Server was installed, and select the Microsoft.VirtualServer.Interop.dll file from the documentation folder.

3. Click OK.

Accessing the Virtual Server COM interfaces from managed code is actually significantly harder than with unmanaged code or VBScript because setting the security impersonation level is quite difficult with managed code. There are, in fact, three possible ways to do this.

The first approach is to use `CoInitializeSecurity`, as with the unmanaged code sample. There are three problems with this approach, however. The first problem is that this method is not officially supported by Microsoft.

The second problem is a bit more complex. `CoInitializeSecurity` can be called only once per process. If you try to call it a second time, you will fail and receive an exception. Unfortunately, the .NET runtime will attempt to call `CoInitializeSecurity` automatically without any input from you (and it will set the security impersonation level too low for accessing Virtual Server). This means that to use `CoInitializeSecurity`, you have to call it as early as possible so that your call gets processed before the .NET runtime uses it (in some cases this is simply not possible).

305

Part VII: Automating Virtual Machine Operations

The third problem is that Visual Studio 2005 uses a method for debugging that stops `CoInitializeSecurity` from working. To address this problem, you will need to open your project and follow these steps:

1. Open the **Project** menu and select to view the project properties (the last entry in the menu).

2. Change to the **Debug** tab.

3. Change the **Configuration** drop-down to **All Configurations**.

4. Clear the **Enable the Visual Studio hosting process** check box.

5. Close the project properties.

I have provided sample code for connecting to Virtual Server using `CoInitializeSecurity` with both Visual Basic .NET and C#. These samples contain three files each. The first file is SetSecurityImpersonationLevel. This file imports the native `CoInitializeSecurity` call so that a managed program can use it. It also defines constants that are normally available to unmanaged programs. The second file is responsible for interacting with Virtual Server. It exposes two methods: one for creating the initial connection to Virtual Server and one for retrieving basic version information from Virtual Server. You can also see that this file is configured to run with an MTA thread apartment model. The final file is the main project file. This file is responsible for calling the SetSecurityImpersonationLevel file as early as possible (during its initialization routine) and calling the Virtual Server file when the user clicks a button.

To create this sample using Visual Basic .NET, follow these steps:

1. Open Microsoft Visual Studio 2005.

2. Open the **File** menu and select **New ⇨ Project**.

3. Select **Visual Basic** from the **Project Types**, select **Windows Application** from the available **Templates**, and specify a name and location for your project. Then click **OK**.

4. Follow the procedures that have already been mentioned to add the references for the Virtual Server COM interface and to disable the Visual Studio hosting process.

5. Open the **Project** menu and select **Add Class**.

6. Enter a file name of **SetSecurityImpersonationLevel.vb** and click **Add**.

7. Use the code listed for **SetSecurityImpersonationLevel.vb** in this file.

8. Open the **Project** menu and select **Add Module**.

9. Enter a file name of **myVS.vb** and click **Add**.

10. Use the code listed for **myVS.vb** in this file.

11. Open the designer view for **Form1.vb**.

12. Drag a **button** from the toolbox onto the form.

13. Double-click the new button and enter the appropriate code from the **Form1.vb** sample.

306

Chapter 16: Using the Virtual Server COM Interface

If you just copy the sample code, and do not double-click the button, Visual Studio will not connect the click event correctly.

14. Open the **Class Name** combo box (it should state **Button1**) and select **Form1**.

15. Open the **Method Name** combo box — it should state **(Declarations)** — and select **New**.

16. Enter the appropriate code from the **Form1.vb** sample.

17. Launch the sample application.

Sample Visual Basic .NET Code

Following is the SetSecurityImpersonationLevel.vb code:

```
Imports System.Reflection
Imports System.Runtime.InteropServices

Public Class SetSecurityImpersonationLevel

    ' Import CoInitializeSecurity from ole32.dll
    <DllImport("ole32.dll", _
        PreserveSig:=False, _
        ExactSpelling:=True, _
        EntryPoint:="CoInitializeSecurity", _
        CallingConvention:=CallingConvention.StdCall, _
        SetlastError:=False)> _
    Private Shared Sub CoInitializeSecurity( _
        ByVal pSD As IntPtr, _
        ByVal cAuthSvc As Int32, _
        ByVal asAuthSvc As IntPtr, _
        ByVal pReserved1 As IntPtr, _
        ByVal dwAuthnlevel As UInt32, _
        ByVal dwImpLevel As UInt32, _
        ByVal pAuthInfo As IntPtr, _
        ByVal dwCapabilities As UInt32, _
        ByVal pvReserved2 As IntPtr)
    End Sub

    'SecurityImpersonationLevel is set to '3' for "impersonate"
    Private Const AuthLevelPktPrivacy As Long = 6
    Private Const SecurityImpersonationLevel As Long = 3
    Private Const EnableDynamicCloaking As Long = 64

    ' Call CoInitializeSecurity with the request to set the
    ' security level to "impersonate"
    Public Sub New()
        CoInitializeSecurity(System.IntPtr.Zero, _
            -1, _
            System.IntPtr.Zero, _
            System.IntPtr.Zero, _
            Convert.ToUInt32(AuthLevelPktPrivacy), _
            Convert.ToUInt32(SecurityImpersonationLevel), _
            System.IntPtr.Zero, _
```

307

Part VII: Automating Virtual Machine Operations

```
                Convert.ToUInt32(EnableDynamicCloaking), _
                System.IntPtr.Zero)
        End Sub
    End Class
```

Here is the myVS.vb code:

```
Imports System.Runtime.InteropServices
Imports Microsoft.VirtualServer.Interop

Module myVS

    'Using a global variable for the main Virtual Server connection
    'without this you would have to reconnect for each call
    Public VSConnection As VMVirtualServer

    'Set the subroutine to run with the MTA thread model
    <MTAThread()> _
    Public Sub Connect(ByVal VSServer As String)

        Try

            If VSServer = "." Then
                'This connects to the local server
                VSConnection = New VMVirtualServerClass
            Else
                Dim typeVSClass As Type
                Dim typeDCOM As Type
                Dim objDCOM As Object

                typeVSClass = GetType(VMVirtualServerClass)
                typeDCOM = Type.GetTypeFromCLSID(typeVSClass.GUID, VSServer, ⤸
True)

                objDCOM = Activator.CreateInstance(typeDCOM)

                VSConnection = CType(Marshal.CreateWrapperOfType(objDCOM, ⤸
typeVSClass), VMVirtualServerClass)
            End If

        Catch ex As Exception
            MsgBox("Cannot connect to Virtual Server", "Error")
            Exit Sub
        End Try
    End Sub

    'Set the subroutine to run with the MTA thread model
    <MTAThread()> _
    Public Sub DisplayInformation()
        ' Display Virtual Server version info
        MsgBox(VSConnection.Name & " version " & VSConnection.Version, ⤸
MsgBoxStyle.OkOnly, "Virtual Server Version Information")
    End Sub
End Module
```

Chapter 16: Using the Virtual Server COM Interface

Here is the `Form1.vb` code:

```
Public Class Form1

    Private Sub Button1_Click(ByVal sender As System.Object, ByVal e As
System.EventArgs) Handles Button1.Click

        'When the user clicks on the button, connect to Virtual Server
        'and display the version information
        myVS.Connect(".")
        myVS.DisplayInformation()

    End Sub

    Public Sub New()

        ' This call is required by the Windows Form Designer.
        InitializeComponent()

        ' Set the Security Impersonation Level as soon as possible
        Dim MySetSecurityImpersonationLevel = New
SetSecurityImpersonationLevel

    End Sub
End Class
```

To create this sample using C#, you need to do the following:

1. Open Microsoft Visual Studio 2005.
2. Open the **File** menu and select **New ⇨ Project**.
3. Select **Visual C#** from the **Project Types**, select **Windows Application** from the available **Templates**, and specify a name and location for your project. Then click **OK**.
4. Follow the procedures that have already been mentioned to add the references for the Virtual Server COM interface and to disable the Visual Studio hosting process.
5. Open the **Project** menu and select **Add Class**.
6. Enter a file name of **Personal.SetSecurityImpersonationLevel.cs** and click **Add**.
7. Use the code listed for **Personal.SetSecurityImpersonationLevel.cs** in this file.
8. Open the **Project** menu and select **Add Class**.
9. Enter a file name of **Personal.VirtualServer.cs** and click **Add**.
10. Use the code listed for **Personal.VirtualServer.cs** in this file.
11. Open the designer view for **Form1.cs**.
12. Drag a **button** from the toolbox onto the form.
13. Double-click the new button and enter the appropriate code from the **Form1.cs** sample.

    If you just copy the sample code, and do not double-click on the button, Visual Studio will not connect the click event correctly.

309

Part VII: Automating Virtual Machine Operations

14. Enter the code from the **Form1.cs** sample for the `public Form1()` section.

15. Launch the sample application.

Sample C# Code

Following is the `Personal.SetSecurityImpersonationLevel.cs` code:

```
using System;
using System.Reflection;
using System.Runtime.InteropServices;

namespace Personal.SetSecurityImpersonationLevel
{

    // Define RPC_C_AUTHN_LEVEL_ constants
    public enum RpcAuthnLevel
    {
        Default = 0,
        None,
        Connect,
        Call,
        Pkt,
        PktIntegrity,
        PktPrivacy
    }

    // Define RPC_C_IMP_LEVEL_ constants
    public enum RpcImpLevel
    {
        Default = 0,
        Anonymous,
        Identify,
        Impersonate,
        Delegate
    }

    // Define EOAC_ constants
    public enum EoAuthnCap
    {
        None = 0x00,
        MutualAuth = 0x01,
        StaticCloaking = 0x20,
        DynamicCloaking = 0x40,
        AnyAuthority = 0x80,
        MakeFullSIC = 0x100,
        Default = 0x800,
        SecureRefs = 0x02,
        AccessControl = 0x04,
        AppID = 0x08,
        Dynamic = 0x10,
        RequireFullSIC = 0x200,
        AutoImpersonate = 0x400,
```

310

Chapter 16: Using the Virtual Server COM Interface

```csharp
        NoCustomMarshal = 0x2000,
        DisableAAA = 0x1000
    }


    public class SetToImpersonate
    {
        // Import CoInitializeSecurity
        [DllImport("Ole32.dll",
            ExactSpelling = true,
            EntryPoint = "CoInitializeSecurity",
            CallingConvention = CallingConvention.StdCall,
            SetLastError = false,
            PreserveSig = false)]

        private static extern void CoInitializeSecurity(
            IntPtr pVoid,
            int cAuthSvc,
            IntPtr asAuthSvc,
            IntPtr pReserved1,
            uint dwAuthnLevel,
            uint dwImpLevel,
            IntPtr pAuthList,
            uint dwCapabilities,
            IntPtr pReserved3);

        // Call CoInitializeSecurity with dwImpLevel set to Impersonate.
        public SetToImpersonate()
        {
            CoInitializeSecurity(IntPtr.Zero,
                -1,
                IntPtr.Zero,
                IntPtr.Zero,
                (uint)RpcAuthnLevel.PktPrivacy,
                (uint)RpcImpLevel.Impersonate,
                IntPtr.Zero,
                (uint)EoAuthnCap.DynamicCloaking,
                IntPtr.Zero);
        }
    }
```

Here is the `Personal.VirtualServer.cs` code:

```csharp
using System;
using System.Runtime.InteropServices;
using Microsoft.VirtualServer.Interop;

namespace Personal.VirtualServer
{

    // This class provides a basic message box

    public class MyMsgBox
```

311

Part VII: Automating Virtual Machine Operations

```csharp
    {
        [ DllImport( "User32.dll", EntryPoint="MessageBox",
                CharSet=CharSet.Auto )]

        public static extern int MsgBox( int hWnd, String text,
            String caption, uint type );
    }

    public class Connection
    {
        // Global variable for Virtual Server connection
        private static VMVirtualServer myVS;

        // Set the thread model to MTA
        [MTAThread]
        public void Connect(string VSServer)
        {
            // Connect locally or remotely
            try
            {
                if (VSServer == ".")
                {
                    // Connect to Virtual Server
                    myVS = new VMVirtualServerClass();
                }

                else
                {
                    Type typeVSClass;
                    Type typeDCOM;
                    object objDCOM;

                    typeVSClass = typeof(VMVirtualServerClass);
                    typeDCOM = Type.GetTypeFromCLSID( typeVSClass.GUID, ⊃
VSServer, true);

                    objDCOM = Activator.CreateInstance(typeDCOM);

                    myVS = ⊃
(VMVirtualServerClass)Marshal.CreateWrapperOfType(objDCOM, typeVSClass);
                }
            }
            catch
            {
             MyMsgBox.MsgBox(0, "Cannot connect to Virtual Server", "Error", 0);
                return;
            }
        }

        // Set the thread model to MTA
        [MTAThread]
        public void displayInformation()
        {
```

Chapter 16: Using the Virtual Server COM Interface

```
                // Get Virtual Server name and version number
                string sName;
                string sVersion;

                sName = myVS.Name;
                sVersion = myVS.Version;

                MyMsgBox.MsgBox(0, sName + " version " + sVersion, "Virtual Server ⤸
Version Information", 0);
            }
        }
    }
```

Here is the `Form1.cs` code:

```
using System;
using System.Collections.Generic;
using System.ComponentModel;
using System.Data;
using System.Drawing;
using System.Text;
using System.Windows.Forms;

namespace vcWinAppVSConnect_CoinitSec
{
    public partial class Form1 : Form
    {
        public Form1()
        {
            InitializeComponent();

            // Set the Security Impersonation level to 'impersonate' as
            // soon as possible
            Personal.SetSecurityImpersonationLevel.SetToImpersonate ⤸
mySetSecurityImpersonationLevel;
            mySetSecurityImpersonationLevel = new ⤸
Personal.SetSecurityImpersonationLevel.SetToImpersonate();
        }

        private void button1_Click(object sender, EventArgs e)
        {
            // When someone clicks on the button, create a new Virtual
            // Server connection, and then display server information
            Personal.VirtualServer.Connection myVSConnection;

            myVSConnection = new Personal.VirtualServer.Connection();

            myVSConnection.Connect(".");
            myVSConnection.displayInformation();
        }
    }
}
```

313

Part VII: Automating Virtual Machine Operations

The next approach for setting the security impersonation level from a managed program is to look at using `CoSetProxyBlanket`. `CoSetProxyBlanket` has advantages and disadvantages when compared to `CoInitializeSecurity`. `CoSetProxyBlanket` is supported by Microsoft, and it can be called repeatedly at any time in the process. It also has no problems with Visual Studio 2005's debugging methods. The first downside of `CoSetProxyBlanket` is that unlike `CoInitializeSecurity`, which you have to call only once for an application, you need to call to `CoSetProxyBlanket` for each object that you create. The second downside is that it is not possible to receive COM events from Virtual Server when using `CoSetProxyBlanket`, which means that you have to poll in order to detect any changes.

`CoSetProxyBlanket` is the most annoying method to use when you're writing code; however, it is the cleanest and best supported method.

As with `CoInitializeSecurity` samples, the `CoSetProxyBlanket` sample has three files. The first file contains the necessary code to import the `CoSetProxyBlanket` call. The second file contains the calls to the Virtual Server COM interface. The third file contains the main program. The big difference here is that the main program does not need to call anything in its initialize routine. Rather it simply calls the Virtual Server interface file when a user clicks on the button. The Virtual Server interface file is then responsible for calling the `CoSetProxyBlanket` file for any objects that it creates.

The following table describes the parameters that `CoSetProxyBlanket` requires.

Parameter	Description
`IntPtr * pProxy`	A pointer to the interface at which the proxy needs to be set.
`UInt32 dwAuthnSvc`	Defines the authentication service to use when connecting to the COM object. A value of RPC_C_AUTHN_WINNT (or 10) says that NTLM authentication should be used. This is the default for COM communication.
`UInt32 dwAuthzSvc`	Defines any extra configuration values that need to be set for the authentication service. When you are using NTLM as your authorization service this value should be set to RPC_C_AUTHZ_NONE (or 0).
`UInt32 * pServerPrincName`	Specifies the server principle name to use when authenticating. Setting this parameter to 0, or null, means that the existing server principle name will be used.
`UInt32 dwAuthnLevel`	Specifies the authentication level to be used. RPC_C _AUTHN_LEVEL_PKT_PRIVACY is a constant defined by_WIN32_DCOM that has a value of 6, which is the most secure authentication level that can be used. It means that all data packets will be authenticated, encrypted, and checked for integrity.

Chapter 16: Using the Virtual Server COM Interface

Parameter	Description
UInt32 dwImpLevel	The parameter that actually specifies the security impersonation level that should be used. RPC_C_IMP_LEVEL _IMPERSONATE is a constant defined by _WIN32 _DCOM that has a value of 3, which sets the security impersonation level to IMPERSONATE.
IntPtr pAuthInfo	Takes a pointer to the handle for the identity of the client. You can set this to null, but that means you will not be able to enable dynamic cloaking.
UInt32 dwCapabilities	Used to specify additional capabilities on the client or server. EOAC_NONE is a constant defined by _WIN32_DCOM that has a value of 0. Setting this parameter to EOAC_NONE means that no additional capabilities will be configured.

To create this sample using Visual Basic .NET you need to do the following:

1. Open Microsoft Visual Studio 2005.

2. Open the **File** menu and select **New ⇨ Project**.

3. Select **Visual Basic** from the **Project Types**, select **Windows Application** from the available **Templates**, and specify a name and location for your project. Then click **OK**.

4. Follow the procedures that have already been mentioned to add the references for the Virtual Server COM interface.

5. Open the **Project** menu and select **Add Class**.

6. Enter a file name of **SetSecurityImpersonationLevel.vb** and click **Add**.

7. Use the code listed for **SetSecurityImpersonationLevel.vb** in this file.

8. Open the **Project** menu and select **Add Module**.

9. Enter a filename of **myVS.vb** and click **Add**.

10. Use the code listed for **myVS.vb** in this file.

11. Open the designer view for **Form1.vb**.

12. Drag a **button** from the toolbox onto the form.

13. Double-click the new button and enter the appropriate code from the **Form1.vb** sample.

    If you just copy the sample code, and do not double-click the button, Visual Studio will not connect the click event correctly.

14. Open the **Class Name** combo-box (it should state **Button1**) and select **Form1**.

15. Open the **Method Name** combo-box — it should state **(Declarations)** — and select **New**.

16. Enter the appropriate code from the **Form1.vb** sample.

17. Launch the sample application.

315

Part VII: Automating Virtual Machine Operations

Sample Visual Basic .NET Code

Following is the `SetSecurityImpersonationLevel.vb` code:

```vbnet
Imports System.Reflection
Imports System.Runtime.InteropServices
Imports Microsoft.VirtualServer.Interop

Public Class SetSecurityImpersonationLevel

    ' Import CoSetProxyBlanket from ole32.dll
    <DllImport("ole32.dll", _
        PreserveSig:=False, _
        ExactSpelling:=True, _
        EntryPoint:="CoSetProxyBlanket", _
        CallingConvention:=CallingConvention.StdCall, _
        SetlastError:=False)> _
    Private Shared Sub CoSetProxyBlanket( _
        ByVal pProxy As IntPtr, _
        ByVal dwAuthnSvc As UInt32, _
        ByVal dwAuthzSvc As UInt32, _
        ByVal pServerPrincName As UInt32, _
        ByVal dwAuthLevel As UInt32, _
        ByVal dwImpLevel As UInt32, _
        ByVal pAuthInfo As IntPtr, _
        ByVal dwCapabilities As UInt32)
    End Sub

    'SecurityImpersonationLevel is set to '3' for "impersonate"
    Private Const SecurityImpersonationLevel As UInt32 = 3
    Private Const RPC_C_AUTHN_WINNT As UInt32 = 10
    Private Const RPC_C_AUTHZ_NONE As UInt32 = 0
    Private Const RPC_C_AUTHN_LEVEL_PKT_PRIVACY As UInt32 = 6
    Private Const EOAC_DYNAMIC_CLOAKING As UInt32 = 64

    ' Call CoSetProxyBlanket with the request to set the
    ' security level to "impersonate"
    Public Sub Secure(ByVal objDCOM As Object)

        Dim dispatchInterface As IntPtr
        Dim comClassType As Type
        Dim fullInterfaceName As String
        Dim interfaceName As String
        Dim interfaceType As Type

        fullInterfaceName = GetType(VMVirtualServer).AssemblyQualifiedName._
Replace( "VMVirtualServer", TypeName(objDCOM))
        comClassType = Type.GetType(fullInterfaceName)

        If TypeName(objDCOM).LastIndexOf("Class") > 0 Then _
            interfaceName = TypeName(objDCOM).Substring(0, _
TypeName(objDCOM).LastIndexOf("Class"))
            interfaceType = comClassType.GetInterface(interfaceName)
            dispatchInterface = Marshal.GetComInterfaceForObject(objDCOM, _
interfaceType)
```

Chapter 16: Using the Virtual Server COM Interface

```
        Else
            dispatchInterface = Marshal.GetComInterfaceForObject(objDCOM, ⤵
comClassType)
        End If

        CoSetProxyBlanket( _
                dispatchInterface, _
                RPC_C_AUTHN_WINNT, _
                RPC_C_AUTHZ_NONE, _
                0, _
                RPC_C_AUTHN_LEVEL_PKT_PRIVACY, _
                SecurityImpersonationLevel, _
                IntPtr.Zero, _
                EOAC_DYNAMIC_CLOAKING _
            )
    End Sub
End Class
```

Here is the myVS.vb code:

```
Imports System.Runtime.InteropServices
Imports Microsoft.VirtualServer.Interop

Module myVS

    'Using a global variable for the main Virtual Server connection
    'without this you would have to reconnect for each call
    Public VSConnection As VMVirtualServer

    'Set the subroutine to run with the MTA thread model
    <MTAThread()> _
    Public Sub Connect()

        Try

            'This connects to the local server
            VSConnection = New VMVirtualServer

            'SetProxyBlanket
            Dim MySetSecurityImpersonationLevel As ⤵
SetSecurityImpersonationLevel = New SetSecurityImpersonationLevel()

            MySetSecurityImpersonationLevel.Secure(VSConnection)

        Catch ex As Exception
            MsgBox("Cannot connect to Virtual Server", "Error")
            Exit Sub
        End Try
    End Sub

    'Set the subroutine to run with the MTA thread model
    <MTAThread()> _
    Public Sub DisplayInformation()
        ' Display Virtual Server version info
```

317

Part VII: Automating Virtual Machine Operations

```
        MsgBox(VSConnection.Name & " version " & VSConnection.Version, ⊃
MsgBoxStyle.OkOnly, "Virtual Server Information")
    End Sub
End Module
```

Here is the `Form1.vb` code:

```
Public Class Form1

    Private Sub Button1_Click(ByVal sender As System.Object, ByVal e As ⊃
System.EventArgs) Handles Button1.Click

        'When the user clicks on the button, connect to Virtual Server
        'and display the version information
        myVS.Connect()
        myVS.DisplayInformation()

    End Sub

    Public Sub New()

        ' This call is required by the Windows Form Designer.
        InitializeComponent()

    End Sub

End Class
```

To create this sample using C#, you need to do the following:

1. Open Microsoft Visual Studio 2005.

2. Open the **File** menu and select **New ⇨ Project**.

3. Select **Visual C#** from the **Project Types**, select **Windows Application** from the available Templates, and specify a name and location for your project. Then click **OK**.

4. Follow the procedures that have already been mentioned to add the references for the Virtual Server COM interface.

5. Open the **Project** menu and select **Add Reference**.

6. Select **Microsoft.VisualBasic** from the **.NET** tab and click **OK**.

   You need to add the reference for `VisualBasic` *as using CoSetProxyBlanket requires the use of the* `Information.TypeName` *API that is available only from* `VisualBasic`.

7. Open the **Project** menu and select **Add Class**.

8. Enter a filename of **Personal.SetSecurity.cs** and click **Add**.

9. Use the code listed for **Personal.SetSecurity.cs** in this file.

10. Open the **Project** menu and select **Add Class**.

11. Enter a filename of **Personal.VirtualServer.cs** and click **Add**.

318

Chapter 16: Using the Virtual Server COM Interface

12. Use the code listed for **Personal.VirtualServer.cs** in this file.

13. Open the designer view for **Form1.cs**.

14. Drag a **button** from the toolbox onto the form.

15. Double-click the new button and enter the appropriate code from the **Form1.cs** sample.

If you just copy the sample code, and do not double-click on the button, Visual Studio will not connect the click event correctly.

16. Enter the code from the **Form1.cs sample** for the `public Form1()` section.

17. Launch the sample application.

Sample C# Code

Following is the `Personal.SetSecurity.cs` code:

```csharp
using System;
using System.Runtime.InteropServices;
using System.Reflection;
using Microsoft.VirtualServer.Interop;

namespace Personal.SetSecurity
{

    public class ProxyBlanket
    {
        // Define useful constants
        const uint EOAC_NONE = 0;
        const uint RPC_C_AUTHN_WINNT = 10;
        const uint RPC_C_AUTHZ_NONE = 0;
        const uint RPC_C_AUTHN_LEVEL_DEFAULT = 0;
        const uint RPC_C_IMP_LEVEL_IMPERSONATE = 3;

        // Import CoSetProxyBlanket
        [DllImport("Ole32.dll",CharSet = CharSet.Auto)]
        private static extern int
        CoSetProxyBlanket(
            IntPtr pProxy,
            uint dwAuthnSvc,
            uint dwAuthzSvc,
            uint pServerPrincName,
            uint dwAuthLevel,
            uint dwImpLevel,
            IntPtr pAuthInfo,
            uint dwCapabilities);

        public int Set(object objDCOM)
        {
            // Generate pointer to COM Interface on object
            string fullInterfaceName = ⤶
 typeof(VMVirtualServer).AssemblyQualifiedName.Replace( "VMVirtualServer", ⤶
Microsoft.VisualBasic.Information.TypeName(objDCOM));
```

Part VII: Automating Virtual Machine Operations

```csharp
                Type comClassType = Type.GetType(fullInterfaceName);
                IntPtr interfacePointer;

                if ⤸
  (Microsoft.VisualBasic.Information.TypeName(objDCOM).LastIndexOf("Class") > 0)
                {
                    string interfaceName = comClassType.Name.Substring(0, ⤸
  comClassType.Name.LastIndexOf("Class"));
                    Type interfaceType = comClassType.GetInterface(interfaceName);
                    interfacePointer = Marshal.GetComInterfaceForObject(objDCOM, ⤸
  interfaceType);
                }
                else
                {
                    interfacePointer = Marshal.GetComInterfaceForObject(objDCOM, ⤸
  comClassType);
                }

                //Set security proxy on COM object
                int hr = CoSetProxyBlanket(
                    interfacePointer,              //pProxy
                    RPC_C_AUTHN_WINNT,             //dwAuthnSvc
                    RPC_C_AUTHZ_NONE,              //dwAuthzSvc
                    0,                             //pServerPrincName
                    RPC_C_AUTHN_LEVEL_DEFAULT,     //dwAuthnLevel
                    RPC_C_IMP_LEVEL_IMPERSONATE,   //dwImpLevel
                    IntPtr.Zero,                   //pAuthInfo
                    EOAC_NONE                      //dwCapabilities
                );
                return hr;
            }
        }
    }
```

Here is the `Personal.VirtualServer.cs` code:

```csharp
using System;
using System.Runtime.InteropServices;
using Microsoft.VirtualServer.Interop;

namespace Personal.VirtualServer
{

    // This class provides a basic message box

    public class MyMsgBox
    {

        [DllImport("User32.dll", EntryPoint = "MessageBox", CharSet = ⤸
  CharSet.Auto)]

        public static extern int MsgBox(int hWnd, String text, String caption, ⤸
  uint type);
```

Chapter 16: Using the Virtual Server COM Interface

```csharp
        }

    public class Connection
    {
        // Global variable for Virtual Server Connection
        private static VMVirtualServer myVS;

        // Set the thread model to MTA
        [MTAThread]
        public void Connect()
        {

            try
            {
                //Connect to Virtual Server
                myVS = new VMVirtualServer();

                //Set Security Impersonation Level
                Personal.SetSecurity.ProxyBlanket myProxyBlanket = new ⊃
Personal.SetSecurity.ProxyBlanket();
                myProxyBlanket.Set(myVS);

            }
            catch
            {
                MyMsgBox.MsgBox(0,"Cannot connect to Virtual Server" , "Error", 0);
                return;
            }
        }

        [MTAThread]
        public void displayInformation()
        {
            // Get Virtual Server name and version number
            string sName;
            string sVersion;

            sName = myVS.Name;
            sVersion = myVS.Version;

            MyMsgBox.MsgBox(0, sName + " version " + sVersion, "Virtual Server ⊃
Version Information", 0);
        }
    }
}
```

Here is the `Form1.cs` code:

```csharp
using System;
using System.Collections.Generic;
using System.ComponentModel;
using System.Data;
using System.Drawing;
```

321

Part VII: Automating Virtual Machine Operations

```
using System.Text;
using System.Windows.Forms;

namespace vcWinAppVSConnect_CoSetProxyBlanket
{
    public partial class Form1 : Form
    {
        public Form1()
        {
            InitializeComponent();
        }

        private void button1_Click(object sender, EventArgs e)
        {
            // When someone clicks on the button, create a new Virtual
            // Server connection, and display the server information
            Personal.VirtualServer.Connection MyVSConnection = new ↵
Personal.VirtualServer.Connection();

            MyVSConnection.Connect();
            MyVSConnection.displayInformation();
        }
    }
}
```

The third option is not to attempt to set your security impersonation level in the process, but rather to change the default level at which programs run on your copy of Windows. This makes it much easier to program against the Virtual Server COM interfaces, but it also lowers the overall security of your computer. As such, you should consider this option only on controlled computers where you know exactly what programs are going to be running.

To do this, follow these steps:

1. Open the **Start** menu and select the **Control Panel**.

2. Open **Administrative Tools** and **Component Services**.

3. Expand **Computer Services** and **Computers**, and then select your computer.

4. Open the **Action** menu and select **Properties**.

5. Change to the **Default Properties** tab.

6. Change the **Default Impersonation Level** to **Impersonate**.

7. Click **OK**.

Once you have done this, you can use the preceding samples without needing to call `CoInitializeSecurity` or `CoSetProxyBlanket`.

322

Chapter 16: Using the Virtual Server COM Interface

Handling the MTA Requirement

In the managed code samples that have been displayed so far, I have handled the requirement that the MTA threading model be used by placing the calls to Virtual Server in a separate file and ensuring that the methods that connect to Virtual Server use the MTA model. This is not the only way that this requirement can be met. Some alternative methods to consider are:

❑ You can simply change the main program to run with the MTA threading model, and make your calls to Virtual Server directly from there. This is definitely easier for the programmer. However, there are a number of cases where the main program needs to run with the STA threading model. (Indeed there will be some samples later in this book that require that the main program run with the STA threading model.)

❑ You can create a second thread for accessing Virtual Server, and configure the thread to use the MTA threading model. This is a bit more flexible, but a lot more complex.

Accessing COM from Windows PowerShell

Microsoft Windows PowerShell is a new command-line shell designed for Windows that offers a rich, scriptable interface. Windows PowerShell is a managed program, so you have to set the security impersonation level appropriately for Virtual Server. PowerShell runs with the correct threading model by default, so you do not need to worry about that. When PowerShell starts, it sets its own security impersonation level to identify. This means that you cannot use `CoInitializeSecurity`. You can use `CoSetProxyBlanket`, but it is a bit tricky.

You will need to create a DLL file that can be loaded by PowerShell in order to get access to `CoSetProxyBlanket`. (This is necessary because, unlike in Visual Basic .NET or C#, PowerShell does not support importing calls to unmanaged libraries directly.) To create the DLL file, use the following `VSWrapperForPS.cs` code:

```
using System;
using System.Runtime.InteropServices;
using System.Reflection;

namespace Microsoft.VirtualServer.Interop
{
    using System;
    using System.Runtime.InteropServices;
    using System.Reflection;

    public class
    Powershell
    {
        const uint EOAC_NONE                     = 0;
        const uint RPC_C_AUTHN_WINNT             = 10;
        const uint RPC_C_AUTHZ_NONE              = 0;
        const uint RPC_C_AUTHN_LEVEL_PKT_PRIVACY = 6;
```

323

Part VII: Automating Virtual Machine Operations

```
       const uint RPC_C_IMP_LEVEL_IMPERSONATE   = 3;

       [DllImport("Ole32.dll", CharSet = CharSet.Auto)]
       public static extern int
       CoSetProxyBlanket(
           IntPtr pProxy,
           uint   dwAuthnSvc,
           uint   dwAuthzSvc,
           uint   pServerPrincName,
           uint   dwAuthLevel,
           uint   dwImpLevel,
           IntPtr pAuthInfo,
           uint   dwCapabilities
       );

       public static int
       SetSecurity(
           object objDCOM
           )
       {
           IntPtr dispatchInterface = Marshal.GetIDispatchForObject(objDCOM);
           int hr = CoSetProxyBlanket(
               dispatchInterface,
               RPC_C_AUTHN_WINNT,
               RPC_C_AUTHZ_NONE,
               0,
               RPC_C_AUTHN_LEVEL_PKT_PRIVACY,
               RPC_C_IMP_LEVEL_IMPERSONATE,
               IntPtr.Zero,
               EOAC_NONE
           );
           return hr;
       }
   }
}
```

Once you have created this file you can compile it into a DLL file by opening a Visual Studio command prompt and running the following:

```
csc /t:library VSWrapperForPS.cs
```

This will generate a DLL file. To load this file into PowerShell, open a PowerShell session and run the following:

```
[System.Reflection.Assembly]::LoadFrom("<<full path and name of DLL>>")
```

After loading the DLL file, you can connect to Virtual Server by running the following:

```
$vs=new-object -com VirtualServer.Application -Strict
[Microsoft.VirtualServer.Interop.Powershell]::SetSecurity($vs)
$vs.Name + " " + $vs.Version
```

Chapter 16: Using the Virtual Server COM Interface

This creates a new object for the connection to Virtual Server (and stores it in $vs). It then sets the proxy blanket on $vs and finally displays the name and version information from Virtual Server.

Accessing COM from ASP.NET

Accessing Virtual Server from an ASP.NET application is very similar to accessing Virtual Server from a managed application. The main differences are that ASP.NET uses the correct thread model by default, and that `CoSetProxyBlanket` is the only option that can be used.

> With Visual Studio 2005, ASP.NET does not allow you to run code early enough to be able to use `CoInitializeSecurity`.

When building an ASP.NET application to control Virtual Server, the first thing you'll need to do is to add the reference libraries for the Virtual Server COM interface to your website under Visual Studio. You can do this under Visual Studio 2005 by opening your website and then following these steps:

1. Open the **Website** menu and select **Add Reference**.
2. Change to the **COM** tab and select **Virtual Server 2005 R2 Type Library**.
3. Click **OK**.

Sample code is provided for connecting to Virtual Server with both Visual Basic .NET and C#-based ASP.NET applications. Each sample has three files. The first file is the class that provides access to `CoSetProxyBlanket`. The second file is the code file for the default web page, which contains the methods that access Virtual Server. The third file is the HTML markup file for the default web page, which calls the code file for the web page.

To create this sample using Visual Basic.Net follow these steps:

1. Open Microsoft Visual Studio 2005.
2. Open the **File** menu and select **New ⇨ Web Site**.
3. Select **ASP.NET Web Site** from the available **Templates**, choose **Visual Basic** as the **Language**, and specify a name and location for your project. Then click **OK**.
4. Follow the procedures that have already been mentioned to add the references for the Virtual Server COM interface.
5. Open the **Website** menu and select **Add New Item**.
6. Select a **Template** of **Class**, enter a filename of **SetSecurityImpersonationLevel.vb**, and click **Add**.
7. Click **Yes** to place the file in the **App_Code** folder.
8. Use the code listed for **SetSecurityImpersonationLevel.vb** in this file.
9. Copy the code listed for **Default.aspx.vb** and **Default.aspx** to the respective files.
10. Launch the sample application.

325

Part VII: Automating Virtual Machine Operations

Sample Visual Basic .NET Code

Following is the `SetSecurityImpersonationLevel.vb` code:

```
Imports System.Reflection
Imports System.Runtime.InteropServices
Imports Microsoft.VirtualServer.Interop

Public Class SetSecurityImpersonationLevel

    ' Import CoSetProxyBlanket from ole32.dll
    <DllImport("ole32.dll", _
        PreserveSig:=False, _
        ExactSpelling:=True, _
        EntryPoint:="CoSetProxyBlanket", _
        CallingConvention:=CallingConvention.StdCall, _
        SetlastError:=False)> _
    Private Shared Sub CoSetProxyBlanket( _
        ByVal pProxy As IntPtr, _
        ByVal dwAuthnSvc As UInt32, _
        ByVal dwAuthzSvc As UInt32, _
        ByVal pServerPrincName As UInt32, _
        ByVal dwAuthLevel As UInt32, _
        ByVal dwImpLevel As UInt32, _
        ByVal pAuthInfo As IntPtr, _
        ByVal dwCapabilities As UInt32)
    End Sub

    'SecurityImpersonationLevel is set to '3' for "impersonate"
    Private Const SecurityImpersonationLevel As UInt32 = 3
    Private Const RPC_C_AUTHN_WINNT As UInt32 = 10
    Private Const RPC_C_AUTHZ_NONE As UInt32 = 0
    Private Const RPC_C_AUTHN_LEVEL_PKT_PRIVACY As UInt32 = 6
    Private Const EOAC_DYNAMIC_CLOAKING As UInt32 = 64

    ' Call CoSetProxyBlanket with the request to set the
    ' security level to "impersonate"
    Public Sub Secure(ByVal objDCOM As Object)

        Dim dispatchInterface As IntPtr
        Dim comClassType As Type
        Dim fullInterfaceName As String
        Dim interfaceName As String
        Dim interfaceType As Type

        fullInterfaceName = ↲
GetType(VMVirtualServer).AssemblyQualifiedName.Replace("VMVirtualServer", ↲
TypeName(objDCOM))
        comClassType = Type.GetType(fullInterfaceName)

        If TypeName(objDCOM).LastIndexOf("Class") > 0 Then
            interfaceName = TypeName(objDCOM).Substring(0, ↲
TypeName(objDCOM).LastIndexOf("Class"))
            interfaceType = comClassType.GetInterface(interfaceName)
            dispatchInterface = Marshal.GetComInterfaceForObject(objDCOM, ↲
```

326

Chapter 16: Using the Virtual Server COM Interface

```
interfaceType)
        Else
            dispatchInterface = Marshal.GetComInterfaceForObject(objDCOM, _
comClassType)
        End If

        CoSetProxyBlanket( _
                dispatchInterface, _
                RPC_C_AUTHN_WINNT, _
                RPC_C_AUTHZ_NONE, _
                0, _
                RPC_C_AUTHN_LEVEL_PKT_PRIVACY, _
                SecurityImpersonationLevel, _
                IntPtr.Zero, _
                EOAC_DYNAMIC_CLOAKING _
            )
    End Sub
End Class
```

Here is the `Default.aspx.vb` code:

```
Imports Microsoft.VirtualServer.Interop

Partial Class _Default
    Inherits System.Web.UI.Page
    'Using a global variable for the main Virtual Server connection
    'without this you would have to reconnect for each call
    Public VSConnection As VMVirtualServer

    'Set the subroutine to run with the MTA thread model
    Public Sub Connect()
        Dim localSecurity As SetSecurityImpersonationLevel

        Try

            'This connects to the local server
            VSConnection = New VMVirtualServer

            'SetProxyBlanket
            localSecurity = New SetSecurityImpersonationLevel()

            localSecurity.Secure(VSConnection)

        Catch ex As Exception
            MsgBox("Cannot connect to Virtual Server", "Error")
            Exit Sub
        End Try
    End Sub

    'Set the subroutine to run with the MTA thread model
    Public Sub DisplayInformation()
        ' Display Virtual Server version info
        Response.Write(VSConnection.Name & " version " & VSConnection.Version)
    End Sub
End Class
```

Part VII: Automating Virtual Machine Operations

Here is the `Default.aspx` code:

```
<%@ Page Language="VB" AutoEventWireup="false" CodeFile="Default.aspx.vb" ⤵
Inherits="_Default" %>

<!DOCTYPE html PUBLIC "-//W3C//DTD XHTML 1.0 Transitional//EN" ⤵
"http://www.w3.org/TR/xhtml1/DTD/xhtml1-transitional.dtd">

<html xmlns="http://www.w3.org/1999/xhtml" >
<head runat="server">
    <title>Untitled Page</title>
</head>
<body>
    <form id="form1" runat="server">
    <div>
    <%
        Connect()
        DisplayInformation()
    %>
    </div>
    </form>
</body>
</html>
```

To create this sample using Visual Basic .NET you need to:

1. Open Microsoft Visual Studio 2005.

2. Open the **File** menu and select **New ⇨ Web Site**.

3. Select **ASP.NET Web Site** from the available **Templates**, choose **Visual C#** as the **Language**, and specify a name and location for your project. Then click **OK**.

4. Follow the procedures that have already been mentioned to add the references for the Virtual Server COM interface.

5. Open the **Website** menu and select **Add Reference**.

6. Select **Microsoft.VisualBasic** from the **.NET** tab and click **OK**.

    You need to add the reference for `VisualBasic` *because using* `CoSetProxyBlanket` *requires the use of the* `Information.TypeName` *API, which is available only from* `VisualBasic`.

7. Open the **Website** menu and select **Add New Item**.

8. Select a **Template** of **Class**, enter a file name of **Personal.SetSecurity.cs**, and click **Add**.

9. Click **Yes** to place the file in the **App_Code** folder.

10. Use the code listed for **Personal.SetSecurity.cs** in this file.

11. Copy the code listed for **Default.aspx.cs** and **Default.aspx** to the respective files.

12. Launch the sample application.

328

Chapter 16: Using the Virtual Server COM Interface

Sample C# Code

Following is the `Personal.SetSecurity.cs` code:

```csharp
using System;
using System.Runtime.InteropServices;
using System.Reflection;
using Microsoft.VirtualServer.Interop;

namespace Personal.SetSecurity
{

    public class ProxyBlanket
    {
        // Define useful constants
        const uint EOAC_NONE = 0;
        const uint RPC_C_AUTHN_WINNT = 10;
        const uint RPC_C_AUTHZ_NONE = 0;
        const uint RPC_C_AUTHN_LEVEL_DEFAULT = 0;
        const uint RPC_C_IMP_LEVEL_IMPERSONATE = 3;

        // Import CoSetProxyBlanket
        [DllImport("Ole32.dll",CharSet = CharSet.Auto)]
        private static extern int
        CoSetProxyBlanket(
            IntPtr pProxy,
            uint dwAuthnSvc,
            uint dwAuthzSvc,
            uint pServerPrincName,
            uint dwAuthLevel,
            uint dwImpLevel,
            IntPtr pAuthInfo,
            uint dwCapabilities);

        public int Set(object objDCOM)
        {
            // Generate pointer to COM Interface on object
            string fullInterfaceName = ⤸
typeof(VMVirtualServer).AssemblyQualifiedName.Replace("VMVirtualServer", ⤸
Microsoft.VisualBasic.Information.TypeName(objDCOM));
            Type comClassType = Type.GetType(fullInterfaceName);
            IntPtr interfacePointer;

            if ⤸
(Microsoft.VisualBasic.Information.TypeName(objDCOM).LastIndexOf(⤸
 "Class") > 0)
            {
                string interfaceName = comClassType.Name.Substring(0, ⤸
comClassType.Name.LastIndexOf("Class"));
                Type interfaceType = comClassType.GetInterface(interfaceName);
                interfacePointer = Marshal.GetComInterfaceForObject(objDCOM, ⤸
interfaceType);
            }
            else
```

329

Part VII: Automating Virtual Machine Operations

```
            {
                    interfacePointer = Marshal.GetComInterfaceForObject(objDCOM, ⏎
    comClassType);
            }

            //Set security proxy on COM object
            int hr = CoSetProxyBlanket(
                interfacePointer,              //pProxy
                RPC_C_AUTHN_WINNT,             //dwAuthnSvc
                RPC_C_AUTHZ_NONE,              //dwAuthzSvc
                0,                             //pServerPrincName
                RPC_C_AUTHN_LEVEL_DEFAULT,     //dwAuthnLevel
                RPC_C_IMP_LEVEL_IMPERSONATE,   //dwImpLevel
                IntPtr.Zero,                   //pAuthInfo
                EOAC_NONE                       //dwCapabilities
            );
            return hr;
        }
    }
}
```

Here is the `Default.aspx.cs` code:

```
using System;
using System.Data;
using System.Configuration;
using System.Web;
using System.Web.Security;
using System.Web.UI;
using System.Web.UI.WebControls;
using System.Web.UI.WebControls.WebParts;
using System.Web.UI.HtmlControls;
using Microsoft.VirtualServer.Interop;

public partial class _Default : System.Web.UI.Page
{
    protected void Page_Load(object sender, EventArgs e)
    {

    }

        // Global variable for Virtual Server connection
        private static VMVirtualServer myVS;

        public void Connect()
        {
            try
            {
                //Connect to Virtual Server
                myVS = new VMVirtualServer();

                //Set Security Impersonation Level
                Personal.SetSecurity.ProxyBlanket myProxyBlanket = new ⏎
    Personal.SetSecurity.ProxyBlanket();
```

Chapter 16: Using the Virtual Server COM Interface

```
        myProxyBlanket.Set(myVS);
    }
    catch
    {
        Response.Write("Cannot connect to Virtual Server");
        return;
    }
}

public void displayInformation()
{
    // Get Virtual Server name and version number
    string sName;
    string sVersion;

    sName = myVS.Name;
    sVersion = myVS.Version;

    Response.Write(sName + " version " + sVersion);
}
}
```

Here is the `Default.aspx` code:

```
<%@ Page Language="C#" AutoEventWireup="true"  CodeFile="Default.aspx.cs" ⤸
Inherits="_Default" %>

<!DOCTYPE html PUBLIC "-//W3C//DTD XHTML 1.0 Transitional//EN" ⤸
"http://www.w3.org/TR/xhtml1/DTD/xhtml1-transitional.dtd">

<html xmlns="http://www.w3.org/1999/xhtml" >
<head runat="server">
    <title>Untitled Page</title>
</head>
<body>
    <form id="form1" runat="server">
    <div>
    <% Connect();
        displayInformation(); %>
    </div>
    </form>
</body>
</html>
```

Accessing Virtual Server Remotely

In each of these samples the code has been connecting to a local instance of Virtual Server. Connecting to a remote instance of Virtual Server is relatively easy. Following, you see the code used to connect local instance with each language and the alternate code that should be used to connect to a remote instance of Virtual Server.

331

Part VII: Automating Virtual Machine Operations

The following VBScript:

```
Set virtualServer = CreateObject("VirtualServer.Application")
```

becomes:

```
Set virtualServer = CreateObject("VirtualServer.Application", "RemoteServer")
```

The following C++ code:

```
hr = CoCreateInstance(classID, NULL, CLSCTX_ALL,
                      IID_IVMVirtualServer, (LPVOID*)ppIVS);
```

becomes:

```
CComBSTR    serverName(pRemoteServer);
MULTI_QI    multiQI = { &IID_IVMVirtualServer, NULL, NOERROR };
COSERVERINFO  serverInfo = { 0, serverName, NULL, 0 };
hr = CoCreateInstanceEx(classID, NULL, CLSCTX_ALL, &serverInfo, 1, &multiQI);

// get interface pointer
  if (SUCCEEDED(hr))
      *ppIVS = (IVMVirtualServer*)(multiQI.pItf);
```

The following Visual Basic .NET code:

```
VSConnection = New VMVirtualServerClass
```

becomes:

```
Dim typeVSClass As Type
Dim typeDCOM As Type
Dim objDCOM As Object

typeVSClass = GetType(VMVirtualServerClass)
typeDCOM = Type.GetTypeFromCLSID(typeVSClass.GUID, "RemoteServer", True)
objDCOM = Activator.CreateInstance(typeDCOM)

VSConnection = CType(Marshal.CreateWrapperOfType(objDCOM, ⊃
typeVSClass), VMVirtualServerClass)
```

The following C# code:

```
myVS = new VMVirtualServerClass();
```

becomes:

```
Type typeVSClass;
Type typeDCOM;
object objDCOM;

typeVSClass = typeof(VMVirtualServerClass);
```

Chapter 16: Using the Virtual Server COM Interface

```
typeDCOM = Type.GetTypeFromCLSID(typeVSClass.GUID, "RemoteServer", true);
objDCOM = Activator.CreateInstance(typeDCOM);
myVS = (VMVirtualServerClass)Marshal.CreateWrapperOfType(objDCOM, typeVSClass);
```

Conclusion

You have now seen how to connect to Virtual Server from a number of different languages and environments. You have learned about the requirements that Virtual Server places on clients that want to access its COM interfaces, both to have the correct threading model and have the right security configuration.

It is possible to control Virtual Server from VBScript, PowerShell, Visual Basic .NET and C# programs as well as from ASP.NET websites. For managed environments, it is necessary to use `CoInitializeSecurity` or `CoSetProxyBlanket` to connect to and control Virtual Server.

The coming chapters build on this knowledge and demonstrate ways to use the Virtual Server COM interfaces.

333

17

Scripting Virtual Server

Chapter 16 demonstrated that using a scripting language such as VBScript to control Virtual Server is quite easy. This chapter goes over the entire Virtual Server COM object model and discusses how VBScript can be used to automate it. Before doing that, you should understand why and when scripting is more appropriate than developing a standard application. There are a number of factors to consider when trying to decide whether to write a script or an application to automate Virtual Server:

❏ **Complexity:** It is possible to perform quite advanced and complex tasks with scripts. However, application development environments usually provide more advanced features for larger programs. You will need to decide whether the problem you are trying to solve can be addressed with a script or requires a full application.

❏ **Interactivity:** Scripts can only take input through command-line parameters and basic user prompts. If the solution you are developing requires extensive and varied user input, an application is a better solution. Alternatively, if you need a solution that is able to run in an unattended mode, scripting may be a better choice.

❏ **Flexibility:** When you develop an application, you produce a single solution for a single problem at the end of the day. If you want to reuse the application to address another problem, you will need to go back to the source code and compile a new application. Scripts are not compiled. Instead, you run the source code directly. This means that making modifications, or making alternate versions of scripts, is very easy and can be done quickly.

❏ **The end user:** It is always possible for the end user to modify a script. If the end user is a technically savvy person, this can be a good thing because scripts enable the end user to immediately correct any issues he encounters, and make modifications appropriate to his environment. If the end user is not technically savvy, it can be a recipe for disaster. If the end user is not familiar with scripting environments, developing a standalone application may be more appropriate.

There are probably other factors that you may want to consider, but these are some of the common ones. Even if you do not plan to use scripting extensively, I recommend you read this chapter. By doing so, you gain an insight into the construction and capabilities of the Virtual Server COM APIs.

Part VII: Automating Virtual Machine Operations

VBScript Best Practices

Before getting too far into scripting, it's a good idea for you to understand some best practices for writing scripts with VBScript.

Use Option Explicit

VBScript has an interesting feature. Typically, it does not require you to declare a variable in order to use it. By just typing the line:

```
Fred = 7
```

VBScript will know to create a variable called "Fred" and assign the value 7 to it. This is very useful when trying to quickly write short scripts, but it can cause problems for larger scripts. If you were using a variable called "Fred" but accidentally typed "Ferd" in your script, VBScript would create a new variable. I have personally seen a large number of broken scripts caused by mistyped variable names. You can avoid this by using the Option Explicit feature. By starting your script with the statement Option Explicit, you are telling VBScript that all variables need to be explicitly declared. If you do this, the preceding script would become:

```
Option Explicit

Dim Fred

Fred = 7
```

Now if you accidentally typed "Ferd" at a later point in the script, VBScript would report this as an error. I strongly recommend you use Option Explicit in all of your scripts to avoid problems with typographical errors in variable names.

Do Not Use "On Error Resume Next"

Okay, that is a bit harsh. You can use On Error Resume Next, but you should do so only with careful consideration. VBScript has a relatively simple error handling model that is quite often misused, to the detriment of the script writer. Normally when VBScript encounters an error, it stops executing the script and provides a description of the error that was hit. In most situations, this behavior is very desirable as it allows you to quickly detect and diagnose any issues with the script. There are, however, times when you will want the script to keep on running even if it encounters an error. To do this, you simply need to run On Error Resume Next. This will cause a VBScript to continue to run when it encounters an error and install the error information in a variable called Err.

The problem with On Error Resume Next is that many script writers call it at the beginning of their scripts and then ignore all errors, which makes it very hard to detect or diagnose any errors in the script. Whenever I receive a script that has On Error Resume Next at the beginning, the first thing I do is remove it. When I run the script, I usually then find at least three or four significant errors with a script that the author was unaware of. Sometimes these hidden errors can have completely unforeseen consequences.

So how should On Error Resume Next be used? It should be used strategically in order to handle known error cases. There are two situations in which On Error Resume Next should be used: when there is potential to encounter an error that should not stop execution of the script, and when there is potential to

Chapter 17: Scripting Virtual Server

encounter a fatal error and you want to provide a friendly explanation of the problem to the end user. If a command is always failing, fix it; do not mask it with `On Error Resume Next`. If you're worried about unknown errors, don't be. Any unknown or unexpected errors that you encounter will cause the script to stop running and provide you with appropriate information about the error. This best enables you to fix the source of the error. Here is an example of how to use `On Error Resume Next` correctly:

```
On Error Resume Next
Set vs = CreateObject("VirtualServer.Application")
If Err.number <> 0 Then
    Wscript.Echo "Unable to connect to Virtual Server."
    Wscript.Quit
End if
On Error Goto 0
```

What this script sample does is call `On Error Resume Next` directly before the line that might fail. It then runs the line that might fail and immediately checks the value of the `Err` variable. `Err.number` will be equal to 0 if no error occurred. If any error occurred, this sample will provide a friendly description of the error and then exit. If no error occurs it calls `On Error Goto 0`, which sets VBScript back to its standard error handling method.

Check Your Execution Environment

Windows scripts can run in one of two environments, wscript or cscript. The wscript environment is a graphical execution environment, and cscript is a command-line–based execution environment. The biggest difference between these two environments is how output is handled. The wscript environment displays any output in graphical message boxes. The cscript environment displays any output as lines of text on the command prompt. This means the scripts run under wscript should provide output only when they want the user to be alerted. Scripts running under cscript can output more regularly. A problem can occur when a script is run under an environment that it was not designed for. For instance, a script designed for cscript would generate far too many graphical message boxes if it were run under wscript. You can check to make sure that the script is running under the execution environment that you intended by running the following code:

```
' Check that the script is running at the command line.
If UCase(Right(Wscript.FullName, 11)) = "WSCRIPT.EXE" Then
    Wscript.Echo "This script must be run under CScript."
    Wscript.Quit
End If
```

Obviously, you should change wscript.exe to cscript.exe if you intend the script to be run under wscript.

Running VBScripts

If you are unfamiliar with running VBScripts on Windows you'll be glad to hear that it is a fairly easy process. To write a VBScript you just need a standard text editor (many people use notepad.exe). Once you have written the code for the script you'll need to save the file with a .vbs extension. You can then run the script by either double-clicking on it or by opening a command prompt and running `CSCRIPT scriptName.vbs` or `WSCRIPT scriptName.vbs`.

337

Part VII: Automating Virtual Machine Operations

VM Task Objects

Many commands on the Virtual Server COM interface run asynchronously. What this means is that you make the request via COM to perform an action and Virtual Server starts performing the action while your code continues to run the next command. This can be very useful, especially for long-running tasks. However, there are many times when you need to wait for a task to complete before attempting to perform the next task. Similarly it is useful to know what tasks are currently being performed on an instance of Virtual Server that you may not have initiated.

Virtual server allows you to do all of this through the use of the VM task object (IVMTask). Whenever you request that Virtual Server perform an action that might take a while, it returns a VM task object that you can use to track the progress of the action. Furthermore, it is possible to get a collection of currently active VM task objects from virtual server so that you can see what other actions are being performed.

The following is a sample VBScript that connects to Virtual Server, retrieves the collection of available VM task objects, and displays the VM task information.

```
Option Explicit

dim vs, tasks, task

'Check that the script is running at the command line.
If UCase(Right(Wscript.FullName, 11)) = "WSCRIPT.EXE" Then
    Wscript.Echo "This script must be run under CScript."
    Wscript.Quit
End If

'Attempt to connect to Virtual Server
On Error Resume Next
Set vs = CreateObject("VirtualServer.Application")
If Err.number <> 0 Then
    Wscript.Echo "Unable to connect to Virtual Server."
    Wscript.Quit
End if
On Error Goto 0

'Retrieve the collection of currently active tasks
Set tasks = vs.Tasks

'Check to see if there are no tasks active
If tasks.Count = 0 Then
    Wscript.Echo "There are no tasks"
Else

'List information about the currently active tasks
    Wscript.Echo "Active tasks: "
    For Each task in tasks
        Wscript.Echo "=================================================="
        Wscript.Echo "    ID:                     " & task.ID
        Wscript.Echo "    Description:            " & task.Description
        Wscript.Echo "    Percent Completed:      " & task.PercentCompleted
```

338

Chapter 17: Scripting Virtual Server

```
        Wscript.Echo "   Is able to be canceled: " & task.IsCancelable
     Next
  End If
```

This script establishes the environment and connects to Virtual Server. It then retrieves the VM task collection from Virtual Server (set tasks = vs.Tasks). Finally, it iterates over each of the VM task objects that are returned and displays the task IDE, description, percent completed, and whether the task can be cancelled.

You can perform a different set of actions on a VM task object that has been returned from an action that you have requested. You can wait for the task to complete, cancel the task, or check the task result once it has completed. If you simply want to wait until the requested task completes, you can use WaitForCompletion, like this:

```
... Other Code ...

set VMTask = ... an action that returns a VMTask object ...

VMTask.WaitForCompletion(-1)

wscript.echo "The task has been completed"
```

WaitForCompletion takes a single parameter, which is the amount of time (in milliseconds) that you want to wait. If you specify –1 for the amount of time to wait, it will wait indefinitely. If you want to wait for a task to complete, but also want to cancel the task if it is taking too long, you can do the following:

```
... Other Code ...

set VMTask = ... an action that returns a VMTask object ...

VMTask.WaitForCompletion(10000)

if VMTask.IsComplete then
   wscript.echo "The task has been completed"
else
   if VMTask.IsCancelable then
      VMTask.Cancel
      wscript.echo "The task has been canceled"
   end if
end if
```

This script section waits for 10 seconds for the task to complete. If the task completes before 10 seconds elapses, the script moves on to the next line of execution, finds that the task is complete, and informs the user of this. Otherwise, after 10 seconds the script moves on and finds that the task is not complete. It then checks to see if the task can be cancelled and will do so if possible.

The last thing to look at on a VM task is the result. WaitForCompletion and IsComplete tell you only whether the task completed or not; they do not tell you whether the task was successful. To find out if a task completed successfully you need to look at the result information. The result information can be

339

Part VII: Automating Virtual Machine Operations

obtained only once the task has completed; attempting to access the result information on a task that has not yet completed results in an error. A result value of 0 indicates success. So a simple check for whether the task completed successfully would look like this:

```
... Other Code ...

set VMTask = ... an action that returns a VMTask object ...

VMTask.WaitForCompletion(10000)

if VMTask.IsComplete then
    if vmTask.Result = 0 then
        Wscript.Echo "The Task completed successfully."
    else
        Wscript.Echo "The Task did not complete successfully."
    end if
else
    Wscript.Echo "The Task has been not completed yet."
end if
```

This script section waits a while for the task to complete and then uses a combination of `IsComplete` and the task result to tell the user what has happened. A more complex solution would examine the result and provide an appropriate error message depending on the value returned:

```
... Other Code ...

set VMTask = ... an action that returns a VMTask object ...
VMTask.WaitForCompletion(10000)

if VMTask.IsComplete then
    Select Case VMTask.Result
        Case 0
            Wscript.Echo("The Task completed successfully")
        Case 1
            Wscript.Echo("The Task was cancelled")
        Case 2
            Wscript.Echo("The Task encountered an unexpected error")
        Case 3
            Wscript.Echo("The Task encountered an out of memory error")
        Case 4
            Wscript.Echo("The Task encountered a disk related error")
        Case 5
            Wscript.Echo("The Task encountered an error due to an incompatible ⤶
saved state")
        Case 6
            Wscript.Echo("The Task encountered a time out error")
        Case 7
            Wscript.Echo("The Task encountered an illegal value error")
        Case 8
            Wscript.Echo("The Task encountered a thread crash error")
    End Select
else
    Wscript.Echo "The Task has been not completed yet."
end if
```

340

Chapter 17: Scripting Virtual Server

The explanation of any constants used by the Virtual Server COM interface can be found in the Microsoft Virtual Server Programmers Guide. They are in the Virtual Server COM Interface Enumerations section of the Microsoft Virtual Server 2005 COM Interface Reference.

The Virtual Server Object

The Virtual Server COM object is the starting point of any interaction with the Virtual Server COM interfaces. Using the Virtual Server COM object, you can either create or connect to all the other COM objects that are available. You can also view and configure properties that map to the entire Virtual Server installation.

Manipulating Virtual Machines

The Virtual Server COM object allows you to perform a number of actions related to virtual machines. You can create new virtual machines, find existing virtual machines, register and unregister virtual machine configurations, find known virtual machine configuration files, and even delete virtual machine configuration files. The following is a sample script that shows you how to do this:

```
Option Explicit

dim vs, vm1, vm2, vm3, knownVMConfFiles, vmConfFile

' Check that the script is running at the command line.
If UCase(Right(Wscript.FullName, 11)) = "WSCRIPT.EXE" Then
    Wscript.Echo "This script must be run under CScript."
    Wscript.Quit
End If

' Attempt to connect to Virtual Server
On Error Resume Next
Set vs = CreateObject("VirtualServer.Application")
If Err.number <> 0 Then
    Wscript.Echo "Unable to connect to Virtual Server."
    Wscript.Quit
End if
On Error Goto 0

set vm1 = vs.CreateVirtualMachine("A new virtual machine", "C:\MyVMs")

set vm2 = vs.RegisterVirtualMachine("Another new virtual machine", "C:\MyVMs")

set vm3 = vs.FindVirtualMachine("A third new virtual machine")

vs.DeleteVirtualMachine(vm1)

vs.UnregisterVirtualMachine(vm2)

knownVMConfFiles = vs.GetVirtualMachineFiles(Array("C:\", "C:\MyVMs"),false)

for each vmConfFile in knownVMConfFiles
    wscript.echo vmConfFile
Next
```

341

Part VII: Automating Virtual Machine Operations

This script starts by exercising the three possible ways to create a virtual machine COM object. `CreateVirtualMachine` takes two parameters: the name of the new virtual machine and the path where the virtual machine files should be stored. I then create a blank virtual machine with these details. `RegisterVirtualMachine` takes the same two parameters, but instead of creating a new virtual machine it adds an existing virtual machine. And finally, `FindVirtualMachine` returns the virtual machine COM object for an existing virtual machine that is already registered with Virtual Server.

`DeleteVirtualMachine` takes a single parameter of a virtual machine COM object and deletes the virtual machine configuration file associated with that virtual machine. (Note that it does not delete any other files associated with the virtual machine, like the virtual hard disk.) `UnregisterVirtualMachine` also takes a single parameter of the virtual machine, `object`. In this case the virtual machine is removed from Virtual Server, but the virtual machine configuration file is not deleted.

`GetVirtualMachineFiles` returns a list of known virtual machine configuration files. It takes two parameters: an array of directories that should be searched for virtual machine configuration files (these paths are combined with the configured search paths in the Virtual Server) and a Boolean value that indicates whether already registered virtual machines should be listed as well (`true` indicates that registered virtual machines should not be listed, and `false` means that they should be listed).

Manipulating Virtual Networks

The same methods that exist on the Virtual Server COM object for manipulating virtual machines also exist for manipulating virtual networks. This sample script demonstrates just how similar they are:

```
Option Explicit

dim vs, vn1, vn2, vn3, knownVNConfFiles, vnConfFile

' Check that the script is running at the command line.
If UCase(Right(Wscript.FullName, 11)) = "WSCRIPT.EXE" Then
    Wscript.Echo "This script must be run under CScript."
    Wscript.Quit
End If


' Attempt to connect to Virtual Server
On Error Resume Next
Set vs = CreateObject("VirtualServer.Application")
If Err.number <> 0 Then
    Wscript.Echo "Unable to connect to Virtual Server."
    Wscript.Quit
End if
On Error Goto 0

set vn1 = vs.CreateVirtualNetwork("A new virtual network", "C:\MyVNs")

set vn2 = vs.RegisterVirtualNetwork("Another new virtual network", "C:\MyVNs")

set vn3 = vs.FindVirtualNetwork("A third new virtual network")

vs.DeleteVirtualNetwork(vn1)

vs.UnregisterVirtualNetwork(vn2)
```

342

Chapter 17: Scripting Virtual Server

```
knownVNConfFiles = vs.GetVirtualNetworkFiles(Array("C:\", "C:\MyVNs"),false)

for each vnConfFile in knownVNConfFiles
    wscript.echo vnConfFile
Next
```

Creating Virtual Hard Disks

Creating virtual hard disks with the Virtual Server COM object is quite different from the process of creating a virtual machine or a virtual network. The first thing to note is that the calls to create a virtual hard disk do not return a virtual hard disk COM object; rather, they return a VMTask object. The reason for this is that creating a new virtual hard disk can be a lengthy operation.

There are four different calls for creating virtual hard disks, one for each type of virtual hard disk. To create a dynamically expanding or fixed size virtual hard disk you need to provide the full path and name of the new virtual hard disk and the size of the virtual hard disk. To create a new differencing virtual hard disk, you need to provide the full name and path of the new virtual hard disk file and of the parent virtual hard disk file. Finally to create a linked virtual hard disk you need to provide the full name and path for the new virtual hard disk, the resource name for the source physical hard disk, and a Boolean indicator as to whether the linked virtual hard disks should be read-only or not.

> You can get the resource name for the source physical hard disk by interrogating the HostInfo object. This is discussed later in this chapter in the "Host Information" section.

Once you've created a virtual hard disk file, you can get a virtual hard disk COM object by calling GetHardDisk with the file name of the virtual hard disk. The final virtual hard disk–specific method that is provided on the Virtual Server COM object is GetHardDiskFiles. This method takes a parameter of an array of paths to search for virtual hard disk files, and returns a collection of virtual hard disk file names.

```
Option Explicit

dim vs, vhdFile, knownVHDs, vmTask1, vmTask2, vmTask3, vmTask4, aVhd

' Check that the script is running at the command line.
If UCase(Right(Wscript.FullName, 11)) = "WSCRIPT.EXE" Then
    Wscript.Echo "This script must be run under CScript."
    Wscript.Quit
End If


' Attempt to connect to Virtual Server
On Error Resume Next
Set vs = CreateObject("VirtualServer.Application")
If Err.number <> 0 Then
    Wscript.Echo "Unable to connect to Virtual Server."
    Wscript.Quit
End if
On Error Goto 0


'Create virtual hard disks
```

343

Part VII: Automating Virtual Machine Operations

```
set vmTask1 = vs.CreateDynamicVirtualHardDisk("C:\MyVHDs\DynamicDisk.vhd", 16384)

vmTask1.WaitForCompletion(-1)

set VMTask2 = vs.CreateFixedVirtualHardDisk("C:\MyVHDs\FixedDisk.vhd", 1024)

vmTask2.WaitForCompletion(-1)

set VMTask3 = vs.CreateDifferencingVirtualHardDisk("C:\MyVHDs\DiffDisk.vhd", ⤵
  "C:\MyVHDs\DynamicDisk.vhd")

vmTask3.WaitForCompletion(-1)

set VMTask4 = vs.CreateHostDriveVirtualHardDisk("C:\MyVHDs\LinkedDisk.vhd", ⤵
  "\\.\PHYSICALDRIVE0",0)

vmTask4.WaitForCompletion(-1)

'Create a virtual hard disk COM object
set aVhd = vs.GetHardDisk("C:\MyVHDs\DynamicDisk.vhd")


'List known virtual hard disks
knownVHDs = vs.GetHardDiskFiles(Array("C:\", "C:\MyVHDs"))

for each vhdFile in knownVHDs
   wscript.echo vhdFile
Next
```

Removable Storage

DVDs and floppies are also treated differently. In this case Virtual Server does not have a COM object for the DVD or floppy media. In fact, for DVDs the only thing the Virtual Server can do is to provide a list of known DVD image files. This is done by using GetDVDFiles which is just like the GetHardDisk method. Known floppy disks can also be enumerated using GetFloppyDiskFiles.

Two additional methods are available for the floppy disk image. CreateFloppyDiskImage allows you to create a new virtual floppy disk image. It takes a parameter of the full name and path of the new virtual floppy disk image and of the format of the new virtual floppy disk image. GetFloppyDiskImageType allows you to determine the format that is used for an existing virtual floppy disk. It takes a single parameter of the full name and path of the virtual floppy disk that you want to know about.

Virtual Server uses what is known as an enumeration to specify the virtual floppy disk type. This is basically a way of associating numeric values with different type definitions. If you were developing a program written in C++ you would import the Virtual Server header file and have access to all of these enumerations natively. When using VBScript you need to manually define enumerations as constants. In the sample that follows, you can see the virtual floppy disk enumeration as defined as constants. Details about all of the Virtual Server enumerations can be found in the Virtual Server programmer's guide.

Although Virtual Server can identify and use six different types of virtual floppy disks, it can only create low-density or high-density floppies.

Chapter 17: Scripting Virtual Server

The following script starts by defining the constants that Virtual Server uses for the different floppy disk image formats. After connecting to Virtual Server it gets a list of the known CD image files and outputs them. The script then does the same thing for known floppy disk images. Finally the script creates a new virtual floppy disk image and examines the type of the new virtual floppy disk image.

```
Option Explicit

dim vs, floppyFile, knownFloppies, cdFile, knownCDFiles

'Setup CONST values for floppy types
CONST vmFloppyDiskImage_Unknown = 0
CONST vmFloppyDiskImage_LowDensity = 1
CONST vmFloppyDiskImage_HighDensity = 2
CONST vmFloppyDiskImage_DMF = 3
CONST vmFloppyDiskImage_LowDensitySingleSided = 4
CONST vmFloppyDiskImage_MediumDensity = 5
CONST vmFloppyDiskImage_HighDensityMSS = 6

' Check that the script is running at the command line.
If UCase(Right(Wscript.FullName, 11)) = "WSCRIPT.EXE" Then
    Wscript.Echo "This script must be run under CScript."
    Wscript.Quit
End If

' Attempt to connect to Virtual Server
On Error Resume Next
Set vs = CreateObject("VirtualServer.Application")
If Err.number <> 0 Then
    Wscript.Echo "Unable to connect to Virtual Server."
    Wscript.Quit
End if
On Error Goto 0

'List known DVD files
knownCDFiles = vs.GetDVDFiles(Array("C:\", "C:\MyVHDs"))

for each cdFile in knownCDFiles
    wscript.echo cdFile
Next

'List known floppy disk files
knownFloppies = vs.GetFloppyDiskFiles(Array("C:\", "C:\MyVHDs"))

for each floppyFile in knownFloppies
    wscript.echo floppyFile
Next

'Create a virtual floppy disk
vs.CreateFloppyDiskImage "C:\MyVHDs\New Virtual Floppy.vfd", ⊃
vmFloppyDiskImage_HighDensity

'Examine existing virtual floppy disk
Select Case vs.GetFloppyDiskImageType("C:\MyVHDs\New Virtual Floppy.vfd")
    Case vmFloppyDiskImage_Unknown
        Wscript.Echo("The floppy disk is an unknown format.")
```

345

Part VII: Automating Virtual Machine Operations

```
        Case vmFloppyDiskImage_LowDensity
            Wscript.Echo("The floppy disk is a low density floppy.")
        Case vmFloppyDiskImage_HighDensity
            Wscript.Echo("The floppy disk is a high density floppy.")
        Case vmFloppyDiskImage_DMF
            Wscript.Echo("The floppy disk is a DMF floppy.")
        Case vmFloppyDiskImage_LowDensitySingleSided
            Wscript.Echo("The floppy disk is a low density single sided floppy.")
        Case vmFloppyDiskImage_MediumDensity
            Wscript.Echo("The floppy disk is a medium density floppy.")
        Case vmFloppyDiskImage_HighDensityMSS
            Wscript.Echo("The floppy disk is a high density MSS floppy.")
    End Select
```

Configuring VMRC

The Virtual Server COM object is also the only place where you can configure VMRC. Information such as the port number that is used, whether VMRC is enabled or not, whether encryption is enabled, what the idle connection timeout is if it is enabled, and what the default resolution should be are all defined through editable properties.

Configuring the authentication type that should be used for VMRC is a bit trickier. vs.VMRCAuthenticator .Name provides the name of the authentication type that is currently being used. But to set a new authentication type you need to iterate over vs.VMRCAuthenticators until you find the authenticator that you want to use and then assign that authenticator to vs.VMRCAuthenticator.

Valid authenticator options are NTLM, Kerberos, or Automatic.

The script that follows connects to Virtual Server, displays the current configuration information for VMRC, and updates the VMRC configuration. The script then displays information about all possible VMRC authenticators, displays the information about the currently configured VMRC authenticator, and finally sets the VMRC authenticator to Automatic.

```
Option Explicit

dim vs, objVMAColl, objAuth


' Check that the script is running at the command line.
If UCase(Right(Wscript.FullName, 11)) = "WSCRIPT.EXE" Then
    Wscript.Echo "This script must be run under CScript."
    Wscript.Quit
End If


' Attempt to connect to Virtual Server
On Error Resume Next
Set vs = CreateObject("VirtualServer.Application")
If Err.number <> 0 Then
    Wscript.Echo "Unable to connect to Virtual Server."
    Wscript.Quit
End if
```

346

Chapter 17: Scripting Virtual Server

```
On Error Goto 0

'Display VMRC Information
wscript.echo "VMRC Information"
wscript.echo "========================="
wscript.echo "VMRCAdminAddress                   : " & vs.VMRCAdminAddress
wscript.echo "VMRCAdminPortNumber                : " & vs.VMRCAdminPortNumber
wscript.echo "VMRCEnabled                        : " & vs.VMRCEnabled
wscript.echo "VMRCEncryptionCertificate          : "
wscript.echo vs.VMRCEncryptionCertificate
wscript.echo "VMRCEncryptionEnabled              : " & vs.VMRCEncryptionEnabled
wscript.echo "VMRCIdleConnectionTimeout          : " & vs.VMRCIdleConnectionTimeout
wscript.echo "VMRCIdleConnectionTimeoutEnabled : " & ⤵
 vs.VMRCIdleConnectionTimeoutEnabled
wscript.echo "VMRCXResolution                    : " & vs.VMRCXResolution
wscript.echo "VMRCYResolution                    : " & vs.VMRCYResolution
wscript.echo ""

'Set VMRC information
vs.VMRCAdminAddress = "192.168.1.10"
vs.VMRCAdminPortNumber = 3390
vs.VMRCEnabled = true
vs.VMRCEncryptionCertificate = ""
vs.VMRCEncryptionEnabled = false
vs.VMRCIdleConnectionTimeout = 15
vs.VMRCIdleConnectionTimeoutEnabled = true
vs.VMRCXResolution = 800
vs.VMRCYResolution = 600

'Display information about possible VMRC Authenticators
Set objVMAColl = vs.VMRCAuthenticators
If objVMAColl.count = 0 Then
    Wscript.Echo "VMRC authenticators: [none]"
Else
    Wscript.Echo "VMRC authenticators: "
    For Each objAuth in objVMAColl
        WScript.Echo "    Name: " & objAuth.Name & " (" & _
        objAuth.Description & ")"
    Next
End If

'Display current VMRC Authenticator
wscript.echo vs.VMRCAuthenticator.Name
wscript.echo vs.VMRCAuthenticator.Description

'Set VMRC Authenticator to Automatic
Set objVMAColl = vs.VMRCAuthenticators
If objVMAColl.count = 0 Then
    Wscript.Echo "VMRC authenticators: [none]"
Else
    Wscript.Echo "VMRC authenticators: "
    For Each objAuth in objVMAColl
        if objAuth.Name = "Automatic" then
```

Part VII: Automating Virtual Machine Operations

```
            vs.VMRCAuthenticator = objAuth
        end if
    Next
End If
```

Read-Only Properties

The Virtual Server COM object also provides a lot of information in the form of read-only properties. Many of these properties are present to allow the Virtual Server Administrative website to determine the correct parameters to offer to the end user (properties such as `MaximumFloppyDrivesPerVM`). These properties will always return the same value on any installation of Virtual Server. Some of the more interesting properties include:

❑   `AvailableSystemCapacity`: This reports the capacity that is available on the system after considering the amount of CPU resource that is reserved by the currently running virtual machines. This value represents the highest reserve that you can place on a virtual machine and still have it power on.

❑   `UpTime` and `Version`: These values are fairly self-explanatory; they show the system uptime for Virtual Server and the version of Virtual Server that is being run.

❑   `Support Drivers`: This is an array of support driver objects. For each object you can display details about the support driver such as the version number, manufacturer, and date it was built on.

```
Option Explicit

dim vs, supportDriver

' Check that the script is running at the command line.
If UCase(Right(Wscript.FullName, 11)) = "WSCRIPT.EXE" Then
    Wscript.Echo "This script must be run under CScript."
    Wscript.Quit
End If


' Attempt to connect to Virtual Server
On Error Resume Next
Set vs = CreateObject("VirtualServer.Application")
If Err.number <> 0 Then
    Wscript.Echo "Unable to connect to Virtual Server."
    Wscript.Quit
End if
On Error Goto 0

'Display VMRC Information
wscript.echo "Virtual Server Information"
wscript.echo "=========================="
wscript.echo "AvailableSystemCapacity        : " & vs.AvailableSystemCapacity
wscript.echo "DefaultVNConfigurationPath     : " & vs.DefaultVNConfigurationPath
wscript.echo "MaximumFloppyDrivesPerVM       : " & vs.MaximumFloppyDrivesPerVM
wscript.echo "MaximumMemoryPerVM             : " & vs.MaximumMemoryPerVM
wscript.echo "MaximumNetworkAdaptersPerVM    : " & vs.MaximumNetworkAdaptersPerVM
wscript.echo "MaximumNumberOfIDEBuses        : " & vs.MaximumNumberOfIDEBuses
```

Chapter 17: Scripting Virtual Server

```
wscript.echo "MaximumNumberOfSCSIControllers : " & ⤴
  vs.MaximumNumberOfSCSIControllers
wscript.echo "MaximumParallelPortsPerVM        : " & vs.MaximumParallelPortsPerVM
wscript.echo "MaximumSerialPortsPerVM          : " & vs.MaximumSerialPortsPerVM
wscript.echo "MinimumMemoryPerVM               : " & vs.MinimumMemoryPerVM
wscript.echo "Name                             : " & vs.Name
wscript.echo "ProductID                        : " & vs.ProductID
wscript.echo "SuggestedMaximumMemoryPerVM      : " & vs.SuggestedMaximumMemoryPerVM
wscript.echo "UpTime                           : " & vs.UpTime
wscript.echo "Version                          : " & vs.Version
wscript.echo ""
wscript.echo "Support Drivers                  : "
wscript.echo "======================="
for each supportDriver in vs.SupportDrivers
wscript.echo supportDriver.Description
wscript.echo "Support Driver Manufacturer      : " & supportDriver.Manufacturer
wscript.echo "Support Driver Provider          : " & supportDriver.Provider
wscript.echo "Support Driver Version           : " & supportDriver.Version
wscript.echo "Support Driver Date              : " & supportDriver.Date
wscript.echo ""
next

' Can't view vs.DefaultLocale in VBScript
```

Managing Paths

You can also configure the default paths through the Virtual Server COM object. The default location for the virtual machine configuration files can be configured through an editable property: `DefaultVMConfigurationPath`. Configuring the search paths requires a bit more work. vs.SearchPaths contains an array of the search paths. While it is easy to create a new array to assign to vs.SearchPaths with VBScript, it is harder to add or remove entries from the existing array. I have provided examples of how to do this that leverage `ReDim`, a command that allows you to change the length of an existing array under VBScript.

```
Option Explicit

dim vs, path, tempArray, tempArray2,  counter, pathToRemove, foundPathToRemove

' Check that the script is running at the command line.
If UCase(Right(Wscript.FullName, 11)) = "WSCRIPT.EXE" Then
    Wscript.Echo "This script must be run under CScript."
    Wscript.Quit
End If

' Attempt to connect to Virtual Server
On Error Resume Next
Set vs = CreateObject("VirtualServer.Application")
If Err.number <> 0 Then
    Wscript.Echo "Unable to connect to Virtual Server."
    Wscript.Quit
End if
On Error Goto 0

'Display Paths
```

349

Part VII: Automating Virtual Machine Operations

```
wscript.echo "Default virtual machine configuration path:"
wscript.echo "=========================================="
wscript.echo vs.DefaultVMConfigurationPath
wscript.echo ""
WScript.echo "File search paths:"
wscript.echo "=================="
for each path in vs.SearchPaths
    Wscript.Echo path
next

'Change default VM Configruation path

vs.DefaultVMConfigurationPath = "L:\Wrox virtual machines"

'Set new set of search paths
tempArray = Array("C:\Path1", "C:\Path2", "C:\Path3")
vs.SearchPaths = tempArray

'Add a new search path
tempArray = vs.SearchPaths
ReDim Preserve tempArray( UBound(tempArray) + 1 )
tempArray ( UBound(tempArray) ) = "C:\MyVHDs"
vs.SearchPaths = tempArray

'Delete a search path
foundPathToRemove = 0
pathToRemove = "C:\MyVHDs"
tempArray2 = vs.SearchPaths

ReDim tempArray( UBound(tempArray2) - 1 )

for counter = 0 to UBound(tempArray2)
    if tempArray2(counter) = pathToRemove then
        foundPathToRemove = 1
    else
        tempArray(counter - foundPathToRemove) = tempArray2(counter)
    end if
next

vs.SearchPaths = tempArray
```

Managing Virtual Server Scripts

Virtual server allows you to associate the scripts with some basic events. The sample code that follows demonstrates how to enable this functionality, query existing scripts that are configured, and configure new scripts.

```
Option Explicit

'Declare event constants
CONST vmEvent_VirtualServerStarted = 0
CONST vmEvent_VirtualServerStopped = 1
CONST vmEvent_VirtualMachineLaunched = 2
CONST vmEvent_VirtualMachineStateRestored = 3
```

Chapter 17: Scripting Virtual Server

```
CONST vmEvent_VirtualMachineStateSaved = 4
CONST vmEvent_VirtualMachineTurnedOff = 5
CONST vmEvent_VirtualMachineTurnedOffByGuest = 6
CONST vmEvent_VirtualMachineReset = 7
CONST vmEvent_VirtualMachineNoHeartbeat = 8
CONST vmEvent_VirtualMachineProcessorError = 9
CONST vmEvent_VirtualMachineHostDiskSpaceWarning = 10
CONST vmEvent_VirtualMachineHostDiskSpaceError = 11

dim vs

' Check that the script is running at the command line.
If UCase(Right(Wscript.FullName, 11)) = "WSCRIPT.EXE" Then
    Wscript.Echo "This script must be run under CScript."
    Wscript.Quit
End If

' Attempt to connect to Virtual Server
On Error Resume Next
Set vs = CreateObject("VirtualServer.Application")
If Err.number <> 0 Then
    Wscript.Echo "Unable to connect to Virtual Server."
    Wscript.Quit
End if
On Error Goto 0

'Display the state of VSScriptsEnabled and VMScriptsEnabled
wscript.echo "VSScriptsEnabled: " & vs.VSScriptsEnabled
wscript.echo "VMScriptsEnabled: " & vs.VMScriptsEnabled

' Enable VSScriptsEnabled and VMScriptsEnabled
vs.VSScriptsEnabled = true
vs.VMScriptsEnabled = true

'Display the configuration for all scripts
wscript.echo "vmEvent_VirtualServerStarted script            : " _
    & vs.FetchScriptByEvent(vmEvent_VirtualServerStarted)
wscript.echo "vmEvent_VirtualServerStopped script            : " _
    & vs.FetchScriptByEvent(vmEvent_VirtualServerStopped)
wscript.echo "vmEvent_VirtualMachineLaunched script          : " _
    & vs.FetchScriptByEvent(vmEvent_VirtualMachineLaunched)
wscript.echo "vmEvent_VirtualMachineStateRestored script     : " _
    & vs.FetchScriptByEvent(vmEvent_VirtualMachineStateRestored)
wscript.echo "vmEvent_VirtualMachineStateSaved script        : " _
    & vs.FetchScriptByEvent(vmEvent_VirtualMachineStateSaved)
wscript.echo "vmEvent_VirtualMachineTurnedOff script         : " _
    & vs.FetchScriptByEvent(vmEvent_VirtualMachineTurnedOff)
wscript.echo "vmEvent_VirtualMachineTurnedOffByGuest script  : " _
    & vs.FetchScriptByEvent(vmEvent_VirtualMachineTurnedOffByGuest)
wscript.echo "vmEvent_VirtualMachineReset script             : " _
    & vs.FetchScriptByEvent(vmEvent_VirtualMachineReset)
wscript.echo "vmEvent_VirtualMachineNoHeartbeat script        : " _
    & vs.FetchScriptByEvent(vmEvent_VirtualMachineNoHeartbeat)
wscript.echo "vmEvent_VirtualMachineProcessorError script     : " _
    & vs.FetchScriptByEvent(vmEvent_VirtualMachineProcessorError)
```

Part VII: Automating Virtual Machine Operations

```
wscript.echo "vmEvent_VirtualMachineHostDiskSpaceWarning script : " _
    & vs.FetchScriptByEvent(vmEvent_VirtualMachineHostDiskSpaceWarning)
wscript.echo "vmEvent_VirtualMachineHostDiskSpaceError script    : " _
    & vs.FetchScriptByEvent(vmEvent_VirtualMachineHostDiskSpaceError)

'Remove the script from VirtualServerStarted
vs.RemoveScriptFromEvent vmEvent_VirtualServerStarted

'Add a script to VirtualServerStopped
vs.AttachScriptToEvent vmEvent_VirtualServerStopped, "C:\Command.cmd"
```

Virtual Machines

The virtual machine COM object can be created from the Virtual Server COM object by using `CreateVirtualMachine`, `RegisterVirtualMachine`, or `FindVirtualMachine`. It allows you to configure devices and settings related to the virtual machine and to perform actions such as turning the virtual machine on or off.

Virtual Machine State Management

A number of state changes can be requested of a virtual machine. It can be turned on (`vm.Startup`), put into a saved state (`vm.Save`), paused and resumed (`vm.Pause` and `vm.Resume`), or turned off (`vm.TurnOff`). With the exception of pause and resume, all state changes return a `VmTask` object.

Shutting down the guest operating system is not performed directly through the virtual machine COM object. This is performed through the guest OS COM object, which is discussed later in this chapter.

```
Option Explicit

dim vs, vm, vmTask

' Check that the script is running at the command line.
If UCase(Right(Wscript.FullName, 11)) = "WSCRIPT.EXE" Then
    Wscript.Echo "This script must be run under CScript."
    Wscript.Quit
End If

' Attempt to connect to Virtual Server
On Error Resume Next
Set vs = CreateObject("VirtualServer.Application")
If Err.number <> 0 Then
    Wscript.Echo "Unable to connect to Virtual Server."
    Wscript.Quit
End if
On Error Goto 0

'Get virtual machine object
set vm = vs.FindVirtualMachine("A virtual machine")

'Start the virtual machine
wscript.echo "Starting the virtual machine..."
```

Chapter 17: Scripting Virtual Server

```
set vmTask = vm.Startup

vmTask.WaitForCompletion(-1)

wscript.sleep(10000)

'Save State the virtual machine
wscript.echo "Saving the virtual machine..."
set vmTask = vm.Save

vmTask.WaitForCompletion(-1)

wscript.sleep(10000)

'Start the virtual machine again
wscript.echo "Starting the virtual machine..."
set vmTask = vm.Startup

vmTask.WaitForCompletion(-1)

wscript.sleep(10000)

'Pause the virtual machine again
wscript.echo "Pause the virtual machine..."
vm.Pause

wscript.sleep(10000)

'Resume the virtual machine again
wscript.echo "Resume the virtual machine..."
vm.Resume

wscript.sleep(10000)

'Turn off the virtual machine again
wscript.echo "Turning off the virtual machine..."
set vmTask = vm.TurnOff

vmTask.WaitForCompletion(-1)
```

Adding and Removing Devices

The virtual machine COM object is used to add and remove devices from the virtual machine. Virtual hard disks, DVD drives, network adapters, and SCSI controllers are the four types of devices that can be added and removed from virtual machines. (All other device types are always present inside a virtual machine — for example, the floppy drive.)

Adding a network adapter or SCSI controller requires no parameters and returns a network adapter COM object or a SCSI controller COM object. Adding a DVD drive requires that you specify the bus type that the DVD drive will be connected to as well as the bus number and the location on the bus.

This is kind of strange given that DVD drives can only be attached to the IDE bus under Virtual Server.

353

Part VII: Automating Virtual Machine Operations

Unlike for network adapters, SCSI controllers, and other devices you do not add a virtual hard disk to the virtual machine. Rather, you create a virtual hard disk connection COM object, which associates the virtual hard disk with the virtual machine. When you create the virtual hard disk connection COM object, you need to provide the details about the virtual hard disk that will be used, the bus type that the virtual hard disk will be connected to, and the bus number and location for the virtual hard disk connection.

Removing each of the devices requires only a single parameter of the COM object for the device that is to be removed.

The script that follows connects to Virtual Server and connects to `"A virtual machine"`. The script then adds an existing virtual hard drive to the virtual machine by creating a new virtual hard disk connection object. The script also uses `AddDVDROMDrive`, `AddNetworkAdapter`, and `AddSCSIController` to add a DVD drive, network adapter, and SCSI controller, respectively. Finally, it removes all these objects.

```
Option Explicit

CONST vmDriveBusType_IDE = 0
CONST vmDriveBusType_SCSI = 1

dim vs, vm, vhdConnection, dvdDrive, netAdapter, scsiController

' Check that the script is running at the command line.
If UCase(Right(Wscript.FullName, 11)) = "WSCRIPT.EXE" Then
    Wscript.Echo "This script must be run under CScript."
    Wscript.Quit
End If


' Attempt to connect to Virtual Server
On Error Resume Next
Set vs = CreateObject("VirtualServer.Application")
If Err.number <> 0 Then
    Wscript.Echo "Unable to connect to Virtual Server."
    Wscript.Quit
End if
On Error Goto 0

'Get virtual machine object
set vm = vs.FindVirtualMachine("A virtual machine")

set vhdConnection = vm.AddHardDiskConnection( _
    "C:\MyVHDs\DynamicDisk.vhd", vmDriveBusType_IDE, 1, 0)

set dvdDrive = vm.AddDVDROMDrive(vmDriveBusType_IDE, 1, 1)

set netAdapter = vm.AddNetworkAdapter

set scsiController = vm.AddSCSIController

'Wait a little bit
Wscript.sleep(10000)

'Remove everything
vm.RemoveHardDiskConnection(vhdConnection)
```

354

Chapter 17: Scripting Virtual Server

```
vm.RemoveDVDROMDrive(dvdDrive)
vm.RemoveNetworkAdapter(netAdapter)
vm.RemoveSCSIController(scsiController)
```

Configuring Virtual Machine Properties

The virtual machine COM object exposes a handful of configurable properties. The virtual machine name, notes, amount of memory, undo disk setting, and default actions when Virtual Server shuts down or for when the guest operating system shuts down with the undo disk present can all be determined and configured through these basic properties. The script that follows connects to Virtual Server and connects to "A virtual machine". The script then displays the current configuration of these properties and updates them with new values.

```
Option Explicit

'Define constants
CONST vmUndoAction_Discard = 0
CONST vmUndoAction_Keep = 1
CONST vmUndoAction_Commit = 2
CONST vmShutdownAction_Save = 0
CONST vmShutdownAction_TurnOff = 1
CONST vmShutdownAction_Shutdown = 2

dim vs, vm

' Check that the script is running at the command line.
If UCase(Right(Wscript.FullName, 11)) = "WSCRIPT.EXE" Then
    Wscript.Echo "This script must be run under CScript."
    Wscript.Quit
End If

' Attempt to connect to Virtual Server
On Error Resume Next
Set vs = CreateObject("VirtualServer.Application")
If Err.number <> 0 Then
    Wscript.Echo "Unable to connect to Virtual Server."
    Wscript.Quit
End if
On Error Goto 0

'Get virtual machine object
set vm = vs.FindVirtualMachine("A virtual machine")

'Display virtual machine information
wscript.echo "Name                  : " & vm.Name
wscript.echo "Notes                 : " & vm.Notes
wscript.echo "Memory                : " & vm.Memory
wscript.echo "Undoable              : " & vm.Undoable
wscript.echo "UndoAction            : " & vm.UndoAction
wscript.echo "ShutdownActionOnQuit  : " & vm.ShutdownActionOnQuit

'Set virtual machine information
vm.Name = "A virtual machine"
vm.Notes = "Notes about something"
```

355

Part VII: Automating Virtual Machine Operations

```
vm.Memory = 256
vm.Undoable = true
vm.UndoAction = vmUndoAction_Discard
vm.ShutdownActionOnQuit = vmShutdownAction_TurnOff
```

Read-Only Virtual Machine Properties

The virtual machine COM object also exposes a number of read-only properties. A number of these properties describe the capabilities of the virtual machine. HasMMX, HasSSE, HasSSE2, Has3DNow, and ProcessorSpeed all provide information about the processor capabilities that are available inside the virtual machine. AccountName reports the name of the user account that the virtual machine is configured to run under (if it is so configured). File reports the name and location of the virtual machine configuration file, and SavedStateFilePath reports the name and location of the virtual machine saves state file.

> *Note that in the script, I enable error handling when checking* SaveStateFilePath. *The reason for this is that you will encounter an error if you check this property when there is no saved state file.*

ConfigID returns the internal identification number that is used by Virtual Server for the virtual machine. AttachedDriveTypes returns an array that describes the type of drives that are attached to the virtual machine. And. finally, state returns the current state of the virtual machine. Checking the value of state is very useful for ensuring that the virtual machine is in the correct state before attempting to perform any operation on it.

The script that follows connects to Virtual Server and connects to "A virtual machine". The script then displays the values of these read-only properties.

```
Option Explicit

'Define constants
CONST vmDriveType_Null = 0
CONST vmDriveType_HardDisk = 1
CONST vmDriveType_DVD = 2
CONST vmVMState_Invalid = 0
CONST vmVMState_TurnedOff = 1
CONST vmVMState_Saved = 2
CONST vmVMState_TurningOn = 3
CONST vmVMState_Restoring = 4
CONST vmVMState_Running = 5
CONST vmVMState_Paused = 6
CONST vmVMState_Saving = 7
CONST vmVMState_TurningOff = 8
CONST vmVMState_MergingDrives = 9
CONST vmVMState_DeleteMachine = 10

dim vs, vm, objDrive

' Check that the script is running at the command line.
If UCase(Right(Wscript.FullName, 11)) = "WSCRIPT.EXE" Then
    Wscript.Echo "This script must be run under CScript."
    Wscript.Quit
```

356

Chapter 17: Scripting Virtual Server

```
End If

' Attempt to connect to Virtual Server
On Error Resume Next
Set vs = CreateObject("VirtualServer.Application")
If Err.number <> 0 Then
    Wscript.Echo "Unable to connect to Virtual Server."
    Wscript.Quit
End if
On Error Goto 0

'Get virtual machine object
set vm = vs.FindVirtualMachine("A virtual machine")

'Display virtual machine information
wscript.echo "AccountName        : " & vm.AccountName
wscript.echo "ConfigID           : " & vm.ConfigID
wscript.echo "File               : " & vm.File

On Error Resume Next
wscript.echo "SavedStateFilePath : " & vm.SavedStateFilePath
If Err.number <> 0 Then
    Wscript.Echo "SavedStateFilePath : No saved state file"
End if

On Error Goto 0
wscript.echo "HasMMX             : " & vm.HasMMX
wscript.echo "HasSSE             : " & vm.HasSSE
wscript.echo "HasSSE2            : " & vm.HasSSE2
wscript.echo "Has3DNow           : " & vm.Has3DNow
wscript.echo "ProcessorSpeed     : " & vm.ProcessorSpeed

Select case vm.State
    case vmVMState_Invalid
        wscript.Echo("State            :" & _
            "The virtual machine is in an invalid state")
    case vmVMState_TurnedOff
        wscript.Echo("State            :" & _
            "The virtual machine is turned off")
    case vmVMState_Saved
        wscript.Echo("State            :" & _
            "The virtual machine is saved")
    case vmVMState_TurningOn
        wscript.Echo("State            :" & _
            "The virtual machine is turning on")
    case vmVMState_Restoring
        wscript.Echo("State            :" & _
            "The virtual machine is restoring")
    case vmVMState_Running
        wscript.Echo("State            :" & _
            "The virtual machine is running")
    case vmVMState_Paused
        wscript.Echo("State            :" & _
            "The virtual machine is pause")
```

Part VII: Automating Virtual Machine Operations

```
      case vmVMState_Saving
         wscript.Echo("State                  :" & _
            "The virtual machine is saving state")
      case vmVMState_TurningOff
         wscript.Echo("State                  :" & _
            "The virtual machine is turning off")
      case vmVMState_MergingDrives
         wscript.Echo("State                  :" & _
            "The virtual machine is mergin undo disks")
      case vmVMState_DeleteMachine
         wscript.Echo("State                  :" & _
            "The virtual machine is being deleted")
   end select

wscript.echo "AttachedDriveTypes : "
for each objDrive in vm.AttachedDriveTypes
Select case objDrive
   case vmDriveType_Null
      wscript.Echo("DriveTypes           : " & _
         "null device")
   case vmDriveType_HardDisk
      wscript.Echo("DriveTypes           : " & _
         "hard disk")
   case vmDriveType_DVD
      wscript.Echo("DriveTypes           : " & _
         "DVD drive")
   end select
next
```

Managing a Virtual Machine Saved State or Undo Disk

In addition to basic virtual machine state management, there are a couple of advanced methods that you can call. `DiscardSavedState` will destroy the saved state of the virtual machine if one exists. The resulting virtual machine will look, feel, and act like it would if the power were cut from the virtual machine at the time that the saved state was taken. The only time you would need to use this method is if you had a corrupted saved state file, or a virtual machine had been saved on another computer and could not be restored on the current computer.

The script that follows connects to Virtual Server and connects to "A virtual machine". The script then discards the saved state file if it exists.

```
Option Explicit

'Define constants
CONST vmVMState_Invalid = 0
CONST vmVMState_TurnedOff = 1
CONST vmVMState_Saved = 2
CONST vmVMState_TurningOn = 3
CONST vmVMState_Restoring = 4
CONST vmVMState_Running = 5
```

358

Chapter 17: Scripting Virtual Server

```
CONST vmVMState_Paused = 6
CONST vmVMState_Saving = 7
CONST vmVMState_TurningOff = 8
CONST vmVMState_MergingDrives = 9
CONST vmVMState_DeleteMachine = 10

dim vs, vm

' Check that the script is running at the command line.
If UCase(Right(Wscript.FullName, 11)) = "WSCRIPT.EXE" Then
    Wscript.Echo "This script must be run under CScript."
    Wscript.Quit
End If

' Attempt to connect to Virtual Server
On Error Resume Next
Set vs = CreateObject("VirtualServer.Application")
If Err.number <> 0 Then
    Wscript.Echo "Unable to connect to Virtual Server."
    Wscript.Quit
End if
On Error Goto 0

'Get virtual machine object
set vm = vs.FindVirtualMachine("A virtual machine")

if vm.state = vmVMState_Saved then
   wscript.echo "Discarding saved state..."
   vm.DiscardSavedState
else
   wscript.echo "There is no saved state to discard..."
end if
```

You can also use `DiscardUndoDisks` to delete any uncommitted undo disks associated with the virtual machine:

```
...

'Get virtual machine object
set vm = vs.FindVirtualMachine("A virtual machine")

if vm.undoable then
   if (vm.state = vmVMState_TurnedOff) then
      wscript.echo "Discarding undo disks..."
      vm.DiscardUndoDisks
   else
      wscript.echo "Can't discard undo disks."
   end if
else
   wscript.echo "Undo disks are not enabled."
end if
```

359

Part VII: Automating Virtual Machine Operations

`MergeUndoDisks` will merge any uncommitted undo disks associated with the virtual machine:

```
...

'Get virtual machine object
set vm = vs.FindVirtualMachine("A virtual machine")

if vm.undoable then
    if (vm.state = vmVMState_TurnedOff) or _
        (vm.state = vmVMState_Saved) then
        wscript.echo "Merging undo disks..."
        set vmtask = vm.MergeUndoDisks
        vmtask.WaitForCompletion(-1)
    else
        wscript.echo "Can't merge undo disks."
    end if
else
    wscript.echo "Undo disks are not enabled."
end if
```

Virtual Machine Identification

Virtual Server allows you to configure a number of the hardware identification strings that are presented inside of the virtual machine. The `BaseBoardSerialNumber`, `BIOSGUID`, `BIOSSerialNumber`, `ChassisAssetTag`, and `ChassisSerialNumber` properties all allow you to configure the respective hardware identification methods inside the virtual machine.

The script that follows connects to Virtual Server and connects to `"A virtual machine"`. The script then displays the current virtual machine identification information, checks to see that the virtual machine is turned off, and, if it is, updates the virtual machine identification information.

```
Option Explicit

'Define constants
CONST vmVMState_TurnedOff = 1

dim vs, vm

' Check that the script is running at the command line.
If UCase(Right(Wscript.FullName, 11)) = "WSCRIPT.EXE" Then
    Wscript.Echo "This script must be run under CScript."
    Wscript.Quit
End If

' Attempt to connect to Virtual Server
On Error Resume Next
Set vs = CreateObject("VirtualServer.Application")
If Err.number <> 0 Then
    Wscript.Echo "Unable to connect to Virtual Server."
    Wscript.Quit
End if
On Error Goto 0

'Get virtual machine object
```

360

Chapter 17: Scripting Virtual Server

```
set vm = vs.FindVirtualMachine("A virtual machine")

'Display current information
wscript.echo vm.name & " identification information"
wscript.echo "--=========================================="
wscript.echo "BaseBoardSerialNumber : " & vm.BaseBoardSerialNumber
wscript.echo "BIOSGUID               : " & vm.BIOSGUID
wscript.echo "BIOSSerialNumber       : " & vm.BIOSSerialNumber
wscript.echo "ChassisAssetTag        : " & vm.ChassisAssetTag
wscript.echo "ChassisSerialNumber    : " & vm.ChassisSerialNumber

'Set information
wscript.echo ""
if vm.state = vmVMState_TurnedOff then
   wscript.echo "Updating identification information."
   vm.BaseBoardSerialNumber = "5779-2158-0120-8892-0505-0317-47"
   vm.BIOSGUID = "{B7532508-1DE4-4002-AC1F-0D8893634777}"
   vm.BIOSSerialNumber = "5779-2158-0120-8892-0505-0317-48"
   vm.ChassisAssetTag = "5779-2158-0120-8892-0505-0317-49"
   vm.ChassisSerialNumber = "5779-2158-0120-8892-0505-0317-50"
else
   wscript.echo "Cannot change identification information while the virtual ⏎
machine is running."
end if
```

If the virtual machine is running a Windows guest operating system you can retrieve this information by using WMI inside the virtual machine. Here is a sample script that does exactly that:

```
Option Explicit

dim WMI, item

' Check that the script is running at the command line.
If UCase(Right(Wscript.FullName, 11)) = "WSCRIPT.EXE" Then
    Wscript.Echo "This script must be run under CScript."
    Wscript.Quit
End If

Wscript.Echo "----------------------------------"
Wscript.Echo "Virtual Machine Identification"
Wscript.Echo "----------------------------------"

Set WMI = GetObject("winmgmts:\\.\root\CIMV2")

For Each item in WMI.ExecQuery("SELECT * FROM Win32_BIOS",,48)
    Wscript.Echo "BIOS Serial Number    : " & item.SerialNumber
Next

For Each item in WMI.ExecQuery("SELECT * FROM Win32_ComputerSystemProduct",,48)
    Wscript.Echo "BIOS GUID             : " & item.UUID
Next

For Each item in WMI.ExecQuery("SELECT * FROM Win32_SystemEnclosure",,48)
    Wscript.Echo "Chassis Serial Number : " & item.SerialNumber
    Wscript.Echo "Chassis Asset Tag     : " & item.SMBIOSAssetTag
```

361

Part VII: Automating Virtual Machine Operations

```
Next

For Each item in WMI.ExecQuery("SELECT * FROM Win32_BaseBoard",,48)
    Wscript.Echo "BaseBoard Serial Number: " & item.SerialNumber
Next
```

Virtual Machine Scripts

Just like with the Virtual Server COM object, the virtual machine COM object allows you to configure scripts that should be launched in response to specific events. The script that follows connects to Virtual Server and connects to "A virtual machine". The script then displays the information about all currently configured scripts, removes any script information that is associated with the VirtualServerStarted event, and associates a new script with the VirtualServerStopped event.

```
Option Explicit

'Declare event constants
CONST vmEvent_VirtualServerStarted = 0
CONST vmEvent_VirtualServerStopped = 1
CONST vmEvent_VirtualMachineLaunched = 2
CONST vmEvent_VirtualMachineStateRestored = 3
CONST vmEvent_VirtualMachineStateSaved = 4
CONST vmEvent_VirtualMachineTurnedOff = 5
CONST vmEvent_VirtualMachineTurnedOffByGuest = 6
CONST vmEvent_VirtualMachineReset = 7
CONST vmEvent_VirtualMachineNoHeartbeat = 8
CONST vmEvent_VirtualMachineProcessorError = 9
CONST vmEvent_VirtualMachineHostDiskSpaceWarning = 10
CONST vmEvent_VirtualMachineHostDiskSpaceError = 11

dim vs, vm

' Check that the script is running at the command line.
If UCase(Right(Wscript.FullName, 11)) = "WSCRIPT.EXE" Then
    Wscript.Echo "This script must be run under CScript."
    Wscript.Quit
End If

' Attempt to connect to Virtual Server
On Error Resume Next
Set vs = CreateObject("VirtualServer.Application")
If Err.number <> 0 Then
    Wscript.Echo "Unable to connect to Virtual Server."
    Wscript.Quit
End if
On Error Goto 0

'Get virtual machine object
set vm = vs.FindVirtualMachine("A virtual machine")

'Display the configuration for all scripts
wscript.echo "vmEvent_VirtualServerStarted script                 : " _
    & vm.FetchScriptByEvent(vmEvent_VirtualServerStarted)
wscript.echo "vmEvent_VirtualServerStopped script                 : " _
```

Chapter 17: Scripting Virtual Server

```
        & vm.FetchScriptByEvent(vmEvent_VirtualServerStopped)
wscript.echo "vmEvent_VirtualMachineLaunched script            : " _
        & vm.FetchScriptByEvent(vmEvent_VirtualMachineLaunched)
wscript.echo "vmEvent_VirtualMachineStateRestored script       : " _
        & vm.FetchScriptByEvent(vmEvent_VirtualMachineStateRestored)
wscript.echo "vmEvent_VirtualMachineStateSaved script          : " _
        & vm.FetchScriptByEvent(vmEvent_VirtualMachineStateSaved)
wscript.echo "vmEvent_VirtualMachineTurnedOff script           : " _
        & vm.FetchScriptByEvent(vmEvent_VirtualMachineTurnedOff)
wscript.echo "vmEvent_VirtualMachineTurnedOffByGuest script     : " _
        & vm.FetchScriptByEvent(vmEvent_VirtualMachineTurnedOffByGuest)
wscript.echo "vmEvent_VirtualMachineReset script               : " _
        & vm.FetchScriptByEvent(vmEvent_VirtualMachineReset)
wscript.echo "vmEvent_VirtualMachineNoHeartbeat script          : " _
        & vm.FetchScriptByEvent(vmEvent_VirtualMachineNoHeartbeat)
wscript.echo "vmEvent_VirtualMachineProcessorError script       : " _
        & vm.FetchScriptByEvent(vmEvent_VirtualMachineProcessorError)
wscript.echo "vmEvent_VirtualMachineHostDiskSpaceWarning script : " _
        & vm.FetchScriptByEvent(vmEvent_VirtualMachineHostDiskSpaceWarning)
wscript.echo "vmEvent_VirtualMachineHostDiskSpaceError script   : " _
        & vm.FetchScriptByEvent(vmEvent_VirtualMachineHostDiskSpaceError)

'Remove the script from VirtualServerStarted
vm.RemoveScriptFromEvent vmEvent_VirtualServerStarted

'Add a script to VirtualServerStopped
vm.AttachScriptToEvent vmEvent_VirtualServerStopped, "C:\Command.cmd"
```

Virtual Machine Automatic Start

You can also use the virtual machine COM object to configure the user account that the virtual machine will be run under (using `SetAccountNameAndPassword` and `RunAsDefinedAccount`), as well as specifying whether the virtual machine should start automatically when Virtual Server starts, and if so, how much the automatic start should be delayed by (in seconds).

The script that follows connects to Virtual Server and connects to `"A virtual machine"`. The script then sets an account name and password to be used to run the virtual machine, enables the option to run the virtual machine as the specified account, and configures the auto start behavior and auto start delay.

```
Option Explicit

'Declare event constants
CONST vmAutoStart_Never = 0
CONST vmAutoStart_Always = 1
CONST vmAutoStart_IfRunningAtQuit = 2

dim vs, vm

' Attempt to connect to Virtual Server
On Error Resume Next
Set vs = CreateObject("VirtualServer.Application")
If Err.number <> 0 Then
    Wscript.Echo "Unable to connect to Virtual Server."
    Wscript.Quit
```

363

Part VII: Automating Virtual Machine Operations

```
End if
On Error Goto 0

'Get virtual machine object
set vm = vs.FindVirtualMachine("A virtual machine")

'Set a username and password to use for running the VM
vm.SetAccountNameAndPassword "Username", "Password"

'Enable the virtual machine to run as the specified account
vm.RunAsDefinedAccount = true

'Configure autolaunch behavior
vm.AutoStartAtLaunch = vmAutoStart_IfRunningAtQuit

'Configure autolaunch delay
vm.AutoStartAtLaunchDelay = 60
```

SCSI Controller

You can get to the SCSI controller COM object by enumerating the SCSIControllers collection available from the virtual machine COM object. Each SCSI controller allows you to configure where the SCSI bus is shared (IsBusShared) and which SCSI ID should be used for the controller (SCSIID).

The script that follows connects to Virtual Server and connects to "A virtual machine". The script then displays how many SCSI controllers the virtual machine currently has, displays configuration information about each of the SCSI controllers, and changes the configuration of the first SCSI controller. (Note that this script will work only if the virtual machine has at least one SCSI controller.)

```
Option Explicit

dim vs, vm, SCSIController, aSCSIController

' Check that the script is running at the command line.
If UCase(Right(Wscript.FullName, 11)) = "WSCRIPT.EXE" Then
    Wscript.Echo "This script must be run under CScript."
    Wscript.Quit
End If

' Attempt to connect to Virtual Server
On Error Resume Next
Set vs = CreateObject("VirtualServer.Application")
If Err.number <> 0 Then
    Wscript.Echo "Unable to connect to Virtual Server."
    Wscript.Quit
End if
On Error Goto 0

'Get virtual machine object
set vm = vs.FindVirtualMachine("A virtual machine")

'Display current SCSI controller data
```

364

Chapter 17: Scripting Virtual Server

```
wscript.echo "The virtual machine has " & _
    vm.SCSIControllers.count & " SCSI Controllers"
wscript.echo ""

for each SCSIController in vm.SCSIControllers
    wscript.echo "SCSI Controller Configuration"
    wscript.echo "============================="
    wscript.echo "IsBusShared : " & SCSIController.IsBusShared
    wscript.echo "SCSI ID     : " & SCSIController.SCSIID
    wscript.echo ""
Next

'Change the first SCSI controller to be shared with a
'SCSI ID of 6.

set aSCSIController = vm.SCSIControllers.item(1)

aSCSIController.Configure true, 6

'This can only be done with undo disks disabled
```

Virtual Hard Disks

You can create a virtual hard disk COM object by calling `GetHardDisk` with a single parameter of the virtual hard disk file that you want to modify. Once you've created the virtual hard disk COM object there are a number of operations you can perform. You can look at the `File`, `Type`, `SizeInGuest`, `SizeOnHost`, `HostFreeDiskSpace`, and `Parent` properties to learn about the state of the virtual hard disk.

`SizeInGuest` reports the size of the virtual hard disk is seen by the guest operating system while `SizeOnHost` reports the actual amount of space that the virtual hard disk file is using on the host operating system. `HostFreeDiskSpace` reports the amount of free space on the hard disk where the virtual hard disk is being kept. The `Parent` property actually returns a virtual hard disk COM object for the parent virtual hard disk of a differencing disk.

Depending on the type of virtual hard disk, you can call the `Compact`, `Convert`, `Merge`, or `MergeTo` methods. Each of these methods returns a `VmTask` object. The following code listing is a relatively detailed VBScript that takes a single command-line parameter of the virtual hard disk file. (It will exit with an error message if no command-line parameter is provided.) It then uses a `case` statement to check the type of the virtual hard disk and display the information about the virtual hard disk file. For each virtual hard disk type, it offers to perform the appropriate actions.

```
Option Explicit

'Define constants
CONST vmDiskType_Dynamic = 0
CONST vmDiskType_FixedSize = 1
CONST vmDiskType_Differencing = 2
CONST vmDiskType_HostDrive = 4

dim vs, aVHD, aVHDFileName, input, vmTask, newVHDFileName

' Check that the script is running at the command line.
```

365

Part VII: Automating Virtual Machine Operations

```
If UCase(Right(Wscript.FullName, 11)) = "WSCRIPT.EXE" Then
    Wscript.Echo "This script must be run under CScript."
    Wscript.Quit
End If


' Attempt to connect to Virtual Server
On Error Resume Next
Set vs = CreateObject("VirtualServer.Application")
If Err.number <> 0 Then
    Wscript.Echo "Unable to connect to Virtual Server."
    Wscript.Quit
End if
On Error Goto 0

If WScript.Arguments.Count = 1 Then
 aVHDFileName = WScript.Arguments.Item(0)
Else
 Wscript.Echo "A single command line argument of the VHD file name should be ↵
 supplied"
 Wscript.Quit
End If

set aVHD = vs.GetHardDisk(aVHDFileName)

select case aVHD.type
  case vmDiskType_Dynamic
     'Display information about the VHD
     wscript.echo "VHD Information:"
     wscript.echo "=================="
     wscript.echo "File Name          : " & aVHD.File
     wscript.echo "Type               : Dynamically Expanding VHD"
     wscript.echo "SizeInGuest        : " & aVHD.SizeInGuest
     wscript.echo "SizeOnHost         : " & aVHD.SizeOnHost
     wscript.echo "HostFreeDiskSpace  : " & aVHD.HostFreeDiskSpace
     wscript.echo ""

     'Offer to perform appropriate actions for a dynamic disk
     wscript.echo "Do you want to (c)ompact the VHD, convert it to a (f)ixed ↵
disk, or (q)uit?"
     input = Wscript.StdIn.Read(1)
     select case input
        case "c"
           'Compact the VHD
           wscript.echo "Compacting the VHD..."
        set VMTask = aVHD.Compact
           vmTask.WaitForCompletion(-1)
           wscript.echo "Done."
        case "f"
           'Convert the VHD
           wscript.echo "Converting the VHD..."
           newVHDFileName = Left(aVHD.File, InStrRev(aVHD.File, ".") - 1) & ↵
" - fixed size.vhd"
           set VMTask = aVHD.Convert(newVHDFileName, vmDiskType_FixedSize)
           vmTask.WaitForCompletion(-1)
           wscript.echo "Done."
```

366

Chapter 17: Scripting Virtual Server

```
        end select

    case vmDiskType_FixedSize
        'Display information about the VHD
        wscript.echo "VHD Information:"
        wscript.echo "=================="
        wscript.echo "File Name          : " & aVHD.File
        wscript.echo "Type               : Fixed Size VHD"
        wscript.echo "SizeInGuest        : " & aVHD.SizeInGuest
        wscript.echo "SizeOnHost         : " & aVHD.SizeOnHost
        wscript.echo "HostFreeDiskSpace  : " & aVHD.HostFreeDiskSpace

        'Offer to perform appropriate actions for a fixed size disk
        wscript.echo "Do you want to (c)onvert the VHD to a dynamic disk, or (q)uit?"
        input = Wscript.StdIn.Read(1)
        select case input
            case "c"
                'Convert the VHD
                wscript.echo "Converting the VHD..."
                newVHDFileName = Left(aVHD.File, InStrRev(aVHD.File, ".") - 1) ⤸
& " - dynamic.vhd"
                set VMTask = aVHD.Convert(newVHDFileName, vmDiskType_Dynamic)
                vmTask.WaitForCompletion(-1)
                wscript.echo "Done."
        end select

    case vmDiskType_Differencing
        'Display information about the VHD
        wscript.echo "VHD Information:"
        wscript.echo "=================="
        wscript.echo "File Name          : " & aVHD.File
        wscript.echo "Type               : Differencing VHD"
        wscript.echo "Parent             : " & aVHD.Parent.File
        wscript.echo "SizeInGuest        : " & aVHD.SizeInGuest
        wscript.echo "SizeOnHost         : " & aVHD.SizeOnHost
        wscript.echo "HostFreeDiskSpace  : " & aVHD.HostFreeDiskSpace

        'Offer to perform appropriate actions for a differencing disk
        wscript.echo "Do you want to (m)erge the VHD to a new file, merge the VHD ⤸
into its (p)arent, or (q)uit?"
        input = Wscript.StdIn.Read(1)
        select case input
            case "m"
                'Merge the VHD to a new file
                wscript.echo "Merging the VHD to a new file..."
                newVHDFileName = Left(aVHD.File, InStrRev(aVHD.File, ".") - 1) & ⤸
" - merged.vhd"
                set VMTask = aVHD.MergeTo(newVHDFileName, aVHD.Parent.Type)
                vmTask.WaitForCompletion(-1)
                wscript.echo "Done."
            case "p"
                'Merge the VHD into the parent disk
                wscript.echo "Merging the VHD into the parent disk..."
                set VMTask = aVHD.Merge
                vmTask.WaitForCompletion(-1)
```

367

Part VII: Automating Virtual Machine Operations

```
                wscript.echo "Done."
        end select

    case vmDiskType_HostDrive
        'Display information about the VHD
        wscript.echo "VHD Information:"
        wscript.echo "=================="
        wscript.echo "File Name          : " & aVHD.File
        wscript.echo "Type               : Linked VHD"
        wscript.echo "HostDriveIdentifier : " & aVHD.HostDriveIdentifier
        wscript.echo "SizeInGuest        : " & aVHD.SizeInGuest
        wscript.echo "SizeOnHost         : " & aVHD.SizeOnHost
        wscript.echo "HostFreeDiskSpace  : " & aVHD.HostFreeDiskSpace

        'Offer to perform appropriate actions for a linke disk
        wscript.echo "Do you want to convert the VHD to a (d)ynamic disk, convert ⤵
the VHD to a (f)ixed size disk or (q)uit?"
        input = Wscript.StdIn.Read(1)
        select case input
            case "d"
                'Convert the VHD
                wscript.echo "Converting the VHD..."
                newVHDFileName = Left(aVHD.File, InStrRev(aVHD.File, ".") - 1) & ⤵
" - dynamic.vhd"
                set VMTask = aVHD.Convert(newVHDFileName, vmDiskType_Dynamic)
                vmTask.WaitForCompletion(-1)
                wscript.echo "Done."
            case "f"
                'Convert the VHD
                wscript.echo "Converting the VHD..."
                newVHDFileName = Left(aVHD.File, InStrRev(aVHD.File, ".") - 1) & ⤵
" - fixed size.vhd"
                set VMTask = aVHD.Convert(newVHDFileName, vmDiskType_FixedSize)
                vmTask.WaitForCompletion(-1)
                wscript.echo "Done."
        end select

end select
```

One thing to note about this script is that the virtual hard disk operations can take a very long period of time. As such, using `vmTask.WaitForCompletion(-1)` may not be appropriate as you have no feedback as to the progress of the task. The following is a replacement script snippet that waits for the tiles to complete but provides a periodic status update.

```
while not VMTask.IsComplete
    wscript.echo vmTask.PercentCompleted & "% complete..."
    wscript.sleep 5000
wend
```

Virtual Hard Disk Connections

As mentioned in the discussion of adding and removing the devices from the virtual machine COM object earlier in this chapter, the virtual hard disk connection is the object that associates a virtual hard

368

Chapter 17: Scripting Virtual Server

disk with the virtual machine. `AddHardDiskConnection` and `RemoveHardDiskConnection` can be used to add or remove virtual hard disk connections. To examine and modify existing virtual hard disk connections, you need to enumerate the `HardDiskConnections` object off the virtual machine COM object. Each connection has a property of the virtual hard disk file name, the type of bus it is connected to, the number of the bus it is connected to, and the location on the bus to which it is connected. To change these properties you'll need to call `SetBusLocation`.

It is not possible to change the virtual hard disk file property of the virtual hard disk connection object. If you want to do this you will need to remove the current virtual hard disk connection object and create a new one.

The script that follows connects to Virtual Server and connects to `"A virtual machine"`. The script then displays all the information about each of the virtual hard disconnections on the virtual machine. Take special note of how the undo-disk file information is handled. If a virtual hard disk connection has no undo disk associated with it, checking the `UndoHardDisk.File` property will return an error so this needs to be wrapped in an `On Error Resume Next` statement. Finally, the script gets the first virtual hard disk connection object and configures it to be connected to the first IDE location on the virtual machine.

```
Option Explicit

'Declare constants
CONST vmDriveBusType_Invalid = -1
CONST vmDriveBusType_IDE = 0
CONST vmDriveBusType_SCSI = 1

dim vs, vm, VHDConnection, aVHDConnection

' Check that the script is running at the command line.
If UCase(Right(Wscript.FullName, 11)) = "WSCRIPT.EXE" Then
    Wscript.Echo "This script must be run under CScript."
    Wscript.Quit
End If

' Attempt to connect to Virtual Server
On Error Resume Next
Set vs = CreateObject("VirtualServer.Application")
If Err.number <> 0 Then
    Wscript.Echo "Unable to connect to Virtual Server."
    Wscript.Quit
End if
On Error Goto 0

'Get virtual machine object
set vm = vs.FindVirtualMachine("A virtual machine")

'Display current VHD Connection data
wscript.echo "The virtual machine has " & _
    vm.HardDiskConnections.count & " VHDs connected"
wscript.echo ""

for each VHDConnection in vm.HardDiskConnections
    wscript.echo "VHD Connection information"
    wscript.echo "=============================="
```

369

Part VII: Automating Virtual Machine Operations

```
    wscript.echo "VHD File name      : " & VHDConnection.HardDisk.File

'This will fail if there is no undo disk - so handle it correctly
On Error Resume Next
    wscript.echo "UndoDisk File name : " & VHDConnection.UndoHardDisk.File
If Err.number <> 0 Then
    Wscript.Echo "UndoDisk File name : No undo disk present"
End if
On Error Goto 0

'Display useful information, instead of the numeric code
select case VHDConnection.BusType
    case vmDriveBusType_Invalid
        wscript.echo "BusType          : Invalid bus type"
    case vmDriveBusType_IDE
        wscript.echo "BusType          : IDE Controller"
    case vmDriveBusType_SCSI
        wscript.echo "BusType          : SCSI Controller"
end select

    wscript.echo "BusNumber        : " & VHDConnection.BusNumber
    wscript.echo "DeviceNumber     : " & VHDConnection.DeviceNumber
    wscript.echo ""
Next

'Select the first VHDConnection
set aVHDConnection = vm.HardDiskConnections(1)

'Connect it to the first location on the first IDE bus
aVHDConnection.SetBusLocation vmDriveBusType_IDE, 0, 0
```

DVD Drive

DVD drives can be added or removed from a virtual machine using `AddDVDROMDrive` and `RemoveDVDROMDrive`. An existing DVD drive can be located by enumerating `DVDROMDrives`. Media can be inserted into a DVD drive by using `AttachHostDrive` or `AttachImage`. If the DVD drive already has media in it, it needs to be released before new media can be attached.

> *You can use* `Attachment`, `ImageFile`, *and* `HostDriveLetter` *to find out what media is currently attached to the DVD drive.*

For existing DVD drives, you can use `SetBusLocation` to change its location on the IDE controller.

> *Remember that a DVD drive can only be attached to an IDE controller.*

The script that follows connects to Virtual Server and connects to `"A virtual machine"`. The script then displays the information about all attached DVD drives by using a case statement to determine the type of DVD drive attachment. Next, the script configures the first DVD drive according to its attachment type. Finally, the script connects the first DVD drive to the second position on the primary IDE controller.

Chapter 17: Scripting Virtual Server

```vbscript
Option Explicit

CONST vmDVDDrive_None = 0
CONST vmDVDDrive_Image = 1
CONST vmDVDDrive_HostDrive = 2

CONST vmDriveBusType_Invalid = -1
CONST vmDriveBusType_IDE = 0
CONST vmDriveBusType_SCSI = 1

dim vs, vm, DVDDrive, aDVDDrive

' Check that the script is running at the command line.
If UCase(Right(Wscript.FullName, 11)) = "WSCRIPT.EXE" Then
    Wscript.Echo "This script must be run under CScript."
    Wscript.Quit
End If

' Attempt to connect to Virtual Server
On Error Resume Next
Set vs = CreateObject("VirtualServer.Application")
If Err.number <> 0 Then
    Wscript.Echo "Unable to connect to Virtual Server."
    Wscript.Quit
End if
On Error Goto 0

'Get virtual machine object
set vm = vs.FindVirtualMachine("A virtual machine")

'Display current DVD drive data
wscript.echo "The virtual machine has " & _
    vm.DVDROMDrives.count & " DVD Drives"
wscript.echo ""

for each DVDDrive in vm.DVDROMDrives
   wscript.echo "DVDROM information"
   wscript.echo "==================="
   select case DVDDrive.Attachment
      case vmDVDDrive_None
         wscript.echo "Media type       : None"
         wscript.echo "BusType          : IDE Controller"
         wscript.echo "BusNumber        : " & DVDDrive.BusNumber
         wscript.echo "DeviceNumber     : " & DVDDrive.DeviceNumber
      case vmDVDDrive_Image
         wscript.echo "Media type       : ISO Image"
         wscript.echo "BusType          : IDE Controller"
         wscript.echo "BusNumber        : " & DVDDrive.BusNumber
         wscript.echo "DeviceNumber     : " & DVDDrive.DeviceNumber
         wscript.echo "ImageFile        : " & DVDDrive.ImageFile
      case vmDVDDrive_HostDrive
         wscript.echo "Media type       : Physical CD / DVD"
         wscript.echo "BusType          : IDE Controller"
         wscript.echo "BusNumber        : " & DVDDrive.BusNumber
         wscript.echo "DeviceNumber     : " & DVDDrive.DeviceNumber
```

371

Part VII: Automating Virtual Machine Operations

```
            wscript.echo "HostDriveLetter : " & DVDDrive.HostDriveLetter & ":"
      end select
      wscript.echo ""
   next

   set aDVDDrive = vm.DVDROMDrives.item(1)

   select case aDVDDrive.Attachment
      case vmDVDDrive_None
         aDVDDrive.AttachHostDrive "J"
      case vmDVDDrive_Image
         aDVDDrive.ReleaseImage
      case vmDVDDrive_HostDrive
         aDVDDrive.ReleaseHostDrive
         aDVDDrive.AttachImage "C:\CDImage.iso"
   end select

   aDVDDrive.SetBusLocation vmDriveBusType_IDE, 0, 1
```

Floppy Drive

Virtual machines always have one, and only one, floppy drive. Despite this, you need to enumerate the `FloppyDrives` collection to access the floppy drive. As with a DVD drive, you can attach a physical drive or floppy image to the floppy drive. You also need to release any existing media before attaching new media.

The script that follows connects to Virtual Server and connects to `"A virtual machine"`. The script then uses a case statement to determine the type of attachment that is currently used for the floppy drive, displays the current configuration information, and updates the attachment.

```
Option Explicit

CONST vmFloppyDrive_None = 0
CONST vmFloppyDrive_Image = 1
CONST vmFloppyDrive_HostDrive = 2

dim vs, vm, aFloppyDrive

' Check that the script is running at the command line.
If UCase(Right(Wscript.FullName, 11)) = "WSCRIPT.EXE" Then
   Wscript.Echo "This script must be run under CScript."
   Wscript.Quit
End If


' Attempt to connect to Virtual Server
On Error Resume Next
Set vs = CreateObject("VirtualServer.Application")
If Err.number <> 0 Then
   Wscript.Echo "Unable to connect to Virtual Server."
   Wscript.Quit
End if
```

Chapter 17: Scripting Virtual Server

```
On Error Goto 0

'Get virtual machine object
set vm = vs.FindVirtualMachine("A virtual machine")

'There is only ever (and always) on floppy drive
set aFloppyDrive = vm.FloppyDrives.item(1)

wscript.echo "Floppy Information"
wscript.echo "=================="
select case aFloppyDrive.Attachment
    case vmFloppyDrive_None
        wscript.echo "FloppyAttachment : No floppy disk attached"
        wscript.echo "DriveNumber      : " & aFloppyDrive.DriveNumber
        wscript.echo ""
        wscript.echo "Attaching floppy disk image..."
        aFloppyDrive.AttachImage("C:\MyVHDs\New Virtual Floppy.vfd")
    case vmFloppyDrive_Image
        wscript.echo "FloppyAttachment : Floppy disk image attached"
        wscript.echo "DriveNumber      : " & aFloppyDrive.DriveNumber
        wscript.echo "ImageFile        : " & aFloppyDrive.ImageFile
        wscript.echo ""
        wscript.echo "Attaching physical floppy disk..."
        aFloppyDrive.ReleaseImage
        aFloppyDrive.AttachHostDrive("A")
    case vmFloppyDrive_HostDrive
        wscript.echo "FloppyAttachment : Physical floppy disk attached"
        wscript.echo "DriveNumber      : " & aFloppyDrive.DriveNumber
        wscript.echo "HostDriveLetter  : " & aFloppyDrive.HostDriveLetter
        wscript.echo ""
        wscript.echo "Removing media..."
        aFloppyDrive.ReleaseHostDrive
end select
```

Virtual Networks

You can create a virtual network COM object by calling `CreateVirtualNetwork`, `RegisterVirtualNetwork` or `FindVirtualNetwork` off the Virtual Server COM object. You can also enumerate the `VirtualNetworks` collection of the Virtual Server COM object. Once you have the virtual network COM object, you can change the name notes and host network adapter connection by editing the `Name`, `Notes`, and `HostAdapter` properties.

> *You can query the `HostInfo` COM object to determine the correct string to use when assigning a host network adapter. This is discussed later in this chapter in the "Host Information" section.*

You can also access information about the name and location of the virtual network configuration file and about general statistics associated with the virtual network. You can view information about packets and bytes that have been dropped, received, and sent. The History properties return an array of their respective statistics information gathered over the last 60 seconds.

Part VII: Automating Virtual Machine Operations

The following script connects to Virtual Server and iterates over all existing virtual networks, displaying the configuration and statistical information for each virtual network. Finally, it selects the first virtual network and updates the name, notes, and host network adapter connection.

```
Option Explicit

dim vs, vn, vn1, item

' Check that the script is running at the command line.
If UCase(Right(Wscript.FullName, 11)) = "WSCRIPT.EXE" Then
    Wscript.Echo "This script must be run under CScript."
    Wscript.Quit
End If


' Attempt to connect to Virtual Server
On Error Resume Next
Set vs = CreateObject("VirtualServer.Application")
If Err.number <> 0 Then
    Wscript.Echo "Unable to connect to Virtual Server."
    Wscript.Quit
End if
On Error Goto 0

'Display current virtual network data
wscript.echo "Virtual Server  has " & _
    vs.VirtualNetworks.count & " Virtual Networks"
wscript.echo ""

for each vn in vs.VirtualNetworks
    wscript.echo "Virtual Network Configuration"
    wscript.echo "=====__==---=================="
    wscript.echo "Name                   :" & vn.Name
    wscript.echo "HostAdapter            :" & vn.HostAdapter
    wscript.echo "Notes                  :" & vn.Notes
    wscript.echo "File                   :" & vn.File
    wscript.echo "PacketsDropped         :" & vn.PacketsDropped
    wscript.echo "PacketsReceived        :" & vn.PacketsReceived
    wscript.echo "PacketsSent            :" & vn.PacketsSent
    wscript.echo "BytesDropped           :" & vn.BytesDropped
    wscript.echo "BytesReceived          :" & vn.BytesReceived
    wscript.echo "BytesSent              :" & vn.BytesSent
    wscript.echo "PacketsDroppedHistory  :"
    for each item in vn.PacketsDroppedHistory
        Wscript.StdOut.Write item
        Wscript.StdOut.Write ", "
    next
    wscript.echo ""
    wscript.echo "PacketsReceivedHistory :"
    for each item in vn.PacketsReceivedHistory
        Wscript.StdOut.Write item
        Wscript.StdOut.Write ", "
    next
    wscript.echo ""
```

374

Chapter 17: Scripting Virtual Server

```
        wscript.echo "PacketsSentHistory     :"
        for each item in vn.PacketsSentHistory
           Wscript.StdOut.Write item
           Wscript.StdOut.Write ", "
        next
        wscript.echo ""
        wscript.echo "BytesDroppedHistory    :"
        for each item in vn.BytesDroppedHistory
           Wscript.StdOut.Write item
           Wscript.StdOut.Write ", "
        next
        wscript.echo ""
        wscript.echo "BytesReceivedHistory   :"
        for each item in vn.BytesReceivedHistory
           Wscript.StdOut.Write item
           Wscript.StdOut.Write ", "
        next
        wscript.echo ""
        wscript.echo "BytesSentHistory       :"
        for each item in vn.BytesSentHistory
           Wscript.StdOut.Write item
           Wscript.StdOut.Write ", "
        next
        wscript.echo ""
        wscript.echo ""
Next

set vn1 = vs.VirtualNetworks.item(1)

vn1.Name = "A Virtual Network"
vn1.Notes = "Some notes"
vn1.HostAdapter = "Intel(R) PRO/1000 PM Network Connection"
```

DHCP Virtual Network Server

Each virtual network has a virtual DHCP server associated with it (this is disabled by default). You can access the virtual DHCP server through the DHCPVirtualNetworkServer object on the virtual network COM object. Setting the IsEnabled property to true enables the virtual DHCP server. You can then use ConfigureDHCPServer (with parameters of the network, subnet mask, DHCP range starting IP, DHCP range ending IP, and the IP address for the DHCP server itself) and ConfigureDHCPLeaseTimes (with parameters of the lease time, the lease renewal time, and the lease rebinding time) to configure the virtual DHCP server.

You can also configure the gateway address, DNS server, and WINS server by editing the appropriate properties. These are not configured by default as you need to have virtual machines that are providing the services in order to have this configured.

The script that follows connects to Virtual Server and iterates over all existing virtual networks, displaying the virtual DHCP configuration information for each virtual network. It then selects the first virtual network and configures the virtual DHCP server for it.

375

Part VII: Automating Virtual Machine Operations

```
Option Explicit

dim vs, vn, vn1

' Check that the script is running at the command line.
If UCase(Right(Wscript.FullName, 11)) = "WSCRIPT.EXE" Then
    Wscript.Echo "This script must be run under CScript."
    Wscript.Quit
End If

' Attempt to connect to Virtual Server
On Error Resume Next
Set vs = CreateObject("VirtualServer.Application")
If Err.number <> 0 Then
    Wscript.Echo "Unable to connect to Virtual Server."
    Wscript.Quit
End if
On Error Goto 0

'Display current SCSI controller data
wscript.echo "Virtual Server  has " & _
    vs.VirtualNetworks.count & " Virtual Networks"
wscript.echo ""

for each vn in vs.VirtualNetworks
    wscript.echo "Virtual Network DHCP Configuration"
    wscript.echo "==================================="
    wscript.echo "IsEnabled             : " & vn.DHCPVirtualNetworkServer.IsEnabled
    wscript.echo "DefaultGatewayAddress : " & ⤴
vn.DHCPVirtualNetworkServer.DefaultGatewayAddress
    wscript.echo "DNSServers            : " & vn.DHCPVirtualNetworkServer.DNSServers
    wscript.echo "EndingIPAddress       : " & ⤴
vn.DHCPVirtualNetworkServer.EndingIPAddress
    wscript.echo "LeaseRebindingTime    : " & ⤴
vn.DHCPVirtualNetworkServer.LeaseRebindingTime
    wscript.echo "LeaseRenewalTime      : " & ⤴
vn.DHCPVirtualNetworkServer.LeaseRenewalTime
    wscript.echo "LeaseTime             : " & vn.DHCPVirtualNetworkServer.LeaseTime
    wscript.echo "Network               : " & vn.DHCPVirtualNetworkServer.Network
    wscript.echo "NetworkMask           : " & ⤴
vn.DHCPVirtualNetworkServer.NetworkMask
    wscript.echo "ServerIPAddress       : " & ⤴
vn.DHCPVirtualNetworkServer.ServerIPAddress
    wscript.echo "StartingIPAddress     : " & ⤴
vn.DHCPVirtualNetworkServer.StartingIPAddress
    wscript.echo "WINSServers           : " & ⤴
vn.DHCPVirtualNetworkServer.WINSServers
    wscript.echo ""
Next

set vn1 = vs.VirtualNetworks.item(1)

vn1.DHCPVirtualNetworkServer.ConfigureDHCPServer _
        "10.240.0.0", _
        "255.255.0.0", _
```

Chapter 17: Scripting Virtual Server

```
        "10.240.0.16", _
        "10.240.255.254", _
        "10.240.0.1"


vn1.DHCPVirtualNetworkServer.ConfigureDHCPLeaseTimes _
        129600, 64800, 97200


vn1.DHCPVirtualNetworkServer.DefaultGatewayAddress = "10.240.0.2"
vn1.DHCPVirtualNetworkServer.DNSServers = "10.240.0.2"
vn1.DHCPVirtualNetworkServer.WINSServers = "10.240.0.2"
vn1.DHCPVirtualNetworkServer.IsEnabled = true
```

Network Adapter

The network adapter object is relatively simple. You can get a network adapter object by enumerating the `NetworkAdapters` collection off of a virtual machine COM object. You can also enumerate `UnconnectedNetworkAdapters` off of the Virtual Server COM object to find any virtual network adapters that are not connected to a virtual network. Each virtual network adapter has a property for the virtual machine and the virtual network to which it is connected. These properties return the COM object for their respective items.

The `IsEthernetAddressDynamic` property allows you to indicate where the Virtual Server should create a dynamic MAC address for the network adapter or if it should accept a static MAC address from the user. If you are using a static MAC address, you can define it using the `EthernetAddress` property. You can detach a virtual network adapter from a virtual network by using the `DetachFromVirtualNetwork` method. To attach a virtual network adapter to a virtual network, use the `AttachToVirtualNetwork` method and pass a parameter of the COM object for the virtual network to which you want to connect.

The network adapter must be disconnected from the virtual network before it can be connected to a new virtual network.

The script that follows connects to Virtual Server and connects to `"A virtual machine"`. The script then iterates over the virtual network adapters that are connected to the virtual machine, iterates over the virtual network adapters that are connected to the second virtual network, and iterates over all unconnected virtual network adapters and displays information about all of these virtual network adapters. The script then disconnects the first virtual network adapter in the virtual machine and connects the first unconnected virtual network adapter to the second virtual network.

```
Option Explicit

dim vs, vm, vNic, aVNic

' Check that the script is running at the command line.
If UCase(Right(Wscript.FullName, 11)) = "WSCRIPT.EXE" Then
    Wscript.Echo "This script must be run under CScript."
    Wscript.Quit
End If


' Attempt to connect to Virtual Server
On Error Resume Next
Set vs = CreateObject("VirtualServer.Application")
```

377

Part VII: Automating Virtual Machine Operations

```
If Err.number <> 0 Then
    Wscript.Echo "Unable to connect to Virtual Server."
    Wscript.Quit
End if
On Error Goto 0

set vm = vs.FindVirtualMachine("A virtual machine")

'Display virtual network adapters that are connected to the virtual machine
wscript.echo "Virtual Network Adapters for " & vm.Name
wscript.echo ""
for each vNic in vm.NetworkAdapters
    wscript.echo "Virtual Network Adapter"
    wscript.echo "======================="
    wscript.echo "EthernetAddress            : " & vNic.EthernetAddress
    wscript.echo "IsEthernetAddressDynamic : " & vNic.IsEthernetAddressDynamic
    wscript.echo "VirtualMachine             : " & vNic.VirtualMachine
    On Error Resume Next
        wscript.echo "VirtualNetwork             : " & vNic.VirtualNetwork.Name
    If Err.number <> 0 Then
        Wscript.Echo "VirtualNetwork             : Not Connected to a virtual network"
    End if
    wscript.echo ""
On Error Goto 0
next

wscript.echo "Virtual Network Adapters for " & vs.VirtualNetworks.item(2).Name
wscript.echo ""
for each vNic in vs.VirtualNetworks.item(2).NetworkAdapters
    wscript.echo "Virtual Network Adapter"
    wscript.echo "======================="
    wscript.echo "EthernetAddress            : " & vNic.EthernetAddress
    wscript.echo "IsEthernetAddressDynamic : " & vNic.IsEthernetAddressDynamic
    wscript.echo "VirtualMachine             : " & vNic.VirtualMachine
    On Error Resume Next
        wscript.echo "VirtualNetwork             : " & vNic.VirtualNetwork.Name
    If Err.number <> 0 Then
        Wscript.Echo "VirtualNetwork             : Not Connected to a virtual network"
    End if
    wscript.echo ""
On Error Goto 0
next

wscript.echo "Virtual Network Adapters with no network connection"
wscript.echo ""
for each vNic in vs.UnconnectedNetworkAdapters
    wscript.echo "Virtual Network Adapter"
    wscript.echo "======================="
    wscript.echo "EthernetAddress            : " & vNic.EthernetAddress
    wscript.echo "IsEthernetAddressDynamic : " & vNic.IsEthernetAddressDynamic
    wscript.echo "VirtualMachine             : " & vNic.VirtualMachine
    wscript.echo "VirtualNetwork             : Not Connected to a virtual network"
    wscript.echo ""
```

Chapter 17: Scripting Virtual Server

```
next

'Configure the first network adapter in the virtual machine
set aVNic = vm.NetworkAdapters.item(1)
aVNic.DetachFromVirtualNetwork
aVNic.IsEthernetAddressDynamic = true

'Configure the first disconnected network adapter
set aVNic = vs.UnconnectedNetworkAdapters.item(1)
aVNic.AttachToVirtualNetwork(vs.VirtualNetworks.item(2))
aVNic.IsEthernetAddressDynamic = false
aVNic.EthernetAddress = "00-22-33-aa-bb-cc"
```

Serial Port

Each virtual machine always has two serial ports, which can be accessed by enumerating the serialPorts collection of the virtual machine COM object. Each serial port can be configured to be disconnected, connected to a physical serial port, connected to a named pipe, or connected to a text file. This can be done by calling the configure method and providing parameters of the type of connection to be used, the name of the object to be connected to, and a Boolean value that indicates whether or not the serial port should be connected to the object immediately upon starting the virtual machine.

The following script connects to Virtual Server and connects to `"A virtual machine"`. The script then displays the current configuration information for both serial ports, connects the first serial port to a named pipe, and connects the second serial port to a physical COM port.

```
Option Explicit

CONST vmSerialPort_HostPort = 0
CONST vmSerialPort_TextFile = 1
CONST vmSerialPort_NamedPipe = 2
CONST vmSerialPort_Null = 3

dim vs, vm, serialPort, aSerialPort

' Check that the script is running at the command line.
If UCase(Right(Wscript.FullName, 11)) = "WSCRIPT.EXE" Then
    Wscript.Echo "This script must be run under CScript."
    Wscript.Quit
End If

' Attempt to connect to Virtual Server
On Error Resume Next
Set vs = CreateObject("VirtualServer.Application")
If Err.number <> 0 Then
    Wscript.Echo "Unable to connect to Virtual Server."
    Wscript.Quit
End if
```

379

Part VII: Automating Virtual Machine Operations

```
On Error Goto 0

set vm = vs.FindVirtualMachine("A virtual machine")

'Display current configuration information
for each serialPort in vm.SerialPorts
    wscript.echo "Serial Port"
    wscript.echo "==========="

    select case serialport.Type
        case vmSerialPort_HostPort
            wscript.echo "Type              : Physical COM port"
        case vmSerialPort_TextFile
            wscript.echo "Type              : Text file"
        case vmSerialPort_NamedPipe
            wscript.echo "Type              : Named pipe"
        case vmSerialPort_Null
            wscript.echo "Type              : Not connected"
    end select

    wscript.echo "Name              : " & serialPort.Name
    wscript.echo "ConnectImmediately : " & serialPort.ConnectImmediately
    wscript.echo ""
Next

'Configure the first serial port to connect to a named pipe
set aSerialPort = vm.serialPorts.item(1)

aSerialPort.configure vmSerialPort_NamedPipe, "\\.\pipe\Pipe1", true

'Configure the second serial port to connect to a physical serial port
set aSerialPort = vm.serialPorts.item(2)

aSerialPort.configure vmSerialPort_HostPort, "COM1", false
```

Parallel Port

Despite the fact that there is a ParallelPorts collection on each virtual machine, you can have only one parallel port per virtual machine. The parallel port object has one property of the name. This can either be set to nothing, meaning that the parallel port is disconnected, or set to LPT1 (378h-37Fh), meaning that the parallel port is connected to LPT1.

Virtual Server supports connecting the parallel port to LPT1 only when it is configured for the port range of 378h–37Fh.

The script that follows connects to Virtual Server and connects to "A virtual machine". The script then displays the current configuration information for parallel port and configures the parallel port to be connected to LPT1.

380

Chapter 17: Scripting Virtual Server

```
Option Explicit

dim vs, vm, parallelPort, aParallelPort

' Check that the script is running at the command line.
If UCase(Right(Wscript.FullName, 11)) = "WSCRIPT.EXE" Then
    Wscript.Echo "This script must be run under CScript."
    Wscript.Quit
End If

' Attempt to connect to Virtual Server
On Error Resume Next
Set vs = CreateObject("VirtualServer.Application")
If Err.number <> 0 Then
    Wscript.Echo "Unable to connect to Virtual Server."
    Wscript.Quit
End if
On Error Goto 0

set vm = vs.FindVirtualMachine("A virtual machine")

'Display current configuration information
for each parallelPort in vm.ParallelPorts
   wscript.echo "Parallel Port"
   wscript.echo "============="
   wscript.echo "Name : " & parallelPort.Name
Next


'Configure the parallel port
set aParallelPort = vm.ParallelPorts.item(1)

aParallelPort.Name = "LPT1 (378h-37Fh)"
```

Display

The display object on a virtual machine provides a lot of interesting information. The `VideoMode` property allows you to tell whether a virtual machine is displaying a text, CGA, VGA, or SVGA screen. The `width` and `height` properties provide you with the details of the current display resolution. The `thumbnail` property returns an array that represents the data for the virtual machine thumbnail that is displayed on the Virtual Server Administrative website.

In this script, I use `Join` *to display the array as a string.*

Finally, if Virtual Machine Additions are present in the virtual machine, the `SetDimensions` method can be used to set the resolution of the virtual machine's display.

```
Option Explicit

CONST vmVideoMode_TextMode = 0
CONST vmVideoMode_CGAMode = 1
CONST vmVideoMode_VGAMode = 2
```

381

Part VII: Automating Virtual Machine Operations

```
CONST vmVideoMode_SVGAMode = 3


dim vs, vm, parallelPort, aParallelPort

' Check that the script is running at the command line.
If UCase(Right(Wscript.FullName, 11)) = "WSCRIPT.EXE" Then
    Wscript.Echo "This script must be run under CScript."
    Wscript.Quit
End If


' Attempt to connect to Virtual Server
On Error Resume Next
Set vs = CreateObject("VirtualServer.Application")
If Err.number <> 0 Then
    Wscript.Echo "Unable to connect to Virtual Server."
    Wscript.Quit
End if
On Error Goto 0

set vm = vs.FindVirtualMachine("A virtual machine")

'Display display information
wscript.echo "Display information"
wscript.echo "===================="

select case vm.Display.VideoMode
   case vmVideoMode_TextMode
      wscript.echo "VideoMode : Text"
   case vmVideoMode_CGAMode
      wscript.echo "VideoMode : CGA"
   case vmVideoMode_VGAMode
      wscript.echo "VideoMode : VGA"
   case vmVideoMode_SVGAMode
      wscript.echo "VideoMode : SVGA"
end select

wscript.echo "Width     : " & vm.Display.width
wscript.echo "Height    : " & vm.Display.height
wscript.echo "Thumbnail : " & Join(vm.Display.Thumbnail)
wscript.echo ""

On Error Resume Next
    vm.Display.SetDimensions 1000,1000
If Err.number <> 0 Then
    Wscript.Echo "Unable to set display, Virtual Machine Additions not loaded."
    Wscript.Quit
End if
On Error Goto 0
```

Chapter 17: Scripting Virtual Server

Keyboard

The keyboard object on the virtual machine allows you to automate the virtual machine by simulating keys being pressed on the virtual keyboard. There are four different ways to automate the virtual keyboard, and each way is needed for different situations. The `PressKey` and `ReleaseKey` methods can be used to specify the state of single keys on the keyboard. The `PressAndReleaseKey` method can be used to simulate the keystroke of a single key on the virtual keyboard. The `TypeKeySequence` method can be used to send a series of key up and key down events, as well as standard keystrokes. Finally, the `TypeAsciiText` method can be used to type a freeform string on the virtual keyboard.

The key code values used for these methods are documented in the Virtual Server Programmers guide.

The `HasExclusiveAccess` and `IsPressed` methods apply only to clients that are connecting to the keyboard COM object. They do not apply to users connected via the VMRC client.

The following script connects to Virtual Server and connects to `"A virtual machine"`. The script then checks the current keyboard state and uses the `PressKey`, `ReleaseKey`, `PressAndReleaseKey`, `TypeKeySequence`, and `TypeAsciiText` methods to demonstrate the different ways of automating the virtual machine's keyboard.

```
Option Explicit

dim vs, vm

' Check that the script is running at the command line.
If UCase(Right(Wscript.FullName, 11)) = "WSCRIPT.EXE" Then
    Wscript.Echo "This script must be run under CScript."
    Wscript.Quit
End If

' Attempt to connect to Virtual Server
On Error Resume Next
Set vs = CreateObject("VirtualServer.Application")
If Err.number <> 0 Then
    Wscript.Echo "Unable to connect to Virtual Server."
    Wscript.Quit
End if
On Error Goto 0

set vm = vs.FindVirtualMachine("A virtual machine")

'Check HasExclusiveAccess on the keyboard
wscript.echo "Checking keyboard state:"
wscript.echo "========================="
wscript.echo "HasExclusiveAccess  : " & vm.keyboard.HasExclusiveAccess
wscript.echo ""

'Try and get exclusive access
vm.keyboard.HasExclusiveAccess = true

'Check key state
wscript.echo "Checking key state:"
wscript.echo "===================="
wscript.echo "Is the A key pressed : " & vm.keyboard.IsPressed("Key_A")
```

383

Part VII: Automating Virtual Machine Operations

```
wscript.echo ""

'Press the A key

vm.keyboard.PressKey("Key_A")

'Release the A key

vm.keyboard.ReleaseKey("Key_A")

'Type "Hello " with PressAndReleaseKey

vm.keyboard.PressAndReleaseKey("Key_Enter")
vm.keyboard.PressAndReleaseKey("Key_H")
vm.keyboard.PressAndReleaseKey("Key_E")
vm.keyboard.PressAndReleaseKey("Key_L")
vm.keyboard.PressAndReleaseKey("Key_L")
vm.keyboard.PressAndReleaseKey("Key_O")
vm.keyboard.PressAndReleaseKey("Key_Space")

'Type "World!" with TypeKeySequence

vm.keyboard.TypeKeySequence("DOWN, Key_LeftShift, Key_W," & _
 "UP, Key_LeftShift, Key_O, Key_R, Key_L, Key_D, DOWN, Key_LeftShift" & _
                          ", Key_1, UP, Key_LeftShift, Key_Enter")
'Type more with TypeAsciiText

vm.keyboard.TypeAsciiText("It is much easier to say Hello World! with this API")
```

Mouse

As with the keyboard you can gather information about, and control, the mouse through the COM interfaces. However, in order to do this, Virtual Machine Additions must be installed and the mouse must be operating in absolute coordinate mode. (This is the default mode of operation when Virtual Machine Additions is installed.)

The following script connects to Virtual Server and connects to `"A virtual machine"`. The script then creates a local copy of the mouse object and tries to enable absolute coordinate mode (this will fail if Virtual Machine Additions is not installed). After this, the script displays information about the current mouse position, updates the mouse position, and demonstrates the two different techniques for clicking a mouse button.

```
Option Explicit

CONST vmMouseButton_Left = 1
CONST vmMouseButton_Right = 2
CONST vmMouseButton_Center = 3

dim vs, vm, vmMouse

' Check that the script is running at the command line.
If UCase(Right(Wscript.FullName, 11)) = "WSCRIPT.EXE" Then
    Wscript.Echo "This script must be run under CScript."
```

384

Chapter 17: Scripting Virtual Server

```
        Wscript.Quit
End If

' Attempt to connect to Virtual Server
On Error Resume Next
Set vs = CreateObject("VirtualServer.Application")
If Err.number <> 0 Then
    Wscript.Echo "Unable to connect to Virtual Server."
    Wscript.Quit
End if
On Error Goto 0

wscript.sleep 5000

set vm = vs.FindVirtualMachine("A virtual machine")

set vmMouse = vm.Mouse

vmMouse.UsingAbsoluteCoordinates = true

'Display information about the mouse
wscript.echo "Mouse information:"
wscript.echo "=================="
if vmMouse.UsingAbsoluteCoordinates then
   wscript.echo "Mouse is configured to use absolute coordinates."
   wscript.echo "HorizontalPosition    : " & vmMouse.HorizontalPosition
   wscript.echo "VerticalPosition      : " & vmMouse.VerticalPosition
   wscript.echo ""
else
   wscript.echo "Mouse is configured to use relative coordinates."
end if

'Control the mouse
if vmMouse.UsingAbsoluteCoordinates then
   vmMouse.HorizontalPosition = 100
   vmMouse.VerticalPosition = 100
end if

vmMouse.click(vmMouseButton_Right)

If not vmMouse.GetButton(vmMouseButton_Right) then
   vmMouse.SetButton vmMouseButton_Right, true
   vmMouse.SetButton vmMouseButton_Right, false
end if

'Turn off absolute mode

vmMouse.UsingAbsoluteCoordinates = false
```

Guest OS

The GuestOS object is available only if the virtual machine is currently running and Virtual Machine Additions is installed. Using the GuestOS object, you can find out the name of the guest operating system (OSName), the version of Virtual Machine Additions that is installed (AdditionsVersion), whether

Part VII: Automating Virtual Machine Operations

the guest operating system can be shut down via Virtual Machine Additions (`CanShutdown`), where the virtual machine additions is reporting a status heartbeat (`IsHeartBeating`), how many heartbeats were received in the last minute (`HeartBeatPercentage`), and whether host time synchronization is enabled (`IsHostTimeSyncEnabled`).

You can shut down the guest operating system by calling the shutdown method, which returns a `VmTask` object. You can enable or disable host time synchronization by directly setting the value of the property `IsHostTimeSyncEnabled`. You can also send data to be stored in the guest operating system's Registry through the `SetParameter` method, which takes a parameter of the Registry entry name to use and the data to be stored.

> *The `GuestOS` object also exposes an `ExecuteCommand` method. This method was available in prerelease versions of Virtual Server and allowed you to execute an arbitrary command inside the virtual machine. This method is present, but disabled, in the release version of Virtual Server. It was disabled because of security concerns with this method.*

The following script connects to Virtual Server and connects to `"A virtual machine"`. The script then tries to access the `GuestOS.OSName` property. If this fails, Virtual Machine Additions is not installed and the script will inform the user of this and initiate the installation process. Otherwise, the script will display the current guest OS information. Next, the script uses `GuestOS.SetParameter` to set a custom parameter, shuts down the guest operating system, and disables host time synchronization.

```
Option Explicit

dim vs, vm, temp, vmTask

' Check that the script is running at the command line.
If UCase(Right(Wscript.FullName, 11)) = "WSCRIPT.EXE" Then
    Wscript.Echo "This script must be run under CScript."
    Wscript.Quit
End If


' Attempt to connect to Virtual Server
On Error Resume Next
Set vs = CreateObject("VirtualServer.Application")
If Err.number <> 0 Then
    Wscript.Echo "Unable to connect to Virtual Server."
    Wscript.Quit
End if
On Error Goto 0

set vm = vs.FindVirtualMachine("A virtual machine")

On Error Resume Next
    temp = vm.GuestOS.OSName
If Err.number <> 0 Then
    Wscript.Echo "The virtual machine needs to be running, " & _
                "and have Virtual Machine Additions Installed."
    vm.GuestOS.InstallAdditions
    Wscript.Quit
End if
```

386

Chapter 17: Scripting Virtual Server

```
On Error Goto 0

'Display information about the GuestOS
wscript.echo "Guest OS Information:"
wscript.echo "======================"
wscript.echo "OSName               : " & vm.GuestOS.OSName
wscript.echo "AdditionsVersion     : " & vm.GuestOS.AdditionsVersion
wscript.echo "CanShutdown          : " & vm.GuestOS.CanShutdown
wscript.echo "IsHeartbeating       : " & vm.GuestOS.IsHeartbeating
wscript.echo "HeartbeatPercentage  : " & vm.GuestOS.HeartbeatPercentage
wscript.echo "IsHostTimeSyncEnabled : " & vm.GuestOS.IsHostTimeSyncEnabled
wscript.echo ""

'Set a Guest OS parameter
vm.GuestOS.SetParameter "Test Parameter", "Some value that needs to be sent"

'Shut down Guest OS
set vmTask = vm.GuestOS.Shutdown

vmTask.WaitForCompletion(10000)

'Disable Time Synchronization (VM needs to be off)
vm.GuestOS.IsHostTimeSyncEnabled = false
```

If you use the `SetParameter` method, you can retrieve the information from inside the virtual machine by examining the Registry. Here is a sample script that does exactly that when run inside of the virtual machine.

```
' Setup constant
const HKEY_LOCAL_MACHINE = &H80000002

' Setup registry object (this is a single line)
Set oReg=GetObject("winmgmts:{impersonationLevel=impersonate}!\\.\root\⟩
default:StdRegProv")

' Set the key path and values to look at
strKeyPath = "SOFTWARE\Microsoft\Virtual Machine\Guest\Parameters"
strValueName1 = "Test Parameter"

' Get the values from the registry
oReg.GetStringValue HKEY_LOCAL_MACHINE, strKeyPath, strValueName1, dwValue1

' Display the results
WScript.Echo "The value for " & strValueName1 & " is: " & dwValue1
```

Accountant

The virtual machine accountant object allows you to view statistics about the virtual machine and to configure CPU resource allocations. CPU resource allocations can be configured by using the `SetSchedulingParameters` method, which takes parameters of the CPU reserve, the CPU maximum, and the relative weight of the virtual machine.

387

Part VII: Automating Virtual Machine Operations

The CPU reserve and maximum are expressed as percentages of the total system resource. So in the script that follows, a reserve of 5 actually equates to 10 percent of a single processor as it was written for a dual processor computer.

All other properties on the virtual machine accountant object are read-only and intended for gathering statistical information. The following script connects to Virtual Server and connects to "A virtual machine". The script then displays all the current information from the accountant object and finishes up by setting new CPU scheduling parameters for the virtual machine.

```
Option Explicit

dim vs, vm, item

' Check that the script is running at the command line.
If UCase(Right(Wscript.FullName, 11)) = "WSCRIPT.EXE" Then
    Wscript.Echo "This script must be run under CScript."
    Wscript.Quit
End If


' Attempt to connect to Virtual Server
On Error Resume Next
Set vs = CreateObject("VirtualServer.Application")
If Err.number <> 0 Then
    Wscript.Echo "Unable to connect to Virtual Server."
    Wscript.Quit
End if
On Error Goto 0

set vm = vs.FindVirtualMachine("A virtual machine")

'Display information about the VM Accountant
wscript.echo "Accountant Information:"
wscript.echo "========================"
wscript.echo "AllowableMaximumSystemCapacity  : " &
vm.Accountant.AllowableMaximumSystemCapacity
wscript.echo "AllowableReservedSystemCapacity : " &
vm.Accountant.AllowableReservedSystemCapacity
wscript.echo "CPUUtilization                  : " & vm.Accountant.CPUUtilization
wscript.echo "DiskBytesRead                   : " & vm.Accountant.DiskBytesRead
wscript.echo "DiskBytesWritten                : " & vm.Accountant.DiskBytesWritten
wscript.echo "MaximumSystemCapacity           : " & ⊃
  vm.Accountant.MaximumSystemCapacity
wscript.echo "NetworkBytesReceived            : " & ⊃
  vm.Accountant.NetworkBytesReceived
wscript.echo "NetworkBytesSent                : " & vm.Accountant.NetworkBytesSent
wscript.echo "RelativeWeight                  : " & vm.Accountant.RelativeWeight
wscript.echo "ReservedSystemCapacity          : " & ⊃
  vm.Accountant.ReservedSystemCapacity
wscript.echo "UpTime                          : " & vm.Accountant.UpTime
wscript.echo "CPUUtilizationHistory           : "
for each item in vm.Accountant.CPUUtilizationHistory
    Wscript.StdOut.Write item
    Wscript.StdOut.Write ", "
next
```

Chapter 17: Scripting Virtual Server

```
wscript.echo ""

'Set CPU resource allocations
vm.Accountant.SetSchedulingParameters 5, 45, 100
```

Security and Access Rights

The Virtual Server, virtual machine, virtual network, and virtual hard disk objects all expose a security object. This object is used to configure the user permissions and access rights for the Virtual Server object. The security object contains the details of the object owner and group and a collection of access right descriptors. Access right descriptors can be managed with the AddEntry, FindEntry, and RemoveEntry methods on the security object.

Once you have an access right descriptor, you can view and modify any of the properties on it to change the rights of the selected user. However, unlike most other COM objects in the Virtual Server COM, API changes made to the security object are not automatically applied to the server. Rather, you need to manually assign your local security object back to the server.

The security object for virtual machines, virtual networks, and virtual hard disks is read-only. If you want to change the security settings for these objects, you need to edit the file access permissions on their associated files.

Access right descriptors come in two forms. You can either have a descriptor that is used to allow access or one that is used to deny access. This is consistent with the Windows security model in general.

The following script connects to Virtual Server and creates a local security object. The script then displays all the information in this security object. (It uses the displayAccessRights subroutine to avoid code duplication.) After this, the script grants access rights to one user and removes access rights for another user. Finally, the script applies the updated security object back to Virtual Server.

```
Option Explicit

CONST vmAccessRights_Allowed = 0
CONST vmAccessRights_Denied = 1

dim vs, vm, securityObject, accessRights, tempAccessRight1, tempAccessRight2

' Check that the script is running at the command line.
If UCase(Right(Wscript.FullName, 11)) = "WSCRIPT.EXE" Then
    Wscript.Echo "This script must be run under CScript."
    Wscript.Quit
End If

' Attempt to connect to Virtual Server
On Error Resume Next
Set vs = CreateObject("VirtualServer.Application")
If Err.number <> 0 Then
    Wscript.Echo "Unable to connect to Virtual Server."
    Wscript.Quit
End if
```

389

Part VII: Automating Virtual Machine Operations

```
On Error Goto 0

set securityObject = vs.Security

'Display information about the security object
wscript.echo "Virtual Server Security Information:"
wscript.echo "====================="
wscript.echo "GroupName : " & securityObject.GroupName
wscript.echo "GroupSid  : " & securityObject.GroupSid
wscript.echo "OwnerName : " & securityObject.OwnerName
wscript.echo "OwnerSid  : " & securityObject.OwnerSid
wscript.echo ""
displayAccessRights securityObject.CurrentUserAccessRights, "Current User"
for each accessRights in securityObject.AccessRights
   wscript.echo ""
   displayAccessRights accessRights, "Virtual Server"
next

'Add a new user to the security object
set tempAccessRight1 = ⊃
 securityObject.AddEntry("DOMAIN\Username",vmAccessRights_Allowed)

'Grant rights to the user
tempAccessRight1.ReadAccess = true
tempAccessRight1.ExecuteAccess = true
tempAccessRight1.WriteAccess = true

'Find another user on the security object
set tempAccessRight2 = ⊃
 securityObject.FindEntry("DOMAIN\Username2",vmAccessRights_Allowed)

'Remove the users access rights
securityObject.RemoveEntry tempAccessRight2

'Apply changes
vs.Security = securityObject

'Subroutine for displaying information about access rights
sub displayAccessRights(anAccessRights, objectName)

   'Display information about the Access Rights object
   wscript.echo objectName & "Access Rights Information:"
   wscript.echo "====================="
   wscript.echo "ChangePermissions : " & anAccessRights.ChangePermissions
   wscript.echo "DeleteAccess      : " & anAccessRights.DeleteAccess
   wscript.echo "ExecuteAccess     : " & anAccessRights.ExecuteAccess
   wscript.echo "Flags             : " & anAccessRights.Flags
   wscript.echo "Name              : " & anAccessRights.Name
   wscript.echo "ReadAccess        : " & anAccessRights.ReadAccess
   wscript.echo "ReadPermissions   : " & anAccessRights.ReadPermissions
   wscript.echo "Sid               : " & anAccessRights.Sid
   wscript.echo "SpecialAccess     : " & anAccessRights.SpecialAccess
   wscript.echo "WriteAccess       : " & anAccessRights.WriteAccess
   if anAccessRights.Type = vmAccessRights_Allowed then
      wscript.echo "Type              : Allowed"
```

Chapter 17: Scripting Virtual Server

```
        else
            wscript.echo "Type             : Denied"
        end if

end sub
```

Host Information

The `HostInfo` object exposes only those read-only properties that provide you with details about the host operating system and the physical hardware. Some of these properties are purely informational while others (such as the NetworkAdapters collection and the HostDrives collection) provide information that you need in order to call other methods. The script that follows connects to Virtual Server and displays all the information that is available from the `HostInfo` object.

```
Option Explicit

dim vs, vm, item

' Check that the script is running at the command line.
If UCase(Right(Wscript.FullName, 11)) = "WSCRIPT.EXE" Then
    Wscript.Echo "This script must be run under CScript."
    Wscript.Quit
End If

' Attempt to connect to Virtual Server
On Error Resume Next
Set vs = CreateObject("VirtualServer.Application")
If Err.number <> 0 Then
    Wscript.Echo "Unable to connect to Virtual Server."
    Wscript.Quit
End if
On Error Goto 0

'Display information about the host information
wscript.echo "Host Information:"
wscript.echo "======================="
wscript.echo "LogicalProcessorCount       : " & vs.HostInfo.LogicalProcessorCount
wscript.echo "Memory                      : " & vs.HostInfo.Memory
wscript.echo "MemoryAvail                 : " & vs.HostInfo.MemoryAvail
wscript.echo "MemoryAvailString           : " & vs.HostInfo.MemoryAvailString
wscript.echo "MemoryTotalString           : " & vs.HostInfo.MemoryTotalString
wscript.echo "MMX                         : " & vs.HostInfo.MMX
wscript.echo "OperatingSystem             : " & vs.HostInfo.OperatingSystem
wscript.echo "OSMajorVersion              : " & vs.HostInfo.OSMajorVersion
wscript.echo "OSMinorVersion              : " & vs.HostInfo.OSMinorVersion
wscript.echo "OSServicePackString         : " & vs.HostInfo.OSServicePackString
wscript.echo "OSVersionString             : " & vs.HostInfo.OSVersionString
wscript.echo "ParallelPort                : " & vs.HostInfo.ParallelPort
wscript.echo "PhysicalProcessorCount      : " & vs.HostInfo.PhysicalProcessorCount
wscript.echo "ProcessorFeaturesString     : " & vs.HostInfo.ProcessorFeaturesString
wscript.echo "ProcessorManufacturerString : " & ⤶
  vs.HostInfo.ProcessorManufacturerString
wscript.echo "ProcessorSpeed              : " & vs.HostInfo.ProcessorSpeed
```

391

Part VII: Automating Virtual Machine Operations

```
wscript.echo "ProcessorSpeedString       : " & vs.HostInfo.ProcessorSpeedString
wscript.echo "ProcessorVersionString     : " & vs.HostInfo.ProcessorVersionString
wscript.echo "SerialPorts                : " & vs.HostInfo.SerialPorts
wscript.echo "SSE                        : " & vs.HostInfo.SSE
wscript.echo "SSE2                       : " & vs.HostInfo.SSE2
wscript.echo "ThreeDNow                  : " & vs.HostInfo.ThreeDNow
wscript.echo "UTCTime                    : " & vs.HostInfo.UTCTime

for each item in vs.HostInfo.DVDDrives
    wscript.echo "DVDDrive                   : " & item
next

for each item in vs.HostInfo.FloppyDrives
    wscript.echo "FloppyDrive                : " & item
next

for each item in vs.HostInfo.NetworkAdapters
    wscript.echo "NetworkAdapter             : " & item
next

for each item in vs.HostInfo.NetworkAddresses
    wscript.echo "NetworkAddress             : " & item
next

for each item in vs.HostInfo.HostDrives
    wscript.echo "HostDrive                  : " & item
    wscript.echo "HostDriveSize              : " & ⤶
 vs.HostInfo.GetHostDriveSize(item)
    wscript.echo "HostDriveIsMounted         : " & ⤶
 vs.HostInfo.IsHostDriveMounted(item)
next
```

Events

The Virtual Server COM API exposes a number of events that relate to the Virtual Server, virtual machine, DVD drive, and floppy drive objects. The following script shows you how to register to receive events using VBScript (by using the `WScript.ConnectObject` call to associate events from objects to methods with specific prefixes). It also shows you how to register for all possible events that are offered by Virtual Server.

This is actually a fascinating script to leave running on the command line as it will generate an audit log of all activity on the server.

```
Option Explicit

'Define constants
CONST vmVMState_Invalid = 0
CONST vmVMState_TurnedOff = 1
CONST vmVMState_Saved = 2
CONST vmVMState_TurningOn = 3
CONST vmVMState_Restoring = 4
CONST vmVMState_Running = 5
```

Chapter 17: Scripting Virtual Server

```
CONST vmVMState_Paused = 6
CONST vmVMState_Saving = 7
CONST vmVMState_TurningOff = 8
CONST vmVMState_MergingDrives = 9
CONST vmVMState_DeleteMachine = 10

Dim vs, vm, dvd, floppy

' Check that the script is running at the command line.
If UCase(Right(Wscript.FullName, 11)) = "WSCRIPT.EXE" Then
    Wscript.Echo "This script must be run under CScript."
    Wscript.Quit
End If

'Jump to the main routine
main()

'=================================================================='

'Virtual Server events

Sub vs_OnEventLogged(eventID)
 wscript.echo "VS Event Loggged : " & CStr(eventID)
end sub

Sub vs_OnHeartbeatStopped(vmConfig)
 wscript.echo "VS VM HeartBeat Stopped : " & vmConfig
end sub

Sub vs_OnServiceEvent (eventID)
 wscript.echo "VS Service Event Loggged : " & CStr(eventID)
end sub

Sub vs_OnVMStateChange(vmConfig, vmstate)
 wscript.echo "VS VM : " & vmConfig & " changed to state : " & ⤶
 displayState(vmstate)
end sub

'Virtual Machine events

Sub vm_OnConfigurationChanged(key, data)

 wscript.echo "VM config : " & key & " changed to : " & CStr(data)
end sub

Sub vm_OnHeartbeatStopped()
 wscript.echo "VM HeartBeat stopped"
end sub

Sub vm_OnRequestShutdown(allowed)
 wscript.echo "VM Shutdown requested"
end sub

Sub vm_OnReset()
 wscript.echo "VM reset"
```

Part VII: Automating Virtual Machine Operations

```
end sub

Sub vm_OnStateChange(vmState)
 wscript.echo "VM changed to state : " & displayState(vmState)
end sub

Sub vm_OnTripleFault()
 wscript.echo "VM tripple faulted"
end sub

'DVD Events

sub dvd_OnMediaEject(mediaPath)
 wscript.echo "DVD media ejected : " & mediaPath
end sub

sub dvd_OnMediaInsert(mediaPath)
 wscript.echo "DVD media inserted : " & mediaPath
end sub

'Floppy Events

sub floppy_OnMediaEject(mediaPath)
 wscript.echo "Floppy media ejected : " & mediaPath
end sub

sub floppy_OnMediaInsert(mediaPath)
 wscript.echo "Floppy media inserted : " & mediaPath
end sub

'================================================================='

function displayState(stateCode)

select case statecode
  case vmVMState_Invalid
     displayState = "Invalid"
  case vmVMState_TurnedOff
     displayState = "Turned off"
  case vmVMState_Saved
     displayState = "Saved state"
  case vmVMState_TurningOn
     displayState = "Turning on"
  case vmVMState_Restoring
     displayState = "Restoring"
  case vmVMState_Running
     displayState = "Running"
  case vmVMState_Paused
     displayState = "Paused"
  case vmVMState_Saving
     displayState = "Saving state"
  case vmVMState_TurningOff
```

Chapter 17: Scripting Virtual Server

```
        displayState = "Turning off"
  case vmVMState_MergingDrives
        displayState = "Merging drives"
  case vmVMState_DeleteMachine
        displayState = "Deleting machine"
end select

end function


'================================================================='

sub main()

' Attempt to connect to Virtual Server
On Error Resume Next
Set vs = CreateObject("VirtualServer.Application")
If Err.number <> 0 Then
    Wscript.Echo "Unable to connect to Virtual Server."
    Wscript.Quit
End if
On Error Goto 0

set vm = vs.FindVirtualMachine("A virtual machine")
set dvd = vm.DVDROMDrives.item(1)
set floppy = vm.FloppyDrives.item(1)

WScript.ConnectObject vs, "vs_"
WScript.ConnectObject vm, "vm_"
WScript.ConnectObject dvd, "dvd_"
WScript.ConnectObject floppy, "floppy_"

do
 WScript.Sleep(500)
loop

end sub
```

Get and Set Configuration Values

The final thing to cover is the `GetConfigurationValue` and `SetConfigurationValue` methods that are exposed on the Virtual Server and virtual machine COM objects. These methods allow you to directly get and set values from the virtual machine or Virtual Server configuration files. You might want to do this for two reasons, both of which are demonstrated in the script that follows.

First, you may want to change a configuration setting that is not exposed through the COM interface. The following script changes the setting for the mouse integration option (this is not exposed through the COM interface).

Second, you may want to extend the configuration file and store your own information in it. The following script demonstrates creating a custom key, storing a value in it, and then retrieving it.

395

Part VII: Automating Virtual Machine Operations

```
Option Explicit

dim vs, vm, key, value

' Check that the script is running at the command line.
If UCase(Right(Wscript.FullName, 11)) = "WSCRIPT.EXE" Then
    Wscript.Echo "This script must be run under CScript."
    Wscript.Quit
End If


' Attempt to connect to Virtual Server
On Error Resume Next
Set vs = CreateObject("VirtualServer.Application")
If Err.number <> 0 Then
    Wscript.Echo "Unable to connect to Virtual Server."
    Wscript.Quit
End if
On Error Goto 0

set vm = vs.FindVirtualMachine("A virtual machine")

'Get the value for a built in key
key = "integration/microsoft/mouse/allow"
value = vm.GetConfigurationValue(key)

Wscript.echo "The state of mouse integration on " & vm.Name & " is: " & value

'Flip the value
if value then
 vm.SetConfigurationValue key, cbool(false)
Else
 vm.SetConfigurationValue key, cbool(true)
End if

'Create a custom key and value
key = "Test_Key/Some_Value"
vm.SetConfigurationValue key, "Hello World"

'Get the value back
Wscript.echo "Fetching custom key: " & key & " value: " & ⊃
vm.GetConfigurationValue(key)
```

Samples

Now that you have seen the extent of the Virtual Server COM API, here are some sample scripts that demonstrate how to solve real-world problems.

Create and Configure a Virtual Machine

This script makes all the necessary calls to create a new virtual machine with a new virtual hard disk. It then configures the memory, notes, network connections, and installation media for the virtual machine and finally starts it running.

Chapter 17: Scripting Virtual Server

```
Option Explicit

'Define constants
CONST vmDiskType_Dynamic = 0
CONST vmDiskType_FixedSize = 1
CONST vmDriveBusType_IDE = 0
CONST vmDriveBusType_SCSI = 1
CONST vmDVDDrive_None = 0
CONST vmDVDDrive_Image = 1
CONST vmDVDDrive_HostDrive = 2

dim vs, vm, vmName, vmLocation, vmVHDType, vmVHDSize
dim vmMemory, vmNotes, vmInstallMedia, vmInstallMediaType
dim vmTask, vmSCSIBoot, vmVHDName, vmStartAfterCreation

' Check that the script is running at the command line.
If UCase(Right(Wscript.FullName, 11)) = "WSCRIPT.EXE" Then
    Wscript.Echo "This script must be run under CScript."
    Wscript.Quit
End If

' Attempt to connect to Virtual Server
On Error Resume Next
Set vs = CreateObject("VirtualServer.Application")
If Err.number <> 0 Then
    Wscript.Echo "Unable to connect to Virtual Server."
    Wscript.Quit
End if
On Error Goto 0

'User provided input
vmName = "A new virtual machine"
vmLocation = "C:\MyVMs"
vmVHDType = vmDiskType_Dynamic
vmVHDSize = 20480
vmMemory = 256
vmNotes = "This VM was generated by a script"
vmSCSIBoot = true
VMInstallMediaType = vmDVDDrive_Image
VMInstallMedia = "C:\OSInstall.iso"
vmStartAfterCreation = true

'Generated values
vmVHDName = vmLocation & "\" & vmName & " - hard disk.vhd"

set vm = vs.CreateVirtualMachine(vmName , vmLocation)

'Configure basic VM properties
vm.Memory = 256
vm.Notes = vmNotes

'Create a new VHD
if vmVHDType = vmDiskType_Dynamic then
    set vmTask = vs.CreateDynamicVirtualHardDisk(vmVHDName , vmVHDSize)
    vmTask.WaitForCompletion(-1)
else
```

397

Part VII: Automating Virtual Machine Operations

```
        set vmTask = vs.CreateFixedVirtualHardDisk(vmVHDName , vmVHDSize)
        vmTask.WaitForCompletion(-1)
    end if

    'Attach VHD to the righ controller
    if vmSCSIBoot then
        vm.AddSCSIController
        vm.AddHardDiskConnection vmVHDName, vmDriveBusType_SCSI, 0, 0
    else
        vm.AddHardDiskConnection vmVHDName, vmDriveBusType_IDE, 0, 0
    end if

    'Connect the first network adapter to the first virtual network
    vm.NetworkAdapters.item(1).AttachToVirtualNetwork vs.VirtualNetworks.item(1)

    'Configure installation CD / DVD
    vm.AddDVDROMDrive vmDriveBusType_IDE, 1, 1
    select case VMInstallMediaType
        case vmDVDDrive_Image
            vm.DVDROMDrives.item(1).AttachImage VMInstallMedia
        case vmDVDDrive_HostDrive
            vm.DVDROMDrives.item(1).AttachHostDrive VMInstallMedia
    end select

    'Start the VM if requested to
    if vmStartAfterCreation then vm.Startup
```

Clone a Base Virtual Machine

This script is a bit more complex. Given the name of an existing virtual machine, this script will create a new virtual machine and then go through and copy all the settings from the source virtual machine to the new virtual machine. It will also create new differencing disks for each virtual hard disk in the source virtual machine and connect them to the new virtual machine.

This script can be used to allow the rapid creation of new virtual machines from a base virtual machine.

```
Option Explicit

CONST vmFloppyDrive_None = 0
CONST vmFloppyDrive_Image = 1
CONST vmFloppyDrive_HostDrive = 2
CONST vmDVDDrive_None = 0
CONST vmDVDDrive_Image = 1
CONST vmDVDDrive_HostDrive = 2

dim vs, sourceVMName, sourceVM, cloneVMName, counter, errorCheck
dim cloneVM, item, item2, aDVDROM, aNetworkAdapter, aSCSIController
dim anAccessRight, aVMTask, newVHDName, newVHD, newVHDConnection

' Check that the script is running at the command line.
If UCase(Right(Wscript.FullName, 11)) = "WSCRIPT.EXE" Then
    Wscript.Echo "This script must be run under CScript."
    Wscript.Quit
```

398

Chapter 17: Scripting Virtual Server

```
End If

' Attempt to connect to Virtual Server
On Error Resume Next
Set vs = CreateObject("VirtualServer.Application")
If Err.number <> 0 Then
    Wscript.Echo "Unable to connect to Virtual Server."
    Wscript.Quit
End if
On Error Goto 0

'Establish virtual machine to be cloned
sourceVMName = " A virtual machine "

set sourceVM = vs.FindVirtualMachine(sourceVMName)

'Warn if the source VM is configured to run as a user account
if sourceVM.RunAsDefinedAccount then
    wscript.echo "WARNING: VM is configured to run as a specific user account. ⊃
 These settings will not be transfered"
end if

'Try to create the VM with the same name as the source,
'but with " - clone 1" appended.  If that fails, increment
'the number until it succeeds.

counter = 1
errorCheck = true

while errorCheck
    cloneVMName = " - clone " & counter
    On Error Resume Next
    set cloneVM = vs.CreateVirtualMachine(sourceVM.Name & cloneVMName, ⊃
 Left(sourceVM.File, InStrRev(sourceVM.File, "\") - 1) & cloneVMName)
    If Err.number <> 0 Then
        counter = counter + 1
    else
        errorCheck = false
    End if
On Error Goto 0
wend

'Remove the network adapter that is created by default
cloneVM.RemoveNetworkAdapter(cloneVM.NetworkAdapters.item(1))

'Clone basic settings
wscript.echo "Cloning basic virtual machine settings"
cloneVM.BaseBoardSerialNumber = sourceVM.BaseBoardSerialNumber
cloneVM.BIOSGUID = sourceVM.BIOSGUID
cloneVM.BIOSSerialNumber = sourceVM.BIOSSerialNumber
cloneVM.ChassisAssetTag = sourceVM.ChassisAssetTag
cloneVM.ChassisSerialNumber = sourceVM.ChassisSerialNumber
cloneVM.Memory = sourceVM.Memory
cloneVM.Notes = sourceVM.Notes
cloneVM.ShutdownActionOnQuit = sourceVM.ShutdownActionOnQuit
cloneVM.Undoable = sourceVM.Undoable
```

399

Part VII: Automating Virtual Machine Operations

```vbscript
   cloneVM.UndoAction = sourceVM.UndoAction

   'Clone Accountant settings
   wscript.echo "Cloning virtual machine scheduling settings"
   cloneVM.Accountant.SetSchedulingParameters ⤶
    sourceVM.Accountant.ReservedSystemCapacity, ⤶
    sourceVM.Accountant.MaximumSystemCapacity ,sourceVM.Accountant.RelativeWeight

   'Clone parallel port settings
   wscript.echo "Cloning parallel port settings"
   cloneVM.ParallelPorts.item(1).Name = sourceVM.ParallelPorts.item(1).Name

   'Clone serial port settings
   wscript.echo "Cloning serial port settings"
   cloneVM.SerialPorts.item(1).Configure sourceVM.SerialPorts.item(1).Type, ⤶
    sourceVM.SerialPorts.item(1).Name, sourceVM.SerialPorts.item(1).ConnectImmediately
   cloneVM.SerialPorts.item(2).Configure sourceVM.SerialPorts.item(2).Type, ⤶
    sourceVM.SerialPorts.item(2).Name, sourceVM.SerialPorts.item(2).ConnectImmediately

   'Clone floppy disk settings
   wscript.echo "Cloning floppy disk settings"
   select case sourceVM.FloppyDrives.item(1).Attachment
      case vmFloppyDrive_Image
         cloneVM.FloppyDrives.item(1).AttachImage ⤶
    sourceVM.FloppyDrives.item(1).ImageFile
      case vmFloppyDrive_HostDrive
         cloneVM.FloppyDrives.item(1).AttachHostDrive ⤶
    sourceVM.FloppyDrives.item(1).HostDriveLetter
   end select

   'Clone DVD drive settings
   wscript.echo "Cloning DVD-ROM drives"
   for each item in sourceVM.DVDROMDrives
      wscript.echo "Cloning DVD-ROM drives - adding DVD-ROM drive"
      set aDVDROM = cloneVM.AddDVDROMDrive(item.BusType, item.BusNumber, ⤶
    item.DeviceNumber)
      select case item.Attachment
         case vmDVDDrive_Image
            aDVDROM.AttachImage item.ImageFile
         case vmDVDDrive_HostDrive
            aDVDROM.AttachHostDrive item.HostDriveLetter
      end select
   next

   'Clone network adapter settings
   wscript.echo "Cloning network adapters"
   for each item in sourceVM.NetworkAdapters
      wscript.echo "Cloning network adapters - adding network adapter"
      set aNetworkAdapter = cloneVM.AddNetworkAdapter()

      'This can fail with an error if the source network adapter is disconnected.
      On Error Resume Next
      aNetworkAdapter.AttachToVirtualNetwork item.VirtualNetwork
      On Error Goto 0

      'Copy the MAC address if it is static, and warn about it.
```

Chapter 17: Scripting Virtual Server

```
    if not item.IsEthernetAddressDynamic then
        wscript.echo "WARNING: Static MAC address has been duplicated.  Both VMs ⊋
cannot be on at the same time."
        aNetworkAdapter.IsEthernetAddressDynamic = false
        aNetworkAdapter.EthernetAddress = item.EthernetAddress
    end if
next


'Clone the SCSI controllers
wscript.echo "Cloning SCSI controllers"
for each item in sourceVM.SCSIControllers
    wscript.echo "Cloning SCSI controllers - adding SCSI controller"
    set aSCSIController = cloneVM.AddSCSIController()
    aSCSIController.Configure item.IsBusShared, item.SCSIID
next



'Clone the hard disks
wscript.echo "Cloning hard disk settings"
for each item in sourceVM.HardDiskConnections
    wscript.echo "Cloning hard disk settings - creating differencing disk"

    'Construct name for new differencing disk
    newVHDName = Left(item.HardDisk.File, InStrRev(item.HardDisk.File, "\") - ⊋
1) & cloneVMName & "\"
    newVHDName = newVHDName & Right(item.HardDisk.File, ⊋
(len(item.HardDisk.File) - InStrRev(item.HardDisk.File, "\")))
    newVHDName = Left(newVHDName, InStrRev(newVHDName, ".") - 1) & cloneVMName &⊋
" - diff.vhd"

    'Create and attach new differencing disk
    set aVMTask = vs.CreateDifferencingVirtualHardDisk(newVHDName,
item.HardDisk.File)
    aVMTask.WaitForCompletion(-1)
    set newVHDConnection = cloneVM.AddHardDiskConnection(newVHDName, ⊋
item.BusType, item.BusNumber, item.DeviceNumber)

next
```

Virtual Machine Automation

The final sample script in this chapter uses a very interesting method to automate virtual machines. It stores the thumbnail data from the virtual machine display object and then uses this to be able to detect when the virtual machine is ready to receive keyboard input. This process actually involves two scripts. The first script gathers the thumbnail data and writes it out to a plain-text file that is defined as a command-line parameter for the script.

```
Option Explicit

dim vs, vm, thumbnailFile, objFSO, objTextStream

' Check that the script is running at the command line.
If UCase(Right(Wscript.FullName, 11)) = "WSCRIPT.EXE" Then
    Wscript.Echo "This script must be run under CScript."
```

401

Part VII: Automating Virtual Machine Operations

```
        Wscript.Quit
End If

' Attempt to connect to Virtual Server
On Error Resume Next
Set vs = CreateObject("VirtualServer.Application")
If Err.number <> 0 Then
    Wscript.Echo "Unable to connect to Virtual Server."
    Wscript.Quit
End if
On Error Goto 0

If WScript.Arguments.Count = 1 Then
  thumbnailFile = WScript.Arguments.Item(0)
Else
  Wscript.Echo "A single command line argument of the thumbnail file ⤸
name should be supplied"
  Wscript.Quit
End If
set vm = vs.FindVirtualMachine("A virtual machine")

Set objFSO = CreateObject("scripting.filesystemobject")
Set objTextStream = objFSO.OpenTextFile(thumbnailFile, 2, True)
objTextStream.WriteLine Join(vm.Display.Thumbnail)
objTextStream.close
```

The second script uses these text files to automate the virtual machine. This script has a function called `checkForThumbnailMatch`. This function takes two parameters: the name of the text file to load the thumbnail data from, and the percentage match that is required. It loads the data back from the text file and uses `Split` to return it to its original array format. It then gets the virtual machine thumbnail every two seconds and compares it to the stored thumbnail. If enough pixels match, it returns success.

It is not always possible to get a 100 percent match because changing data is displayed on the screen, like the clock in the Windows taskbar.

This script uses this function combined with the keyboard APIs to start a virtual machine, log in, open the Start menu, launch Notepad, and type a basic string. It then shuts down the virtual machine.

```
Option Explicit

dim vs, vm, savedThumbnail, savedThumbnailArray, newThumbnail, counter, ⤸
  matchCounter, notMatchCounter, entry, objFSO, objTextStream

' Check that the script is running at the command line.
If UCase(Right(Wscript.FullName, 11)) = "WSCRIPT.EXE" Then
    Wscript.Echo "This script must be run under CScript."
    Wscript.Quit
End If

' Attempt to connect to Virtual Server
On Error Resume Next
Set vs = CreateObject("VirtualServer.Application")
If Err.number <> 0 Then
    Wscript.Echo "Unable to connect to Virtual Server."
```

```
    Wscript.Quit
End if
On Error Goto 0

set vm = vs.FindVirtualMachine("A virtual machine")

'Start the virtual machine
vm.startup

'Wait for the login screen
checkForThumbnailMatch "loginScreen.txt", 95

'Send CTRL+ALT+DEL
vm.keyboard.TypeKeySequence("DOWN, Key_LeftCtrl, DOWN, Key_LeftAlt, DOWN, ↵
 Key_Delete, UP, Key_Delete, UP, Key_LeftAlt, UP, Key_LeftCtrl")

'Wait for the next screen
checkForThumbnailMatch "loginScreen2.txt", 95

'Enter password and hit enter
vm.keyboard.TypeAsciiText("password")
vm.keyboard.PressAndReleaseKey("Key_Enter")

'Wait for desktop
checkForThumbnailMatch "desktop.txt", 95

'Open Start menu and wait for it
vm.keyboard.PressAndReleaseKey("Key_LeftWindows")

checkForThumbnailMatch "startmenu.txt", 95

'Navigate the Start menu and launch notepad
vm.keyboard.PressAndReleaseKey("Key_P")

checkForThumbnailMatch "programs.txt", 95

vm.keyboard.PressAndReleaseKey("Key_Enter")

checkForThumbnailMatch "accessories.txt", 95

vm.keyboard.PressAndReleaseKey("Key_N")

'Once notepad is up, type in some text
checkForThumbnailMatch "notepad.txt", 95

vm.keyboard.TypeAsciiText("Hello World!")

'Shutdown the guest OS
vm.GuestOS.Shutdown

'Wait for a shutdown confirmation and accept it
checkForThumbnailMatch "shutdown.txt", 95

vm.keyboard.PressAndReleaseKey("Key_E")

Function checkForThumbnailMatch(thumbnailFile, percentageMatch)
```

Part VII: Automating Virtual Machine Operations

```
        checkForThumbnailMatch = false

        'Open requested thumbnail file
        Set objFSO = CreateObject("scripting.filesystemobject")
        Set objTextStream = objFSO.OpenTextFile(thumbnailFile, 1, True)
        savedThumbnail = objTextStream.ReadLine
        objTextStream.close

        'Return the savedThumbnail back to an array
        savedThumbnailArray = Split(savedThumbnail)

        'Poll for matching thumbnail
        do until checkForThumbnailMatch
            counter = 0
            matchCounter = 0
            notMatchCounter = 0
            newThumbnail = vm.Display.Thumbnail

            for each entry in savedThumbnailArray
                if CStr(savedThumbnailArray(counter)) = CStr(newThumbnail(counter)) then
                    matchCounter = matchCounter + 1
                else
                    notMatchCounter = notMatchCounter + 1
                end if
                counter = counter + 1
            next

            if ((matchCounter/(matchCounter + notMatchCounter))*100) >= ↲
        percentageMatch then
                checkForThumbnailMatch = true
            end if

            wscript.echo "Percentage match: " & ((matchCounter/(matchCounter + ↲
        notMatchCounter))*100)

            wscript.sleep(2000)

        loop

    end Function
```

Conclusion

Virtual Server exposes a very rich and powerful COM API that you can use to control all aspects of Virtual Server. You have now seen the full scope of the Virtual Server COM API, including all of the information about the Virtual Server, virtual machine, and virtual network COM objects (as well as many other associated objects).

VBscript is a very powerful tool for systems administrators and for users who wish to perform ad hoc automation of Virtual Server.

You have also seen samples of how the Virtual Server COM API can be scripted in order to address real-world problems.

404

18

Using PowerShell to Control Virtual Server

Windows PowerShell is a new command-line and scripting environment provided by Microsoft. It is a managed application, which means it is a bit more difficult to create an initial connection to the Virtual Server COM interface. For the most part, PowerShell scripts are written for the same reason as VBScripts: They provide an elegant way to repeatedly perform unattended operations.

One of the big advantages that PowerShell scripting has over VBScript is its object-oriented nature. Imagine a situation in which you have two scripts that interact with virtual hard disks and you want to chain these scripts together. In VBScript, the first script would create a virtual hard disk COM object and perform any needed operations on the virtual hard disk COM object, but when the first script went to call the second script, the first script would only be able to provide the virtual hard disk file string, and then the second script would need to create its own virtual hard disk COM object. With a PowerShell script, the first script is able to directly pass the virtual hard disk COM object to the second script.

Another advantage of the PowerShell environment is that it is possible to casually access and interact with the Virtual Server COM interface in an ad hoc manner directly from the command line, once the initial connection is established.

One downside to using PowerShell for scripting is that, at the moment, it cannot connect to COM objects on remote computers, which means you can connect only to Virtual Server on the local computer.

Setting Up the PowerShell Environment

Before you get going with using PowerShell to control Virtual Server, there are a couple of basic configuration changes to make that will make your life a lot easier.

Part VII: Automating Virtual Machine Operations

Configuring Set-ExecutionPolicy

The first thing you need to do is to configure `Set-ExecutionPolicy` on PowerShell. `Set-ExecutionPolicy` has four possible settings:

❑ `Restricted`: This is the default setting for Windows PowerShell. With this setting no configuration files or scripts are allowed to run.

❑ `AllSigned`: This setting requires that all scripts in configuration files be signed by a trusted publisher in order to be run.

❑ `RemoteSigned`: This setting requires that any scripts or configuration files that you download from the Internet be signed by a trusted publisher, but it allows you to run unsigned scripts or configuration files that have been created locally. This is most likely the setting that you'll end up using. It is also the setting that I recommend that you use to run the scripts provided in this chapter.

❑ `Unrestricted`: This setting allows you to run any script whether it is signed or unsigned, local or remote. You'll still be prompted if you attempt to run an unsigned script that was obtained from a remote source.

To change your `Set-ExecutionPolicy` setting, you'll need to open a PowerShell command window and run the following:

```
Set-ExecutionPolicy {new execution policy setting}
```

For example, to set the policy to `RemoteSigned` you would run the following:

```
Set-ExecutionPolicy RemoteSigned
```

Note that if you are doing this on a computer running Windows Vista, you need to launch PowerShell as administrator in order to run this command. Once set, this policy applies to all the users on the computer.

Configuring Basic Scripts

Using the DLL that is discussed in Chapter 16, creating a virtual machine COM object under PowerShell involves the following commands:

```
PS C:\Users\Benjamin>
[System.Reflection.Assembly]::loadfrom("C:\FULLPath\VSWrapperForPS.dll")
PS C:\Users\Benjamin> $vs = new-object -com VirtualServer.Application -strict
PS C:\Users\Benjamin>
[Microsoft.VirtualServer.Interop.PowerShell]::SetSecurity($vs)
PS C:\Users\Benjamin> $vm = $vs.FindVirtualMachine("A virtual machine")
PS C:\Users\Benjamin>
[Microsoft.VirtualServer.Interop.PowerShell]::SetSecurity($vm)
```

Obviously, this is far more typing than you want to do if you're regularly interacting with the Virtual Server COM interface. Thankfully this can be made much easier through the use of two simple shell scripts. The first shell script (named `SetSecurity.ps1`) takes an object as a parameter, loads the CoSetProxyBlanket DLL, and calls the SetSecurity routine on the DLL:

406

Chapter 18: Using PowerShell to Control Virtual Server

```
Param($object)
$result = ⊃
  [System.Reflection.Assembly]::loadfrom("C:\[PATH]\VSWrapperForPS.dll")
[Microsoft.VirtualServer.Interop.PowerShell]::SetSecurity($object)
```

Note that this script loads the interop DLL every time. This is not necessary, as it needs to be loaded only once, but loading it multiple times does not cause any problems or errors.

The next script (named newVSObject.ps1) creates a new Virtual Server COM object. It simply makes the call to establish the COM object and then calls SetSecurity.ps1 on it:

```
$global:vs = new-object -com VirtualServer.Application -strict
$result = SetSecurity($vs)
```

$global:vs needs to be used instead of $vs for this script. Typically, it is not possible to access a variable from a script once the script has finished running. Using $global: ensures that the variable can be accessed once the script has finished running.

Some of the lines in these scripts store the command output in $result. This is done so that the user doesn't see any unnecessary output. Under PowerShell, any information that is not stored in a parameter is printed on the console.

By creating these scripts, and placing them in a folder that is referenced by your path environment variable, you can now create a virtual machine COM object by typing in the following:

```
PS C:\Users\Benjamin> newVSObject
PS C:\Users\Benjamin> $vm = $vs.FindVirtualMachine("A virtual machine")
PS C:\Users\Benjamin> SetSecurity($vm)
```

Yes, that is much easier.

Customizing the PowerShell Profile

If you wanted to go a step further you could add a call to newVSObject.ps1 as part of your shell profile. This way, every PowerShell command window that you open will have the $vs object already created. To configure this for your user account, open a PowerShell command window and run the following:

```
notepad $profile
```

If you already have a profile script, this command will open it; otherwise, it will create a new one for you and open it. You can then just add newVSObject to the beginning of this script.

If you want to have this setting apply to all users on the computer you will need to create %windir%\system32\WindowsPowerShell\v1.0\Microsoft.PowerShell _profile.ps1 and add newVSObject to the beginning of this script.

407

Part VII: Automating Virtual Machine Operations

Accessing Virtual Server Directly from the PowerShell Command Line

One of the most interesting things about using PowerShell with Virtual Server is that you can perform pretty much any operation directly from the command line without actually needing to write a script. For example, if I want to save state a virtual machine and wait for the operation to complete, all I need to do is run the following commands:

```
PS C:\Users\Benjamin> newVSObject
PS C:\Users\Benjamin> $vm = $vs.FindVirtualMachine("A virtual machine")
PS C:\Users\Benjamin> SetSecurity($vm)
PS C:\Users\Benjamin> $vmTask = $vm.Save()
PS C:\Users\Benjamin> setsecurity($vmTask)
PS C:\Users\Benjamin> $vmTask.WaitForCompletion(-1)
```

In fact, there are a number of features of PowerShell that make this form of interaction even easier. The first thing to be aware of is PowerShell's support for tab completion. If you take any COM object, you can easily use tab completion to see all the properties and methods that it exposes. For example, if you had run the preceding set of commands, you could type in $vm. and then press Tab to cycle through the properties and methods that are available on the virtual machine COM object.

When using Tab to look at the properties and methods of an object, the properties and methods are displayed in alphabetical order, with the properties first and the methods second.

Objects, Properties, and Methods

Most of the time in PowerShell, you are handling objects. When you have an object, such as a virtual machine COM object, you can see a basic summary of its properties by just entering the name of the object on the command line and running it. Here is the output from a virtual machine COM object that is displayed when you run $vm:

```
Name                     : A Virtual Machine
ConfigID                 : {A2E3651E-CA59-4C05-8667-FB2407BF5782}
File                     : E:\My Virtual Machines\A Virtual Machine\A Virtual
Machine.vmc
Accountant               : System.__ComObject
GuestOS                  : System.__ComObject
Display                  : System.__ComObject
Keyboard                 : System.__ComObject
Mouse                    : System.__ComObject
State                    : 5
AutoStartAtLaunch        : 2
AutoStartAtLaunchDelay   : 0
ShutdownActionOnQuit     : 0
SavedStateFilePath       :
BIOSGUID                 : {08543F2C-B21E-430D-A7B2-737724098C3C}
BIOSSerialNumber         : 5813-3261-6366-5593-0151-5649-14
BaseBoardSerialNumber    : 5813-3261-6366-5593-0151-5649-14
ChassisSerialNumber      : 5813-3261-6366-5593-0151-5649-14
ChassisAssetTag          : 5813-3261-6366-5593-0151-5649-14
```

Chapter 18: Using PowerShell to Control Virtual Server

```
HardDiskConnections    : System.__ComObject
Undoable               : True
UndoAction             : 1
DVDROMDrives           : System.__ComObject
FloppyDrives           : System.__ComObject
NetworkAdapters        : System.__ComObject
SerialPorts            : System.__ComObject
SCSIControllers        : System.__ComObject
ParallelPorts          : System.__ComObject
ProcessorSpeed         : 2010
HasMMX                 : True
HasSSE                 : True
HasSSE2                : True
Has3DNow               : True
Notes                  : These are some notes...
Memory                 : 128
AttachedDriveTypes     : {1, 0, 2, 0...}
RunAsDefinedAccount    : False
AccountName            :
Security               : System.__ComObject
```

It is important to remember that what is being displayed here is just a summary of the property. For some properties, such as integers or relatively short strings, the summary does match the value. For other properties, such as the preceding `AttachedDriveTypes` property, the summary is just a partial representation of the actual property. When you see a summary value of `System.__ComObject`, this tells you that the property in question returns a COM object. Finally, a property that displays no summary value is either null or uninitialized, or an error was encountered while trying to gather the property.

> **If you have requested a summary of a COM object and have received nothing but null values returned, it is highly likely that you have not set the COM security impersonation level on this object. You can easily confirm this by trying to get the value for a specific property on the object. If it returns null then the object was correctly returning nulls. If it returns an error, then this is most likely the cause of the problem.**

If you want to access a subobject of an existing object, you will need to assign it to a new variable and then set the COM security impersonation level on the new object, like this:

```
PS C:\Users\Benjamin> $anAccountant = $vm.Accountant
PS C:\Users\Benjamin> SetSecurity($anAccountant)
0
PS C:\Users\Benjamin> $anAccountant


reservedSystemCapacity          : 0
AllowableReservedSystemCapacity : 50
MaximumSystemCapacity           : 50
AllowableMaximumSystemCapacity  : 50
relativeWeight                  : 100
CPUUtilization                  : 4
CPUUtilizationHistory           : {3, 1, 1, 17...}
DiskBytesRead                   : 19302400
```

409

Part VII: Automating Virtual Machine Operations

```
DiskBytesWritten           : 62464
NetworkBytesReceived       : 0
NetworkBytesSent           : 0
UpTime                     : 1536
```

Unfortunately, it is not possible to access the subobject directly (for example, get a summary of `$vm.Accountant` directly). The reason for this is that it is not possible to set the COM security impersonation level on a subobject.

To see the value of property, just execute it (for example, `$vm.notes`) and the full value will be displayed. For simple properties, the value can be updated by using the = operator. For example:

```
PS C:\Users\Benjamin> $vm.notes
These are some notes...
PS C:\Users\Benjamin> $vm.notes = "These are my new notes..."
PS C:\Users\Benjamin> $vm.notes
These are my new notes...
PS C:\Users\Benjamin> $vm.UndoAction
1
PS C:\Users\Benjamin> $vm.UndoAction = 2
PS C:\Users\Benjamin> $vm.UndoAction
2
PS C:\Users\Benjamin> $vm.Undoable
True
PS C:\Users\Benjamin> $vm.Undoable = $false
Exception setting "Undoable": "The configuration value could not be set. The
property cannot be changed while the virtual machine is saved or running."
At line:1 char:5
+ $vm.U <<<< ndoable = $false
```

The last attempt to set a property failed because the virtual machine was running, and that property can be changed only when the virtual machine is turned off. As you can see, PowerShell provides a fairly descriptive error message whenever an error is encountered. It should also be noted that the $ symbol is a special marker for PowerShell. $ is placed in front of all your variables. It is also used to indicate special values such as `$true` and `$false`.

If you execute a method with no parentheses or parameters, PowerShell will display a description of the method, including the types of parameters it takes and the objects it returns. If you execute a method with the appropriate parameters specified, it will be called and the appropriate objects will be returned. Here is an example of what this looks like for the `GetConfigurationValue` method on a virtual machine COM object:

```
PS C:\Users\Benjamin> $vm.GetConfigurationValue

MemberType          : Method
OverloadDefinitions : {Variant GetConfigurationValue (string)}
TypeNameOfValue     : System.Management.Automation.PSMethod
Value               : Variant GetConfigurationValue (string)
Name                : GetConfigurationValue
IsInstance          : True

PS C:\Users\Benjamin> $vm.GetConfigurationValue("integration/microsoft/
mouse/allow")
True
```

410

Chapter 18: Using PowerShell to Control Virtual Server

When a method or a property returns a value, PowerShell displays it on the command line by default. Sometimes this is useful but more often you'll want to store it in an object so that you can perform further operations on it. Furthermore, you have to store COM objects returned by Virtual Server in an object so you can set the COM security impersonation level before accessing them. Storing the output in an object is simply done by prepending the call with $objectname =. Here is an example:

```
PS C:\Users\Benjamin> $vm.save

MemberType          : Method
OverloadDefinitions : {IVMTask Save ()}
TypeNameOfValue     : System.Management.Automation.PSMethod
Value               : IVMTask Save ()
Name                : Save
IsInstance          : True

PS C:\Users\Benjamin> $vm.save()

PercentCompleted :
Description      :
Result           :
IsCancelable     :
ID               :
IsComplete       :

PS C:\Users\Benjamin> $aVMTask = $vm.Startup()
PS C:\Users\Benjamin> SetSecurity($aVMTask)
0
PS C:\Users\Benjamin> $aVMTask

PercentCompleted : 100
Description      : The virtual machine "A Virtual Machine" is being restored.
Result           : 0
IsCancelable     : False
ID               : 5
IsComplete       : True
```

To get a complete list of the properties and methods associated with an object, execute `$object.PSObject.Members`.

Understanding Pipelining

PowerShell introduces the concept of *pipeline execution*. In this mode you can execute multiple commands and have the objects that are returned by one command automatically provided as input for the next command. This is very useful as it allows you to take small scripts and string them together in an ad-hoc fashion. In many situations, you do not need to use scripts at all, but can instead just string together a series of commands. Unfortunately, because of the issues with the COM security impersonation level, this is rarely possible with Virtual Server, but pipelining can still be used effectively with scripts.

411

Part VII: Automating Virtual Machine Operations

Here is a `waitForTaskPipeline.ps1` script that is a very useful example of how to use pipelining:

```
$vmTask = $($input)
$result = setSecurity($vmTask)
$vmTask.WaitForCompletion(-1)
```

`$input` represents the input received from the pipeline. It is an array of objects. `$($input)` will return a single object if only one object is present in the input array; if multiple objects are present, you need to iterate over the input array. Once the `VMTask` object has been extracted from the pipeline, the script sets the COM security impersonation level on it and calls `WaitForCompletion`. Here is an example of how this script can be used: If you wanted to save state a virtual machine, merge the undo disks, and restore the virtual machine, you would need to wait for multiple `VMTask` objects. This can be done in a simple script by using pipelining, as shown in the following `saveMergeAndRestore.ps1` sample:

```
$vm.Save() | ./waitForTaskPipeline
$vm.MergeUndoDisks() | ./waitForTaskPipeline
$vm.Startup() | ./waitForTaskPipeline
```

If you want a script to output an object for the next script in the pipeline to use, you just need to execute the object at the end of the script in question.

Variable Declaration and Error Handling

Chapter 17 made a big deal about the correct usage of variable declaration and error handling with VBScript. When scripting PowerShell both of these items are handled completely differently.

It is always possible to dynamically declare a variable with PowerShell, and there is no way to disable this behavior. So be on the lookout for spelling mistakes and variable names! With PowerShell scripting you can use the command `set-psdebug –strict`, which stops you from performing operations with uninitialized variables but does not stop you from accidentally creating new variables.

Error handling is also significantly different in PowerShell scripting. You can configure the PowerShell error handling logic by setting the `$erroractionpreference` variable. The options are as follows:

❑ `SilentlyContinue`: This option tells PowerShell to silently ignore any errors and continue running the script. I would not recommend using this option, as it will hide any errors and make it very hard to debug problems.

❑ `Continue`: This option calls PowerShell to display error messages, but to continue running anyway. This is the default setting, and for most situations is appropriate.

❑ `Inquire`: I really like this option. This will cause PowerShell to prompt you when an error occurs and allow you to decide whether the script should continue running or not.

❑ `Stop`: This option tells PowerShell to stop the script on any error.

To set your script to use a different error-handling setting than the default, run something like the following in your script:

```
$erroractionpreference = "Inquire"
```

412

Functions and Script Parameters

Two other concepts to quickly discuss are functions and script parameters. Earlier in this chapter, SetSecurity.ps1 took a single parameter by using the `Param($object)` command. The parameter block can specify multiple parameters and the type of parameter to be received. `Param($object, [String]$aString)` indicates that a script takes two parameters: a generic object and a string.

If no type is specified for a parameter, the `[Object]` type is used.

Unfortunately, this form of passing parameters is not compatible with the method used for pipelining. This can be easily dealt with, however. Here is the `waitForTaskPipeline.ps1` script modified to accept both parameters and pipeline input:

```
Param([Object]$vmTask)

if ($vmTask -eq $null)
{
    $vmTask = $($input)
}

$result = setSecurity($vmTask)
$vmTask.waitForCompletion(-1)
```

This script first checks to see if a parameter has been provided, and if it does not find a parameter it checks the input pipeline.

Functions are a common concept of most programming languages. In PowerShell scripting, functions serve the same purpose as in most languages (to help you to organize large blocks of code into smaller, more manageable and easy-to-reuse blocks of code, and to help formalize the contract between different sections of code). There is one extra piece of functionality provided by functions in PowerShell. Typically, a function like the following is accessible only by code and running in the same script as the function itself:

```
function getVHD ([String]$string)
{
$returnedVHD = $vs.GetHardDisk($string)
$result = SetSecurity($returnedVHD)
$returnedVHD
}
```

But PowerShell allows you to declare functions in a global scope, which means you can call the functions from other scripts, all from the command line itself, once the function has been loaded into memory. To change a normal function to a global function you just need to change the declaration as follows:

```
function global:getVHD ([String]$string)
{
$returnedVHD = $vs.GetHardDisk($string)
$result = SetSecurity($returnedVHD)
$returnedVHD
}
```

Part VII: Automating Virtual Machine Operations

Using this method, you can use the function capability of PowerShell to define a large number of common tasks with a single script. You may even want to use functions as part of your profile script to define commands that you commonly use.

Sample Scripts

Now it is time to look at some sample PowerShell scripts that interact with Virtual Server. The first script, `CreateVirtualMachine.ps1`, creates, and potentially starts, a new virtual machine according to the parameters provided.

```
# Define constants
set-variable -name vmDiskType_Dynamic -value 0 -option constant
set-variable -name vmDiskType_FixedSize -value 1 -option constant
set-variable -name vmDriveBusType_IDE -value 0 -option constant
set-variable -name vmDriveBusType_SCSI -value 1 -option constant
set-variable -name vmDVDDrive_None -value 0 -option constant
set-variable -name vmDVDDrive_Image -value 1 -option constant
set-variable -name vmDVDDrive_HostDrive -value 2 -option constant

# User provided input
$vmName = "A new virtual machine"
$vmLocation = "C:\MyVMs\A new virtual machine"
$vmVHDType = $vmDiskType_Dynamic
$vmVHDSize = 20480
$vmMemory = 256
$vmNotes = "This VM was generated by a script"
$vmSCSIBoot = $true
$VMInstallMediaType = $vmDVDDrive_Image
$VMInstallMedia = "F:\Windows Server 2003 Standard.iso"
$vmStartAfterCreation = $true

# Generated values
$vmVHDName = $vmLocation + "\" + $vmName + " - hard disk.vhd"

# Create new virtual machine
$vm = $vs.CreateVirtualMachine($vmName, $vmLocation)
$result = SetSecurity($vm)

# Configure basic VM properties
$vm.Memory = 256
$vm.Notes = $vmNotes

# Create a new VHD
if ($vmVHDType -eq $vmDiskType_Dynamic)
{
    $vmTask = $vs.CreateDynamicVirtualHardDisk($vmVHDName, $vmVHDSize)
    $result = SetSecurity($vmTask)
    $vmTask.WaitForCompletion(-1)
}
else
{
```

414

Chapter 18: Using PowerShell to Control Virtual Server

```
    $vmTask = $vs.CreateFixedVirtualHardDisk($vmVHDName, $vmVHDSize)
    $result = SetSecurity($vmTask)
    $vmTask.WaitForCompletion(-1)
}

# Attach VHD to the right controller
if ($vmSCSIBoot)
{
    $aSCSIController = $vm.AddSCSIController()
    $vhdConnection = $vm.AddHardDiskConnection($vmVHDName, $vmDriveBusType_SCSI, ↵
 0, 0)
}
else
{
    $vhdConnection = $vm.AddHardDiskConnection($vmVHDName, $vmDriveBusType_IDE, ↵
 0, 0)
}

# Connect the first network adapter to the first virtual network

# First get the first virtual network
$vNets = $vs.VirtualNetworks
$result = SetSecurity($vNets)

$vNet1 = $vNets.item(1)
$result = SetSecurity($vNet1)

# Then get the first virtual network adapter
$vNics = $vm.NetworkAdapters
$result = SetSecurity($vNics)

$vNic1 = $vNics.item(1)
$result = SetSecurity($vNic1)

# Now connect them
$vNic1.AttachToVirtualNetwork($vNet1)

# Configure installation CD / DVD
$aDVDDrive = $vm.AddDVDROMDrive($vmDriveBusType_IDE, 1, 1)
$result = SetSecurity($aDVDDrive)

if ($VMInstallMediaType -eq $vmDVDDrive_Image)
{
    $aDVDDrive.AttachImage($VMInstallMedia)
}
else
{
    $aDVDDrive.AttachHostDrive($VMInstallMedia)
}

# Start the VM if requested to
if ($vmStartAfterCreation)
{
    $vmTask = $vm.Startup()
}
```

415

Part VII: Automating Virtual Machine Operations

There are a couple of things to highlight here:

❑ Declaring constants under PowerShell is rather clunky. You can see that the terminology that needs to be used is set-variable -name constant name -value constant name -option constant. It is worthwhile noting that when the set-variable command is used, you do not put a $ in front of the variable name.

❑ Attaching the first virtual network adapter to the first virtual network is complicated by the need to secure all the objects along the way. Unfortunately, this is unavoidable. For both the virtual network adapter and the virtual network, the object needs to be retrieved from a collection (which in turn is an object itself). This means that this action ends up creating four separate COM objects that need to be secured.

The next script to look at is a virtual hard disk utility script. It takes a single parameter of the virtual hard disk file name, displays information about the virtual hard disk, prompts the user for an action, and finally performs the requested action on the virtual hard disk. The interesting thing about this script is that it uses a number of functions, which are declared as global functions and can therefore be used separately after running the script. The functions include the following:

❑ getVHD: Takes a single parameter of the virtual hard disk file name and returns a secured virtual hard disk object.

❑ displayVHDInfo: Takes a single parameter of a secured virtual hard disk object and outputs information about the virtual hard disk to the console.

❑ editVHD: Takes a single parameter of a secured virtual hard disk object and prompts the user for an action and then performs it.

❑ convertVHDtoDynamic: Takes a single parameter of a secured virtual hard disk object and attempts to convert the virtual hard disk to a dynamically expanding virtual hard disk.

❑ convertVHDtoFixed: Takes a single parameter of a secured virtual hard disk object and attempts to convert the virtual hard disk to a fixed-size virtual hard disk.

❑ mergeVHDToNewFile: Takes a single parameter of a secured virtual hard disk object and attempts to merge it into a new virtual hard disk file.

❑ mergeVHDToParent: Takes a single parameter of a secured virtual hard disk object and attempts to merge it into the parent virtual hard disk.

❑ compactVHD: Takes a single parameter of a secured virtual hard disk object and attempts to compact it.

❑ waitForVMTask: Takes a single parameter of an unsecured VMTask object, secures it, displays its description, and then waits for it to complete while periodically displaying updates.

Here is a sample VHDUtility.ps1 script:

```
Param([String]$vhdName)

# Define constants
set-variable -name vmDiskType_Dynamic -value 0 -option constant
set-variable -name vmDiskType_FixedSize -value 1 -option constant
set-variable -name vmDiskType_Differencing -value 2 -option constant
```

Chapter 18: Using PowerShell to Control Virtual Server

```powershell
set-variable -name vmDiskType_HostDrive -value 4 -option constant

# Check to make sure that a VHD parameter was provided
if ($vhdName -eq "")
{
    write-host "You need to specify a VHD to examine"
    return
}

# Function to return a VHD object given the file name
function global:getVHD ([String]$string)
{
    $returnedVHD = $vs.GetHardDisk($string)
    $result = SetSecurity($returnedVHD)
    $returnedVHD
}

# Function to display information about a VHD object
function global:displayVHDInfo([object]$aVHDObject)
{
    write-host "VHD Information:"
    write-host "================="
    write-host "File Name        : " $aVHDObject.File
    write-host "SizeInGuest      : " $aVHDObject.SizeInGuest
    write-host "SizeOnHost       : " $aVHDObject.SizeOnHost
    write-host "HostFreeDiskSpace : " $aVHDObject.HostFreeDiskSpace

    switch ($aVHDObject.type)
    {
        $vmDiskType_Dynamic
        {
            write-host "Type             :  Dynamically Expanding VHD"
        }

        $vmDiskType_FixedSize
        {
            write-host "Type             :  Fixed Size VHD"
        }

        $vmDiskType_Differencing
        {
            $parentVhd = $aVHDObject.Parent
            $result = SetSecurity($parentVhd)

            write-host "Type             :  Differencing VHD"
            write-host "Parent           : " $parentVhd.File
        }

        $vmDiskType_HostDrive
        {
            write-host "Type             :  Linked VHD"
            write-host "HostDriveIdentifier : " $aVHDObject.HostDriveIdentifier
        }
    }
```

417

Part VII: Automating Virtual Machine Operations

```
}

# Function to prompt a user about what to do with a VHD object
function global:editVHD([object]$aVHDObject)
{
    switch ($aVHDObject.type)
    {
        $vmDiskType_Dynamic
        {
            # Offer to perform appropriate actions for a dynamic disk
            write-host ""
            write-host "Do you want to (c)ompact the VHD, convert it to a (f)ixed ⊋
disk, or (q)uit?"
            $userInput = read-host
            switch ($userInput)
            {
                "c" {compactVHD($aVHDObject)}
                "f" {convertVHDtoFixed($aVHDObject)}
                "q" {return}
            }
        }

        $vmDiskType_FixedSize
        {
            # Offer to perform appropriate actions for a fixed disk
            write-host ""
            write-host "Do you want to (c)onvert the VHD to a dynamic disk, or ⊋
(q)uit?"
            $userInput = read-host
            switch ($userInput)
            {
                "c" {convertVHDtoDynamic($aVHDObject)}
                "q" {return}
            }
        }

        $vmDiskType_Differencing
        {
            # Offer to perform appropriate actions for a differencing disk
            write-host ""
            write-host "Do you want to (m)erge the VHD to a new file, merge the ⊋
VHD into its (p)arent, or (q)uit?"
            $userInput = read-host
            switch ($userInput)
            {
                "m" {mergeVHDToNewFile($aVHDObject)}
                "p" {mergeVHDToParent($aVHDObject)}
                "q" {return}
            }
        }

        $vmDiskType_HostDrive
        {
            # Offer to perform appropriate actions for a linked disk
            write-host ""
```

Chapter 18: Using PowerShell to Control Virtual Server

```
        write-host "Do you want to convert the VHD to a (d)ynamic disk, ⊃
convert the VHD to a (f)ixed size disk or (q)uit?"
        $userInput = read-host
        switch ($userInput)
        {
            "d" {convertVHDtoDynamic($aVHDObject)}
            "f" {convertVHDtoFixed($aVHDObject)}
            "q" {return}
        }
    }
  }
}

# Converts a VHD to a dynamic disk
function global:convertVHDtoDynamic([object]$aVHDObject)
{
   $newVHDFileName = $aVHDObject.File.substring(0,
$aVHDObject.File.lastindexofany(".")) + " - dynamic.vhd"
   $vmTask = $aVHDObject.Convert($newVHDFileName, $vmDiskType_Dynamic)
   waitForVMTask($vmTask)
}

# Converts a VHD to a fixed disk
function global:convertVHDtoFixed([object]$aVHDObject)
{
   $newVHDFileName = $aVHDObject.File.substring(0, ⊃
$aVHDObject.File.lastindexofany(".")) + " - fixed.vhd"
   $vmTask = $aVHDObject.Convert($newVHDFileName, $vmDiskType_Fixed)
   waitForVMTask($vmTask)
}

# Merges a VHD to a new file
function global:mergeVHDToNewFile([object]$aVHDObject)
{
   $parentVhd = $aVHDObject.Parent
   $result = SetSecurity($parentVhd)

   $newVHDFileName = $aVHDObject.File.substring(0, ⊃
$aVHDObject.File.lastindexofany(".")) + " - merged.vhd"
   $vmTask = $aVHDObject.MergeTo($newVHDFileName, $parentVhd.Type)
   waitForVMTask($vmTask)
}

# Merges a VHD to the parent VHD
function global:mergeVHDToParent([object]$aVHDObject)
{
   $vmTask = $aVHDObject.Merge()
   waitForVMTask($vmTask)
}

# Compacts a VHD
function global:compactVHD([object]$aVHDObject)
{
   $vmTask = $aVHDObject.Compact()
   waitForVMTask($vmTask)
```

419

Part VII: Automating Virtual Machine Operations

```
    }

    # Waits for a VMTask and displays progress
    function global:waitForVMTask([object]$vmTask)
    {
        SetSecurity($vmTask)
        write-host "TasK:" $vmTask.Description
        while ($vmTask.IsComplete -eq $false)
        {
            write-host $vmTask.PercentCompleted "% complete..."
            Start-Sleep -m 1000
        }
        write-host "Done."
    }

    # The actual execution of the script
    $aVHD = getVHD($vhdName)
    displayVHDInfo($aVHD)
    editVHD($aVHD)
```

Conclusion

PowerShell provides a very interesting scripting environment, and its object-oriented nature lends itself well to scripting Virtual Server. Furthermore the ability to directly navigate the Virtual Server COM interface from the command-line interface is very attractive for administrators and power users. As long as you are looking to only interact with the local installation of Virtual Server you should spend some time getting familiar with PowerShell and what it can do for you.

Functions and pipelining can also provide an easy way to build up more complex scripts using smaller components.

Part VIII

Developing Software for Virtual Server

Chapter 19: Developing Managed Applications for Virtual Server

Chapter 20: Developing ASP.NET Applications with Virtual Server

19

Developing Managed Applications for Virtual Server

In Chapter 17, you learned how to write VBScripts to automate pretty much every aspect of Virtual Server. In this chapter, you'll be seeing a couple of targeted examples that highlight how to interact with Virtual Server from managed applications. Developing an application, rather than writing a script, is advantageous when you need to have significant user interaction in the process. Most people who choose to develop applications to control Virtual Server are primarily interested in providing a customized user experience when interacting with the virtual machines themselves.

Creating a VMRC Client

Connecting to the Virtual Server COM interface for a managed application enables you to perform all of the functions highlighted in Chapter 17 with a managed application. Above and beyond this, managed applications can actually host the VMRC client and provide a way for users to interact directly with the virtual machine. This section shows you how to create a basic application that hosts the VMRC client and highlights some of the common issues that are encountered with such applications.

Start by opening Visual Studio 2005 and creating a new Windows application project (you can use either Visual Basic or Visual C#). Then follow these steps:

1. Open the **Project** menu and select **Add Reference**.
2. Change to the **COM** tab and select **Microsoft Virtual Server VMRC Control**, and then click **OK**.

Part VIII: Developing Software for Virtual Server

*If you can't find this entry, go to the **Browse** tab, browse to the **Documentation** folder under the **Virtual Server** installation folder, and select **Microsoft.VMRCClientControl.Interop.dll**. Then click **OK**.*

3. Open the **Tools** menu and select **Choose Toolbox Items**.

4. Change to the **COM** components tab and select **Microsoft Virtual Server VMRC Control**, and then click **OK**.

   If you're doing this on Windows Vista you'll need to run `regsvr32 VMRCActiveXClient.dll` *from an administrative command prompt.*

5. There should now be a **Microsoft Virtual Server VMRC Control** entry in the **General** section of the toolbox. Select this item and drag it onto the windows form.

   You may need to resize the Windows form to fit the new control.

6. Select the newly created VMRC control.

7. In the **Properties** section, set **ServerAddress** to the name of the Virtual Server instance that you want to connect to.

8. Set **ServerPort** to **5900**.

   *If you're doing this on Windows Vista, you'll need to run this Visual Studio **as administrator** to connect to the VMRC control. You will not need to run your application **as administrator**.*

At this stage, you should be able to launch the application and have it successfully load the VMRC client and connect to the Virtual Server. But numerous things need to be cleaned up before this can be really usable for the average user, such as being able to specify the server and virtual machine to connect to, as well as being able to control the state of the virtual machines.

If you publish the application and try to run it outside of the development environment, you will need to make sure that VMRCActiveXClient.dll is in the same directory as the application.

Adding the VMRC ActiveX Control

In order for this option to appear on the COM components tab the Microsoft Virtual Server VMRC ActiveX control needs to have been installed on your system. It will also need to be installed on any computers that you want to run this application on. You can install the Microsoft Virtual Server VMRC ActiveX control in two ways:

❑ Use VMRC on the Virtual Server Administrative website on the target computer. This is certainly easy for a single computer case but can be problematic if you want to roll your application out on many computers.

❑ Locate VMRCActiveXClient.CAB (it will be in WebSite\VirtualServer\activex under the Virtual Server installation directory), open it, and copy the contents to a known location and then run `regsvr32 VMRCActiveXClient.dll`.

Chapter 19: Developing Managed Applications for Virtual Server

Specifying the Server and Virtual Machine

At this stage you are only connecting to a single instance of Virtual Server and showing the VMRC administrative display.

> *The VMRC administrative display is the page displayed by VMRC when it is not connected to an active virtual machine. It displays a list of available virtual machines and allows you to click on one to control it.*

Ideally, you want to be able to specify the Virtual Server instance and the virtual machine to connect to when the application is started. To do this, you'll need to add three new items to your project. The first item is the `CoSetProxyBlanket` module/class discussed in Chapter 16. The second item is for the prompt to display to allow the user to enter the server to connect to. The third item is the displayed prompt that enables the user to select which virtual machine to connect to.

You can follow the directions in Chapter 16 to create the `CoSetProxyBlanket` module/class (you do not need to use the other two files from Chapter 16, just the file that sets the COM security level). To create the other items, open the **Project** menu and select **Add New Item**. Select **Windows Form** and enter a name of **SelectServerPrompt**. Then repeat this process and enter a name of **SelectVirtualMachinePrompt**.

> *You will also need to follow the directions from Chapter 16 on adding the Virtual Server COM reference to the project.*

Open the visual designer for SelectServerPrompt and follow these steps:

1. Select the main form and view its **Properties**.

2. Select **Appearance** ⇨ **FormBorderStyle** and choose **FixedDialog**.

3. Select **Appearance** ⇨ **Text** and enter **Select the server**.

4. Select **Window Style** ⇨ **ControlBox** and choose **False**.

5. Select **Window Style** ⇨ **ShowInTaskbar** and choose **False**.

6. Drag a **Label** object from **Toolbox** onto the top section of the form.

7. With the new Label object selected, choose **Appearance** ⇨ **Text** and type **Please enter the name of a Virtual Server instance to connect to:**.

8. With the Label still selected, choose **Layout** ⇨ **AutoSize** and then choose **False**. Resize the Label as desired.

9. Drag a **TextBox** object from the **Toolbox** onto the form, under the Label.

10. With the new TextBox object selected, choose **Design** ⇨ **(Name)** and set it to **VirtualServerNameTextBox**.

> *You can leave the item names at the default settings. However, I find it easier to program when the item names are actually meaningful.*

11. Drag two **Buttons** from the **Toolbox** onto the form, side by side under the text box.

12. Select the left button, select **Design** ⇨ **(Name)**, and name the button **OKButton**.

13. With the left button still selected, choose **Appearance** ⇨ **Text** and enter **OK**.

425

Part VIII: Developing Software for Virtual Server

14. Select the right button, select **Design ⇨ (Name),** and name the button **ExitButton**.
15. With the right button still selected, choose **Appearance ⇨ Text** and enter **Cancel**.
16. Select the main form and view its **Properties**.
17. Select **Misc ⇨ AcceptButton** and enter **OKButton**. Then select **Misc ⇨ CancelButton** and enter **ExitButton**.

    The AcceptButton is automatically activated if the user presses Enter anywhere on the Windows form. The CancelButton is automatically activated if the user presses Esc anywhere on the Windows form, and the form is closed if this button is activated.

    > **Do not give your buttons the names AcceptButton or CancelButton, as this will cause significant problems with Visual Studio.**

18. Resize and arrange the dialog to your preferences.

When you are done you should have a form similar to the one displayed in Figure 19-1.

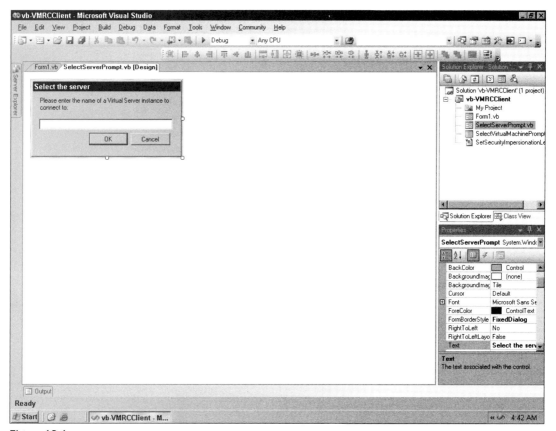

Figure 19-1

Chapter 19: Developing Managed Applications for Virtual Server

You now need to edit SelectServerPrompt. The following code enables the prompt to attempt to connect to the Virtual Server instance specified when the OK button is clicked. If it fails to connect to the Virtual Server instance specified, or it fails to set the security impersonation level, it reports an error to the user and allows them to try another Virtual Server instance. If it connects successfully, or the user presses Cancel, it exits. The code also needs to store the Virtual Server COM object and Virtual Server name in public variables so that the main program can easily retrieve these values.

Remember that for the button click events you need to double-click the button in the designer view and enter the code in the routine that gets created by this process.

Here's the code as it would appear in Visual Basic .NET:

```vb
Imports Microsoft.VirtualServer.Interop
Imports System.Reflection
Imports System.Runtime.InteropServices

Public Class SelectServerPrompt

    'Create public variable so that main program can access it
    Public VSConnection As VMVirtualServer = Nothing
    Public VSName As String = Nothing

    'Set threading apartment model
    <MTAThread()> _
    Private Sub OKButton_Click(ByVal sender As System.Object, ByVal e As _
System.EventArgs) Handles OKButton.Click

        Dim typeVSClass As Type
        Dim typeDCOM As Type
        Dim objDCOM As Object
        Dim SetSecurity As New SetSecurityImpersonationLevel

        VSName = VirtualServerNameTextBox.Text

        Try
            'Attempt to connect to Virtual Server over DCOM
            typeVSClass = GetType(VMVirtualServerClass)
            typeDCOM = Type.GetTypeFromCLSID(typeVSClass.GUID, VSName, True) _
            objDCOM = Activator.CreateInstance(typeDCOM)
            VSConnection = CType(Marshal.CreateWrapperOfType(objDCOM, _
typeVSClass), VMVirtualServerClass)

            'Attempt to set security impersonation level
            SetSecurity.Secure(VSConnection)

        Catch ex As Exception
            'Display error if failed
            MsgBox("Cannot connect to Virtual Server on: '" & VSName & "'", _
MsgBoxStyle.Critical, "Error")
            'Clean up public variables
            VSConnection = Nothing
            VSName = Nothing
            Exit Sub
```

427

Part VIII: Developing Software for Virtual Server

```
            End Try

            'Exit if succeeded
            Me.Close()

        End Sub

    End Class
```

Here's the code in C#:

```csharp
using System;
using System.Collections.Generic;
using System.ComponentModel;
using System.Data;
using System.Drawing;
using System.Text;
using System.Windows.Forms;
using Microsoft.VirtualServer.Interop;
using System.Runtime.InteropServices;
using System.Reflection;


namespace vc_VMRCClient
{


    public partial class SelectServerPrompt : Form
    {
        // Public variable so that the main program can access it
        public VMVirtualServerClass myVS;
        public string myVSName;

        public SelectServerPrompt()
        {
            InitializeComponent();
        }

        // Set the thread model to MTA
        [MTAThread]
        private void OKButton_Click(object sender, EventArgs e)
        {

            myVSName = VirtualServerNameTextBox.Text;

            try
            {
                //Connect to Virtual Server
                Type typeVSClass;
                Type typeDCOM;
                object objDCOM;

                typeVSClass = typeof(VMVirtualServerClass);
                typeDCOM = Type.GetTypeFromCLSID(typeVSClass.GUID, myVSName, true);
                objDCOM = Activator.CreateInstance(typeDCOM);
```

Chapter 19: Developing Managed Applications for Virtual Server

```
            myVS = (VMVirtualServerClass)Marshal.CreateWrapperOfType⤸
(objDCOM, typeVSClass);

                //Set Security Impersonation Level
                Personal.SetSecurity.ProxyBlanket myProxyBlanket = new ⤸
Personal.SetSecurity.ProxyBlanket();
                myProxyBlanket.Set(myVS);

        }
        catch
        {
                //Display error message if failed
                MessageBox.Show("Cannot connect to Virtual Server: '" + ⤸
myVSName + "'", "Error");
                myVSName = null;
                myVS = null;
                return;
        }

        //Close prompt
        this.Close();

    }
    }
}
```

Now open the visual designer for SelectVirtualMachinePrompt and follow these steps:

1. Select the main form and view its **Properties**.

2. Select **Appearance** ⇨ **FormBorderStyle** and choose **FixedDialog**.

3. Select **Appearance** ⇨ **Text** and enter **Select the virtual machine**.

4. Select **Window Style** ⇨ **ControlBox** and choose **False**.

5. Select **Window Style** ⇨ **ShowInTaskbar** and choose **False**.

6. Drag a **Label** object from the **Toolbox** onto the top section of the form.

7. With the new Label object selected, choose **Appearance** ⇨ **Text** and enter **Select a virtual machine to connect to:**.

8. With the Label still selected, choose **Layout** ⇨ **AutoSize** and then choose **False**. Resize the Label as desired.

9. Drag a **ListBox** from the **Toolbox** onto the form, just below the Label.

10. With the new ListBox object selected, choose **Design** ⇨ **(Name)** and enter **VirtualMachineListBox**.

11. Drag two **Buttons** from the **Toolbox** onto the form, side by side under the ListBox.

12. Select the left button, choose **Design** ⇨ **(Name)**, and enter **OKButton**.

13. With the left button still selected, choose **Appearance** ⇨ **Text** and enter **OK**.

14. With the left button still selected, choose **Behavior** ⇨ **Enabled** and then choose **False**.

15. Select the right button and choose **Design** ⇨ **(Name)** and enter **ExitButton**.

429

16. With the right button still selected, choose **Appearance ⇨ Text**, and enter **Cancel**.
17. Select the main form and view its **Properties** again.
18. Select **Misc ⇨ AcceptButton** and enter **OKButton**. Then select **Misc ⇨ CancelButton** and enter **ExitButton**.
19. Resize and arrange the dialog according to your preferences.

When you are done, you should have a form similar to the one displayed in Figure 19-2.

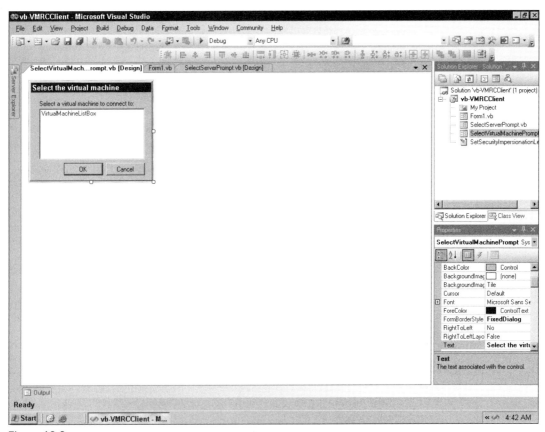

Figure 19-2

Following is the necessary code for providing a Virtual Server COM object to enumerate the available virtual machines and add their names to the virtual machine list box. The code to do this is stored in the routine called populateVMList, which is called once the form has finished being drawn (on the shown event). The OK button is enabled only once the list has been populated. Clicking OK will cause a virtual machine COM object to be created for the virtual machine that was selected from the list. Once again the virtual machine COM object is stored in a public variable so that the calling program can retrieve the value.

Chapter 19: Developing Managed Applications for Virtual Server

Here's the code as it would appear in Visual Basic .NET:

```vb
Imports Microsoft.VirtualServer.Interop

Public Class SelectVirtualMachinePrompt

    'Create public variable so that main program can access it
    Public VSConnection As VMVirtualServer = Nothing
    Public VirtualMachine As VMVirtualMachine = Nothing
    Private SetSecurity As New SetSecurityImpersonationLevel

    Private Sub populateVMList()
        'Exit if VSConnection is not setup
        If VSConnection Is Nothing Then Exit Sub

        Dim VM As VMVirtualMachine
        Dim VMs As IVMVirtualMachineCollection
        Dim index As Integer

        'Clear the list box - just in case
        VirtualMachineListBox.Items.Clear()

        'Populate VMs and set security on it
        VMs = VSConnection.VirtualMachines
        SetSecurity.Secure(VMs)

        'Make sure that there are actually virtual machines
        If VMs.Count > 0 Then

            'Go through each virtual machine and add it to the list
            For index = 1 To VMs.Count
                VM = VMs.Item(index)
                SetSecurity.Secure(VM)
                VirtualMachineListBox.Items.Add(VM.Name)
            Next

            'Select the fist entry
            VirtualMachineListBox.SelectedIndex = 0

            'Enable the OK button
            OKButton.Enabled = True

        Else
            'If there are no virtual machines, alert and exit
            MsgBox("There are no virtual machines on the server.", ⤶
 MsgBoxStyle.Critical, "Error")
            VirtualMachine = Nothing
            Me.Close()
        End If

    End Sub

    Private Sub SelectVirtualMachinePrompt_Shown(ByVal sender As Object, ⤶
ByVal e As System.EventArgs) Handles Me.Shown
        'Call PopulateVMList as soon as the prompt is drawn
```

431

Part VIII: Developing Software for Virtual Server

```
            populateVMList()
    End Sub

    Private Sub OKButton_Click(ByVal sender As System.Object, ByVal e As ⤶
System.EventArgs) Handles OKButton.Click
        'Try to Set virtual machine
        Try
            VirtualMachine = VSConnection.FindVirtualMachine(⤶
VirtualMachineListBox.SelectedItem.ToString)
            SetSecurity.Secure(VirtualMachine)
        Catch
            MsgBox("Failed to connect to virtual machine.", ⤶
MsgBoxStyle.Critical, "Error")
            VirtualMachine = Nothing
        End Try

        'Close the prompt when finished
        Me.Close()
    End Sub
End Class
```

Here's the code as it would appear in C#:

```csharp
using System;
using System.Collections.Generic;
using System.ComponentModel;
using System.Data;
using System.Drawing;
using System.Text;
using System.Windows.Forms;
using Microsoft.VirtualServer.Interop;

namespace vc_VMRCClient
{
    public partial class SelectVirtualMachinePrompt : Form
    {

        public VMVirtualServer myVS = null;
        public VMVirtualMachine myVM = null;
        private Personal.SetSecurity.ProxyBlanket myProxyBlanket = new ⤶
Personal.SetSecurity.ProxyBlanket();

        public SelectVirtualMachinePrompt()
        {
            InitializeComponent();

            //Connect event handler for 'shown' event
            this.Shown += new EventHandler(SelectVirtualMachinePrompt_Shown);
        }

        private void populateVMList()
        {

        // Exit if myVS is not setup
        if (myVS == null)
```

432

Chapter 19: Developing Managed Applications for Virtual Server

```csharp
            {
                return;
            }

        //Clear the list box - just in case
        VirtualMachineListBox.Items.Clear();

        //Populate VMs and set security on it
        IVMVirtualMachineCollection VMs = myVS.VirtualMachines;
        myProxyBlanket.Set(VMs);

        //Make sure that there are actually virtual machines
        if (VMs.Count > 0)
        {
            VMVirtualMachine VM;

            //Go through each virtual machine and add it to the list
            for (int index = 1; index <= VMs.Count; index++)
            {
                VM = VMs[index];
                myProxyBlanket.Set(VM);
                VirtualMachineListBox.Items.Add(VM.Name);
            }

            //Select the fist entry
            VirtualMachineListBox.SelectedIndex = 0;

            //Enable the OK button
            OKButton.Enabled = true;
        }
        else
        {
            //If there are no virtual machines, alert and exit
            MessageBox.Show("There are no virtual machines on the ⊃
    server.","Error");
            myVM = null;
            this.Close();
        }

    }

    private void SelectVirtualMachinePrompt_Shown(object sender, EventArgs e)
    {
        populateVMList();
    }

    private void OKButton_Click(object sender, EventArgs e)
    {
    //Try to Set myVM
    try
        {
            string selectedVMName = ⊃
VirtualMachineListBox.SelectedItem.ToString();
            myVM = myVS.FindVirtualMachine(selectedVMName);
            myProxyBlanket.Set(myVM);
        }
```

433

Part VIII: Developing Software for Virtual Server

```csharp
        catch
            {
                MessageBox.Show("Failed to connect to virtual machine.", "Error");
                myVM = null;
            }

        //Close the prompt when finished
        this.Close();
        }
    }
}
```

Finally, you'll need to return to the main application. You next see the appropriate code to tell the application to wait until the form has finished displaying before displaying the two prompts. A couple of things to highlight in the code that follows are that once again the Virtual Server COM object, virtual machine COM object, and Virtual Server name are stored in public variables. I'm handling it this way because I will use this application as a component in the next application discussed in this chapter. Apart from that, the code is fairly straightforward. New `SelectServerPrompt` and `SelectVirtualMachinePrompt` objects are created and displayed in order. After each prompt is displayed, the program checks to see if the public variables contain valid data; if they do, it copies the values to local public variables. If they don't, it exits.

Here's the code as it would appear in Visual Basic .NET:

```vbnet
Imports Microsoft.VirtualServer.Interop

Public Class Form1

    Public VSConnection As VMVirtualServer = Nothing
    Public VSName As String = Nothing
    Public VirtualMachine As VMVirtualMachine = Nothing
    Private SetSecurity As New SetSecurityImpersonationLevel

    Private Sub SelectVMToConnectTo()

        'Check to see if the values have been prepopulated
        If VSConnection Is Nothing Or _
           VirtualMachine Is Nothing Or _
           VSName Is Nothing Then

            Dim serverPrompt As New SelectServerPrompt
            Dim VMPrompt As New SelectVirtualMachinePrompt

            'Set the starting location and show the first dialog
            serverPrompt.StartPosition = FormStartPosition.CenterParent
            serverPrompt.ShowDialog(Me)

            'If the server prompt fails, exit the application
            If serverPrompt.VSConnection Is Nothing Then
                Me.Close()
            Else
                'Store the information from the server prompt
                'and then clear it out.
                VSConnection = serverPrompt.VSConnection
                VSName = serverPrompt.VSName
```

434

Chapter 19: Developing Managed Applications for Virtual Server

```vb
            serverPrompt = Nothing

            'Give the VM prompt the VS COM object and start it up
            VMPrompt.VSConnection = VSConnection
            VMPrompt.StartPosition = FormStartPosition.CenterParent
            VMPrompt.ShowDialog(Me)

            'Exit if the VM prompt fails
            If VMPrompt.VirtualMachine Is Nothing Then
                Me.Close()
            Else
                'Store the information from the VM prompt
                'and then clear it out.
                VirtualMachine = VMPrompt.VirtualMachine
                VMPrompt = Nothing

                'Connect to the VM
                ConnectToVM()
            End If
        End If
    Else
        'Connect to the VM
        ConnectToVM()
    End If

End Sub

Private Sub ConnectToVM()

    'Make sure all variables are populated
    If VSConnection Is Nothing Or _
        VirtualMachine Is Nothing Or _
        VSName Is Nothing Then
        Exit Sub
    Else

        'Configure the VMRC client and connect
        AxVMRCClientControl1.ServerAddress = VSName
        AxVMRCClientControl1.ServerPort = VSConnection.VMRCAdminPortNumber
        AxVMRCClientControl1.ServerDisplayName = VirtualMachine.Name
        AxVMRCClientControl1.Connect()

        'Update the window title
        Me.Text = VirtualMachine.Name & " on " & VSName

    End If

End Sub

Private Sub Form1_Shown(ByVal sender As Object, ByVal e As ⤶
System.EventArgs) Handles Me.Shown
    'Once the form is loaded - start showing dialogs
    SelectVMToConnectTo()
End Sub
End Class
```

435

Part VIII: Developing Software for Virtual Server

Here's the code as it would appear in C#:

```csharp
using System;
using System.Collections.Generic;
using System.ComponentModel;
using System.Data;
using System.Drawing;
using System.Text;
using System.Windows.Forms;
using System.Runtime.InteropServices;
using System.Reflection;
using Microsoft.VirtualServer.Interop;

namespace vc_VMRCClient
{

    public partial class Form1 : Form
    {

        //Declare global variables
        public VMVirtualServerClass myVS = null;
        public string myVSName = null;
        public VMVirtualMachine myVM = null;

        public Form1()
        {
            InitializeComponent();
            //Connect event handler for 'shown' event
            this.Shown += new EventHandler(Form1_Shown);
        }

        private void Form1_Shown(object sender, EventArgs e)
        {
            //Check to see if the values have been prepopulated
            if (myVS == null || myVM == null || myVSName == null)
            {
                //Set the starting location and show the first dialog
                SelectServerPrompt serverPrompt = new SelectServerPrompt();

                serverPrompt.StartPosition = FormStartPosition.CenterParent;
                serverPrompt.ShowDialog(this);

                //If the server prompt fails, exit the application
                if (serverPrompt.myVS == null)
                {
                    this.Close();
                }
                else
                {
                    //Store the information from the server prompt
                    //and then clear it out.
                    myVS = serverPrompt.myVS;
                    myVSName = serverPrompt.myVSName;
```

Chapter 19: Developing Managed Applications for Virtual Server

```csharp
            serverPrompt = null;

            //Give the VM prompt the VS COM object and start it up
            SelectVirtualMachinePrompt VMPrompt = new
SelectVirtualMachinePrompt();

            VMPrompt.StartPosition = FormStartPosition.CenterParent;
            VMPrompt.myVS = myVS;
            VMPrompt.ShowDialog(this);

            //Exit if the VM prompt fails
            if (VMPrompt.myVM == null)
            {
                this.Close();
            }
            else
            {
                //Store the information from the VM prompt
                //and then clear it out.
                myVM = VMPrompt.myVM;
                VMPrompt = null;

                //Connect to the VM
                connectToVM();
            }
        }
    }
    else
    {
        //Connect to the VM
        connectToVM();
    }
}

private void connectToVM()
{
    //Make sure all variables are populated
    if (myVS == null || myVM == null || myVSName == null)
        {
            return;
        }
        else
        {
            //Configure the VMRC client and connect
            axVMRCClientControl1.ServerAddress = myVSName;
            axVMRCClientControl1.ServerPort = myVS.VMRCAdminPortNumber;
            axVMRCClientControl1.ServerDisplayName = myVM.Name;
            axVMRCClientControl1.Connect();

            //Update the window title
            this.Text = myVM.Name + " on " + myVSName;
        }

    }
  }
}
```

437

Part VIII: Developing Software for Virtual Server

Once this is all done, go back to the designer view of the main application, select the VMRC control, and change the ServerAddress field to be blank. This way. the VMRC control won't connect to a server until the user specifies one.

Handling Display Size Changes

The next common problem to look at is how to correctly handle display size changes. The issue here is that the virtual machine can display any arbitrary resolution; furthermore, it can change its resolution at any stage. Lucky for us, this is relatively easy to handle. First, open the designer view for the main application and edit the properties of the main form. Set **FormBorderStyle** to **Fixed3D** and **MaximizeBox** to **False**.

Then select the VMRC client control and make sure that the **Location** property is set to **0,0**.

This ensures that the VMRC client control is correctly aligned with the rest of the application.

Now you simply add code to resize the main form whenever that VMRC client control changes its size. Following is the code that you need to add to the main application to do this:

The order of the routines is not important.

Here's the code as it would appear in Visual Basic .NET:

```
...

    Private Sub ConnectToVM()

        'Make sure all variables are populated
        If VSConnection Is Nothing Or _
           VirtualMachine Is Nothing Or _
           VSName Is Nothing Then
            Exit Sub
        Else

            'Configure the VMRC client and connect
            AxVMRCClientControl1.ServerAddress = VSName
            AxVMRCClientControl1.ServerPort = VSConnection.VMRCAdminPortNumber
            AxVMRCClientControl1.ServerDisplayName = VirtualMachine.Name
            AxVMRCClientControl1.Connect()

            'Update the window title
            Me.Text = VirtualMachine.Name & " on " & VSName

            'Resize the form after connecting to the virtual machine
            resizeForm1()
        End If

    End Sub

    Private Sub AxVMRCClientControl1_SizeChanged(ByVal sender As Object, ByVal ⤶
  e As System.EventArgs) Handles AxVMRCClientControl1.SizeChanged
        resizeForm1()
```

438

Chapter 19: Developing Managed Applications for Virtual Server

```vb
        End Sub

    Private Sub resizeForm1()
        'Calculate the extra padding to add
        Dim heightPad As Integer = Me.Height - Me.ClientSize.Height
        Dim widthPad As Integer = Me.Width - Me.ClientSize.Width

        'Resize the form
        Me.Height = AxVMRCClientControl1.Height + heightPad
        Me.Width = AxVMRCClientControl1.Width + widthPad
    End Sub
End Class
```

Here's the code as it would appear in C#:

```csharp
...
    public Form1()
    {
        InitializeComponent();
        //Connect event handler for 'shown' event
        this.Shown += new EventHandler(Form1_Shown);

        //Connect event handler for VMRC resize
        axVMRCClientControl1.Resize += new ⤶
EventHandler(axVMRCClientControl1_Resize);
    }

...

    private void connectToVM()
    {
        //Make sure all variables are populated
        if (myVS == null || myVM == null || myVSName == null)
            {
                return;
            }
        else
            {
                //Configure the VMRC client and connect
                axVMRCClientControl1.ServerAddress = myVSName;
                axVMRCClientControl1.ServerPort = myVS.VMRCAdminPortNumber;
                axVMRCClientControl1.ServerDisplayName = myVM.Name;
                axVMRCClientControl1.Connect();

                //Update the window title
                this.Text = myVM.Name + " on " + myVSName;

                //Resize the form after connecting to the vm
                resizeForm1();
            }

    }

    private void axVMRCClientControl1_Resize(object sender, EventArgs e)
    {
```

439

Part VIII: Developing Software for Virtual Server

```
            resizeForm1();
    }

    private void resizeForm1()
    {
        //Calculate the extra padding to add
        int heightPad = this.Height - this.ClientSize.Height;
        int widthPad = this.Width - this.ClientSize.Width;

        //Resize the form
        this.Height = axVMRCClientControl1.Height + heightPad;
        this.Width = axVMRCClientControl1.Width + widthPad;
    }
```

This code adds a new routine, resizeForm1, which resizes the form correctly for the new size of the VMRC client. It does this by first calculating how much pad it needs to add to the VMRC client size. It looks at the current height and width of the form as compared to the height and width of the drawable area inside of the form (ClientSize) to determine the amount to pad by. It then resizes the form to the VMRC client size plus appropriate pad. This routine is called when the VMRC client first connects to the virtual machine and whenever the VMRC client is resized.

Locking Down the VMRC Client

As you have seen by now, VMRC provides an administrative display that allows you to see and connect all virtual machines on an instance of Virtual Server. While there are times when this is convenient, many times you want to make sure that the user never sees this display. You've also probably noticed a black menu bar at the top of the VMRC client. Users can use this menu bar to access information about the VMRC connection and to connect to another server. This can also present problems in a controlled environment.

The first step to locking down these options is to open the main form in the designer view, select the VMRC client, and configure the following properties:

1. Set **AdministratorMode** to **False**.
2. Set **MenuEnabled** to **False**.

Unfortunately, even with these changes made, things are not bulletproof. If a user is connected to a virtual machine via VMRC and the virtual machine shuts down, the VMRC client returns to the administrative display even if this option is disabled. Also, even with the menu disabled, a user can still press the host key plus c to bring up a connection dialog box that allows them to connect to any virtual machine on any Virtual Server instance.

Given these issues, you need to be prepared to reactively handle situations where the VMRC client is connected to the wrong display. You can do this with the following code.

Here's the code in Visual Basic .NET:

```
...
    Private Sub ConnectToVM()

        'Make sure all variables are populated
```

Chapter 19: Developing Managed Applications for Virtual Server

```vb
        If VSConnection Is Nothing Or _
            VirtualMachine Is Nothing Or _
            VSName Is Nothing Then
            Exit Sub
        Else

            'Configure the VMRC client and connect
            AxVMRCClientControl1.ServerAddress = VSName
            AxVMRCClientControl1.ServerPort = VSConnection.VMRCAdminPortNumber
            AxVMRCClientControl1.ServerDisplayName = VirtualMachine.Name
            AxVMRCClientControl1.Connect()

            'Update the window title
            Me.Text = VirtualMachine.Name & " on " & VSName

            'Display the VMRC client control
            AxVMRCClientControl1.Visible = True

            'Resize the form after connecting to the virtual machine
            resizeForm1()
        End If

    End Sub

...

    Private Sub AxVMRCClientControl1_OnSwitchedDisplay(ByVal sender As Object, ↩
  ByVal e As AxMicrosoft.VMRCClientControl.Interop._IVMRCClientControlEvents_↩
OnSwitchedDisplayEvent) Handles AxVMRCClientControl1.OnSwitchedDisplay
        If (Not AxVMRCClientControl1.ServerAddress = VSName Or _
            Not AxVMRCClientControl1.ServerDisplayName = VirtualMachine.Name) And _
            AxVMRCClientControl1.Visible Then
            AxVMRCClientControl1.Disconnect()
            AxVMRCClientControl1.Visible = False
        End If
    End Sub

...
```

Here's the code in C#:

```csharp
...

        public Form1()
        {
            InitializeComponent();
            //Connect event handler for 'shown' event
            this.Shown += new EventHandler(Form1_Shown);

            //Connect event handler for VMRC resize
            axVMRCClientControl1.Resize += new ↩
    EventHandler(axVMRCClientControl1_Resize);

            //Connect event handler for VMRC OnSwitchedDisplay
```

Part VIII: Developing Software for Virtual Server

```
                axVMRCClientControl1.OnSwitchedDisplay += delegate { ⤵
    axVMRCClientControl1_OnSwitchedDisplay(); };
            }

    ...

        private void connectToVM()
        {
            //Make sure all variables are populated
            if (myVS == null || myVM == null || myVSName == null)
            {
                return;
            }
            else
            {
                //Configure the VMRC client and connect
                axVMRCClientControl1.ServerAddress = myVSName;
                axVMRCClientControl1.ServerPort = ⤵
    myVS.VMRCAdminPortNumber;
                axVMRCClientControl1.ServerDisplayName = myVM.Name;
                axVMRCClientControl1.Connect();

                //Update the window title
                this.Text = myVM.Name + " on " + myVSName;

                //Display the VMRC client control
                axVMRCClientControl1.Visible = true;

                //Resize the form after connecting to the vm
                resizeForm1();
            }

        }

    ...

        public void axVMRCClientControl1_OnSwitchedDisplay()
        {
        if ((axVMRCClientControl1.ServerAddress != myVSName || ⤵
  axVMRCClientControl1.ServerDisplayName != myVM.Name) && ⤵
axVMRCClientControl1.Visible)
            {
            axVMRCClientControl1.Disconnect();
            axVMRCClientControl1.Visible = false;
            }
        }
    }
}
```

The two code changes here are that the routine to connect to the virtual machine now changes the VMRC client to be visible, and that there is now an event handler for the OnSwitchedDisplay event on the VMRC client. The OnSwitchedDisplay event handler checks to see that the Virtual Server instance and virtual machine connection being used by the VMRC client match the values that are stored in the global variables. If they did not match it will disconnect the VMRC client and change it to not be visible.

Chapter 19: Developing Managed Applications for Virtual Server

On Visual Basic .NET event handlers are assigned through the Handles *parameter on the subroutine declaration. C# does this by manually assigning an event handler. It is also possible to manually add an event handler with Visual Basic .NET by using the* AddHandler *command.*

The one problem with this approach is that when you connect to a virtual machine that is not currently running, Virtual Server starts the virtual machine automatically and then connects you to it. While the virtual machine is starting, you are momentarily connected to the VMRC administrative display. This approach results in the connection getting dropped in this situation — which leads us to the next topic of discussion.

Handling the Virtual Machine State

The standard VMRC client will always start a virtual machine when you attempt to connect to it. It then provides no way to perform state operations such as stopping the virtual machine or putting it into a saved state. To address this, follow these steps:

1. Open the designer view for the main application.

2. Drag a **MenuStrip** from the **Toolbox** onto the main form.

3. Select the VMRC control and change the **Location** property to **0,24**.

24 comes from the height of the MenuStrip. You should check your MenuStrip control to ensure that it has the same height. You'll also need to edit the resizeForm1 routine to include this extra 24 pixels in its padding calculation.

4. Click the **Type Here** box and enter **Action**.

5. Select the newly created action menu and add entries for **Start**, **Turn Off**, **Save State**, **Shut Down**, **Pause**, and **Resume**.

If you want to enter a line break to break up the list just press the - key for an entry name.

6. Select each of the newly created menu entries and change the **Enabled** property to **False**.

When you are done, you should have a form similar to the one displayed in Figure 19-3.

Now a lot of code needs to be written. You first need to hook up clicked events for each of the menu items. If you look at each of the subroutines for handling the menu click events, you'll notice a couple of things.

First, the pause and resume commands do not return VMTask objects. These operations happen instantaneously. Second, the shut down command needs to check the GuestOS object to ensure that it can shut down before calling the shut down method. Finally you'll notice that I do not use WaitForCompletion; instead, I use a while loop that checks the IsComplete status. The reason for doing this is that some of these tasks can take a long time. If I used WaitForCompletion, the user interface would be unresponsive while the task was completing. This could cause user confusion and even result in users thinking that the application had hung. Using a while loop, which calls Application.DoEvents, you can ensure that the user interface remains responsive.

443

Part VIII: Developing Software for Virtual Server

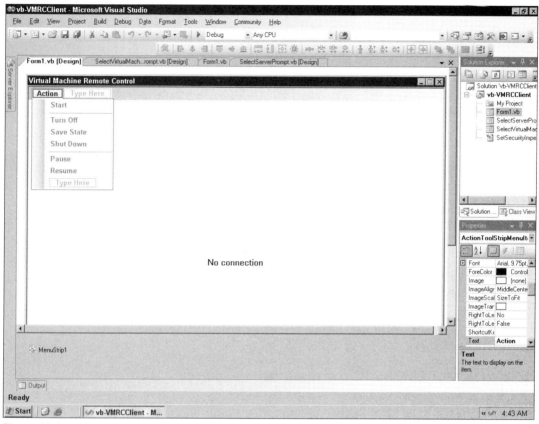

Figure 19-3

Next you need to make a routine to check the state of the virtual machine and enable and disable the appropriate menu entries. In the code provided, the `checkVirtualMachineState` does this by using a case statement on the virtual machine state. You'll notice that the `checkVirtualMachineState` routine is called when the initial connection is made to the virtual machine and whenever a user changes the virtual machine state using the **Action** menu.

> *Unfortunately, because `CoSetProxyBlanket` is being used, it is not possible to receive events from the virtual machine object. This means that if someone else connects to Virtual Server and changes the virtual machine state, it will not be reflected in this menu. It would be possible to implement some sort of polling routine to provide a solution for this.*

The last change is that the `ConnectToVM` routine needs to be updated to check to see if the virtual machine is running before attempting to connect the VMRC control.

> *If you start the virtual machine from the action menu, `ConnectToVM` will be called again.*

The complete source code that is now present in the main application is shown in the following code blocks for Visual Basic .NET and C#.

Chapter 19: Developing Managed Applications for Virtual Server

Here is the code in Visual Basic .NET:

```
Imports Microsoft.VirtualServer.Interop

Public Class Form1

    'Declare global variables
    Public VSConnection As VMVirtualServer = Nothing
    Public VSName As String = Nothing
    Public VirtualMachine As VMVirtualMachine = Nothing

    'Create SetSecurity for internal use
    Private SetSecurity As New SetSecurityImpersonationLevel

    Public Sub New()

        ' This call is required by the Windows Form Designer.
        InitializeComponent()

        ' Add any initialization after the InitializeComponent() call.

    End Sub

    Private Sub SelectVMToConnectTo()

        'Check to see if the values have been prepopulated
        If VSConnection Is Nothing Or _
           VirtualMachine Is Nothing Or _
           VSName Is Nothing Then

            Dim serverPrompt As New SelectServerPrompt
            Dim VMPrompt As New SelectVirtualMachinePrompt

            'Set the starting location and show the first dialog
            serverPrompt.StartPosition = FormStartPosition.CenterParent
            serverPrompt.ShowDialog(Me)

            'If the server prompt fails, exit the application
            If serverPrompt.VSConnection Is Nothing Then
                Me.Close()
            Else
                'Store the information from the server prompt
                'and then clear it out.
                VSConnection = serverPrompt.VSConnection
                VSName = serverPrompt.VSName
                serverPrompt = Nothing

                'Give the VM prompt the VS COM object and start it up
                VMPrompt.VSConnection = VSConnection
                VMPrompt.StartPosition = FormStartPosition.CenterParent
                VMPrompt.ShowDialog(Me)

                'Exit if the VM prompt fails
                If VMPrompt.VirtualMachine Is Nothing Then
                    Me.Close()
```

445

Part VIII: Developing Software for Virtual Server

```
                Else
                    'Store the information from the VM prompt
                    'and then clear it out.
                    VirtualMachine = VMPrompt.VirtualMachine
                    VMPrompt = Nothing

                    'Update the action menu
                    checkVirtualMachineState()

                    'Connect to the VM
                    ConnectToVM()
                End If
            End If
        Else
            'Connect to the VM
            ConnectToVM()
        End If

    End Sub

    Private Sub ConnectToVM()

        'Make sure all variables are populated
        If VSConnection Is Nothing Or _
           VirtualMachine Is Nothing Or _
           VSName Is Nothing Then
            Exit Sub
        Else

            'Check that the virtual machine is running
            If VirtualMachine.State = VMVMState.vmVMState_Running Then

                'Configure the VMRC client and connect
                AxVMRCClientControl1.ServerAddress = VSName
                AxVMRCClientControl1.ServerPort = VSConnection.VMRCAdminPortNumber
                AxVMRCClientControl1.ServerDisplayName = VirtualMachine.Name⤵
                AxVMRCClientControl1.Connect()

                'Update the window title
                Me.Text = VirtualMachine.Name & " on " & VSName

                'Display the VMRC client control
                AxVMRCClientControl1.Visible = True

                'Resize the form after connecting to the virtual machine
                resizeForm1()
            End If
        End If

    End Sub

    Private Sub Form1_Shown(ByVal sender As Object, ByVal e As ⤵
System.EventArgs) Handles Me.Shown
        'Once the form is loaded - start showing dialogs
        SelectVMToConnectTo()
```

Chapter 19: Developing Managed Applications for Virtual Server

```vbnet
End Sub

Private Sub resizeForm1()
    'Calculate the extra padding to add
    Dim heightPad As Integer = Me.Height - Me.ClientSize.Height + 24
    Dim widthPad As Integer = Me.Width - Me.ClientSize.Width

    'Resize the form
    Me.Height = AxVMRCClientControl1.Height + heightPad
    Me.Width = AxVMRCClientControl1.Width + widthPad
End Sub

Private Sub checkVirtualMachineState()

    If Not VirtualMachine Is Nothing Then
        Select Case VirtualMachine.State
            Case VMVMState.vmVMState_TurnedOff
                'Configure menu entries
                StartToolStripMenuItem.Enabled = True
                TurnOffToolStripMenuItem.Enabled = False
                SaveStateToolStripMenuItem.Enabled = False
                ShutDownToolStripMenuItem.Enabled = False
                PauseToolStripMenuItem.Enabled = False
                ResumeToolStripMenuItem.Enabled = False

            Case VMVMState.vmVMState_Saved
                'Configure menu entries
                StartToolStripMenuItem.Enabled = True
                TurnOffToolStripMenuItem.Enabled = False
                SaveStateToolStripMenuItem.Enabled = False
                ShutDownToolStripMenuItem.Enabled = False
                PauseToolStripMenuItem.Enabled = False
                ResumeToolStripMenuItem.Enabled = False

            Case VMVMState.vmVMState_Running
                'Configure menu entries
                StartToolStripMenuItem.Enabled = False
                TurnOffToolStripMenuItem.Enabled = True
                SaveStateToolStripMenuItem.Enabled = True
                ShutDownToolStripMenuItem.Enabled = True
                PauseToolStripMenuItem.Enabled = True
                ResumeToolStripMenuItem.Enabled = False

            Case VMVMState.vmVMState_Paused
                'Configure menu entries
                StartToolStripMenuItem.Enabled = False
                TurnOffToolStripMenuItem.Enabled = False
                SaveStateToolStripMenuItem.Enabled = False
                ShutDownToolStripMenuItem.Enabled = False
                PauseToolStripMenuItem.Enabled = False
                ResumeToolStripMenuItem.Enabled = True

            Case Else
                'Configure menu entries
                StartToolStripMenuItem.Enabled = False
                TurnOffToolStripMenuItem.Enabled = False
```

447

Part VIII: Developing Software for Virtual Server

```vbnet
                SaveStateToolStripMenuItem.Enabled = False
                ShutDownToolStripMenuItem.Enabled = False
                PauseToolStripMenuItem.Enabled = False
                ResumeToolStripMenuItem.Enabled = False

        End Select
    End If
End Sub

Private Sub StartToolStripMenuItem_Click(ByVal sender As System.Object, ⤶
ByVal e As System.EventArgs) Handles StartToolStripMenuItem.Click
    If Not VirtualMachine Is Nothing Then
        Dim aVMTask As VMTask

        'Start the virtual machine
        aVMTask = VirtualMachine.Startup()

        'Update menu
        checkVirtualMachineState()

        'Wait for task to complete
        SetSecurity.Secure(aVMTask)
        While Not aVMTask.IsComplete
            Application.DoEvents()
            Threading.Thread.Sleep(100)
        End While

        'Update the menu again
        checkVirtualMachineState()

        'Connect to the VM
        ConnectToVM()
    End If
End Sub

Private Sub TurnOffToolStripMenuItem_Click(ByVal sender As System.Object, ⤶
ByVal e As System.EventArgs) Handles TurnOffToolStripMenuItem.Click
    If Not VirtualMachine Is Nothing Then
        Dim aVMTask As VMTask

        'Stop the virtual machine
        aVMTask = VirtualMachine.TurnOff()

        'Update menu
        checkVirtualMachineState()

        'Wait for task to complete
        SetSecurity.Secure(aVMTask)
        While Not aVMTask.IsComplete
            Application.DoEvents()
            Threading.Thread.Sleep(100)
        End While

        'Update the menu again
        checkVirtualMachineState()
```

Chapter 19: Developing Managed Applications for Virtual Server

```vb
        End If
    End Sub

    Private Sub SaveStateToolStripMenuItem_Click(ByVal sender As System.Object _
    , ByVal e As System.EventArgs) Handles SaveStateToolStripMenuItem.Click
        If Not VirtualMachine Is Nothing Then
            Dim aVMTask As VMTask

            'Save state the virtual machine
            aVMTask = VirtualMachine.Save()

            'Update menu
            checkVirtualMachineState()

            'Wait for task to complete
            SetSecurity.Secure(aVMTask)
            While Not aVMTask.IsComplete
                Application.DoEvents()
                Threading.Thread.Sleep(100)
            End While

            'Update the menu again
            checkVirtualMachineState()

        End If
    End Sub

    Private Sub ShutDownToolStripMenuItem_Click(ByVal sender As System.Object, _
    ByVal e As System.EventArgs) Handles ShutDownToolStripMenuItem.Click
        If Not VirtualMachine Is Nothing Then

            Dim GuestOS As VMGuestOS

            GuestOS = VirtualMachine.GuestOS

            SetSecurity.Secure(GuestOS)

            If GuestOS.CanShutdown Then
                Dim aVMTask As VMTask

                'Shutdown the guest OS
                aVMTask = GuestOS.Shutdown()

                'Update menu
                checkVirtualMachineState()

                'Wait for task to complete
                SetSecurity.Secure(aVMTask)
                While Not aVMTask.IsComplete
                    Application.DoEvents()
                    Threading.Thread.Sleep(100)
                End While

                'Update the menu again
                checkVirtualMachineState()
```

449

Part VIII: Developing Software for Virtual Server

```vbnet
            Else
                MsgBox("The virtual machine needs to have Virtual Machine ↩
    Additions installed and running to shut down", MsgBoxStyle.Information, ↩
    "Information")
            End If
        End If
    End Sub

    Private Sub PauseToolStripMenuItem_Click(ByVal sender As System.Object, ↩
    ByVal e As System.EventArgs) Handles PauseToolStripMenuItem.Click
        If Not VirtualMachine Is Nothing Then
            'Pause the virtual machine - note this does not
            'return a VMTask object
            VirtualMachine.Pause()
            checkVirtualMachineState()
        End If
    End Sub

    Private Sub ResumeToolStripMenuItem_Click(ByVal sender As System.Object, ↩
    ByVal e As System.EventArgs) Handles ResumeToolStripMenuItem.Click
        If Not VirtualMachine Is Nothing Then
            'Resume the virtual machine - note this does not
            'return a VMTask object
            VirtualMachine.Resume()
            checkVirtualMachineState()
        End If
    End Sub

    Private Sub AxVMRCClientControl1_OnSwitchedDisplay(ByVal sender As Object, ↩
    ByVal e As AxMicrosoft.VMRCClientControl.Interop._IVMRCClientControlEvents↩
    _OnSwitchedDisplayEvent) Handles AxVMRCClientControl1.OnSwitchedDisplay
        'Check to see if the VMRC is visible and connected to the wrong thing
        If (Not AxVMRCClientControl1.ServerAddress = VSName Or _
            Not AxVMRCClientControl1.ServerDisplayName = VirtualMachine.Name) And _
            AxVMRCClientControl1.Visible Then
            'If it is, disconnect and hide it.
            AxVMRCClientControl1.Disconnect()
            AxVMRCClientControl1.Visible = False
        End If
    End Sub

    Private Sub AxVMRCClientControl1_SizeChanged(ByVal sender As Object, ByVal ↩
    e As System.EventArgs) Handles AxVMRCClientControl1.SizeChanged
        resizeForm1()
    End Sub
End Class
```

Here is the code in C#:

```csharp
using System;
using System.Collections.Generic;
using System.ComponentModel;
using System.Data;
using System.Drawing;
using System.Text;
```

450

Chapter 19: Developing Managed Applications for Virtual Server

```csharp
using System.Windows.Forms;
using System.Runtime.InteropServices;
using System.Reflection;
using Microsoft.VirtualServer.Interop;

namespace vc_VMRCClient
{

    public partial class Form1 : Form
    {

        //Declare global variables
        public VMVirtualServerClass myVS = null;
        public string myVSName = null;
        public VMVirtualMachine myVM = null;
        private Personal.SetSecurity.ProxyBlanket myProxyBlanket = new ⟳
Personal.SetSecurity.ProxyBlanket();


        public Form1()
        {
            InitializeComponent();
            //Connect event handler for 'shown' event
            this.Shown += new EventHandler(SelectVMToConnectTo);

            //Connect event handler for VMRC resize
            axVMRCClientControl1.Resize += new ⟳
EventHandler(axVMRCClientControl1_Resize);

            //Connect event handler for VMRC OnSwitchedDisplay
            axVMRCClientControl1.OnSwitchedDisplay += delegate { ⟳
 axVMRCClientControl1_OnSwitchedDisplay(); };

            //Connect action menu event handlers
            startToolStripMenuItem.Click += new ⟳
EventHandler(StartToolStripMenuItem_Click);
            turnOffToolStripMenuItem.Click += new ⟳
 EventHandler(TurnOffToolStripMenuItem_Click);
            shutDownToolStripMenuItem.Click += new ⟳
 EventHandler(ShutDownToolStripMenuItem_Click);
            saveStateToolStripMenuItem.Click += new ⟳
EventHandler(SaveStateToolStripMenuItem_Click);
            pauseToolStripMenuItem.Click += new ⟳
EventHandler(PauseToolStripMenuItem_Click);
            resumeToolStripMenuItem.Click += new ⟳
 EventHandler(ResumeToolStripMenuItem_Click);
        }

        private void SelectVMToConnectTo(object sender, EventArgs e)
        {
            //Check to see if the values have been prepopulated
            if (myVS == null || myVM == null || myVSName == null)
            {
                //Set the starting location and show the first dialog
```

451

Part VIII: Developing Software for Virtual Server

```csharp
            SelectServerPrompt serverPrompt = new SelectServerPrompt();

            serverPrompt.StartPosition = FormStartPosition.CenterParent; ⤸
            serverPrompt.ShowDialog(this);

            //If the server prompt fails, exit the application
            if (serverPrompt.myVS == null)
            {
                this.Close();
            }
            else
            {
                //Store the information from the server prompt
                //and then clear it out.
                myVS = serverPrompt.myVS;
                myVSName = serverPrompt.myVSName;
                serverPrompt = null;

                //Give the VM prompt the VS COM object and start it up
                SelectVirtualMachinePrompt VMPrompt = new ⤸
SelectVirtualMachinePrompt();

                VMPrompt.StartPosition = FormStartPosition.CenterParent;
                VMPrompt.myVS = myVS;
                VMPrompt.ShowDialog(this);

                //Exit if the VM prompt fails
                if (VMPrompt.myVM == null)
                {
                    this.Close();
                }
                else
                {
                    //Store the information from the VM prompt
                    //and then clear it out.
                    myVM = VMPrompt.myVM;
                    VMPrompt = null;

                    //Update the action menu
                    checkVirtualMachineState();

                    //Connect to the VM
                    connectToVM();
                }
            }
        }
        else
        {
            //Connect to the VM
            connectToVM();
        }
    }

    private void connectToVM()
    {
```

Chapter 19: Developing Managed Applications for Virtual Server

```csharp
            //Make sure all variables are populated
            if (myVS == null || myVM == null || myVSName == null)
            {
                return;
            }
            else
            {
                //Check that the virtual machine is running
                if (myVM.State == VMVMState.vmVMState_Running)
                {

                    //Configure the VMRC client and connect
                    axVMRCClientControl1.ServerAddress = myVSName;
                    axVMRCClientControl1.ServerPort = myVS.VMRCAdminPortNumber;
                    axVMRCClientControl1.ServerDisplayName = myVM.Name;
                    axVMRCClientControl1.Connect();

                    //Update the window title
                    this.Text = myVM.Name + " on " + myVSName;

                    //Display the VMRC client control
                    axVMRCClientControl1.Visible = true;

                    //Resize the form after connecting to the vm
                    resizeForm1();
                }
            }

        }

        private void axVMRCClientControl1_Resize(object sender, EventArgs e)
        {
            resizeForm1();
        }

        private void resizeForm1()
        {
            //Calculate the extra padding to add
            int heightPad = this.Height - this.ClientSize.Height;
            int widthPad = this.Width - this.ClientSize.Width;

            //Resize the form
            this.Height = axVMRCClientControl1.Height + heightPad;
            this.Width = axVMRCClientControl1.Width + widthPad;
        }

        private void checkVirtualMachineState()
        {
                if (myVM != null)
            {
            switch (myVM.State)
            {
                case VMVMState.vmVMState_TurnedOff:
                    //Configure menu entries
                    startToolStripMenuItem.Enabled = true;
```

453

Part VIII: Developing Software for Virtual Server

```csharp
                turnOffToolStripMenuItem.Enabled = false;
                saveStateToolStripMenuItem.Enabled = false;
                shutDownToolStripMenuItem.Enabled = false;
                pauseToolStripMenuItem.Enabled = false;
                resumeToolStripMenuItem.Enabled = false;
                break;

            case VMVMState.vmVMState_Saved:
                //Configure menu entries
                startToolStripMenuItem.Enabled = true;
                turnOffToolStripMenuItem.Enabled = false;
                saveStateToolStripMenuItem.Enabled = false;
                shutDownToolStripMenuItem.Enabled = false;
                pauseToolStripMenuItem.Enabled = false;
                resumeToolStripMenuItem.Enabled = false;
                break;

            case VMVMState.vmVMState_Running:
                //Configure menu entries
                startToolStripMenuItem.Enabled = false;
                turnOffToolStripMenuItem.Enabled = true;
                saveStateToolStripMenuItem.Enabled = true;
                shutDownToolStripMenuItem.Enabled = true;
                pauseToolStripMenuItem.Enabled = true;
                resumeToolStripMenuItem.Enabled = false;
                break;

            case VMVMState.vmVMState_Paused:
                //Configure menu entries
                startToolStripMenuItem.Enabled = false;
                turnOffToolStripMenuItem.Enabled = false;
                saveStateToolStripMenuItem.Enabled = false;
                shutDownToolStripMenuItem.Enabled = false;
                pauseToolStripMenuItem.Enabled = false;
                resumeToolStripMenuItem.Enabled = true;
                break;

            default:
                //Configure menu entries
                startToolStripMenuItem.Enabled = false;
                turnOffToolStripMenuItem.Enabled = false;
                saveStateToolStripMenuItem.Enabled = false;
                shutDownToolStripMenuItem.Enabled = false;
                pauseToolStripMenuItem.Enabled = false;
                resumeToolStripMenuItem.Enabled = false;
                break;

            }
        }
    }

    private void StartToolStripMenuItem_Click(System.Object sender, ⮐
System.EventArgs e)
    {
        if (myVM != null)
```

Chapter 19: Developing Managed Applications for Virtual Server

```
        {
            VMTask aVMTask;

            //Start the virtual machine
            aVMTask = myVM.Startup();

            //Update menu
            checkVirtualMachineState();

            //Wait for task to complete
            myProxyBlanket.Set(aVMTask);
            while (!aVMTask.IsComplete)
            {
                Application.DoEvents();
                System.Threading.Thread.Sleep(100);
            }

            //Update the menu again
            checkVirtualMachineState();

            //Connect to the VM
            connectToVM();
        }
    }

    private void TurnOffToolStripMenuItem_Click(System.Object sender, ⤵
System.EventArgs e)
    {
        if (myVM != null)
        {
            VMTask aVMTask;

            //Stop the virtual machine
            aVMTask = myVM.TurnOff();

            //Update menu
            checkVirtualMachineState();

            //Wait for task to complete
            myProxyBlanket.Set(aVMTask);
            while (!aVMTask.IsComplete)
            {
                Application.DoEvents();
                System.Threading.Thread.Sleep(100);
            }

            //Update the menu again
            checkVirtualMachineState();
        }
    }

    private void SaveStateToolStripMenuItem_Click(System.Object sender, ⤵
System.EventArgs e)
    {
        if (myVM != null)
```

Part VIII: Developing Software for Virtual Server

```csharp
    {
        VMTask aVMTask;

        //Save state the virtual machine
        aVMTask = myVM.Save();

        //Update menu
        checkVirtualMachineState();

        //Wait for task to complete
        myProxyBlanket.Set(aVMTask);
        while (!aVMTask.IsComplete)
        {
            Application.DoEvents();
            System.Threading.Thread.Sleep(100);
        }

        //Update the menu again
        checkVirtualMachineState();
    }
}

private void ShutDownToolStripMenuItem_Click(System.Object sender, ⊃
System.EventArgs e)
{
    if (myVM != null)
    {
        VMTask aVMTask;
        VMGuestOS guestOS;

        guestOS = myVM.GuestOS;
        myProxyBlanket.Set(guestOS);

        if (guestOS.CanShutdown)
        {
            //Shutdown the guest OS
            aVMTask = guestOS.Shutdown();

            //Update menu
            checkVirtualMachineState();

            //Wait for task to complete
            myProxyBlanket.Set(aVMTask);
            while (!aVMTask.IsComplete)
            {
                Application.DoEvents();
                System.Threading.Thread.Sleep(100);
            }

            //Update the menu again
            checkVirtualMachineState();
        }
        else
        {
```

Chapter 19: Developing Managed Applications for Virtual Server

```csharp
                    MessageBox.Show("The virtual machine needs to have Virtual⤶
Machine Additions installed and running to shut down", "Information");
                }
            }
        }

        private void PauseToolStripMenuItem_Click(System.Object sender, ⤶
System.EventArgs e)
        {
            if (myVM != null)
            {
                //Pause the virtual machine - note this does not
                //return a VMTask object
                myVM.Pause();
                checkVirtualMachineState();
            }
        }

        private void ResumeToolStripMenuItem_Click(System.Object sender, ⤶
System.EventArgs e)
        {
            if (myVM != null)
            {
                //Resume the virtual machine - note this does not
                //return a VMTask object
                myVM.Resume();
                checkVirtualMachineState();
            }
        }

        private void axVMRCClientControl1_OnSwitchedDisplay()
        {
            //Check to see if the VMRC is visible and connected to the
            //wrong thing
            if ((axVMRCClientControl1.ServerAddress != myVSName || ⤶
axVMRCClientControl1.ServerDisplayName != myVM.Name) && ⤶
axVMRCClientControl1.Visible)
            {
                //If it is, disconnect and hide it.
                axVMRCClientControl1.Disconnect();
                axVMRCClientControl1.Visible = false;
            }
        }
    }
}
```

Creating a Management Application

This section demonstrates how to use the Virtual Server COM interface to create a simple management application that can manage multiple instances of Virtual Server. For this sample, I use `CoInitializeSecurity`.

Part VIII: Developing Software for Virtual Server

You should follow the directions in Chapter 16 on how to configure a managed application to use `CoInitializeSecurity`.

This sample also loads the VMRC client from the previous sample. So you should have the first sample compiled and handy before working on this one.

To get started, create a new Windows Application under Visual Studio and follow these steps:

1. Open the visual designer for the main application.
2. Drag a **MenuStrip** onto the main form.
3. Give the first menu entry a name of **Add Server**.
4. Drag a **ListView** object onto the main form (and size it appropriately).
5. Edit the properties for the **ListView**.
6. Select **Appearance ⇨ FullRowSelect** and set it to **True**.
7. Select **Appearance ⇨ GridLines** and set it to **True**.
8. Select **Appearance ⇨ View** and set it to **Details**.
9. On the columns item, click the . . . button.
10. Create three new columns.
11. Set the column **Name** to **vmName**, **vmHost**, and **vmState**.
12. Set the column **Text** to **VM Name**, **VM Host**, and **VM State**.
13. Click **OK**.
14. Select **Behavior ⇨ MultiSelect** and set it to **False**.
15. Select **Design ⇨ (Name)** and enter **VMListView**.

Now you'll need to copy the SelectServerPrompt files from the previous sample, as you will be reusing this prompt. Use the **Add Existing Item** option on the project menu to do this.

Now it is time to write the code that will allow you to connect to multiple Virtual Servers and list the virtual machines that are on them. The code that follows uses a custom structure (`VSEntry`) that contains the name of the Virtual Server and the Virtual Server COM object. I then create an array of these structures. This array is used to store multiple Virtual Server references.

`CoInitializeSecurity` is called as soon as possible (in the creation routine).

`AddServerToolStripMenuItem_Click` is called when the user clicks the **Add Server** menu. It uses SelectServerPrompt to get the Virtual Server name and COM object, which is then stored in a `VSentry` in the `VSEntries` array. Event handlers are registered on the Virtual Server COM object for `OnVMStateChange` and `OnEventLogged`, and then `updateVMList` is called.

`VMstateChange` calls `updateVMList` when any of the virtual machines on the registered Virtual Servers change their state. `VSEventLogged` calls `updateVMList` when log messages are filed for a virtual machine being created, registered, or deleted.

458

Chapter 19: Developing Managed Applications for Virtual Server

Unfortunately there is no documentation about what log message IDs map to which events. If you want to monitor for another type of event you'll need to put a breakpoint on this routine and before the event you want to monitor, and see what log message ID is sent.

Finally, `updateVMList` enumerates all the virtual machines on all registered Virtual Servers and creates list entries for them.

Here is the code in Visual Basic .NET:

```vb
Imports Microsoft.VirtualServer.Interop

Public Class Form1

    'Personal structure for tracking VS instances
    Private Structure VSEntry
        Public VSName As String
        Public VSConnection As VMVirtualServer
    End Structure

    'Array of VSEntry structures
    Private VSEntries() As VSEntry = New VSEntry() {}

    Public Sub New()

        ' This call is required by the Windows Form Designer.
        InitializeComponent()

        ' Add any initialization after the InitializeComponent() call.

        ' Set the Security Impersonation Level as soon as possible
        Dim MySetSecurityImpersonationLevel = New SetSecurityImpersonationLevel

    End Sub

    Private Sub AddServerToolStripMenuItem_Click(ByVal sender As System.Object _
    , ByVal e As System.EventArgs) Handles AddServerToolStripMenuItem.Click

        'Create and display server prompt
        Dim serverPrompt As New SelectServerPrompt
        Dim newVSEntry As VSEntry

        serverPrompt.StartPosition = FormStartPosition.CenterParent
        serverPrompt.ShowDialog(Me)

        'Check that the values are populated, and exit if they are not
        If serverPrompt.VSConnection Is Nothing Then
            Exit Sub
        End If

        'Populate new VSEntry
        newVSEntry.VSName = serverPrompt.VSName
        newVSEntry.VSConnection = serverPrompt.VSConnection

        'Grow VSEntries and add the new VSEntry
        ReDim Preserve VSEntries(VSEntries.Length)
```

459

Part VIII: Developing Software for Virtual Server

```vb
            VSEntries(VSEntries.Length - 1) = newVSEntry

            serverPrompt = Nothing

            'Add event handlers
            AddHandler newVSEntry.VSConnection.OnVMStateChange, AddressOf VMstateChange
            AddHandler newVSEntry.VSConnection.OnEventLogged, AddressOf VSEventLogged

            'Update the VM list
            updateVMList()
    End Sub

    Private Sub VMstateChange(ByVal virtualMachineConfig As String, ByVal ⌐
virtualMachineState As Microsoft.VirtualServer.Interop.VMVMState)
            updateVMList()
    End Sub

    Private Sub VSEventLogged(ByVal logMessageID As Integer)
            'Remove VM  = event 16843783
            'Add existing virtual machine = event 16843782
            'Create new virtual machine  = event 16843780

            If logMessageID = 16843783 Or _
               logMessageID = 16843782 Or _
               logMessageID = 16843780 Then
                updateVMList()
            End If
    End Sub

    Private Sub updateVMList()
            Dim VM As VMVirtualMachine
            Dim aVSentry As VSEntry
            Dim anItem As ListViewItem

            'Start the update process
            VMListView.BeginUpdate()

            'Clear existing items
            VMListView.Items.Clear()

            For Each aVSentry In VSEntries
                'Add new items for each virtual machine
                For Each VM In aVSentry.VSConnection.VirtualMachines
                    anItem = VMListView.Items.Add(VM.Name)
                    anItem.SubItems.Add(aVSentry.VSName)
                    Select Case VM.State
                        Case VMVMState.vmVMState_DeleteMachine
                            anItem.SubItems.Add("Deleting virtual machine")
                        Case VMVMState.vmVMState_Invalid
                            anItem.SubItems.Add("Invalid state")
                        Case VMVMState.vmVMState_MergingDrives
                            anItem.SubItems.Add("Merging undo disks")
                        Case VMVMState.vmVMState_Paused
                            anItem.SubItems.Add("Paused")
                        Case VMVMState.vmVMState_Restoring
```

Chapter 19: Developing Managed Applications for Virtual Server

```
                        anItem.SubItems.Add("Restoring saved state")
                Case VMVMState.vmVMState_Running
                    anItem.SubItems.Add("Running")
                Case VMVMState.vmVMState_Saved
                    anItem.SubItems.Add("Saved")
                Case VMVMState.vmVMState_Saving
                    anItem.SubItems.Add("Saving state")
                Case VMVMState.vmVMState_TurnedOff
                    anItem.SubItems.Add("Turned off")
                Case VMVMState.vmVMState_TurningOff
                    anItem.SubItems.Add("Turning off")
                Case VMVMState.vmVMState_TurningOn
                    anItem.SubItems.Add("Turning on")
            End Select
        Next
    Next

        'Complete update process
        VMListView.EndUpdate()

    End Sub
End Class
```

Here is the code in C#:

```csharp
using System;
using System.Collections.Generic;
using System.ComponentModel;
using System.Data;
using System.Drawing;
using System.Text;
using System.Windows.Forms;
using Microsoft.VirtualServer.Interop;

namespace vc_VMManagement
{
    public partial class Form1 : Form
    {
        //Personal structure for tracking VS instances
        private struct vsEntry
        {
            public string vsName;
            public VMVirtualServerClass vsConnection;
        }

        //Array of VSEntry structures
        private vsEntry[] vsEntries = new vsEntry[0];

        public Form1()
        {
            InitializeComponent();

            // Set the Security Impersonation Level as soon as possible
            Personal.SetSecurityImpersonationLevel.SetToImpersonate mySecurity;
```

461

Part VIII: Developing Software for Virtual Server

```csharp
            mySecurity = new ⤶
Personal.SetSecurityImpersonationLevel.SetToImpersonate();

            //Add event handlers
            addServerToolStripMenuItem.Click += new ⤶
EventHandler(addServerToolStripMenuItem_Click);

        }

        private void addServerToolStripMenuItem_Click(System.Object sender , ⤶
    System.EventArgs e)
        {
            //Create and display server prompt
            SelectServerPrompt serverPrompt = new SelectServerPrompt();
            vsEntry newVSEntry;

            serverPrompt.StartPosition = FormStartPosition.CenterParent;
            serverPrompt.ShowDialog(this);

            //Check that the values are populated, and exit if they are not
            if (serverPrompt.myVS == null)
            {
                return;
            }

            //Populate new VSEntry
            newVSEntry.vsName = serverPrompt.myVSName;
            newVSEntry.vsConnection = serverPrompt.myVS;

            //Grow VSEntries and add the new VSEntry
            vsEntry[] temp = new vsEntry[vsEntries.Length + 1];
            if (vsEntries != null)
                Array.Copy(vsEntries, temp, vsEntries.Length);
            vsEntries = temp;

            vsEntries[vsEntries.Length - 1] = newVSEntry;

            serverPrompt = null;

            //Add Event handlers
            newVSEntry.vsConnection.OnVMStateChange += new Microsoft.Virtual⤶
Server.Interop.IVMVirtualServerEvents_OnVMStateChangeEventHandler(vmStateChange);
            newVSEntry.vsConnection.OnEventLogged += new Microsoft.Virtual⤶
Server.Interop.IVMVirtualServerEvents_OnEventLoggedEventHandler(vsEventLogged);

            //Update the VM list
            updateVMList();
        }

        private void vmStateChange(String virtualMachineConfig, ⤶
Microsoft.VirtualServer.Interop.VMVMState virtualMachineState)
        {
            updateVMList();
        }

        private void vsEventLogged(int logMessageID)
```

Chapter 19: Developing Managed Applications for Virtual Server

```
        {
            //Remove VM  = event 16843783
            //Add existing virtual machine = event 16843782
            //Create new virtual machine  = event 16843700

            if (logMessageID == 16843783 || logMessageID == 16843782 ||
logMessageID == 16843780)
            {
                updateVMList();
            }
        }
    }

    private void updateVMList()
        {

            ListViewItem anItem;

            //Start the update process
            VMListView.BeginUpdate();

            //Clear existing items
            VMListView.Items.Clear();

            //Go through each known VS Server
            foreach (vsEntry aVSentry in vsEntries)
            {
                //Add new items for each virtual machine
                foreach (VMVirtualMachine VM in
aVSentry.vsConnection.VirtualMachines)
                {
                    anItem = VMListView.Items.Add(VM.Name);
                    anItem.SubItems.Add(aVSentry.vsName);
                    switch (VM.State)
                    {
                        case VMVMState.vmVMState_DeleteMachine:
                            anItem.SubItems.Add("Deleting virtual machine");
                            break;

                        case VMVMState.vmVMState_Invalid:
                            anItem.SubItems.Add("Invalid state");
                            break;

                        case VMVMState.vmVMState_MergingDrives:
                            anItem.SubItems.Add("Merging undo disks");
                            break;

                        case VMVMState.vmVMState_Paused:
                            anItem.SubItems.Add("Paused");
                            break;

                        case VMVMState.vmVMState_Restoring:
                            anItem.SubItems.Add("Restoring saved state");
                            break;

                        case VMVMState.vmVMState_Running:
```

463

Part VIII: Developing Software for Virtual Server

```
                        anItem.SubItems.Add("Running");
                        break;

                    case VMVMState.vmVMState_Saved:
                        anItem.SubItems.Add("Saved");
                        break;

                    case VMVMState.vmVMState_Saving:
                        anItem.SubItems.Add("Saving state");
                        break;

                    case VMVMState.vmVMState_TurnedOff:
                        anItem.SubItems.Add("Turned off");
                        break;

                    case VMVMState.vmVMState_TurningOff:
                        anItem.SubItems.Add("Turning off");
                        break;

                    case VMVMState.vmVMState_TurningOn:
                        anItem.SubItems.Add("Turning on");
                        break;
                }
            }
        }

        //Complete update process
        VMListView.EndUpdate();

        }
    }
}
```

Adding Virtual Machine Information

To add the ability to display detailed information about a virtual machine when it is selected from the list, follow these steps:

1. Resize the VMListView and then drag a new **GroupBox** onto the main form, under the **ListView**.

2. Change the **GroupBox Text** property to **Virtual Machine Information**.

3. Drag a **PictureBox** into the **GroupBox**.

4. Change the **PictureBox BorderStyle** property to **FixedSingle**.

5. Change the **PictureBox Size** property to **128, 96**.

6. Change the **PictureBox (Name)** property to **VMThumbNailPictureBox**.

7. Change the **PictureBox SizeMode** property to **StretchImage**.

8. Drag a **Label** into the **GroupBox**.

Chapter 19: Developing Managed Applications for Virtual Server

9. Change the **Label Text** property to **Virtual machine notes:**.

10. Drag a **RichTextBox** into the **GroupBox**, under the **Label**.

11. Change the **RichTextBox ReadOnly** property to **True**.

12. Change the **RichTextBox (Name)** property to **VMNotesRichTextBox**.

The following code is needed to update the values for these objects whenever a virtual machine is selected. VMListView_SelectedIndexChanged gets called whenever the selection is changed on the VMListView. It collects the information from the VMListView and uses it to create a virtual machine COM object. It then calls updateVMNotes and updateThumbnail with the virtual machine COM object as a parameter.

UpdateVMNotes simply copies the virtual machine's notes information to the RichTextBox text. UpdateThumbnail gets the virtual machine's thumbnail data, converts it to a bitmap, and assigns it to VMThumbNailPictureBox.

Here's the code in Visual Basic .NET:

```
    . . .

    Private Sub VMListView_SelectedIndexChanged(ByVal sender As System.Object, ⤶
    ByVal e As System.EventArgs) Handles VMListView.SelectedIndexChanged

        Dim aVM As VMVirtualMachine
        Dim vmName, vmHost As String
        Dim aVSEntry As VSEntry

        'Check to see if something is selected
        If VMListView.SelectedItems.Count = 1 Then

            vmName = VMListView.SelectedItems.Item(0).SubItems(0).Text
            vmHost = VMListView.SelectedItems.Item(0).SubItems(1).Text

            'Create VM object
            For Each aVSEntry In VSEntries
                If aVSEntry.VSName = vmHost Then
                    aVM = aVSEntry.VSConnection.FindVirtualMachine(vmName)
                End If
            Next

            'Update VM information
            updateVMNotes(aVM)
            updateThumbnail(aVM)

        End If

    End Sub

    Private Sub updateThumbnail(ByVal aVM As VMVirtualMachine)

        Dim pixelArray As Object()
```

465

Part VIII: Developing Software for Virtual Server

```vbnet
        Dim bmp As New Bitmap(64, 48)
        Dim i As Integer = 0

        'Get thumbnail data
        pixelArray = aVM.Display.Thumbnail

        'Iterate over the data and convert it to a BMP
        For y As Integer = 0 To 47
            For x As Integer = 0 To 63

                Dim uiPixel As UInteger = CUInt(pixelArray(i))
                Dim red, green, blue As Integer

                red = CInt((uiPixel >> 8) Mod 256)
                green = CInt((uiPixel >> 16) Mod 256)
                blue = CInt((uiPixel >> 24) Mod 256)

                bmp.SetPixel(x, y, Color.FromArgb(red, green, blue))
                i = i + 1
            Next
        Next

        'Update the thumbnail image
        VMThumbNailPictureBox.Image = bmp
        VMThumbNailPictureBox.Refresh()

    End Sub

    Private Sub updateVMNotes(ByVal aVM As VMVirtualMachine)

        'Update the virtual machine notes
        VMNotesRichTextBox.Text = aVM.Notes

    End Sub
End Class
```

Here's the code in C#:

```csharp
...

        public Form1()
        {
            InitializeComponent();

            // Set the Security Impersonation Level as soon as possible
            Personal.SetSecurityImpersonationLevel.SetToImpersonate mySecurity;
            mySecurity = new ⤸
    Personal.SetSecurityImpersonationLevel.SetToImpersonate();

            //Add event handlers
            addServerToolStripMenuItem.Click += new ⤸
    EventHandler(addServerToolStripMenuItem_Click);
```

Chapter 19: Developing Managed Applications for Virtual Server

```
                VMListView.SelectedIndexChanged += new ⤶
EventHandler(VMListView_SelectedIndexChanged);

        }


...


        private void VMListView_SelectedIndexChanged(System.Object sender, ⤶
System.EventArgs e)
        {
            VMVirtualMachine aVM = null;

            //Check to see if something is selected
            if (VMListView.SelectedItems.Count == 1)
            {

                String vmName = VMListView.SelectedItems[0].SubItems[0].Text;
                String vmHost = VMListView.SelectedItems[0].SubItems[1].Text;

                //Create VM object
                foreach(vsEntry aVSEntry in vsEntries)
                {
                    if (aVSEntry.vsName == vmHost)
                    {
                        aVM = aVSEntry.vsConnection.FindVirtualMachine(vmName);
                    }
                }

                if (aVM != null)
                {
                //Update VM information
                updateVMNotes(aVM);
                updateThumbnail(aVM);
                }
            }

        }

    private void updateThumbnail(VMVirtualMachine aVM)
    {
        Bitmap bmp = new Bitmap(64, 48);
        int i = 0;

        //Get thumbnail data
        Object pixelArrayObject = aVM.Display.Thumbnail;
        Array pixelArray = (Array)pixelArrayObject;

        //Iterate over the data and convert it to a BMP
        for (int y = 0; y < 48; y += 1)
        {
            for (int x = 0; x < 64; x += 1)
            {
                uint uiPixel = (uint)pixelArray.GetValue(i);
                int red, green, blue;

                red = (int)(uiPixel >> 8) % 256;
```

Part VIII: Developing Software for Virtual Server

```
                green = (int)(uiPixel >> 16) % 256;
                blue = (int)(uiPixel >> 24) % 256;

                bmp.SetPixel(x, y, Color.FromArgb(red, green, blue));
                i = i + 1;
            }
        }

        //Update the thumbnail image
        VMThumbNailPictureBox.Image = bmp;
        VMThumbNailPictureBox.Refresh();
    }

    private void updateVMNotes(VMVirtualMachine aVM)
    {
        //Update the virtual machine notes
        VMNotesRichTextBox.Text = aVM.Notes;
    }
    }
}
```

Launching the VMRC Client

To add the ability to launch the VMRC client created in the previous example from this management console, follow these steps:

1. Open the **Project** menu and select **Add Reference**.

2. Select the **Browse** tab and locate the executable for the VMRC client; then click **OK**.

3. Drag a **Button** into the Virtual Machine Information **GroupBox**.

4. Change the **Button (Name)** property to **OpenVMRCButton**.

5. Change the **Button Text** property to **Open VMRC control**.

The OpenVMRCButton_Click routine creates a new VMRCClient object, prepopulates Virtual Server and virtual machine COM objects on the VMRC client, and launches it.

Here's the code in Visual Basic .NET:

```
    Private Sub OpenVMRCButton_Click(ByVal sender As System.Object, ByVal e As ⤴
  System.EventArgs) Handles OpenVMRCButton.Click
        'Create new VMRCClient object
        Dim VMRCClient As New vb_VMRCClient.Form1
        Dim vmName, vmHost As String
        Dim aVSEntry As VSEntry
        Dim aVSConnection As VMVirtualServer
        Dim aVM As VMVirtualMachine

        'Check to see if something is selected
        If VMListView.SelectedItems.Count = 1 Then

            vmName = VMListView.SelectedItems.Item(0).SubItems(0).Text
```

468

Chapter 19: Developing Managed Applications for Virtual Server

```vb
            vmHost = VMListView.SelectedItems.Item(0).SubItems(1).Text

            'Create VM object
            For Each aVSEntry In VSEntries
                If aVSEntry.VSName = vmHost Then
                    aVM = aVSEntry.VSConnection.FindVirtualMachine(vmName)
                    aVSConnection = aVSEntry.VSConnection
                End If
            Next

            'Prepopulate public variables
            VMRCClient.VSConnection = aVSConnection
            VMRCClient.VSName = vmHost
            VMRCClient.VirtualMachine = aVM

            'Show VMRCClient
            VMRCClient.Show(Me)
        End If

    End Sub
```

Here's the code in C#:

```csharp
    ...

        public Form1()
        {
            InitializeComponent();

            // Set the Security Impersonation Level as soon as possible
            Personal.SetSecurityImpersonationLevel.SetToImpersonate mySecurity;
            mySecurity = new ⤸
Personal.SetSecurityImpersonationLevel.SetToImpersonate();

            //Add event handlers
            addServerToolStripMenuItem.Click += new ⤸
 EventHandler(addServerToolStripMenuItem_Click);
            VMListView.SelectedIndexChanged += new ⤸
 EventHandler(VMListView_SelectedIndexChanged);
            OpenVMRCButton.Click += new EventHandler(OpenVMRCButton_Click);

        }

    ...

        private void OpenVMRCButton_Click(System.Object sender, System.EventArgs e)
        {
            //Check to see if something is selected
            if (VMListView.SelectedItems.Count == 1)
            {
                //Create new VMRCClient object
                vc_VMRCClient.Form1 VMRCClient = new vc_VMRCClient.Form1();

                VMVirtualServerClass aVSConnection = null;
```

469

Part VIII: Developing Software for Virtual Server

```
        VMVirtualMachine aVM = null;

        String vmName = VMListView.SelectedItems[0].SubItems[0].Text;
        String vmHost = VMListView.SelectedItems[0].SubItems[1].Text;

        //Create VM object
        foreach (vsEntry aVSEntry in vsEntries)
        {
            if (aVSEntry.vsName == vmHost)
            {
                aVM = aVSEntry.vsConnection.FindVirtualMachine(vmName);
                aVSConnection = aVSEntry.vsConnection;
            }
        }

        //Prepopulate public variables
        VMRCClient.myVS = aVSConnection;
        VMRCClient.myVSName = vmHost;
        VMRCClient.myVM = aVM;

        //Show VMRCClient
        VMRCClient.Show(this);
    }
}
```

Integrating with the Virtual Server Administrative Website

When developing management tools, programmers often overlook the ability to integrate the Virtual Server Administrative website into the management tool. This is very useful as it means you do not have to implement all the functionality of the Virtual Server Administrative website, but instead you can just focus on the areas that are important to you. Follow these steps:

1. Drag a **TabControl** onto the main form.

2. Move all of the existing controls on to the first page of the **TabControl**.

3. Delete the second **TabPage** from the **TabControl**.

4. Change the **TabPage Text** property to **Virtual Machines**.

5. Drag two new buttons into the Virtual Machine Information **GroupBox**.

6. Change the first **Button (Name)** property to **OpenVMSettingsButton**.

7. Change the first **Button Text** property to **Open VM Settings**.

8. Change the second **Button (Name)** property to **OpenVSWebSiteButton**.

9. Change the second **Button Text** property to **Open VS WebSite**.

When you are done, you should have a form similar to the one displayed in Figure 19-4.

470

Chapter 19: Developing Managed Applications for Virtual Server

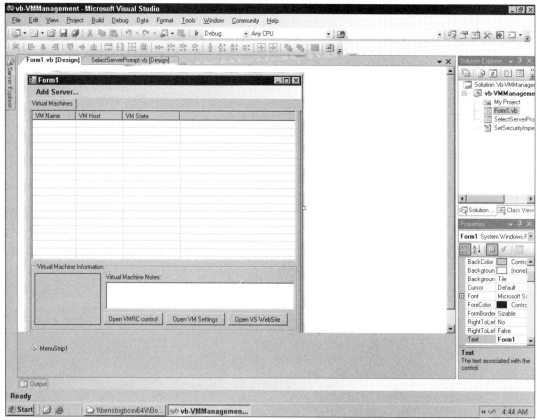

Figure 19-4

In the following code, `OpenVMSettingsButton_Click` and `OpenVSWebSiteButton_Click` are both very similar. They create a new TabPage, place a web browser and button control on it, construct a URL to load on the web page, and finally put it all together and switch to the active tab. When the TabPage is created, an event handler is created for the new button so that it can be used to close the tab. In this way, you can quickly open, close, and switch between multiple tabs containing different sections of the Virtual Server Administration website.

Here's the code in Visual Basic .NET:

```
Private Sub OpenVMSettingsButton_Click(ByVal sender As System.Object, ByVal e _
  As System.EventArgs) Handles OpenVMSettingsButton.Click
        Dim aUri As System.Uri
        Dim aNewTabPage As New TabPage
        Dim aNewWebBrowser As New WebBrowser
        Dim aButton As New Button
        Dim systemURL As String
        Dim vmName, vmHost As String

        'Check to see if something is selected
```

471

Part VIII: Developing Software for Virtual Server

```vb
        If VMListView.SelectedItems.Count = 1 Then

            vmName = VMListView.SelectedItems.Item(0).SubItems(0).Text
            vmHost = VMListView.SelectedItems.Item(0).SubItems(1).Text

            'Construct URL
            systemURL = "http://" & vmHost &
"/VirtualServer/vswebapp.exe?view=2&vm=" & vmName

            aUri = New System.Uri(systemURL)

            'Create new webbrowser object
            aNewWebBrowser.Url = aUri
            aNewWebBrowser.Refresh()
            aNewWebBrowser.Location = New Point(0, 0)
            aNewWebBrowser.Width = TabControl1.SelectedTab.ClientSize.Width
            aNewWebBrowser.Height = TabControl1.SelectedTab.ClientSize.Height - 24

            'Create new button
            aButton.Text = "Close Tab"
            aButton.Location = New Point(TabControl1.SelectedTab.ClientSize.
Width - 100 , TabControl1.SelectedTab.ClientSize.Height - 24)
            aButton.Width = 100
            aButton.Height = 24

            'Create new tab with controls
            aNewTabPage.Text = vmName & " Settings"
            aNewTabPage.Controls.Add(aNewWebBrowser)
            aNewTabPage.Controls.Add(aButton)

            'Add the new tab and switch to it
            TabControl1.TabPages.Add(aNewTabPage)
            TabControl1.SelectTab(aNewTabPage)

            'Add event handler for the close button
            AddHandler aButton.Click, AddressOf aButton_Click

        End If

    End Sub

    Private Sub OpenVSWebSiteButton_Click(ByVal sender As System.Object, ByVal
  e As System.EventArgs) Handles OpenVSWebSiteButton.Click
        Dim aUri As System.Uri
        Dim aNewTabPage As New TabPage
        Dim aNewWebBrowser As New WebBrowser
        Dim aButton As New Button
        Dim systemURL As String
        Dim vmHost As String

        'Check to see if something is selected
        If VMListView.SelectedItems.Count = 1 Then

            vmHost = VMListView.SelectedItems.Item(0).SubItems(1).Text

            'Construct URL
```

Chapter 19: Developing Managed Applications for Virtual Server

```
        systemURL = "http://" & vmHost & "/VirtualServer/vswebapp.exe"

        aUri = New System.Uri(systemURL)

        'Create new webbrowser object
        aNewWebBrowser.Url = aUri
        aNewWebBrowser.Refresh()
        aNewWebBrowser.Location = New Point(0, 0)
        aNewWebBrowser.Width = TabControl1.SelectedTab.ClientSize.Width
        aNewWebBrowser.Height = TabControl1.SelectedTab.ClientSize.Height - 24

        'Create new button
        aButton.Text = "Close Tab"
        aButton.Location = New Point(TabControl1.SelectedTab.ClientSize. ⤶
Width - 100 , TabControl1.SelectedTab.ClientSize.Height - 24)
        aButton.Width = 100
        aButton.Height = 24

        'Create new tab with controls
        aNewTabPage.Text = vmHost & " Website"
        aNewTabPage.Controls.Add(aNewWebBrowser)
        aNewTabPage.Controls.Add(aButton)

        'Add the new tab and switch to it
        TabControl1.TabPages.Add(aNewTabPage)
        TabControl1.SelectTab(aNewTabPage)

        'Add event handler for the close button
        AddHandler aButton.Click, AddressOf aButton_Click

    End If

  End Sub

  Private Sub aButton_Click(ByVal sender As System.Object, ByVal e As ⤶
System.EventArgs)
      'Close the tab that controls the button
      TabControl1.TabPages.Remove(sender.Parent)
  End Sub
```

Here's the code in C#:

```
...

    public Form1()
    {
        InitializeComponent();

        // Set the Security Impersonation Level as soon as possible
        Personal.SetSecurityImpersonationLevel.SetToImpersonate mySecurity;
        mySecurity = new ⤶
Personal.SetSecurityImpersonationLevel.SetToImpersonate();

        //Add event handlers
        addServerToolStripMenuItem.Click += new ⤶
EventHandler(addServerToolStripMenuItem_Click);
```

Part VIII: Developing Software for Virtual Server

```
            VMListView.SelectedIndexChanged += new ⤸
    EventHandler(VMListView_SelectedIndexChanged);
            OpenVMRCButton.Click += new ⤸ EventHandler(OpenVMRCButton_Click);
            OpenVMSettingsButton.Click += new ⤸
    EventHandler(OpenVMSettingsButton_Click);
            OpenVSWebSiteButton.Click += new ⤸
    EventHandler(OpenVSWebSiteButton_Click);
        }

...

        private void OpenVMSettingsButton_Click(System.Object sender, ⤸
    System.EventArgs e)
        {
            TabPage aNewTabPage = new TabPage();
            WebBrowser aNewWebBrowser = new WebBrowser();
            Button aButton = new Button();

            //Check to see if something is selected
            if (VMListView.SelectedItems.Count == 1)
            {

                String vmName = VMListView.SelectedItems[0].SubItems[0].Text;
                String vmHost = VMListView.SelectedItems[0].SubItems[1].Text;

                //Construct URL
                String systemURL = "http://" + vmHost + ⤸
     "/VirtualServer/vswebapp.exe?view=2&vm=" + vmName;

                System.Uri aUri = new System.Uri(systemURL);

                //Create new webbrowser object
                aNewWebBrowser.Url = aUri;
                aNewWebBrowser.Refresh();
                aNewWebBrowser.Location = new Point(0, 0);
                aNewWebBrowser.Width = tabControl1.SelectedTab.ClientSize.Width;
                aNewWebBrowser.Height = tabControl1.SelectedTab.ClientSize. ⤸
    Height - 24;

                //Create new button
                aButton.Text = "Close Tab";
                aButton.Location = new Point(tabControl1.SelectedTab. ⤸
    ClientSize.Width - 100 , tabControl1.SelectedTab.ClientSize.Height - 24);
                aButton.Width = 100;
                aButton.Height = 24;

                //Create new tab with controls
                aNewTabPage.Text = vmName + " Settings";
                aNewTabPage.Controls.Add(aNewWebBrowser);
                aNewTabPage.Controls.Add(aButton);

                //Add the new tab and switch to it
                tabControl1.TabPages.Add(aNewTabPage);
```

Chapter 19: Developing Managed Applications for Virtual Server

```csharp
            tabControl1.SelectTab(aNewTabPage);

            //Add event handler for the close button
            aButton.Click += new EventHandler(aButton_Click);

        }

    }

    private void OpenVSWebSiteButton_Click(System.Object sender, ⊃
System.EventArgs e)
    {
        TabPage aNewTabPage = new TabPage();
        WebBrowser aNewWebBrowser = new WebBrowser();
        Button aButton = new Button();

        //Check to see if something is selected
        if (VMListView.SelectedItems.Count == 1)
        {

            String vmHost = VMListView.SelectedItems[0].SubItems[1].Text;

            //Construct URL
            String systemURL = "http://" + vmHost + ⊃
 "/VirtualServer/vswebapp.exe";

            System.Uri aUri = new System.Uri(systemURL);

            //Create new webbrowser object
            aNewWebBrowser.Url = aUri;
            aNewWebBrowser.Refresh();
            aNewWebBrowser.Location = new Point(0, 0);
            aNewWebBrowser.Width = tabControl1.SelectedTab.ClientSize.Width;
            aNewWebBrowser.Height = tabControl1.SelectedTab.ClientSize. ⊃
Height - 24;

            //Create new button
            aButton.Text = "Close Tab";
            aButton.Location = new Point(tabControl1.SelectedTab. ⊃
ClientSize.Width - 100, tabControl1.SelectedTab.ClientSize.Height - 24);
            aButton.Width = 100;
            aButton.Height = 24;

            //Create new tab with controls
            aNewTabPage.Text = vmHost + " Website";
            aNewTabPage.Controls.Add(aNewWebBrowser);
            aNewTabPage.Controls.Add(aButton);

            //Add the new tab and switch to it
            tabControl1.TabPages.Add(aNewTabPage);
            tabControl1.SelectTab(aNewTabPage);

            //Add event handler for the close button
```

Part VIII: Developing Software for Virtual Server

```
        aButton.Click += new EventHandler(aButton_Click);

    }

}

private void aButton_Click(System.Object sender, System.EventArgs e)
{
    //Close the tab that controls the button
    Button aButton = (Button)sender;
    tabControl1.TabPages.Remove((TabPage)aButton.Parent);
}
```

Conclusion

Developing managed applications that use the Virtual Server COM interface can provide for a highly customized user experience. All the functionality that you need to create a user interface that controls all aspects of Virtual Server is available in the COM interface. Managed applications can provide a much more detailed user experience than scripts can.

In this chapter you have seen how to integrate the VMRC client in a managed application and how to build a fully functional management tool for Virtual Server with Visual Studio.

20

Developing ASP.NET Applications with Virtual Server

The development of ASP.NET solutions that control Virtual Server opens up a number of interesting avenues for usage of Virtual Server. In a typical ASP.NET solution, you have a web-based application that users connect to remotely. They can then use this application to control Virtual Server. These sorts of solutions are usually the most attractive in development, training, and demonstration environments.

Using ASP.NET with Virtual Server has two main advantages. First, there is no need for users to install any software on their end computer. All their interaction is handled through a web browser (if they are directly controlling virtual machines through VMRC they will need to install the ActiveX control, but the browser should do this automatically for them).

The second advantage is that by utilizing a service account model it is possible to achieve a very high level of control over the exact privileges that the end user has. Figure 20-1 shows the usual mode of operation for Virtual Server.

Part VIII: Developing Software for Virtual Server

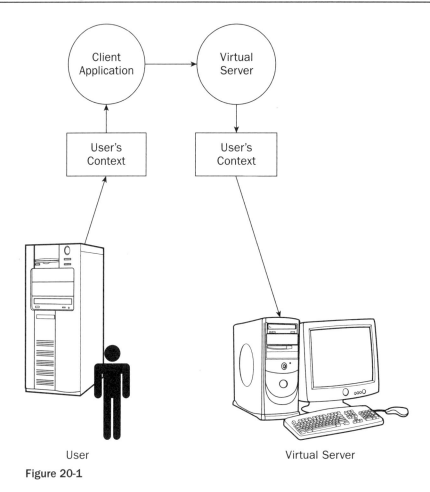

Figure 20-1

With ASP.NET, it is possible to configure the system such that the web application always runs under a specific user account. This way the end user does not need to have any specific privileges on the Virtual Server, and the web application can determine what operations each user is allowed to perform. Figure 20-2 outlines what this configuration looks like.

This chapter steps you through a sample self-provisioning web application. This application enables users to create virtual machines from existing virtual machine templates. Users can make minor changes to the virtual machines, control the virtual machine state, and delete virtual machines that they've created. They will not be able to make virtual machines that are not based on the templates provided, nor will they be able to change any of the settings of Virtual Server.

Chapter 20: Developing ASP.NET Applications with Virtual Server

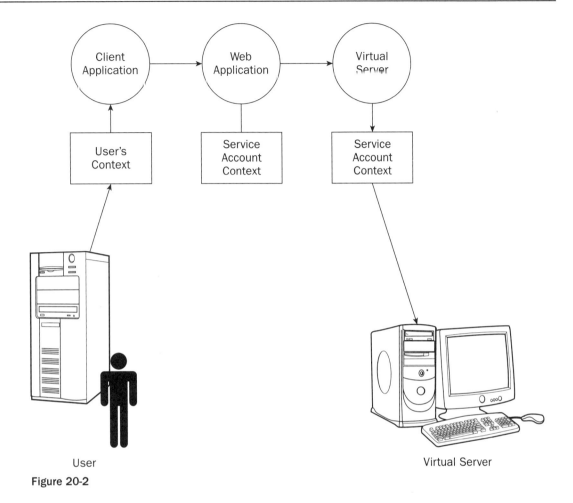

Figure 20-2

Creating Template Virtual Machines

For this project you need to create a set of template virtual machines (by following the process in Chapter 5). You need to be able to identify these virtual machines as templates, as compared to standard virtual machines, and to access extended information about the templates. To do this, you use `SetConfigurationValue` and `GetConfigurationValue` to extend the virtual machine configuration with this information. The template virtual machine should be an entire virtual machine (configuration and virtual hard disk) that is ready to be cloned for use by the end user.

Following are two scripts: a VBScript and PowerShell script that extend the virtual machine configuration.

479

Part VIII: Developing Software for Virtual Server

Here is the `extendVM.vbs` script:

```
Option Explicit

dim vs, vm, input, key, error

' Check that the script is running at the command line.
If UCase(Right(Wscript.FullName, 11)) = "WSCRIPT.EXE" Then
    Wscript.Echo "This script must be run under CScript."
    Wscript.Quit
End If

' Attempt to connect to Virtual Server
On Error Resume Next
Set vs = CreateObject("VirtualServer.Application")
If Err.number <> 0 Then
    Wscript.Echo "Unable to connect to Virtual Server."
    Wscript.Quit
End if
On Error Goto 0

error = 1

while error = 1
    wscript.echo "Please enter the name of the virtual machine that you want to ⊃
 be a template:"
    input = Wscript.StdIn.ReadLine

    set vm = vs.FindVirtualMachine(input)

    On Error Resume Next
    input = vm.name
    If Err.number <> 0 Then
        Wscript.Echo "Please insert a valid VM name."
    Else
        error = 0
    End if
    On Error Goto 0

wend

'Create a custom key and value
key = "Template_Key/IsTemplate"
vm.SetConfigurationValue key, true

wscript.echo "Please enter the name for the virtual machine that you want the ⊃
 user to see:"
input = Wscript.StdIn.ReadLine

'Create a custom key and value
key = "Template_Key/Template_Name"
vm.SetConfigurationValue key, cstr(input)

wscript.echo "Do you want the user to be able to change the memory? (y/n)"
input = Wscript.StdIn.Read(1)
```

480

Chapter 20: Developing ASP.NET Applications with Virtual Server

```
Wscript.StdIn.Readline

key = "Template_Key/Fixed_Memory"

select case Left(input,1)
   case "y"
      vm.SetConfigurationValue key, false
   case "n"
      vm.SetConfigurationValue key, true
end select

wscript.echo "Do you want the user to be able to change the network setting? (y/n)"
input = Wscript.StdIn.Read(1)
Wscript.StdIn.Readline

key = "Template_Key/Fixed_Network"

select case Left(input,1)
   case "y"
      vm.SetConfigurationValue key, false
   case "n"
      vm.SetConfigurationValue key, true
end select
```

Here is the `extendVM.ps1` script:

```
write-host "Please enter the name of the virtual machine that you want to be a ⊃
  template:"
$input = read-host

$vm = $vs.FindVirtualMachine($input)
SetSecurity($vm)

$key = "Template_Key/IsTemplate"
$vm.SetConfigurationValue($key, $true)

write-host "Please enter the name for the virtual machine that you want the ⊃
  user to see:"
$input = read-host

$key = "Template_Key/Template_Name"
$vm.SetConfigurationValue($key, $input)

write-host "Do you want the user to be able to change the memory? (y/n)"
$input = read-host

$key = "Template_Key/Fixed_Memory"

if ($input -eq "y")
{
    $vm.SetConfigurationValue($key, $false)
}
else
{
    $vm.SetConfigurationValue($key, $true)
```

481

Part VIII: Developing Software for Virtual Server

```
}

write-host "Do you want the user to be able to change the network setting? (y/n)"
$input = read-host

$key = "Template_Key/Fixed_Network"

if ($input -eq "y")
{
    $vm.SetConfigurationValue($key, $false)
}
else
{
    $vm.SetConfigurationValue($key, $true)
}
```

These scripts ask you to provide the name of the virtual machine that you want to use as a template, and then set the `"Template_Key/IsTemplate"` configuration key to true. They also configure a number of other custom keys. `"Template_Key/Template_Name"` is used to store a friendly name that will be displayed to the end user for this template (as opposed to using the virtual machine name). `"Template_Key/Fixed_Memory"` and `"Template_Key/Fixed_Network"` are used to indicate whether the user should be allowed to change the memory and network settings when creating a new virtual machine from this template virtual machine. The virtual machine will need to be turned off when you run these scripts.

Please note that while I've chosen to create custom keys for memory and networking in this sample application, there is no reason why you cannot provide a similar functionality for any of the configuration options for a virtual machine.

Understanding ASP.NET Thread Identity

In order for this solution to work, it is important that the various components are running under the correct user contexts. When it comes to determining the context that is being used for an ASP.NET application, things can get rather tricky. In an ASP.NET application, there are actually three different identity contexts that are tracked. `"HttpContext"` represents the context of the user that is using the web session. `"WindowsIdentity"` is the context of the user that the ASP.NET framework is aware of. And finally there is the user context under which the ASP.NET application threads run. Each of these identity contexts are affected by a number of configuration options.

HttpContext can be retrieved programmatically by looking at the `HttpContext.Current.User` object. WindowsIdentity can be retrieved by calling `WindowsIdentity.GetCurrent()`, and the user context that the ASP.NET application threads run under can be retrieved by looking at Thread.CurrentPrincipal.

IIS can be configured to authenticate the user in a number of different ways. ASP.NET can then be configured to also authenticate the user in a number of different ways. And finally, ASP.NET has its own impersonation functionality, which also has an effect.

While IIS has many authentication options, most of them do not affect the identity contexts for ASP.NET. In fact, the only one that has any effect is *anonymous authentication*. If IIS is configured to use anonymous

Chapter 20: Developing ASP.NET Applications with Virtual Server

authentication and ASP.NET is configured to use the Windows authentication mode, there will be no identity context set for the HttpContext object and the ASP.NET application thread.

ASP.NET provides the option to use Windows or Forms authentication modes. If ASP.NET is using Windows authentication, then the current user's credentials will be automatically used (if the website security is configured to allow this, otherwise the user will be presented with an authentication dialog box in order to provide user credentials). With Forms authentication it is up to the ASP.NET application to gather the user credentials and provide them to the ASP.NET Framework. Either way this identity information is used to set the "HttpContext" and the ASP.NET application thread context.

> *The ASP.NET authentication mode can be configured by editing the web.config file. (If your project does not have this file, Visual Studio will offer to create it the first time you attempt to debug the program.) Open this file and find the line that says:*
>
> ```
> <authentication mode="Windows"/>
> ```
>
> *and configure as you wish.*

Finally, there is ASP.NET impersonation. This can be enabled by editing the web.config file and adding a line that says:

```
<identity impersonate="true"/>
```

ASP.NET impersonation affects the WindowsIdentity object that is used by the ASP.NET framework. If it is not enabled, the ASP.NET framework will use a generic service account. If it is enabled, the ASP.NET framework will use the user account provided by the user. It is also possible to configure ASP.NET impersonation such that a hard-coded user account is always used to run the ASP.NET framework.

So what settings are needed for this project? Well, the HttpContext needs to be that of the user that is accessing the website. This happens for all configuration options except when IIS anonymous authentication is used in combination with ASP.NET Windows authentication. The WindowsIdentity is not important, but the ASP.NET application thread context needs to be configured to use the service account that you create for this project. Now if you read back over this section carefully, you'll see that there is no way to hard code the user account that is used for the ASP.NET application thread context. Luckily there is another way to configure this.

IIS and Application Pools

When you use IIS as your web server, ASP.NET application threads run in what is called an *application pool*. It is possible to configure these application pools to always run with a specified user account. Doing this requires some configuration under both Visual Studio and IIS. Before you get started you need to create a user account to run the web application. This does not need to have administrative privilege, but it does need to be granted full control of Virtual Server. Once you have done so, open Visual Studio and follow these steps:

   1. Open the **File** menu, select **New**, and then select **Web Site**.

   2. Select **ASP.NET Web Site**.

   3. Change **Location:** to **HTTP** and click the **Browse** button.

483

Part VIII: Developing Software for Virtual Server

4. Select **Local IIS**, and then create a new web application to use.

*You need to be running Visual Studio as a user that has administrative access to IIS. If you're running on Windows Vista this means that you have to launch Visual Studio **as administrator**.*

If you do not create the project on the local installation of IIS, Visual Studio will use its own built-in web server to run the web application. Unfortunately, it is not possible to configure the application pool identity with this built-in web server, so this is not a suitable configuration for this project.

5. Select the **Language:** that you want to use and click **OK**.

Now you'll need to create a new application pool for your web application. To do this under IIS on Windows XP or Windows Server 2003, follow these steps:

1. Open the **Start** menu, select **Control Panel**, open **Administrative Tools**, and open **Internet Information Services (IIS) Manager**.

2. Select the node for your computer and then select the **Application Pools** node.

3. Open the **Action** menu, select **New**, and then select **Application Pool**.

4. Provide an appropriate name for the application pool, and use the default settings for new application pools.

5. Select the newly created application pool, open the **Action** menu, and select **Properties**.

6. Change to the **Identity** tab, select **Configurable**, and enter the details for the user account you created earlier. Click **OK** when you are done.

7. Expand the **Web Sites** node and select the entry for the web application that you created earlier.

8. Open the **Action** menu and select **Properties**.

9. Change to the **Home Directory** tab.

10. Change the **Application pool** to the pool that you just created.

11. Click **OK** and exit the **Internet Information Services (IIS) Manager**.

To configure this under IIS on Windows Vista, follow these steps:

1. Open the **Start** menu and select **Control Panel**.

2. Select **System and Maintenance** and then **Administrative Tools**.

3. Open **Internet Information Services (IIS) Manager**.

4. Select the node for your computer and then select the **Application Pools** node.

5. Click **Add Application Pool** in the **Actions** pane.

6. Enter an appropriate name for the application pool and accept the default settings.

7. Select the newly created application pool and click **Advanced Settings** in the **Actions** pane.

8. Under the **Process Model** section of the **Advanced Settings**, change the **Identity** entry to **SpecificUser**.

9. Configure the **Identity SpecificUser Credentials** entry, and then click **OK** to exit.

484

Chapter 20: Developing ASP.NET Applications with Virtual Server

10. Expand the **Web Sites** node and select the entry for the web application that you created earlier.

11. Click **Advanced Settings** in the **Actions** pane.

12. Under the **Behavior** section, change the **Application Pool** entry to the application pool that you've just created.

13. Click **OK** and exit the **Internet Information Services (IIS) Manager**.

Now everything is ready for you to begin development on the application.

ASP.NET Application Overview

The sample application consists of four ASPX pages. The primary page (Default.aspx) displays a list of available template virtual machines that the user can use to create new virtual machines from. It also displays a list of virtual machines that have been created by the user and allows them to start, stop, control, and delete the virtual machines. Secondary pages are used to change the virtual machine state (changeState.aspx), create new virtual machines from templates (createNewVM.aspx), and control the virtual machines (vmrc.aspx).

To allow the user to control the virtual machine through VMRC, the application grants the user read permission to the virtual machine when the user tries to access it. Returning to the primary page causes this permission to be revoked.

To keep things simple, this application uses very basic HTML.

You will need to use the code provided in Chapter 16 to be able to interact with the Virtual Server COM APIs. Also remember to add a project reference for the Virtual Server COM Interop.

Default.aspx

Default.aspx is the standard starting page for ASP.NET applications. You'll need to open the designer view for this page and follow these steps:

1. Drag a **Label** onto the page, and then change the label **ID** to **WelcomeLabel**.

2. Change the label **Text** to **Welcome**.

3. Drag a second **Label** onto the page, under the first one.

4. Set the **Text** of this label to Error message, the **ID** to **ErrorLabel**, and the **ForeColor** to **Red**.

5. Now drag a **Horizontal Rule** under these two labels.

6. Drag another **Label** onto the page and set its **Text** to **Available Virtual Machines:**.

7. Drag a **ListBox** onto the page, under the **Available Virtual Machines** label.

8. Change the ListBox **ID** to **AvailableVMListBox**, and resize the ListBox to be large enough to display the virtual machine names.

9. Drag three **Buttons** onto the page, under the ListBox.

485

Part VIII: Developing Software for Virtual Server

10. Change the first button's **Text** to **Change State**; the second button's **Text** to **View**; and the third button's **Text** to **Delete**.

11. Change the first button's **ID** to **ChangeStateButton**; the second button's **ID** to **ViewButton**; and the third button's **ID** to **DeleteButton**.

12. Place another **Horizontal Rule** on the page.

13. Drag a **Label** onto the page and set its **Text** to **Available Templates:**.

14. Drag a **ListBox** onto the page, under the **Available Templates** label.

15. Change the ListBox **ID** to **AvailableTemplateListBox**, and resize the ListBox to be large enough to display the virtual machine template names.

16. Drag a **Button** onto the page, under the ListBox.

17. Change the button **Text** to **Create** and the ID to **CreateButton**.

This should generate the following ASPX code as it appears in Visual Basic .NET:

```
<%@ Page Language="VB" AutoEventWireup="false" CodeFile="Default.aspx.vb"
 Inherits="_Default" %>

<!DOCTYPE html PUBLIC "-//W3C//DTD XHTML 1.0 Transitional//EN"
 "http://www.w3.org/TR/xhtml1/DTD/xhtml1-transitional.dtd">

<html xmlns="http://www.w3.org/1999/xhtml" >
<head id="Head1" runat="server">
    <title>Untitled Page</title>
</head>
<body>
    <form id="form1" runat="server">
    <div>
        <asp:Label ID="WelcomeLabel" runat="server" Text="Welcome"></asp:Label>
        <br />
        <asp:Label ID="ErrorLabel" runat="server" ForeColor="Red" Text="Error
message"></asp:Label><br />
        <hr />
    </div>
        <asp:Label ID="Label1" runat="server" Text="Available Virtual
Machines:"></asp:Label><br />
        <asp:ListBox ID="AvailableVMListBox" runat="server"
Width="400px"></asp:ListBox> <br />
        <asp:Button ID="ChangeStateButton" runat="server" Text="Change State"
Width="104px" />
        <asp:Button ID="ViewButton" runat="server" Text="View" />
        <asp:Button ID="DeleteButton" runat="server" Text="Delete" />
        <br />
        <hr />
        <asp:Label ID="Label2" runat="server" Text="Available
Templates:"></asp:Label><br />
        <asp:ListBox ID="AvailableTemplateListBox" runat="server"
Width="400px"></asp:ListBox><br />
        <asp:Button ID="CreateButton" runat="server" Text="Create..." />
```

Chapter 20: Developing ASP.NET Applications with Virtual Server

```
         

    </form>
</body>
</html>
```

Here's the code in C#:

```
<%@ Page Language="C#" AutoEventWireup="true"  CodeFile="Default.aspx.cs"
 Inherits="_Default" %>

<!DOCTYPE html PUBLIC "-//W3C//DTD XHTML 1.0 Transitional//EN"
 "http://www.w3.org/TR/xhtml1/DTD/xhtml1-transitional.dtd">

<html xmlns="http://www.w3.org/1999/xhtml" >
<head runat="server">
    <title>Untitled Page</title>
</head>
<body>
    <form id="form1" runat="server">
    <div>
        <asp:Label ID="WelcomeLabel" runat="server" Text="Welcome"></asp:Label>
 <br />
        <asp:Label ID="ErrorLabel" runat="server" ForeColor="Red" Text="Error
message"></asp:Label>
        <hr />

    </div>
        <asp:Label ID="Label1" runat="server" Text="Available Virtual
Machines:"></asp:Label>
        <br />
        <asp:ListBox ID="AvailableVMListBox" runat="server"
Width="400px"></asp:ListBox><br />
        <asp:Button ID="ChangeStateButton" runat="server"
OnClick="ChangeStateButton_Click"
            Text="Change State" />
        <asp:Button ID="ViewButton" runat="server" OnClick="ViewButton_Click"
Text="View" />
        <asp:Button ID="DeleteButton" runat="server"
OnClick="DeleteButton_Click" Text="Delete" />
        <hr />
        <asp:Label ID="Label2" runat="server" Text="Available
Templates:"></asp:Label><br />
        <asp:ListBox ID="AvailableTemplateListBox" runat="server"
Width="400px"></asp:ListBox><br />
        <asp:Button ID="CreateButton" runat="server"
OnClick="CreateButton_Click" Text="Create..." />
    </form>
</body>
</html>
```

The result of running this code is shown in Figure 20-3.

487

Part VIII: Developing Software for Virtual Server

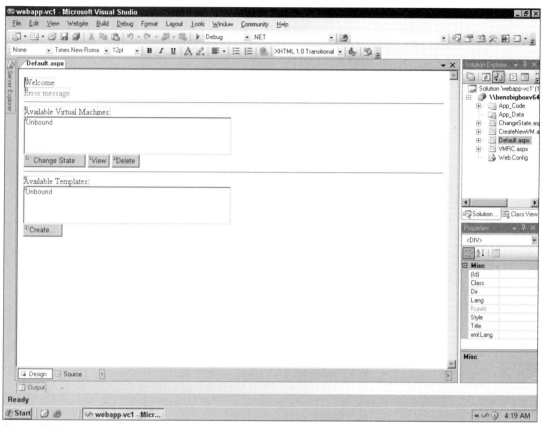

Figure 20-3

The Default.aspx page needs code associated with it that consists of the following routines:

- `Connect`: This routine is used to establish the primary Virtual Server COM object and the `LocalSecurity` object that will be used to call `CoSetProxyBlanket`. Because it is not possible to pass objects between ASPX pages, every ASPX page has this routine and needs to establish its own connection to Virtual Server. Both the objects that are created in this routine are stored in global variables so that other routines can access them.

  It is worth pointing out the different method for error handling that is used here. It is not possible to use a message box to display an error message as this routine may be called before the web page has finished loading. Instead, an error in this routine will cause all the controls on the page to be hidden and an error message to be displayed.

- `populateListBoxes`: This routine iterates over all of the virtual machines on the server and then performs three operations. First, it checks to see if the user has any permissions on the virtual machine configuration file, and removes them if he or she does. Then it checks each virtual machine to see if it has a custom key that indicates that this virtual machine was created by the user. If the key is present it adds the virtual machine name to the available virtual machines ListBox. (It also appends the state of the virtual machine to the virtual machine name.) Finally, it checks to see if the virtual machine is marked as a template and, if it is, it adds the template name to the available templates ListBox.

Chapter 20: Developing ASP.NET Applications with Virtual Server

The Virtual Server security settings are modified through the COM API, but Virtual Server does not allow you to modify the virtual machine security settings in this way. Rather you need to edit the access control lists (ACLs) of the virtual machine configuration file directly.

This code is a check that ensures that security changes are not applied to a specified user account (DOMAIN\UserName). The purpose of this is to allow you to test the application with your own account and not worry about losing your security privileges.

❏ Page_Load: This routine is called when the page loads. It calls the Connect and populateListBoxes routines. It also checks to see if anyone called this page with an error message. If it finds an error message, it displays the error message label with the appropriate information; otherwise it hides the error message label. It also updates the Welcome label to include the user's name.

> **Putting the user's name in the Welcome label is not just friendly and personal, but helps with debugging issues when the wrong user identity is being used.**

Code that is called by the page load event runs before the webpage is displayed. Because this application is using simple static HTML, this is the best time to update any data on the page.

❏ ChangeStateButton_Click: This routine checks to see that a valid selection has been made in the available virtual machines ListBox. If the selection is valid, it strips the virtual machine state information from the ListBox entry (in order to just get the virtual machine name) and then calls changeState.aspx with the virtual machine name as a parameter. If there is no valid selection, it reloads the page and indicates an error.

❏ ViewButton_Click: This routine checks to see that a valid selection has been made, and that the selected virtual machine is running. If either of these requirements is not met, it reloads the page and indicates an error. Otherwise, it grants the user read access to the virtual machine and calls VMRC.aspx.

The user needs to have read access on the virtual machine in order to control it over VMRC. By granting the user read access only, and removing all access that the user has when Default.aspx is loaded, you are able to effectively restrict the user from interacting with Virtual Server outside of the web application.

> **Not all people use VMRC in these kinds of solutions. If the virtual machines are guaranteed to be connected to a public network, and their network name is known, you can use Remote Desktop to connect to the virtual machines. This way the user never needs to have any permissions under Virtual Server.**

❏ DeleteButton_click: This routine checks to see that a valid selection has been made and then iterates over all of the virtual machine's virtual hard disks and tries to delete them (as well as any associated undo disks). It then stores the location of the virtual machine configuration file, deletes the virtual machine, and deletes the virtual machine folder if no files are left in it. Deleting a virtual machine under Virtual Server will not delete any virtual hard disks, or the

489

Part VIII: Developing Software for Virtual Server

virtual machine folder, which is why it is necessary to do these things manually. You have to be careful about ordering here because once the virtual machine is deleted it is not possible to find out what virtual hard disks it had, or where it was stored.

Strictly speaking, I should be checking to ensure that the virtual machine is not running before trying to delete it. I should also be checking to see if undo disks are enabled before trying to delete them. But given that there is always the possibility of failure when performing file operations I have taken the easier path of just writing code to get any exceptions and indicate an error if it happens.

One important thing to know is that you should not place `Response.Redirect` **inside of a** `try . . . catch` **statement. The reason for this is that** `Response` `.Redirect` **causes an abnormal thread termination that will be detected as an error case.**

❑ `CreateButton_Click`: This routine simply checks to see the valid selection has been made in the AvailableTemplateListBox and calls `createNewVM.aspx` with the template name as a parameter. If there is no valid selection it reloads the page and indicates an error.

Remember that the purpose of this page is to display a list of available template virtual machines that the user can use to create new virtual machines. The application also displays a list of virtual machines that have been created by the user and allows them to start, stop, control, and delete the virtual machines.

Here is the code in Visual Basic .NET:

```vbnet
Imports Microsoft.VirtualServer.Interop

Partial Class _Default
    Inherits System.Web.UI.Page
    'Using a global variable for the main Virtual Server connection
    'without this you would have to reconnect for each call
    Public VSConnection As VMVirtualServer = Nothing
    Public LocalSecurity As SetSecurityImpersonationLevel

    'Define constants
    Const vmVMState_Invalid = 0
    Const vmVMState_TurnedOff = 1
    Const vmVMState_Saved = 2
    Const vmVMState_TurningOn = 3
    Const vmVMState_Restoring = 4
    Const vmVMState_Running = 5
    Const vmVMState_Paused = 6
    Const vmVMState_Saving = 7
    Const vmVMState_TurningOff = 8
    Const vmVMState_MergingDrives = 9
    Const vmVMState_DeleteMachine = 10

    Public Sub Connect()

        'SetProxyBlanket
```

Chapter 20: Developing ASP.NET Applications with Virtual Server

```vb
            localSecurity = New SetSecurityImpersonationLevel

        Try
            'This connects to the local server
            VSConnection = New VMVirtualServer

            'Secure the VS Connection object, if we have one.
            localSecurity.Secure(VSConnection)

        Catch ex As Exception
            'If a failure occurs - state so on the page and hide the controls
            ErrorLabel.Visible = True
            ErrorLabel.Text = "ERROR: Failed to connect to Virtual Server"
            AvailableVMListBox.Visible = False
            AvailableTemplateListBox.Visible = False
            ChangeStateButton.Visible = False
            ViewButton.Visible = False
            DeleteButton.Visible = False
            CreateButton.Visible = False
            Exit Sub
        End Try
    End Sub

    Public Sub populateListBoxes()
        ' Display Virtual Server version info
        Dim VMs As IVMVirtualMachineCollection
        Dim aVM As VMVirtualMachine
        Dim aVMSecurity As VMSecurity
        Dim aVMAccessRight As VMAccessRights
        Dim entryName As String = ""
        Dim counter As Integer
        Dim fSecurity As System.Security.AccessControl.FileSecurity
        Dim ident As System.Security.Principal.IdentityReference

        'Do not continue if VSConnection has not been populated
        If VSConnection Is Nothing Then
            Exit Sub
        End If

        'Create secure VirtualMachines COM object
        VMs = VSConnection.VirtualMachines
        localSecurity.Secure(VMs)

        'Populate AvailableVMListBox and AvailableTemplateListBox
        For counter = 1 To VMs.Count
            'Create and secure a VM object for each entry in VMs
            aVM = VMs.Item(counter)
            localSecurity.Secure(aVM)

            If Not (LCase(HttpContext.Current.User.Identity.Name) = ⊃
    LCase("DOMAIN\UserName")) Then

                'Remove any access the user has to any of the virtual machine
                ident = New ⊃
    System.Security.Principal.NTAccount(HttpContext.Current.User.Identity.Name)
                fSecurity = System.IO.File.GetAccessControl(aVM.File)
```

491

Part VIII: Developing Software for Virtual Server

```vb
        fSecurity.PurgeAccessRules(ident)

        ' Set the new access settings.
        System.IO.File.SetAccessControl(aVM.File, fSecurity)

        'Create VS security COM object
        aVMSecurity = VSConnection.Security
        LocalSecurity.Secure(aVMSecurity)

        'Look for and remove any Virtual Server privileges the user has
        aVMAccessRight = Nothing
        aVMAccessRight = ⮑
aVMSecurity.FindEntry(HttpContext.Current.User.Identity.Name, ⮑
VMAccessRightsType.vmAccessRights_Allowed)

        If Not aVMAccessRight Is Nothing Then
            LocalSecurity.Secure(aVMAccessRight)
            aVMSecurity.RemoveEntry(aVMAccessRight)
        End If

        aVMAccessRight = Nothing
        aVMAccessRight = ⮑
aVMSecurity.FindEntry(HttpContext.Current.User.Identity.Name, ⮑
VMAccessRightsType.vmAccessRights_Denied)
        If Not aVMAccessRight Is Nothing Then
            LocalSecurity.Secure(aVMAccessRight)
            aVMSecurity.RemoveEntry(aVMAccessRight)
        End If

        'Update VS security settings
        VSConnection.Security = aVMSecurity
    End If

    Try
        'Does the VM have a "Template_Key/UserName" that maps
        'to the current user?
        If aVM.GetConfigurationValue("Template_Key/UserName") _
            = HttpContext.Current.User.Identity.Name Then

            'Append the VM name with the state.  '/' is used as
            'a special character here
            Select Case aVM.State
                Case vmVMState_Invalid
                    entryName = aVM.Name & " / invalid state"
                Case vmVMState_TurnedOff
                    entryName = aVM.Name & " / turned off"
                Case vmVMState_Saved
                    entryName = aVM.Name & " / saved"
                Case vmVMState_TurningOn
                    entryName = aVM.Name & " / turning on"
                Case vmVMState_Restoring
                    entryName = aVM.Name & " / restoring"
                Case vmVMState_Running
                    entryName = aVM.Name & " / running"
                Case vmVMState_Paused
                    entryName = aVM.Name & " / paused"
```

Chapter 20: Developing ASP.NET Applications with Virtual Server

```vb
                    Case vmVMState_Saving
                        entryName = aVM.Name & " / saving state"
                    Case vmVMState_TurningOff
                        entryName = aVM.Name & " / turning off"
                    Case vmVMState_MergingDrives
                        entryName = aVM.Name & " / merging undo disks"
                    Case vmVMState_DeleteMachine
                        entryName = aVM.Name & " / being deleted"
                End Select

                'Add the entry to the list box
                AvailableVMListBox.Items.Add(entryName)
            End If
        Catch
            'The VM did not have the "Template_Key/UserName" key at all
        End Try

        Try
            'Is the VM marked as a template?
            If aVM.GetConfigurationValue("Template_Key/IsTemplate") Then
                'Add the template name, not the VM name, to the list
                AvailableTemplateListBox.Items.Add( _
                    aVM.GetConfigurationValue("Template_Key/Template_Name"))
            End If
        Catch
            'The VM did not have this key at all
        End Try
    Next

End Sub

Protected Sub Page_Load(ByVal sender As Object, ByVal e As ↵
System.EventArgs) Handles Me.Load
    'Call Connect and populateListBoxes
    Connect()
    populateListBoxes()

    'Set the welcome text to show the current user (useful for debugging)
    WelcomeLabel.Text = "Welcome " & HttpContext.Current.User.Identity.Name

    'Display an error message if one was provided
    If Request.QueryString.Item("error") Is Nothing Then
        ErrorLabel.Visible = False
    Else
        ErrorLabel.Visible = True
        ErrorLabel.Text = Request.QueryString.Item("error")
    End If
End Sub

Protected Sub ViewButton_Click(ByVal sender As Object, ByVal e As ↵
System.EventArgs) Handles ViewButton.Click
    Dim vmName As String
    Dim vm As VMVirtualMachine
    Dim aVMSecurity As VMSecurity
    Dim aVMAccessRight As VMAccessRights
    Dim fSecurity As System.Security.AccessControl.FileSecurity
```

493

Part VIII: Developing Software for Virtual Server

```vb
        Dim accessRule As System.Security.AccessControl.FileSystemAccessRule

    'Make sure that a valid selection is available
    If AvailableVMListBox.SelectedIndex >= 0 Then

        'Strip off the VM state information to just get the VM name
        vmName = AvailableVMListBox.SelectedItem.Text
        vmName = Left(vmName, InStrRev(vmName, "/") - 2)

        'Check that the virtual machine is runnning
        vm = VSConnection.FindVirtualMachine(vmName)
        localSecurity.Secure(vm)

        If vm.State = VMVMState.vmVMState_Running Then

            'Give the user read abilty on the virtual machine
            fSecurity = System.IO.File.GetAccessControl(vm.File)
            accessRule = New ⤸
System.Security.AccessControl.FileSystemAccessRule(HttpContext.Current.User. ⤸
Identity.Name, System.Security.AccessControl.FileSystemRights.Read, ⤸
 System.Security.AccessControl.AccessControlType.Allow)
            fSecurity.AddAccessRule(accessRule)

            ' Set the new access settings.
            System.IO.File.SetAccessControl(vm.File, fSecurity)

            'Create VS security COM object
            aVMSecurity = VSConnection.Security
            localSecurity.Secure(aVMSecurity)

            'Add security entry for the actual user
            aVMAccessRight = Nothing
            aVMAccessRight = ⤸
aVMSecurity.FindEntry(HttpContext.Current.User.Identity.Name, ⤸
VMAccessRightsType.vmAccessRights_Allowed)
            LocalSecurity.Secure(aVMAccessRight)

            If aVMAccessRight Is Nothing Then
                aVMAccessRight = ⤸
aVMSecurity.AddEntry(HttpContext.Current.User.Identity.Name, ⤸
VMAccessRightsType.vmAccessRights_Allowed)
                LocalSecurity.Secure(aVMAccessRight)
            End If

            'Grant read access for VirtualServer
            aVMAccessRight.ReadAccess = True

            'Update VS security object
            VSConnection.Security = aVMSecurity

            'Redirect to the VMRC page, with the VM name as a parameter
            Response.Redirect("vmrc.aspx?vm=" & vmName, True)
        Else
            'If the VM is not running reload the page with an error message
            Response.Redirect("Default.aspx?error=ERROR: You can only view ⤸
a running virtual machine.")
```

Chapter 20: Developing ASP.NET Applications with Virtual Server

```vb
            End If
        Else
            'If there is not a valid selection - just reload the current page
            Response.Redirect("Default.aspx?error=ERROR! You need to select a ↵
virtual machine to view.")
        End If
    End Sub

    Protected Sub CreateButton_Click(ByVal sender As Object, ByVal e As ↵
System.EventArgs) Handles CreateButton.Click

        'Make sure that a valid selection is available
        If AvailableTemplateListBox.SelectedIndex >= 0 Then
            Response.Redirect("createNewVM.aspx?vm=" & ↵
AvailableTemplateListBox.SelectedItem.Text, True)
        Else
            'If there is not a valid selection - just reload the current page
            Response.Redirect("Default.aspx?error=ERROR: You need to select a ↵
template to create a virtual machine from.")
        End If
    End Sub

    Protected Sub DeleteButton_Click(ByVal sender As Object, ByVal e As ↵
System.EventArgs) Handles DeleteButton.Click
        Dim aVM As VMVirtualMachine
        Dim hardDiskConnections As IVMHardDiskConnectionCollection
        Dim hardDiskConnection As VMHardDiskConnection
        Dim aVHD As VMHardDisk
        Dim undoDisk As VMHardDisk
        Dim vmName As String
        Dim vmDirectory As String
        Dim vmDirectoryFiles() As String

        'Make sure that a valid selection is available
        If AvailableVMListBox.SelectedIndex >= 0 Then

            Try
                'Strip off the VM state information to just get the VM name
                vmName = AvailableVMListBox.SelectedItem.Text
                vmName = Left(vmName, InStrRev(vmName, "/") - 2)

                'Create and Secure a virtual machine COM object
                aVM = VSConnection.FindVirtualMachine(vmName)
                localSecurity.Secure(aVM)

                'Create and Secure a virtual hard disk connections COM object
                hardDiskConnections = aVM.HardDiskConnections
                localSecurity.Secure(hardDiskConnections)

                'Go over each connection and delete the virtual hard disk
                For Each hardDiskConnection In hardDiskConnections
                    localSecurity.Secure(hardDiskConnection)
                    aVHD = hardDiskConnection.HardDisk
                    localSecurity.Secure(aVHD)
```

495

Part VIII: Developing Software for Virtual Server

```vbnet
                System.IO.File.Delete(aVHD.File)

                'Also try to delete any associated VHD
                Try
                    undoDisk = hardDiskConnection.UndoHardDisk
                    localSecurity.Secure(undoDisk)
                    System.IO.File.Delete(undoDisk.File)
                Catch ex As Exception
                    'Most likely there was no undo disk
                End Try
            Next

            'Need to record the directory before deleting the VM
            vmDirectory = Left(aVM.File, InStrRev(aVM.File, "\") - 1)

            'Delete the virtual machine configuration file
            VSConnection.DeleteVirtualMachine(aVM)

            'Note - the VM folder will still be left around
            vmDirectoryFiles = System.IO.Directory.GetFiles(vmDirectory)

            'If there are no files left in the VM directory - delete it
            If vmDirectoryFiles.Length = 0 Then
                System.IO.Directory.Delete(vmDirectory)
            End If

        Catch
            Response.Redirect("Default.aspx?error=ERROR: An error occurred ⤶
while trying to delete the virtual machine.", True)
        End Try
    Else
        'If there is not a valid selection - just reload the current page
        Response.Redirect("Default.aspx?error=ERROR: You need to select a ⤶
virtual machine to delete.", True)
    End If

    'Reload the main page
    Response.Redirect("Default.aspx", True)

End Sub

Protected Sub ChangeStateButton_Click(ByVal sender As Object, ByVal e As ⤶
System.EventArgs) Handles ChangeStateButton.Click
    Dim vmName As String

    'Make sure that a valid selection is available
    If AvailableVMListBox.SelectedIndex >= 0 Then

        'Strip off the VM state information to just get the VM name
        vmName = AvailableVMListBox.SelectedItem.Text
        vmName = Left(vmName, InStrRev(vmName, "/") - 2)

        'Load the change state page
        Response.Redirect("changeState.aspx?vm=" & vmName, True)
    Else
        'If there is not a valid selection - just reload the current page
```

Chapter 20: Developing ASP.NET Applications with Virtual Server

```
                Response.Redirect("Default.aspx?error=ERROR: You need to select a ⊃
    virtual machine to change state on.")
            End If
        End Sub
    End Class
```

Here is the code in C#:

```csharp
using System;
using System.Data;
using System.Configuration;
using System.Web;
using System.Web.Security;
using System.Web.UI;
using System.Web.UI.WebControls;
using System.Web.UI.WebControls.WebParts;
using System.Web.UI.HtmlControls;
using Microsoft.VirtualServer.Interop;

public partial class _Default : System.Web.UI.Page
{
    // Using a global variable for the main Virtual Server connection
    // without this you would have to reconnect for each call
    public VMVirtualServer VSConnection = null;
    public Personal.SetSecurity.ProxyBlanket LocalSecurity;

    private void Connect()
    {
        //CoSetProxyBlanket
        LocalSecurity = new Personal.SetSecurity.ProxyBlanket();

        try
        {
            //This connects to the local server
            VSConnection = new VMVirtualServer();

            //Secure the VS Connection object.
            LocalSecurity.Set(VSConnection);
        }
        catch
        {
            //If a failure occurs - state so on the page and hide the controls
            ErrorLabel.Visible = true;
            ErrorLabel.Text = "ERROR: Failed to connect to Vitual Server";
            AvailableVMListBox.Visible = false;
            AvailableTemplateListBox.Visible = false;
            ChangeStateButton.Visible = false;
            ViewButton.Visible = false;
            DeleteButton.Visible = false;
            CreateButton.Visible = false;
            return;
        }
    }

    private void populateListBoxes()
```

497

Part VIII: Developing Software for Virtual Server

```csharp
    {

        IVMVirtualMachineCollection VMs;
        VMVirtualMachine aVM;
        VMSecurity aVMSecurity;
        VMAccessRights aVMAccessRight;
        string entryName = "";
        System.Security.AccessControl.FileSecurity fSecurity;
        System.Security.Principal.IdentityReference ident;

        //Do not continue if VSConnection has not been populated
        if (VSConnection == null)
        {
            return;
        }

        //Create secure VirtualMachines COM object
        VMs = VSConnection.VirtualMachines;
        LocalSecurity.Set(VMs);

        //Populate AvailableVMListBox and AvailableTemplateListBox
        for (int counter = 1; counter <= VMs.Count; counter++)
        {
            //Create and secure a VM object for each entry in VMs
            aVM = VMs[counter];
            LocalSecurity.Set(aVM);

            string exemptUser = "DOMAIN\\UserName";
            string currentUser = HttpContext.Current.User.Identity.Name;
            if (currentUser.ToLower() != exemptUser.ToLower())
            {

                // Remove any access the user has to any of the virtual machine
                ident = new ⊃
System.Security.Principal.NTAccount(HttpContext.Current.User.Identity.Name);
                fSecurity = System.IO.File.GetAccessControl(aVM.File);
                fSecurity.PurgeAccessRules(ident);

                // Set the new access settings.
                System.IO.File.SetAccessControl(aVM.File, fSecurity);

                // Create VS security COM object
                aVMSecurity = VSConnection.Security;
                LocalSecurity.Set(aVMSecurity);

                // Look for and remove any Virtual Server privileges the user has
                aVMAccessRight = null;
                aVMAccessRight = ⊃
aVMSecurity.FindEntry(HttpContext.Current.User.Identity.Name, ⊃
VMAccessRightsType.vmAccessRights_Allowed);

                if (aVMAccessRight != null)
                {
                    LocalSecurity.Set(aVMAccessRight);
                    aVMSecurity.RemoveEntry(aVMAccessRight);
```

498

Chapter 20: Developing ASP.NET Applications with Virtual Server

```
            }

            aVMAccessRight = null;
            aVMAccessRight =
aVMSecurity.FindEntry(HttpContext.Current.User.Identity.Name,
VMAccessRightsType.vmAccessRights_Denied);
            if (aVMAccessRight != null)
            {
                LocalSecurity.Set(aVMAccessRight);
                aVMSecurity.RemoveEntry(aVMAccessRight);
            }

            // Update VS security settings
            VSConnection.Security = aVMSecurity;
        }

        try
        {
            // Does the VM have a "Template_Key/UserName" that maps
            // to the current user?
            if
(aVM.GetConfigurationValue("Template_Key/UserName").ToString() ==
HttpContext.Current.User.Identity.Name)
            {
                // Append the VM name with the state.  '/' is used as
                // a special character here
                switch (aVM.State)
                {
                    case VMVMState.vmVMState_Invalid:
                        entryName = aVM.Name + " / invalid state";
                        break;

                    case VMVMState.vmVMState_TurnedOff:
                        entryName = aVM.Name + " / turned off";
                        break;

                    case VMVMState.vmVMState_Saved:
                        entryName = aVM.Name + " / saved";
                        break;

                    case VMVMState.vmVMState_TurningOn:
                        entryName = aVM.Name + " / turning on";
                        break;

                    case VMVMState.vmVMState_Restoring:
                        entryName = aVM.Name + " / restoring";
                        break;

                    case VMVMState.vmVMState_Running:
                        entryName = aVM.Name + " / running";
                        break;

                    case VMVMState.vmVMState_Paused:
                        entryName = aVM.Name + " / paused";
```

Part VIII: Developing Software for Virtual Server

```
                              break;

                    case VMVMState.vmVMState_Saving:
                        entryName = aVM.Name + " / saving state";
                        break;

                    case VMVMState.vmVMState_TurningOff:
                        entryName = aVM.Name + " / turning off";
                        break;

                    case VMVMState.vmVMState_MergingDrives:
                        entryName = aVM.Name + " / merging undo disks";
                        break;

                    case VMVMState.vmVMState_DeleteMachine:
                        entryName = aVM.Name + " / being deleted";
                        break;
                }

                // Add the entry to the list box
                AvailableVMListBox.Items.Add(entryName);
            }
        }
        catch
        {
            // The VM did not have the "Template_Key/UserName" key at all
        }

        try
        {
            // Is the VM marked as a template?
            string isTemplate = ⤸
aVM.GetConfigurationValue("Template_Key/IsTemplate").ToString();
            if (isTemplate == "True")
            {
                // Add the template name, not the VM name, to the list
                string template_name = ⤸
aVM.GetConfigurationValue("Template_Key/Template_Name").ToString();
                AvailableTemplateListBox.Items.Add(template_name);
            }
        }
        catch
        {
            // The VM did not have this key at all
        }
    }
}

protected void Page_Load(object sender, EventArgs e)
{
    // Call Connect and populateListBoxes
    Connect();
    populateListBoxes();

    // Set the welcome text to show the current user (useful for debugging)
```

Chapter 20: Developing ASP.NET Applications with Virtual Server

```csharp
        WelcomeLabel.Text = "Welcome " + HttpContext.Current.User.Identity.Name;

        // Display an error message if one was provided
        if (Request.QueryString["error"] == null)
        {
            ErrorLabel.Visible = false;
        }
        else
        {
            ErrorLabel.Visible = true;
            ErrorLabel.Text = Request.QueryString["error"];
        }
    }

    protected void ChangeStateButton_Click(object sender, EventArgs e)
    {
        //Make sure that a valid selection is available
        if (AvailableVMListBox.SelectedIndex >= 0)
        {
            // Strip off the VM state information to just get the VM name
            String vmName = AvailableVMListBox.SelectedItem.Text;
            vmName = vmName.Substring(0, vmName.LastIndexOf("/") - 1);

            // Load the change state page
            Response.Redirect("changeState.aspx?vm=" + vmName, true);
        }
        else
        {
            // If there is not a valid selection - just reload the current page
            Response.Redirect("Default.aspx?error=ERROR: You need to select a ⤵
virtual machine to change state on.");
        }
    }
    protected void ViewButton_Click(object sender, EventArgs e)
    {
        System.Security.AccessControl.FileSecurity fSecurity;
        System.Security.AccessControl.FileSystemAccessRule accessRule;

        //Make sure that a valid selection is available
        if (AvailableVMListBox.SelectedIndex >= 0)
        {
            // Strip off the VM state information to just get the VM name
            String vmName = AvailableVMListBox.SelectedItem.Text;
            vmName = vmName.Substring(0, vmName.LastIndexOf("/") - 1);

            // Check that the virtual machine is runnning
            VMVirtualMachine aVM = VSConnection.FindVirtualMachine(vmName);
            LocalSecurity.Set(aVM);

            if (aVM.State == VMVMState.vmVMState_Running)
            {
                // Give the user read abilty on the virtual machine
                fSecurity = System.IO.File.GetAccessControl(aVM.File);
                accessRule = new ⤵
System.Security.AccessControl.FileSystemAccessRule(HttpContext.Current.User. ⤵
```

501

Part VIII: Developing Software for Virtual Server

```
Identity.Name, System.Security.AccessControl.FileSystemRights.Read, ⟲
  System.Security.AccessControl.AccessControlType.Allow);
                fSecurity.AddAccessRule(accessRule);

                // Set the new access settings.
                System.IO.File.SetAccessControl(aVM.File, fSecurity);

                // Create VS security COM object
                VMSecurity aVMSecurity = VSConnection.Security;
                LocalSecurity.Set(aVMSecurity);

                // Add security entry for the actual user
                VMAccessRights aVMAccessRight = null;
                aVMAccessRight = ⟲
aVMSecurity.FindEntry(HttpContext.Current.User.Identity.Name, ⟲
VMAccessRightsType.vmAccessRights_Allowed);
                LocalSecurity.Set(aVMAccessRight);

                if (aVMAccessRight == null)
                {
                    aVMAccessRight = ⟲
aVMSecurity.AddEntry(HttpContext.Current.User.Identity.Name, ⟲
VMAccessRightsType.vmAccessRights_Allowed);
                    LocalSecurity.Set(aVMAccessRight);
                }

                // Grant read access for VirtualServer
                aVMAccessRight.ReadAccess = true;

                // Update VS security object
                VSConnection.Security = aVMSecurity;

                // Redirect to the VMRC page, with the VM name as a parameter
                Response.Redirect("vmrc.aspx?vm=" + vmName, true);
            }
            else
            {
                // If the VM is not running reload the page with an error message
                Response.Redirect("Default.aspx?error=ERROR: You can only view ⟲
a running virtual machine.");
            }
        }
        else
        {
            // If there is not a valid selection - just reload the current page
            Response.Redirect("Default.aspx?error=ERROR: You need to select a ⟲
virtual machine to view.");
        }
    }
    protected void DeleteButton_Click(object sender, EventArgs e)
    {

        //Make sure that a valid selection is available
        if (AvailableVMListBox.SelectedIndex >= 0)
        {
```

Chapter 20: Developing ASP.NET Applications with Virtual Server

```
try
{
    // Strip off the VM state information to just get the VM name
    String vmName = AvailableVMListBox.SelectedItem.Text;
    vmName = vmName.Substring(0, vmName.LastIndexOf("/") - 1);

    // Check that the virtual machine is runnning
    VMVirtualMachine aVM = VSConnection.FindVirtualMachine(vmName);
    LocalSecurity.Set(aVM);

    //Create and Secure a virtual hard disk connections COM object
    IVMHardDiskConnectionCollection hardDiskConnections = 🡒
aVM.HardDiskConnections;
    LocalSecurity.Set(hardDiskConnections);

    // Go over each connection and delete the virtual hard disk
    foreach (VMHardDiskConnection hardDiskConnection in 🡒
hardDiskConnections)
    {
        LocalSecurity.Set(hardDiskConnection);
        VMHardDisk aVHD = hardDiskConnection.HardDisk;
        LocalSecurity.Set(aVHD);
        System.IO.File.Delete(aVHD.File);

        // Also try to delete any associated VHD
        try
        {
            VMHardDisk undoDisk = hardDiskConnection.UndoHardDisk;
            LocalSecurity.Set(undoDisk);
            System.IO.File.Delete(undoDisk.File);
        }
        catch
        {
            // Most likely there was no undo disk
        }
    }

    // Need to record the directory before deleting the VM
    String vmDirectory = aVM.File.Substring(0, 🡒
aVM.File.LastIndexOf("\\"));

    // Delete the virtual machine configuration file
    VSConnection.DeleteVirtualMachine(aVM);

    // Note - the VM folder will still be left around
    string[] vmDirectoryFiles = 🡒
System.IO.Directory.GetFiles(vmDirectory);

    // If there are no files left in the VM directory - delete it
    if (vmDirectoryFiles.Length == 0)
    {
        System.IO.Directory.Delete(vmDirectory);
    }
}
catch
```

Part VIII: Developing Software for Virtual Server

```
            {
                    Response.Redirect("Default.aspx?error=ERROR: An error occurred ⊃
        while trying to delete the virtual machine.", true);
            }
        }
        else
        {
            // If there is not a valid selection - just reload the current page
            Response.Redirect("Default.aspx?error=ERROR: You need to select a ⊃
        virtual machine to delete.", true);
        }

        // Reload the main page
        Response.Redirect("Default.aspx", true);
    }
    protected void CreateButton_Click(object sender, EventArgs e)
    {
        // Make sure that a valid selection is available
        if (AvailableTemplateListBox.SelectedIndex >= 0)
        {
            Response.Redirect("createNewVM.aspx?vm=" + ⊃
    AvailableTemplateListBox.SelectedItem.Text, true);
        }
        else
        {
            // If there is not a valid selection - just reload the current page
            Response.Redirect("Default.aspx?error=ERROR: You need to select a ⊃
        template to create a virtual machine from.");
        }
    }
}
```

CreateNewVM.aspx

CreateNewVM.aspx is responsible for creating a new virtual machine, given a template virtual machine and some input from the user (on memory configuration, network configuration, and virtual machine name).

Follow these steps to create CreateNewVM.aspx:

1. In Visual Studio, open the **Website** menu.

2. Select **Add New Item**.

3. Choose **Web Form** and specify a name of **CreateNewVM.aspx**.

4. Ensure that the right **Language** is selected and that the **Place code in separate file** option is checked.

5. Click **Add**.

6. Open the designer view for CreateNewVM.aspx.

504

Chapter 20: Developing ASP.NET Applications with Virtual Server

7. Drag a **Label** onto the page and set its **Text** to **Configure Virtual Machine:**.

8. Drag a **Horizontal Rule** underneath this label.

9. Drag another **Label** onto the page, and then change the label **ID** to **VMNameLabel**.

10. Change the label **Text** to **Virtual machine name:**.

11. Drag a **TextBox** onto the page, next to the label, and then change the TextBox **ID** to **VMNameTextBox**.

12. Drag a **Label** onto the page, underneath the last one, and then change the label **ID** to **MemoryLabel**.

13. Change the label **Text** to **Memory:**.

14. Drag a **TextBox** onto the page, next to the label, and then change the TextBox **ID** to **MemoryTextBox**.

15. Drag another **Label** onto the page, underneath the last one, and then change the label **ID** to **NetworkingLabel**.

16. Change the label **Text** to **Network Connection:**.

17. Drag a **DropDownList** onto the page, next to the label, and then change the DropDownList **ID** to **NetworkDropDownList**.

18. Drag two **Buttons** onto the page, under everything else.

19. Change the first button's **Text** to **Create VM**, and change the second button's **Text** to **Cancel**.

20. Set the first button's **ID** to **CreateVMButton**; and set the second button's **ID** to **CancelButton**.

This should generate the following ASPX code, as displayed in Visual Basic .NET:

```
<%@ Page Language="VB" AutoEventWireup="false" CodeFile="createNewVM.aspx.vb" ⤵
 Inherits="createNewVM" %>

<!DOCTYPE html PUBLIC "-//W3C//DTD XHTML 1.0 Transitional//EN" ⤵
 "http://www.w3.org/TR/xhtml1/DTD/xhtml1-transitional.dtd">

<html xmlns="http://www.w3.org/1999/xhtml" >
<head runat="server">
    <title>Untitled Page</title>
</head>
<body>
    <form id="form1" runat="server">
    <div>
        <asp:Label ID="Label1" runat="server" Text="Configure Virtual ⤵
Machine:"></asp:Label>
        <hr />

    </div>
        <asp:Label ID="VMNameLabel" runat="server" Text="Virtual machine ⤵
name:"></asp:Label>
        <asp:TextBox ID="VMNameTextBox" runat="server"></asp:TextBox><br />
        <asp:Label ID="MemoryLabel" runat="server" Text="Memory:"></asp:Label>
```

505

Part VIII: Developing Software for Virtual Server

```
        <asp:TextBox ID="MemoryTextBox" runat="server"></asp:TextBox>
        <br />
        <asp:Label ID="NetworkingLabel" runat="server" Text="Network ⟳
Connection:"></asp:Label> 
        <asp:DropDownList ID="NetworkDropDownList" runat="server" Width="167px">
        </asp:DropDownList><br />
        <asp:Button ID="CreateVMButton" runat="server" Text="Create VM" />
        <asp:Button ID="CancelButton" runat="server" Text="Cancel" />
    </form>
</body>
</html>
```

Here's the code as it is displayed in C#:

```
<%@ Page Language="C#" AutoEventWireup="true" CodeFile="CreateNewVM.aspx.cs" ⟳
  Inherits="CreateNewVM" %>

<!DOCTYPE html PUBLIC "-//W3C//DTD XHTML 1.0 Transitional//EN" ⟳
  "http://www.w3.org/TR/xhtml1/DTD/xhtml1-transitional.dtd">

<html xmlns="http://www.w3.org/1999/xhtml" >
<head runat="server">
    <title>Untitled Page</title>
</head>
<body>
    <form id="form1" runat="server">
    <div>
        <asp:Label ID="Label1" runat="server" Text="Configure Virtual ⟳
Machine:"></asp:Label>
        <hr />

    </div>
        <asp:Label ID="VMNameLabel" runat="server" Text="Virtual machine ⟳
name:"></asp:Label>
        <asp:TextBox ID="VMNameTextBox" runat="server"></asp:TextBox><br />
        <asp:Label ID="MemoryLabel" runat="server" Text="Memory:"></asp:Label>
        <asp:TextBox ID="MemoryTextBox" runat="server"></asp:TextBox><br />
        <asp:Label ID="NetworkingLabel" runat="server" Text="Network ⟳
Connection:"></asp:Label>
        <asp:DropDownList ID="NetworkDropDownList" runat="server" Width="156px">
        </asp:DropDownList><br />
         <asp:Button ID="CreateVMButton" runat="server" Text="Create VM" ⟳
OnClick="CreateVMButton_Click" />
        <asp:Button ID="CancelButton" runat="server" Text="Cancel" ⟳
OnClick="CancelButton_Click" />
    </form>
</body>
</html>
```

The preceding code should result in a screen that looks like Figure 20-4.

Chapter 20: Developing ASP.NET Applications with Virtual Server

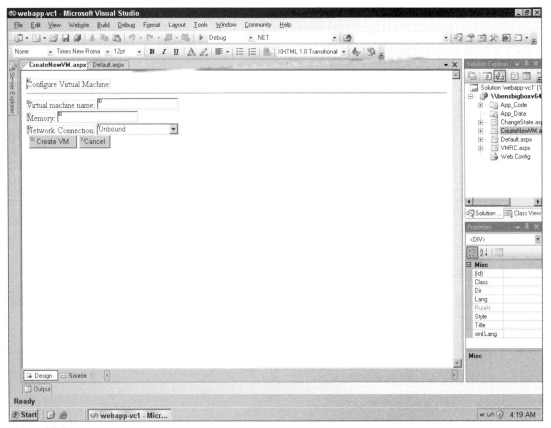

Figure 20-4

The CreateNewVM.aspx page needs to have code listed associated with it that consists of the following routines:

- `Connect`: This is very similar to the connect routine from Default.aspx. The biggest difference is that if an error is detected it redirects to Default.aspx and displays an appropriate error message.

- `Page_Load`: This routine first checks to ensure that a valid template virtual machine name has been provided. It then connects to Virtual Server and iterates over the virtual machines until it finds one with a matching template name. Once it has the virtual machine object, it checks to see if the user is allowed to configure the memory and network settings for the new virtual machine. Depending on what it finds, it either enables or disables the appropriate controls and pre-populates them with data.

  Calling GetConfigurationValue to retrieve a value that is not present in the virtual machine configuration file throws an exception. Unfortunately, there is no safe way to determine whether a key is present or not, so you just need to be prepared to handle the exception.

- `CancelButton_Click`: This is a simple routine that just reloads Default.aspx.

Part VIII: Developing Software for Virtual Server

❑ `CreateVMButton_Click`: This routine is rather large because CoSetProxyBlanket cannot be used on subobjects of a COM object. This means that every COM object needs to be stored in its own variable. The first section of this routine declares all the necessary variables, creates the new virtual machine, and creates and secures all of the appropriate COM objects. After this is done, it is a fairly straightforward operation to copy the settings from the source virtual machine to the new virtual machine. Differencing virtual hard disks are created against the source virtual machines virtual hard disks and attached to the new virtual machine.

Not everyone uses differencing virtual hard disks for this kind of solution. Doing a full copy of the virtual hard disk can provide high performance for the virtual machine but makes the process of creating a new virtual machine from a template much longer.

Remember that CreateNewVM.aspx is responsible for creating a new virtual machine, given a template virtual machine and some input from the user (on memory configuration, network configuration, and virtual machine name).

Here is the code in Visual Basic .NET:

```vbnet
Imports Microsoft.VirtualServer.Interop

Partial Class createNewVM
    Inherits System.Web.UI.Page
    'Using a global variable for the main Virtual Server connection
    'without this you would have to reconnect for each call
    Public VSConnection As VMVirtualServer
    Public LocalSecurity As SetSecurityImpersonationLevel
    Public sourceVM As VMVirtualMachine

    Const vmFloppyDrive_None = 0
    Const vmFloppyDrive_Image = 1
    Const vmFloppyDrive_HostDrive = 2
    Const vmDVDDrive_None = 0
    Const vmDVDDrive_Image = 1
    Const vmDVDDrive_HostDrive = 2

    Public Sub Connect()

        'SetProxyBlanket
        LocalSecurity = New SetSecurityImpersonationLevel

        Try

            'This connects to the local server
            VSConnection = New VMVirtualServer
            LocalSecurity.Secure(VSConnection)

        Catch ex As Exception
            'Return to the main page if not able to connect to Virtual Server
            Response.Redirect("Default.aspx?error=ERROR: Failed to connect to ↵
Virtual Server.", True)
            Exit Sub
```

508

Chapter 20: Developing ASP.NET Applications with Virtual Server

```vbnet
        End Try

    End Sub

    Protected Sub Page_Load(ByVal sender As Object, ByVal e As System.EventArgs)
) Handles Me.Load
        'Get the vmName parameter
        Dim vmName As String = Request.QueryString.Item("vm")

        Dim VMs As IVMVirtualMachineCollection
        Dim VNs As IVMVirtualNetworkCollection
        Dim aVM As VMVirtualMachine
        Dim aVN As VMVirtualNetwork
        Dim counter As Integer

        'Check that a valid VM name was provided
        If vmName Is Nothing Then
            Response.Redirect("Default.aspx?error=ERROR: Need to specify
virtual machine.", True)
        End If

        'Connect to Virtual Server
        Connect()

        'Try to find the VM given the VM template name
        Try
            'Create VM collection object
            VMs = VSConnection.VirtualMachines
            localSecurity.Secure(VMs)

            'Create virtual network collection object
            VNs = VSConnection.VirtualNetworks
            localSecurity.Secure(VNs)

            'Iterate the VMs looking for the VM with the given template name
            For counter = 1 To VMs.Count
                aVM = VMs.Item(counter)
                localSecurity.Secure(aVM)
                Try
                    If aVM.GetConfigurationValue("Template_Key/Template_Name")
= vmName Then

                        sourceVM = aVM
                    End If
                Catch
                    'The VM did not have this key at all
                End Try
            Next

            'Display or hide the memory controls depending on the configuration
            If sourceVM.GetConfigurationValue("Template_Key/Fixed_Memory") Then
                MemoryLabel.Visible = False
                MemoryTextBox.Visible = False
            End If
            MemoryTextBox.Text = sourceVM.Memory

            'Display or hide the network controls depending on the configuration
```

509

Part VIII: Developing Software for Virtual Server

```vb
            If sourceVM.GetConfigurationValue("Template_Key/Fixed_Network") Then
                NetworkingLabel.Visible = False
                NetworkDropDownList.Visible = False
            Else
                'Iterate over virtual networks and populate NetworkDropDownList1
                For counter = 1 To VNs.Count
                    aVN = VNs.Item(counter)
                    localSecurity.Secure(aVN)
                    NetworkDropDownList.Items.Add(aVN.Name)
                Next
            End If
        Catch
            Response.Redirect("Default.aspx?error=ERROR: An error occurred ↩
while trying to find template.", True)
        End Try

    End Sub

    Protected Sub CancelButton_Click(ByVal sender As Object, ByVal e As ↩
System.EventArgs) Handles CancelButton.Click
        'Return to main page
        Response.Redirect("Default.aspx", True)
    End Sub

    Protected Sub CreateVMButton_Click(ByVal sender As Object, ByVal e As ↩
System.EventArgs) Handles CreateVMButton.Click
        'Declare a whole bunch of variables that will be needed to clone template
        Dim cloneVM As VMVirtualMachine
        Dim sourceVNics, cloneVNics As IVMNetworkAdapterCollection
        Dim sourceAccountant, cloneAccountant As VMAccountant
        Dim sourceParallelPortCollection, cloneParallelPortCollection As ↩
IVMParallelPortCollection
        Dim sourceParallelPort, cloneParallelPort As VMParallelPort
        Dim sourceSerialPorts, cloneSerialPorts As IVMSerialPortCollection
        Dim sourceSerialPort1, sourceSerialPort2, cloneSerialPort1, ↩
cloneSerialPort2 As VMSerialPort
        Dim sourceFloppyDrives, cloneFloppyDrives As IVMFloppyDriveCollection
        Dim sourceFloppyDrive, cloneFloppyDrive As VMFloppyDrive
        Dim sourceDVDs, cloneDVDs As IVMDVDDriveCollection
        Dim sourceSCSIControllers, cloneSCSIControllers As ↩
IVMSCSIControllerCollection
        Dim aVN As VMVirtualNetwork
        Dim sourceDVDROM, cloneDVDROM As VMDVDDrive
        Dim sourceNetworkAdapter, cloneNetworkAdapter As VMNetworkAdapter
        Dim sourceSCSIController, cloneSCSIController As VMSCSIController
        Dim aVMTask As VMTask
        Dim sourceVHD As VMHardDisk
        Dim sourceVHDConnection, cloneVHDConnection As VMHardDiskConnection
        Dim newVHDName, cloneVMName As String
        Dim userName As String = HttpContext.Current.User.Identity.Name
        Dim userVMName As String = VMNameTextBox.Text
        Dim vmMemory As String = MemoryTextBox.Text
        Dim vmNetwork As String = Nothing

        If NetworkDropDownList.SelectedIndex >= 0 Then
```

Chapter 20: Developing ASP.NET Applications with Virtual Server

```
                vmNetwork = NetworkDropDownList.SelectedItem.Text
        End If

        'Create Clone VM name (combination of template name and new VM name)
        cloneVMName = Left(sourceVM.File, InStrRev(sourceVM.File, "\") - 1) & _
" - " & userVMName
        Try
            'Create new virtual machine
            cloneVM = VSConnection.CreateVirtualMachine(userVMName, cloneVMName)
            localSecurity.Secure(cloneVM)
        Catch
            'Return to main page with error message
            Response.Redirect("Default.aspx?error=ERROR: An error occurred _
while creating the new VM, most likely this is because the VM name is already _
in use.", True)
        End Try

        Try
            'Setup Clone COM objects
            cloneVNics = cloneVM.NetworkAdapters
            cloneAccountant = cloneVM.Accountant
            cloneParallelPortCollection = cloneVM.ParallelPorts
            cloneSerialPorts = cloneVM.SerialPorts
            cloneFloppyDrives = cloneVM.FloppyDrives
            cloneDVDs = cloneVM.DVDROMDrives
            cloneSCSIControllers = cloneVM.SCSIControllers

            'Secure new clone objects
            LocalSecurity.Secure(cloneVNics)
            LocalSecurity.Secure(cloneAccountant)
            LocalSecurity.Secure(cloneParallelPortCollection)
            LocalSecurity.Secure(cloneSerialPorts)
            LocalSecurity.Secure(cloneFloppyDrives)
            LocalSecurity.Secure(cloneDVDs)
            LocalSecurity.Secure(cloneSCSIControllers)

            'Setup secondary COM objects
            cloneParallelPort = cloneParallelPortCollection.Item(1)
            cloneSerialPort1 = cloneSerialPorts.Item(1)
            cloneSerialPort2 = cloneSerialPorts.Item(2)
            cloneFloppyDrive = cloneFloppyDrives.Item(1)

            'Secure secondary COM objects
            LocalSecurity.Secure(cloneParallelPort)
            LocalSecurity.Secure(cloneSerialPort1)
            LocalSecurity.Secure(cloneSerialPort2)
            LocalSecurity.Secure(cloneFloppyDrive)

            'Setup source COM objects
            sourceVNics = sourceVM.NetworkAdapters
            sourceAccountant = sourceVM.Accountant
            sourceParallelPortCollection = sourceVM.ParallelPorts
            sourceSerialPorts = sourceVM.SerialPorts
            sourceFloppyDrives = sourceVM.FloppyDrives
            sourceDVDs = sourceVM.DVDROMDrives
```

511

Part VIII: Developing Software for Virtual Server

```
        sourceSCSIControllers = sourceVM.SCSIControllers

        'Secure new source objects
        LocalSecurity.Secure(sourceVNics)
        LocalSecurity.Secure(sourceAccountant)
        LocalSecurity.Secure(sourceParallelPortCollection)
        LocalSecurity.Secure(sourceSerialPorts)
        LocalSecurity.Secure(sourceFloppyDrives)
        LocalSecurity.Secure(sourceDVDs)
        LocalSecurity.Secure(sourceSCSIControllers)

        'Setup secondary COM objects
        sourceParallelPort = sourceParallelPortCollection.Item(1)
        sourceSerialPort1 = sourceSerialPorts.Item(1)
        sourceSerialPort2 = sourceSerialPorts.Item(2)
        sourceFloppyDrive = sourceFloppyDrives.Item(1)

        'Secure secondary COM objects
        LocalSecurity.Secure(sourceParallelPort)
        LocalSecurity.Secure(sourceSerialPort1)
        LocalSecurity.Secure(sourceSerialPort2)
        LocalSecurity.Secure(sourceFloppyDrive)

        'Remove the network adapter that is created by default
        cloneNetworkAdapter = cloneVNics.Item(1)
        LocalSecurity.Secure(cloneNetworkAdapter)
        cloneVM.RemoveNetworkAdapter(cloneNetworkAdapter)

        'Clone basic settings (the VM needs to have been turned on once)
        cloneVM.BIOSGUID = sourceVM.BIOSGUID
        cloneVM.Notes = sourceVM.Notes
        cloneVM.ShutdownActionOnQuit = sourceVM.ShutdownActionOnQuit
        cloneVM.Undoable = sourceVM.Undoable
        cloneVM.UndoAction = sourceVM.UndoAction
        cloneVM.Memory = CInt(vmMemory)

        'These settings may be null if the template has never been started
        Try
            cloneVM.BIOSSerialNumber = sourceVM.BIOSSerialNumber
            cloneVM.BaseBoardSerialNumber = sourceVM.BaseBoardSerialNumber
            cloneVM.ChassisAssetTag = sourceVM.ChassisAssetTag
            cloneVM.ChassisSerialNumber = sourceVM.ChassisSerialNumber
        Catch ex As Exception
            'Null setting
        End Try

        'Clone Accountant settings
        cloneAccountant.SetSchedulingParameters(sourceAccountant ⤸
    .reservedSystemCapacity, _
            sourceAccountant.MaximumSystemCapacity, sourceAccountant.relativeWeight)

        'Clone parallel port settings
        cloneParallelPort.Name = sourceParallelPort.Name

        'Clone serial port settings
        cloneSerialPort1.Configure(sourceSerialPort1.Type, ⤸
```

Chapter 20: Developing ASP.NET Applications with Virtual Server

```
sourceSerialPort1.Name, sourceSerialPort1.connectImmediately)
            cloneSerialPort2.Configure(sourceSerialPort2.Type, ↵
sourceSerialPort2.Name, sourceSerialPort2.connectImmediately)

            'Clone floppy disk settings
            Select Case sourceFloppyDrive.Attachment
                Case vmFloppyDrive_Image
                    cloneFloppyDrive.AttachImage(sourceFloppyDrive.ImageFile)
                Case vmFloppyDrive_HostDrive
                    cloneFloppyDrive.AttachHostDrive(sourceFloppyDrive.HostDriveLetter)
            End Select

            'Clone DVD drive settings
            For Each sourceDVDROM In sourceDVDs
                LocalSecurity.Secure(sourceDVDROM)
                cloneDVDROM = cloneVM.AddDVDROMDrive(sourceDVDROM.busType, ↵
sourceDVDROM.busNumber, sourceDVDROM.deviceNumber)
                LocalSecurity.Secure(cloneDVDROM)
                Select Case sourceDVDROM.Attachment
                    Case vmDVDDrive_Image
                        cloneDVDROM.AttachImage(sourceDVDROM.ImageFile)
                    Case vmDVDDrive_HostDrive
                        cloneDVDROM.AttachHostDrive(sourceDVDROM.HostDriveLetter)
                End Select
            Next

            'Clone network adapter settings
            For Each sourceNetworkAdapter In sourceVNics
                LocalSecurity.Secure(sourceNetworkAdapter)

                cloneNetworkAdapter = cloneVM.AddNetworkAdapter()
                LocalSecurity.Secure(cloneNetworkAdapter)

                'Use the specified virtual network, otherwise use the source
                'virtual network
                If NetworkDropDownList.SelectedIndex >= 0 Then
                    aVN = VSConnection.FindVirtualNetwork(vmNetwork)
                Else
                    aVN = sourceNetworkAdapter.virtualNetwork
                End If

                LocalSecurity.Secure(aVN)

                'This can fail with an error if the source network adapter is
                'disconnected.
                Try
                    cloneNetworkAdapter.AttachToVirtualNetwork(aVN)
                Catch
                    'Disconnected network adapter
                End Try

                'Copy the MAC address if it is static.
                If Not sourceNetworkAdapter.IsEthernetAddressDynamic Then
                    cloneNetworkAdapter.IsEthernetAddressDynamic = False
                    cloneNetworkAdapter.EthernetAddress = ↵
sourceNetworkAdapter.EthernetAddress
```

Part VIII: Developing Software for Virtual Server

```vb
                    End If
            Next

            'Clone the SCSI controllers
            For Each sourceSCSIController In sourceSCSIControllers
                LocalSecurity.Secure(sourceSCSIController)
                cloneSCSIController = cloneVM.AddSCSIController()
                LocalSecurity.Secure(cloneSCSIController)
                cloneSCSIController.Configure(sourceSCSIController.isBusShared, ⤸
sourceSCSIController.SCSIID)
            Next

            'Clone the hard disks
            For Each sourceVHDConnection In sourceVM.HardDiskConnections
                LocalSecurity.Secure(sourceVHDConnection)

                sourceVHD = sourceVHDConnection.HardDisk
                LocalSecurity.Secure(sourceVHD)

                'Construct name for new differencing disk
                newVHDName = Left(sourceVHD.File, InStrRev(sourceVHD.File, "\") ⤸
- 1) & " - " & userVMName & "\"
                newVHDName = newVHDName & Right(sourceVHD.File, ⤸
 (Len(sourceVHD.File) - InStrRev(sourceVHD.File, "\")))
                newVHDName = Left(newVHDName, InStrRev(newVHDName, ".") - 1) ⤸
& userVMName & " - diff.vhd"

                'Create and attach new differencing disk
                aVMTask = ⤸
VSConnection.CreateDifferencingVirtualHardDisk(newVHDName, sourceVHD.File)
                LocalSecurity.Secure(aVMTask)
                aVMTask.WaitForCompletion(-1)
                cloneVHDConnection = cloneVM.AddHardDiskConnection(newVHDName, ⤸
sourceVHDConnection.busType, sourceVHDConnection.busNumber, ⤸
sourceVHDConnection.deviceNumber)
            Next

            'Add template keys
            cloneVM.SetConfigurationValue("Template_Key/UserName", userName)
            cloneVM.SetConfigurationValue("Template_Key/Fixed_Memory", ⤸
sourceVM.GetConfigurationValue("Template_Key/Fixed_Memory"))
            cloneVM.SetConfigurationValue("Template_Key/Fixed_Network", ⤸
sourceVM.GetConfigurationValue("Template_Key/Fixed_Network"))

        Catch
            'Return to main page with error message
            Response.Redirect("Default.aspx?error=ERROR: An error occurred ⤸
while creating the new VM.", True)
        End Try

        'Return to the main page without an error
        Response.Redirect("Default.aspx", True)
    End Sub
End Class
```

514

Chapter 20: Developing ASP.NET Applications with Virtual Server

Here is the code in C#:

```csharp
using System;
using System.Data;
using System.Configuration;
using System.Collections;
using System.Web;
using System.Web.Security;
using System.Web.UI;
using System.Web.UI.WebControls;
using System.Web.UI.WebControls.WebParts;
using System.Web.UI.HtmlControls;
using Microsoft.VirtualServer.Interop;

public partial class CreateNewVM : System.Web.UI.Page
{
    public VMVirtualServer VSConnection = null;
    public Personal.SetSecurity.ProxyBlanket LocalSecurity;
    public VMVirtualMachine sourceVM;

    private void Connect()
    {
        //CoSetProxyBlanket
        LocalSecurity = new Personal.SetSecurity.ProxyBlanket();

        try
        {
            //This connects to the local server
            VSConnection = new VMVirtualServer();

            //Secure the VS Connection object.
            LocalSecurity.Set(VSConnection);
        }
        catch
        {
            //Return to the main page if not able to connect to Virtual Server
            Response.Redirect("Default.aspx?error=ERROR: Failed to connect to ⤶
Virtual Server.", true);
        }
    }

    protected void Page_Load(object sender, EventArgs e)
    {
        // Get the vmName parameter
        String vmName = Request.QueryString["vm"];

        VMVirtualMachine aVM;
        VMVirtualNetwork aVN;

        // Check that a valid VM name was provided
        if (vmName == null)
        {
            Response.Redirect("Default.aspx?error=ERROR: Need to specify ⤶
virtual machine.", true);
```

515

Part VIII: Developing Software for Virtual Server

```csharp
        }

        // Connect to Virtual Server
        Connect();

        // Try to find the VM given the VM template name
        try
        {
            // Create VM collection object
            IVMVirtualMachineCollection VMs = VSConnection.VirtualMachines;
            LocalSecurity.Set(VMs);

            // Create virtual network collection object
            IVMVirtualNetworkCollection VNs = VSConnection.VirtualNetworks;
            LocalSecurity.Set(VNs);

            // Iterate the VMs looking for the VM with the given template name
            for (int counter = 1; counter <= VMs.Count; counter++)
            {
                aVM = VMs[counter];
                LocalSecurity.Set(aVM);
                try
                {
                    if ⊃
(aVM.GetConfigurationValue("Template_Key/Template_Name").ToString() == vmName)
                    {
                        sourceVM = aVM;
                    }
                }
                catch
                {
                    // The VM did not have this key at all
                }
            }

            // Display or hide the memory controls depending on the template
            // configuration
            if ⊃
(sourceVM.GetConfigurationValue("Template_Key/Fixed_Memory").ToString() == "True")
            {
                MemoryLabel.Visible = false;
                MemoryTextBox.Visible = false;
            }
            MemoryTextBox.Text = sourceVM.Memory.ToString();

            // Display or hide the network controls depending on the template
            // configuration
            if ⊃
(sourceVM.GetConfigurationValue("Template_Key/Fixed_Network").ToString() == "True")
            {
                NetworkingLabel.Visible = false;
                NetworkDropDownList.Visible = false;
            }
            else
            {
```

Chapter 20: Developing ASP.NET Applications with Virtual Server

```csharp
                // Iterate over virtual networks and populate NetworkDropDownList1
                for (int counter = 1; counter <= VNs.Count; counter++)
                {
                    aVN = VNs[counter];
                    LocalSecurity.Set(aVN);
                    NetworkDropDownList.Items.Add(aVN.Name);
                }
            }
        }
        catch
        {
            Response.Redirect("Default.aspx?error=ERROR: An error occurred ⟳
while trying to find template.", true);
        }
    }
    protected void CreateVMButton_Click(object sender, EventArgs e)
    {
        String userName = HttpContext.Current.User.Identity.Name;
        String userVMName = VMNameTextBox.Text;
        String vmMemory = MemoryTextBox.Text;
        String vmNetwork = null;
        VMVirtualMachine cloneVM;
        VMVirtualNetwork aVN;

        if (NetworkDropDownList.SelectedIndex >= 0)
        {
            vmNetwork = NetworkDropDownList.SelectedItem.Text;
        }

        //Create Clone VM name (combination of template name and new VM name)
        string cloneVMName = sourceVM.File.Substring(0, ⟳
sourceVM.File.LastIndexOf("\\")) + " - " + userVMName;
        try
        {
            //Create new virtual machine
            cloneVM = VSConnection.CreateVirtualMachine(userVMName, cloneVMName);
            LocalSecurity.Set(cloneVM);
        }
        catch
        {
            //Return to main page with error message
            Response.Redirect("Default.aspx?error=ERROR: An error occurred ⟳
while creating the new VM, most likely this is because the VM name is already ⟳
in use.", true);
            return;
        }

        try
        {
            //Setup Clone COM objects
            IVMNetworkAdapterCollection cloneVNics = cloneVM.NetworkAdapters;
            VMAccountant cloneAccountant = cloneVM.Accountant;
            IVMParallelPortCollection cloneParallelPortCollection = ⟳
cloneVM.ParallelPorts;
            IVMSerialPortCollection cloneSerialPorts = cloneVM.SerialPorts;
```

517

Part VIII: Developing Software for Virtual Server

```
            IVMFloppyDriveCollection cloneFloppyDrives = cloneVM.FloppyDrives;
            IVMDVDDriveCollection cloneDVDs = cloneVM.DVDROMDrives;
            IVMSCSIControllerCollection cloneSCSIControllers = ⊃
    cloneVM.SCSIControllers;

            //Secure new clone objects
            LocalSecurity.Set(cloneVNics);
            LocalSecurity.Set(cloneAccountant);
            LocalSecurity.Set(cloneParallelPortCollection);
            LocalSecurity.Set(cloneSerialPorts);
            LocalSecurity.Set(cloneFloppyDrives);
            LocalSecurity.Set(cloneDVDs);
            LocalSecurity.Set(cloneSCSIControllers);

            //Setup secondary COM objects
            VMParallelPort cloneParallelPort = cloneParallelPortCollection[1];
            VMSerialPort cloneSerialPort1 = cloneSerialPorts[1];
            VMSerialPort cloneSerialPort2 = cloneSerialPorts[2];
            VMFloppyDrive cloneFloppyDrive = cloneFloppyDrives[1];

            //Secure secondary COM objects
            LocalSecurity.Set(cloneParallelPort);
            LocalSecurity.Set(cloneSerialPort1);
            LocalSecurity.Set(cloneSerialPort2);
            LocalSecurity.Set(cloneFloppyDrive);

            //Setup source COM objects
            IVMNetworkAdapterCollection sourceVNics = sourceVM.NetworkAdapters;
            VMAccountant sourceAccountant = sourceVM.Accountant;
            IVMParallelPortCollection sourceParallelPortCollection = ⊃
    sourceVM.ParallelPorts;
            IVMSerialPortCollection sourceSerialPorts = sourceVM.SerialPorts;
            IVMFloppyDriveCollection sourceFloppyDrives = sourceVM.FloppyDrives;
            IVMDVDDriveCollection sourceDVDs = sourceVM.DVDROMDrives;
            IVMSCSIControllerCollection sourceSCSIControllers = ⊃
    sourceVM.SCSIControllers;

            //Secure new source objects
            LocalSecurity.Set(sourceVNics);
            LocalSecurity.Set(sourceAccountant);
            LocalSecurity.Set(sourceParallelPortCollection);
            LocalSecurity.Set(sourceSerialPorts);
            LocalSecurity.Set(sourceFloppyDrives);
            LocalSecurity.Set(sourceDVDs);
            LocalSecurity.Set(sourceSCSIControllers);

            //Setup secondary COM objects
            VMParallelPort sourceParallelPort = sourceParallelPortCollection[1];
            VMSerialPort sourceSerialPort1 = sourceSerialPorts[1];
            VMSerialPort sourceSerialPort2 = sourceSerialPorts[2];
            VMFloppyDrive sourceFloppyDrive = sourceFloppyDrives[1];

            //Secure secondary COM objects
            LocalSecurity.Set(sourceParallelPort);
            LocalSecurity.Set(sourceSerialPort1);
            LocalSecurity.Set(sourceSerialPort2);
```

Chapter 20: Developing ASP.NET Applications with Virtual Server

```
        LocalSecurity.Set(sourceFloppyDrive);

        //Remove the network adapter that is created by default
        VMNetworkAdapter cloneNetworkAdapter = cloneVNics[1];
        LocalSecurity.Set(cloneNetworkAdapter);
        cloneVM.RemoveNetworkAdapter(cloneNetworkAdapter);

        //Clone basic settings (the VM needs to have been turned on once)
        cloneVM.BIOSGUID = sourceVM.BIOSGUID;
        cloneVM.Notes = sourceVM.Notes;
        cloneVM.ShutdownActionOnQuit = sourceVM.ShutdownActionOnQuit;
        cloneVM.Undoable = sourceVM.Undoable;
        cloneVM.UndoAction = sourceVM.UndoAction;
        cloneVM.Memory = Convert.ToInt32(vmMemory);

        //These settings may be null if the template has never been started
        try
        {
            cloneVM.BIOSSerialNumber = sourceVM.BIOSSerialNumber;
            cloneVM.BaseBoardSerialNumber = sourceVM.BaseBoardSerialNumber;
            cloneVM.ChassisAssetTag = sourceVM.ChassisAssetTag;
            cloneVM.ChassisSerialNumber = sourceVM.ChassisSerialNumber;
        }
        catch
        {
            //Null setting
        }

        //Clone Accountant settings

cloneAccountant.SetSchedulingParameters(sourceAccountant.reservedSystem⊃
Capacity, sourceAccountant.MaximumSystemCapacity, sourceAccountant.relativeWeight);

        //Clone parallel port settings
        cloneParallelPort.Name = sourceParallelPort.Name;

        //Clone serial port settings
        cloneSerialPort1.Configure(sourceSerialPort1.Type, ⊃
sourceSerialPort1.Name, sourceSerialPort1.connectImmediately);
        cloneSerialPort2.Configure(sourceSerialPort2.Type, ⊃
sourceSerialPort2.Name, sourceSerialPort2.connectImmediately);

        //Clone floppy disk settings
        switch (sourceFloppyDrive.Attachment)
        {
            case VMFloppyDriveAttachmentType.vmFloppyDrive_Image:
                cloneFloppyDrive.AttachImage(sourceFloppyDrive.ImageFile);
                break;

            case VMFloppyDriveAttachmentType.vmFloppyDrive_HostDrive:
              cloneFloppyDrive.AttachHostDrive(sourceFloppyDrive.HostDriveLetter);
                break;
        }

        //Clone DVD drive settings
```

Part VIII: Developing Software for Virtual Server

```
            foreach (VMDVDDrive sourceDVDROM in sourceDVDs)
            {
                LocalSecurity.Set(sourceDVDROM);
                VMDVDDrive cloneDVDROM = ⤸
cloneVM.AddDVDROMDrive(sourceDVDROM.busType, sourceDVDROM.busNumber, ⤸
sourceDVDROM.deviceNumber);
                LocalSecurity.Set(cloneDVDROM);
                switch (sourceDVDROM.Attachment)
                {
                    case VMDVDDriveAttachmentType.vmDVDDrive_Image:
                        cloneDVDROM.AttachImage(sourceDVDROM.ImageFile);
                        break;

                    case VMDVDDriveAttachmentType.vmDVDDrive_HostDrive:
                        cloneDVDROM.AttachHostDrive(sourceDVDROM.HostDriveLetter);
                        break;

                }
            }

            //Clone network adapter settings
            foreach (VMNetworkAdapter sourceNetworkAdapter in sourceVNics)
            {
                LocalSecurity.Set(sourceNetworkAdapter);

                cloneNetworkAdapter = cloneVM.AddNetworkAdapter();
                LocalSecurity.Set(cloneNetworkAdapter);

                //Use the specified virtual network, otherwise use the source
                //virtual network
                if (NetworkDropDownList.SelectedIndex >= 0)
                {
                    aVN = VSConnection.FindVirtualNetwork(vmNetwork);
                }
                else
                {
                    aVN = sourceNetworkAdapter.virtualNetwork;
                }

                LocalSecurity.Set(aVN);

                //This can fail with an error if the source network adapter is
                //disconnected.
                try
                {
                    cloneNetworkAdapter.AttachToVirtualNetwork(aVN);
                }
                catch
                {
                    //Disconnected network adapter
                }

                //Copy the MAC address if it is static.
                if (sourceNetworkAdapter.IsEthernetAddressDynamic == false)
                {
```

Chapter 20: Developing ASP.NET Applications with Virtual Server

```csharp
                        cloneNetworkAdapter.IsEthernetAddressDynamic = false;
                        cloneNetworkAdapter.EthernetAddress =
sourceNetworkAdapter.EthernetAddress;
                    }
                }

            //Clone the SCSI controllers
            foreach (VMSCSIController sourceSCSIController in
sourceSCSIControllers)
                {
                    LocalSecurity.Set(sourceSCSIController);
                    VMSCSIController cloneSCSIController = cloneVM.AddSCSIController();
                    LocalSecurity.Set(cloneSCSIController);
                    cloneSCSIController.Configure(sourceSCSIController.isBusShared,
sourceSCSIController.SCSIID);
                }

            //Clone the hard disks
            foreach (VMHardDiskConnection sourceVHDConnection in
sourceVM.HardDiskConnections)
                {
                    LocalSecurity.Set(sourceVHDConnection);

                    VMHardDisk sourceVHD = sourceVHDConnection.HardDisk;
                    LocalSecurity.Set(sourceVHD);

                    //Construct name for new differencing disk
                    string newVHDName = sourceVHD.File.Substring(0,
sourceVHD.File.LastIndexOf("\\")) + " - " + userVMName + "\\";
                    newVHDName = newVHDName +
sourceVHD.File.Substring(sourceVHD.File.LastIndexOf("\\") + 1,
sourceVHD.File.Length - sourceVHD.File.LastIndexOf("\\") - 1);
                    newVHDName = newVHDName.Substring(0, newVHDName.LastIndexOf("."));
                    newVHDName = newVHDName + " - " + userVMName + " - diff.vhd";

                    //Create and attach new differencing disk
                    VMTask aVMTask =
VSConnection.CreateDifferencingVirtualHardDisk(newVHDName, sourceVHD.File);
                    LocalSecurity.Set(aVMTask);
                    aVMTask.WaitForCompletion(-1);
                    VMHardDiskConnection cloneVHDConnection =
cloneVM.AddHardDiskConnection(newVHDName, sourceVHDConnection.busType,
sourceVHDConnection.busNumber, sourceVHDConnection.deviceNumber);
                }

            //Add template keys
            cloneVM.SetConfigurationValue("Template_Key/UserName", userName);
            cloneVM.SetConfigurationValue("Template_Key/Fixed_Memory",
sourceVM.GetConfigurationValue("Template_Key/Fixed_Memory"));
            cloneVM.SetConfigurationValue("Template_Key/Fixed_Network",
sourceVM.GetConfigurationValue("Template_Key/Fixed_Network"));
        }
        catch
        {
            //Return to main page with error message
```

521

Part VIII: Developing Software for Virtual Server

```
            Response.Redirect("Default.aspx?error=ERROR: An error occurred ⤵
while creating the new VM.", true);
        }

        //Return to the main page without an error
        Response.Redirect("Default.aspx", true);
    }
    protected void CancelButton_Click(object sender, EventArgs e)
    {
        //Return to main page
        Response.Redirect("Default.aspx", true);
    }
}
```

ChangeState.aspx

Follow these steps to create ChangeState.aspx:

1. In Visual Studio, open the **Website** menu.

2. Select **Add New Item**.

3. Choose **Web Form** and specify a name of **ChangeState.aspx**.

4. Ensure that the right **Language** is selected and that the **Place** code in separate file option is checked.

5. Click **Add**.

6. Open the designer view for ChangeState.aspx.

7. Drag a **Label** onto the page, and then change the label **ID** to **HeaderLabel**.

8. Change the label **Text** to **The virtual machine "" is currently ""**.

9. Drag another **Label** onto the page and set its **Text** to **Select an action to perform:**.

10. Drag a **DropDownList** onto the page, and then change the DropDownList **ID** to **ActionDropDownList**.

11. Drag two **Buttons** onto the page.

12. Change the first button's **Text** to **Go**, and change the second button's **Text** to **Cancel**.

13. Set the first button's **ID** to **GoButton**, and set the second button's **ID** to **CancelButton**.

This should generate the following ASPX code, as displayed in Visual Basic .NET:

```
<%@ Page Language="VB" AutoEventWireup="false" CodeFile="changeState.aspx.vb" ⤵
Inherits="changeState" %>

<!DOCTYPE html PUBLIC "-//W3C//DTD XHTML 1.0 Transitional//EN" ⤵
"http://www.w3.org/TR/xhtml1/DTD/xhtml1-transitional.dtd">

<html xmlns="http://www.w3.org/1999/xhtml" >
<head runat="server">
```

522

Chapter 20: Developing ASP.NET Applications with Virtual Server

```
    <title>Untitled Page</title>
</head>
<body>
    <form id="form1" runat="server">
    <div>
        <asp:Label ID="HeaderLabel" runat="server" Text='The virtual machine ⤶
"" is currently "".'></asp:Label>
          
        <br />
        <asp:Label ID="Label1" runat="server" Text="Select an action to ⤶
perform:"></asp:Label><br />
        <asp:DropDownList ID="ActionDropDownList" runat="server" Width="177px">
        </asp:DropDownList>
        <asp:Button ID="GoButton" runat="server" Text="Go" />
        <asp:Button ID="CancelButton" runat="server" Text="Cancel" /></div>
    </form>
</body>
</html>
```

Here's the code in C#:

```
<%@ Page Language="C#" AutoEventWireup="true" CodeFile="ChangeState.aspx.cs" ⤶
Inherits="ChangeState" %>

<!DOCTYPE html PUBLIC "-//W3C//DTD XHTML 1.0 Transitional//EN" ⤶
"http://www.w3.org/TR/xhtml1/DTD/xhtml1-transitional.dtd">

<html xmlns="http://www.w3.org/1999/xhtml" >
<head runat="server">
    <title>Untitled Page</title>
</head>
<body>
    <form id="form1" runat="server">
    <div>
        <asp:Label ID="HeaderLabel" runat="server" Text='The virtual machine ⤶
"" is currently ""'></asp:Label><br />
        <asp:Label ID="Label1" runat="server" Text="Select an action to ⤶
perform:"></asp:Label><br />
        <asp:DropDownList ID="ActionDropDownList" runat="server" Width="206px">
        </asp:DropDownList>
        <asp:Button ID="GoButton" runat="server" OnClick="GoButton_Click" ⤶
Text="Go" />
        <asp:Button ID="CancelButton" runat="server" ⤶
OnClick="CancelButton_Click" Text="Cancel" /><br />

    </div>
    </form>
</body>
</html>
```

The preceding code should result in a screen that looks like Figure 20-5.

Part VIII: Developing Software for Virtual Server

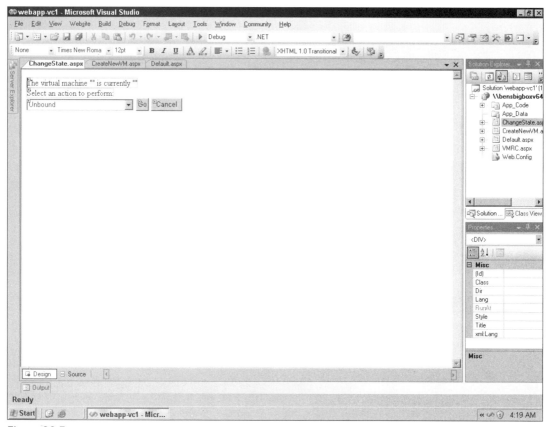

Figure 20-5

The ChangeState.aspx page will need to have code associated with it that consists of the following routines:

- `Connect`: This is the same as the connect routine from CreateNewVM.aspx.

- `Page_Load`: This routine first checks to ensure that a valid virtual machine name has been provided. It then connects to Virtual Server and to the virtual machine specified. It then examines the virtual machine state, updates the HeaderLabel text appropriately, and populates the ActionDropDownList with available actions.

- `GoButton_Click`: This routine performs the appropriate actions depending on what was selected in the ActionDropDownList, and then reloads Default.aspx.

In order to keep this as simple as possible this routine waits for any VMTask objects that are returned to complete on the main thread. To the end user, it will appear as though it takes a long time to load the default.aspx page for some operations. A more elegant solution would provide a way to continue using the web application while providing status updates on outstanding tasks.

- `CancelButton_Click`: This is a simple routine that just reloads Default.aspx.

Chapter 20: Developing ASP.NET Applications with Virtual Server

Remember that the purpose of ChangeState.aspx is to allow the user to start, stop, save state, pause, and resume a selected virtual machine.

Here is the code in Visual Basic .NET:

```vbnet
Imports Microsoft.VirtualServer.Interop

Partial Class changeState
    Inherits System.Web.UI.Page
    Private aVM As VMVirtualMachine
    Private GuestOS As VMGuestOS
    Public VSConnection As VMVirtualServer
    Public LocalSecurity As SetSecurityImpersonationLevel

    'Define constants
    Const vmVMState_Invalid = 0
    Const vmVMState_TurnedOff = 1
    Const vmVMState_Saved = 2
    Const vmVMState_TurningOn = 3
    Const vmVMState_Restoring = 4
    Const vmVMState_Running = 5
    Const vmVMState_Paused = 6
    Const vmVMState_Saving = 7
    Const vmVMState_TurningOff = 8
    Const vmVMState_MergingDrives = 9
    Const vmVMState_DeleteMachine = 10

    Public Sub Connect()

        'SetProxyBlanket
        LocalSecurity = New SetSecurityImpersonationLevel

        Try

            'This connects to the local server
            VSConnection = New VMVirtualServer
            LocalSecurity.Secure(VSConnection)

        Catch ex As Exception
            'Return to the main page if not able to connect to Virtual Server
            Response.Redirect("Default.aspx?error=ERROR: Failed to connect to ⮑
Virtual Server.", True)
            Exit Sub
        End Try

    End Sub

    Protected Sub Page_Load(ByVal sender As Object, ByVal e As ⮑
System.EventArgs) Handles Me.Load
        'Get the vmName parameter
        Dim vmName = Request.QueryString.Item("vm")

        'Check that a valid VM name was provided
        If vmName Is Nothing Then
```

525

Part VIII: Developing Software for Virtual Server

```vbnet
                Response.Redirect("Default.aspx?error=ERROR: Need to specify ↵
virtual machine.", True)
        End If

        'Connect to Virtual Server
        Connect()

        Try

            'Connect to virtual machine
            aVM = VSConnection.FindVirtualMachine(vmName)
            LocalSecurity.Secure(aVM)

            'Connect to GuestOS object
            GuestOS = aVM.GuestOS
            LocalSecurity.Secure(aVM)

            'Set the VM name label
            HeaderLabel.Text = "The virtual machine " & Chr(34) & aVM.Name & ↵
Chr(34) & " is currently " & Chr(34)

            'Switch on the VM state
            Select Case aVM.State
                Case vmVMState_Invalid
                    'There are no possible actions for this state
                    HeaderLabel.Text = HeaderLabel.Text & "invalid" & Chr(34) & "."
                    ActionDropDownList.Enabled = False
                    GoButton.Enabled = False
                Case vmVMState_TurnedOff
                    'There is only one option for a turned off virtual machine
                    HeaderLabel.Text = HeaderLabel.Text & "turned off" & ↵
Chr(34) & "."
                    ActionDropDownList.Items.Add("Start")
                Case vmVMState_Saved
                    'Set the options for a saved virtual machine
                    HeaderLabel.Text = HeaderLabel.Text & "saved" & Chr(34) & "."
                    ActionDropDownList.Items.Add("Start")
                    ActionDropDownList.Items.Add("Discard Saved State")
                Case vmVMState_TurningOn
                    'There are no possible actions for this state
                    HeaderLabel.Text = HeaderLabel.Text & "turning on" & ↵
Chr(34) & "."
                    ActionDropDownList.Enabled = False
                    GoButton.Enabled = False
                Case vmVMState_Restoring
                    'There are no possible actions for this state
                    HeaderLabel.Text = HeaderLabel.Text & "restoring" & ↵
Chr(34) & "."
                    ActionDropDownList.Enabled = False
                    GoButton.Enabled = False
                Case vmVMState_Running
                    HeaderLabel.Text = HeaderLabel.Text & "running" & Chr(34) & "."
                    'Check to see if undo disks need to be handled
                    If aVM.Undoable Then
```

Chapter 20: Developing ASP.NET Applications with Virtual Server

```
                              ActionDropDownList.Items.Add("Turn off & delete undo ⤶
disks")
                              ActionDropDownList.Items.Add("Turn off & keep undo disks")
                              ActionDropDownList.Items.Add("Turn off & commit undo ⤶
disks")
                              ActionDropDownList.Items.Add("Save State & keep undo ⤶
disks")
                              ActionDropDownList.Items.Add("Save State & commit undo ⤶
disks")
                              ActionDropDownList.Items.Add("Pause")
                              'Check to see if the GuestOS can be shut down
                              If GuestOS.CanShutdown Then
                                  ActionDropDownList.Items.Add("Shut down & keep ⤶
undo disks")
                                  ActionDropDownList.Items.Add("Shut down & commit ⤶
undo disks")
                              End If
                          Else
                              ActionDropDownList.Items.Add("Turn off")
                              ActionDropDownList.Items.Add("Save State")
                              ActionDropDownList.Items.Add("Pause")
                              'Check to see if the GuestOS can be shut down
                              If GuestOS.CanShutdown Then
                                  ActionDropDownList.Items.Add("Shut Down")
                              End If
                          End If
                      Case vmVMState_Paused
                          'There is only one option for a paused virtual machine
                          HeaderLabel.Text = HeaderLabel.Text & "paused" & Chr(34) & ⤶
"."
                          ActionDropDownList.Items.Add("Resume")
                      Case vmVMState_Saving
                          'There are no possible actions for this state
                          HeaderLabel.Text = HeaderLabel.Text & "saving state" & ⤶
Chr(34) & "."
                          ActionDropDownList.Enabled = False
                          GoButton.Enabled = False
                      Case vmVMState_TurningOff
                          'There are no possible actions for this state
                          HeaderLabel.Text = HeaderLabel.Text & "turning off" & ⤶
Chr(34) & "."
                          ActionDropDownList.Enabled = False
                          GoButton.Enabled = False
                      Case vmVMState_MergingDrives
                          'There are no possible actions for this state
                          HeaderLabel.Text = HeaderLabel.Text & "merging undo disks" ⤶
& Chr(34) & "."
                          ActionDropDownList.Enabled = False
                          GoButton.Enabled = False
                      Case vmVMState_DeleteMachine
                          'There are no possible actions for this state
                          HeaderLabel.Text = HeaderLabel.Text & "being deleted" & ⤶
Chr(34) & "."
                          ActionDropDownList.Enabled = False
                          GoButton.Enabled = False
```

Part VIII: Developing Software for Virtual Server

```vbnet
                End Select

        Catch
                Response.Redirect("Default.aspx?error=ERROR: An error occurred ⤸
trying to create page", True)
        End Try

    End Sub

    Protected Sub GoButton_Click(ByVal sender As Object, ByVal e As ⤸
System.EventArgs) Handles GoButton.Click

        Dim aVMTask As VMTask

        Try
            'Switch on the selection of the action drop down list
            Select Case ActionDropDownList.SelectedItem.Text

                Case "Resume"
                    'Resume is a simple case
                    aVM.Resume()

                Case "Turn off"
                    'Turn off returns a task to wait for
                    aVMTask = aVM.TurnOff
                    LocalSecurity.Secure(aVMTask)
                    aVMTask.WaitForCompletion(-1)

                Case "Save State"
                    'Save state returns a task to wait for
                    aVMTask = aVM.Save
                    LocalSecurity.Secure(aVMTask)
                    aVMTask.WaitForCompletion(-1)

                Case "Shut Down"
                    'Shut down is performed on the GuestOS - not the VM
                    aVMTask = GuestOS.Shutdown
                    LocalSecurity.Secure(aVMTask)
                    aVMTask.WaitForCompletion(-1)

                Case "Pause"
                    'Pause is also a simple case
                    aVM.Pause()

                Case "Start"
                    'Startup returns a task to wait for
                    aVMTask = aVM.Startup
                    LocalSecurity.Secure(aVMTask)
                    aVMTask.WaitForCompletion(-1)

                Case "Discard Saved State"
                    'Another simple case
                    aVM.DiscardSavedState()

                Case "Turn off & delete undo disks"
```

Chapter 20: Developing ASP.NET Applications with Virtual Server

```
                    'Perform turn off
                    aVMTask = aVM.TurnOff
                    LocalSecurity.Secure(aVMTask)
                    aVMTask.WaitForCompletion(-1)
                    'And then discard undo disks
                    aVM.DiscardUndoDisks()

            Case "Turn off & keep undo disks"
                    'No action is required to keep undo disks
                    aVMTask = aVM.TurnOff
                    LocalSecurity.Secure(aVMTask)
                    aVMTask.WaitForCompletion(-1)

            Case "Turn off & commit undo disks"
                    'Perform turn off
                    aVMTask = aVM.TurnOff
                    LocalSecurity.Secure(aVMTask)
                    aVMTask.WaitForCompletion(-1)

                    'Merge undo disks - returns a task (and can take a while)
                    aVMTask = aVM.MergeUndoDisks
                    LocalSecurity.Secure(aVMTask)
                    aVMTask.WaitForCompletion(-1)

            Case "Save State & keep undo disks"
                    'Same as just save state
                    aVMTask = aVM.Save
                    LocalSecurity.Secure(aVMTask)
                    aVMTask.WaitForCompletion(-1)

            Case "Save State & commit undo disks"
                    'Save state
                    aVMTask = aVM.Save
                    LocalSecurity.Secure(aVMTask)
                    aVMTask.WaitForCompletion(-1)

                    'And then merge undo disks
                    aVMTask = aVM.MergeUndoDisks
                    LocalSecurity.Secure(aVMTask)
                    aVMTask.WaitForCompletion(-1)

            Case "Shut down & keep undo disks"
                    'Same as just shut down
                    aVMTask = GuestOS.Shutdown
                    LocalSecurity.Secure(aVMTask)
                    aVMTask.WaitForCompletion(-1)

            Case "Shut down & commit undo disks"
                    'Shut down
                    aVMTask = GuestOS.Shutdown
                    LocalSecurity.Secure(aVMTask)
                    aVMTask.WaitForCompletion(-1)

                    'And then merge undo disks
                    aVMTask = aVM.MergeUndoDisks
                    LocalSecurity.Secure(aVMTask)
```

Part VIII: Developing Software for Virtual Server

```
                        aVMTask.WaitForCompletion(-1)

                End Select

            Catch
                'If there is an error, return to the main page with an error message
                Response.Redirect("Default.aspx?error=ERROR: Failed to change the ⤵
    virtual machine state.", True)
            End Try

                'Return to the main page when done
                Response.Redirect("Default.aspx")

        End Sub

        Protected Sub CancelButton_Click(ByVal sender As Object, ByVal e As ⤵
    System.EventArgs) Handles CancelButton.Click
                'Return to main page
                Response.Redirect("Default.aspx", True)
        End Sub
    End Class
```

Here is the code in C#:

```csharp
using System;
using System.Data;
using System.Configuration;
using System.Collections;
using System.Web;
using System.Web.Security;
using System.Web.UI;
using System.Web.UI.WebControls;
using System.Web.UI.WebControls.WebParts;
using System.Web.UI.HtmlControls;
using Microsoft.VirtualServer.Interop;


public partial class ChangeState : System.Web.UI.Page
{
    public VMVirtualServer VSConnection = null;
    public Personal.SetSecurity.ProxyBlanket LocalSecurity;
    public VMVirtualMachine aVM;
    public VMGuestOS GuestOS;

    private void Connect()
    {
        //CoSetProxyBlanket
        LocalSecurity = new Personal.SetSecurity.ProxyBlanket();

        try
        {
            //This connects to the local server
            VSConnection = new VMVirtualServer();

            //Secure the VS Connection object.
```

Chapter 20: Developing ASP.NET Applications with Virtual Server

```csharp
                LocalSecurity.Set(VSConnection);
        }
        catch
        {
            //Return to the main page if not able to connect to Virtual Server
            Response.Redirect("Default.aspx?error=ERROR: Failed to connect to
Virtual Server.", true);
        }
    }

    protected void Page_Load(object sender, EventArgs e)
    {
        //Get the vmName parameter
        string vmName = Request.QueryString["vm"];

        //Check that a valid VM name was provided
        if (vmName == null)
        {
            Response.Redirect("Default.aspx?error=ERROR: Need to specify
virtual machine.", true);
        }

        //Connect to Virtual Server
        Connect();

        try
        {
            //Connect to virtual machine
            aVM = VSConnection.FindVirtualMachine(vmName);
            LocalSecurity.Set(aVM);

            //Connect to GuestOS object
            GuestOS = aVM.GuestOS;
            LocalSecurity.Set(aVM);

            //Set the VM name label
            HeaderLabel.Text = "The virtual machine \"" + aVM.Name + "\" is
currently \"";

            //Switch on the VM state
            switch (aVM.State)
            {
                case VMVMState.vmVMState_Invalid:
                    //There are no possible actions for this state
                    HeaderLabel.Text = HeaderLabel.Text + "invalid\".";
                    ActionDropDownList.Enabled = false;
                    GoButton.Enabled = false;
                    break;

                case VMVMState.vmVMState_TurnedOff:
                    //There is only one option for a turned off virtual machine
                    HeaderLabel.Text = HeaderLabel.Text + "turned off\".";
                    ActionDropDownList.Items.Add("Start");
                    break;

                case VMVMState.vmVMState_Saved:
```

531

Part VIII: Developing Software for Virtual Server

```csharp
            //Set the options for a saved virtual machine
            HeaderLabel.Text = HeaderLabel.Text + "saved\".";
            ActionDropDownList.Items.Add("Start");
            ActionDropDownList.Items.Add("Discard Saved State");
            break;

        case VMVMState.vmVMState_TurningOn:
            //There are no possible actions for this state
            HeaderLabel.Text = HeaderLabel.Text + "turning on\".";
            ActionDropDownList.Enabled = false;
            GoButton.Enabled = false;
            break;

        case VMVMState.vmVMState_Restoring:
            //There are no possible actions for this state
            HeaderLabel.Text = HeaderLabel.Text + "restoring\".";
            ActionDropDownList.Enabled = false;
            GoButton.Enabled = false;
            break;

        case VMVMState.vmVMState_Running:
            HeaderLabel.Text = HeaderLabel.Text + "running\".";
            //Check to see if undo disks need to be handled
            if (aVM.Undoable)
            {
                ActionDropDownList.Items.Add("Turn off + delete undo
disks");
                ActionDropDownList.Items.Add("Turn off + keep undo disks");
                ActionDropDownList.Items.Add("Turn off + commit undo
disks");
                ActionDropDownList.Items.Add("Save State + keep undo
disks");
                ActionDropDownList.Items.Add("Save State + commit undo
disks");
                ActionDropDownList.Items.Add("Pause");
                //Check to see if the GuestOS can be shut down
                if (GuestOS.CanShutdown)
                {
                    ActionDropDownList.Items.Add("Shut down + keep
undo disks");
                    ActionDropDownList.Items.Add("Shut down + commit
undo disks");
                }
            }
            else
            {
                ActionDropDownList.Items.Add("Turn off");
                ActionDropDownList.Items.Add("Save State");
                ActionDropDownList.Items.Add("Pause");
                //Check to see if the GuestOS can be shut down
                if (GuestOS.CanShutdown)
                {
                    ActionDropDownList.Items.Add("Shut Down");
```

Chapter 20: Developing ASP.NET Applications with Virtual Server

```
                }
            }
            break;

        case VMVMState.vmVMState_Paused:
            //There is only one option for a paused virtual machine
            HeaderLabel.Text = HeaderLabel.Text + "paused\".";
            ActionDropDownList.Items.Add("Resume");
            break;

        case VMVMState.vmVMState_Saving:
            //There are no possible actions for this state
            HeaderLabel.Text = HeaderLabel.Text + "saving state\".";
            ActionDropDownList.Enabled = false;
            GoButton.Enabled = false;
            break;

        case VMVMState.vmVMState_TurningOff:
            //There are no possible actions for this state
            HeaderLabel.Text = HeaderLabel.Text + "turning off\".";
            ActionDropDownList.Enabled = false;
            GoButton.Enabled = false;
            break;

        case VMVMState.vmVMState_MergingDrives:
            //There are no possible actions for this state
            HeaderLabel.Text = HeaderLabel.Text + "merging undo disks\".";
            ActionDropDownList.Enabled = false;
            GoButton.Enabled = false;
            break;

        case VMVMState.vmVMState_DeleteMachine:
            //There are no possible actions for this state
            HeaderLabel.Text = HeaderLabel.Text + "being deleted\".";
            ActionDropDownList.Enabled = false;
            GoButton.Enabled = false;
            break;

        }
    }

    catch
    {
        Response.Redirect("Default.aspx?error=ERROR: An error occurred ⤶
trying to create page", true);
    }
}
protected void GoButton_Click(object sender, EventArgs e)
{
    VMTask aVMTask;

    try
    {
        //Switch on the selection of the action drop down list
```

533

Part VIII: Developing Software for Virtual Server

```
switch (ActionDropDownList.SelectedItem.Text)
{

    case "Resume":
        //Resume is a simple case
        aVM.Resume();
        break;

    case "Turn off":
        //Turn off returns a task to wait for
        aVMTask = aVM.TurnOff();
        LocalSecurity.Set(aVMTask);
        aVMTask.WaitForCompletion(-1);
        break;

    case "Save State":
        //Save state returns a task to wait for
        aVMTask = aVM.Save();
        LocalSecurity.Set(aVMTask);
        aVMTask.WaitForCompletion(-1);
        break;

    case "Shut Down":
        //Shut down is performed on the GuestOS - not the VM
        aVMTask = GuestOS.Shutdown();
        LocalSecurity.Set(aVMTask);
        aVMTask.WaitForCompletion(-1);
        break;

    case "Pause":
        //Pause is also a simple case
        aVM.Pause();
        break;

    case "Start":
        //Startup returns a task to wait for
        aVMTask = aVM.Startup();
        LocalSecurity.Set(aVMTask);
        aVMTask.WaitForCompletion(-1);
        break;

    case "Discard Saved State":
        //Another simple case
        aVM.DiscardSavedState();
        break;

    case "Turn off + delete undo disks":
        //Perform turn off
        aVMTask = aVM.TurnOff();
        LocalSecurity.Set(aVMTask);
        aVMTask.WaitForCompletion(-1);

        //And then discard undo disks
        aVM.DiscardUndoDisks();
```

Chapter 20: Developing ASP.NET Applications with Virtual Server

```
            break;

    case "Turn off + keep undo disks":
        //No action is required to keep undo disks
        aVMTask = aVM.TurnOff();
        LocalSecurity.Set(aVMTask);
        aVMTask.WaitForCompletion(-1);
        break;

    case "Turn off + commit undo disks":
        //Perform turn offf
        aVMTask = aVM.TurnOff();
        LocalSecurity.Set(aVMTask);
        aVMTask.WaitForCompletion(-1);

        //Merge undo disks - returns a task (and can take a while)
        aVMTask = aVM.MergeUndoDisks();
        LocalSecurity.Set(aVMTask);
        aVMTask.WaitForCompletion(-1);
        break;

    case "Save State + keep undo disks":
        //Same as just save state
        aVMTask = aVM.Save();
        LocalSecurity.Set(aVMTask);
        aVMTask.WaitForCompletion(-1);
        break;

    case "Save State + commit undo disks":
        //Save state
        aVMTask = aVM.Save();
        LocalSecurity.Set(aVMTask);
        aVMTask.WaitForCompletion(-1);

        //And then merge undo disks
        aVMTask = aVM.MergeUndoDisks();
        LocalSecurity.Set(aVMTask);
        aVMTask.WaitForCompletion(-1);
        break;

    case "Shut down + keep undo disks":
        //Same as just shut down
        aVMTask = GuestOS.Shutdown();
        LocalSecurity.Set(aVMTask);
        aVMTask.WaitForCompletion(-1);
        break;

    case "Shut down + commit undo disks":
        //Shut down
        aVMTask = GuestOS.Shutdown();
        LocalSecurity.Set(aVMTask);
        aVMTask.WaitForCompletion(-1);

        //And then merge undo disks
        aVMTask = aVM.MergeUndoDisks();
```

535

Part VIII: Developing Software for Virtual Server

```
                LocalSecurity.Set(aVMTask);
                aVMTask.WaitForCompletion(-1);
                break;


        }
    }
    catch
    {
        //if there is an error, return to the main page with an error message
        Response.Redirect("Default.aspx?error=ERROR: Failed to change the ⤵
virtual machine state.", true);
    }

    //Return to the main page when done
    Response.Redirect("Default.aspx");
}
protected void CancelButton_Click(object sender, EventArgs e)
{
    //Return to main page
    Response.Redirect("Default.aspx", true);
}
}
```

VMRC.aspx

Follow these steps to create VMRC.aspx:

1. In Visual Studio, open the **Website** menu.

2. Select **Add New Item**.

3. Choose **Web Form** and specify a name of **VMRC.aspx**.

4. Ensure that the right **Language** is selected and that the **Place** code in separate file option is checked.

5. Click **Add**.

6. Open the designer view for VMRC.aspx.

7. Drag a single **Button** onto the page.

8. Set the button **ID** to **CancelButton** and the button **Text** to **Return to Main Page**.

9. Change to the source view of VMRC.aspx.

10. Do one of the following:

❑ If you are using Visual Basic .NET, insert this line after the `<body>` line:

```
<% loadVMRC %>
```

❑ If you are using C#, insert this line after the `<body>` line:

```
<% loadVMRC(); %>
```

Chapter 20: Developing ASP.NET Applications with Virtual Server

This should generate the following ASPX code, as it appears in Visual Basic .NET:

```
<%@ Page Language="VB" AutoEventWireup="false" CodeFile="vmrc.aspx.vb"
Inherits="vmrc" %>

<!DOCTYPE html PUBLIC " //W3C//DTD XHTML 1.0 Transitional//EN"
"http://www.w3.org/TR/xhtml1/DTD/xhtml1-transitional.dtd">

<html xmlns="http://www.w3.org/1999/xhtml" >
<head runat="server">
    <title>Untitled Page</title>
</head>
<body>
    <% loadVMRC %>
    <form id="form1" runat="server">
    <div>
        <asp:Button ID="CancelButton" runat="server" Text="Return to Main
Page" /></div>
    </form>
</body>
</html>
```

Here's the code in C#:

```
<%@ Page Language="C#" AutoEventWireup="true" CodeFile="VMRC.aspx.cs"
Inherits="VMRC" %>

<!DOCTYPE html PUBLIC "-//W3C//DTD XHTML 1.0 Transitional//EN"
 "http://www.w3.org/TR/xhtml1/DTD/xhtml1-transitional.dtd">

<html xmlns="http://www.w3.org/1999/xhtml" >
<head runat="server">
    <title>Untitled Page</title>
</head>
<body>
<% loadVMRC(); %>
    <form id="form1" runat="server">
    <div>
        <asp:Button ID="CancelButton" runat="server" Text="Return to Main
Page" OnClick="CancelButton_Click" /></div>
    </form>
</body>
</html>
```

The preceding code should result in a screen that looks like Figure 20-6.

The VMRC.aspx page will need to have code associated with it that consists of the following routines:

❑   loadVMRC: This routine constructs the HTML that needs to be loaded in order to load the VMRC ActiveX control on the web page. It takes a number of parameters. One parameter is the location of VMRCActiveXClient.cab. This is located in the ActiveX directory under the default Virtual Server installation. You can just reference this location, or you can copy this file to another web location. The administratorMode, reducedColors, and menuEnabled parameters are all set to zero, which means that these options are disabled.

❑   CancelButton_Click: This is a simple routine that just reloads Default.aspx.

537

Part VIII: Developing Software for Virtual Server

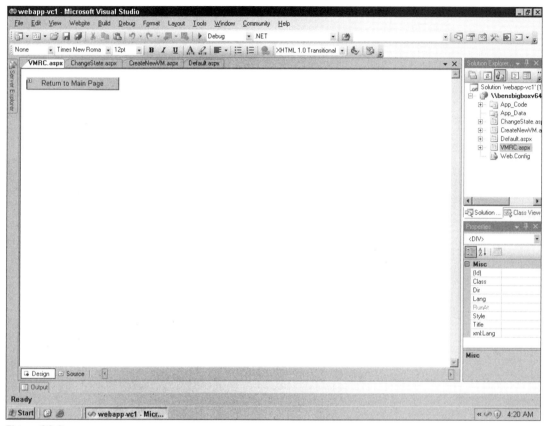

Figure 20-6

Here is the code in Visual Basic .NET:

```
Partial Class vmrc
    Inherits System.Web.UI.Page

    Public Sub loadVMRC()
        Dim objectHtml As String

        'The ID is what ever you want it to be
        Dim id = "VSClientControl"

        'This CAB file can be placed where ever you want
        Dim codebase = _
"http://myVSServer/VirtualServer/activex/VMRCActiveXClient.cab"

        'The VS instance you are connecting to
        Dim serverIP = "myVSServer"

        'The VMRC port to use
```

Chapter 20: Developing ASP.NET Applications with Virtual Server

```vb
        Dim port = "5900"

        'This gathers to VM name that was passed to this page as a parameter
        Dim vmName = Request.QueryString.Item("vm")

        'Disable administratorMode
        Dim administratorMode = "0"

        'Do not reduce colors
        Dim reducedColors = "0"

        'Do not display the menu
        Dim menuEnabled = "0"


        objectHtml = "<object ID=" & Chr(34) & id & Chr(34) & " codebase=" &
Chr(34) & codebase & Chr(34) & " classID=" & Chr(34) & "CLSID:7C896371-4B7F-
4B34-95B1-24851F5DED24" & Chr(34) & ">\r\n"
        objectHtml += "\t<PARAM NAME=" & Chr(34) & "ServerAddress" & Chr(34) &
" VALUE=" & Chr(34) & serverIP & Chr(34) & ">\r\n"
        objectHtml += "\t<PARAM NAME=" & Chr(34) & "ServerPort" & Chr(34) & "
VALUE=" & Chr(34) & port & Chr(34) & ">\r\n"
        objectHtml += "\t<PARAM NAME=" & Chr(34) & "ServerDisplayName" &
Chr(34) & " VALUE=" & Chr(34) & vmName & Chr(34) & ">\r\n"
        objectHtml += "\t<PARAM NAME=" & Chr(34) & "AdministratorMode" &
Chr(34) & " VALUE=" & Chr(34) & administratorMode & Chr(34) & ">\r\n"
        objectHtml += "\t<PARAM NAME=" & Chr(34) & "menuEnabled" & Chr(34) & "
VALUE=" & Chr(34) & menuEnabled & Chr(34) & ">\r\n"
        objectHtml += "\t<PARAM NAME=" & Chr(34) & "ReducedColorsMode" &
Chr(34) & " VALUE=" & Chr(34) & reducedColors & Chr(34) & ">\r\n"
        objectHtml += "</object>"

        Response.Write(objectHtml)
    End Sub

    Protected Sub CancelButton_Click(ByVal sender As Object, ByVal e As
System.EventArgs) Handles CancelButton.Click
        Response.Redirect("Default.aspx")
    End Sub
End Class
```

Here is the code in C#:

```csharp
using System;
using System.Data;
using System.Configuration;
using System.Collections;
using System.Web;
using System.Web.Security;
using System.Web.UI;
using System.Web.UI.WebControls;
using System.Web.UI.WebControls.WebParts;
using System.Web.UI.HtmlControls;

public partial class VMRC : System.Web.UI.Page
```

539

Part VIII: Developing Software for Virtual Server

```
{
    public void loadVMRC()
    {
        String objectHtml;

        //The ID is what ever you want it to be
        String id = "VSClientControl";

        //This CAB file can be placed where ever you want
        String codebase = ⤶
"http://myVSServer/VirtualServer/activex/VMRCActiveXClient.cab";

        //The VS instance you are connecting to
        String serverIP = "myVSServer";

        //The VMRC port to use
        String port = "5900";

        //This gathers to VM name that was passed to this page as a parameter
        String vmName = Request.QueryString["vm"];

        //Disable administratorMode
        String administratorMode = "0";

        //Do not reduce colors
        String reducedColors = "0";

        //Do not display the menu
        String menuEnabled = "0";


        objectHtml = "<object ID=\"" + id + "\" codebase=\"" + codebase + "\" ⤶
classID=\"" + "CLSID:7C896371-4B7F-4B34-95B1-24851F5DED24\"" + ">\r\n";
        objectHtml += "\t<PARAM NAME=\"" + "ServerAddress\"" + " VALUE=\"" + ⤶
serverIP + "\">\r\n";
        objectHtml += "\t<PARAM NAME=\"" + "ServerPort\"" + " VALUE=\"" + port ⤶
+ "\">\r\n";
        objectHtml += "\t<PARAM NAME=\"" + "ServerDisplayName\"" + " VALUE=\"" ⤶
+ vmName + "\">\r\n";
        objectHtml += "\t<PARAM NAME=\"" + "AdministratorMode\"" + " VALUE=\"" ⤶
+ administratorMode + "\">\r\n";
        objectHtml += "\t<PARAM NAME=\"" + "menuEnabled\"" + " VALUE=\"" + ⤶
menuEnabled + "\">\r\n";
        objectHtml += "\t<PARAM NAME=\"" + "ReducedColorsMode\"" + " VALUE=\"" ⤶
+ reducedColors + "\">\r\n";
        objectHtml += "</object>";

        Response.Write(objectHtml);
    }

    protected void Page_Load(object sender, EventArgs e)
    {

    }
```

Chapter 20: Developing ASP.NET Applications with Virtual Server

```
protected void CancelButton_Click(object sender, EventArgs e)
{
    //Return to main page
    Response.Redirect("Default.aspx", true);
}
}
```

As you can see, there is a lot of power and potential in developing ASP.NET solutions for Virtual Server. This sample solution has been a very simple case, but here are some more advanced ideas that you may want to explore:

❑ Implementing and tracking quotas that would allow you to control how many virtual machines a single user had configured, or how much memory or CPU resource a single user was allowed to use.

❑ Providing more detail and functionality in the virtual machine template. Also providing more automation in the virtual machine creation, which would allow users to get up and running with the desired configuration quicker.

❑ Creating session-based virtual machines, where a new virtual machine would be created when a user connects, and the virtual machine would then be deleted when they disconnect. This is a good solution for an environment that uses anonymous authentication.

And there are many other possibilities for this sort of environment.

Conclusion

In this chapter, you have seen how to configure ASP.NET and IIS thread identity and application pools to allow for the creation of a self-service virtual machine website.

You've also created a fully functional self-service virtual machine website that allows users to create new virtual machines from preconfigured templates, control and interact with these virtual machines, and delete the virtual machines — all while restricting the access privileges that they need to have to Virtual Server itself.

541

Part IX

Development and Debugging in Virtual Machines

Chapter 21: Application Debugging with Virtual Server

Appendix A: Common Problems and Solutions

Appendix B: Virtual Server Clustering Script: HAVM.VBS

21

Application Debugging with Virtual Server

You have now seen how applications that control Virtual Server can be developed. But Virtual Server can also be used to help greatly in the development of other applications. Virtual machines can be used to provide clean, trustworthy testing environments that can be rapidly provisioned. Beyond this, virtual machines can help developers while testing and debugging their applications.

Note that this chapter is not intended to be a primer on debugging; I assume you are familiar with how to debug software in general. This chapter applies those principles to Virtual Server.

Virtual machines bring two big advantages. First they provide an always-clean and trustworthy testing environment for the developer. As you're developing an application, it is not uncommon to make changes to system settings or shared libraries that affect your application in ways you do not realize. When testing your application in a virtual machine you can be sure that it is not being influenced by any unknown customization of the environment. The other advantage of virtual machines is that they make it much easier to test applications that are being developed for multiple platforms. The reality for most developers who need to support multiple platforms is that, because of the difficulty involved in testing their application and all the various platforms, they usually just develop and test on one platform and only test other platforms once development has finished. Discovering problems at this stage of development is much more costly than discovering them earlier on, when they would be easier to fix.

This chapter details how to set up virtual machines for application and kernel debugging to help developers working in these environments.

Application Debugging

Visual Studio 2005 has built-in support for remote debugging of applications. You can use this with virtual machines to provide an integrated application debugging solution. You first need to install the Visual Studio 2005 remote debugging components inside the virtual machine. If you

Part IX: Development and Debugging in Virtual Machines

have Visual Studio 2005 on a DVD, the remote debugging components files are in the vs/Remote Debugger folder. If you have CDs, the files are in the Remote Debugger folder on the last CD in the set. You need to start rdbgsetup.exe and accept the defaults for the installer.

> **If you have the Windows firewall enabled, the remote debugging components installer will create appropriate exceptions for remote debugging. If you are using a different firewall you'll, need to configure the firewall manually. For details on how to do this go to** `http://msdn2.microsoft.com/en-us/library/bt727f1t(VS.80).aspx`.

To launch the remote debugger, open the Start menu, select All Programs ⇨ Microsoft Visual Studio 2005 ⇨ Visual Studio Tools ⇨ Visual Studio 2005 Remote Debugger.

> **By default the remote debugger is configured to allow administrators to remotely debug programs. You can allow other users to do this by opening the Tools menu on the Visual Studio Remote Debugging Monitor and selecting Permissions.**

Manual Remote Debugging

Once the remote debugging tools are installed and running you can manually remotely debug the program by executing the following steps:

1. Build the program that you want to debug on the host computer.
2. Copy the files that are built by Visual Studio to the virtual machine.

   Most likely you will do this over the network.

3. Launch the program on the virtual machine.
4. On the host operating system, under Visual Studio, open the **Debug** menu.
5. Select **Attach to Process**.
6. Enter the network name of the virtual machine in the **Qualifier** field.
7. Select the program from the **Available Processes** list, and click **Attach**.

   If the Windows firewall is configured on the host operating system, visual studio will offer to configure it to allow remote debugging. This works only if you're running as an administrative user.

You should now be able to set breakpoints and remotely debug the program in the virtual machine from the host operating system.

In order to remotely debug a program you need to using the same user credentials on both computers, or you need to be using a user account that has administrative privilege on the remote computer.

Chapter 21: Application Debugging with Virtual Server

Automated Remote Debugging

With a bit more work, it is possible to set things up so that the application starts on the virtual machine, and the remote debugger attaches automatically when you select to run the application from under Visual Studio on the host operating system. The first thing you need to do is to create a network share that is accessible by the host operating system and the virtual machine.

The network share can be on the host operating system itself.

Once you have done this you need to configure Microsoft.Net to allow programs to be run off of this network share. In order to do this, follow these steps:

1. Run **MMC.exe**.

2. Open the **File** menu and select **Add/Remove Snap-in**.

3. Click the **Add** button.

4. Select the **.Net Framework 2.0 Configuration** snap-in and click **Add**. If you are using a different version of the .NET Framework you'll see a different version number available, and you should select that instead.

5. Return to the main console and expand the **.Net Framework 2.0 Configuration** entry.

6. Expand **My Computer ⇨ Runtime Security Policy ⇨ Machine ⇨ Code Groups ⇨ All_Code**, and select **LocalIntranet_Zone**.

7. Open the **Action** menu and select **New**.

8. Define an appropriate name and description for the new code group.

9. In the **Choose the condition for this code group** drop-down list, select **URL**.

10. Enter the URL for your file share in the format of `file://\\<network share>\folder`.

11. On the **Assign a Permission Set to the Code Group** page, select **FullTrust** from the **Use existing permission set** drop-down list.

12. Complete the wizard and close the MMC console.

Repeat this process on both the virtual machine and the host operating system. Once this is done, and the remote debugger is installed and configured in the virtual machine, you need to do the following:

1. Copy your project to the network share that you've just created.

   If you are doing this before creating a project you'll just need to create the new project on the network share.

2. Open the project from the network share with Visual Studio. Visual studio will warn you that the project is running from an untrusted location. This is not correct and the warning can be safely ignored.

3. Select the drop down next to the start button (which usually says "Debug"). Click the entry that says **Configuration Manager**.

4. Click on the **Active solution configuration** drop down and select **<New>**.

5. Enter an appropriate name for the new configuration (such as the name of the virtual machine that you will be using).

547

Part IX: Development and Debugging in Virtual Machines

6. Select to **Copy settings from** the **Debug** configuration and click **OK**.

7. Close the **Configuration Manager**.

8. Select your project from the **Solution Explorer** (not the solution), open the **Project** menu, and select **Properties**.

9. Change to the **Debug** tab.

10. Select the configuration that you created in Steps 4 and 5.

11. Check **Use remote machine** and enter the network name of the virtual machine that you'll be using.

At this stage, you should be able to select to run the program and have it automatically launch on the virtual machine and have remote debugging connected. You can easily change your configuration selection to run the program locally. You can even set up multiple configurations for multiple virtual machines, enabling you to quickly and easily test the program on different platforms.

> *You still need to have the virtual machines running with the remote debugger launched ahead of time for this to work.*

Kernel Debugging

The majority of developers do not do kernel-level development. Kernel-level development is usually reserved for people who are developing hardware drivers, or software that emulates hardware. There are a few notable exceptions to this rule.

Given that virtual machines always have a static set of hardware and it is unlikely that you are going to be developing hardware drivers that can run inside a virtual machine, you may be wondering why anyone would want to debug kernel-level code in a virtual machine. There are a couple of reasons. Developing and debugging kernel-level code is complex, and if you make any mistakes you may render your computer unusable (until it is rebooted). Doing this sort of work inside a virtual machine is very attractive as any mistakes will be confined to the virtual machine, and you'll be able to continue using the host machine with no disruption.

You may wish to write kernel-level code to run inside a virtual machine because you are developing software that emulates hardware, or because you want to use it as a safe learning environment for kernel-level development that you're planning to do on real hardware. Otherwise, you might be investigating a problem and be looking to find out more information about what is happening in the kernel of the operating system.

With physical hardware you perform kernel-level debugging by having a second physical computer connected to the first computer that runs the debugging software. These computers can be connected by either a serial cable, USB cable, or IEEE1394 cable. You can kernel debug a guest operating system in a virtual machine in exactly the same manner as you would for a physical computer by using a null-modem cable connected to the serial port. However, this is by far the least elegant method for kernel debugging with virtual machines.

Virtual Server supports mapping a virtual machine serial port to a named pipe on the host operating system. A second virtual machine can be configured to connect its serial port to the same named pipe.

Chapter 21: Application Debugging with Virtual Server

In this configuration, the two virtual machines behave as if they have a virtual null-modem cable running between them, and the second virtual machine can act as the kernel debugger. Even better, you can install the kernel debugging software on the host operating system and have it connect directly to the named pipe that is being used by the virtual machine's serial port, making the host operating system the kernel debugger for the guest operating system.

> *It is possible to connect the virtual machine to a named pipe that already exists on another physical computer. However, the virtual machine cannot create this named pipe and will need to rely on another program to create the named pipe (or a virtual machine on the remote computer can create the named pipe).*

> *This section talks about situations where the kernel debugger is on the same physical computer as the virtual machine. However, named pipes are accessible over the network, which means that the kernel debugger could easily be running on a remote network–connected computer.*

Configuring the Guest Operating System for Kernel Debugging

The steps to configure the guest operating system for kernel debugging vary for the different versions of Windows.

For Windows NT 4.0 and Windows 2000, do the following:

1. Boot the virtual machine and log into the guest operating system.
2. Open the **Start** menu and select **Run**.
3. Run `cmd`.
4. Change directory to the root of the boot drive (this will usually be C:\).
5. Run `attrib -s -h -r boot.ini`.
6. Run `notepad boot.ini`.
7. Under the [operating systems] section you should see a line like this:

   ```
   multi(0)disk(0)rdisk(0)partition(1)\WINNT="Microsoft Windows 2000 Advanced Server"
   /fastdetect
   ```

8. Make a copy of this line and place it immediately underneath the original entry.
9. Add `/debug /debugport=COM1 /baudrate=115200` to the end of the new line.
10. Change the name in quotes to indicate that debugging is enabled (I usually add - `debug` to the end of the name).
11. Close boot.ini and save changes.
12. Run `attrib +s +h +r boot.ini`.
13. Shut down the guest operating system.

For Windows XP and Windows Server 2003, use the following steps:

1. Boot the virtual machine and log into the guest operating system.
2. Open the **Start** menu, right-click on **My Computer**, and select **Properties**.

549

Part IX: Development and Debugging in Virtual Machines

Checking Your Settings

You can confirm that Windows Vista has the correct settings by running `bcdedit /enum all` and reviewing the debugger settings section. This should read:

```
Debugger Settings
-----------------
identifier              {dbgsettings}
debugtype               Serial
debugport               1
baudrate                115200
```

---

3. Change to the **Advanced** tab.

4. Click on the **Settings** button in the **Startup and Recovery** section.

5. Click the **Edit** button.

6. Follow Steps 7 through 11 from the process for Windows NT 4.0 and Windows 2000.

7. Shut down the guest operating system.

You can use the process for Windows NT 4.0 and Windows 2000 with Windows XP and Windows Server 2003 as well.

Follow these steps for Windows Vista:

1. Boot the virtual machine and log into the guest operating system.

2. Open the **Start** menu, click **All Programs** and then **Accessories**.

3. Right-click on **Command Prompt** and select **Run as administrator**.

4. Accept the **User Account Control** prompt.

5. Windows Vista should have the correct settings for kernel debugging set by default.

6. Create a new boot entry by running `bcdedit /copy {current} /d DebugEntry`.

7. This command displays the unique identifier for the new boot entry in the format of `{xxxxxxxx-xxxx-xxxx-xxxx-xxxxxxxxxxxx}`. You need this identifier for the next couple of commands.

8. Update the boot menu by running `bcdedit /displayorder {current} {ID}`. Where `{ID}` is the value displayed by the previous command.

9. Enable debugging on the new boot entry by running `bcdedit /debug {ID} on`.

10. Shut down the guest operating system.

Connecting the Virtual Serial Port to a Named Pipe

To connect the virtual machine's serial port to a named pipe, follow these steps:

1. Open the Virtual Server Administrative website.

2. Click **Configure** from the **Virtual Machines** section of the navigation panel, and select the virtual machine in question.

550

Chapter 21: Application Debugging with Virtual Server

> ### Naming Named Pipes
>
> Named pipes are named with the following syntax:
>
> ```
> \\<servername>\pipe\<pipename>
> ```
>
> If the named pipe is being created on the local computer, a period (.) can be used for the server name. So a named pipe called VMDebug on the local computer would be:
>
> ```
> \\.\pipe\VMDebug
> ```

3. Click **COM ports**.

4. Change the **Attachment** for **COM port 1** to **Named pipe:**.

5. Enter the named pipe name that you want to use and click **OK**.

Connecting a Kernel Debugger from Another Virtual Machine

To debug one virtual machine from another virtual machine, you need to have both virtual machines configured to use the same named pipe for their serial port connection. Once you have done this, you should boot the virtual machine that will be running the debugger software (not the virtual machine that you wish to debug). In this virtual machine you will need to download the debugging tools that are available at www.microsoft.com/whdc/devtools/debugging/debugstart.mspx.

Next, decide how you're going to be getting the symbols needed for debugging. You can manually download symbols for the platforms that you'll be debugging from www.microsoft.com/whdc/devtools/debugging/symbolpkg.mspx. Alternatively, you can configure the Windows debuggers to automatically download the correct symbols when they connect to the target virtual machine.

> *The latter option is almost always preferable as there is no risk of having the wrong symbols for the platform that you're trying to debug. The only drawback is that you need to have an active Internet connection at the time that you want to debug the virtual machine (although this can be addressed through caching).*

If you decide to have the symbols automatically downloaded, you'll need to run the following command from the location where the debugging tools were installed:

```
kd -y srv*C:\WebSymbols*http://msdl.microsoft.com/download/symbols -k
com:port=1,baud=115200
```

> *If you run this command on a system without Internet connectivity, you will receive error messages about being unable to open files.*

If you decide to manually download the symbols, you'll need to run the following command:

```
kd -y C:\MySymbols -k com:port=1,baud=115200
```

> *where* C:\MySymbols *is the location that you saved the symbols files to.*

551

Part IX: Development and Debugging in Virtual Machines

-y is used to indicate where the symbols will be located. `srv*C:\WebSymbols*http://msdl`
`.microsoft.com/download/symbols` tells the debugger to download the needed symbols from
`http://msdl.microsoft.com/download/symbols` and to keep a local copy of the symbols at
`C:\WebSymbols`. This way you can debug virtual machines when you don't have an Internet connection, as long as you've connected to them before when you did have an Internet connection.

-k is used to indicate the parameters of the connection. The meaning of the values used here should be
fairly obvious.

> **kd is a command-line tool. If you would prefer to use a graphical debugging tool
> you can use windbg with exactly the same parameters specified previously.**

Once you have run the command that is appropriate for your configuration you should get a message
that it is waiting to reconnect. At this stage you can boot the virtual machine that is going to be debugged,
and select the debug option from the boot menu. While the target virtual machine is booting you should
see the debugger reporting that it has connected successfully and loaded the symbols. At this stage you
can test that the kernel debugger is working correctly by typing Ctrl+C (if you are using kd) or Ctrl+
Break (if you are using windbg). This should display a message indicating that the debugger has requested
that the system break. You can now run any commands that you wish (`!process 00` is a simple command that shows information about the active process). When you are done, run g to allow the target
machine to continue running.

You are now completely configured for kernel debugging.

Connecting a Kernel Debugger from the Host Operating System

Connecting a kernel debugger from the host operating system is very similar to doing it from another
virtual machine. You need to download and install the debugging tools on your host operating system
and decide how you'll be managing symbols. The only real difference is that rather than connecting to a
serial port you'll be connecting to a named pipe. You can do this with the following command:

```
kd -y srv*c:\websymbols*http://msdl.microsoft.com/download/symbols -k
com:pipe,port=\\.\pipe\<pipeName>,resets=0,reconnect
```

-k com:pipe,port=\\.\pipe\<pipeName> specifies that a named pipe should be used, and the name
of the named pipe to be used. `resets=0,reconnect` is required in order to be compatible with Virtual
Server.

You can also use this command with a local symbols store or with windbg.

Conclusion

Virtual Server provides a powerful tool that allows developers to rapidly test their applications on different platforms, in isolated safe environments, on a single piece of hardware. By using Virtual Server in

Chapter 21: Application Debugging with Virtual Server

the configurations outlined in this chapter it is possible to more readily identify and correct problems earlier in the development process — saving time, money, and many hours of frustration.

You can use Virtual Server with Visual Studio's remote debugging functionality to provide a very useful development tool. And Virtual Server's support for kernel debugging virtual machines over a named pipe is invaluable for users who are beginning to get involved in the world of kernel development.

Common Problems and Solutions

The host operating system crashes or freezes when running virtual machines under Virtual Server.

Virtual Server does not have any known issues that cause the host operating system to crash. It does, however, heavily utilize the physical computer and may expose problems with drivers or hardware in the host operating system. If your system is freezing or crashing when running virtual machines under Virtual Server, try checking for updated drivers for the hardware and your computer, checking for BIOS updates for your computer, and testing the physical memory in your computer. Microsoft has provided a tool to allow you to test your physical memory, the Windows Memory Diagnostic tool. You can download a copy of it from http://oca.microsoft.com/en/windiag.asp.

When running Virtual Server on a Windows XP computer that is not joined to a domain, you receive an accessed-denied error when trying to open the Virtual Server Administrative website.

In order for this configuration to work correctly you need to disable the simple file sharing support in Windows XP. To do this, follow these steps:

1. Open the **Start** menu and select **My Computer**.
2. Open the **Tools** menu and select **Folder Options**.
3. Change to the **View** tab.
4. Scroll to the bottom of the **Advanced settings:** box and uncheck **Use simple file sharing (Recommended)**.
5. Click **OK** to apply the settings changes.

Part IX: Development and Debugging in Virtual Machines

When shutting down the host computer when virtual machines are running that are configured to save state when the host shuts down, the virtual machines do not always save state.

Saving state of a large number of virtual machines can take a significant amount of time. If Virtual Server takes too long to try and shut down, Windows will forcefully stop it. When this happens, any virtual machine that is not yet finished saving state will be turned off. For details on what can be done to stop this from happening, check out `http://support.microsoft.com/kb/888745/en-us`.

Accessing the Virtual Server Administrative website when connected to the host operating system over remote desktop results in an accessed-denied, or page-cannot-be-displayed, error.

Accessing the Virtual Server Administrative website from the hosting computer works only when it is done from session 0. Remote desktop usually uses session 1 or higher. In order for this to work, you should either run the Virtual Server Administrative website by using Internet Explorer on your computer (and not using Internet Explorer on the Virtual Server), or start the remote desktop client by running `mstsc /console`. This causes remote desktop to use session 0.

After moving a virtual machine that is configured to automatically start as a specified user account to another host computer, the virtual machine is no longer able to start.

When you configure a virtual machine to start automatically as a specified user account, the user account credentials are stored in a secure credential store on the host operating system. When you move the virtual machine to another host operating system, this credential information is not moved. You'll need to reconfigure the user account in the virtual machine settings. Follow these steps:

1. Open the Virtual Server Administrative website.

2. Select **Configure** from the **Virtual Machines** section of the **Navigation** pane, and select the virtual machine that you need to correct.

3. Select **General properties**.

4. Uncheck **Run virtual machine under the following user account** and click **OK**.

5. Select **General properties** again.

6. Check **Run virtual machine under the following user account**, enter the user account information, and click **OK**.

You experience slow network performance/intermittent network connectivity issues when using virtual machines.

There are known issues with Virtual Server networking and some advanced features on some network cards. The article at `http://support.microsoft.com/kb/888750` discusses how to configure the network cards to correct this issue.

Virtual Server fails to add an existing virtual machine with an error message that it is already registered, even though it is not.

When you register a virtual machine with Virtual Server, it creates a shortcut to the virtual machine configuration file in %allusersprofile%\Application Data\Microsoft\Virtual Server\Virtual Machines on Windows Server 2003 and Windows XP; on Windows Vista it is created in `%allusersprofile%\`

556

Appendix A: Common Problems and Solutions

`Microsoft\Virtual Server\Virtual Machines`. If you delete or move a virtual machine configuration without first removing the virtual machine with Virtual Server, the shortcut is left behind. This will stop the virtual machine from being registered again. You'll need to go to the above folder and delete the shortcut, and then register the virtual machine. To do this, follow these steps:

1. Open the Virtual Server Administrative website.

2. Select **Add** from the **Virtual Machines** section of the **Navigation** pane.

3. Enter the fully qualified path for the virtual machine configuration file (VMC) and click **OK**.

One of the virtual machines is no longer being displayed on the Virtual Server Administrative website, and an error is displayed stating "The configuration value could not be retrieved because the key could not be found."

The virtual machine configuration file for this computer has been corrupted. You'll need to remove the virtual machine and create a new configuration file. You can reuse the existing virtual hard disk to ensure that you don't lose any data. To do this:

1. Open the Virtual Server Administrative website.

2. Hover your mouse over the name of the problematic virtual machine, and select **Remove** from the contextual menu that is displayed.

3. Locate the virtual machine configuration file (VMC) on the hard disk and delete it.

4. Select **Create** from the **Virtual Machines** section of the **Navigation** pane.

5. Enter the full path and name for the virtual machine configuration file (VMC).

6. Select **Use an existing virtual hard disk** and enter the full path and name for the virtual hard disk file (VHD).

7. Click **OK**.

8. Select **Configure** from the **Virtual Machines** section of the **Navigation** pane, and select the virtual machine that was just created.

9. Update any other settings that need to be changed to match the previous virtual machine's configuration.

When trying to compact a dynamically expanding virtual hard disk, you receive an error that there is not enough space available.

When dynamically expanding a compacted virtual hard disk, it is actually copied to a temporary file and then copied back. This means that you have to have enough space available for two copies of the entire virtual hard disk.

Virtual Server reports errors about SPNs not being registered.

This usually happens when Virtual Server is installed on a domain controller, but it can happen with other configurations. Typically, Virtual Server configures this during installation, but if this fails, you can manually configure it by following the steps outlined at `http://support.microsoft.com/kb/890893`.

Part IX: Development and Debugging in Virtual Machines

When configuring a Windows NT 4.0 virtual machine with multiple network adapters, only the first one is detected by Windows.

The network driver that is included in Windows NT 4.0 for the Virtual Server emulated network adapter does not support multiple network adapters. To get this to work, you will need to install the updated network driver that is included with Virtual Server. To do this, follow these steps:

1. On the Virtual Server administrative website, select **Configure** from the **Virtual Machines** section of the **Navigation** pane, and then click on your virtual machine.

2. Click on **Floppy Drive**.

3. Select the **NT4 Network Driver.vfd** entry from the **Known floppy disks** drop-down list and click **OK**.

4. Log in to the guest operating system with an administrative user account.

5. Right-click on **Network Neighborhood** on the desktop and select **Properties**.

6. Change to the **Adapters** tab.

7. **Remove** any existing network adapters.

8. Click on **Add** and then click on **Have Disk.**

9. Make sure A: is specified and click **OK**.

10. Select DEC PCI Fast Ethernet DECchip 21140 and click OK three times.

Then remove **NT4 Network Driver.vfd** from the floppy drive and reboot the virtual machine.

Accessing the Virtual Server Administrative website does not work.

There are a couple of reasons why this happens, and a couple of solutions to try. The first thing to try is adding the URL for the Virtual Server Administrative website to your trusted sites under Internet Explorer. The next thing to try is using some alternative URLs. By default, Virtual Server uses the fully qualified domain name for the URL (for example, mycomputer.mydomain.com). Alternatively, you can try using the NetBIOS name (for example, mycomputer) followed by localhost, followed by the host IP address or 127.0.0.1.

Installing Virtual Machine Additions for Linux fails.

Installation of Virtual Machine Additions for Linux may fail for a number of reasons. You should make sure that your virtual machine is configured to meet all the prerequisites for installing Virtual Machine Additions for Linux, as defined in the Readme text file that is included with Virtual Machine Additions for Linux.

This information is documented on the download site for the Virtual Machine Additions for Linux at www.microsoft.com/windowsserversystem/virtualserver/evaluation/linuxguestsupport/default.mspx.

If the installation is still failing, you can obtain more details about what is causing the failure by reading the installation log file from /var/log/vmadd-install.log.

Appendix A: Common Problems and Solutions

When using Linux virtual machines you are seeing repeated keystrokes inside of the virtual machine.

This is a known issue that is caused by the way in which certain Linux distributions calculate time. Details on how to configure your Linux virtual machine to address this problem are available at http://support.microsoft.com/?kbid=918461.

B

Virtual Server Clustering Script: HAVM.VBS

```
'Used with permission, Copyright Microsoft(c) 2005
'*****************************************************************************
'*************************************************************************
'Global variables
'*****************************************************************************
'*************************************************************************
'Script Version
ScriptVersion = "1.0"

'Flagged TRUE if the virtual machine has ever responded to an additions
heartbeat.
VirtualMachineHasHeartbeat = FALSE

'Used by Terminate() to make failure recovery decisions.
VirtualMachineFailedOnline = FALSE

'Time in milliseconds to wait to save/restore state.
Timeout = 300000

'Stores the percentage of received heartbeats over 1 time block at which the
guest is considered dead.
AdditionsIsAliveHeartbeatThreshold = 0

'*****************************************************************************
'*************************************************************************
'Open()
'
'Check to see if "Virtual Server" service is running. If not attempt to start
it.
'
'Check to see if the following private properties exist. If not, create/set
them:
```

Part IX: Development and Debugging in Virtual Machines

```
'    VirtualMachineName - Stores the name of the virtual machine that is made highly
available by this resource. (User has to set it explicitly)
'    UseAdditionsIsAlive - 1 to use the additions heartbeat code path in IsAlive(),
0 to not use that code path. (Default is 1)
'    AdditionsIsAliveFailureRecoveryAction - 1 to turn off vm, 0 to save state.
(Default is 1)
'*********************************************************************************
*********************************************************************
Function Open()

    On Error Resume Next
    Resource.LogInformation("Entering Open() for Virtual Server Host Clustering
Generic Script Version " & ScriptVersion)
    Set wmiProvider = GetObject("winmgmts:/root/cimv2")
    Set vsService = wmiProvider.Get("win32_service='Virtual Server'")
    vsServiceState = vsService.State

    If uCase(vsServiceState) <> "RUNNING" Then
        returnValue = vsService.StartService()
        'Check if the call to start the service succeeded or not. 0 or 10 means it
did.
        If (returnValue <> 0) and (returnValue <> 10) Then
            Resource.LogInformation("Attempt to start 'Virtual Server' service on
this machine failed with error " & returnValue)
            Open = returnValue
            Exit Function
        End If
    End If

    If Resource.PropertyExists("VirtualMachineName") = FALSE Then
        Resource.AddProperty("VirtualMachineName")
    End If

    If Resource.PropertyExists("UseAdditionsIsAlive") = FALSE Then
        Resource.AddProperty("UseAdditionsIsAlive")
        Resource.UseAdditionsIsAlive = 1
    End If

    If Resource.PropertyExists("AdditionsIsAliveFailureRecoveryAction") = FALSE
Then
        Resource.AddProperty("AdditionsIsAliveFailureRecoveryAction")
        Resource.AdditionsIsAliveFailureRecoveryAction = 1
    End If

End Function


'*********************************************************************************
*********************************************************************
'Online()
'
'Issue a start control to the virtual machine.
'
'If the virtual machine is already in "Running" state, this can either mean the
virtual machine has very recently failed, or it is really up and running.
```

Appendix B: Virtual Server Clustering Script: HAVM.VBS

```
'Handle the worst case by setting VirtualMachineFailedOnline = TRUE, which will
cause Terminate() to attempt to save the state.
'*********************************************************************************
*********************************************************************
Function Online( )

    On Error Resume Next
    If Resource.VirtualMachineName = "" Then
        Resource.LogInformation("The VirtualMachineName private property is blank.
Please run the following command on any one node of the cluster to correct the
problem: cluster.exe res """ & Resource.Name & """ /priv VirtualMachineName=" &
"""name of virtual machine""" )
        Online = 13 '13 - The data is invalid.
        Exit Function
    Else
        Resource.LogInformation("Entering Online() for " &
Resource.VirtualMachineName)
    End If

    Set virtualServer = CreateObject("VirtualServer.Application")
    Set vm = virtualserver.FindVirtualMachine(Resource.VirtualMachineName)
    Set state = vm.Startup()

    Select Case err.number <> 0
        Case err.number = "-1610349312"
            'Handle the case where the virtual machine is already in "Running"
state at the time the resource is brought online.
            If vm.state = 5 Then
                Resource.LogInformation("Startup() was called for virtual machine "
& Resource.VirtualMachineName & ", however it was already in the started state.
Setting VirtualMachineFailedOnline = TRUE")
                VirtualMachineFailedOnline = TRUE
                Online = 1
                Exit Function
            End If
        Case err.number = "2147614729"
            If vm.state = 5 Then
                Resource.LogInformation("Startup() was called for virtual machine "
& Resource.VirtualMachineName & ", however it was already in the started state.
Setting VirtualMachineFailedOnline = TRUE")
                VirtualMachineFailedOnline = TRUE
                Online = 1
                Exit Function
            End If
        Case err.number = "2684617984"
            If vm.state = 5 Then
                Resource.LogInformation("Startup() was called for virtual machine "
& Resource.VirtualMachineName & ", however it was already in the started state.
Setting VirtualMachineFailedOnline = TRUE")
                VirtualMachineFailedOnline = TRUE
                Online = 1
                Exit Function
            End If
        Case Else
            Resource.LogInformation("Startup() for virtual machine " &
Resource.VirtualMachineName & " failed with error " & err.number)
```

Part IX: Development and Debugging in Virtual Machines

```
                Online = err.number
                Exit Function
        End Select

        Call state.WaitForCompletion(Timeout)
        If state.IsComplete = TRUE Then
            Online = 0
        End If

End Function


'******************************************************************************
'*********************************************************************
'LooksAlive()
'
'Return success
'******************************************************************************
'*********************************************************************
Function LooksAlive()
    LooksAlive = TRUE
End Function


'******************************************************************************
'*********************************************************************
'IsAlive()
'
'If UseAdditionsIsAlive = 1 and if VirtualMachineHasHeartbeat = TRUE and if
'vm.GuestOS.HeartbeatPercentage =< AdditionsIsAliveHeartbeatThreshold set IsAlive to
'FALSE and exit function.
'If UseAdditionsIsAlive = 1 and if VirtualMachineHasHeartbeat = TRUE and if
'vm.GuestOS.heartbeatpercentage > AdditionsIsAliveHeartbeatThreshold set IsAlive to
'TRUE and exit function.
'If UseAdditionsIsAlive <> 1 or if VirtualMachineHasHeartbeat <> TRUE, then attempt
'to set VirtualMachineHasHeartbeat and do basic IsAlive.
'******************************************************************************
'*********************************************************************
Function IsAlive()

    On Error Resume Next
    IsAlive = FALSE

    Set virtualServer = CreateObject("VirtualServer.Application")
    Set vm = virtualserver.FindVirtualMachine(Resource.VirtualMachineName)

    If (Resource.UseAdditionsIsAlive = 1) Then
        If VirtualMachineHasHeartbeat = TRUE Then
            If vm.GuestOS.HeartbeatPercentage <= AdditionsIsAliveHeartbeatThreshold
Then
                IsAlive = FALSE
                Exit Function
            Else
                IsAlive = TRUE
                Exit Function
```

Appendix B: Virtual Server Clustering Script: HAVM.VBS

```vbnet
                End If
            End If
        End If

        'Set VirtualMachineHasHeartbeat
        VirtualMachineHasHeartbeat = vm.GuestOS.IsHeartbeating

        'Do basic IsAlive check
        If vm.state = 3 or vm.state = 4 or vm.state = 5 Then
            IsAlive = TRUE
        End If

End Function


'*****************************************************************************
'*********************************************************************
'Offline()
'
'Issue a save state control to the virtual machine.
'
'If the virtual machine is not already in the "Running" state, assume success.
'*****************************************************************************
'*********************************************************************
Function Offline()

    On Error Resume Next
    Resource.LogInformation("Entering Offline() for " &
Resource.VirtualMachineName)

    Set virtualServer = CreateObject("VirtualServer.Application")
    Set vm = VirtualServer.FindVirtualMachine(Resource.VirtualMachineName)
    Set state = vm.Save()

    Select Case err.number <> 0
        'Handle the case where the virtual machine is not already in the "Running"
state at the time the resource is taken offline.
        Case err.number = "2684617222"
            Resource.LogInformation("Save() was called for virtual machine " &
Resource.VirtualMachineName & ", however it was not in the started state.")
        'Handle another case where the virtual machine is not already in the
"Running" state at the time the resource is taken offline.
        Case err.number = "-1610350074"
            Resource.LogInformation("Save() was called for virtual machine " &
Resource.VirtualMachineName & ", however it was not in the started state.")
        Case Else
            Resource.LogInformation("Save() for virtual machine " &
Resource.VirtualMachineName & " failed with error " & err.number)
            Offline = err.number
            Exit Function
    End Select

    Call state.WaitForCompletion(Timeout)
    If state.IsComplete = TRUE Then
        Offline = 0
```

Part IX: Development and Debugging in Virtual Machines

```vb
        End If

End Function


'*********************************************************************************
'*************************************************************************
'Terminate()
'
'If Online() failed because the virtual machine was already "Running"
(VirtualMachineFailedOnline = FALSE), then Terminate() needs to attempt to save
state.
'If UseAdditionsIsAlive = 1 and VirtualMachineHasHeartbeat = TRUE, then take
failure action specified by AdditionsIsAliveFailureRecoveryAction.
'*********************************************************************************
'*************************************************************************
Function Terminate()

    On Error Resume Next
    Set virtualServer = CreateObject("VirtualServer.Application")
    Set vm = virtualserver.FindVirtualMachine(Resource.VirtualMachineName)

    If VirtualMachineFailedOnline = TRUE Then
        Set state = vm.Save()
        Call state.WaitForCompletion(Timeout)
        Exit Function
    End If

    If Resource.UseAdditionsIsAlive = 1 AND virtualMachineHasHeartbeat = TRUE Then
        If Resource.AdditionsIsAliveFailureRecoveryAction = 0 Then
            Set state = vm.Save()
            Call state.WaitForCompletion(Timeout)
            Exit Function
        Else
            Set state = vm.TurnOff()
            Call state.WaitForCompletion(Timeout)
            Exit Function
        End If
    End If

End Function


'*********************************************************************************
'*************************************************************************
'Close()
'
'Return success
'*********************************************************************************
'*************************************************************************
Function Close()
    Close = 0
End Function
```

Index

SYMBOLS AND NUMERICS

1-Gbit network, 86–88
2.4 kernel Linux, 42, 456
2D video card, 32
3DNow!, 290
/3GB boot parameter, 78
24-bit color modes, 43
32-bit operating systems, 77–78
64-bit operating systems, 77–78
100-Mbit network, 86, 87
802.3 (Ethernet) standard, 31
802.5 (Token Ring) standard, 31

A

abstraction
  hardware, 6
  virtual machines, 4
AcceptButton, **426**
access
  to administrative website, 558
  to BIOS, 32
  COM. See COM API access
  from PowerShell, 408
  restricting, 165–168
  to virtual machine, 165–168
access control list (ACL), 166, 489

access restriction, 165–168
access right descriptors, 389
accessed-denied error, 72, 555
accountant, virtual machine, 387–389
ACL (access control list), 166, 489
ACPI (Advanced Configuration and Power
    Interface), 250
activation, grace period for, 58
Active Directory
  Domains and Trusts, 73
  environment, 20
  server backup, 191
active mode (FTP), 151
ActiveX control, VMRC, 19, 424
Adaptec SCSI controller, 89
AddDVDROMDrive, **370**
Additional Commands (Sysprep)
  discussed, 122
  with Windows 2000 server, 61
ADDLOCAL, 17
Administration Agent (ADS), 221
Administrative website. See Virtual Server
    Administrative website
administrator password (Sysprep)
  discussed, 55
  encryption of, 60
  with Windows 2000 server, 60–61, 64
  with Windows Vista, 68
administrators group, local, 70
ADS. See Automated Deployment Services
Advanced Configuration and Power Interface
    (ACPI), 250

Advanced Programmable Interrupt Controller

Advanced Programmable Interrupt Controller (APIC), 250

Allocated MB, 107

Allocated Pages, 108

`AllSigned` **setting, 405**

AMD

hardware virtualization, 78

NUMA, 95

Opteron 246 processors, 86

anonymous authentication, 482–483

answer file (Sysprep 2.0)

defined, 54

discussed, 61–63

viewing, 56–58

with Windows 2000 server, 61

with Windows NT, 64

antispyware software, 147–148

antivirus software, 147–148

apartments, threading, 301

APIC (Advanced Programmable Interrupt Controller), 250

application debugging

automated remote debugging, 547–548

discussed, 545–546

manual remote debugging, 546

approval, automatic, 120–121

Approve for Detection, 120, 123

Approve for Installation, 120, 123

ASP.NET

advantages of, 477

authentication with, 482–483

ChangeState.aspx, 522–536

COM API access with, 325–331

CreateNewVM.aspx, 504–522

Default.aspx, 485–504

discussed, 477–479

identity in, 482–483

IIS and, 483–485

impersonation in, 483

solutions with, 541

thread identity in, 482–483

user account in, 478

VMRC.aspx, 536–541

ASPX pages, 485

ASR backup. *See Automated System Recovery backup*

assumeeyes, 142

`AttachedDriveTypes`, **356**

`AttachHostDrive`, **370**

`AttachImage`, **370**

`AttachToVirtualNetwork`, **377**

Audit options, 58

AUOptions, 133

authentication

anonymous, 482–483

with ASP.NET, 482–483

Basic Authentication, 184, 185

choosing type of, 183–185

configuring, 184–185

discussed, 183–185

IIS and, 482–483

NTLM, 20, 183–185

options for, 346

types of, 183

user, 182

VMRC, 182

AutoInstallMinorUpdates, 133

automated backup, 193

Automated Deployment Services (ADS)

Administration Agent, 221

booting to, 233

Deployment Agent, 233, 234

discussed, 215

setup for, 217–219

static IP address for, 218

in VSMT, 234–235

automated remote debugging, 547–548

automated setup, 54

Automated System Recovery (ASR) backup

with NTBackup, Advanced mode, 239

with NTBackup, Wizard mode, 238–239

restoring, to virtual machine, 239–241

for Windows Server 2003, 238–245

for Windows Server XP, 238–245

automated updating

discussed, 116–117

with WSUS, 117–136

with YUM, 137–144

automated virtual machine library, 51–52

automatic approval (WSUS), 120–121

automatic detection, 265

automatic grouping, 112

automatic restart (WSUS), 128–129

automatic start

problems with, 556

virtual machine COM object, 363–364

automatic update. *See automated backup*

automatic updates, 126

automation, 401–404

`AvailableSystemCapacity`, **348**

568

B

Background Intelligent Transfer Service (BITS), 117, 118

backing up
Active Directory server, 191
automated, 193
with Backup Wizard, 195–199
base virtual machines, 144
with command-line interface, 201–203
detailed log for, 198
discussed, 187, 212
to DVD drives, 239
files, 189–193, 240
full system, 241–243
graphical interface for, 194
guest operating system, 191
incremental, 190
inside virtual machine, 193–208
locating file for, 240
log for, 198
machine file-based, 193–194
for manual migration, 241–243, 244–245
problems with, 193–194
in Red Hat Enterprise Linux 4, 205–208
from remove backup server, 208–209
for resiliency, 8
scheduling, 199–201
software for, 238–245
strategies for, 211
for Sysprep, 144
with VHDMount, 187–188
of virtual machine files, 189–193
of Virtual Server, 210–211
VMC and, 189
with VSS, 203, 209–210
with Windows 2000, 203, 241–243
with Windows NT 4.0, 203–204
with Windows Server 2003, 194–203, 241–243
with Windows Vista, 204–205
with Windows XP, 194–203, 205, 241–243
backup log, summary, 198
Backup Reports dialog box, 197
backup software, 238–245
Backup tab, 196
Backup Type tab, 198
Backup Wizard, 195–199
bandwidth, 82

base virtual machine
backup for, 144
cloning, 398–401
languages for, 122
Linux, 70–72
passwords for, 55
Sysprep for, 53
updating of, 144
Basic Authentication, 184, 185
BIOS
NUMA and, 96
with virtual network, 32
BITS (Background Intelligent Transfer Service), 117, 118
"block level" clone, 25
boot failures, 230–231
boot loader, 46
boot parameter, /3GB, 78
boot partitions, multiple, 217
boot policy, 231
Branding (OEM), 61
"broken" virtual machines, 9
"brute force" attack, 184
buttons, naming issues with, 426

C

cache memory, 95
CancelButton_Click, **426, 507, 524, 537**
candidate selection, 98–99
casual virtual machine library, 49–50
CD/DVD drive
imaging, 246
physical, 29
as storage, 22–29
centralized virtual machine library, 50–51
chaining (WSUS), 118
change permissions, 165
ChangeState.aspx, 485, 522–536
ChangeStateButton_Click, **490**
checking process, 227
checkpointing, 113
cleanup, 264–266
client virtual machine
emulated SCSI and, 281–282
in WSUS, 123–131
client-side targeting, 127

clock=pit option

`clock=pit` **option, 42, 46**
cloning
  base virtual machine, 398–401
  "block level," 25
  SCVMM and, 112
  support for, 112
  of virtual machine, 112
cluster group, 280, 293–295
cluster network, private, 275
cluster node
  pinging, 275
  preparation for, 272–274
  preparing, 272–275
  SCSI setup for, 275–282
  on virtual machine, 294
cluster resource script, 294–295
cluster service, 278–280
cluster user account, 275–276
ClusterDC, 271
clustered Virtual Server, 291–292
clustering. See also Virtual Server clustering
  configuration of, 285–286
  dynamically expanding virtual hard disk, 277
  with emulated SCSI, 269–282
  with iSCSI, 5, 282–286, 285–286
  public network, 270
  Share SCSI bus, 276
  support for, 5
  of virtual machine, 5, 269–286
`CoInitializeSecurity`, **302–303, 314, 458**
color
  24-bit mode, 43
  in Linux, 43, 46
COM (Component Object Model) API
  constants used in, 341
  defined, 299
  discussed, 299, 333
  impersonation in, 300
  security with, 300–301
  summary request, 409
  tabbing through, 408
  threading apartments in, 301
  VM task objects, 338
COM API access
  from ASP.NET, 325–331
  C# code, sample, 310–315, 329–331
  from managed code, 305–323
  from Microsoft Windows PowerShell, 323–325
  from native code, 302–305
  remotely, 331–333

  requirements for, 300–301
  from VBScript, 301–302
  Visual Basic .NET code, sample, 307–310,
    319–323, 326–328
COM objects. See also virtual machine COM object;
  Virtual Server COM object
  discussed, 299–300
  .NET framework for, 305–307
  for removable storage, 344
  for virtual networks, 373–375
COM ports, 32
command, YUM, 143
command line-based installation, 17
command-line interface
  backing up with, 201–203
  of PowerShell, 408
compacting
  dynamically expanding virtual hard disk, 24–25, 557
  imaging for, 25
compatibility issues, 223
complexity, 335
Component Object Model API. See under COM API
compressed tar archives, 208
computer groups (WSUS), 119
computer name, static, 55. See also static IP
  address
computer name (Sysprep)
  discussed, 55
  with Windows 2000 server, 60, 63
`ConfigID`, **356**
configuration values, 395–396
`Connect` **routine, 488, 507, 524**
connected virtual network adapter, 30
connections
  kernel debugging of, 550–552
  problems with, 556
consistency, 193
consolidation, 7
constants
  in COM API, 341
  in PowerShell, 416
constrained delegation, 73
context switch
  discussed, 79
  Host-to-VMM, 108
`Continue` **option, 412**
control permission, 165
conversion
  of dynamically expanding virtual hard disk, 26
  VSMT for, 234

CORE 1.5 (WMI), 216
`CoSetProxyBlanket,` **314–315, 323, 406, 444**
CPU allocation, 82
CPU load, 82, 86
crashes
 solutions for, 555
 virtual machine, 4
 VSMT and, 230–231
`CreateButton_Click,` **491**
`CreateFloppyDiskImage,` **344**
CreateNewVM.aspx, 485, 504–522
`CreateVirtualMachine,` **342**
`CreateVirtualNetwork,` **373**
`CreateVMButton_Click,` **508**
critical devices, 249
critical updates, 120
cscript, 337
Cumulative Guest Run Time, 108
custom installation, 16
Customize the Software (Sysprep), 60

D

DACL (discretionary access control list), 165
DAG archive, 140
daily schedule setting, 199
DCOM (Distributed COM), 182–183
debugging
 application, 545–548
 automated remote debugging, 547–548
 discussed, 545
 firewalls and, 546
 kernel, 548–552
 manual remote debugging, 546
 remote debugging, 546–548
 symbols for, 551
 virtual machine, 545
DEC 21140 network adapter, 29
Decline update, 123
default settings, 98
Default.aspx, 485–504
definition updates, 121
defragmentation, 93
delegation, constrained, 73
`DeleteButton_Click,` **490–491**
demonstrations, 9–10
Deployment Agent (DA), 233, 234

Description of service, 154
`DetachFromVirtualNetwork,` **377**
detailed backup log, 198
Details tab, 123
Detection, Approve for, 120, 123
DetectionFrequency, 133
DetectionFrequencyEnabled, 133
Device Manager, 292
DHCP server
 configuration, 219–220, 272
 for domain joining, 56, 61
 IP addresses for, 272
 network, 375–377
 for physical to virtual migration, 219–220
 virtual, 30, 375–377
Diagram option (MOM), 111
differencing virtual hard disk
 creating, 343
 discussed, 26–28, 89
 full copies vs., 52
 for new virtual machines, 144
 for virtual machine library, 52
differential tar archives, 207
`DiscardSavedState,` **358–359**
`DiscardUndoDisks,` **359**
Disconnect idle connections setting, 181
discretionary access control list (DACL), 165
disk write failure, 24
display object, 381–382
display settings, 54
display size changes, 438–440
Distributed COM (DCOM), 182–183
DNS server, 375
Documentation and Developer Resources, 16
Domain (Sysprep)
 discussed, 55–56
 with Windows 2000 server, 61
Domain Administrator password, 271
domain controller
 setup, with emulated SCSI, 271–272
 static IP address for, 271–272
domain joining
 DHCP for, 56, 61
 of virtual machine, 69
"Don't reset grace period for activation" option, 58
DOS-based networking, 247
driver
 F6 floppy driver, 37
 HAL, 231
 IDE. See IDE drivers

driver (continued)

driver (continued)
  SCSI. *See* SCSI drivers
  storage. *See* storage drivers
  VMM, 108
  in Windows 2000, 265
  in Windows NT 4.0, 265
  WSUS, 121
"dry runs," 8
dual processing computer, 83–86
DVD drives. *See also* **CD/DVD drive**
  backing up to, 239
  floppies vs., 344
  on IDE controller, 370
  location changing, 370
  scripting, 370–372
  as storage, 22–29
dynamic MAC address, 29–30, 377
dynamically expanding virtual hard disk
  in clustering, 277
  compacting, 24–25, 557
  conversion of, 26
  creating, 343
  discussed, 24, 39, 89
  errors in, 24
  fixed-size virtual hard disk and, 23, 26
  maximum size of, 26
  problems with, 557
  space in, 24
  undo disks and, 92

E

EFS (Encrypting File System), 169
802.5 (Token Ring) standard, 31
802.3 (Ethernet) standard, 31
ElevateNonAdmins, 132
emulated device(s)
  discussed, 21, 30
  for networking, 29–31
  for storage, 22–29
  in Virtual Server 2005, 21–30
emulated SCSI
  application setup, 280–281
  client virtual machines and, 281–282
  cluster node preparation for, 272–274
  cluster node setup for, 275–282
  cluster service and, 278–280

  clustering with, 269–282
  discussed, 269
  domain controller setup with, 271–272
  shared disk configuration for, 276–278
  testing with, 281–282
  Virtual Server setup with, 269–271
Enabled configuration, 127
Encrypting File System (EFS), 169
encryption
  SSL and, 174
  of Sysprep administrator password, 60
end user, 335
end user license agreement (EULA), 38
error(s)
  access-denied error, 72, 555
  with added virtual machine, 556–557
  configuration value, 557
  in dynamically expanding virtual hard disk, 24
  from failure. *See* failure
  in migration, 233
  moving disks, 294
  page-cannot-be-displayed error, 556
  on SPNs, 557
  unknown/unexpected, 337
  unregistered SPNs, 557
error handling
  in MOM, 110
  in PowerShell, 410, 412
  in VBScript, 336–337
Ethernet (802.3) standard, 31
EthernetAddress, **377**
EULA (end user license agreement), 38
event
  classes of, 104
  display of, 104
  ID for, 107
  scripting, 392–395
event handlers, .NET, 443
event log
  display of, 104
  monitoring with, 106–107
Exceptions, VMM, 108
Exchange server, 6, 53
Exchange Server (Microsoft), 53
Exclude Files option, 198–199
exclude option, 142
execute permissions, 166
ExecuteCommand, **386**
execution, pipeline, 411–412
expand.exe, 248

graphical interface

express installation files, **122**
external firewall, **148**
external firewalls, **182–183**
External Port number, **154**

F

F6 floppy driver, **37**
Factory and Audit options, **58**
failure. *See also* error
  boot failures, 230–231
  at deployment, 233
  disk write failure, 24
  error messages lacking at, 233
  of migration, 234–235
  resiliency to, 8
  system, 8
  of virtual hard disk, 38
  of Virtual Machine Additions, 558
FAT partitions, **217**
feature packs (WSUS), **121**
file(s)
  backing up, 189–193
  for backing up, 240
  VHD, 22
  VMC, 18
  VSV, 189
  VUD, 189
  in web-based interface, 36
  for WSUS, 122
  XML, 229
file permissions, **165–167**
file transfer protocol (FTP), **151**
filter(s)
  configuring, 160
  inbound, 157, 160
  for network traffic, 160–161
  outbound, 157, 160
FindVirtualNetwork, **373**
firewall(s)
  configuration of, 15–16
  debugging and, 546
  external, 148, 182–183
  on host operating system, 546
  inside virtual machine, 148
  network connections through, 149
  for network security, 148–149

  for TCP connections, 183
  visual studio and, 546
fixed-size virtual hard disk
  creating, 313
  discussed, 23, 39, 89
  dynamically expanding virtual hard disk and, 23, 26
  undo disks disabled on, 92
flexibility, **4, 335**
floppy drives
  disk images, 29
  DVD drives vs, 344
  F6, 37
  scripting, 372–373
formal virtual machine library, **50**
forwarding
  with Internet Connection Sharing, 153–154
  port, 153–154, 158
  with RRAS, 158
fragmentation, **93**
FTP (file transfer protocol), **151**
full copies, **52**
full format
  quick format vs., 38
  reformatting and, 39
full permission, **165**
full system backup
  for manual migration, 241–243
  with Windows Server 2003, 241–243
  with Windows XP, 241–243
full system recovery, **193**
fully automated setup, **54**
functions, PowerShell, **413–414**

G

gateway address, **375**
Gatherhw.exe, **219**
GetConfigurationValues, **395**
GetDVDFiles, **344**
GetFloppyDiskFiles, **344**
GetHardDisk, **343**
GetHardDiskFiles, **344**
GetVirtualMachineFiles, **342**
global function, PowerShell, **413**
GoButton_Click, **524**
grace period, **58**
graphical interface, **194**

573

Group Policy (WSUS)

Group Policy (WSUS), 119, 123–124
grouping, 112
GRUB boot loader, 46
guest CPU load, 82, 86
Guest External Interrupts, 108
guest operating system
  backing up, 191
  defined, 11
  discussed, 35, 47
  for kernel debugging, 549–550
  Red Hat Enterprise Linux 4, 41–46
  Windows Server 2003, 36–41
GuestOS object, 385–387

H

HAL. *See* hardware abstraction layer
hard disk
  physical, 246
  SAT A, 91
  virtual. *See* virtual hard disk
hardware
  abstraction of, 6
  emulated. *See* emulated device(s)
  identification strings, 360
  non-plug and play, 59
  performance of, 78–81
  for Virtual Server 2005, 12
  virtualization, 78
  virtualization of, 78–81
hardware abstraction layer (HAL)
  ACPI, 250
  APIC, 250
  configuration of, 249
  defined, 225
  discussed, 250–251
  drivers, 231
  loading, 263
  migration and, 254–256
  MP, 250–251
  Non-ACPI, 250
  PIC, 250
  types of, 250–251
  unsupported type, 231
  UP, 250–251
  in VSMT, 225
  wrong installation of, 225

havm.vbs, 561–566
HBA (Hot Bus Adapter) cards, 282
health information, in MOM 2005, 110–111
History properties, 373
host CPU load, 82, 86
"host key"
  defined, 37
  for log in, 39
host name, Linux, 71
host operating system
  defined, 11
  firewall on, 546
  kernel debugging connection for, 552
HostInfo object, 373, 391–392
Host-to-VMM context switch, 108
Host-to-VMM context switches, 108
Hot Bus Adapter (HBA) cards, 282
hotfix files, 229
HttpContext, 482, 483
HVM mode, 108
HVM-VP, 108
hyper-threaded processors, 88

I

IDE controller
  DVD drives on, 370
  PCI, 252
  SCSI controller vs., 89
  storage, 22
IDE disk
  configuration changes, 36
  Linux on, 41
  performance, 90
  Virtual Machine Additions and, 92
IDE drivers
  loading, 251–254, 262
  in Windows 2000, 253
  in Windows NT, 254
  in Windows Server 2003, 251–252
  in Windows XP, 251–252
identification, COM object for, 360–362
Identification String (OEM Duplicator String)
  discussed, 122
  hardware, 360
  with Windows 2000 server, 61
identity, in ASP.NET, 482–483

574

iSCSI

IIS. *See* Internet Information Server
IIS configuration. *See* Internet Information Server configuration
IIS Lockdown tool, 172
image encryption, 235
image file configuration (CD/DVD), 29
imaging
blank, 29
CD/DVD drive, 246
for compacting disks, 25
ISO, 116
for manual physical to virtual migration, 245–256
migration and, 249–256
over network, 247
of physical into virtual, 245–256
prepared, 237
unprepared, 237
VHDMount and, 247
virtual floppy disk, 29
of Windows systems, 247–248
in Windows Vista, 264
impersonation
in ASP.NET, 483
in COM, 300
discussed, 72, 163
inbound filters, 157, 160
incremental backups, 190
incremental tar archives, 207–208
Inquire option, 412
Install Printers, 122
"Install Updates and Shut Down," 124–125
Installation, Approve for, 120, 123
installation (Microsoft Virtual Server 2005)
advanced options for, 16–17
command line-based, 17
custom, 16
discussed, 14
firewall configuration, 15–16
MSI-based, 16–17
options for, 16–17
speed of, 80
website configuration, 15
Integrated Windows Authentication, 183
Integrated Windows Automatic, 183
Intel, hardware virtualization by, 78
Intel 21140 network adapter, 29, 39, 81
Intelide.sys, 235
intelligent placement technology, 113
interactivity, 335

internal firewall, 148
internal networking, 88
Internal Port number, 154
Internet Connection Sharing
discussed, 151–153
for network security, 151–154
port forwarding with, 153–154
Internet Explorer (Microsoft)
running, as administrator, 18
Trusted Sites, 231
Internet Information Server (IIS)
ASP.NET and, 483–485
authentication and, 482–483
default website of, removing, 173–174
Lockdown tool, 172
remote, 12
security with, 169–174
self-signed SSL certificates from, 179–180
SSL and, 174, 176
for web-based interface, 12
website configuration with, 15
Windows XP with, 173
Internet Information Server (IIS) configuration
securing, for Virtual Server, 171–174
on separate computers, 169–171
on Windows Codenamed Longhorn Server, 14
on Windows Server 2003, 13
on Windows Vista, 13–14
on Windows XP, 13
Internet Information Server (IIS) Lockdown tool, 172
Internet sharing, with NAT router, 151
Intranet, updating via, 126–127
IP address. *See also* static IP address
connectivity, 275
for DHCP server, 272
with NAT, 158
static, 218
with VSMT, 231
IsComplete, 339, 340, 443
iSCSI
cluster configuration with, 285–286
clustering with, 5, 282–286
defined, 282
discussed, 282–283
HBA cards, 282
preparation for, 283–284
shared data drive configuration for, 284–285
software-based target of, 284
targets, 282

575

IsEthernetAddressDynamic property

`IsEthernetAddressDynamic` **property, 377**
ISO imaging, 116
isolation, 4
ISORecorder, 116

K

Kerberos, 20, 181, 184, 185
kernel
discussed, 249
loading, 263
migration preparation of, 254–256
uniprocessor, 249
kernel debugging
connections, 550–552
discussed, 548–549
guest operating system for, 549–550
host operating system connection for, 552
named pipes and, 550–551
virtual machine connection for, 551–552
virtual serial port and, 550–551
kernel (ring 0) mode, 79
kernel mode code, 79, 80
kernel-level development, 548
keyboard object, 383–384
keystroke repetition, 559
Kudzu, 264

L

learning applications, 9
legacy applications, 8
LeoStream, 103
license agreement, end user, 38
Licensing Mode
discussed, 55
with Windows 2000 server, 60
LiLO boot loader, 46
line breaks, 443
linked virtual hard disk, 26, 343
Linux base virtual machines. *See also* **Red Hat**
Enterprise Linux 4
2.4 kernel, 42, 456
background of, 46

colors and, 43, 46
discussed, 70–72
failure of, 558
keystrokes repeated in, 559
PIT in, 42
problems with, 559
SIDs and, 70
Virtual Machine Addition installation, 558
"zero out" free space on, 25
Linux Yellow dog Updater, Modified (YUM), 137–144
automated updating with, 137–144
commands for, 143
configuring, 141–143
creating, 137–141
discussed, 137
offline, 141
using, 143
`loadVMRC`, **537**
Local Administrator
adding users to groups, 70
password, 271
"local computer" option, 107
log in
"host key" for, 39
with Windows NT, 66
log message IDs, 459
log out, of user, 70
logical unit number (LUN), 288–289
LPT port, 32
LPT1 port, 380
LUN (logical unit number), 288–289

M

MAC address
configuration, 29–30
dynamic, 29–30, 377
finding, 221
management of, 29
migration and, 225
of network card, 221
static, 377
machine file-based backup, 193–194
managed applications
creating, 457–476
discussed, 423
Virtual Server Administrative website and, 470–476
VMRC client for, 423–457, 468–470

migration

managed code, 305–323
manual physical to virtual migration
  with backup software, 238–245
  clean up after, 264–266
  with complete PC backup, 244–245
  discussed, 237–238, 266
  with full system backup, 241–243
  imaging, 245–256
  for Red Hat Enterprise Linux 4, 256, 264
  success rate of, 238
  with system image, unprepared, 256–264
  for Windows 2000, 241–243, 256–261, 265
  for Windows NT server, 253–254, 261–263, 265
  for Windows Server 2003, 238–243, 251–252,
    256–261, 264
  for Windows Vista, 244–245, 264
  for Windows XP server, 238–245, 251–253,
    256–261, 264
manual remote debugging, 546
manual updating, 116
mapping, to serial port, 548
maximum capacity, 97
MB, Allocated, 107
memory
  amount of, 94–95
  for cache, 94–95
  configuration settings for, 18
  non-uniform, 95–96
  PerfMon for, 95
  performance and, 5, 94–97
  utilization of, 94
  for virtual machine, 94
`MergeUndoDisks,` **360**
methods, PowerShell, 408–411
Microsoft
  licensing by, 187
  products of. *See specific types, e.g.:* Windows Server
    2003
  support policy of, 11
Microsoft Exchange server, 6, 53
Microsoft installer package (MSI), 16–17
Microsoft installer package-based (MSI-based)
  installation, 16–17
Microsoft Internet Explorer
  running, as administrator, 18
  Trusted Sites, 231
Microsoft (MS) Loopback Adapter
  discussed, 149
  for network security, 150–151
Microsoft Operations Manager (MOM) 2005
  Diagram option in, 111
  discussed, 108

  error handling in, 110
  health information in, 110–111
  for monitoring, 108–111
  Operator Console, 111
  performance monitoring with, 111
  reporting capabilities of, 111
  rules of, 111
  tasks in, 109
  virtualization reports with, 111
Microsoft SMS, 16
Microsoft SQL Server, 53
Microsoft SQL Server Desktop Edition, 217
Microsoft Virtual Hard Disk, 10
Microsoft Virtual Server 2005
  backing up, 210–211
  clustering of, 269–286
  configuring host environment of, 12–14
  creating virtual machines in, 17–19
  discussed, 11–23
  emulated devices in, 21–30
  hardware requirements for, 12
  host environment configuration with, 12–14
  installing, 14–17, 290–291
  PowerShell and, 408
  previous versions of, 5
  on separate computers, 169–171
  setup, with emulated SCSI, 269–271
  Virtual Machine Additions in, 33
  virtual machines and, 17–20
  virtual networks in, 31–33
Microsoft Virtual Server Programmers Guide, 341
Microsoft Windows PowerShell. *See* **PowerShell**
Microsoft Windows SQL Server 2000 Desktop
  Engine (WMSDE), 118
Microsoft Windows Update Catalog, 116
migration
  errors in, 233
  failure of, 234–235
  of HAL, 254–256
  imaging and, 249–256
  of kernel, 254–256
  MAC address and, 225
  manual. See manual physical to virtual migration
  physical to virtual. See physical to virtual migration
  SCVMM and, 112
  of storage drivers, 251–252, 251–254
  support for, 112
  of virtual machine, 112
  Windows NT 4.0, 232
  of Windows Server 2003, 251–252

577

migration (continued)

migration (continued)
Windows systems, 249, 251
of Windows XP, 251–252
Mini-Setup, 59
minor updates, WSUS for, 129–130
mixed capacity, 98
MMX, 193
modify permissions, 165
MOM 2005. *See* **Microsoft Operations Manager 2005**
MOM Operator Console, 111
monitoring (managing)
with MOM 2005, 108–111
with PerfMon, 107–108
with SCVMM, 112–113
SCVMM for, 112–113
with web interface, 103–106
with Windows event log, 106–107
monthly schedule setting, 199
mount points, NTFS, 289
mouse, scripting, 384–385
Move computers task, 119
MP (multiprocessor), 250–251
MSDE, 118
MSI (Microsoft installer package), 16–17
MSI-based (Microsoft installer package-based) installation, 16–17
Msvmscsi.sys, 235
MTA model. *See* **multithreaded apartment model**
multiple boot partitions, 217
multiprocessor (MP), 250–251
multithreaded apartment (MTA) model
defined, 301
handling, 322–323

N

named pipe
for COM port, 32
kernel debugging and, 550–551
virtual serial port to, 550–551
NAT. *See* **Network Address Translation router**
native code, COM API access from, 302–305
.NET framework
for COM objects, 305–307
event handlers, 443
for WSUS, 118
NetBIOS, 275

Netbootdisk.com, 247
NetDom, 69, 70
network adapter
DEC 21140, 29
Intel 21140, 29, 39, 81
isolating, 164
object, 377
on physical computer, 30
scripting, 377–379
security with, 164
virtual, 19
Network Address Translation (NAT) router
Internet sharing with, 151
ports in, 153–154
RRAS for, 156–157
security with, 152
network card
enabling, 232
MAC address of, 221
network connection
configuration, 30
routing, 149–161
security with, 149–161
through firewall, 149
network DHCP server, 375–377
network notes, virtual, 30
network performance, 556
network security
discussed, 148
with firewalls, 148–149
with Internet Connection Sharing, 151–154
with MS Loopback Adapter, 150–151
by routing network connections, 149–161
with RRAS, 155–161
Network Service, 106, 170
Network Settings (Sysprep), 61
network storage, 72–73
network traffic, 160–161
network-based scripting, 70
network-based tape drives, 194
networking
custom options for, 39
DOS-based, 247
emulated devices for, 29–31
internal, 88
MAC address configuration, 29–30
network connection configuration, 30
performance and, 81–88
performance of, 5
virtual networks and, 30–31
Networking Components, 55

578

performance

NewSID, 53
"no media" configuration, 28
NoAutoRebootWithLoggedOnUsers, 133
NoAutoUpdate, 134
Non-ACPI (Non-Advanced Configuration and Power Interface), 250
Non-Advanced Configuration and Power Interface (Non-ACPI), 250
non-plug and play hardware, 59
Non-Uniform Memory Architecture (NUMA), 94–96
"NoSIDGen," 59
Not Configured, 125, 128, 129
NSR, 238
NTBackup
   Advanced mode, 239
   modes of, 194
   NSR creation with, 238
   options for, 196–197
   at startup, 196
   VSS and, 209
   in Windows Vista, 205
   Wizard mode, 238–239
NTFS mount points, 289
Ntkrnlpa.exe, 255
NTLM authentication, 20, 183–185
NUMA (Non-Uniform Memory Architecture), 94–96
NUMA ratio, 95, 96

O

OEM Branding, 61
OEM Duplicator String. *See Identification String*
On Error Resume Next, 336–337
OnSwitchedDisplay **event handler, 442**
operating system. *See also specific types,*
   e.g.: Windows XP
   32-bit, 77–78
   64-bit, 77–78
   guest, 11, 191
   host, 11
Operator Console (MOM), 111
OptionExplicit, 336
options setting, 119–120
OSI layer 3, 29, 31, 148
outbound filters, 157, 160

P

P2V migration. *See Physical to virtual migration*
P2Vdrivers.xml, 230
packet filtering, static, 157, 160
page file (Windows), 94
page-cannot-be-displayed error, 556
Page_Load, 490, 507, 524
Pages, Allocated, 108
parallel port, 380–381
ParallelPorts collection, 380
"parent" disk, 26
parser, script, 106
passive mode (FTP), 151
password
   administrator, 55, 60–61, 64
   for base virtual machine, 55
   changing, 70
   for Domain Administrator, 271
   for Local Administrator, 271
   user account, 70
pause **command, 443**
PCI IDE controller, 252
Pciidex.sys, 235
PerfMon (Performance Monitor)
   for memory, 95
   monitoring with, 107–108
performance
   in 32-bit operating systems, 77–78
   in 64-bit operating systems, 77–78
   at 100%, 82
   candidate selection for, 98–99
   defragmentation, 93
   discussed, 77, 93
   fragmentation for, 93
   of hardware, 78–81
   hardware virtualization, 78–81
   IDE disk, 90
   of internal networking, 88
   memory and, 5, 94–97
   network, 556
   networking, 5, 81–88
   resource allocations for, 97–98
   slow, 556
   storage, 88–93
   testing, 6
   Virtual Machine Additions for, 33
   virtualization and, 5–6

579

Performance Monitor (PerfMon)

Performance Monitor (PerfMon)
for memory, 95
monitoring with, 107–108
permission
change, 165
control, 165
execute, 166
file system, 165
full, 165
modify, 165
read, 166
remove, 165
special, 165
for VHD files, 166
view, 165
for VNC, 166–167
physical CD/DVD drive, 29
physical clusters
preparation for, 288–290
Virtual Server installation on, 290–291
physical computer serial port, 32
physical hard disk
mounted, 246
virtual hard disk vs., 38
physical to virtual (P2V) migration. *See also* **manual**
physical to virtual migration
checking process for, 227
compatibility issues with, 223
deployment, 227
DHCP configuration for, 219–220
discussed, 215, 236
process of, 222–227
script file generation for, 223–226
SCVMM and, 113, 235
server setup for, 217–219
source computer and, 216–217, 222, 226–227
source server information for, 222–223
System Center Virtual Machine Manager and, 235
tools for, 113
Virtual Server configuration for, 221–222
with VSMT, 215–216, 227–235
physical Virtual Server clustering, 288–291
PIC (Programmable Interrupt Controller), 250
pinging, cluster node, 275
pipeline execution, 411–412
PIT (Programmable Interval Timer), 42
PlateSpin, 103
"PnP," 59
`populateListBoxes`, **488**

port(s)
for administrative website, 15
in NAT router, 153–154
parallel, 380–381
scripting, 380–381
serial, 548
for website, 15
port 21, 153, 154
port 80, 15, 182
port 135, 15
port 443, 182
port 1024, 15, 182, 183
port 5900, 36
Port 5900 (TCP), 182
port forwarding
with Internet Connection Sharing, 153–154
with RRAS, 158
portability, 193
PortsInternetAvailable, 183
post-deployment commands, 69–70
power
management settings, 201
processing, 82
PowerShell
accessing Virtual Server from, 408
advantages of, 405
COM API access from, 323–325
command line of, 408
constants in, 416
discussed, 405
environment for, 405–407
error handling in, 410, 412
functions of, 413–414
global function in, 413
integration of, 113
methods of, 408–411
objects of, 408–411
pipeline execution in, 411–412
pipelining execution in, 411–412
profile of, 407
properties of, 408–411
script configuration on, 406–407
script parameters of, 413–414
in SCVMM, 113
set up for, 405–407
Set-ExecutionPolicy on, 406
variable declaration in, 412
VBScript vs., 405
Virtual Server and, 408

580

remove permissions

Index

"Pre-activated" option, 58
"preferred" node, 96
prepared system image, 237
PressAndReleaseKey, **383**
PressKey, **383**
print servers, 4
printers, install, **122**
private network
  cluster, 275
  IP addresses on, 158
problems, 555–559
processing power, 82
product key, 54
product type specifications, **121–122**
ProductID (Sysprep), 63
Programmable Interrupt Controller (PIC), 250
Programmable Interval Timer (PIT), 42
programmatical shutdown, 193
provisioning
  SVCMM and, 113
  virtualization for, 4
proxy option, 143
proxy server, 122
public network
  clustering, 270
  VMRC on, 174
PXE, 226

Q

quick format, 38

R

R2 SP1, Virtual Server. *See Virtual Server R2 SP1*
RAID storage, 88
Raise Domain Functional Level, 73
rbfg.exe, 226
read permissions, 166
read-only properties
  of virtual machine, 356–357
  Virtual Server COM object, 348–349

"Reanalyzing cluster," 279
rebooting, 70
RebootRelaunchTimeout, **134**
RebootRelaunchTimeoutEnabled, **134**
RebootWarning, **134**
RebootWarningTimeout, **134**
recovery, full system, 193
Red Hat Enterprise Linux 4
  backing up in, 205–208
  configuring, after installation, 46
  guest operating system of, 41–46
  host name in, 71
  on IDE disk, 41
  installing, 41–46
  manual migration for, 256, 264
  SCSI and, 41
  on SCSI disk, 41
  speed of, 80
  tar archives in, 206–208
  Virtual Machine Additions for, 44–46, 558
refresh rate, of administrative website, 104
REG files (Sysprep), 65–66
Regional Settings, 56
RegisterVirtualMachine, **342**
RegisterVirtualNetwork, **373**
Registry
  editing, 131, 247–248
  offline editing, 247–248
  Windows, 247–248
  WSUS with, 131–135
relative weight, 97
relative weight-based capacity, 98
ReleaseKey, **383**
reliability, 191
remote access, to COM API, 331–333
Remote Boot Floppy (Windows), 231
Remote Control, 106
remote debugging
  automated, 547–548
  manual, 546
Remote Desktop, 490
remote IIS, 12
Remote Procedure Calls, 15
RemoteSigned setting, 405
removable storage. *See also specific types, e.g.:*
    CD/DVD drive
  COM objects for, 344
  for Virtual Server COM object, 344–346
remove permissions, 165

581

RemoveDVDROMDrive

`RemoveDVDROMDrive`, **370**
reports (MOM 2005), 111
repository metadata file, 140
re-prompt delays, 130–131
RescheduleWaitTime, 134
RescheduleWaitTimeEnabled, 134
Reseal option, 58, 59
reservation based capacity, 98
reserved capacity, 97
resiliency, 8
resource(s)
 allocating, 97–98
 moving, 294
 multiple, 294
Resource Kit (Windows NT 4.0), 70
resource script, cluster, 294–295
`Response.Redirect`, **491**
restart
 automatic, 128–129
 delays, 130
Restore and Manage Media, 196
Restore tab, 198
`Restricted` **setting, 405**
`resume` **command, 443**
retries option, 142
Revisions to Updates, 120
ring 0 (kernel) mode, 79
ring 3 (run user mode) code, 79
router
 NAT. *See* Network Address Translation router
 RRAS as, 158–160
 for traffic, 149
Routing and Remote Access Services (RRAS)
 discussed, 155
 for filtering network traffic, 160–161
 for NAT routing, 156–157
 for network security, 155–161
 port forwarding with, 158
 as standard router, 158–160
RPM, 138–140
RRAS. *See* Routing and Remote Access Services
rsync, 140, 141
`Run as Administrator`, **18**
Run Once, 122
run user mode (ring 3 code) code, 79

S

S3 Trio 32/64 video adapter, 32
SAN (storage area network), 288–289
SAT A hard disk, 91
saved state, 192, 193
 discard, 358
 discussed, 192, 193
 problems with, 556
 at shutdown, 556
scalability, 6
Schedule Jobs tab, 196–197
Schedule Task setting, 199
scheduled system scans, 148
ScheduledInstallDay, 126, 135
ScheduledInstallTime, 126, 135
schedules
 backing up, 199–201
 daily schedule setting, 199
 multiple, 199
 options for, 199
 timing of, 199
 WSUS, 121
script file generation, 223–226
script parser, 106
scripting. *See also* VBScript
 cluster resource script, 294–295
 complexity, 335
 cscript, 337
 DVD drives, 370–372
 end user, 335
 events, 392–395
 flexibility, 335
 floppy drives, 372–373
 GuestOS object, 385–387
 interactivity, 335
 keyboard objects, 383–384
 launching, 106
 network adapters, 377–379
 network-based, 70
 PowerShell, 406–407, 413–414
 SCSI controller, 364–365
 virtual hard disk, 365–370
 virtual machine COM object, 362–363
 for Virtual Server clustering, 291
 Virtual Server COM object, 350–352
 wscript, 337

solutions

SCSI adapter
install confirmation for, 274
shared, 277
VSMT and, 232–233

SCSI controller
from Adaptec, 89
IDE controllers vs., 89
scripting, 364–365
storage, 22
virtual, 22
VM-SCSI, 89

SCSI disk
configuration for, 36
emulated. *See* emulated SCSI
Linux and, 41
Linux on, 41

SCSI drivers
disk attachment for, 252
loading, 252, 254, 262–263
in Windows NT, 254
in Windows Server 2003, 252

SCSIControllers collection, 364

SCVMM. *See* **System Center Virtual Machine Manager**

SDK, VSS, 209

search paths, 349

second virtual hard disk, 247

Secure Sockets Layer. *See under* **SSL**

security. *See also* **network security**
with access restriction, 165–168
with antivirus/antispyware software, 147–148
with authentication, 183–185
with COM API, 300–301
discussed, 72, 147, 163–164
with EFS, 169
with external firewalls, 182–183
with IIS, 169–174
with NAT routers, 152
with network adapters, 164
with RRAS over NAT, 157
with SSL, 20, 174–180
with VMRC, 181–182

security identifiers (SIDs)
discussed, 53
in Linux, 70
regeneration of, 59

security object, 389–391

security updates (WSUS), 121

SecurityAnonymous (COM), 300
SecurityDelegation (COM), 300
SecurityIdentification (COM), 300
SecurityImpersonation (COM), 300, 306, 314
self-service provisioning tool, 113
self-signed SSL certificates
discussed, 179
for IIS, 179–180
for VMRC, 180–181

SelfSSL, 179
serial port
mapping to, 548
physical, 32
scripting, 379–380
virtual, 550–551

server consolidation, 7
service packs (WSUS), 121
`SetBusLocation`, **370**
`SetConfigurationValues`, **395**
`SetDimensions`, **381**
`Set-ExecutionPolicy`, **406**
`SetParameter`, **387**
`SetSchedulingParameters`, **387**
Setting Change category, 106
Setup Manager, 54
Setup.exe, 14
Share SCSI bus, 276
shared data drive, 284–285
shared disk, emulated SCSI and, 276–278
shared SCSI adapter, 277
shutdown
discussed, 59
programmatical, 193
saved state at, 556
of virtual machine, 192
in Windows Server 2003, 59

SIDs. *See* **Security identifiers**
`SilentlyContinue`, **412**
single processing computer, 83–86
single threaded apartment (STA) model, 301
single user interface (SCVMM), 112
64-bit operating systems, 77–78
slicing, time, 78
SMS (Microsoft), 16
snapshot, VSS, 209
software, antivirus/antispyware, 147–148
software development, 8
solutions, 555–559

583

source computer

source computer
capturing, 226–227
migration and, 216–217, 222, 226–227
migration requirements for, 216–217
preparing, for migration, 222
source server information, 222–223
special permissions, 165
SPNs, errors on, 557
SQL Server (Microsoft), 53, 118, 217
SQL Server Desktop Edition (Microsoft), 217
SSE2, 193
SSL (Secure Sockets Layer)
configuring, 174–180
encryption and, 174
IIS and, 174
security with, 20, 174–180
on Virtual Server Administrative web site, 174–176
on VMRC, 174, 177–179
SSL certificates
assigning, 175, 177
existing, 176–179
requesting, 174–175, 177
requiring, for IIS, 176
self-signed, 179–181
workaround for, 178–179
STA (single threaded apartment) model, 301
StarWind software, 284
state
discard, 358
restoration to, 193
saved, 192, 193, 358
saving, 192
Static Ethernet (MAC), 29
static IP address. See also IP address
for ADS, 218
discussed, 55
for domain controller, 271–272
MS Loopback Adapter and, 151
static MAC address, 377
static packet filtering, 157, 160
Status tab, 123
Stop **option, 412**
storage
CD/DVD drives, 22–29
emulated devices for, 22–29
floppy drives, 29
fragmentation of, 93
network, 72–73
performance and, 88–93

performance of, 5
RAID, 88
removable, 344
SCSI controller, 22
virtual hard disk, 72–73
of virtual hard disk, 72–73
virtual hard disks, 22–28
storage area network (SAN), 288–289
storage drivers
migration of, 251–254
of Windows 2000, 252–253
of Windows NT 4.0, 253–254
of Windows Server 2003, 251–252
of Windows XP, 251–252
subnet, 156
summary backup log, 198
summary request, COM API, 409
Support Drivers, **348**
support policy (Microsoft), 11
symbols, for debugging, 551
synchronization (WSUS), 121–122
Sysprep
answer file of, 56–58, 61–63
backup, 144
for base virtual machine, 53
discussed, 53
drawbacks of, 65–66
running, 58–59, 63, 66
user interface for, 59
with Windows 2000 server, 60–63
for Windows base virtual machines, 53–69
with Windows NT, 64–66
with Windows Server 2003, 53–59
with Windows Vista, 66–69
with Windows XP, 53–59
System Center Virtual Machine Manager (SCVMM)
migration and, 112
for monitoring, 112–113
physical to virtual migration and, 113, 235
PowerShell in, 113
system failures, 8
system file loading, 248–249
system imaging
prepared, 237
unprepared, 237
in Windows Vista, 264
system scans, scheduled, 148
System State option, 195

584

T

tape archives. See tar archives
tape drives, network-based, 194
tar archives (tape archives), 206–208
  compressed, 208
  creating, 206–207
  differential, 207
  incremental, 207–208
  restoring, 206–207
TargetGroup, 132
TargetGroupEnabled, 132
TCP
  defining, 154
  firewall for, 183
TCP Port 5900, 182
TCP/IP, 31, 275
Telephony, 56
template virtual machine, 479–482
TESTCLUSTER node, 280
testing
  advantages for, 545
  with emulated SCSI, 281–282
  performance, 6
text file (COM), 32
third-party firewalls, 15
32-bit operating systems, 77–78
thread identity (ASP.NET), 482–483
threading apartments, 301
"three machine problem," 72
/3GB boot parameter, 78
throttle option, 143
time slicing, 78
Time Stamp Counter (TSC), 42
time zone settings, 54
timeout option, 143
TimeZone (Sysprep), 67
Titanium processors, 11
Token Ring (802.5) standard, 31
tolerant option, 142
tools
  for physical to virtual migration, 113
  WSUS, 121
traffic routing, 149
training applications, 9
troubleshooting VSMT, 227–234
Trusted Sites (Internet Explorer), 231
try...catch statement, 491
TSC (Time Stamp Counter), 42

24-bit color modes, 43
2D video card, 32
2.4 kernel-based Linux, 42, 456
TypeAsciiText, 383
TypeKeySequence, 383

U

UDP, 154
undo disks
  discussed, 28, 89
  dynamically expanding disks and, 92
  fixed-size virtual hard disks and, 92
uniprocessor (UP), 250–251
uniprocessor kernel, 249
unprepared system image, 237
unregistered SPNs, 557
Unrestricted setting, 405
UP (uniprocessor), 250–251
Update Catalog (Microsoft Windows), 116
update CD, 116
update detection frequency (WSUS), 129
update rollups (WSUS), 121
Update Tasks panel, 123
updating
  automated. See automated updating
  of base virtual machines, 144
  declining, 123
  of definitions, 121
  discussed, 115
  with Intranet, 126–127
  lack of, 115–116
  manual, 116
  minor, 129–130
  nonexistant, 115–116
  WSUS, 120, 121, 129–130
UpTime, 348
URLScan tool, 172–173
UseInternetPorts, 183
user account
  in ASP.NET, 478
  cluster, 275–276
  password for, 70
user authentication, VMRC, 182
user interface (Sysprep 2.0), 59
UseWUServer, 135

variable declaration, in PowerShell

V

variable declaration, in PowerShell, 412
VBScript
  best practices for, 336–337
  COM API access from, 301–302
  discussed, 335
  error handling in, 336–337
  On Error Resume Next, 336–337
  execution environments of, 337
  OptionExplicit, 336
  PowerShell vs., 405
  running, 337
  Virtual Server COM object and, 341–352
  VM task objects, 338–341
  in Windows, 337
VHD files
  discussed, 189
  EFS on, 169
  functions for, 416
  permissions for, 166
  virtual hard disk as, 22
VHDMount
  backing up with, 187–188
  discussed, 148
  imaging, 247
video
  performance of, 5
  virtual network for, 32
  VMRC for, 32
video adapter, S3 Trio 32/64, 32
video card, 2D, 32
`VideoMode`, **381**
view permissions, 165
`ViewButton_Click`, **490**
virtual DHCP server, 30
Virtual Disk Operation, 107
Virtual Disk Service, 188
virtual floppy disk images, 29
virtual hard disk
  calls for, 343
  configuration settings for, 18–19
  creating, 343
  differencing, 26–28
  discussed, 22–28
  dynamically expanding, 23–26
  failure of, 38
  fixed-size, 23
  linked, 26
  network storage of, 72–73

  physical hard disk vs., 38
  scripting, 365–370
  second, 247
  size of, 190
  storing, 72–73
  undo disks, 28
  as VHD files, 22
  Virtual Server COM object for, 343–344
Virtual Hard Disk (Microsoft), 10
virtual hard disk COM object, 300
virtual machine. *See also* base virtual machine
  abstraction, 4
  additional, 556–557
  advantages of, 545
  ASR backups for, 239–241
  automatic grouping of, 112
  automation, 401–404
  backing up inside, 193–208
  "broken," 9
  checkpointing, 113
  cloning of, 112
  on cluster nodes, 294
  on clustered Virtual Server, 291–292
  clustering and, 5, 269–286, 291–292
  columnar display of, 104
  content determination for, 52–53
  crashes, 4
  creating, 17–19, 396–398
  debugging, 545
  display list, 104
  domain joining to, 69
  file backups, 189–193
  firewall inside, 148
  first, 17–20
  kernel debugging and, 551–552
  memory for, 94
  on Microsoft Virtual Server 2005, 17–20
  migration of, 112
  read-only properties, 356–357
  renaming, 70
  restricting access to, 165–168
  shutdown of, 192
  size of, 190
  starting, 19–20
  starting, in Virtual Server, 19–20
  template, 479–482
  Virtual Server and, 17–20
  Virtual Server COM object, 341–342
  viruses in, 152
  VMRC access to, 35

Virtual Server Administrative website

virtual machine accountant, 387–389
Virtual Machine Additions
  on 2.4 kernel-based Linux, 456
  IDE virtual hard disks and, 92
  Installation of, 40
  installer for, 41
  for mouse, 384
  for performance, 33
  for Red Hat Enterprise Linux 4, 44–46, 558
  VSMT and, 234–235
  in Windows 2000, 33
  in Windows Codenamed Longhorn Server, 33
  in Windows NT, 33
  in Windows Server 2003, 33, 40–41
  in Windows Vista, 33
  in Windows XP, 33
virtual machine category, 107
virtual machine COM object
  adding devices, 353–355
  automatic start, 363–364
  defined, 300
  DiscardSavedState, 358–359
  DiscardUndoDisks, 359–360
  discussed, 352
  for identification, 360–362
  property configuration, 355–357
  removing devices, 353–355
  scripting, 362–363
  state management with, 352–353
virtual machine configuration (VMC)
  backing up and, 189
  undo disk files in, 28
virtual machine file backup
  discussed, 189–190
  problems with, 190–191
  saved state for, 191–193
  shut down for, 191–193
virtual machine library
  advantages of, 50
  automated, 51–52
  casual, 49–50
  centralized, 50–51
  content determination for, 52–53
  defined, 49
  differencing disks for, 52
  disadvantages of, 50
  discussed, 49
  formal, 50
  full copies of, 52

  managed, 112
  types of, 49–52
virtual machine name, 18
Virtual Machine Remote Control Client (VMRC)
  access, to virtual machine, 35
  ActiveX control, 19, 424
  administrative display, 425
  display size changes, 438–440
  in installation, 16
  for interaction, 35
  locking down, 440–443
  for managed applications, 423–457, 468–470
  on public network, 174
  securing, 181–182
  security with, 181–182
  self-signed SSL certificates for, 379–380
  SSL on, 174, 177–179
  at startup, 19
  state handling, 443–457
  user authentication, 182
  for video, 32
  Virtual Server COM object and, 346–348
  web interface and, 35
virtual network
  BIOS access with, 32
  clustering and, 292–293
  COM objects for, 373–375
  COM ports in, 32
  discussed, 30
  LPT ports in, 32
  name of, 30
  for networking emulated devices, 30–31
  operation of, 31–33
  for video, 32
  in Virtual Server, 31–33
  Virtual Server COM object, 342–343
virtual network adapter, 19, 30
virtual network COM object, 300
Virtual Network Computer (VNC)
  discussed, 189
  file permissions for, 166–167
  TCP Port 5900, 182
virtual network notes, 30
virtual SCSI controller, 22
virtual serial port, 550–551
Virtual Server Administrative website
  access to, 558
  accessed-denied error, 555
  configuration of, 15

587

Virtual Server Administrative website (continued)

Virtual Server Administrative website (continued)
- on desktop operating systems, 15
- discussed, 15, 231, 470–476
- IIS, 173–174
- with IIS, 15
- page-cannot-be-displayed error, 556
- ports for, 15
- problems with, 557, 558
- refresh rate of, 104
- removing, 173–174
- SSL on, 174–176
- of VSMT, 231
- Windows Server 2003 and, 173, 179
- on Windows XP, 179
- for WSUS, 119

Virtual Server category, 107

Virtual Server clustering
- advantages of, 287
- cluster group for, 293–295
- disadvantages of, 287
- havm.vbs, 561–566
- layered, 288
- physical, 288–291
- preparation for, 288–290
- script for, 291
- virtual machines and, 288, 291–292
- virtual network configuration, 292–293

Virtual Server COM object
- accessing, 305
- discussed, 341
- path management with, 349–350
- read-only properties, 348–349
- removable storage for, 344–346
- scripting and, 350–352
- VBScript and, 341–352
- for virtual hard disks, 343–344
- for virtual machine manipulation, 341–342
- for virtual network manipulation, 342–343
- VMRC configuration and, 346–348

Virtual Server Host Clustering Step-By-Step Guide, 291

Virtual Server Migration Toolkit (VSMT)
- administrative website of, 231
- ADS Deployment Agent in, 234–235
- advanced options for, 234–235
- boot failures and, 230–231
- boot policy for, 231
- for conversion, 234
- crashes and, 230–231

- Hardware Abstraction Layer drivers in, 231
- image encryption and, 235
- IP address issues with, 231
- long migration and, 233
- network card enabling for, 232
- physical to virtual migration with, 215–216, 227–235
- problems with, 233–234
- SCSI adapter enabling, 232–233
- server setup for, 217–219
- software incompatibilities with, 228–230
- support for, 216
- troubleshooting, 227–234
- Virtual Machine Additions and, 234–235
- for Vmware conversion, 234

Virtual Server R2 SP1
- discussed, 5, 19, 41, 77
- for scanning, 148
- Virtual Server Host Clustering Step-By-Step Guide, 291
- VSS in, 209

Virtual Server Scripts, 105–106

Virtual Server Service, 16

Virtual Server Web Application, 16

virtualization
- for availability, 5
- benefits of, 3–5
- for consolidation, 7
- for demonstrating solutions, 9–10
- for demonstrations, 9–10
- in development and testing, 7–8
- drawbacks of, 5–6
- for flexibility, 4
- hardware, 78–81
- hardware abstraction and, 6
- for learning applications, 9
- with legacy applications, 8
- performance and, 5–6
- physical world vs., 4
- for provisioning, 4
- for resiliency to system failures, 8
- scalability of, 6
- for server consolidation, 7
- for system isolation, 4
- for training applications, 9
- uses of, 7–10
- for utilization increases, 3
- in web-based interface, 10

virtualization reports (MOM 2005), 111

virus, in virtual machine, 152
Visual Studio 2005, 305–306, 325, 484, 545–546
VM task objects, 338–341
VMC (virtual machine configuration)
  file, 18, 166, 189
  folder, 166
  undo disk files in, 28
VMList, 430
VMM driver, 108
VMM Exceptions, 108
vmm.sys, 78
VMRC. See Virtual Machine Remote Control Client
VMRC ActiveX control, 19, 424
VMRC.aspx, 485, 536–541
VMRCAuthenticator, 346
Vmscript, 228
VmScript.exe, 223
VM-SCSI controller, 89
Vmsrvc.sys, 235
Vmware conversion, 234
VNC. See Virtual Network Computer
Volume Shadow Copy Services (VSS)
  backing up with, 203, 209–210
  NTBackup and, 209
  SDK, 209
  snapshot, 209
  in Virtual Server R2 SP1, 209
  Writer, 107
vsftpd, 137, 138
VSMT. See Virtual Server Migration Toolkit
Vsmt_ide.inf, 235
Vsmt_scsi.inf, 235
VSS. See Volume Shadow Copy Services
VSS SDK, 209
VSS snapshot, 209
VSS Writer, 107
VSV file, 189
VUD files, 189

WaitForCompletion, 339, 443
web-based interface. See also Virtual Server Administrative website
  disadvantages of, 104
  files in, 36
  IIS for, 12

  for monitoring, 103–106
  problems with, 35
  Virtual Server Scripts in, 105–106
  virtualization in, 10
  VMRC and, 35
weekly schedule setting, 199
welcome dialog box, 14
Welcome tab, 196
Windows 2000
  backing up in, 203
  cleanup requirements of, 265
  drivers in, 265
  full system backup with, 241–243
  IDE drivers in, 253
  manual migration for, 241–243, 256–261, 265
  storage drivers of, 252–253
  Sysprep 2.0 with, 60–63
  Virtual Machine Additions in, 33
Windows AIK (Windows Automated Installation Kit), 67
Windows Automated Installation Kit (Windows AIK), 67
Windows base virtual machines
  discussed, 53
  post-deployment commands for, 69–70
  Sysprep 2.0 for, 53–69
Windows Codenamed Longhorn Server
  IIS configuration on, 14
  Virtual Machine Additions in, 33
  Virtual Server on, 11
Windows Complete PC Backup, 204–205
Windows event log. See event log
Windows firewall, 15
Windows Management Instrumentation (WMI)
  CORE 1.5, 216
  interface, 183
Windows Memory Diagnostic Tool, 555
Windows NT 4.0
  automatic detection in, 265
  backing up in, 203–204
  drivers in, 265
  IDE drivers in, 254
  log in with, 66
  manual migration for, 253–254, 261–263, 265
  migrating, 232
  multiple network adapters, 558
  problems with, 558
  SCSI drivers in, 254
  storage drivers of, 253–254
  Sysprep 2.0 with, 63–66
  Virtual Machine Additions in, 33

589

Windows NT 4.0 Resource Kit

Windows NT 4.0 Resource Kit, 70
Windows Performance Monitor (PerfMon)
for memory, 95
monitoring with, 107–108
Windows PowerShell. *See* **PowerShell**
Windows Remote Boot Floppy, 231
Windows Server 2003
ASM backup for, 238–245
backing up in, 194–203
full system backup with, 241–243
guest operating system of, 36–41
IDE drivers in, 251–252
IIS configuration on, 13
installing, 36–41
manual migration for, 238–243, 251–252,
   256–261, 264
migration of, 251–252
Mini-Setup on, 59
plug and play hardware in, 59
SCSI drivers in, 252
shutdown in, 59
SID regeneration in, 59
storage drivers of, 251–252
Sysprep 2.0 with, 53–59
Virtual Machine Additions in, 33, 40–41
"virtual server" in, 280
Virtual Server on, 8, 11
websites and, 173, 179
WSUS on, 117
Windows Server Update Service (WSUS)
administration of, 119
automated updating with, 117–136
automatic approval options of, 120–121
automatic restart option of, 128–129
chaining, 118
classifications, 120–122
client virtual machine configuration in, 123–131
client-side targeting in, 127
computer groups in, 119
configuring, 119
discussed, 117, 136
drivers, 121
files for, 122
"Install Updates and Shut Down" option of,
   124–125
installing, 118–119
Internet connection, without, 135–136
with Intranet, 126–127
languages for, 122

for minor updates, 129–130
options setting in, 119–120
preparation for installation of, 117–118
product type specifications, 121–122
with proxy server, 122
with registry, 131–135
re-prompt delays with, 130–131
rescheduling, 127–128
restart delays with, 130
scheduling, 121
synchronization options, 121–122
update detection frequency in, 129
with update source, 122
updates for, 120
using, 122–123
website for, 119
Windows Update and, 131
Windows SQL Server 2000 Desktop Engine
   (WMSDE), 118
Windows System Image Manager, 66–69
Windows systems
imaging of, 247–248
migrating, 249, 251
system files in, 248–249
VBscripts in, 337
Windows Task Manager, 94
Windows Update
timing of, 129
WSUS and, 131
Windows Update Catalog (Microsoft), 116
Windows Vista
backing up in, 204–205
cache memory, 95
IIS configuration on, 13–14
manual migration for, 244–245, 264
NTBackup in, 205
system imaging in, 264
Virtual Machine Additions in, 33
Virtual Server on, 11
Windows XP
ASR backup for, 238–245
backing up in, 194–203, 205
full system backup with, 241–243
IDE drivers in, 251–252
with IIS 5.1, 173
IIS configuration on, 13
manual migration for, 238–245, 251–253,
   256–261, 264
migration of, 251–252

590

Mini-Setup on, 59
plug and play hardware in, 59
shutdown in, 59
SID regeneration in, 59
storage drivers of, 251–252
Sysprep 2.0 with, 53–59
Virtual Machine Additions in, 33
Virtual Server on, 11
websites on, 179
WINS server, 375
WMI (Windows Management Instrumentation)
  CORE 1.5, 216
  interface, 183
WMSDE (Microsoft Windows SQL Server 2000 Desktop Engine), 118
Workgroup (Sysprep)
  discussed, 55
  with Windows 2000 server, 61
Writer, VSS, 107
wscript, 337

WSUS. *See* **Windows Server Update Service**
WUServer, 132
WUStatusServer, 132

X

xcopy, 203–204
XML files, 229

Y

Yellow dog Updater, Modified (YUM).
    See **Linux Yellow dog Updater, Modified**

Programmer to Programmer™

BROWSE BOOKS | P2P FORUM | FREE NEWSLETTER | ABOUT WROX

Get more Wrox at Wrox.com!

Special Deals
Take advantage of special offers every month

Free Chapter Excerpts
Be the first to preview chapters from the latest Wrox publications

Unlimited Access. . .
. . . to over 70 of our books in the Wrox Reference Library (see more details online)

Forums, Forums, Forums
Take an active role in online discussions with fellow programmers

Meet Wrox Authors!
Read running commentaries from authors on their programming experiences and whatever else they want to talk about

Browse Books
.NET XML
SQL Server Visual Basic
Java C# / C++

Join the community!

Sign-up for our free monthly newsletter at
newsletter.wrox.com

Programmer to Programmer™

Take your library wherever you go.

Now you can access more than 70 complete Wrox books online, wherever you happen to be! Every diagram, description, screen capture, and code sample is available with your subscription to the **Wrox Reference Library**. For answers when and where you need them, go to wrox.books24x7.com and subscribe today!

Find books on
- ASP.NET
- C#/C++
- Database
- General
- Java
- Mac
- Microsoft Office
- .NET
- Open Source
- PHP/MySQL
- SQL Server
- Visual Basic
- Web
- XML

www.wrox.com